THE HUGUENOTS:

THEIR

SETTLEMENTS, CHURCHES, AND INDUSTRIES

IN ENGLAND AND IRELAND.

By SAMUEL SMILES,

AUTHOR OF "SELF-HELP," "LIVES OF THE ENGINEERS," ETC.

WITH AN APPENDIX RELATING TO

THE HUGUENOTS IN AMERICA.

University Press of the Pacific
Honolulu, Hawaii

The Huguenots:
Their Settlements, Churches, and Industries in
England and Ireland

by
Samuel Smiles

ISBN: 1-4102-0358-1

Copyright © 2002 by University Press of the Pacific

Reprinted from the 1874 edition

University Press of the Pacific
Honolulu, Hawaii
http://www.universitypressofthepacific.com

All rights reserved, including the right to reproduce this book, or portions thereof, in any form.

In order to make original editions of historical works available to scholars at an economical price, this facsimile of the original edition of 1874 is reproduced from the best available copy and has been digitally enhanced to improve legibility, but the text remains unaltered to retain historical authenticity.

PREFACE.

The geographical position of Britain has, from the earliest times, rendered it a country of refuge. Fronting Europe, yet separated from it by a deep sea-moat, the proscribed of other lands have by turns sought the protection of the island fortress, and made it their home. To the country of the Britons the Saxons brought their industry, the Northmen their energy, and the Flemings and French their skill and spirit of liberty; and out of the whole has come the English nation.

The early industry of England was almost entirely pastoral. Down to a comparatively recent period it was a great grazing country, and its principal staple was wool. The English people being as yet unskilled in the arts of manufacture, the wool was bought up by foreign merchants, and exported abroad in large quantities, principally to Flanders and France, there to be manufactured into cloth, and partly returned in that form for sale in the English markets.

The English kings, desirous of encouraging home industry, held out repeated inducements to foreign artisans to come over and settle in the country for the purpose of instructing their subjects in the industrial arts. This policy was pursued during many successive reigns, more particularly in that of Edward III.; and, by the middle of the fourteenth century, large numbers of Flemish artisans, driven out of the Low Countries by the tyranny of the trades-unions as well as by civil war, embraced the offers held out to them, settled in various parts of England, and laid the foundations of English skilled industry.*

But by far the most important migrations of skilled foreigners out of Europe were occasioned by the religious persecutions which prevailed in Flanders and France for a considerable period after the Reformation. Two great waves of foreign population then flowed over from the Continent into England—probably the largest in point of numbers which have occurred since the date of the Saxon settlement. The first took place in the latter half of the sixteenth century, and consisted partly of French, but principally of Flemish Protestants; the second, toward the end of the seventeenth century, consisted almost entirely of French Huguenots.

The second of these emigrations, consequent on the religious persecutions which followed the Revocation of the Edict of Nantes by Louis XIV., was of extraordinary magnitude. According to Sismondi, the loss which it occasioned to France was not far short of a million of persons, and those her best and most industrious subjects. Although the circumstances connected with this remarkable exodus, as well as the events which flowed from them, exercised an important influence on the political as well as industrial history of Northern Europe, they have as yet, viewed in this connection, received but slight notice at the hands of the historian.

It is the object of the following book more particularly to give an account of the causes which led to this last great migration of foreign Protestants from France into England, and to describe its effects upon English industry as well as English history. The author merely offers the book as a contribution to the subject, which seems to him to be one well worthy of farther investigation.

LONDON, *July*, 1867.

---

* See APPENDIX for account of the "Early Settlement of Foreign Artisans in England."

CONTENTS.

CHAPTER I.
INVENTION OF PRINTING.—RISE OF THE HUGUENOTS.
Invention of Printing.—Dearness of MS. Books.—Power conferred on Educated Men by Printing.—Coster, Gutenburg, Schœffer.—The first printed Bible.—Faust of Mainz.—Diffusion of Printing.—Spread of printed Bibles.—Opposed by the Priests.—Effects of reading the Bible.—Luther's Translation.—Bibles printed at Antwerp.—Eager Demand for the Scriptures.—Ecclesiastical Abuses assailed.—The Reformation at Meaux.—Jacques Lefevre.—Resistance of the Sorbonne.—Burning of Bibles and Printers.—Rise of the Huguenots.................................. Page 13

CHAPTER II.
EPISODE IN THE LIFE OF BERNARD PALISSY.
The Life of Palissy illustrative of his Epoch.—His Birth and Education.—Travels through France, Germany, and Flanders.—The prevailing Excitement.—Palissy joins "The Religion."—Life at Saintes.—His pursuit of the Secret of the Enamel.—His Sufferings.—Calvin at Saintonge.—Palissy begins a Reformed Church at Saintes.—The early Gospellers.—Philebert Hamelin.—Progress of "The Religion."—The Persecutions at Saintes.—Palissy employed by the Duke of Montmorency.—Imprisoned at Bordeaux.—Liberated and made Royal Potter.—Dies for his Religion in the Bastile... 31

CHAPTER III.
PERSECUTIONS OF THE REFORMED IN FRANCE AND FLANDERS.
Huguenot Men of Genius.—Spread of "The Religion."—Charles IX. and Catharine de Medicis.—A National Council held.—The Chancellor de l'Hôpital.—Catharine's Letter to the Pope.—Outbreak of Persecution.—Massacre of Vassy.—The Duke of Guise: Triumph of his Policy.—Massacres throughout France.—Civil War.—The Iconoclasts.—Treaty of Peace.—Council of Trent.—Catharine de Medicis and the Duke of Alva.—Ignatius Loyola.—Persecutions in Flanders.—Philip II. of Spain.—Devastation of the Low Countries and Flight of the Protestants.—Mar-

riage of Henry of Navarre and Margaret of France.—Attempted Assassination of Admiral Coligny.—Massacre of Saint Bartholomew.—Rejoicings at Rome.—Death of Charles IX.—Flight of Huguenots.—Renewed Civil War.—Accession of Henry IV.—The Edict of Nantes....... Page 50

CHAPTER IV.
RELATIONS OF ENGLAND WITH FRANCE AND SPAIN.

England at the Accession of Elizabeth.—The Pope denies the Queen's Legitimacy.—Plots against her Life.—The English Asylum granted to the Foreign Protestants a cause of Offense abroad.—Demands that the Fugitives be expelled the Kingdom.—The Pope denounces the Refugees.—Bishop Jewel's Defense of them.— French and Spanish Plots against Elizabeth.—Mary Queen of Scots.—The Pope's Bull against Elizabeth.—The Bishop of Ross and Ridolfi.—Conference at Madrid.—The Plots defeated.—News of the Massacre of Saint Bartholomew arrive in England.—Reception of the French Embassador by Elizabeth.—Execution of the Queen of Scots.—Continued Flight of the Refugees from Flanders.—Defeat of the Sacred Armada.—The Reigns of Philip II. and Elizabeth contrasted.. 71

CHAPTER V.
SETTLEMENTS AND INDUSTRIES OF THE PROTESTANT REFUGEES IN BRITAIN.

Early English Industry.—The Woolen Manufacture.—Extensive Immigrations of Flemish Protestant Artisans.—Landings at Sandwich, Rye, and Dover.—Their Settlement at Sandwich.—Cloth-making and Gardening introduced.—The Flemings in London.—Their Industries.—Dye-works at Bow.—Native Jealousy.—The Flemish Merchants.—Numbers of the Immigrants.—Settlement at Norwich.—Protected by Queen Elizabeth.—Establishment of the Cloth Manufacture.—Flemish Lace-makers.—Workers in Iron and Steel.—Fishing Settlement at Yarmouth.—Drainers of the Fen-lands.—Settlements in Ireland.—Flemings in Scotland.—Reactionary Policy of Charles I. summarily checked.................................. 85

CHAPTER VI.
EARLY WALLOON AND FRENCH CHURCHES IN ENGLAND.

Desire of the Refugees for Freedom of Worship.—The first Walloon and French Churches in London.—Dutch Church in Austin Friars.—French Church in Threadneedle Street.—Churches at Sandwich, Rye, Norwich.—"God's House" at Southampton.—Register of their Church.—Their Fasts and Thanksgivings.—Walloon Church at Canterbury.—Memorial of the Refugees.—The Undercroft in Canterbury Cathedral.—The Lady Chapel.—Occupation of the Undercroft by the Walloons.—The French Church still in Canterbury Cathedral.. 113

CHAPTER VII.

RENEWAL OF THE PERSECUTIONS IN FRANCE.—REVOCATION OF THE EDICT OF NANTES.

Assassination of Henry IV.—Marie de Medicis.—Renewal of Civil War in France.—Cardinal Richelieu.—Siege of Rochelle.—The Huguenots suppressed as a Political Body.—Edict of Pardon.—Loyalty of the Huguenots.—Their Industry.—Their Manufactures.—Their Integrity as Merchants.—Colbert —Absolutism of Louis XIV.—His Ambition.—His Extravagance.—His Enmity to the Huguenots.—The Persecution renewed. —Emigration prohibited. — Cruel Edicts of Louis. — His Amours and "Conversion."—Madame de Maintenon.—Attempt to purchase Huguenot Consciences.—Abduction of Protestant Children.—The Dragonnades. —Wholesale Conversions.— The Protestant Churches destroyed.— Incident at Saintonge.—Dragonnades in Bearn.—Louis XIV. revokes the Edict of Nantes, and marries Madame de Maintenon............. Page 128

CHAPTER VIII.

RENEWED FLIGHT OF THE HUGUENOTS FROM FRANCE.

Rejoicings at Rome on the Revocation of the Edict.—Bossuet's and Massillon's praises of Louis XIV.—Consequences of the Revocation.—The Military Jacquerie.—Demolition of Protestant Churches.—Employment of the Huguenots proscribed.—Pursued beyond Death.—M. de Chenevix.— Conversion or Flight.—Escape of Literary and Scientific Men.—Schomberg, Ruvigny, Duquesne.— The Banished Pastors. — Historical Significance of the Exodus.—General Flight of the Huguenots.—Closing of the Frontier.— Capture and Punishment of the Detected.—Flight in Disguise. —Flight of Women.—Jean Marteilhe of Bergerac.—The Captured condemned to the Galleys.—Louis de Marolles.—John Huber.—The Flight by Sea.—Count de Marancé.—The Lord of Castelfranc.—The Misses Raboteau.—Case of a French Gentlewoman Refugee.—Fumigation of Ships' Holds.—Numbers of the Fugitives from France.—A Death-blow given to French Industry... 152

CHAPTER IX.

THE HUGUENOTS AND THE ENGLISH REVOLUTION OF 1688.

The Counties of the Refuge.—The Asylum of Geneva.—The Huguenots in Switzerland; in Brandenburg and Germany.—Holland "The Great Ark of the Fugitives."—Eminent Refugees in the Low Countries.—Their Hospitable Reception by the Dutch.—Refugee Soldiers and Sailors.—William, Prince of Orange: his Relation to the English Throne.—The Stuart Kings and the Protestant Refugees.—Accession of James II.: compared with Louis XIV.—Attempts to suppress Protestantism.—Popular Reaction.—William of Orange invited over to England.—French Huguenot Officers and Soldiers in the Dutch Army.—Marshal Schomberg....... 171

x   *CONTENTS.*

CHAPTER X.
DUMONT DE BOSTAQUET.—HIS ESCAPE FROM FRANCE INTO HOLLAND.

Dumont de Bostaquet, a Protestant Gentleman of Normandy: his Church at Lindebœuf demolished.—Dragonnades in Normandy.—Scenes at Rouen.—Soldiers quartered in Protestant Families.—De Bostaquet promises Abjuration.—His Family pretend to abjure.—They meditate Flight from France.—Attempted Escape.—Journey to the Sea-coast.—Attacked by the Coast-guard.—De Bostaquet Wounded.—His Flight through Picardy, and Sufferings.—Refuge in Holland .... Page 192

CHAPTER XI.
DE BOSTAQUET IN ENGLAND.—THE IRISH CAMPAIGNS OF 1689-90.

Expedition of William of Orange to England.—The Flotilla sets sail.—Voyage along the English Coast.—Landing at Torbay.—Advance to Exeter and London.—Revolution of 1688.—The Exiles in London.—The Marquis de Ruvigny at Greenwich.—De Bostaquet's Family in England.—Huguenot Regiments sent into Ireland.—The Irish Campaign of 1689.—Losses of the Army at Dundalk.—Landing of James II. in Ireland with a French Army.—Huguenot Regiments recruited in Switzerland.—William III. takes the Field in Person.—Campaign of 1690.—Battle of the Boyne.—Death of Marshal Schomberg 205

CHAPTER XII.
HUGUENOT OFFICERS IN THE BRITISH SERVICE.

Henry, Second Marquis de Ruvigny, distinguishes himself at the Battle of Aughrim, and is created Earl of Galway —War in Savoy.—Earl of Galway placed in Command.—Appointed Lord Justice in Ireland.—Founding of Portarlington.—Earl of Galway takes Command of the Army in Spain.—Bravery of the Huguenot Soldiers.—Jean Cavalier, the Camisard Leader.—The War of the Blouses.—Cavalier enters the Service of William III.—His Desperate Valor at the Battle of Almanza in Spain.—Made Governor of Jersey and Major General.—Rapin-Thoyras, the Soldier-Historian.—John de Bodt, the Engineer.—Field Marshal Lord Ligonier.—The Huguenot Sailors.—The Admirals Gambier 217

CHAPTER XIII.
HUGUENOT SETTLERS IN ENGLAND.—MEN OF SCIENCE AND LEARNING.

The Huguenot Refugees for Liberty.—The Emigration a Protest against Intellectual and Religious Tyranny.—Eminent Refugees.—Solomon de Caus.—Denis Papin, his Scientific Eminence.—Dr. Desaguliers.—Abraham de Moivre.—Refugee Literati.—Refugee Pastors: Abbadie; Saurin; Allix; Pineton, his Escape from France.—Refugee Graduates of Oxford.—The Du Moulins.—James Capell.—Claude de la Mothe.—Armand du Bourdieu 230

CHAPTER XIV.

HUGUENOT SETTLEMENTS IN ENGLAND.—MEN OF INDUSTRY.

Flight of the Manufacturing Class from France.—Districts from which they chiefly came.—Money brought by them into England.—Measures taken for the relief of the Destitute.—French Relief Committee.—The Huguenots self-helping and helpful of each other.—Their Benefit Societies.—Their settlements in Spitalfields and other parts of London.—Introduce new branches of Industry from France.—Establishment of the Silk Manufacture.—Silk Stocking Trade.—Glass-works.—Paper-mills.—The De Portal Family.—Henry de Portal, the Paper-maker.—Manufactures at Canterbury, Norwich, and Ipswich.—Lace-making.—Refugee Industry in Scotland.. Page 250

CHAPTER XV.

THE HUGUENOT CHURCHES IN ENGLAND.

Large number of Refugee Churches in London.—French Church of Threadneedle Street.—Church of the Savoy.—Swallow Street Church, Piccadilly.—French Churches in Spitalfields.—Churches in Suburban Districts.—The Malthouse Church, Canterbury.—"God's House," Southampton.—French Churches at Bristol, Plymouth, Stonehouse, Dartmouth, and Exeter. — Church at Thorpe-le-Soken, Essex. — Gradual Decadence of the Churches.—Sermon of the Rev. M. Bourdillon.—Founding of the French Hospital.—Governors and Directors of the Institution................... 270

CHAPTER XVI.

HUGUENOT SETTLEMENTS IN IRELAND.

Attempts to establish the Linen-trade in Ireland by Refugees.—The Duke of Ormond.—Efforts of William III. to promote Irish Industry.—Refugee Colony at Dublin.—Settlement at Lisburn, near Belfast.—Louis Crommelin appointed "Overseer of Royal Linen Manufactory of Ireland."—His Labors crowned with Success.—Peter Goyer.—Settlements at Kilkenny and Cork.—Life and Adventures of James Fontaine in England and Ireland.—Settlement at Youghal.—Refugee Colony at Waterford.—The French Town of Portarlington: its Inhabitants and their Descendants 283

CHAPTER XVII.

DESCENDANTS OF THE REFUGEES.

The Descendants of the Refugee Flemings and French still recognizable in England.—Changes of Name by the Flemings.—The Des Bouveries Family.—Hugessens.—Houblons.—Eminent Descendants of Flemish Refugees.—The Grote Family.—Changes of French Names.—Names still preserved.—The Queen's Descent from a Huguenot.—The Trench Family.—Peers descended from Huguenots.—Peerages of Taunton, Eversley, and

Romilly.—The Lefevres.—Family of Romilly.—Baronets descended from Huguenots.—Members of Parliament.—Eminent Scholars: Archdeacon Jortin, Maturin, Dutens, Rev. William Romaine.—Eminent Lawyers descended from Refugees.—Eminent Literary Men of the same Origin.—The Handloom-weavers of Spitalfields.—The Dollonds.—Lewis Paul, inventor of Spinning by Rollers.—Migration from Spitalfields.—The last Persecutions in France.—The Descendants of the Huguenot Refugees become British.. Page 307

CHAPTER XVIII.
CONCLUSION.—THE FRENCH REVOLUTION.

Effects of the Persecutions in Flanders and France.—Suppression of Protestantism and Liberty.—Disappearance of Great Men in France after the Revocation.—Triumph of the Jesuits.—Aggrandizement of the Church.—Hunger and Emptiness of the People.—Extinction of Religion.—The Church assailed by Voltaire.—Persecution of the Clergy.—The Reign of Terror.—Flight of the Nobles and Clergy from France into Germany and England.—The Dragonnades of the Huguenots repeated in the Noyades of the Royalists.—Louis XVI. and Marie Antoinette the Victims of Louis XIV.—Relation of the Revocation of the Edict of Nantes to the French Revolution.—Conclusion 340

APPENDIX.

I. Early Settlement of Foreign Artisans in England........................ 353

II. Registers of French Protestant Churches in England................. 368

III. Huguenot Refugees and their Descendants............................. 397

THE HUGUENOTS IN AMERICA... 427

INDEX.. 443

THE HUGUENOTS.

CHAPTER I.

INVENTION OF PRINTING.—RISE OF THE HUGUENOTS.

Of all inventions, probably none has exercised a greater influence upon modern civilization than that of printing. While it has been the mother and preserver of many other inventions which have changed the face of society, it has also afforded facilities for the intercourse of mind with mind —of living men with each other, as well as with the thinkers of past generations—which have evoked an extraordinary degree of mental activity, and exercised a powerful influence on the development of modern history.

Although letters were diligently cultivated long before the invention of printing, and many valuable books existed in manuscript, and seminaries of learning flourished in all civilized countries, knowledge was for the most part confined to a comparatively small number of persons. The manuscripts which contained the treasured thoughts of the ancient poets, scholars, and men of science, were so scarce and dear that they were frequently sold for double or treble their weight in gold. In some cases they were considered so precious that they were conveyed by deed like landed estate. In the thirteenth century a manuscript copy of the *Romance of the Rose* was sold at Paris for over £33 sterling. A copy of the Bible cost from £40 to £60 for the writing only, for it took an expert copyist about ten months' labor to make one.* Such being the case, it will be obvious that books were then for the most part the luxury of the rich, and comparatively inaccessible to the great body of the people.

Even the most advanced minds could exercise but little influence on their age. They were able to address themselves to only a very limited number of their fellow-men, and in most cases their influence died with them. The results of study, investigation, and experience remaining unrecorded, knowledge was for the most part transmitted orally, and often inaccurately. Thus many arts and inventions discovered by individuals became lost to the race, and a point of social stagnation was arrived at, beyond which farther progress seemed improbable.

This state of things was entirely changed by the introduction of printing. It gave a new birth to letters; it enabled books to be perpetually renovated and multipled at a comparatively moderate cost, and to diffuse the light which they contained over a much larger number of minds. It gave a greatly increased power to the individual and to society, by facilitating the intercourse of educated men of all countries with each other. Active thinkers were no longer restricted by the limits of their town or parish, or even of their nation or epoch; and the knowledge that their printed

* It is difficult to form an accurate idea of the relative value of money to commodities in the thirteenth century, compared with present prices; but it may be mentioned that in 1445 (according to Fleetwood's *Chronicon Pretiosum*, 1707) the price of wheat was 4s. 6d. the quarter, and oats 2s.; bullocks and heifers sold for 5s., and sheep for 2s. 5½d. each. In 1460 a gallon of ale sold for a penny, which was also the ordinary day's wage of laborers and servants, in addition to meat and drink. As late as 1558, a good sheep sold for 2s. 10d. In 1414 the ordinary salary of chaplains was five or six marks a year (the mark being equal to 13s. 4d.), and of resident parish priests eight marks; so that for about £5 10s. a year a single man was expected to live cleanly and decently. These prices multiplied by about twelve would give something approaching their equivalent in modern money. It is true, manuscripts were in many cases sold at fancy prices, as books are now. But copying had become a regular branch of business: at Milan, in the fourteenth century, about fifty persons earned their living by it. The ordinary charge for making a copy of the Bible was 80 Bologna livres, or equal to 53 gold florins.

words would have an effect where their spoken words did not reach, could not fail to stimulate the highest order of minds into action. The permanency of invention and discovery was thus secured; the most advanced point of one generation became the starting-point of the next; and the results of the labors of one age were carried forward into all the ages that succeeded.*

The invention of printing, like most others, struggled slowly and obscurely into life. The wooden blocks or tablets of Laurence Coster were superseded by separate types of the same material. Gutenberg, of Mentz, next employed large types cut in metal, from which the impressions were taken. And, finally, Gutenberg's associate, Schœffer, cut the characters in a matrix, after which the types were cast, and thus completed the art as it now remains.

It is a remarkable circumstance, that the first book which Gutenberg undertook to print with his cut metal types was a folio edition of the Bible in the Latin Vulgate, consisting of 641 leaves. When the immense labor involved in carrying out such a work is considered — the cutting by hand, with imperfect tools, of each separate type required for the setting of a folio page, and the difficulties to be overcome with respect to vellum, paper, ink, and press-work—one can not but feel astonished at the boldness of the undertaking; nor can it be matter of surprise that the execution of the work occupied Gutenberg and his associates a period of from seven to eight years.†

---

* See BABBAGE, *Ninth Bridgewater Treatise*, 52-6. Lord Bacon observes: "If the invention of ships was thought so noble, which carrieth riches and commodities from place to place, how much more are letters to be magnified, which, as ships, pass through the vast seas of time, and make ages so distant to participate of the wisdom, illuminations, and inventions, the one of the other."

† The first Bible printed by Gutenberg is known as the Mazarin Bible, from a copy of it having been found in Cardinal Mazarin's library at Paris about the middle of last century. Johnson, in his *Typographia* (p. 17), says: "It was printed with large cut metal types, and published in 1450." Others give the date of publication as five years later, in 1455. Mr. Hallam inclines to think that it was printed with cast-metal types; but there is reason to believe that the casting of the types by a matrix was invented at

We do not, however, suppose that Gutenberg and his associates were induced to execute this first printed Bible through any more lofty motive than that of earning a considerable sum of money by the enterprise. They were, doubtless, tempted to undertake it by the immense prices for which manuscript copies of the Bible then sold; and they merely sought to produce, by one set of operations, a number of duplicates in imitation of the written character, which they hoped to be able to sell at the manuscript prices. But, as neither Gutenberg nor Schœffer were rich men, and as the work involved great labor and expense while in progress, they found it necessary to invite some capitalist to join them; and hence their communication of the secret to John Faust, the wealthy goldsmith of Mentz, who agreed to join them in their venture, and supply them with the necessary means for carrying out the undertaking.

The first edition of the printed Bible having been disposed of, without the secret having transpired, Faust and Schœffer brought out a second edition in 1462, which they again offered for sale at the manuscript prices. Faust carried a number of copies to Paris to dispose of, and sold several of them for 500 or 600 crowns, the price then paid for manuscript Bibles. But great was the astonishment cf the Parisian copyists when Faust, anxious to dispose of the remainder, lowered his price to 60 and then to 30 crowns! The copies sold having been compared with each other, were found to be exactly uniform! It was immediately inferred

a subsequent period. Mr. Hallam says: "It is a very striking circumstance that the high-minded inventors of this great art tried at the very outset so bold a flight as the printing an entire Bible, and executed it with astonishing success. It was Minerva leaping on earth in her divine strength and radiant armor, ready at the moment of her nativity to subdue and destroy her enemies. The Mazarin Bible is printed, some copies on vellum, some on paper of choice quality, with strong, black, and tolerably handsome characters, but with some want of uniformity, which has led, perhaps unreasonably, to doubt whether they were cast in a matrix. We may see in imagination this venerable and splendid volume leading up the crowded myriads of its followers, and imploring, as it were, a blessing on the new art, by dedicating its first-fruits to the service of Heaven."—*Literary History*, edition 1864, p. 156–7.

that these Bibles must be produced by magic, as such an extraordinary uniformity was considered entirely beyond the reach of human contrivance. Information was forthwith given to the police against Faust as a magician. His lodgings were searched, when a number of Bibles were found there complete. The red ink with which they were embellished was supposed to be his blood. It was seriously believed that he was in league with the devil; and he was carried off to prison, from which he was only delivered upon making a full revelation of the secret.*

Several other books, of less importance, were printed by Gutenberg and Schœffer at Mentz: two editions of the Psalter, a Catholicon, a Codex Psalmorum, and an edition of Cicero's Offices; but they were printed in such small numbers, and were sold at such high prices, that, like the manuscripts which they superseded, they were only purchasable by kings, nobles, collegiate bodies, and rich ecclesiastical establishments. It was only after the lapse of many years, when the manufacture of paper had become improved, and Schœffer had invented his method of cutting the characters in a matrix, and casting the type in quantity, that books could be printed in such forms as to be accessible to the great body of the people.

In the mean while, the printing establishments of Gutenberg and Schœffer were for a time broken up by the sack and plunder of Mentz by the Archbishop Adolphus in 1462, when, their workmen becoming dispersed, and being no longer bound to secrecy, they shortly after carried with them the invention of the new art into nearly every country in Europe.

Wherever the printers set up their trade, they usually began by issuing an edition of the Latin Bible. There was no author class in those days to supply "copy" enough to keep their presses going. Accordingly, they fell back upon the

* Such is supposed to be the origin of the tradition of "The Devil and Dr. Faustus." It is believed that Faust died of the plague at Paris in 1466.

B

ancient authors, issuing editions of Livy, Horace, Sallust, Cicero, and portions of Aristotle, with occasional devotional manuals; but their favorite book, most probably because it was the one most in demand, was the Bible. Only twenty-four books were published in Germany during the ten years that followed the sack of Mentz; but of these five were Latin and two were German Bibles. Translators were at the same time busily engaged upon it in different countries, and year by year the Bible became more accessible. Thus an Italian version appeared in 1471, a Bohemian in 1475, a Dutch in 1477, a French in 1477, and a Spanish (Valencian) in 1478.*

The Bible, however, continued a comparatively scarce and dear book, being little known to the clergy generally, and still less to the people. By many of the former it was regarded with suspicion, and even with hostility. At length, the number of editions of the Bible which were published in Germany, as if heralding the approach of the coming Reformation, seriously alarmed the Church; and in 1486 the Archbishop of Mentz placed the printers of that city, which had been the cradle of the printing-press, under strict censorship. Twenty-five years later, Pope Alexander VI. issued a bull prohibiting the printers of Cologne, Mentz, Treves, and Magdeburg from publishing any books without the express license of their archbishops. Although these measures were directed against the printing of religious works generally, they were more particularly directed against the publication of the Scriptures in the vulgar tongue.†

* Lord Spencer's famous library contains twenty editions of the Bible in Latin, printed between the appearance of the Mazarin Bible in 1450-5 and the year 1480 inclusive. It also contains nine editions of the German Bible printed before the year 1495.—See EDWARDS *on Libraries*, p. 430.

† HALLAM—*Literary History*, ed. 1864, i., 254. No translation of the Bible was permitted to appear in England during the fifteenth century; and the reading of Wycliffe's translation was prohibited under penalty of excommunication and death. Tyndale's translation of the New Testament was first printed at Antwerp. The government tried to suppress the book, and many copies were seized and burnt. John Tyndale, a merchant of London, brother of the translator, having been convicted of reading the New Testament, was sentenced by the excellent Sir Thomas More "that he should be set upon a horse with his face to the tail, and have a paper pinned upon his

The printers, nevertheless, continued to print the Bible, regardless of these prohibitions — the Old Testament in Hebrew, the new in Greek, and both in Latin, German, French, and other modern languages. Finding that the reading of the Bible was extending, the priests began to inveigh against the practice from the pulpit. "They have now found out," said a French monk, "a new language called Greek; we must carefully guard ourselves against it. That language will be the mother of all sorts of heresies. I see in the hands of a great number of persons a book written in this language, called 'The New Testament;' it is a book full of brambles, with vipers in them. As to the Hebrew, whoever learns that becomes a Jew at once."*

The fears of the priests increased as they saw their flocks becoming more intent upon reading the Scriptures, or hearing them read, than attending mass; and they were especially concerned at the growing disposition of the people to call in question the infallibility of the Church and the sacred character of the priesthood. It was every day becoming clearer to them that if the people were permitted to resort to books, and pray to God direct in their vulgar tongue, instead of through the priests in Latin, the authority of the mass would fall, and the Church itself would be endangered.† A most

head, and many sheets of New Testaments sewn to his cloak, to be afterward thrown into a great fire kindled in Cheapside, and then pay to the king a fine which should ruin him."

* SISMONDI—*Histoire des Français*, xvi., 364.

† Lord Herbert, in his *Life of Henry VII.* (p. 147), supposed Cardinal Wolsey to have stated the effects of printing to the pope in the following terms: "That his holiness could not be ignorant what deverse effects the new invention of printing had produced; for it had brought in and restored books and learning; so together it hath been the occasion of those sects and schisms which daily appear in the world, but especially in Germany; where men begin now to call in question the present faith and tenets of the Church, and to examine how far religion is departed from its primitive institution. And that, which particulaily was most to be lamented, they had exhorted lay and ordinary men to read the Scriptures, and to pray in their vulgar tongue; and if this was suffered, besides all other dangers, the common people at last might come to believe that there was not so much use of the clergy. For if men were persuaded once they could make their own way to God, and that prayers in their native and ordinary language might pierce heaven as well as Latin, how much would the authority of the mass fall!

forcible expression was given to this view by the Vicar of Croydon in a sermon preached by him at Paul's Cross, in which he boldly declared that "we must root out printing, or printing will root out us."

But printing could not be rooted out any more than the hand of Time could be put back. This invention, unlike every other, contained within itself a self-preserving power which insured its perpetuation. Its method had become known, and was recorded by itself. Printed books were now part of the inheritance of the human race; and though they might be burnt, as vast numbers of Bibles were, so that they might be kept out of the hands of the people, so long as a single copy remained it was not lost, but was capable of immediate restoration and of infinite multiplication.

The intense interest which the publication of the Bible excited, and the emotion it raised in the minds of those who read it, are matters of history. At this day, when Bibles are common in almost every household, it is perhaps difficult to appreciate the deep feeling of awe and reverence with which men for the first time perused the sacred volume. We have become so familiar with it, that we are apt to look upon it merely as one among many books — as part of the current literature of the day, or as a record of ancient history, to be checked off by the arithmetician and analyzed by the critic.

It was far different in those early times, when the Bible was rare and precious. Printing had brought forth the Book, which had lain so long silent in manuscript beneath the dust of old libraries, and laid it before the people, to be read by them in their own tongue. It was known to be the very charter and title-deed of Christianity—the revelation of God's own will to man; and now, to read it, or hear it read, was like meeting God face to face, and listening to His voice speaking directly to them.

For this purpose, since printing could not be put down, it was best to set up learning against learning; and by introducing all persons to dispute, to suspend the laity between fear and controversy. This, at most, would make them attentive to their superiors and teachers."

At first it could only be read to the people; and in the English cathedrals, where single copies were placed, chained to a niche, eager groups gathered round to drink in its living truths. But as the art of printing improved, and copies of the Bible became multiplied in portable forms, it could then be taken home into the study or the chamber, and read and studied in secret. It was found to be an ever-fresh gushing spring of thought, welling up, as it were, from the Infinite. No wonder that men pondered over it with reverence, and read it with thanksgiving! No wonder that it moved their hearts, influenced their thoughts, gave a color to their familiar speech,* and imparted a bias to their whole life!

To the thoughtful, the perusal of the Bible gave new views of life and death; showed them man, standing on the narrow isthmus of time which divides the eternity of the past from the eternity of the future—a weak, helpless, and sinful creature, yet the object of God's unceasing care. Its effect was to make those who pondered its lessons more solemn; it made the serious more earnest, and impressed them with a deeper sense of responsibility and duty. To the poor, the suffering, and the struggling, it was the aurora of a new world. With this Book in their hands, what to them were the afflictions of time, which were but for a moment, working out for them "a far more exceeding and eternal weight of glory?"

It was the accidental sight of a copy of one of Gutenberg's Bibles in the library of the convent of Erfurt, where Luther was in training for a monk, that fixed his destiny for life.†

* The perusal and study of the Bible in the fifteenth and sixteenth centuries exercised an important influence on literature in all countries. The great writers of the period unconsciously adopted Bible phraseology to a large extent—the thoughts of Scripture clothing themselves in language which became habitual to all who studied it closely. This tendency is noticeable in the early foreign as well as English writers—in Latimer, Bradford, Jewell, More, Brown, Bacon, Milton, and others. Coleridge has said, "Intense study of the Bible will keep any writer from being vulgar in point of style."

† "I was twenty years old," said Luther, "before I had even seen the Bi-

He opened it, and read with inexpressible delight the history of Hannah and her son Samuel. "O God!" he murmured, "could I but have one of these books, I would ask no other treasure!" A great revolution forthwith took place in his soul. He read, and studied, and meditated, until he fell seriously ill. Dr. Staupitz, a man of rank in the Church, was then inspecting the convent at Erfurt, in which Luther had been for two years. He felt powerfully attracted toward the young monk, and had much confidential intercourse with him. Before leaving, Staupitz presented Luther with a copy of the Bible—a Bible all to himself, which he could take with him to his cell and study there. "For several years," said Luther afterward, "I read the whole Bible twice in every twelvemonth. It is a great and powerful tree, each word of which is a mighty branch; each of these branches have I shaken, so desirous was I to learn what fruit they every one of them bore, and what they could give me."*

This Bible of Luther's was, however, in the Latin Vulgate, a language known only to the learned. Several translations had been printed in Germany by the end of the fifteenth century; but they were unsatisfactory versions, unsuited for popular reading, and were comparatively little known. One of Luther's first thoughts, therefore, was to translate the Bible into the popular speech, so that the people at large might have free access to the unparalleled book. Accordingly, in 1521, he began the translation of the New Testament during his imprisonment in what he called his Patmos, the castle of Wartburg. It was completed and published in the following year; and two years later his Old Testament appeared.

---

ble. I had no notion that there existed any other gospels or epistles than those in the service. At last I came across a Bible in the library at Erfurt, and used often to read it to Dr. Staupitz with still increasing wonder."—TISCHREDEN—*Table-Talk* (Frankfort, 1568), p. 255. And again, "Dr. Usinger, an Augustan monk, who was my preceptor at the convent of Erfurt, used to say to me, 'Ah! brother Martin, why trouble yourself with the Bible? Rather read the ancient doctors, who have collected for you all its marrow and honey. The Bible itself is the cause of all our troubles.'"—TISCHREDEN, p. 7.   * TISCHREDEN, p. 311.

None valued more than Luther did the invention of printing. "Printing," said he, "is the latest and greatest gift by which God enables us to advance the things of the Gospel." Printing was, indeed, one of the prime agents of the Reformation. The ideas had long been born, but printing gave them wings. Had the writings of Luther and his fellow-laborers been confined only to such copies as could have been made by hand, they would have remained few in number, been extremely limited in their effects, and could easily have been suppressed and destroyed by authority. But the printing-press enabled them to circulate by thousands all over Germany.* Luther was the especial favorite of the printers and booksellers. The former took pride in bringing out his books with minute care, and the latter in circulating them. A large body of ex-monks lived by traveling about and selling them all over Germany. They also flew abroad, into Switzerland, Bohemia, France, and England.†

The printing of the Bible was also carried on with great activity in the Low Countries. Besides versions in French and Flemish for the use of the people in the Walloon provinces, where the new views extensively prevailed, various versions in foreign tongues were printed for exportation abroad. Thus Tyndale, unable to get his New Testament printed in England, where its perusal was forbidden, had the first edition printed at Antwerp in 1526,‡ as well as two sub-

* At Nuremberg, at Strasburg, even at Mentz, there was a constant struggle for Luther's least pamphlets. The sheet, yet wet, was brought from the press under some one's cloak, and passed from shop to shop. The pedantic bookmen of the German trades-unions, the poetical tinmen, the literary shoemakers, devoured the good news. Worthy Hans Sachs raised himself above his wonted commonplace; he left his shoe half made, and with his most high-flown verses, his best productions, he sang, in under tones, "The Nightingale of Wittenberg," and the song was taken up and resounded all over the land.—MICHELET—*Life of Luther*, 70, 71.

† Works printed in Germany or in the Flemish provinces, where at first the administration connived at the new religion, were imported into England, and read with that eagerness and delight which always compensate the risk of forbidden studies.—HALLAM—*Hist. of England*, i., p. 82.

‡ A complete edition of the English Bible, translated partly by Tyndale and partly by Coverdale, was printed at Hamburg in 1535; and a second edition, edited by John Rogers, under the name of "Thomas Matthew," was

sequent editions at the same place. Indeed, Antwerp seems at that time to have been the head-quarters of Bible-printing. No fewer than thirteen editions of the Bible and twenty-four editions of the New Testament, in the Flemish or Dutch language, were printed there within the first thirty-six years of the sixteenth century, besides various other editions in English, French, Danish, and Spanish.*

An eager demand for the Scriptures had by this time sprung up in France. Several translations of portions of the Bible appeared there toward the end of the fifteenth century; but these were all superseded by a version of the entire Scriptures, printed at Antwerp, in successive portions, between the years 1512 and 1530. This translation was the work of Jacques le Fevre or Faber, of Estaples, and it formed the basis of all subsequent editions of the French Bible.

The effects were the same wherever the Book appeared, and was freely read by the people. It was followed by an immediate reaction against the superstition, indifferentism, and impiety which generally prevailed. There was a sudden awakening to a new religious life, and an anxious desire for a purer faith, less overlaid by the traditions, inventions, and corruptions which impaired the efficacy, and obscured the simple beauty of Christianity. The invention of print-

---

printed at Marlborow, in Hesse, in 1537. Tyndale suffered martyrdom at Vilvorde, near Brussels, in 1536, yet he died in the midst of victory, for before his death no fewer than fourteen editions of the New Testament, several of them of two thousand copies each, had been printed; and at the very time that he died the first edition of the Scriptures printed in England was passing through the press. Cranmer's Bible, so called because revised by Cranmer, was published in 1539-40. In the year 1542, Henry VIII. issued a proclamation directing a large Bible to be set up in every parish church, while at the same time Bibles were authorized to be publicly sold. The Spencer collection contains copies of fifteen English editions of the Bible printed between 1536 and 1581, showing that the printing-press was by that time actively at work in England. Wycliffe's translation, though made in 1380, was not printed until 1731.

* "There can be no sort of comparison," says Mr. Hallam, "between the number of these editions, and consequently the eagerness of the people of the Low Countries for biblical knowledge, considering the limited extent of their language, and any thing that could be found in the Protestant states of the empire."—*Literary History*, i., 387.

ing had also its political effects; and for men to be able to read books, and especially the Scriptures, in the common tongue, was itself a revolution. It roused the hearts of the people in all lands, producing commotion, excitement, and agitation. Society became electric, and was stirred to its depths. The sentiment of Right was created, and the long down-trodden peasants—along the Rhine, in Alsace, and Suabia—raised their cries on all sides, demanding freedom from serfdom, and to be recognized as Men. Indeed, this electric fervor and vehement excitement throughout society was one of the greatest difficulties that Luther had to contend with in guiding the Reformation in Germany to a successful issue.

The ecclesiastical abuses, which had first evoked the indignation of Luther, were not confined to Germany, but prevailed all over Europe. There were Tetzels also in France, where indulgences were things of common traffic. Money must thus be raised, for the building of St. Peter's at Rome had to be paid for. . Each sin had its price, each vice its tax. There was a regular tariff for peccadilloes of every degree, up to the greatest crimes.* The Bible, it need scarcely be said, was at open war with this monstrous state of things; and the more extensively it was read and its precepts became known, the more strongly were these practices condemned. Hence the alarm occasioned at Rome by the rapid extension of the art of printing and the increasing circulation of the Bible. Hence also the prohibition of printing which shortly followed, and the burning of the printers who printed the Scriptures, as well as the persons who were found guilty of reading them.

The first signs of the Reformation in France showed themselves in the town of Meaux, about fifty miles northeast of Paris, and not far distant from the then Flemish frontier. It

* The well-known book entitled *Taxes of the Roman Chancery* sets forth the various crimes for which absolution might be given, and the price charged in each case. Numerous instances are quoted *verbatim* in PUAUX—*Histoire de la Réformation Française*, i., 15. The book, it must be added, is now repudiated by Roman Catholics, though it was issued from the Romish press.

was a place full of working-people—mechanics, wool-carders, fullers, cloth-makers, and artisans. The proximity to Flanders, and the similarity of their trade to that of the larger Flemish towns, occasioned a degree of intercourse between them, which doubtless contributed to the propagation of the new views at Meaux, where the hearts of the poor artisans were greatly moved by the tidings of the Gospel which reached them from the North.

At the same time, men of learning in the Church had long been meditating over the abuses which prevailed in it, and devising the best means for remedying them. Among the most earnest of these was Jacques Lefevre, a native of Etaples in Picardy. He was a man of great and acknowledged learning, one of the most distinguished professors in the University of Paris. The study of the Bible produced the same effect upon his mind that it had done on that of Luther; but he was a man of far different temperament—gentle, retiring, and timid, though no less devoted to the cause of truth. He was, however, an old man of seventy; his life was fast fleeting; yet here was a world lying in wickedness around him. What he could do he nevertheless did. He translated the four Gospels into French in 1523; had them printed at Antwerp; and put them into circulation. He found a faithful follower in Guillaume Farel—a young, energetic, and active man—who abounded in those qualities in which the aged Lefevre was so deficient. Another coadjutor shortly joined them—no other than Guillaume Briçonnet, count of Montbrun and bishop of Meaux, who also became a convert to the new doctrines.

The bishop, on taking charge of his diocese, had been shocked by the disorders which prevailed there, by the licentiousness of the clergy, and their general disregard for religious life and duty. As many of them were non-resident, he invited Lefevre, Farel, and others, to occupy their pulpits and preach to the people, the bishop preaching in his turn; and the people flocked to hear them. The bishop also distributed the four Gospels gratuitously among the poor, and very soon a copy was to be found in almost every workshop in Meaux. A reformation of manners shortly followed. Blasphemy, drunkenness, and disorder disappeared; and the movement spread far and near.

It must not be supposed, however, that the supporters of the old Church were indifferent to these proceedings. At first they had been stunned by the sudden spread of the new views and the rapid increase of the Gospellers, as they were called, throughout the northern provinces; but they speedily rallied from their stupor. They knew that power was on their side — the power of kings and Parliaments, and their agents; and these they loudly called to their help for the purpose of preventing the spread of heresy. At the same time, Rome, roused by her danger, availed herself of all methods for winning back her wandering children, by force if not by suasion. The Inquisition was armed with new powers; and wherever heresy appeared, it was crushed, unsparingly, unpityingly. No matter what the rank or learning of the suspected heretic might be, he must satisfy the tribunal before which he was brought, or die at the stake.

The priests and monks of Meaux, though mostly absentees, finding their revenues diminishing, appealed for help to the Sorbonne, the Faculty of Theology at Paris, and the Sorbonne called upon Parliament at once to interpose with a strong hand. The result was, that the Bishop of Meaux was heavily fined, and he shrank thenceforward out of sight, and ceased to give farther cause of offense. But his disciples were less pliant, and continued boldly to preach the Gospel. Jean Leclerc was burnt alive at Metz, and Jacques Pavent and Louis de Berguin on the Place de Grève at Paris. Farel escaped into Switzerland, and there occupied himself in printing copies of Lefevre's New Testament, thousands of which he caused to be disseminated throughout France by the hands of peddlers.

The Sorbonne then proceeded to make war against books

and the printers of them. Bibles and New Testaments were seized wherever found, and burnt; but more Bibles and Testaments seemed to rise, as if by magic, from their ashes. The printers who were convicted of printing Bibles were next seized and burnt. The *Bourgeois de Paris*[*] gives a detailed account of the human sacrifices offered up to ignorance and intolerance in that city during the six months ending June, 1534, from which it appears that twenty men and one woman were burnt alive. One was a printer of the Rue Saint Jacques, found guilty of having "printed the books of Luther." Another, a bookseller, was burnt for "having sold Luther." In the beginning of the following year, the Sorbonne obtained from the king an ordinance, which was promulgated on the 26th of February, 1535, for the suppression of printing!

But it was too late. The art was now full born, and could no more be suppressed than light, or air, or life. Books had become a public necessity, and supplied a great public want; and every year saw them multiplying more abundantly.[†]

The same scenes were enacted all over France, wherever the Bible had penetrated and found followers. In 1545 the massacre of the Vaudois of Provence was perpetrated, accompanied by horrors which it is impossible to describe. This terrible persecution, however, did not produce its intended effect, but, on the other hand, was followed by a strong reaction in the public mind against the fury of the persecutors. The king, Francis I., complained that his orders

---

[*] MICHELET says the *Bourgeois de Paris* (Paris, 1854) was not the publication of a Protestant, which might be called in question, but of a "very zealous Catholic."—*Histoire de France au Seizième Siecle*, viii., p. 411.

[†] It has been calculated (by Daunon, Petit, Rudel, Taillandier, and others) that by the end of the fifteenth century four millions of volumes had been printed, the greater part in folio; and that between 1500 and 1536 eighteen more millions of volumes had been printed. After that it is impossible to number them. In 1533 there had already been eighteen editions of the German Bible printed at Wittemberg, thirteen at Augsburg, thirteen at Strasburg, twelve at Basle, and so on. Schœffer, in his *Influence of Luther on Education*, says that Luther's Catechism soon ran to 100,000 copies. Printing was at the same time making rapid strides in France, England, and the Low Countries.

had been exceeded; but he was sick and almost dying at the time, and had not the strength to prosecute the assassins.

There was, however, a lull for a time in the violence of the persecutions, during which the new views made rapid progress; and men of rank, of learning, and of arms, ranged themselves on the side of "The Religion." Then arose the Huguenots or French Protestants,* who shortly became so numerous as to constitute a considerable power in the state, and to exercise, during the next hundred years, a most important influence on the political history of France.

The origin of the term *Huguenot* is extremely obscure. It was at first applied to them as a nickname, and, like the *Gueux* of Flanders, they assumed and bore it with pride. Some suppose the term to be derived from *Huguon*, a word used in Touraine to signify persons who walk at night in the streets—the early Protestants, like the early Christians, having chosen that time for their religious assemblies. Others are of opinion that it was derived from a French and faulty pronunciation of the German word *Eidgenossen*, or confederates, the name given to those citizens of Geneva who entered into an alliance with the Swiss cantons to resist the attempts of Charles III., duke of Savoy, against their liberties. The confederates were called *Eignots*, and hence, probably, the derivation of the word Huguenots. A third surmise is, that the word was derived from one *Hugues*, the name of a Genevese Calvinist.

Farther attempts continued to be made by Rome to check the progress of printing. In 1599, Pope Paul IV. issued the first *Index Expurgatorius*, containing a list of the books expressly prohibited by the Church. It included all Bibles printed in modern languages, of which forty-eight editions were enumerated; while sixty-one printers were put under a

---

* The followers of the new views called themselves at first *Gospellers* (from their religion being based on the reading of the Gospel), *Religionaries*, or *Those of the Religion*. The name *Protestant* was not applied to them until the end of the seventeenth century, that term originally characterizing the disciples of the Lutheran Reformation in Germany.

general ban, and all works of every description issued from their presses were forbidden. Notwithstanding, however, these and similar measures, such as the wholesale burning of Bibles wherever found, the circulation of the Scriptures rapidly increased, and the principles of the Reformation more and more prevailed throughout all the northern nations.

CHAPTER II.

EPISODE IN THE LIFE OF PALISSY.

AT the time when the remarkable movement we have rapidly sketched was sweeping round the frontiers of France, from Switzerland to Brabant, and men were every where listening with eagerness to the promulgation of the new ideas, there was wandering along the Rhine a poor artisan, then obscure, but afterward famous, who was seeking to earn a living by the exercise of his trade. He could glaze windows, mend furniture, paint a little on glass, draw portraits rudely, gild and color images of the Virgin, or do any sort of work requiring handiness and dexterity. On an emergency he would even undertake to measure land, and was ready to turn his hand to any thing that might enable him to earn a living, and at the same time add to his knowledge and experience. This wandering workman was no other than Bernard Palissy—afterward the natural philosopher, the chemist, the geologist, and the artist—but more generally known as the great Potter.

Fortunately for our present purpose, Palissy was also an author; and though the works he left behind him are written in a quaint and simple style, it is possible to obtain from certain passages in them a more vivid idea of the times in which he lived, and of the trials and sufferings of the Gospellers, of whom he was one of the most illustrious, than from any other contemporary record. The life of Palissy, too, is eminently illustrative of his epoch; and provided we can but accurately portray the life of any single man in relation to his epoch, then biography becomes history in its truest sense; for history, after all, is but accumulated biography.

From the writings of Palissy,* then, we gather the following facts regarding this remarkable man's life and career. He was born about the year 1510, at La Chapelle Biron, a poor village in Perigord, where his father brought him up to his own trade of a glazier. The boy was by nature quick and ingenious, with a taste for drawing, designing, and decoration, which he turned to account in painting on glass and decorating images for the village churches in his neighborhood. Desirous of improving himself at the same time that he earned his living, he resolved on traveling into other districts and countries, according to the custom of skilled workmen in those days. Accordingly, so soon as his term of apprenticeship had expired, he set out upon his "wanderschaft," at about the age of twenty-one. He first went into the country adjacent to the Pyrenees; and his journeyings in those mountain districts awoke in his mind that love for geology and natural history which he afterward pursued with so much zeal. After settling for a time at Tarbes, in the High Pyrenees, he proceeded northward, through Languedoc, Dauphiny, part of Switzerland, Alsace, the duchies of Cleves and Luxemburg, and the provinces of the Lower Rhine, to Ardennes and Flanders.

It will be observed that Palissy's line of travel lay precisely through the provinces in which the people had been most deeply moved by the recent revolt of Luther from Rome. In 1517 the Reformer had publicly denounced the open sale of indulgences "by the profligate monk Tetzel," and affixed his celebrated propositions to the outer pillars of the great church of Wittemberg. The propositions were at once printed in thousands, devoured, and spread abroad in every direction. In 1518 Luther appeared, under the safe-conduct of the Elector of Saxony, before the Pope's legate at Augsburg; and in 1520 he publicly burnt the Pope's bull at

---

* *Œuvres Complètes de Bernard Palissy*, édition conforme aux textes originaux imprimés du vivant de l'auteur; avec des notes et une Notice Historique. Par PAUL-ANTOINE CAP, Paris, 1844.

Wittemberg, amid the acclamations of the people. All Germany was now in a blaze, and Luther's books and pamphlets were every where in demand. It was shortly after this time that Palissy passed through the excited provinces. Wherever he went he heard of Luther, the Bible, and the new revelation which it had brought to light. The men of his own class, with whom he most freely mixed in the course of his travels—artists, mechanics, and artisans*—were full of the new ideas which were stirring the heart of Germany. These were embraced with especial fervor by the young and the energetic. Minds formed and grown old in the established modes of thought were unwilling to be disturbed, and satisfied to rest as they were: "too old for change" was their maxim. But it was different with the young, the ardent, and the inquiring, who looked before rather than behind—to the future rather than the past. These were, for the most part, vehement in support of the doctrines of the Reformation.

Palissy was then of an age at which the mind is most open to receive new impressions. He was, moreover, by nature a shrewd observer and an independent thinker, and he could not fail to be influenced by the agitation which stirred society to its depths. Among the many things which Palissy learned in the course of his travels was the art of reading printed books; and one of the books which he learned to read, and most prized, was the printed Bible, the greatest marvel of his time. It was necessarily read in secret, for the ban of the Church was upon it; but the prohibition was disregarded, and probably gave even an additional zest to the study of the forbidden book. Men recognized each other's love for it as by a secret sympathy; and they gathered together in workshops and dwellings to read and meditate over it, and exhort one another from its pages. Among these was Palissy, who, by the time he was thirty years old, had become

* An old Roman Catholic historian says, "Above all, painters, watchmakers, sculptors, goldsmiths, booksellers, printers, and others, who, from their callings, have some nobility of mind, were among the first easily surprised."—REMOND—*Histoire de l'Heresie de ce Siecle*, book vii., 931.

a follower of the Gospel, and a believer in the religion of the open Bible.*

Palissy returned to France in 1539, at a time when persecution was at the hottest; when printing had been suppressed by royal edict; when the reading of the Bible was prohibited on pain of death, and when many were being burnt alive for reading and believing it. The persecution especially raged in Paris and the neighborhood, which may account for Palissy's avoidance of that city, where an artist so skilled as he was would naturally have desired to settle, and his proceeding to the remote district of Saintonge, in the southwest corner of France. There he married, and began to pursue his manifold callings, more particularly glass-painting, portrait-painting, and land-measuring. He had a long and hard fight for life. His employment was fitful, and he was often reduced to great straits. Some years after his settlement at Saintes, while still struggling with poverty, chance threw in his way an enameled cup of Italian manufacture, of great beauty, which he had no sooner seen than he desired to imitate; and from that time the determination to discover the art by which it was enameled possessed him like a passion.

The story of Palissy's heroic ardor in prosecuting his researches in connection with this subject is well known: how he built furnace after furnace, and made experiments with them again and again, only to end in failure; how he was all the while studying the nature of earths and clays, and learning chemistry, as he described it, "with his teeth;" how he reduced himself to a state of the most distressing poverty, which he endured amid the expostulations of his friends, the

---

* We can not learn from Palissy's writings what his creed was. He never once mentions the names of either Luther or Calvin; but he often refers to the "teachings of the Bible," and "the statutes and ordinances of God as revealed in his Word." Here, for example, is a characteristic passage:

"Je n'ay trouvé rien meilleur que suivre le conseil de Dieu, ses esdits, statuts et ordonnances : et en regardant quel estoit son vouloir, j'ay trouvé que, par testament dernier, il a commandé à ses héritiers qu'ils eussent à manger le pain au labeur de leurs corps, et qu'ils eussent à multiplier les talens qu'ils leur avoit laissez par son testament."—*Recepte Véritable*, 1563.

bitter sarcasms of his neighbors, and, what was still worse to bear, the reproaches of his wife and children. But he was borne up throughout by his indomitable determination, his indefatigable industry, and his irrepressible genius.

On one occasion he sat by his furnace for six successive days and nights without changing his clothes. He made experiment after experiment, and still the enamel did not melt. At his last and most desperate experiment, when the fuel began to run short, he rushed into his house, seized and broke up sundry articles of furniture, and hurled them into the furnace to keep up the heat. No wonder that his wife and children, as well as his neighbors, thought the man had gone mad. Bnt he himself was in a measure compensated by the fact that the last great burst of heat had melted the enamel; for, when the common clay jars, which had been put in brown, were taken out after the furnace had cooled, they were found covered with the white glaze of which he had been so long and so furiously in search. By this time, however, he had become reduced to a state of the greatest poverty. He had stripped his dwelling, he had beggared himself, and his children wanted food. "I was in debt," said he, "at many places, and when two children were at nurse I was unable to pay the nurse's wages. No one helped me. On the contrary, people mocked me, saying, 'He will rather let his children die of hunger than mind his own business.'" Others said of him that he was "seeking to make false money." These jeerings of the town's folk reached his ears as he passed along the streets of Saintes, and cut him to the heart.

Like Brindley the engineer, Palissy betook himself to his bed to meditate upon his troubles, and study how to find a way out of them. "When I had lain for some time in bed," says he, "and considered that if a man has fallen into a ditch his first duty is to try and raise himself out of it, I, being in like case, rose and set to work to paint some pictures, and by this and other means I endeavored to earn a little money.

Then I said to myself that all my losses and risks were over, and there was nothing now to hinder me from making good pieces of ware; and so I began again, as before, to work at my old art."* But he was still very far from success, and continued to labor on for years amid misfortune, privation, and poverty. "All these failures," he continues, "occasioned me such labor and sadness of spirit that before I could render my various enamels fusible at the same degree of heat, I was obliged, as it were, to roast myself to death at the door of the sepulchre; moreover, in laboring at such work, I found myself, in the space of about ten years, so worn out that I was shrunk almost to a skeleton; there was no appearance of muscle on my arms or legs, so that my stockings fell about my feet when I walked abroad."

His neighbors would no longer have patience with him, and he was despised and mocked by all. Yet he persevered with his art, and proceeded to make vessels of divers colors, which he at length began to be able to sell, and thus earned a slender maintenance for his family. "The hope which inspired me," says he, "enabled me to proceed with my work, and when people came to see me I sometimes contrived to entertain them with pleasantry, while I was really sad at heart. . . . Worst of all, the sufferings I had to endure were the mockeries and persecutions of those of my household, who were so unreasonable as to expect me to execute work without the means of doing so. For years my furnaces were without any covering or protection, and while attending to them I have been exposed for nights, at the mercy of the wind and the rain, without any help or consolation, save it might be the meauling of cats on the one side, and the howling of dogs on the other. Sometimes the tempest would beat so furiously against the furnaces that I was compelled to leave them, and seek shelter within doors. Drenched by rain, and in no better plight than if I had been dragged

---

* PALISSY—*De l'Art de Terre:* Œuvres Completes, p. 318.

through mire, I have gone to lie down at midnight, or at daybreak, stumbling into the house without a light, and reeling from one side to another as if I had been drunken, my heart filled with sorrow at the loss of my labor after such long toiling. But, alas! my home proved no refuge for me; for, drenched and besmeared as I was, I found in my chamber a second persecution worse than the first, which makes me even now marvel that I was not utterly consumed by my many sorrows."*

In the midst of his great distress, religion came to Palissy as a consoler. He found comfort in recalling to mind such passages of the Bible as he carried in his memory, and which from time to time gave him fresh hope. "You will thus observe," he afterward wrote, "the goodness of God to me: when I was in the depth of suffering because of my art, He consoled me with His Gospel; and when I have been exposed to trials because of the Gospel, then it has been with my art that He has consoled me." When wandering abroad in the fields about Saintes, at the time of his greatest troubles, Palissy's attention was wont to be diverted from his own sorrows by the wonderful beauty and infinite variety of nature, of which he was a close and accurate observer. What were his petty cares and trials in sight of the marvelous works of God, which spoke in every leaf, and flower, and plant, of His infinite power, and goodness, and wisdom? "When I contemplated these things," says Palissy, "I have fallen upon my face, and, adoring God, cried to Him in spirit, 'What is man, that Thou art mindful of him? Not to us, Lord, not to us, but to Thy name be the honor and the glory.'"†

There were already many followers of the Gospel in Saintes and the adjoining districts. It so happened that Calvin had, at an early period in his life, visited Saintonge, and sowed its seeds there. Calvin was a native of Noyon,

---

* PALISSY—*De l'Art de Terre:* Œuvres Completes, p. 321.
† PALISSY—*Recepte Véritable:* Œuvres Completes, 116–17.

in Picardy, and had from his childhood been destined for the priesthood. When only twelve years old he was provided with a benefice, but by the time he grew to man's estate a relative presented him with a copy of the Bible, and he became a religious reformer. He began, almost involuntarily, to exhort others from its pages, and proceeded to preach to the people at Bourges, at Paris, and in the adjoining districts. From thence he went into Poitou and Saintonge on the same errand, holding his meetings late at night or early in the morning, in retired places—in a cellar or a garret—in a wood or in the opening of a rock in a mountain-side; a hollow place of this sort, near Poitiers, in which Calvin and his friends secretly celebrated the Lord's Supper, being still known as " Calvin's Cave."

We are not informed by Palissy whether he ever met Calvin in the course of his mission in Saintonge, which occurred shortly after the former had settled at Saintes; but certain it is that he was one of the first followers and teachers of the new views in that neighborhood. Though too poor himself to possess a copy of the Bible, Palissy had often heard it read by others as well as read it himself while on his travels, and his retentive memory enabled him to carry many of its most striking passages in his mind,* which he was accustomed to reproduce in his ordinary speech. Hence the style of his early writings, which is strongly marked by Biblical terms and similitudes. He also contrived to obtain many written extracts from the Old and New Testament, for the purpose of reading them to others, and they formed the texts from which he exhorted his fellow Gospellers. For Palissy was one of the earliest preachers of the Reformed Church in the

---

* The Vaudois peasantry knew the Bible almost by heart. Raids were from time to time made into their district by the agents of the Romish Church for the purpose of seizing and burning all such copies of the Bible as they could lay hands on. Knowing this, the peasants formed societies of young persons, each of whom was appointed to preserve in his memory a certain number of chapters; and thus, though their Bibles were seized and burnt, the Vaudois were still enabled to refer to their Bibles through the memories of the young minds in which the chapters were preserved.

town of Saintes, if he was not indeed its founder. In one of his earliest works* he gives an account of the origin of the movement, which is all the more interesting as being that of the principal actor in the transactions which he describes:

"Some time before this," says he, writing of the year 1557, "there was in this town a certain artisan, poor and miserable to the last degree, who had so great a desire for the advancement of the Gospel, that he spoke of it one day to another artisan as poor as himself, and who knew as little of it as he did, for both knew scarcely any thing. Nevertheless, the one urged upon the other that if he would but engage to make some sort of exhortation, great benefit might arise from it; and though this last felt himself to be utterly destitute of knowledge, the advice gave him courage. So, some days later, he drew together one Sunday morning some nine or ten persons, and seeing that he was badly instructed in letters, he had extracted several passages from the Old and New Testament, having put them in writing. And when they had assembled he read to them the passages or authorities, saying, 'Let every one, as he has received good gifts, distribute them to others;' and 'Every tree that beareth not fruit shall be cut down and cast into the fire.' He also read another passage taken from Deuteronomy, wherein it is said, 'Thou shalt proclaim my law when seated in thy house, when walking by the way, when lying down, and when rising up.' He further propounded the parable of the talents, and cited a number of passages, making practical application of them; and urging, first, that to every man appertains the right of speaking of the statutes and ordinances of God, to the end that his Word may not be set at naught, notwithstanding our unworthiness; and, second, that certain of his hearers should be incited to follow his example. Accordingly, they agreed together that six among them should exhort the others in rotation; that is to say, that each should take his turn once in every six weeks, on Sundays only. And as they were undertaking a duty, for the due performance of which they had received no special instruction, it was arranged that they should put their exhortations in writing, and read them to the assembly. Now all these things were done in accordance with the good example, counsel, and doctrine of the worthy Philebert Hamelin.†

---

* PALISSY—*Recepte Véritable, par laquelle tous les hommes de la France pourront apprendres a multiplier et augmenter leur thresois.*—Œuvres Completes, 106–7.

† In a previous part of the treatise (*Recepte Véritable*) in which the above passage occurs, Palissy gives an interesting account of Philebert Hamelin, one of the early martyrs to the Reformed faith in the south of France. Hamelin, like Calvin, had been educated for the priesthood, and, like him, was converted to the new views by reading and studying the Bible. He joined the Calvinist Church at Geneva, where he learned the art of printing, and proceeded to set up a press for the purpose of printing Bibles.

"Such," continues Palissy, "was the beginning of the Reformed Church at Saintes. I am confident that when the members first began to meet they did not number more than five persons. While the church was thus small, and Master Philebert was in prison, there came to us a minister named De la Place, who had been sent to preach at Allevert; but the procureur of Allevert arrived at Saintes on the same day about the matter of the baptism celebrated by Philebert at the former place, on account of which many of the

---

From that time Hamelin went about from place to place throughout France, selling Bibles and other religious books, and every where finding persons ready to help him in his work. The book-hawkers, or *colporteurs*, were among the most active agents of the Reformation. De Felicé, in his *History of the Protestants of France*, says, "They were called bale-bearers, basket or literary carriers. They belonged to different classes of society; many were students in theology, or even ministers of the Gospel. Staff in hand, basket on back, through heat and cold, by lonely ways, through mountain ravines and dreary morasses, they went from door to door, often ill received, always at the hazard of their lives, and not knowing in the morning where to lay their head at night. It was chiefly through them that the Bible penetrated into the manor of the noble as well as the hut of the peasant."

Of such was Philebert Hamelin, who expounded as well as sold the Bible. He frequently visited the town of Saintes, where he had several friends and disciples, of whom Palissy was one. Though feeble in frame, and suffering from ill health, Hamelin made all his journeys on foot. Friends offered to lend him their horses to ride on; but he preferred walking alone and unarmed, merely with a staff in his hand, and thus he traveled into all parts without fear.

At Hamelin's last visit to Saintes, some seven or eight of his friends received him, and after praying with them and counseling them to meet and exhort one another frequently, he set out on foot for Allevert. There he publicly preached to many people. He also publicly baptized an infant. This latter circumstance having come to the ears of the Bishop of Saintes, he required the magistrates immediately to pursue and apprehend Hamelin, who was shortly after taken at the house of a gentleman, and, to Palissy's horror and indignation, lodged in the common jail with thieves and malefactors. "He was so perfect in his walk," says Palissy, "that even his enemies themselves were constrained to acknowledge, though not approving of his doctrine, that his was a most pure and holy life. I am, indeed, quite amazed that any men should have dared to pronounce sentence of death upon him, seeing that they well knew, for they had heard, his godly conversation. No sooner was I informed of his imprisonment than I had the hardihood (perilous though the times then were!) to go and remonstrate with six of the principal judges and magistrates of the town of Saintes, that they had put in prison a prophet, an angel of God, sent to proclaim His message and the judgment of condemnation to men in these latter times, assuring them that during the eleven years I had known the said Philebert Hamelin he was of so pure and holy a way of life that it seemed to me that other men were altogether wicked compared with him."—*Recepte Véritable*, 106.

Palissy's remonstrances, made at the peril of his own life, were, however, of no avail. Hamelin was sent to Bordeaux in the custody of the provost-marshal. There he was tried for the fatal crime of heresy, sentenced to death, and—to use Palissy's words—"hanged like a common thief."

persons there present were liable to heavy penalties. This was the occasion of our taking the said De la Place to administer to us the Word of God, and he remained with us until Monsieur de la Boissiere came, who is our minister at the present time.* But ours is indeed a pitiable case, for, although we have a good will, we have not the means of supporting ministers. De la Place, during the time he was with us, was principally maintained at the expense of gentlefolks, who often kept him at their houses; but fearing that our ministers might thereby be corrupted, Monsieur de la Boissiere was desired not to leave the town at the instance of the gentry, without leave, excepting in cases of emergency. Such being the case, the poor man was as closely confined as any prisoner; very often he had to eat apples and drink water for his dinner, and to use his chemise in lieu of a table-cloth; for there were very few people of any means who belonged to our little congregation, and we had not wherewithal to pay him his stipend. . . . .

"Thus was the church first set up among us by a few poor and despised people, with great difficulty, and amid many perils. Great was the detraction we had to encounter from wicked and perverse calumniators. Some said if our doctrines were good we ought to preach them in public. Others alleged that we met in secret merely for purposes of wantonness, and that at our meetings the women were in common. Again, notwithstanding these unfounded scandals, God prospered our efforts so much, that although our assemblies were for the most part held at midnight, and our enemies heard us passing along the streets, God kept them bridled in such sort that we were preserved for a time under His protection. And when God willed that his Church should at length make a public manifestation in open day, then was a great work done in our town; for though two of our principal men, who went to Toulouse, were unable to obtain permission for us to hold our assemblies in public, we nevertheless had the courage to take the market-house for the purpose."†

The meetings of the little congregation soon became more popular in Saintes. The people of the town went at first out of curiosity to observe their proceedings, and were gradually attracted by the earnestness of the worshipers. The members of "The Religion" were known throughout the town to be persons of blameless lives, peaceable, well-disposed, and industrious, who commanded the respect even of their ene-

* The *Recepte Véritable*, in which Palissy gives this account, is supposed to have been written by him in prison at Bordeaux, where he was confined for the crime of heresy, as will be hereafter explained, in the year 1559–60. The treatise was printed at La Rochelle in 1563.
† *Recepte Véritable*, 106–9.

mies. At length the Roman Catholics of Saintes began to say to their monks and priests, "See these ministers of the new religion; they make prayers; they lead a holy life; why can not you do the like?" The monks and priests, not to be outdone by the men of The Religion, then began to pray and to preach like the ministers; "so that in those days," to use the words of Palissy, "there were prayers daily in this town, both on one side and the other." So kindly a spirit began to spring up under the operation of these influences, that the religious exercises of both parties—of the old and the new religion—were for a short time celebrated in some of the churches by turns; one portion of the people attending the prayers of the old church, and another portion the preaching of the new; so that the Catholics, returning from celebrating the mass, were accustomed to meet the Huguenots on their way to hear the exhortation,* as is usual in Holland at this day. The effects of this joint religious action on the morals of the people are best described in Palissy's own words:

"The progress made by us was such, that in the course of a few years, by the time that our enemies rose up to pillage and persecute us, lewd plays, dances, ballads, gormandizings, and superfluities of dress and head-gear, had almost entirely ceased. Scarcely was any bad language to be heard on any side, nor were there any more crimes and scandals. Lawsuits greatly diminished; for no sooner had any two persons of The Religion fallen out, than means were found to bring them to an agreement; moreover, very often, before beginning any lawsuit, the one would not begin it before first exhorting the other. When the time for celebrating Easter drew near, many differences, discussions, and quarrels were thus stayed and settled. There were then no questions among them, but only psalms, prayers, and spiritual canticles;† nor was there any more desire for lewd and dissolute songs.

---

* ALFRED DUMESNIL—*Bernard Palissy, Le Potier de Terre*; Paris, Gressart, p. 120.

† The Reformers early enlisted music in their service, and it exercised a powerful influence in extending the new movement among the people. "Music," said Luther, "is the art of the prophets. It is one of the most magnificent and delightful presents that God has given us. Satan can not make head against music." Luther was a poet as well as a musician; his *Ein' feste Burg ist unser Gott* (one of the themes of Meyerbeer's *Huguenots*), which rang through all Germany, was the "Marseillaise" of the Reformation.

Indeed, The Religion made such progress, that even the magistrates began to prohibit things that had grown up under their authority. Thus they forbade inn-keepers to permit gambling or dissipation to be carried on within their premises, to the enticement of men away from their own homes and families.

"In those days might be seen, on Sundays, bands of work-people walking abroad in the meadows, the groves, and the fields, singing psalms and spiritual songs, or reading to and instructing one another. There might also be seen girls and maidens seated in groups in the gardens and pleasant places, singing songs on sacred themes; or boys accompanied by their teachers, the effects of whose instruction had already been so salutary, that those young persons not only exhibited a manly bearing, but a manful steadfastness of conduct. Indeed, these various influences, working one with another, had already effected so much good, that not only had the habits and modes of life of the people been reformed, but their very countenances themselves seemed to be changed and improved."*

But this happy state of affairs did not last long. While the ministers of the new religion and priests of the old (with a few exceptions) were working thus harmoniously together at Saintes, events were rapidly drawing to a crisis in other parts of France. The heads of the Roman Catholic Church saw with alarm the rapid strides which the new religion was making, and that a large proportion of the population were day by day escaping from their control. Pope Pius IV., through his agents, urged the decisive interference of the

Luther had improved both the words and the music two days before his appearance at the Diet of Worms. As he was journeying toward that city, he caught sight of its bell-towers in the distance, on which he rose up in his chariot and sang the noble song.

The French Reformers also enlisted music in their service at an early period. The psalms were translated by Clement Marot and Theodore de Beza, set to attractive music, and sung in harmony in family worship, in the streets and fields, and in congregational meetings. During a lull in the persecution at Paris in 1558, thousands of persons assembled at the Pré-aux-Clercs to listen to the psalms sung by the men of "The Religion" as they marched along. But when the persecution revived, the singing of psalms was one of the things most strictly interdicted, even on pain of death.

Calvin also, at Geneva, took great care to have the psalms set to good music. He employed, with that object, the best composers, and distributed printed copies of the music throughout all the churches. Thus psalmody, in which the whole people could join, every where became an essential part of the service of the Reformed Church; the chants of the Roman Catholics having, until then, been sung only by the priests or by hired performers.

* PALISSY—Œuvres Complètes: *Recepte Véritable*, 108.

secular authority to stay the progress of heresy; and Philip II. of Spain supported him with all his influence. The Huguenots had, by virtue of their increasing numbers, become a political power; and many of the leading politicians of France embraced the Reformed cause, not because they were impressed by the truth of the new views, but because they were capable of being used as an instrument for party warfare. Ambitious men, opposed to the court party, arrayed themselves on the side of the Huguenots, caring perhaps little for their principles, but mainly actuated by the desire of promoting their own personal ends. Thus political and religious dissension combined together to fan the fury of the contending parties into a flame; the councils of state became divided and distracted; there was no controlling mediating power; the extreme partisans were alike uncompromising; and the social outbreak, long imminent, at length took place. The head of the Church in France alarmed the king with fears for his throne and his life. "If the secular arm," said the Cardinal de Lorraine to Henry II., "fails in its duty, all the malcontents will throw themselves into this detestable sect. They will first destroy the ecclesiastical power, after which it will be the turn of the royal power." The secular arm was not slow to strike. In 1559, a royal edict was published declaring the crime of heresy punishable by death, and forbidding the judges to remit or mitigate the penalty. The fires of persecution, which had long been smouldering, again burst forth all over France. The provincial Parliament instituted *Chambres ardentes*, so called because they condemned to the fire all who were accused and convicted of the crime of heresy. Palissy himself has vividly narrated the effect of these relentless measures in his own district of Saintes:

"The very thought of the evil deeds of those days," says he, "when wicked men were let loose upon us to scatter, overwhelm, ruin, and destroy the followers of the Reformed faith, fills my mind with horror. That I might be out of the way of their frightful and execrable tyrannies, and in order not to be a witness of the cruelties, robberies, and murders perpetrated in this rural neighborhood, I concealed myself at home, remaining there for the space of two months. It seemed to me as if during that time hell itself had broken loose, and that raging devils had entered into and taken possession of the town of Saintes. For in the place where I had shortly before heard only psalms and spiritual songs, and exhortations to pure and honest living, I now heard nothing but blasphemies, assaults, threatenings, tumults, abominable language, dissoluteness, and lewd and disgusting songs, of such sort that it seemed to me as if all purity and godliness had become completely stifled and extinguished. Among other horrors of the time, there issued forth from the Castle of Taillebourg a band of wicked imps who worked more mischief even than any of the devils of the old school. On their entering the town accompanied by certain priests, with drawn swords in their hands, they shouted, 'Where are they? let us cut their throats instantly!' though they knew well enough that there was no resistance to them, those of the Reformed Church having all taken to flight. To make matters worse, they met an innocent Parisian in the street, reported to have money about him, and him they set upon and killed without resistance, first stripping him to his shirt before putting him to death. Afterward they went from house to house, stealing, plundering, robbing, gormandizing, mocking, swearing, and uttering foul blasphemies both against God and man."*

During the two months that Palissy remained secluded at home, he busily occupied himself in perfecting the secret of the enamel, after which he had been so long in search. For, notwithstanding his devotion to the exercises of his religion, he continued to devote himself with no less zeal to the practice of his art; and his fame as a potter already extended beyond the bounds of his district. He had, indeed, been so fortunate as by this time to attract the notice of a powerful noble, the Duke of Montmorency, Constable of France, then engaged in building the magnificent château of Ecouen, at St. Denis, near Paris. Specimens of Palissy's enameled tiles had been brought under the duke's notice, who admired them so much that he at once gave Palissy an order to execute the pavement for his new residence. He even advanced a sum of money to the potter, to enable him to enlarge his works, so as to complete the order with dispatch.

Palissy's opinions were of course well known in his dis-

* PALISSY—Œuvres Completes: *Recepte Veritable*, 111.

trict, where he had been the founder, and was in a measure the leader, of the Reformed sect. The duke was doubtless informed of the danger which his potter ran on the outbreak of the persecution, and accordingly used his influence to obtain a safeguard for him from the Duke of Montpensier, who then commanded the royal army in Saintonge. But even this protection was insufficient; for, as the persecution waxed hotter, and the search for heretics became keener, Palissy found his workshop no longer safe. At length he was seized, dragged from his home, and hurried off by night to Bordeaux, to be put upon his trial for the crime of heresy. And this first great potter of France — this true man of genius, religion, and virtue—would certainly have been tried and burnt, as hundreds more were, but for the accidental circumstance that the Duke of Montmorency was in urgent want of enameled tiles for his castle floor, and that Palissy was the only man in France capable of executing them.

In the epistle dedicatory to the *Recepte Véritable*, Palissy, addressing the duke, says, with much apparent simplicity, "I assure you, in all truth, that my enemies have really no cause against me, except that I have many times shown them certain passages of Scripture, wherein it is written that he is miserable and accursed who drinks the milk, and clothes himself with the wool of the flock, but gives them no pasture. And although my doing so ought to have incited them to love me, it only had the effort of inducing them to destroy me as a malefactor."* It is not improbable that the

* In his prefatory address to "the reader" he also says: "Je voudrois prier la noblesse de France, ausquels le pourtrait pourroit beaucoup seruir, qu' après que j'auray employé mon temps pour leur faire service, qu'ils leur plaise ne me rendre mal pour bien, comme ont fait les Ecclesiastiques Romains de cette ville, lesquels m'ont voulu faire pendre pour leur avoir pourchassé le plus grand bien que iamais leur pourroit aduenir, qui est pour les avoir voulu inciter à paistre leur troupeaux suivant le commandement de Dieu. Et sauroit-on dire que iamais ie leur eusse fait aucun tort? Mais parce que ie leur auois remonstré leur perdition au dixhuitième de l'Apocalypse, tendant à fin de une authorité escrite au prophete Ieremie, où il dit: Malediction sur vous, Pasteurs, qui mangez le lait et vestissez la laine, et laissez mes brebis esparses par les montagnes! Ic les redemanderay de nostre main. Eux voyans telle chose, au lieu de s'amender, ils se sont endur-

sending of Palissy to Bordeaux, to be tried there instead of at Saintes, was a ruse on the part of the Duke of Montpensier, to gain time until the Constable could be informed of the danger which threatened the life of his potter; for Palissy adds, "It is a certain truth that, had I been tried by the judges of Saintes, they would have caused me to die before I could have obtained from you any help." He proceeds:

"I would have taken very good care not to have fallen into the sanguinary hands of my enemies, had it not been that I relied upon their having respect for your work on which I was engaged, as well as on the protection of my lord the Duke of Montpensier, who gave me a safeguard, prohibiting them from taking notice of or interfering with me, or with my house, well knowing, as he did, that no one could execute your tiles but myself. So, being in their hands a prisoner, the Seigneur de Burie, the Seigneur de Jarnac, and the Seigneur de Ponts made every effort toward my deliverance, in order that your work might be completed. Nevertheless, my enemies sent me by night to Bordeaux by roundabout roads, having no regard either for your dignity or your desires. This I found very strange, seeing that the Count Rochefoucauld, although for the time he took the part of your adversaries, nevertheless felt so much pride in your honor that he did not wish any other work than yours to be proceeded with in my pottery, because of your commands; while my persecutors, on the contrary, had no sooner made me prisoner than they broke into my workshop and made a public place of part thereof, for they had come to a resolution in the Maison de Ville to raze my work to the ground, though it had been partly erected at your expense; and this resolution they would have carried out had it not been that the Seigneur de Ponts and his lady entreated the aforesaid persons not to commit such an outrage. I have set down all these things in writing in order that you may see that I was not committed to prison as a thief or a murderer. I know that you will bear these things in remembrance both as to time and place, seeing that your work must cost you much more than it otherwise would have done, through the injury you have sustained in my person; nevertheless I hope that, following the counsel of God, you will render good for evil, which is my desire, while for my part I will en-

---

cis, et se sont bandez contre la lumière, à fin de cheminer le surplus de leurs iours en tenebres, et ensuyvans leurs voluptez et desirs charnels accoustumez. Ie n'eusse iamais pensé que par là ils eussent voulu prendre occasion de me faire mourir. Dieu m'est temoin que le mal qu'ils m'ont fait n'a esté pour autre occasion que pour la susdite. Ce neantmoins, ie prie Dieu qu'ils les veuille amender."—*Preface*, p. 11, 12.

deavor to the best of my power to repay the many benefits which you have been pleased to confer upon me."*

To return to the narrative. No sooner did Montmorency hear of the peril into which his potter had fallen, and find that unless he bestirred himself Palissy would be burnt and his tiles for Ecouen remain unfinished, than he at once used his influence with Catharine de Medicis, the queen-mother, with whom he was then all-powerful, and had him forthwith appointed "Inventor of Rustic Figulines to the King." This appointment had the immediate effect of withdrawing Palissy from the jurisdiction of the Parliament of Bordeaux, and transferring him to that of the Grand Council of Paris, which was tantamount to an indefinite adjournment of his case. The now royal potter was accordingly released from prison, and returned to Saintes to find his workshop roofless and devastated. He at once made arrangements for leaving the place; and, shaking the dust of Saintes from his feet, he shortly after removed to the Tuileries† at Paris, where he long continued to carry on the manufacture of his famous pottery.

It is not necessary to pursue the career of Palissy farther than to add that the circumstance of his being employed by the bigoted Catharine de Medicis had not the slightest effect in inducing him to change his religion. He remained a Huguenot, and stoutly maintained his opinions to the last—so stoutly, indeed, that toward the close of his life, when an old man of seventy-eight, he was again arrested as a heretic and imprisoned in the Bastile. He was threatened with death unless he recanted. But, though he was feeble, and trembling on the verge of the grave, his spirit was as brave as ever. He was as obstinate now in holding to his religion as he had been more than thirty years before in hunting out

---

* Preface to *Recepte Véritable*, addressed by Palissy to "Monseigneur le Duc de Montmorency, Pair et Connestable de France."
† Tuileries—so called from the tile-works originally established there by Francis I. in 1518.

the secret of the enamel. Mathieu de Launay, minister of state, one of the sixteen members of council, insisted that Palissy should be publicly burnt; but the Duc de Mayenne, who protected him, contrived to protract the proceedings and delay the sentence.

The French historian D'Aubigné, in his *Universal History*, describes Henry III. as visiting Palissy in person, with the object of inducing him to abjure his faith. "My good man," said the king, " you have now served my mother and myself for forty-five years. We have put up with your adhering to your religion amid fires and massacres. But now I am so pressed by the Guise party, as well as by my own people, that I am constrained to leave you in the hands of your enemies, and to-morrow you will be burnt unless you become converted." "Sire," answered the unconquerable old man, "I am ready to give my life for the glory of God. You have said many times that you have pity on me; now I have pity on you, who have pronounced the words 'I am constrained.' It is not spoken like a king, sire ; it is what you, and those who constrain you, the Guisards and all your people, can never effect upon me, for I know how to die."

Palissy was not burnt, but died in the Bastile, after about a year's imprisonment, courageously persevering to the end, and glorying in being able to lay down his life for his faith. Thus died a man of truly great and noble character, of irrepressible genius, indefatigable industry, heroic endurance, and inflexible rectitude — one of France's greatest and noblest sons.

D

CHAPTER III.

PERSECUTIONS OF THE REFORMED IN FRANCE AND FLANDERS.

PALISSY was not the only man of genius in France who embraced the Reformed faith. The tendency of books and the Bible was to stimulate inquiry on the part of all who studied them; to extend the reign of thought, and emancipate the mind from the dominion of mere human authority. Hence we find such men as Peter Ramus and Joseph Justus Scaliger, the philosophers; Charles Dumoulin, the jurist; Ambrose Paré, the surgeon; Henry Stephens (or Estienne), the printer and scholar;* Jean Goujon, the sculptor; Charles Goudimel, the musical composer; and Oliver de Serre, the agriculturist, were all Protestants. These were among the very first men of their time in France.

Persecution did not check the spread of the new views; on the contrary, it extended them. The spectacle of men and women publicly suffering death for their faith, expiring under the most cruel tortures rather than deny their convictions, attracted the attention even of the incredulous. Their curiosity was roused; they desired to learn what there was in the forbidden Bible to inspire such constancy and endurance; and they too read the book, and in many cases became followers of The Religion.

Thus the new views spread rapidly all over France. They not only became established in all the large towns, but penetrated the rural districts, more especially in the south and

---

* The Stephenses, being threatened with persecution by the Sorbonne because of the editions of the Bible and New Testament printed by them, were under the necessity of leaving Paris for Geneva, where they settled, and a long succession of illustrious scholars and printers handed down the reputation of the family.

southeast of France. The social misery which pervaded those districts doubtless helped the spread of the new doctrines among the lower classes; for "there was even more discontent abroad," said Brantome, "than Huguenotism." But they also extended among the learned and the wealthy. The heads of the house of Bourbon, Antoine, duke of Vendôme, and Louis, prince of Condé, declared themselves in favor of the new views. The former became the husband of the celebrated Jeanne D'Albret, queen of Navarre, daughter of the Protestant Margaret of Valois, and the latter became the recognized leader of the Huguenots. The head of the Coligny family took the same side. The Montmorencies were divided; the Constable halting between the two opinions, waiting to see which should prove the stronger; while others of the family openly sided with the Reformed. Indeed it seemed at one time as if France were on the brink of becoming Protestant. In 1561 the alarmed Cardinal de Sainte-Croix wrote to the Pope, "The kingdom is already half Huguenot."

When Charles IX. succeeded to the throne in 1560, he was a boy only ten years old, and entirely under the control of Catharine de Medicis, his mother. The finances of the kingdom were found to be in a deplorable state, and the public purse was almost empty. Society was distracted by the feuds of the nobles, over whom, as in Scotland about the same period, the monarch exercised no effective control.

France had, however, her Parliament or States-General, which in a measure placed the king's government *en rapport* with the nation. On its assembling in December, 1560, the Chancellor de L'Hôpital exhorted men of all parties to rally round the young king; and, while condemning the odious punishments which had recently been inflicted on persons of the Reformed faith, he announced the intended holding of a national council, and expressed the desire that thenceforward France should recognize neither Huguenots nor Papists, but only Frenchmen.

This was the first utterance of the voice of conciliation. The Protestants heard it with joy, their enemies with rage. Jean Quintin, the representative of the clergy, demanded that measures should be taken to deliver France from heresy, and that Charles IX. should vindicate his claim to the title of "Most Christian King." Lange, the spokesman of the Tiers Etat, on the other hand, declared against "the three principal vices of the ecclesiastics—pride, avarice, and ignorance," and urged that they should return to the simplicity of the primitive Church. The nobles, divided among themselves, demanded, some that the preaching of the Gospel should be forbidden, and others that there should be general freedom of worship; but all who spoke were unanimous in acknowledging the necessity for a reform in the discipline of the Church.*

While the state of religion thus occupied the deputies, an equally grave question occupied the court. There was no money in the exchequer; the rate of interest was twelve per cent., and forty-three millions of francs were required to be raised from an impoverished nation. The deputies were alarmed at the appalling figure which the chancellor specified, and, declaring that they had not the requisite power to vote the required sum, they broke up amid agitation, leaving De L'Hôpital at variance with the Parliament, which refused to register the edict of amnesty to the Protestants which the king had proclaimed.

The king's minister was, however, desirous of bringing all parties to an agreement, if possible, and especially of allaying the civil discord which seemed to be fast precipitating France into civil war. He accordingly, with the sanction of the queen-mother, arranged for a conference between the heads of the religious parties, which took place at Vassy, in the presence of the king and his court, in August, 1561. Pope Pius IV. was greatly exasperated when informed of the intended conference, and declared himself to have been betray-

* PUAUX—*Histoire de la Réformation Française*, ii., 82.

ed by Catharine de Medicis.* The granting of such a conference was a recognition of the growing power of heresy in France—the same heresy which had already deprived Rome of her dominion over the mind of England and half Germany. The Pope's fears were, doubtless, not without foundation; and had France at that juncture possessed a Knox or a Luther — a Regent Murray or a Lord Burleigh — the results would have been widely different. But as it was, the Reformed party had no better leader than the scholarly and pious Theodore de Beza; and the conference had no other result than to drive the contending parties more widely asunder than before.

Although a royal edict was published in January, 1562, guaranteeing to the Protestants liberty of worship, the concession was set at defiance by the Papal party, whose leaders urged on the people in many districts to molest and attack

* PUAUX (ii., 98) quotes a remarkable letter written at this time by Catharine de Medicis to the Pope, defending herself for having sanctioned the conference, and urging the necessity for a reform in the Church. "The number of those who have separated themselves from the Roman Church," she said, "is so great that they can no longer be restrained by severity of law or force of arms. They have become so powerful by reason of the nobles and magistrates who have joined the party, they are so firmly united, and daily acquire such strength, that they are becoming more and more formidable in all parts of the kingdom. In the mean time, by the grace of God, there are among them neither Anabaptists nor libertines, nor any partisans of odious opinions. All admit the twelve articles of the Creed as they have been explained by Pius III. and the œcumenical councils. Thus many of the most zealous Catholics believe that it is not necessary to curtail the communion of the Church, although they think differently on other points, wherein they consider change may be tolerated, and which might be a step toward the reunion of the Greek with the Latin Church. Many persons of great piety indulge the hope that if they can terminate in some such manner the differences of religion, God, who always helps his people, will dissipate the darkness, and make his light and truth to shine in the eyes of all men." The queen-mother farther proceeded to specify the abuses which had crept into public worship in the Church, and requested the Pope to banish the use of the Latin tongue. "If the people do not understand what is said," she observed, with much reason, "how can they intelligently respond with the 'Amen' or 'Ainsi soit-il?'" The Pope concealed his indignation on receipt of this letter, but dispatched as his legate to Paris the Cardinal de Ferrara, of infamous origin, grandson of Roderic Borgia, and son of Roderic's daughter Lucretia. The papal legate had usually been welcomed at Paris by the ringing of all the church-bells, but on this occasion it was matter of general remark that the bells were mute.

the followers of the new faith. The Papists denounced the heretics, and called upon the government to extirpate them; the Huguenots, on their part, denounced the corruptions of the Church, and demanded their reform. There was no dominant or controlling power in the state, which drifted steadily in the direction of civil war. Both parties began to arm; and in such a state of things a spark may kindle a conflagration. The queen-mother, though inclining to the side of the Reformed, did not yet dare to take a side; but she sounded Coligny as to the number of followers that he could, in event of need, place at the service of the king. His answer was, "We have two thousand and fifty churches, and four hundred thousand men able to bear arms, without taking into account our secret adherents.* Such was the critical state of affairs when matters were precipitated to an issue by the action of the Duke of Guise, the leader of the Catholic party.

On Christmas day, 1562, the Protestants of Vassy, in Champagne, met to the number of about three thousand, to listen to the preaching of the Word, and to celebrate the sacrament according to the practice of their Church. Vassy was one of the possessions of the Guises, the mother of whom, Antoinette de Bourbon, an ardent Roman Catholic, could not brook the idea of the vassals of the family daring to profess a faith different from that of their feudal superior. Complaint had been made to her grace, by the Bishop of Châlons, of the offense done to religion by the proceedings of the people of Vassy, and she threatened them, if they persisted in their proceedings, with the vengeance of her son, the Duke of Guise.

Undismayed by this threat, the Protestants of Vassy continued to meet publicly and listen to their preachers, believing themselves to be under the protection of the law, according to the terms of the royal edict. On the 1st of March, 1563, they held one of their meetings, at which about

* *Mémoires de Conde.* ii., 587.

twelve hundred persons were present in a large barn which served for a church. The day before, the Duke of Guise, accompanied by the duchess his wife, the Cardinal of Guise, and about two hundred men armed with arquebuses and poniards, set out for Vassy. They rested during the night at Dampmarten, and next morning marched direct upon the congregation assembled in the barn. The minister, Morel, had only begun his opening prayer, when two shots were fired at the persons on the platform. The congregation tried in vain to shut the doors; the followers of the Duke of Guise burst in, and precipitated themselves on the unarmed men, women, and children. For an hour they fired, hacked, and stabbed among them, the duke coolly watching the carnage. Sixty persons of both sexes were left dead on the spot, more than two hundred were severely wounded, and the rest contrived to escape. After the massacre the duke sent for the local judge, and severely reprimanded him for having permitted the Huguenots of Vassy thus to meet. The judge intrenched himself behind the edict of the king. The duke's eyes flashed with rage, and, striking the hilt of his sword with his hand, he said, "The sharp edge of this will soon cut your edict to pieces."[*]

The massacre of Vassy was the match applied to the charge which was now ready to explode. It was the signal to Catholic France to rise in mass against the Huguenots. The clergy glorified the deed from the pulpit, and compared the duke to Moses, in ordering the extermination of all who had bowed the knee to the golden calf. A fortnight later the duke entered Paris in triumph, followed by about twelve hundred noblemen and gentlemen, mounted on horses richly caparisoned. The provost of merchants went out to meet and welcome him at the Porte Saint-Denis, and the people received him with immense acclamations as the defender of the faith and the savior of the country.

Theodore de Beza, overwhelmed with grief, waited on his

[*] DAVILA—*Histoire des Guerres Civiles de France*, liv. ii., p. 379.

majesty to complain of the gross violation of the terms of the royal edict of which the Guise party had been guilty. But the king and the queen-mother were powerless amid the whirlwind of excitement which prevailed throughout Paris. They felt that their own lives were not safe, and they at once secretly departed for Fontainebleau. The Duke of Guise followed them, accompanied by a strong escort. Arrived there, and admitted to an interview, the duke represented to Catharine that, in order to prevent the Huguenots obtaining possession of the king's person, it was necessary that he should accompany them to Melun, but the queen-mother might remain if she chose. She determined to accompany her son. After a brief stay at Vincennes, the court was again installed in the Louvre on the 6th of April. The queen-mother was vanquished.

The court waverers and the waiters on fortune at once arrayed themselves on the side of the strong. The old Constable de Montmorency, who had been halting between the two opinions, signalized his readherence to the Church of Rome by a characteristic act. Placing himself at the head of the mob, whose idol he was ambitious to be, he led them to the storming of the Protestant church outside the Porte Saint-Jacques, called the "Temple of Jerusalem." Bursting in the doors of the empty place, they tore up the seats, and, placing them and the Bibles in a pile upon the floor, they set the whole on fire, amid great acclamations. After this exploit the Constable made a sort of triumphal entry into Paris, as if he had won some great battle. Not content, he set out on the same day to gather more laurels at the village of Popincourt, where he had the Protestant church there set on fire; but the conflagration extending to the adjoining houses, many of them were also burnt down. For these two great exploits, however, the Constable, if we except the acclamations of the mob, received no other acknowledgment than the nickname of "Captain Burnbenches!"*

* *Mémoires de Condé*, iii., p. 187.

More appalling, however, than the burning of churches, were the massacres which followed that of Vassy all over France—at Paris, at Senlis, at Amiens, at Meaux, at Châlons, at Troyes, at Bar-sur-Seine, at Epernay, at Nevers, at Mans, at Angers, at Blois, and many other places. At Tours the number of the slain was so great that the banks of the Loire were almost covered with the corpses of men, women, and children. The persecution especially raged in Provence, where the Protestants were put to death after being subjected to a great variety of tortures.* Any detail of these events would present only a hideous monotony of massacre. We therefore pass them by.

The Huguenots, taken unawares, were at first unable to make head against their enemies. But the Prince of Condé took the field, and numbers at once rallied to his standard. Admiral Coligny at first refused to join them, but, yielding to the entreaties of his wife, he at length placed himself by the side of Condé. A period of fierce civil war ensued, in which the worst passions were evoked on both sides, and frightful cruelties were perpetrated, to the shame of religion, in whose name these things were done. The Huguenots revenged themselves on the assassins of their co-religionists by defacing and destroying the churches and monasteries. In their iconoclastic rage they hewed and broke the images, the carvings, and the richly-decorated work of the cathedrals at Bourges, at Lyons, at Orleans, at Rouen, at Caen, at Tours, and many other places. They tore down the crucifixes, and dragged them through the mud of the streets. They violated the tombs alike of saints and sovereigns, and profaned the shrines which were the most sacred in the eyes of the Roman Catholics. "It was," says Henri Martin, "as if a blast of the infernal trumpet had every where awakened

---

* PUAUX, ii., p. 152. This writer says that although the massacre of Saint Bartholomew is usually cited as the culminating horror of the time, the real Saint Bartholomew was not that of 1572, but of 1562—which year contains by far the most dolorous chapter in the history of French Protestantism.

the spirit of destruction, and the delirious fury grew and became drunk with its own excess." All this rage, however, was but the inevitable reaction against the hideous cruelties of which the Huguenots had so long been merely the passive victims. They decapitated beautiful statues of stone, it is true, but the Guises had decapitated the living men.

It is not necessary, in our rapid sketch, to follow the course of the civil war. The Huguenots were every where outnumbered. They fought bravely, but they fought as rebels, the king and the queen-mother being now at the head of the Guise party. In nearly all the great battles fought by them, they were defeated—at Dreux,* at St. Denis, at Jarnac, and at Montcontour. But they always rallied again, sometimes in greater numbers than before; and at length Coligny was enabled to collect such re-enforcements as seriously to threaten Paris. France had now been devastated throughout by the contending armies, and many of the provinces were reduced almost to a state of desert. The combatants on both sides were exhausted, though their rancor remained unabated. Peace, however, had at last become a necessity; and a treaty was signed at St. Germain's in 1570, by which the Protestants were guaranteed liberty of worship, equality before the law, and admission to the universities, while the four principal towns of Rochelle, Montauban, Cognac, and La Charité were committed to them as a pledge of safety. Under the terms of this treaty France enjoyed a state of quiet for about two years, but it was only the quiet that preceded the outbreak of another storm.

At the famous Council of Trent, which met in 1545, and

* This was nearly a drawn battle; and that it was decided in favor of the Guise party was almost entirely due to the Swiss infantry, who alone resisted the shock of Condé's cavalry. When Condé and Coligny withdrew their forces in good order, 8000 men lay dead on the field. Montluc, one of the Guise generals, says, in his Commentaries, "If this battle had been lost, what would have become of France? Its government would have been changed as well as its religion, for with a young king parties can do what they will." When the news of the victory reached the Council of Trent, then sitting, it occasioned the prelates as much joy as when they had heard of the death of Luther.

MEETING OF CATHARINE AND ALVA.

continued its sittings for sixteen years, during which the events thus rapidly described were in progress, the laws of the Roman Catholic Church were carefully codified, and measures were devised for the more effectual suppression of heresy wherever it showed itself. Shortly after the close of the council sittings, an interview took place at Bidassoa, on the frontier of Spain, between Catharine de Medicis, the queen-mother, and the Duke of Alva, the powerful minister of Philip II. of Spain, of sinister augury for the Protestants. When Philip succeeded to the throne of his father, Charles V., he inherited from him two passions—hatred of the Reformed Church, and jealousy of France. To destroy the one and humiliate the other constituted the ambition of his life; and to accomplish both objects, he spared neither the gold of the New World nor the blood of his subjects. His first desire, however, was to crush Protestantism; and it was to devise measures with that object that the meeting between his favorite minister and Catharine de Medicis took place at Bidassoa.

The queen-mother had by this time gone entirely round to the Guise party, and she had carried Charles IX., her son, with her. She had become equally desirous with the Duke of Alva to destroy heresy; but while the Duke urged extermination of the Huguenots,[*] in accomplishing which he promised the help of a Spanish army, Catharine, on the contrary, was in favor of temporizing with them. It might be easy for Philip to extirpate heresy by force in Spain or Italy, where the Protestants were few in number; but the case was different in France, where the Huguenots had shown themselves able to bring large armies into the field, led by veteran generals, and actually held in possession many of the strongest places in France. She assured the duke, nevertheless, of her ardent desire to effect the ruin of the Reformed

---

[*] The saying of the Duke of Alva is said to have alarmed the queen-mother. "Better," he said, "a head of salmon than ten thousand heads of frogs."

party, her only difficulty consisting in the means by which it was to be accomplished.*

Shortly before this time there had risen up in the bosom of the old Church a man in all respects as remarkable as Luther, who exercised as extraordinary an influence, though in precisely the opposite direction, on the religious history of Europe. This was Ignatius Loyola, the founder of the Jesuits, who infused into his followers a degree of zeal, energy, devotion, and, it must be added, unscrupulousness—stopping not to consider the means, provided the ends could be compassed—which told most powerfully in the struggle of Protestantism for life or death throughout Northern Europe.

Loyola was born in 1491; he was wounded at the siege of Pampeluna in 1520; after a period of meditation and mortification, he devoted himself, in 1522, to the service of the Church; and in 1540, the Order of the Jesuits was recognized at Rome and established by papal bull. The society early took root in France, where it was introduced by the Cardinal de Lorraine; and it shortly acquired almost supreme influence in the state. Under the Jesuits, the Romish Church, reorganized and redisciplined, became one of the most complete of spiritual machines. They enjoined implicit submission and obedience. Against liberty they set up authority. To them the individual was nothing, the Order every thing. They were vigilant sentinels, watching night and day over the interests of Rome. One of the first works to which they applied themselves was the extirpation of the heretics who had strayed from her fold. The principal instrument which they employed with this object was the Inquisition; and wherever they succeeded in establishing themselves, that institution was set up, or was armed with fresh powers. They tolerated no half measures. They were unsparing and unpitying; and wherever a heretic was brought before them, and they had the power to deal with him, he must recant or die.

* PUAUX, ii., p. 228.

The first great field in which the Jesuits put forth their new-born strength was Flanders, which then formed part of the possessions of Spain. The provinces of the Netherlands had reached the summit of commercial and manufacturing prosperity. They were inhabited by a hard-working, intelligent, and enterprising people—great as artists and merchants, painters and printers, architects and iron-workers—as the decayed glories of Antwerp, Bruges, and Ghent testify to this day. Although the two latter cities never completely recovered from the injuries inflicted on them by the tyranny of the trades-unions, there were numerous other towns, where industry had been left comparatively free, in which the arts of peace were cultivated in security. Under the mild sway of the Burgundian dukes, Antwerp became the centre of the commerce of Northern Europe; and more business is said to have been done there in a month than at Venice in two years when at the summit of its grandeur. About the year 1550, it was no uncommon sight to see as many as 2500 ships in the Scheldt, laden with merchandise for all parts of the world.

Such was the prosperity of Flanders, and such the greatness of Antwerp, when Philip II. of Spain succeeded to the rich inheritance of Burgundy on the resignation of Charles V. in the year 1556. Had his subjects been of the same mind with himself in religious matters, Philip might have escaped the infamy which attaches to his name. But a large proportion of the most skilled and industrious people in the Netherlands had imbibed the new ideas as to a reform in religion which had swept over Northern Europe. They had read the newly-translated Bible with avidity; they had formed themselves into religious communities, and appointed preachers of their own; in a word, they were Protestants.

Philip had scarcely succeeded to the Spanish throne than he ordered a branch of the Inquisition to be set up in Flanders, with the Cardinal Grenvelle as Inquisitor General. The institution excited great opposition among all classes, Catholic as well as Protestant; and it was shortly followed by hostility and resistance, which eventually culminated in civil war. Sir Thomas Gresham, writing to Cecil from Antwerp in 1566, said, "There are above 40,000 Protestants in this toune, which will die rather than the Word of God should be put to silence."

The struggle which now began was alike fierce and determined on both sides, and extended over many years. The powerful armies which the king directed against his revolted subjects were led by able generals, by the Duke of Alva, by Alexander Farnese, prince of Parma, and many more; and although they did not succeed in establishing the Inquisition in the Netherlands, they succeeded in either exterminating or banishing the greater part of the Protestants south of the Scheldt, at the same time that they ruined the industry of Flanders, destroyed its trade, and reduced the Catholics themselves to beggary. Bruges and Ghent became crowded with thieves and paupers. The busy quays of Antwerp were deserted, and its industrious artisans, tradesmen, and merchants fled from the place, leaving their property behind them a prey to the spoiler.*

The Duchess of Parma, writing to Philip in 1567, said that "in a few days 100,000 men had already left the country with their money and goods, and that more were following every day." Clough, writing to Gresham from Antwerp in the same year, said, "It is marveylus to see how the pepell packe away from hense; some for one place, and some for another; as well the papysts as the Protestants; for it is thought that howsomever it goeth, it can not go well here; for that presently all the welthy and rich men of both sydes, who should be the stay of matters, make themselves away."†

The Duke of Alva carried on this frightful war of extermination and persecution for six years, during which he boast-

* It is said that for some years the plunder of the murdered and proscribed Protestants of the Low Countries brought into the royal treasury of Philip twenty millions of dollars annually.
† *Flanders Correspondence.*—State-Paper Office.

ed that he had sent 18,000 persons to the scaffold, besides the immense numbers destroyed in battles and sieges, and in the unrecorded acts of cruelty perpetrated on the peasantry by the Spanish soldiery. Philip heard of the depopulation and ruin of his provinces without regret; and though Alva was recalled, the war was carried on with increased fury by the generals who succeeded him. What mainly comforted Philip was, that the people who remained were at length becoming terrified into orthodoxy. The ecclesiastics assured the Duke of Parma, the governor, that, notwithstanding the depopulation of the provinces, more people were coming to them for confession and absolution at the last Easter than had ever come since the beginning of the revolt. Parma immediately communicated the consoling intelligence to Philip, who replied, "You can not imagine my satisfaction at the news you give me concerning last Easter."*

The flight of the Protestants from the Low Countries continued for many years. All who were strong enough to fly, fled; only the weak, the helpless, and the hopeless, remained. The fugitives turned their backs on Flanders, and their faces toward Holland, Germany, and England, and fled thither with their wives and children, and what goods they could carry with them, to seek new homes. Several hundred thousands of her best artisans—clothiers, dyers, weavers, tanners, cutlers, and iron-workers of all kinds—left Flanders, carrying with them into the countries of their adoption their skill, their intelligence, and their spirit of liberty. The greater number of them went directly into Holland, then gallantly struggling with Spain for its independent existence. There they founded new branches of industry, which eventually proved a source of wealth and strength to the United Provinces. Many others passed over into England, hailing it as "Asylum Christi," and formed the settlements of which some account will be given in succeeding chapters.

* MOTLEY—*History of the United Netherlands* (i., 490), where the story of Philip's war against his subjects in the Low Countries will be found related with remarkable power.

Having thus led the reader up to the period at which the exodus of Protestants from the Low Countries took place, we return to France, where Catharine de Medicis was stealthily maturing her plans for stamping out heresy in the dominions of her son. The treaty of 1570 was still observed; the Protestants were allowed to worship God after their own forms, and France was slowly recovering from the wounds which she had received during the recent civil war. At this time Catharine de Medicis artfully contrived a marriage between her daughter Margaret and Henry of Bearn, king of Navarre, chief of all the Huguenots. Henry's mother, Jeanne D'Albret, and the Admiral Coligny, concurred in the union, in the hope that it would put an end to the feuds which existed between the rival religious parties. Pope Pius V., however, refused to grant the necessary dispensation to enable the marriage to be celebrated according to the rites of the Roman Catholic Church; but the queen-mother got over this little difficulty by causing a dispensation to be forged in the Pope's name.*

As Catharine de Medicis had anticipated, the heads of the Reformed party, regarding the marriage as an important step toward national reconciliation, resorted to Paris in large numbers to celebrate the event and grace the royal nuptials. Among those present were Admiral Coligny and his family. Some of the Huguenot chiefs were not without apprehensions for their personal safety, and even urged the admiral to quit Paris. But he believed in the pretended friendship of the queen-mother and her son, and insisted on staying until the ceremony was over. The marriage was celebrated with great splendor in the cathedral church of Notre Dame on the 18th of August, 1572, the principal members of the nobility, Protestant as well as Roman Catholic, being present on the occasion. It was followed by a succession of feasts and gayeties, in which the leaders of both parties alike participated,

---

* VAUVILLIERS—*Historie de Jeanne d'Albret.*

and the fears of the Huguenots were thus completely disarmed.

On the day after the marriage a secret council was held, at which it was determined to proclaim a general massacre of the Huguenots. The king was now willing to give 50,000 crowns for the head of Coligny. To earn the reward, one Maurevert lay in wait for the admiral, on the 22d of August, in a house situated near the church of Saint Germain l'Auxerrois, between the Louvre and the Rue Béthisy. As the admiral passed, Maurevert fired and wounded him in the hand. Coligny succeeded in reaching his hotel, where he was attended by Ambrose Paré, who performed upon him a painful operation. The king visited the wounded man at his hotel, professed the greatest horror at the dastardly act which had been attempted, and vowed vengeance against the assassin.

Meanwhile, the day fixed by the queen-mother for the general massacre of the Huguenots drew near. Between two and three o'clock in the morning of the 24th of August, 1572, as the king sat in his chamber with his mother and the Duke of Anjou, the great bell of the church of St. Auxerrois rang to early prayer. It was the arranged signal for the massacre to begin! Almost immediately after, the first pistol-shot was heard. Three hundred of the royal guard, who had been held in readiness during the night, rushed out into the streets, shouting "For God and the king." To distinguish themselves in the darkness, they wore a white sash on their left arm, and a white cross in their hats.

Before leaving the palace, a party of the guard murdered the retinue of the young King of Navarre, then the guests of Charles IX. in the Louvre. They had come in the train of their chief, to be present at the celebration of his marriage with the sister of the King of France. One by one they were called from their rooms, marched down unarmed into the quadrangle, where they were hewed down before the very eyes of their royal host. A more perfidious butchery is probably not to be found recorded in history.

At the same time, mischief was afoot throughout Paris. Le Charron, provost of the merchants, and Marcel, his ancient colleague, had mustered a large number of desperadoes, to whom respective quarters had been previously assigned, and they now hastened to enter upon their frightful morning's work. The Duke of Guise determined to anticipate all others in the murder of Coligny. Hastening to his hotel, the duke's party burst in the outer door, and the admiral was roused from his slumber by the shots fired at his followers in the court-yard below. He rose from his couch, and though scarce able to stand, fled to an upper chamber. There he was tracked by his assassins, who stabbed him to death as he stood leaning against the wall. His body was then thrown out of the window into the court-yard. The Duke of Guise, who had been waiting impatiently below, hurried up to the corpse, and wiping the blood from the admiral's face, said, "I know him—it is he;" then, spurning the body with his foot, he called out to his followers, "Courage, comrades, we have begun well; now for the rest; the king commands it." They then rushed out again into the street.

Firing was now heard in every quarter throughout Paris. The houses of the Huguenots, which had long been marked, were broken into, and men, women, and children were sabred or shot down. It was of no use trying to fly. The fugitives were slaughtered in the streets. The king himself seized his arquebus, and securely fired upon his subjects from the windows of the Louvre. For three days the massacre continued. Corpses blocked the doorways; mutilated bodies lay in every lane and passage; and thousands were cast into the Seine, then swollen by a flood. At length, on the fourth day, when the fury of the assassins had become satiated, and the Huguenots were for the most part slain, a dead silence fell upon the streets of Paris.

These dreadful events at the capital were almost immediately followed by similar deeds all over France. From fifteen to eighteen hundred persons were killed at Lyons, and the dwellers on the Rhone below that city were horrified by the sight of the dead bodies floating down the river. Six hundred were killed at Rouen, and many more at Dieppe and Havre. The numbers killed during the massacre throughout France have been variously estimated. Sully says 70,000 were slain, though other writers estimate the victims at 100,000.

Catharine de Medicis wrote in triumph to Alva, to Philip II., and to the Pope, of the results of the three days' dreadful work in Paris. When Philip heard of the massacre, he is said to have laughed for the first and only time in his life. Rome was thrown into a delirium of joy at the news. The cannon were fired at St. Angelo; Gregory XIII. and his cardinals went in procession from sanctuary to sanctuary to give God thanks for the massacre. The subject was ordered to be painted, and a medal was struck, with the Pope's image on one side, and the destroying angel on the other immolating the Huguenots. Cardinal Orsini was dispatched on a special mission to Paris to congratulate the king; and on his passage through Lyons, the assassins of the Huguenots there, the blood on their hands scarce dry, knelt before the holy man in the cathedral and received his blessing. At Paris, the triumphant clergy celebrated the massacre by a public procession; they determined to consecrate to it an annual jubilee on the day of St. Bartholomew; and they too had a medal struck in commemoration of the event, bearing the legend, "Piety has awakened justice!"

As for the wretched young King of France, the terrible crime to which he had been a party weighed upon his mind to the last moment of his life. The recollection of the scenes of the massacre constantly haunted him, and he became restless, haggard, and miserable. He saw his murdered guests sitting by his side at bed and at board. "Ambrose,"* said

* Ambrose Paré had won the confidence and friendship of Charles IX. by saving him from the effects of a wound inflicted by a clumsy surgeon in performing the operation of venesection. Paré, though a Huguenot, held the important office of surgeon in ordinary to the king, and was constantly about

he to his confidential physician, "I know not what has happened to me these two or three days past, but I feel my mind and body as much at enmity with each other as if I was seized with a fever. Sleeping or waking, the murdered Huguenots seem ever present to my eyes, with ghastly faces, and weltering in blood. I wish the innocent and helpless had been spared." He died in tortures of mind impossible to be described—attended in his last moments, strange to say, by a Huguenot physician and a Huguenot nurse; one of the worst horrors that haunted him being that his own mother was causing his death by slow poisoning, an art in which he knew that great bad woman to be fearfully accomplished.

To return to the surviving Huguenots, and the measures adopted by them for self-preservation. Though they were at first stunned by the massacre, they were not slow to associate themselves together, in those districts in which they were sufficiently strong, for purposes of self-defense. Along the western sea-board, at points where they felt themselves unable to make head against their persecutors, they put to sea in ships and boats, and made for England, where they landed in great numbers—at Rye, at Hastings, at Southampton, and the numerous other ports on the south coast. This

his person To this circumstance he owed his escape from the massacre, the king concealing him during the night in a private room adjoining his own chamber. Palissy, of whom we have already spoken, most probably also owed his escape to the circumstance of his being in the immediate employment of Catharine de Medicis. But even employment at court did not secure the Huguenots in all cases against assassination. Thus Jean Goujon, the sculptor, sometimes styled "the French Phidias," was shot from below while employed on a scaffold in executing the decorative work of the old Louvre. Some of the greatest early artists of France were Huguenots like Goujon; for example, Jean Cousin, founder of the French school of painting; Barthélemy Prieur, sculptor; and Jean Bullant, Debrosses, and Du Cerceau, the celebrated architects. Goudimel the musical composer, and Ramus the philosopher, were also slain in the massacre. Before this time Ramus's house had been pillaged and his library destroyed. Dumoulin, the great jurisconsult, had previously escaped by death. "The execrable day of Saint Bartholomew," said the Catholic Chateaubriand, "only made martyrs; it gave to philosophical ideas an advantage over religious ideas which has never since been lost."

was particularly the case with the artisans and skilled labor class, whose means of living are invariably imperiled by a state of civil war; and they fled into England to endeavor, if possible, to pursue their respective callings in peace, while they worshiped God according to their conscience.

But the Huguenot nobles and gentry would not and could not abandon their followers to destruction. They gathered together in their strong places, and prepared to defend themselves by force against force. In the Cevennes, Dauphiny, and other quarters, they betook themselves to the mountains for refuge. In the plains of the south, fifty towns closed their gates against the royal troops. Wherever resistance was possible it showed itself. The little town of Sancerre held out successfully for ten months, during which the inhabitants, without arms, heroically defended themselves with slings, called "the arquebuses of Sancerre," enduring meanwhile the most horrible privations, and reduced to eat moles, snails, bread made of straw mixed with scraps of horse-harness, and even the parchment of old title-deeds. The Roman Catholics, under the Duke of Anjou, also attacked Rochelle, and after great suffering and heroism on both sides, the assailants were repulsed and compelled to retire from the siege. While this civil war was in progress, the king died and was succeeded by Henry III., the same Duke of Anjou who had been repulsed from Rochelle. Henry of Navarre and the Prince of Condé now assumed the leadership of the Huguenots, and the wars of the League began, which kept France in a state of anarchy for many years, and were only brought to a conclusion by the succession of Henry IV. to the throne in 1594.

So powerful, however, was the Roman Catholic party in France, that Henry found it necessary to choose between his religion and his crown. In that age of assassination, he probably felt that unless he reconciled himself to the old Church, his life was not safe for a day. Henry's religion at all times clung to him but loosely; indeed, he was not a religious man in any sense; for, though magnanimous, large-hearted, and brave, he was given up, like most kings in those days, to the pleasures of the senses. He had become a Huguenot through political rather than religious causes, and it cost him little sacrifice to become a Catholic. For sake of peace, therefore, as well as for the sake of his own life, Henry conformed. But, though he governed France ably and justly for a period of sixteen years, his apostasy did not protect him; for, after repeated attempts upon his life by emissaries of the Jesuits, he was eventually assassinated by Francis Ravaillac, a lay-brother of the monastery of St. Bernard, on the 14th of May, 1610.

One of Henry's justest and greatest acts was the promulgation, in 1598, of the celebrated Edict of Nantes. By that edict, the Huguenots, after sixty years of persecution, were allowed at last comparative liberty of conscience and freedom of worship. What the Roman Catholics thought of it may be inferred from the protest of the Pope, Clement VIII., who wrote to say that "a decree which gave liberty of conscience to all was the most accursed that had ever been made."

Persons of the Reformed faith were now admitted to public employment; their children were afforded access to the schools and universities; they were provided with equal representation in some of the provincial Parliaments, and permitted to hold a certain number of places of surety in the kingdom. And thus was a treaty of peace at length established for a time between the people of the contending faiths throughout France.

CHAPTER IV.

RELATIONS OF ENGLAND WITH FRANCE AND SPAIN.

WHILE the rulers of France and Spain were making these desperate efforts to crush the principles of the Reformation in their dominions, the Protestants of England regarded their proceedings with no small degree of apprehension and alarm. Though the Reformed faith had made considerable progress in the English towns at the period of Elizabeth's accession to the throne in 1558, it was still in a considerable minority throughout the country.* The great body of the nobility, the landed gentry, and the rural population adhered to the old religion, while there was a considerable middle class of Gallios, who were content to wait the issue of events before declaring themselves on either side.

During the reigns which had preceded that of Elizabeth, the country had been ill governed and the public interests neglected. The nation was in debt and unarmed, with war raging abroad. But Elizabeth's greatest difficulty consisted in the fact of her being a Protestant, and the successor of a Roman Catholic queen who had reigned with undisputed

* Soames, in his *Elizabethan Religious History*, says that at the accession of Elizabeth two thirds of the people were Catholics. Butler, in his *Memoirs of the Catholics*, holds the same view. On the other hand, Mr. Hallam, in his *Constitutional History*, estimates that in 1559 the Protestants were two thirds of the population. Mr. Buckle, in an able posthumous paper which appeared in *Fraser's Magazine* (February, 1867), inclines to the view that the Protestants were still in the minority. "Of the two great parties," he says, "one occupied the north and the other the south, and a line drawn from the Humber (to the mouth of the Severn?) formed the boundary of their respective dominions. The Catholics of the north were headed by the great families (of the Percies and Nevilles), and had on their side all those advantages which the prescription of ages alone can give. To the south were the Protestants, who, though they could boast of none of those great historical names which reflected a lustre on their opponents, were supported by the authority of the government, and felt that enthusiastic confidence which only belongs to a young religion."

power during the five years which preceded her accession to the throne. No sooner had she become queen than the embarrassment of her position was at once felt. The Pope denied her legitimacy, and refused to recognize her authority. The bishops refused to crown her. The two universities united with Convocation in presenting to the House of Lords a declaration in favor of the papal supremacy. The King of France openly supported the claim of Mary Queen of Scots to the English throne; and a large and influential body of the nobility and gentry were her secret, if not her avowed partisans.

From the day of her ascending the throne Elizabeth was the almost constant object of plots formed to destroy her and pave the way for the re-establishment of the old religion. Elizabeth might possibly have escaped from her difficulties by accepting the hand of Philip II. of Spain, which was offered her. She refused, and determined to trust to her people. But her enemies were numerous, powerful, and active in conspiring against her authority, and they had their emissaries constantly at the French and Spanish courts, and at the camp of Alva in the Netherlands, urging the invasion of England and the overthrow of the English queen.

One of the circumstances which gave the most grievous offense to the French and Spanish monarchs was the free asylum which Elizabeth offered in England to the Protestants flying from their persecutions abroad. Though those rulers would not permit their subjects to worship according to conscience in their own country, neither would they tolerate their leaving it to worship in freedom elsewhere. Conformity, not depopulation, was their object, but conformity by force if not by suasion. All attempts made by the persecuted to leave France or Flanders were accordingly interdicted. They were threatened with confiscation of their property and goods if they fled, and with death if they were captured. The hearts of the kings were hardened, and they " would not let the people go!" But the sea was a broad and free road that could not be closed, and from all parts of the coasts of France and Flanders the tidings reached the monarchs of the escape of their subjects, whom they had failed either to convert or to kill. They could then but gnash their teeth and utter threats against the queen and the nation that had given their persecuted people asylum.

The French king formally demanded that Elizabeth should banish his fugitive subjects from her realm as rebels and heretics; but he was impotent to enforce his demands, and the fugitives remained. The Spanish monarch then called upon the Pope to interfere, and he, in his turn, tried to close the ports of England against foreign heretics. In a communication addressed by him to Elizabeth, the Pope proclaimed the fugitives to be "drunkards and sectaries"—*ebriosi et sectarii* —and declared "that all such as were the worst of the people resorted to England, and were by the queen received into safe protection"—*ad quam velut ad asylum omnium impestissimi perfugium invenerunt.*

The Pope's denunciations of the refugees were answered by Bishop Jewell, who vindicated their character, and held them up as examples of industry and orderly living. "Is it not lawful," he asked, "for the queen to receive strangers without the Pope's warrant?" Quoting the above-cited Latin passages, he proceeded: "Thus he speaketh of the poor exiles of Flanders, France, and other countries, who either lost or left behind them all that they had, goods, lands, and houses —not for adultery, or theft, or treason, but for the profession of the Gospel. It pleased God here to cast them on land; the queen, of her gracious pity, hath granted them harbor. Is it so heinous a thing to show mercy?" The bishop proceeded to retort upon the Pope for harboring 6000 usurers and 20,000 courtesans in his own city of Rome; and he desired to know whether, if the Pope was to be allowed to entertain such "servants of the devil," the Queen of England was to be denied the liberty of receiving "a few servants of God?" "They are," he continued, "our brethren; they live not idly. If they have houses of us, they pay rent for them. They hold not our grounds but by making due recompense. They beg not in our streets, nor crave any thing at our hands but to breathe our air and to see our sun. They labor truefully, they live sparingly. They are good examples of virtue, travail, faith, and patience. The towns in which they abide are happy, for God doth follow them with his blessings."*

When the French and Spanish monarchs found that Elizabeth continued to give an asylum to their Protestant subjects, they proceeded to compass her death. Their embassadors at the English court acted as spies upon her proceedings, organized plots against her, and stirred up discontent on all sides. They found a ready instrument in the Queen of Scots, then confined in Tutbury Castle. Mary was not, however, held so strict a prisoner as to be precluded from carrying on an active correspondence with her partisans in England and Scotland, with the Duke of Guise and others in France, and with the Duke of Alva and Philip II. in Flanders and Spain. Guilty though the Queen of Scots had been of the death of her husband, the Roman Catholics of England regarded her as their rightful head, and were ready to rise in arms in her cause.

Mary was an inveterate intriguer. We find her entreating the courts of France and Spain to send her soldiers, artillerymen, and arms; and the King of Spain to set on foot the in-

* BISHOP JEWELL'S *Works* (Parker Society), p. 1148, 1149. The refugee Flemings also, in 1567, defended themselves against the charges made against them, in a letter to the Bishop of London, inclosed by him to Cecil (as preserved in the State Paper Office), in which they referred to "the murders, pillories, massacres, imprisonments, re-baptisms of little children, banishments, confiscations, and all sorts of 'desbordements' executed against the faithful subjects of the king in the Low Countries, and supplicating grace and license" "a touts gentilshommes, borgeois, marchants, et artizants des Pays Bas de povoir librement venir en cestun vostre royaume, et ses retirer en villes lesquelles ils vous plaira de nommer et designer a cest effect et quelles il leur soit permit de librement demeurer negotier et exercer toutes sortes de stils et mestiers chascun selon sa sorte et qualite ou quelque aultre quil estimera plus convenable en regard au particuliers commodites des lieux et la charge touttefois en condition que chascun apporte certificate a l'apprusment du consistoire de l'Eglise de v're ville de Londres," etc.—*State Papers*, vol. xliii., 29.

vasion of England, with the object of dethroning Elizabeth and restoring the Roman Catholic faith. Her importunities, as well as the fascinations of her person, were not without their effect upon those under her immediate influence; and she succeeded in inducing the Duke of Norfolk, who cherished the hope of becoming her fourth husband, to undertake a scheme for her liberation. A conspiracy of the leading nobles was formed, at the head of which were the Earls of Northumberland and Westmoreland; and in the autumn of 1568 they raised the standard of revolt in the northern counties, where the power of the Roman Catholic party was the strongest.* But the rising was speedily suppressed; some of its leaders fled into Scotland, and others into foreign countries; the Duke of Norfolk was sent to the Tower; and the queen's authority was for the time upheld.

The Pope next launched against Elizabeth the most formidable missile of the Church—a bull of excommunication—in which he declared her to be cut off, as the minister of iniquity, from the community of the faithful, and forbade her subjects to recognize her as their sovereign. This document was found nailed up on the Bishop of London's door on the morning of the 15th of May, 1570. The French and Spanish courts now considered themselves at liberty to compass the life of Elizabeth by assassination.† The Cardinal de Lor-

---

* After having written to Pope Pius V., the Spanish embassador, and the Duke of Alva, to request their assistance, and to advise that a port should be seized on the eastern coast of England, where it would be easy to disembark troops, . . . they left Brancepath on the 14th of November, at the head of 500 horsemen, and marched toward Durham. The insurrection was entirely Catholic. They had painted Jesus Christ on the cross, with his five bleeding wounds, upon a banner borne by old Norton, who was inspired by the most religious enthusiasm. The people of Durham opened their gates and joined the rebels. Thus made masters of the town, the insurgents proceeded to the cathedral, burned the Bible, destroyed the Book of Common Prayer, broke in pieces the Protestant communion-table, and restored the old form of worship.—MIGNET—*History of Mary Queen of Scots*, Lond. ed., 1851, ii., 100.

† Assassination was in those days regarded as the readiest method of getting rid of an adversary; and in the case of an excommunicated person, it was regarded almost in the light of a religious duty. When the Regent Murray (of Scotland) was assassinated by Bothwellhaugh, in 1570, Mary of

raine, head of the Church in France, and the confidential adviser of the queen-mother, hired a party of assassins in the course of the same year for the purpose of destroying Elizabeth, because of the encouragement she had given to Coligny and the French Huguenots. Again, the Duke of Alva, in his correspondence with Mary Queen of Scots and the leaders of the Roman Catholic party in England, insisted throughout that the first condition of sending a Spanish army to their assistance was the death of Elizabeth.

Such was the state of affairs when the Bishop of Ross, one of Mary's most zealous partisans, set on foot a conspiracy for the destruction of the queen. The principal agent employed in communicating with foreign powers on the subject was one Ridolfi, a rich Florentine banker in London, director of the company of Italian merchants, and an ardent papist Minute instructions were drawn up and intrusted to Ridolfi, to be laid by him before Pope Pius V. and Philip II. of Spain. On his way to Rome through the Low Countries he waited on the Duke of Alva, and presented to him a letter from Mary Queen of Scots, beseeching him to furnish her with prompt assistance, with the object of "laying all this island" under perpetual obligations to his master the King of Spain as well as to herself, as the faithful executor of his commands.*

At Rome Ridolfi was welcomed by the Pope, who eagerly adopted his plans, and furnished him with a letter to Philip II., conjuring that monarch, by his fervent piety toward God, to furnish all the means he might judge most suitable for carrying them into effect. Ridolfi next proceeded to Madrid

---

Scots gave him a pension. Many attempts were about the same time made on the life of William of Orange, surnamed "The Silent." One made at Mechlin, in 1572, proved a failure; but he was finally assassinated at Delft, in 1585, by Balthazar Gerard, an avowed agent of Philip II. and the Jesuits; Philip having afterward ennobled the family of the assassin. The wife of William of Orange, in whose arms he expired, was a daughter of Admiral Coligny.

* Prince Labanoff's Collection, iii., 216–220, cited by MIGNET—*History of Mary Queen of Scots*, ii., 135.

to hold an interview with the Spanish court and arrange for the murder of the English queen. He was received to a conference with the Council of State, at which were present the Pope's nuncio, the Cardinal Archbishop of Seville (Inquisitor General); the Grand Prior of Castile, the Duke of Feria, the Prince of Eboli, and other high ministers of Spain. Ridolfi proceeded to lay his plan for assassinating Elizabeth before the council.* He said "the blow would not be struck in London, because that city was the strong-hold of heresy, but while she was traveling." On the council proceeding to discuss the expediency of the proposed murder, the Pope's nuncio at once undertook to answer all objections. The one sufficient pretext, he said, was the bull of excommunication. The vicar of God had deprived Elizabeth of her throne, and the soldiers of the Church were the instruments of his decree to execute the sentence of heaven against the heretical tyrant. On this, one Chapin Vitelli, who had come from Flanders to attend the council, offered himself as the assassin. He said, if the matter was intrusted to him, he would take or kill the queen. The councilors of state present then severally stated their views, which were placed on record, and are still to be seen in the archives at Simancas.

Philip II. concurred in the plot, and professed himself ready to undertake the conquest of England by force if it failed; but he suggested that the Pope should supply the necessary money. Philip, however, was a man of hesitating purpose; and, foreseeing the dangers of the enterprise, he delayed embarking in it, and eventually resolved on leaving the matter to the decision of the Duke of Alva.†

While these measures against the life of Elizabeth were being devised abroad, Mary Queen of Scots was diligently

* The minutes of this remarkable meeting of council were fully written out by Zayas, Secretary of State, and are preserved in the archives of Simancas (Inglaterra, fol. 823). We follow the account given by Mignet in his *History of Mary Queen of Scots*, published in 1851, since fully confirmed by Mr. Froude in his recently published *History of England from the Fall of Wolsey to the Death of Elizabeth*, vol. iv.

† MIGNET—*History of Mary Queen of Scots.*

occupied at Chatsworth in encouraging a like plot at home with the same object. Lord Burleigh, however, succeeded in gaining a clew to the conspiracy, on which the principal agents in England were apprehended, and the queen was put upon her guard. The Spanish embassador, Don Gerau, being found in secret correspondence with Mary, was warned to depart the realm; his last characteristic act being to hire two bravoes to assassinate Burleigh, and he lingered upon the road to Dover, hoping to hear that the deed had been done. But the assassins were detected in time, and, instead of taking Burleigh's life, they only lost their own.

The Protestant party were from time to time thrown into agonies of alarm by the rumor of these plots against the life of their queen, and by the reported apprehension of agents of foreign powers arriving in England for the purpose of stirring up rebellion and preparing the way for the landing of the Duke of Alva and his army. The intelligence brought by the poor hunted Flemings, who had by this time landed in England in large numbers, and settled in London and the principal towns of the south, and the accounts which they spread abroad of the terrors of Philip's rule in the Low Countries, told plainly enough what the English Protestants had to expect if the threatened Spanish invasion succeeded.

The effect of these proceedings was to rouse a general feeling of indignation against the foreign plotters and persecutors, and to evoke an active and energetic public opinion in support of the queen and her government. A large proportion of the English people were probably still in a great measure undecided as to their faith; but their feeling of nationality was intense. The conduct of Elizabeth herself was doubtless influenced quite as much by political as religious considerations; and in the midst of the difficulties by which she was surrounded, her policy doubtless seemed tortuous and inconsistent. The nation was, indeed, in one of the greatest crises of its fate; and the queen, her ministers, and the nation at large, every day more clearly recognized in the great questions at stake not merely the cause of Protestantism against Popery, but of English nationality against foreign ascendency, and of resistance to the threatened yoke of Rome, France, and Spain.

The massacre of St. Bartholomew, which shortly followed, exercised a powerful influence in determining the sympathies of the English people. The news of its occurrence called forth a general shout of execration. The Huguenot fugitives who crowded for refuge into the southern ports brought with them accounts of the barbarities practiced on their fellow-countrymen which filled the mind of the nation with horror. The people would have rushed willingly into a war to punish the perfidy and cruelty of the French Roman Catholics, but Elizabeth forbade her subjects to take up arms except on their own account as private volunteers.

What the queen's private feelings were may be inferred from the reception which she gave to La Mothe Fénélon, the French embassador, on his first appearance at court after the massacre. For several days she refused to see him, but at length admitted him to an audience. The lords and ladies in waiting received him in profound silence. They were dressed in deep mourning, and grief seemed to sit on every countenance. They did not deign to salute, or even to look at the embassador, as he advanced toward the queen, who received him with a severe and mournful countenance; and, stammering out his odious apology, he hastened from her presence. Rarely, if ever, had a French embassador appeared at a foreign court ashamed of the country he represented; but on this occasion La Mothe Fénélon declared, in the bitterness of his heart, that he blushed to bear the name of Frenchman.

The massacre of Saint Bartholomew most probably sealed the fate of Mary Stuart. She herself rejoiced in it as a bold stroke for the faith, and, it might be, the signal for a like enterprise on her own behalf. Accordingly, she went on plotting as before, and in 1581 she was found engaged in a conspiracy with the Duke of Lennox for the re-establishment of popery in Scotland, under the auspices of the Jesuits.* These intrigues of the Queen of Scots at length became intolerable. Her repeated and urgent solicitations to the King of Spain to invade England with a view to the re-establishment of the old religion—the conspiracies against the life of Elizabeth in which she was from time to time detected†—excited the vehement indignation of the English nation, and eventually led to her trial and execution; for it was felt that so long as Mary Stuart lived the life of the English queen, as well as the liberties of the English people, were in daily jeopardy.

It is doubtless easy to condemn the policy of Elizabeth in this matter, now that we are living in the light of the nineteenth century, and peacefully enjoying the freedom won for us through the suffering and agony of our forefathers. But, in judging of the transactions of those times, it is right that allowance should be made for the different moral sense which then prevailed, as well as the circumstances amid which the nation carried on its life-and-death struggle for independent existence. Right is still right, it is true; but the times have

* MIGNET—*History of Mary Queen of Scots*, ii., 207-12.

† One of such conspiracies against the life of Elizabeth was that conducted by John Ballard, a Roman Catholic priest, in 1586. The principal instrument in the affair was one Anthony Babington, who had been for two years the intermediary correspondent between Mary Stuart, the Archbishop of Glasgow, and Paget and Morgan, his co-conspirators. Ballard, Babington, and the rest of the gang were detected, watched, and eventually captured and condemned, through the vigilance of Elizabeth's ever-watchful minister Walsingham. Mary had been kept fully advised of all their proceedings. Babington wrote to her in June, 1587, explaining the intention of the conspirators, and enumerating all the means for getting rid of Elizabeth. "Myself in person," he said, "with ten gentlemen and a hundred others of our company and suite, will undertake the deliverance of your royal person from the hands of your enemies. As regards getting rid of the usurper, from subjection to whom we are absolved by the act of excommunication issued against her, there are six gentlemen of quality, all of them my intimate friends, who, for the love they bear to the Catholic cause and to your majesty's service, will undertake the tragic execution." In the same letter Babington requested Mary Stuart to appoint persons to act as her lieutenants, and raise the populace in Wales, and in the counties of Lancashire, Derby, and Stafford. This letter, with others to a like effect, duly came into the possession of Walsingham.—See MIGNET—*History of Mary Queen of Scots*.

become completely changed, and public opinion has changed with them.

In the mean while, religious persecutions continued to rage abroad with as much fury as before, and fugitives from Flanders and France continued to take refuge in England, where they received protection and asylum. Few of the refugees brought any property with them; the greater number were entirely destitute. But very many of them brought with them that kind of wealth which money could not buy—intelligence, skill, virtue, and the spirit of independence; those very qualities which made them hateful to their persecutors, rendering them all the more valuable subjects in the countries of their adoption.

A large part of Flanders, before so rich and so prosperous, had by this time become reduced almost to a state of desert. The country was eaten bare by the Spanish armies. Wild beasts infested the abandoned dwellings of the peasantry, and wolves littered their young in the deserted farm-houses. Bruges and Ghent became the resort of thieves and paupers. The sack of Antwerp in 1585 gave the last blow to the staggering industry of that great city; and though many of its best citizens had already fled from it into Holland and England, one third of the remaining merchants and workers in silks, damasks, and other stuffs shook the dust of the Low Countries from their feet, and left the country forever.

Philip of Spain at length determined to take summary vengeance upon England. He was master of the most powerful army and navy in the world, and he believed that he could effect by force what he had been unable to compass by intrigue. The most stern and bigoted of kings, the great colossus of the Papacy, the duly-appointed Defender of the Faith, he resolved, at the same time that he pursued and punished his recreant subjects who had taken refuge in England, to degrade and expel the sacrilegious occupant of the English throne. Accordingly, in 1588, he prepared and launched his Sacred Armada, one of the most powerful armaments that ever put to sea. It consisted of 130 ships, besides transports, carrying 2650 great guns and 33,000 soldiers and sailors, besides 180 priests and monks under a Vicar General of the Holy Inquisition. It was also furnished with chains and instruments of torture, and with smiths to set them to work —destined for the punishment of the pestilent heretics who had so long defied the power of Spain.

This armament was to be joined in its progress by another equally powerful off the coast of Flanders, consisting of an immense fleet of flat-bottomed boats, carrying an army of 100,000 men, equipped with the best weapons and materials of war, who were to be conveyed to the mouth of the Thames under the escort of the great Spanish fleet.

The expedition was ably planned. The Pope blessed it, and promised to co-operate with his money, pledging himself to advance a million of ducats so soon as the expedition reached the British shores. At the same time, the bull issued by Pope Pius V., excommunicating Elizabeth and dispossessing her of her throne, was confirmed by Sixtus V., and reissued with additional anathemas. Setting forth under such auspices, it is not surprising to find that Catholic Europe entertained the conviction that the expedition must necessarily be successful, and that Elizabeth and Protestantism in England were doomed to inevitable destruction.

No measure could, however, have been better calculated than this to weld the English people of all ranks and classes, Catholics as well as Protestants, into one united nation. The threatened invasion of England by a foreign power—above all, by a power so hated as Spain—roused the patriotic feeling in all hearts. There was a general rising and arming by land and by sea. Along the south coast the whole maritime population arrayed themselves in arms; and every available ship, sloop, and wherry was manned and sent forth to meet and fight the Spaniards.

The result is matter of history. The Sacred and Invincible Armada was shattered by the ships of Drake, Hawkins, and Howard, and finally scattered by the tempests of the Almighty. The free asylum of England was maintained; the hunted exiles were thenceforward free to worship and to labor in peace; and beneficent effects of the addition of so many skilled, industrious, and free-minded men to our population are felt in England to this day.

Philip II. of Spain died in 1598, the same year in which Henry IV. of France promulgated the Edict of Nantes. At his accession to the Spanish throne in 1556, Philip was the most powerful monarch in Europe, served by the ablest generals and admirals, with an immense army and navy at his command. At his death, Spain was distracted and defeated, with a bankrupt exchequer; Holland was free, and Flanders in ruins. The intellect and energies of Spain were prostrate; but the priests were paramount. The only institution that flourished throughout the dominions of Philip, at his death, was the Inquisition.

Elizabeth of England, on the other hand, succeeded, in 1558, to an impoverished kingdom, an empty exchequer, and the government of a distracted people, one half of whom denied, and were even ready to resist, her authority. England was then without weight in the affairs of Europe. She had no army, and her navy was contemptible. After a reign of forty-five years, the aspect of affairs had become completely changed. The nation was found firmly united, content, free, and prosperous. An immense impulse had been given to industry. The intellect of the people had become awakened, and a literature sprang up which is the wonder even of modern times. The power of England abroad was every where recognized. The sceptre of the seas was wrested from Spain, and England thenceforward commanded the high road to America and the Indies.

The queen was supported by able ministers, though not more able than those who surrounded the King of Spain. But the spirit that moved them was wholly different—the English monarch encouraging freedom, the Spanish repressing it. As the one was the founder of modern England, so the other was of modern Spain.

It is true, Elizabeth did not rise to the high idea of complete religious liberty. But no one then did—not even the most advanced thinker. Still, the foundations of such liberty were laid, while industry was fostered and protected. It was accomplishing much to have done this. The rest was the work of experience working under an atmosphere of freedom.

CHAPTER V.

SETTLEMENTS AND INDUSTRIES OF THE PROTESTANT REFUGEES.

THE early English were a pastoral and agricultural, and by no means a manufacturing people. In the thirteenth and fourteenth centuries, most articles of clothing, excepting such as were produced by ordinary domestic industry, were imported from Flanders, France, and Germany.* The great staple was wool, which was sent abroad in vast quantities. "The ribs of all people throughout the world," wrote Matthew Paris, "are kept warm by the fleeces of English wool." The wool and its growers were on one side of the Channel, and the skilled workmen who dyed and wove it into cloth were on the other. When war broke out, and communication between the two shores was interrupted, as much distress was occasioned in Flanders as was lately experienced in Lancashire by the stoppage of the supply of cotton from the United States. On one occasion, in the fourteenth century, when the export of wool from England was prohibited, the effect was to reduce the manufacturing population throughout the Low Countries to destitution and despair.

* Besides the cloth of Flanders, England was also supplied with most of its finer fabrics from abroad, the names of the articles to this day indicating the places where they were manufactured. Thus there was the mechlin lace of Mechlin, the duffle of Duffel, the diaper of Ypres (d'Ypres), the cambric of Cambray, the arras of Arras, the tulle of Tulle, the damask of Damascus, and the dimity of Diametta. Besides these, we imported delph ware from Delft, venetian glass from Venice, cordovan leather from Cordova, and milanery from Milan. The Milaners of London were a special class of general dealers. They sold not only French and Flemish cloths, but Spanish gloves and girdles, Milan caps and cutlery, silk, lace, needles, pins for ladies' dresses (before which skewers were used), swords, knives, daggers, brooches, glass, porcelain, and various articles of foreign manufacture. The name of "milliner" (from Milaner) is now applied only to dealers in ladies' caps and bonnets.

"Then might be seen throughout Flanders," says the local historian, "weavers, fullers, and others living by the woolen manufacture, either begging, or, driven by debt, tilling the soil."*

At the same time, like distress overtook the English woolgrowers, who lost the market for their produce, on which they had been accustomed to rely. It naturally occurred to the English kings that it would be of great advantage to this country to have the wool made into cloth by the hands of their own people, instead of sending it abroad for the purpose. They accordingly held out invitations to the distressed Flemish artisans to come and settle in England, where they would find abundant employment at remunerative wages; and as early as the reign of Edward III. a large number of Flemings came over and settled in London, Kent, Norfolk, Devon, Somerset, Yorkshire, Lancashire, and Westmoreland.†

The same policy was pursued by successive English kings, down to the reign of Henry VIII., who encouraged skilled artisans of all kinds to settle in England, as armorers, cutlers, miners, brewers, and ship-builders; the principal craftsmen employed by the court being Flemings and Germans. The immigration of foreigners persecuted for conscience' sake began in the reign of his successor Edward VI., after which there was no longer any necessity for holding out invitations to skilled artisans of other countries to settle among us. Latimer, preaching before the king on one occasion, shrewdly observed of the distressed foreigners then beginning to flow into the country—"I wish that we could collect together such valuable persons in this kingdom as it would be the means of insuring its prosperity." Very few years passed before Latimer's wish was fully realized; and there was scarcely a town of any importance in England in which foreign artisans were not found settled and diligently pursuing their several callings.

* Meyer—*Annales Flandriæ*, p. 137.
† Appendix—*Early Settlement of Foreign Artisans in England.*

The immigration of the Protestant Flemings in Edward VI.'s reign was so considerable, that in 1550 the king gave them the church in Austin Friars, Broad Street, "to have their service in, and for avoiding all sects of Anabaptists and the like." The influx continued at such a rate as to interfere with the employment of the native population, who occasionally showed a disposition to riot, and even to expel the foreigners by violence. In a letter written by Francis Peyto to the Earl of Warwick, then at Rome, the following passage occurs: "Five or six hundred men waited upon the mayor and aldermen, complaining of the late influx of strangers, and that, by reason of the great dearth, they can not live for these strangers, whom they were determined to kill up through the realm if they found no remedy. To pacify them, the mayor and aldermen caused an esteame to be made of all strangers in London, which showed an amount of forty thousand, besides women and children, for the most part heretics fled out of other countries."* Although this estimate was probably a gross exaggeration, there can be no doubt that by this time a large number of the exiles had arrived and settled in London and other English towns.

The influx of the persecuted Protestants, however, did not fully set in until about ten years later, about the beginning of the reign of Elizabeth. The fugitives, in the extremity to which they were reduced, naturally made for that part of the English coast which lay the nearest to Flanders and France. In 1561, a considerable body of fugitive Flemings landed near Deal, and subsequently settled at the then decayed town of Sandwich. The queen was no sooner informed of their landing than she wrote to the mayor, jurats, and commonalty of the burgh, enjoining them to give liberty to the foreigners to settle there and carry on their respective trades. She recommended the measure as calculated to greatly benefit the town by "plantynge in the same men of knowledge in sundry handycrafts," in which they "were very skilful;"

* *Calendar of State Papers*, Foreign Series, 1547-53.

and her majesty more particularly enjoined that the trades the foreign artisans were to carry on were "the makinge of says, bays, and other cloth, which hath not been used to be made in this our realme of Englonde."

Other landings of Flemings took place about the same time at Harwich, at Yarmouth, at Dover, and other towns on the southeast coast. Some settled at the places where they had landed, and began to pursue their several branches of industry, while others proceeded to London, Norwich, Maidstone, Canterbury, and other inland towns, where the local authorities gave them like protection and succor.

The year after the arrival of the Flemings at Sandwich, the inhabitants of the little sea-port of Rye, on the coast of Sussex, were thrown into a state of commotion by the sudden arrival of a number of destitute French people from the opposite coast. Some came in open boats, others in sailing vessels. They were of all classes and conditions, and among them were many women and children. They had fled from their own country in great haste, and were nearly all alike destitute. Some crossed the Channel in mid-winter, braving the stormiest weather; and when they reached the English shore they usually fell upon their knees and thanked God for their deliverance.

In May, 1562, we find John Young, mayor of Rye, writing to Sir William Cecil, the queen's chief secretary, as follows: "May it please your honor, there is daily great resort of Frenchmen here, insomuch as already there is esteemed to be 500 persons; and we be in great want of corn for their and our sustentation, by reason the country adjoining is barren. . . . . Also may it please your honor, after night and this day is come two shippis of Dieppe into this haven, full of many people."*

It will be remembered that Rye is situated at the southwestern extremity of the great Romney Marsh; and as no corn was grown in the neighborhood, the wheat consumed in

* *Domestic State Papers*—Elizabeth, 1562. No. 35.

the place was all brought thither by sea, or from a distance inland over the then almost impassable roads of Sussex. The townspeople of Rye nevertheless bestirred themselves in aid of the poor refugees. They took them into their houses, fed them, and supplied their wants as well as they could; but the fugitives continued to arrive in such numbers that the provisions of the place soon began to run short.

These landings continued during the summer of 1562; and even as late as November the mayor again wrote to Cecil: "May it please your honor to be advertised that the third day of the present month, at twelve of the clocke, there arrived a bote from Dieppe, with Frenchmen, women, and children, to the number of a hundred and fiftye; there being a great number also which were here before." And as late as the 10th of December, the French people still flying for refuge, though winter had already set in severely, the mayor again wrote that another boat had arrived with "maney poor people, as well men and women as children, which were of Rouen and Dieppe."

Six years passed, and again, in 1568, we find another boat-load of fugitives from France landing at Rye: "Monsieur Gamayes, with his wife and children and ten strangers; and Captain Sows, with his wife and two servants, who had all come out of France, as they said, for the safeguard of their lives." Four years later, in 1572, there was a farther influx of refugees at Rye, the mayor again writing to Lord Burleigh, informing him that between the 27th of August and the 4th of November no fewer than 641 had landed. The records have been preserved of the names and callings of most of the immigrants, from which it appears that they were of all ranks and conditions, including gentlemen, merchants, doctors of physic, ministers of religion, students, schoolmasters, tradesmen, mechanics, artisans, shipwrights, mariners, and laborers. Among the fugitives were also several widows, who had fled with their children across the sixty miles of sea which there divide France and England, sometimes by night in open boats, braving the fury of the winds and waves in their eagerness to escape.*

The mayor of Rye made appeals to the queen for help, and especially for provisions, which from time to time ran short, and the help was at once given. Collections were made for the relief of the destitute refugees in many of the churches in England, as well as Scotland;† and, among others, we find the refugee Flemings at Sandwich giving out of their slender means "a benefaction to the poor Frenchmen who have left their country for conscience' sake."‡

These landings continued for many years. The people came flying from various parts of France and Flanders — cloth-makers from Bruges and Antwerp, lace-makers from Valenciennes, cambric-makers from Cambray, glass-makers from Paris, stuff-weavers from Meaux, merchants and tradesmen from Rouen, and shipwrights and mariners from Dieppe and Havre. As the fugitives continued to land, they were sent inland as speedily as possible, to make room for newcomers, as the household accommodation of the little towns along the English coast was but limited. From Rye, many proceeded to London to join their countrymen who had settled there; others went forward to Canterbury, to Southampton, to Norwich, and the other towns where Walloon congregations had already been established. A body of them settled at Winchelsea, an ancient town, formerly of much importance,§ on the south coast, though now left high and dry inland.

* W. DURRANT COOPER—Paper in *Sussex Archæological Collections*, vol. xiii., p. 179, entitled "The Protestant Refugees in Sussex."
† James Melville, in his diary, mentions that subscriptions were raised for French Protestants in indigent circumstances in 1575; and Calderwood has a similar notice in 1622.   ‡ Borough Records of Sandwich, 1572.
§ It will be remembered that Thackeray, who was fond of visiting Winchelsea, laid the early scenes of his novel of *Denis Duval* among the French immigrants of the place. Winchelsea, now a village amid ruins, was once a flourishing sea-port. The remains of the vaults and warehouses where the merchants' goods were stored are still pointed out, and the wharves may still be seen where ships discharged their cargoes, lying with their broadsides to the shore. The place is now some miles from the sea, and sheep and cattle graze over a wide extent of marsh-land, over which the tide formerly washed.

Many fugitives also landed at Dover, which was a convenient point for both France and Flanders. Some of the immigrants passed through to Canterbury and London, while others settled permanently in the place. Early in the seventeenth century a census was taken of the foreigners residing in Dover, when it was found that there were seventy-eight persons "which of late came out of France by reason of the troubles there." The description of them is interesting, as showing the classes to which the exiles principally belonged. There were two "preachers of God's Word;" three physicians and surgeons; two advocates; two esquires; three merchants; two schoolmasters; thirteen drapers, grocers, brewers, butchers, and other trades; twelve mariners; eight weavers and wool-combers; twenty-five widows, "makers of bone-lace and spinners;" two maidens; one woman, designated as the wife of a shepherd; one button-maker; one gardener; and one undescribed male.* There were at the same time settled in Dover thirteen Walloon exiles, of whom five were merchants, three mariners, and the others of different trades.

In the mean time, the body of Flemings who had first settled at Sandwich began to show signs of considerable prosperity. The local authorities had readily responded to the wishes of Queen Elizabeth, and did what she required. They appointed two markets to be held weekly for the sale of their cloths, in making which we very shortly find them busily occupied. When Archbishop Parker visited Sandwich in 1563, he took notice of "the French and Dutche, or both," who had settled in the town, and wrote to a friend at court that the refugees were as godly on the Sabbath days as they were industrious on week-days; observing that such "profitable and gentle strangers ought to be welcome, and not to be grudged at."†

Before the arrival of the Flemings, Sandwich had been a poor and decayed place. It was originally a town of consider-

* *Dom. Col.*—James I., 1622. † Strype's *Parker*, p. 139.

able importance, and one of the Cinque Ports. But when the River Stour became choked with silt, the navigation, on which it had before depended, was so seriously impeded that its trade soon fell into decay, and the inhabitants were reduced to great poverty. No sooner, however, had the first colony of Flemings, above four hundred in number, settled there under the queen's protection, than the empty houses were occupied, the town became instinct with new life, and was more than restored to its former importance. The artisans set up their looms, and began diligently to work at the manufacture of sayes, bayes, and other kinds of cloth, which met with a ready sale, the London merchants resorting to the bi-weekly markets, and buying up the goods at remunerative prices.

The native population also shared in the general prosperity, learning from the strangers the art of cloth-making, and becoming competitors with them for the trade. Indeed, before many years had passed, the townspeople, forgetful of the benefits they owed to the foreign artisans, became jealous, and sought to impose upon them special local taxes. On this the Flemings memorialized the queen, who again stood their friend; and, on her intercession, the corporation were at length induced to relieve them of the unjust burden.* At this time they constituted about one third of the entire population of the town; and when Queen Elizabeth visited Sandwich in 1573, it is recorded that "against the school-house, upon the new turfed wall, and upon a scaffold made upon

* The memorial, which is still preserved among the town records, concludes with the following prayer: "Which condition (viz., the local imposition on the foreign settlers) is suche, that by means of their chardges they should finally be secluded and syndered from the hability of those manifolde and necessary contributions which yet in this our exile are practised amongst us, as well towards the maintenance of the ministry of God's word as lykewise in the sustentation of our poore, besydes the chardges first above rehearsed: performyng therefore our foresayde humble petition, we shall be the more moved to directe our warmest prayers to our mercyfull God, that of his heavenly grace he will beatify your common weall more and more, grauntynge to ytt his spiritual and temporal blessyngs, which he gracefully powreth uppon them that showe favour and consolation to the poore afflicted straungers."—Boys' *History of Sandwich*, p. 744.

the wall of the school-house yard, were divers children, to the number of a hundred or six score, all spinning of fine bag yarn, a thing well liked of both her Majesty and of the Nobility and Ladies."*

The Protestant exiles at Sandwich did not, however, confine themselves to cloth-making,† but engaged in various other branches of industry. Some of them were millers, who erected the first wind-mills near the town in which they plied their trade. Two potters from Delft began the pottery manufacture. Others were smiths, brewers, hatmakers, carpenters, or shipwrights. Thus trade and population increased; new buildings arose on all sides, until Sandwich became almost transformed into a Flemish town; and to this day, though fallen again into comparative decay, the quaint, foreign-looking aspect of the place never fails to strike the modern visitor with surprise.

Among other branches of industry introduced by the Flemings at Sandwich, that of gardening is worthy of notice. The people of Flanders had long been famous for their horticulture, and one of the first things which the foreign settlers did on arriving in the place was to turn to account the excellent qualities of the soil in the neighborhood, so well suited for gardening purposes. Though long before practiced by the monks, gardening had become almost a lost art in England; and it is said that Katherine, queen of Henry VIII., unable to obtain a salad for her dinner in all England, had her table supplied from the Low Countries.‡ The first Flemish gar-

* *Antiquarian Repertory*, iv., 65.

† The principal trades which they followed were connected with the manufacture of cloths of different kinds. Thus, of 351 Flemish householders resident in Sandwich in 1582, 86 were bay-makers, 74 bay-weavers, 17 fullers, 24 linsey-wolsey weavers, and 24 wool-combers.

‡ Vegetables were formerly so scarce that they were salted down. Even in the sixteenth century a cabbage from Holland was deemed an acceptable present (Fox's *Life of James II.*, 205). Hull then carried on a thriving import trade in cabbages and onions. The rarity of vegetables in the country may be inferred from the fact that in 1595 a sum equal to twenty shillings was paid at that port for six cabbages and a few carrots by the purveyor for the Clifford family (WHITAKER—*History of Craven*, 321). Hartlib, writing in 1650, says that an old man then living remembered "the first gardener

dens proved highly successful. The cabbage, carrots, and celery produced by the foreigners met with so ready a sale, and were so much in demand in London itself, that a body of gardeners shortly removed from Sandwich and settled at Wandsworth, Battersea, and Bermondsey, where many of the rich garden-grounds first planted by the Flemings continue to this day the most productive in the neighborhood of the metropolis.

As might naturally be expected, by far the largest proportion of the Protestant exiles—Flemish and French—settled in London—London, the world's asylum—the refuge of the persecuted in all lands, whether for race, or politics, or religion—a city of Celts, Danes, and Saxons—of Jews, Germans, French, and Flemings, as well as of English—an aggregate of men of all European countries, and probably one of the most composite populations to be found in the world. Large numbers of French, Germans, and Flemings, of the industrious classes, had already taken refuge in London from the political troubles which had long raged abroad. About the beginning of the reign of Henry VIII. so many foreigners had settled in the western parts of London that "Tottenham is turned French" passed into a proverb;* and now the relig-

who came into Surrey to plant cabbages and cauliflowers, and to sow turnips, carrots, and parsnips, and to sow early pease—all of which at that time were great wonders, we having few or none in England but what came from Holland or Flanders." It is also supposed, though it can not be exactly ascertained, that the Protestant Walloons introduced the cultivation of the hop in Kent, bringing slips of the plant with them from Artois. The old distich—
"Hops, Reformation, Bays, and Beer,
Came into England all in one year"—
marks the period (about 1524) when the first English hops were planted. There is a plot of land at Bourne, near Canterbury, where there is known to have been a hop-plantation in the reign of Elizabeth. Reginald Scot, the author of *The Perfite Platforme of a Hoppe Garden*, speaks of "the trade of the Flemminge" (*i.e.*, his method of culture), and his "ostes at Poppering" as "a profytable patterne and a necessarie instruction for as manie as shall have to doe therein." Another kind of crop introduced by the Flemings at Sandwich was canary-grass, which still continues to be grown on the neighboring farms, and is indeed almost peculiar to the district. It may be added that to this day the "Sandwich celery" maintains its reputation.

* *Tottenham is turned French.*—About the beginning of Henry VIII. French mechanics swarmed in England, to the great prejudice of English artisans,

ious persecutions which raged abroad compelled foreigners of various nations to take refuge in London in still greater numbers than at any former period.

Fortunately for London, as for England, the men who now fled thither for refuge were not idle, dissolute, and ignorant, but peaceable, gentle, and laborious. Though they were poor, they were not pauperized, but were thrifty and self-helping, and, above all things, eager in their desire to earn an honest living. They were among the most skilled and intelligent inhabitants of the countries which had driven them forth. Had they been weak men, they would have gone with the stream as others did, and conformed; but they were men with convictions, earnest and courageous, and ready to brave all perils in their determination to find some land of refuge in which they might be permitted to worship God according to the dictates of their conscience.

Of the Flemings and French who settled in London, the greater part congregated in special districts, for the convenience of carrying on their trades together. Thus a large number of the Flemings settled in Southwark and Bermondsey, and began many branches of industry which continue there to this day, Southwark being still the principal manufacturing district of London. There was a quarter in Bermondsey, known as "The Borgeney," or "Petty Burgundy," because of the foreigners who inhabited it. Joiner's Street, which still exists in name, lay in the district, and was so called because of its being almost wholly occupied by Flemish joiners, who were skilled in all kinds of carpentry.* Another branch of trade begun by the Flemings in Bermondsey

---

which caused the insurrection in London on Ill-Mayday, 1517.—*England's Worthies in Church and State*, Lond., 1684, p. 471.

* "At St. Olave's, in Southwark, you shall learn, among the joyners, what inlayes and marquetrie weare. Inlaye (as the word imports) is a laying of coloured wood in their wainscot works, bedsteads, cupboards, chayres, and the like."—Bolton, *Elements of Armories*, 1610.

"The Flemish burying-ground," appropriated to the foreigners as a place of sepulture, was situated near the south end of London Bridge. It is now covered by the approach to the London Bridge Railway Station.

was the manufacture of felts or hats. Tanneries and breweries were also started by them, and carried on with great success. Henry Leek, originally Hoek or Hook,* from Wesel, was one of the principal brewers of his time, to whose philanthropic bequest Southwark owes the foundation of the excellent free-school of St. Olave's—one of the best of its class.

Another important settlement of the Flemings was that at Bow, where they established dye-works on a large scale. Before their time, white cloth of English manufacture was usually sent abroad to be dyed, after which it was reimported and sold as Flemish cloth. The best known among the early dyers were Peter de Croix and Dr. Kepler, the latter of whom established the first dye-work in England; and cloth of "Bow dye" soon became famous. Another body of the refugees settled at Wandsworth, and began several branches of industry, such as the manufacture of felts, and the making of brass plates for culinary utensils, which Aubrey says they "kept a mystery." One Fromantel introduced the manufacture of pendulum or Dutch clocks, which shortly came into common use. At Mortlake the French exiles began the manufacture of arras, and at Fulham of tapestry. The art of printing paper-hangings was introduced by some artisans from Rouen, where it had been originally practiced; and many other skilled workers in metal settled in different parts of the metropolis, as cutlers, jewelers, and makers of mathematical instruments, in which the French and Flemish workmen then greatly excelled.†

The employment given to the foreign artisans seems to

---

* Many of the foreigners adopted names of English sound, so that it is now difficult to trace them amid the population in which they have become merged. Thus, in the parish church of Allhallows, Barking, we find the monument of a distinguished Fleming, one Roger Haestrecht, who changed his name to James. He was the founder of the family of James, of Ightham Court, in Kent.

† A French refugee, named Briot, was the first to introduce the coining-press, which was a French invention, into England. He was appointed chief engraver to the Mint; and forty years after his time, in the reign of Charles II., another Frenchman, named Blondeau, was selected to superintend the stamping of our English money.

have excited considerable discontent among the London tradesmen, who from time to time beseeched the interference of the corporations and of Parliament. Thus, in 1576, we find the London shoemakers petitioning for a commission of inquiry as to the alien shoemakers who were carrying on their trade in the metropolis. In 1586, the London apprentices raised a riot in the city against the foreigners; and several youths of the Plasterer's Company were apprehended and committed to Newgate by order of the queen and council. A few years later, in 1592, the London freemen and shopkeepers complained to Parliament that the strangers were spoiling their trades, and a bill was brought in for the purpose of restraining them. The bill was strongly supported by Sir Walter Raleigh, who complained bitterly of the strangers; but it was opposed by Cecil and the queen's ministers; and though it passed the Commons, it failed through the dissolution of Parliament, so that the refugees were left to the enjoyment of their former protection and hospitality.*

Many of the foreigners established themselves as merchants in the city, and soon became known as leading men in commercial affairs. Several of them had already been distinguished as merchants in their own country, and they brought with them a spirit and enterprise which infused quite a new life into London business. Among the leading foreign merchants of Elizabeth's time we recognize the names of Houblon, Palavicino, De Malines, Corsellis, Van Peine, Tryan, Buskell, Cursini, De Best, and Cotett. And that they prospered by the exercise of their respective callings may be inferred from the circumstance that when, in 1588, Queen Elizabeth proceeded to raise a loan in the city by voluntary subscriptions, thirty-eight of the foreign merchants subscribed among themselves £5000 in sums of £100 and upward.

The accounts given of the numbers of the exiles from Flanders and France who then settled in London are very imperfect, yet they enable us to form some idea of the extensive

* BURN—*History of the Protestant Refugees*, p. 10.

character of the immigration. Thus, a return of the population, made in 1571, the year before the massacre of St. Bartholomew, shows that in the city of London alone (exclusive of the large number of strangers settled in Southwark, at Bow, and outside the liberties) there were, of foreigners belonging to the English Church, 889; to the Dutch, French, and Italian churches, 1763; certified by their elders, but not presented by the wards, 1828; not yet joined to any particular church, 2663; "strangers that do confesse themselves that their comyng hether was onlie to seek worck for their lyvinge," 2561; or a total of 9704 persons.* From another return of about the same date, in which the numbers are differently given, we obtain some idea of the respective nationalities of the refugees. Out of the 4594 strangers then returned as resident in the city of London, 3643 are described as Dutch (*i. e.*, Flemings); 657 French; 233 Italians; and 53 Spaniards and Portuguese.†

That the foreign artisans continued to resort to England in increasing numbers is apparent from a farther census taken in 1621, from which it appears that there were then 10,000 strangers in the city of London alone, carrying on 121 different trades. Of 1343 persons whose occupations are specified, there were found to be 11 preachers, 16 schoolmasters, 349 weavers, 183 merchants, 148 tailors, 64 sleeve-makers, 43 shoemakers, 39 dyers, 37 brewers, 35 jewelers, 25 diamond-cutters, 22 cutlers, 20 goldsmiths, 20 joiners, 15 clock-makers, 12 silk-throwsters, 10 glass-makers, besides hemp-dressers, thread-makers, button-makers, coopers, engravers, gun-makers, painters, smiths, watch-makers, and other skilled craftsmen.‡

Numerous other settlements of the refugees took place

---

* *State Papers, Dom.—Elizabeth*, vol. 84, anno 1571. It appears from the Bishop of London's certificate of 1567 (four years before), that the number of persons of foreign birth then settled in London was 4851, and 512 French. There were at the same time in London 36 Scots, 128 Italians, 23 Portuguese, 54 Spaniards, 10 Venetians, 2 Blackamoors, and 2 Greeks.

† *State Papers, Dom.—Elizabeth*, vol. 82, anno 1571.

‡ *Lists of Foreign Protestants and Aliens resident in England*, 1618–88. Edited by William Durrant Cooper, F.S.A., Camden Society's Papers, 1862.

throughout England, more particularly in the southern counties. "The foreign manufacturers," says Hasted, "chose their situations with great judgment, distributing themselves with the queen's license throughout England, so as not to interfere too much with each other."* One of the most important of such settlements was that formed at Norwich, where they founded and carried on many important branches of trade.

Although Norwich had been originally indebted mainly to foreign artisans for its commercial and manufacturing importance, the natives of this city were among the first to turn upon their benefactors. The local guilds, in their usual narrow spirit, passed stringent regulations directed against the foreign artisans, who had originally taught them their trade. The jealousy of the native workmen was also roused, and riots were stirred up against the Flemings, many of whom left Norwich for Leeds and Wakefield in Yorkshire, where they prosecuted the woolen-manufacture free from the restrictions of the trades-unions,† while others left the country for Holland, to carry on their trades in the free towns of that country.

The consequence was that Norwich, left to its native enterprise and industry, gradually fell into a state of stagnation and decay. Its population rapidly diminished; a large proportion of the houses stood empty; riots among the distressed workpeople were of frequent occurrence; and it was even mooted in Parliament whether the place should not be razed. Under such circumstances, the corporation determined to call to their aid the skill and industry of the exiled Protestant artisans now flocking into the country. In the year 1564, a deputation of the citizens, headed by the mayor, waited on

* Hasted, *History of Kent*, x., p. 160.
† In the reign of Henry VII. an attempt was made by a body of Flemings to establish the manufacture of felt hats at Norwich. To evade the fiscal regulations of the guilds, they settled outside the boundaries of the city. But an act having been passed enjoining that hats were only to be manufactured in some city, borough, or market-town, the Flemings were thereby brought under the bondage of the guilds; the making of hats by them was suppressed; and the Flemish hat-makers left the neighborhood.

the Duke of Norfolk at his palace in the city, and asked his
assistance in obtaining a settlement in the place of a body of
Flemish workmen. The duke used his influence with this
object, and succeeded in inducing some 300 Dutch and Walloon families to settle in the place at his charge, and to carry
on their trades under a license granted by the queen.

The exiles were very shortly enabled not only to maintain
themselves by their industry, but to restore the city to more
than its former prosperity. The houses which had been
standing empty were again tenanted, the native population
were again fully employed, and the adjoining districts shared
in the general prosperity. In the course of a few years, as
many as 3000 of the foreign workmen had settled in the city,
and many entirely new branches of trade were introduced
and successfully carried on by them. Besides the manufacture of sayes, bayes, serges, arras, mouchade, and bombazines,
they introduced the striping and flowering of silks and damasks, which shortly became one of the most thriving branches
of trade in the place. The manufacture of beaver and felt
hats, before imported from abroad, was also successfully established. One Anthony Solen introduced the art of printing, for which he was awarded the freedom of the city. Two
potters from Antwerp, Jasper Andries and Jacob Janson,
started a pottery, though in a very humble way.* Other
Flemings introduced the art of gardening in the neighbor-

---

* Stowe makes the following reference to these men in his *Survey of London:* "About the year 1567 Jasper Andries and Jacob Janson, potters, came away from Antwerp to avoid the persecution there, and settled themselves in Norwich, where they followed their trade, making galley paving-tiles and apothecaries' vessels, and others, very artificially. Anno 1570 they removed to London. They set forth, in a petition to Queen Elizabeth, that they were the first that brought in and exercised the said science in this realm, and were at great charges before they could find the materials in the realm. They beseeched her, in recompense of their great cost and charges, that she would grant them house-room in or without the liberties of London by the water-side." The brothers Elers, afterward, in 1688, began the manufacture of a better sort of pottery in Staffordshire. They were natives of Nuremberg in Germany. In 1710 they removed from Staffordshire, and settled in Lambeth or Chelsea. To these brothers is ascribed the invention of the salt-glaze.

hood, and culinary stuffs became more plentiful in Norwich than in any other town or city in England. The general result was abundant employment, remunerative trade, cheap food, and great prosperity; Bishop Parkhurst declaring his persuasion that "these blessings from God have happened by reason of the godly exiles who were here so kindly harbored."

But not so very kindly after all. As before, the sour native heart grew jealous; and notwithstanding the admitted prosperity of the place, the local population began to mutter discontent against the foreigners, who had been mainly its cause. Like Jeshurun, the people had waxed fat and they kicked. It is true, the numbers of Dutch, French, and Walloons in Norwich had become very considerable, by reason of the continuance of the persecutions abroad, which drove them across the Channel in increasing numbers. But who so likely to give them succor and shelter as their own countrymen, maintaining themselves by the exercise of their skill and industry in the English towns? The opposition which displayed itself against the foreign artisans is even said to have been encouraged by some of the "gentlemen" of the neighborhood, who in 1570 set on foot a conspiracy, with the object of expelling them by force from the city and realm. But the conspiracy was discovered in time. Its leader and instigator, John Throgmorton, was seized and executed, with two others; and the strangers were thenceforward permitted to pursue their respective callings in peace.

Whatever may have been the shortcomings of Elizabeth in other respects, she certainly proved herself the steadfast friend and protector of the Protestant exiles from first to last. Her conduct with reference to the Norwich conspiracy clearly shows the spirit which influenced her. In a letter written by her from the palace at Greenwich, dated the 19th of March, 1570, she strongly expostulated with the citizens of Norwich against the jealousy entertained by them against the authors of their prosperity. She reminded them of the advantages they had derived from the settlement among them of so many skilled artisans, who were inhabiting the houses which had before stood desolate, and were furnishing employment to large numbers of persons who must otherwise have remained unemployed. She therefore entreated and enjoined them to continue their favors " to the poor men of the Dutch nation, who, seeing the persecution lately begun in their country for the trewe religion, hath fledd into this realm for succour, and be now placed in the city of Norwich, and hath hitherto been favourablye and jintely ordered, which the Queen's Majestie, as a mercifull and religious Prince, doth take in very good part, praeing you to continue your favour unto them so long as they shall lyve emongste you quyetlye and obedyently to God's trewe religion, and to Her Majesty's lawes, for so one chrystian man (in charitie) is bound to help another, especially them who do suffer afflixion for the gospelle's sake."*

---

* The following is a copy of a document in the State Paper Office (Dom. Eliz., 1561), giving an account of "the benefite receyved by the strangers in Norwich for the space of tenne yeres." Several passages of the paper have been obliterated by age:

"*In primis*, They brought a grete comoditie thether—viz., the making of bayes, moucades, grograynes, all sorts of tufts, &c.—wch were not made there before, whereby they do not onely set on worke their owne people, but [do also] set on worke o^r owne people wthin the cittie, as alsoe a gi ete nomber of people nere xx^{ti} myles aboute the cittie, to the grete relief of the [poorer] sorte theie.

"*Item*, By their means o^r cittie [is well inhabited, o^r] decayed houses reedified & repaired that [were in rewyn and more wolde be]. And now good rents [are] paide for the same.

"*Item*, The marchants by their comoditi[es have] and maye have grete trade as well wthin the realme as wthoute the [realme], being in good estimacon in all places.

"*Item*, It cannot be, but whereas a number of people be but the one receyve comoditie of the other as well of the cittie as men of the countrie.

"*Item*, They be contributors to all paym^{ts}, as subsidies, taskes, watches, contribusions, mynisters' wagis, etc.

"*Item*, O^r owne people do practice & make suche comodities as the strangers do make, whereby the youthe is set on worke and kept from idlenes.

"*Item*, They digge & delve a number of acres of grounde, & do sowe flaxe & do make it out in lynnen clothe, wch set many on worke.

"*Item*, They digge & delve a grete quantitie of grounde for rootes, [w^{ch}] is a grete succor & sustenance for the [pore], both for themselves as for all others of cittie and countrie.

A census was shortly after taken of the foreigners settled in Norwich, when it was ascertained that they amounted to about 4000, including women and children; and that they were effectually protected in the exercise of their respective callings, and continued to prosper, may be inferred from the circumstance that, when the numbers were again taken, about ten years later, it was found that the foreign community had increased to 4679 persons.

It would occupy too much space to enter into a detailed account of the settlement of the industrious strangers throughout the country, and to describe the various branches of manufacture which they introduced in addition to those already described. "The persecution for religion in Brabant and Flanders," says Hasted, "communicated to all the Protestant parts of Europe the paper, woollen and other valuable manufactures of Flanders and France, almost peculiar at that time to these countries, and till then in vain practised elsewhere."* Although the manufacture of cloth had already made some progress in England, only the coarser sorts were produced, the best being imported from abroad; and it was not until the settlement among us of the Flemish weavers that this branch of industry became one of national importance. They spread themselves through the towns and villages in the west of England, as well as throughout the north, and wherever the woolen weavers set up their looms they carried on a prosperous trade.† Among other places in the

"*Item*, They live holy of themselves w[th]out [o[r] chardge], and do begge of no man, & do sustayne [all their owne] poore people.

"And to conclude, they for the [moste pte feare] God & diligently & laboriously attende upon their several occupations, they obay all maiestratis & all good lawes & ordynances, they live peaceblie amonge themselves & towards all men, & we thinke o[r] cittie happy to enioye them."

* HASTED, *History of Kent*, x., p. 160.
† Fuller specifies the following textile manufactures as having been established by the immigrants:

In Norwich, cloths, fustians, etc.
" Sudbury, baizes.
" Colchester, sayes and serges
" Kent, Kentish broad-cloths..
" Devonshire, kerseys.

In Gloucestershire } cloths.
" Worcestershire }
" Wales, Welsh friezes.
" Westmoreland, Kendal cloth.
" Lancashire, coatings or cottons.

west, they settled at Worcester, Evesham, Droitwitch, Kidderminster, Stroud, and Glastonbury.* In the east they settled at Colchester,† Hertford, Stamford, and other places. In the north we find them establishing themselves at Manchester, Bolton, and Halifax, where they made "coatings ;"‡ and at Kendal, where they made cloth caps and woolen stockings. The native population gradually learned to practice the same branches of manufacture; new sources of employment were opened up to them; and in the course of a few years, England, instead of depending upon foreigners for its supply of cloth, was not only able to produce sufficient for its own use, but to export the article in considerable quantities abroad.

Other Flemings introduced the art of thread and lace making. A body of them who settled at Maidstone in 1567 car-

---

In Yorkshire, Halifax cloths. In Berks } cloth.
" Somerset, Taunton serges. " Sussex }
" Hants, cloth.

* A settlement of Flemish woolen-weavers took place at Glastonbury as early as 1549, through the influence of the Duke of Somerset, who advanced them money to buy wool, at the same time providing them with houses and small allotments of land from the domain of the Abbey, which the king had granted him. After the fall of the duke the weavers were protected by the Privy Council, and many documents relating to them are to be found in the State Paper Office.—(Edwd. VI., Dom. xiii., 71-77, and xiv., 2-14 and 55.)

† Colchester became exceedingly prosperous in consequence of the settlement of the Flemish artisans there. In 1609 it contained as many as 1300 Walloons and other persons of foreign parentage, and every house was occupied.

‡ The "coatings" or "cottons" of Lancashire were in the first instance but imitations in woolen of the goods known on the Continent by that name; the importation of cotton wool from the Levant having only begun, and that in small quantities, about the middle of the seventeenth century. "There is one fact," says the editor of the *Shuttleworth Papers*, "which seems to show that the Flemings, after their immigration, had much to do with the fulling-mill at Manchester; for its ordinary name was the 'walken-milne'—*walche* being the Flemish name for a fulling-mill. So persistent do we find this name, that a plot of land occupied by a mill on the banks of the Irk still retains its old name of the Walker's Croft (*i. e.*, the fuller's field or ground), and in the earlier Manchester directories the fullers were styled 'walkers.'"—*House and Home Accounts of the Shuttleworth Family* (Chetham Society Papers, 1856-8), p. 637-8. [The name of Walker, so common in Yorkshire, Lancashire, and the clothing districts of the west of England, doubtless originated in this calling, which was followed by so considerable a portion of the population.]

ried on the thread manufacture, flax spun for the thread-man being still known there as "Dutch work." Some lace-makers from Alencon and Valenciennes settled at Cranfield, in Bedfordshire, in 1568; after which others settled at Buckingham, Stony Stratford, and Newport-Pagnell, from whence the manufacture gradually extended over the shires of Oxford, Northampton, and Cambridge. About the same time the manufacture of bone-lace, with thread obtained from Antwerp, was introduced into Devonshire by the Flemish exiles, who settled in considerable numbers at Honiton, Colyton, and other places, where the trade continued to be carried on by their descendants almost to our own time—the Flemish and French names of Stocker, Murch, Spiller, Genest, Maynard, Gerard, Raymunds, Rochett, Kettel, etc., being still common in the lace-towns of the west.

Besides these various branches of textile manufacture, the immigrants applied themselves to mining, working in metals, salt-making, fish-curing, and other arts, in which they were much better skilled than the English then were. Thus we find a body of them from the neighborhood of Liege establishing themselves at Shotley Bridge, in the neighborhood of Newcastle-on-Tyne, where they introduced the making of steel, and became celebrated for the swords and edge-tools which they manufactured. The names of the settlers, some of which have been preserved—Ole, Mohl, Vooz, etc.—indicate their origin, and some of their descendants are still to be found residing in the village, under the names of Oley, Mole, and such like.

Mr. Spencer read a paper on the "Manufacture of Steel" at the meeting of the British Association at Newcastle in 1863, in which he thus referred to these early iron-workers:

"In the wall of an old two-story dwelling-house, the original materials of which are hidden under a coat of rough-cast, there still exists a stone above the doorway with an inscription in bad German, to the following effect: DES. HERREN. SECEN. MACHET. REICH. OHN. ALLF. SORC. WAN. DVZVGLEICH. IN. DEINLM. STAND. TREVW. VND-LLEISIC. BIST. VND. DVEST. WAS. DIR. BE·

LOHLEN. IST. 1691, of which the following is a fiee translation, showing that the original importers of the steel manufacture to the district were probably good Lutherans, who had suffered persecution for conscience' sake: "The blessing of the Lord makes rich without care, so long as you are industrious in your vocation, and do what is ordered you."

There is, however, a much earlier reference to the immigrants in the parish register of Ebchester Church, which contains the entry of a baptism in 1628 of the daughter of one Mathias Wrightson Ole or Oley—the name indicating a probable marriage of the grandfather of the child into a native family of the name of Wrightson, and thereby marking the third generation in the neighborhood.

Another body of skilled workers in iron and steel settled at Sheffield under the protection of the Earl of Shrewsbury, on condition that they should take English apprentices and instruct them in their trade. What the skill of the Low Country iron-workers was will be understood by any one who has seen the beautiful specimens of ancient iron-work to be met with in Belgium, as, for instance, the exquisite iron canopy over the draw-well in front of the cathedral at Antwerp, or the still more elaborate iron gates inclosing the little chapels behind the high altar of the cathedral of St. Bavon, at Ghent. Only the Nurembergers, in all Germany, could then vie with the Flemings in such kind of work. The effects of the instruction given by the Flemish artisans to their Sheffield apprentices were soon felt in the impulse which the improvement of their manufactures gave to the trade of the town; and Sheffield acquired a reputation for its productions in steel and iron which it retains to this day.

A body of refugees of the seafaring class established themselves at Yarmouth in 1568, with the queen's license, and there carried on the business of fishing with great success. Before then, the fish along the English coasts were mostly caught by the Dutch, who cured them in Holland, and brought them back for sale in the English markets. But shortly after the establishment of the fishery at Yarmouth by the Flemings, the home demand was almost entirely supplied by their industry. They also introduced the arts of salt-making and herring-curing, originally a Flemish invention; and the trade gradually extended to other places, and furnished employment to a large number of persons.

By the enterprise chiefly of the Flemish merchants settled in London, a scheme was set on foot for the reclamation of the drowned lands in Hatfield Chase and the great level of the Fens,* and a large number of laborers assembled under Cornelius Vermuyden to execute the necessary works. They were, however, a very different class of men from the modern "navvies," for wherever they went they formed themselves into congregations, erected churches, and appointed ministers to conduct their worship. Upward of two hundred Flemish families settled on the land reclaimed by them in the Isle of Axholm; the ships which brought the immigrants up the Humber to their new homes being facetiously hailed as "the navy of Tarshish." The reclaimers afterward prosecuted their labors, under Vermuyden, in the great level of the Fens, where they were instrumental in recovering a large extent of drowned land, before then a mere watery waste, but now among the richest and most fertile land in England. In short, wherever the refugees settled they acted as so many missionaries of skilled work, exhibiting the best practical examples of diligence, industry, and thrift, and teaching the English people in the most effective manner the beginnings of those various industrial arts in which they have since acquired so much distinction and wealth.

Besides the numerous settlements of the foreigners throughout England, others passed over into Ireland, and settled in Dublin, Waterford, Limerick, Belfast, and other towns. Sir Henry Sidney, in the "Memoir of his Government in Ireland," written in 1590, thus speaks of the little colony of refugees settled at Swords, near Dublin: "I caused to plant and inhabit there about fourtie families of the Reformed Churches

* *Lives of the Engineers*, i., 15-65.

of the Low Countries, flying thence for religion's sake, in one ruinous town called Swords; and truly, sir, it would have done any man good to have seen how diligently they wrought, how they re-edified the quite spoiled ould castell of the same town, and repayred almost all the same, and how godlie and cleanly they, their wiefs, and children lived. They made diaper and tickes for beddes, and other good stuffes for man's use; and as excellent leather of deer skynnes, goat and sheep fells, as is made in Southwarke."*

In the early part of the reign of James I. many Flemings and French obtained grants of naturalization in Ireland; and it was about this time that the Derenzie (now De Rinzy), Olfertson (now Olferts), Vanhomrigh, and Vandeleur families settled in that country. The unsettled state of Ireland was not encouraging to industry; nevertheless, the strangers seem eventually to have obtained a footing and made steady progress.

When the Earl of Strafford was appointed chief deputy in the reign of Charles I., he applied himself with much energy to the establishment of the linen manufacture; sending to Holland for flax-seed, and inviting Flemish and French artisans to settle in Ireland. In order to stimulate the new industry, the earl himself embarked in it, and expended not less than £30,000 of his private fortune in the enterprise. It was afterward made one of the grounds of his impeachment that "he had obstructed the industry of the country by introducing new and unknown processes into the manufacture of flax."† It was nevertheless greatly to the credit of the earl that he should have endeavored to improve the industry of Ireland by introducing the superior processes employed by the foreign artisans; and had he not attempted to turn the improved flax manufacture to his own advantage by erecting it into a personal monopoly, he might have been entitled to regard as a genuine benefactor of Ireland.‡

* See *Ulster Journal of Archæology*, v., p. 306.
† FOSTER, *Lives of Eminent British Statesmen*, ii., 385.
‡ The first Duke of Ormonde, imitating the example of Strafford, in like

Not many of the refugees found their way into Scotland.* That country was then too poor to hold out much encouragement to the banished artisans. An attempt was, however, made about the beginning of the seventeenth century to introduce into Scotland the manufacture of cloth; and in 1601, seven Flemings were engaged to settle in the country and set the work agoing—six of them for serges, and one for broadcloth. But disputes arose among the boroughs as to the towns in which the settlers were to be located, during which the strangers were "entertained in meat and drink."† At length, in 1609, a body of Flemings became settled in the Canongate of Edinburg under one Joan Van Hedan, where they engaged in "making, dressing, and litting of stuffis, giving great licht and knowledge of their calling to the country people."‡

An attempt was also made to introduce the manufacture of paper in Scotland about the middle of the seventeenth century, and French workmen were introduced for the instruction of the natives. The first mill was erected at Dalry, on the Water of Leith; but, though they succeeded in making gray and blue paper, the speculation does not seem to have answered, as we find Alexander Daes, one of the principal proprietors, shortly after occupied in showing an elephant about the country!—the first animal of the kind that had been seen north of the Tweed.§

manner established about five hundred immigrants at Chapel Izod, in Kilkenny, under Colonel Richard Lawrence. He there built houses for the weavers, supplying them with looms and raw material, and a considerable trade in cordage, sail-cloth, and linen shortly grew up. The duke also settled large colonies of Walloons at Clonmel, Kilkenny, and Carrick-on-Suir, where they established, and for some time successfully carried on, the manufacture of woolen cloths.

* Michelet, the French historian, says he found at Holyrood the decayed tomb-stone of a Frenchman, who had been the first paviour in Edinburg, and probably in Scotland.

† CHAMBERS—*Domestic Annals of Scotland*, i., p. 351. ‡ *Ibid.*, i., p. 421.

§ *Ibid.*, ii., p. 390–410. The art of paper-making was not successfully established in Scotland until the middle of the following century. Literature must then have been at a low ebb north of the Tweed. In 1683 there was only *one* printing-press in all Scotland; and when it was proposed to license a second printer, the widow of Andrew Anderson, who held the only license,

Although the number of foreigners who had migrated from Flanders, France, and other European countries into England, down to about the middle of the seventeenth century, had been very large, it had by no means ceased. Every fresh outburst of persecution abroad was followed by renewed landings of the persecuted on our shores. Whereas the number of persons of foreign birth established in the city of London in 1567 included 4851 Flemings and 512 French, it was found, ten years later, that the foreigners were more than treble the number; and a century later, there were estimated to be not fewer than 13,500 refugees of French birth in London alone.

The policy adopted by the early English kings, and so consistently pursued by Queen Elizabeth throughout her reign, of succoring and protecting industrious exiles flying into England for refuge, was followed by James I. and by the later Stuarts. An attempt was indeed made by Bishop Laud, in the reign of Charles I., in 1622, to compel the refugees, who were for the most part Calvinists, to conform to the English Liturgy. On this, the foreign congregations appealed to the king, pleading the hospitality extended to them by the nation when they had fled from papal persecution abroad, and the privileges and exemptions granted to them by Edward VI., which had been confirmed by Elizabeth and James, and even by Charles I. himself. The utmost concession that the king would grant was, that those who were born aliens might still enjoy the use of their own church service, but that all their children born in England should regularly attend the parish churches. Even this small concession was limited only to the congregation at Canterbury, and measures were taken to enforce conformity in the other dioceses.*

endeavored to keep the new printer (one David Lindsay) out of the trade, alleging that she had been previously invested with the sole privilege, and that "*one press is sufficiently able to supply all Scotland!*"

* The policy of Laud, by which Charles I. was mainly guided, was essentially reactionary. His object seemed to be to establish a great ecclesiastical hierarchy in England, with himself as pope. On his appointment as Primate of England in 1633, he proceeded to assimilate the ritual and ceremonies of the Church to the Roman model. Strict rules were enjoined with

The refugees thus found themselves exposed to the same kind of persecution from which they had originally fled into England, and, rather than endure it, several thousands of them left the country, abandoning their new homes, and again risking the loss of all rather than give up their religion. The result was the emigration of about a hundred and forty families from Norwich into Holland, where the Dutch received them hospitably, and gave them house-accommodation free, with exemption from taxes for seven years, during which they instructed the natives in the woolen manufacture, of which they had before been ignorant. But the greater number of the nonconformist foreigners emigrated with their families to North America, and swelled the numbers of the little colony already formed in Massachusetts Bay, which eventually laid the foundation of the great New England States.

respect to the dress of the clergy, and the use of surplices and hoods, copes, albs, stoles, and chasubles. Careful attention was paid to ritual, and to the attitudes and postures, the crossings and genefluxions, with which it was to be accompanied. Candles were introduced on the communion table, which was railed in and called the altar, after the manner of Rome; while the communion became a more or less disguised mass. Laud would admit of no Low-Churchism or Dissent, against both of which he hurled excommunications and anathemas. Under his rule, the poor foreign Protestants felt themselves like toads under a harrow. When they humbly expostulated with him by petition, and prayed for that liberty of worship which they had enjoyed in past reigns, he told them that his course was not to be stopped by the letters-patent of Edward VI., or by any arguments they might use; that their churches were nests of schism; that it were better there should be no foreigners in England than that they should be permitted to prejudice and endanger the Church government of the realm; and that they must conform at their peril by the time appointed. While Laud was thus rigid in matters of religion, he was equally uncompromising in matters of literature. He instituted a strict censorship of the press, and if any book was published without his *imprimatur*, the author and printer were liable to be flogged, fined, placed in the pillory, and have their ears cropped. The reprinting of old books was also prohibited; even such works as those of the Protestant Bishop Jewell being interdicted. The tendency of all this was obvious. Laud was carrying the English Church back to Rome as fast as the nation would let him. The Pope offered him a cardinal's hat, and repeated the offer, but the time for accepting it never arrived. A few weeks after the meeting of the Long Parliament, in 1640, Laud was impeached of high treason, condemned, and sentenced to death; and he was beheaded on the 10th of January following. The injustice as well as illegality of the sentence is now, we believe, generally admitted; but the Long Parliament had the upper hand, and the struggle had become one not only for liberty, but for life.

After the lapse of a few years, the reactionary course on which Archbishop Laud and Charles I. had entered was summarily checked, as all readers of history know. The foreign refugees were again permitted to worship God according to conscience, and the right of free asylum in England was again recognized and established.

CHAPTER VI.

THE EARLY WALLOON AND FRENCH CHURCHES IN ENGLAND.

THE chief object which the foreign Protestants had in view in flying for refuge into England was to worship God according to conscience. For that they had sacrificed all—possessions, home, and country. Accordingly, no sooner did they settle in any place than they formed themselves into congregations for the purpose of worshiping together. While their numbers were small, they were content to meet in each other's houses, or in workshops or other roomy places; but, as the influx of refugees increased with the increase of persecution abroad, and as many pastors of eminence came with them, the strangers besought the government to grant them conveniences for holding their worship in public. This was willingly conceded to them, and as early as the reign of Edward VI. churches were set apart for their use in London, Norwich, Southampton, and Canterbury.

The first Walloon and French churches in London owed their origin to the young King Edward VI., and to the protection of the Duke of Somerset and Archbishop Cranmer. On the 24th of July, 1550, the King issued royal letters patent, appointing John A' Lasco, a learned Polish gentleman,*

* In 1544, John A' Lasco gave up the office of provost of the church of Gnezne in Posen, of which his uncle was archbishop, to go and found a Protestant church at Embden, in East Friesland. An order of Charles V. obliged him to leave that town four years later, when he came over to England, in the year 1548, and placed himself in communication with Cecil, who recommended him to the Duke of Somerset and Archbishop Cranmer. During his residence in England, A' Lasco was actively engaged in propagating the new views. He established the first French printing-house in London for the publication of religious books, of which he produced many; and he also published others, written in French by Edward VI. himself. During the reign of Mary, when Protestantism in all its forms was temporarily suppressed, A' Lasco fled for his life, and took refuge in Switzerland, where he died. The foreign churches in Austin Friars and Threadneedle Street were reopened on the accession of Elizabeth.

H

superintendent of the refugee Protestant churches in England; and at the same time he assigned to such of the strangers as had settled in London the church in Austin Friars called the Temple of Jesus, wherein to hold their assemblies and celebrate their worship according to the custom of their country. Of this church Walter Deloen and Martin Flanders, François de la Riviere and Richard François, were appointed the first ministers; the two former of the Dutch or Flemish part of the congregation, and the two latter of the French. The king further constituted the superintendent and the ministers into a body politic, and placed them under the safeguard of the civil and ecclesiastical authorities of the kingdom. The number of refugees settled in London had by this time become so great that one church was found insufficient for their accommodation, although the Dutch and French met at alternate hours during the day. In the course of a few months, therefore, a second place of worship was granted for the French-speaking part of the refugees; and the church of St. Anthony's Hospital, in Threadneedle Street, was set apart for their use.*

Walloon and French congregations were also formed at Sandwich, Rye, Winchelsea, Southampton, and the other ports at which the refugees first landed; at Yarmouth, where they established their fishing-station; and at Colchester, Stamford, Thetford, Glastonbury, and the inland towns, where they carried on the cloth manufacture. At Sandwich, the old church of St. Peter's was set apart for their special use; but, at the same time, they were enjoined not to dispute openly concerning their religion.† At Rye they were allowed the use of

---

* Both these churches were subsequently destroyed by fire. The church in Austin Friars was burnt down quite recently, and has since been restored. The church in Threadneedle Street was burnt down during the great fire of London, and was afterward rebuilt; but it has since been demolished to make way for the approaches to the new Royal Exchange, when it was removed to the new French church in St. Martin's-le-Grand.

† This church long continued to flourish. The Rev. Gerard de Gols, rector of St. Peter's, and minister of the Dutch congregation in Sandwich between 1713 and 1737, was highly esteemed in his day as an author, and so

the parish church during one part of the day, until a special place of worship could be provided for their accommodation. At Norwich, where the number of the settlers was greater in proportion to the population than in most other towns, the choir of Friars Preachers Church, on the east side St. Andrew's Hall, was assigned for the use of the Dutch, and the Bishop's Chapel, afterward the church of St. Mary's Tombland, was appropriated for the use of the French and Walloons.

Two of the most ancient and interesting of the churches founded by the refugees are those of Southampton and Canterbury, both of which survive to this day. Southampton was resorted to at an early period by the fugitives from the persecutions in Flanders and France. Many came from the Channel Islands, where they had first fled for refuge, on account of the proximity of these places to the French coast. This appears from the register of the church, a document of great interest, preserved among the records of the Register General at Somerset House.* Like the two foreign Protestant churches in London already named, that at Southampton was established in the reign of Edward VI.,† when an old chapel in Winkle Street, near the harbor, called Domus Dei, or "God's House," forming part of an ancient hospital founded by two merchants in the reign of Henry III., was set apart for the accommodation of the refugees. The hospital and chapel had originally been dedicated to St. Julian, the patron of travelers, and was probably used in ancient times by pil-

much respected by his fellow-townsmen that he was one of the persons selected by the corporation to support the canopies at the coronation of George II. and Queen Caroline.

* See Appendix, *Registers of French Protestant Churches in England.*

† The original grant of the chapel for the use of the Protestant refugees is usually attributed to Elizabeth, who merely confirmed the grant made by Edward VI. Mr. Burn (*Hist. of Foreign Protestant Refugees*, p. 80) quotes a petition addressed by the settlers to the mayor and aldermen of Southampton in Queen Elizabeth's time (Brit. Mus. Vesp., F. ix.), asking "to have a church assigned to them, and to have sacraments and sermons as used in the time of Edward VI." They at the same time asked permission to use their various crafts in the town, and "to employ their own countrymen and maidens in their trades."

grims passing through Southampton to and from the adjoining monastic establishments of Netley and Beaulieu, and the famous shrines of Winchester, Wells, and Salisbury.

There are no records of this early French church beyond what can be gathered from their register,* which, however, is remarkably complete and well preserved, and presents many points of curious interest. The first entries are dated 1567, when the register began to be kept; and they are continued, with occasional intermissions, down to the year 1797. From the first list of communicants given, it appears that their number in 1567 was fifty-eight, of whom eight were distinguished as "Anglois." The callings of the members were various, medical men being comparatively numerous; while others are described as weavers, bakers, cutlers, and brewers. The places from which the refugees had come are also given, those most frequently occurring being Valenciennes, Lisle, Dieppe, Gernése (Guernsey), and Jersé. It further appears from the entries that satisfactory evidence was required of the character and religious standing of the new refugees who from time to time arrived from abroad, before they were admitted to the privileges of membership; the words "avec attestation," "témoinage par ecrit," or simply "témoinage," being attached to a large number of names. Many of the fugitives, before they succeeded in making their escape, appear to have been forced to attend mass; and their first care on landing seems to have been to seek out the nearest pastor, confess their sins, and take the sacrament according to the rites of their church. On the 3d of July, 1574 (more than a year after the massacre of St. Bartholomew), occurs this entry: "Tiebaut de Béfroi, his wife, his son, and his daughter, after having made their public acknowledgment of having been at the mass, were all received to the sacrament."

One of the most interesting portions of the register is the record of fasts and thanksgivings held at God's House, in the

* Register of the Church of St. Julian, or God's House, of Southampton. Archives of Registrar General at Somerset House. See Appendix.

course of which we see the poor refugees anxiously watching the course of events abroad, deploring the increasing ferocity of the persecutors, praying God to bridle the strong and wicked men who sought to destroy His Church, and to give the help of His outstretched arm to its true followers and defenders. The first of such fasts (jeûsnes) relates to the persecutions in the Netherlands by the Duke of Alva, and runs as follows:* "The year 1568, the third day of September, was celebrated a public fast; the occasion was that Monseignor the Prince of Orange had descended from Germany into the Low Countries to try with God's help to deliver the poor churches there from affliction; and now to beseech the Lord most fervently for the deliverance of His people, this fast was celebrated."

Another fast was held in 1570, on the occasion of the defeat of the Prince of Condé at the battle of Jarnac, when the little church at Southampton again beseeched help for their brethren against the calamities which threatened to overwhelm them. Two years later, on the 25th of September, 1572, we find them again entreating help for the Prince of Orange, who had entered the Low Countries from Germany with a new army, to deliver the poor churches there from the hands of the Duke of Alva, "that cruel tyrant; and also, principally, for that the churches of France have suffered a marvelous and extremely horrible calamity—a horrible massacre having been perpetrated at Paris on the 24th day of August last, in which a great number of nobles and of the faithful were killed in one night, about twelve or thirteen thousand; preaching forbidden throughout the kingdom, and all the property of the faithful given up to pillage throughout the kingdom. Now, for the consolation of them and of the Low Countries, and to pray the Lord for their deliverance, was celebrated this solemn fast."†

Other fasts were held, to pray God to maintain her majesty the queen in good friendship and accord with the Prince

* For the words in the original, see Appendix. † *Id. ibid.*

of Orange,* to uphold the Protestant churches in France, to stay the ravages of the plague, to comfort and succor the poor people of Antwerp driven out of that city on its destruction by the Spaniards,† and to help and strengthen the churches of the refuge established in England. Several of these fasts were appointed to be held by the conference (colloque) of the churches, the meetings of which were held annually in London, Canterbury, Norwich, Southampton, and other places, so that at the same time the same fast was being held in all the foreign churches throughout the kingdom.

In one case the shock of an earthquake is recorded. The entry runs as follows: "The 28th of April, 1580, a fast was celebrated to pray God to preserve us against his anger, since on the sixth of this month we have been appalled by a great trembling of the earth, which has not only been felt throughout all this kingdom, but also in Picardy and the Low Countries of Flanders; as well as to preserve us against war and plague, and to protect the poor churches of Flanders and France against the assaults of their enemies, who have joined their forces to the great army of Spain for the purpose of working their destruction." Another fast commemorates the appearance of a comet, which was first seen on the 8th of October, and continued in sight until the 12th of December, in the year 1581.

A subsequent entry relates to the defeat of the great Spanish Armada. On this occasion the little church united in a public thanksgiving. The record is as follows: "The 29th of November, 1588, thanks were publicly rendered to God for the wonderful dispersion of the Spanish fleet, which had descended upon the coast of England with the object of conquering the kingdom and bringing it under the tyranny of the Pope." And on the 5th of December following, another public fast was held for the purpose of praying the Lord that he would be pleased to grant to the churches of France and of Flanders a like happy deliverance as had been vouchsafed

* Fast, 29th August, 1576. † Fast, 22d November, 1576.

to England. A blessing was also sought upon the English navy, which had put to flight the Armada of Spain.

Other fasts and thanksgivings relate to the progress of the arms of Henry of Navarre, and his subsequent ascent of the French throne, when the right of the French Protestants to liberty of worship became legally recognized.* In the midst of these events Queen Elizabeth visited Southampton with her court, on which occasion the refugees sought to obtain access to her majesty, to thank her for the favor and protection they had enjoyed at her hands. They were unable to obtain an interview with the queen until she had set out on her way homeward, when a deputation of the refugees waited for her outside the town and craved a brief interview. This she graciously accorded, when their spokesman thanked her for the tranquillity and rest which they had enjoyed during the twenty-four years that they had lived in the town, to which the queen replied very kindly, giving praise to God who had given her the opportunity and the power of welcoming and encouraging the poor foreigners.†

A considerable proportion of the fasts relate to the plague, which was a frequent and unwelcome visitor—on one occasion sweeping away almost the entire settlement. In 1583 the communicants were reduced to a very small number, but those who remained met daily at "God's House" to pray for the abatement of the pestilence. It returned again in 1604, and again swept away a large proportion of the congregation, which had considerably increased in the interval. One hundred and sixty-one persons are set down as having died of plague in that year, the number of deaths amounting to four and five a day. The greater part of the inhabitants of Southampton abandoned their dwellings, and the clergy seem

* On the 7th of September, 1589, the French Protestant refugees in London sent an address to Henry IV., on his accession to the French throne, exhorting him to continue steadfast in his support of the Church, showing that the poor French emigrants had neither forgotten their native country, nor the cause of their coming hither.—*State Paper Office;* Foreign Correspondence—France.

† Entry in Register of God's House, Southampton. See Appendix.

to have accompanied them; for on the 23d of July, 1665, an English child was brought to the French church to be baptized, by authority of the mayor, and the ceremony was performed by M. Courand, the pastor. Shortly after, Courand died at his post, after registering with his own hand the deaths of the greater part of his flock. On the 21st of September, 1665, the familiar handwriting of the pastor ceases, and the entry is made by another hand: "Monsieur Courand, notre pasteur—peste." While death was thus busy, marrying and giving in marriage nevertheless went on. Some couples were so impatient to be united that they could not wait for the return of the English clergy, who had all left the town, but proceeded to be married at "God's House," as we find by the register.

Another highly-interesting memorial of the asylum given to the persecuted Protestants of Flanders and France so many centuries ago, is presented by the Walloon or French church which exists to this day in Canterbury Cathedral. It was formed at a very early period, some suppose as early as the reign of Edward VI., like those of London and Southampton; but the first record preserved of its existence is early in the reign of Elizabeth. Shortly after the landings of the foreign Protestants at Sandwich and Rye, a body of them proceeded to Canterbury, and sought permission of the mayor and aldermen to settle in the place. They came principally from Lisle, Nuelle, Turcoing, Waterloo, Darmentiéres, and other places situated along the present French frontier.

The first arrivals of the fugitives consisted of eighteen families, led by their pastor, Hector Hamon, "minister verbi Dei." They are described as having landed at Rye, and temporarily settled at Winchelsea, from which place they came across the country to Canterbury. Persecution had made these poor exiles very humble. All that they sought was freedom to worship and to labor. They had no thought but to pursue their several callings in peace and quiet—to bring up their children virtuously—and to lead a diligent, sober, and religious life, according to the dictates of conscience. Men such as these are the salt of the earth in all times; yet they had been forced by a ruthless persecution from their homes, and driven forth as wanderers on the face of the earth.

In their memorial to the mayor and aldermen in 1564, they set forth that they had, for the love of religion (which they earnestly desired to hold fast with a free conscience), relinquished their country and their worldly goods; and they humbly prayed that they might be permitted the free exercise of their religion within the city, and allowed the privilege of a temple to hold their worship in, together with a place of sepulture for their dead. They farther requested that lest, under the guise of religion, profane and evil-minded men should seek to share in the privileges which they sought to obtain, none should be permitted to join them without giving satisfactory evidences of their probity of character. And, in order that the young persons belonging to their body might not remain untaught, they also asked permission to maintain a teacher for the purpose of instructing them in the French tongue. Finally, they declared their intention of being industrious citizens, and proceeding, under the favor and protection of the magistrates, to make Florence, serges, bombazine, Orleans, silk, bayes, mouquade, and other stuffs.*

---

* The following is the memorial, as given in the appendix to SOMNER'S *Antiquities of Canterbury*, and which he entitles "The articles granted to the French strangers by the Mayor and Aldermen of the City:"

Dignissimis Dominis Domino Maiori et Fratribus Consiliariis Urbis Cantuariensis Salutem.

Supplicant humilimè extranei vestra libertate adm si in ista urbe Cantuariensi quat' velitis sequentes articulos illis concedere.

Prior Articulus.

1. Quia religionis amore (quam libera conscientia tenere percupiunt) patriam et propria bona reliquerunt, orant sibi liberum exercitium suæ religionis permitti in hac urbe, quod ut fiat commodius sibi assignari templum et locum in quo poterint sepelire mortuos suos.

Secundus Articulus.

2. Et ne sub eorum umbra et titulo religionis profani et malè morati homines sese in hanc urbem intromittant per quos tota societas malè audiret apud cives vestros; supplicant nemini liberam mansionem in hac urbe permitti, nisi prius suæ probitatis sufficiens testimonium vobis dederit.

Canterbury was fortunate in being appealed to by the fugitives for an asylum, bringing with them, as they did, skill, industry, and character; and the authorities at once cheerfully granted them all that they asked, in the terms of their own memorial. The mayor and aldermen gave them permission to carry on their trades within the precincts of the city. At the same time, the liberal-minded Matthew Parker, then Archbishop of Canterbury, with the sanction of the queen, granted to the exiles the free use of the Under Croft of the cathedral, where "the gentle and profitable strangers," as the archbishop styled them, not only celebrated their worship and taught their children, but set up their looms and carried on their several trades.

The Under Croft, or Crypt, extends under the choir and high altar of Canterbury Cathedral, and is of considerable extent. The body of Thomas à Becket was buried first in the Under Croft, and lay there for fifty years, until it was translated with great ceremony to the sumptuous shrine prepared by Stephen Langton, his successor, at the east end of the cathedral. Part of the Under Croft, immediately under the cross aisle of the choir, was dedicated and endowed as a

Tertius Articulus.

3. Et ne inventus inculta maneat, requirunt permissionem dari præceptori quem secum adduxerunt instruendi juvenes, tum eos quos secum adduxerunt, tum eos qui volunt linguam Gallicum discere.

Quartus Articulus.

4. Artes ad quas exercendas sunt vocari, et in quibus laborare cupit tota societas sub vestro favore et protectione sunt Florenci, Serges, Bombasin, D. of Ascot Serges, etc., of Orleance, Frotz, Silkwever, Mouquade, Mauntes, Bazes, &c., Stofe Mouquades.

Nomina supplicantium sunt.

HECTOR HAMON, Minister verbi Dei.
VINCENTIUS PRIMONT, Institutor Juventutis.
EGIDIUS COUSIN, Magister operum, et conductor totius congregationis in opere.

MICHAEL COUSIN.   JOHANNES LE PELU.
JACOBUS QUERIN.   JOHANNES DE LA FORTERYE.
PETRUS DU BOSE.   NOEL LESTENE.
ANTONIUS DU VERDIER.   NICHOLAUS DUBUISSON.
PHILIPPUS DE NEUZ.   PETRUS DESPORTES.
ROBERTUS JOVELIN.   JACOBUS BOUDET.
              TRES VIDUÆ.

chapel by Edward the Black Prince; and another part of the area was inclosed by rich Gothic stone-work, and dedicated to the Virgin.*

The Lady Undercroft Chapel was one of the most gorgeous shrines of its time. It was so rich and of such high esteem, that Somner says "the sight of it was debarred to the vulgar, and reserved only for persons of great quality." Erasmus, who by especial favor (Archbishop Warham recommending him) was brought to the sight of it, describes it thus: "There," said he, "the Virgin-mother hath a habitation, but somewhat dark, inclosed with a double Sept or Rail of Iron for fear of Thieves. For indeed I never saw a thing more laden with Riches. Lights being brought, we saw a more than Royal Spectacle. In beauty it far surpasseth that of Walsingham. This Chapel is not showed but to Noblemen and especial Friends."† Over the statue of the Virgin, which was in pure gold, there was a royal purple canopy, starred with jewels and precious stones; and a row of silver lamps was suspended from the roof in front of the shrine.

All these decorations were, however, removed by Henry VIII., who took possession of the greater part of the gold, and silver, and jewels of the cathedral, and had them con-

---

* Canterbury Cathedral contains an interesting Huguenot memorial of about the same date as the settlement of the Walloons in the Under Croft. The visitor to the cathedral observes behind the high altar, near the tomb of the Black Piince, a coffin of brick plastered over in the form of a sarcophagus. It contains the ashes of Cardinal Odo Coligny, brother of the celebrated Admiral Coligny, one of the first victims of the massacre of St. Bartholomew. In 1568 the cardinal visited Queen Elizabeth, who received him with maiked respect, and lodged him sumptuously at Sheen. Thiee years later he died at Canterbury after a brief illness. Strype, and nearly all subsequent writers, allege that he died of poison, administered by one of his attendants because of his supposed conversion to Protestantism. From a full report of his death made to Burghley and Leicester, preserved in the State Paper Office, there does not, however, appear sufficient ground for the popular belief. His body was not interred, but was placed in the brick coffin behind the high altar, in order that it might be the more readily removed for interment in the family vault in France when the religious troubles which then prevailed had come to an end. But the massacre of St. Bartholomew shoitly followed; the Coligny family were thereby almost destroyed; and hence the body of Odo Coligny has not been buried to this day.

† SOMNER—*Antiquities of Canterbury*, 1703, p. 97.

verted into money.* The Under Croft became deserted; the chapels it contained were disused; and it remained merely a large, vaulted, ill-lighted area, until permission was granted to the Walloons to use it by turns as a weaving-shed, a school, and a church. Over the capitals of the columns on the north side of the crypt are several texts of Scripture still to be seen in old French, written up for the benefit of the scholars, and doubtless taught them by heart. The texts are from the Psalms, the Proverbs, and the New Testament.

Desolate, gloomy, and sepulchral though the place was— with the ashes of former archbishops and dignitaries of the cathedral mouldering under their feet — the exiles were thankful for the refuge it afforded them in their time of need, and they daily made the vaults resound with their prayer and praise. Morning and night they "sang the Lord's song in a strange land, and wept when they remembered Zion." During the daytime the place was busy with the sound of labor; the floor was covered with looms, through which the shuttles went flashing; and the exiles were cheered at the thought of being able thus honestly to earn their living, though among foreigners.

The refugees worked, worshiped, and prospered. They succeeded in maintaining themselves; they supported their own poor; and they were able, out of their small means, to entend a helping hand to the numerous fugitives who continued to arrive in England, fleeing from the persecutions in Flanders and France. Their numbers so increased, that in the course of a few years the French congregation consisted of several hundred persons. Every corner of the Under Croft was occupied, and, as more immigrants continued to

* One of the richest parts of the treasure taken from the Cathedral was the shrine of Thomas à Becket, thus described by Stow in his *Annals* (in Henry VIII.): "The timber-work of this Shrine on the outside was covered with plates of Gold, damasked and embossed with Wires of Gold, garnished with Brooches, Images, Angels, Chains, Precious Stones, and great Orient Pearls, the Spoil of which Shrine (in Gold and Jewels of an inestimable value) filled two great Chests, one of which six or eight strong men could do no more than convey out of the Church—all which was taken to the King's use."

arrive, the place became too small to accommodate them. Somner, writing in 1639, thus refers to the exiles:

"Let me now lead you to the Under Croft—a place fit, and haply (as one cause) fitted to keep in memory the subterraneous Temples of the Primitives in the times of Persecution. The West part whereof, being spacious and lightsome, for many years hath been the strangers' church: A congregation for the most part of distressed Exiles, grown so great, and yet daily multiplying, that the place in short time is likely to prove a Hive too little to contain such a Swarm. So great an alteration is there since the time the first of the Tribe came hither, the number of them then consisting of but eighteen families, or thereabouts."[*]

The exiles remained unmolested in the exercise of their worship until the period when Laud became archbishop, when the attempt was made to compel them to conform to the English ritual, and they began to fear lest they should again have to fly and seek refuge elsewhere. But the attention of the archbishop was shortly diverted from them by the outbreak of the Scottish war; and although there were riots and disturbances in the cathedral[†]—the popular indignation being greatly excited by the retrograde movement then on foot in religious and political affairs—it does not appear that the foreigners were farther molested. They were protected throughout the period of the Commonwealth and the Protectorate, and afterward by Charles II. Their num-

[*] SOMNER—*Antiquities of Canterbury*, Part i., 97.
[†] In the preface to the new edition of Somner's *Antiquities of Canterbury*, the editor, Nicolas Battely, M.A., thus refers to these riots: "Mr. William Somner collected the Antiquities of Canterbury in a time of Peace, while (as yet) the Church flourished under the Government of King Charles I., and under the conduct of Archbishop Laud, to whose Patronage he dedicated this Work, which he published Anno 1640. But before this Year was ended a dismal Storm did arise, which did shake and threaten with a final overthrow the very Foundations of this Church: For upon the Feast of the Epiphany, and the Sunday following, there was a riotous disturbance raised by some disorderly People, in the time of Divine Service, in the Quire of this Church: And altho' by the care of the Prebendaries a stop was put to these Disorders for a time, yet afterwards the Madness of the People did rage, and prevail beyond resistance. The venerable Dean and Canons were turned out of their Stalls, the beautiful and new-erected Font was pulled down, the Inscriptions, Figures, and Coats of Arms, engraven upon Brass, were torn off from the ancient Monuments; and whatsoever there was of beauty or decency in the Holy Place was despoiled by the outrages of Sacrilege and Profaneness."

bers were greatly increased by the arrival of a body of silk and stuff weavers from Tours, until, in 1665, they numbered 126 master-weavers and above 1300 workpeople, who carried on the trades of silk and stuff weaving, dyeing, loom and wheel making, and various other branches of skilled industry. At the same time, they gave employment to a large number of the townspeople, who gradually learned the various branches of trade pursued by the foreigners. In 1676 the king granted the weavers a charter, under which they formed themselves into a company, entitled "The Masters, Wardens, Assistants, and Fellowship of Weavers;" and in the course of a few more years they had a thousand looms at work.

The exiles continued to prosper and the trade of Canterbury to thrive until after the revocation of the Edict of Nantes, which was followed by another immense influx of refugee Protestants from France into various parts of England. A large number of them settled in Spitalfields, and there established various branches of the silk manufacture; and the advantages of concentrating the trade shortly after induced the greater part of the Canterbury settlers to remove to London. The consequence was, that the French church at Canterbury gradually declined; and though many of the French exiles and their descendants remained in the city, and are traceable to this day, they have long ceased to form a distinctive part of the population.

But it is a remarkable circumstance that the original French Calvinist church still continues to exist in Canterbury Cathedral. Three hundred years have passed since the first body of exiled Walloons met to worship there — three hundred years, during which generations have come and gone, and revolutions have swept over Europe; and still that eloquent memorial of the religious history of the Middle Ages survives, bearing testimony alike to the rancor of the persecutions abroad, the heroic steadfastness of the foreign Protestants, the large and liberal spirit of the English Church, and the glorious asylum which England has in all times given to foreigners flying for refuge against oppression and tyranny.

The visitor to the cathedral, in passing through the Under Croft, has usually pointed out to him the apartment still used as "the French church." It is walled off from the crypt in the south side-aisle; and through the windows which overlook the interior the arrangements of the place can easily be observed. It is plainly fitted up with pews, a pulpit, and precentor's desk, like a dissenting place of worship; and, indeed, it is a dissenting place of worship, though forming part of the High Cathedral of Canterbury. The place also contains a long table, at which the communicants sit when receiving the sacrament of the Lord's Supper, after the manner of the Geneva brethren.

And here the worship still continues to be conducted in French, and the psalms are sung to the old Huguenot tunes, almost within sound of the high choral service of the Established Church of England overhead. "Here," says the German Dr. Pauli, "the early refugees celebrated the services of their church; and here their descendants, who are now reduced to a very small number, still carry on their Presbyterian mode of worship in their own tongue, immediately below the south aisle of the high choir, where the Anglican ritual is observed in all its prescribed form—a noble and touching concurrence, the parallel to which can not be met with in any other cathedral church in England."*

The French church at Canterbury would doubtless long since have become altogether extinct, like the other churches of the refugees, but for an endowment of about £200 a year, which has served to keep it alive. The members do not now amount to more than twenty, of whom two are elders and four deacons. But, though the church has become reduced to a mere vestige and remnant of what it was, it nevertheless serves to mark an epoch of memorable importance to England.

* PAULI—*Pictures of Old England*, 29.

CHAPTER VII.

RENEWAL OF THE PERSECUTIONS IN FRANCE.—REVOCATION OF THE EDICT OF NANTES.

THE Huguenots did not long enjoy the privileges conceded to them by the Edict of Nantes. Twelve years after its promulgation by Henry IV., that monarch was assassinated by Ravaillac, on which the elements of discord again broke loose. Although the edicts of toleration were formally proclaimed by his successor, they were practically disregarded and violated. Marie de Medicis, the queen regent, was, like all her race, the bitter enemy of Protestantism. She was governed by Italian favorites, who inspired her policy. They distributed among themselves the public treasure with so lavish a hand that the Parisians rose in insurrection against them, murdered Concini, whom the queen had created Marshal d'Ancre, and afterward burned his wife as a sorceress; the young king, Louis XIII., then only about sixteen years old, joining in the atrocities.

Civil war shortly broke out between the court and the country factions, which soon became embittered by the old religious animosities. There was a great massacre of the Huguenots in Bearn, where their worship was suppressed, and the Roman Catholic priests were installed in their places. Other massacres followed, and occasioned general alarm among the Protestants. In those towns where they were the strongest they shut their gates against the king's forces, and determined to resist force by force. In 1621, the young king set out with his army to reduce the revolted towns, and first attacked St. Jean d'Angely, which he captured after a siege of twenty-six days. He next assailed Montauban, but, after

SIEGE OF ROCHELLE.

a siege of two months, he was compelled to retire from the place defeated, with tears in his eyes.

In 1622, the king called to his councils Armand Duplessis de Richelieu, the queen's favorite adviser, whom the Pope had recently presented with a cardinal's hat. His force of character was soon felt, and in all affairs of government the influence of Richelieu became supreme. One of the first objects to which he applied himself was the suppression of the anarchy which prevailed throughout France, occasioned in a great measure by the abuse of the feudal powers still exercised by the ancient noblesse. Another object which he considered essential to the unity and power of France was the annihilation of the Protestants as a political party. Accordingly, shortly after his accession to office, he advised the attack of Rochelle, the head-quarters of the Huguenots, and regarded as the citadel of Protestantism in France. His advice was followed, and a powerful army was assembled and marched on the doomed place, Richelieu combining in himself the functions of bishop, prime minister, and commander-in-chief. The Huguenots of Rochelle defended themselves with great bravery for more than a year, during which they endured the greatest privations. But their resistance was in vain; for on the 28th of October, 1628, Richelieu rode into Rochelle by the king's side, in velvet and cuirass, at the head of the royal army; after which he proceeded to perform high mass in the great church of St. Margaret, in celebration of his victory.

The siege of Rochelle, while in progress, excited much interest among the Protestants throughout England, and anxious appeals were made to Charles I. to send help to the besieged. This he faithfully promised to do; and he dispatched a fleet and army to their assistance, commanded by his favorite, the Duke of Buckingham. The fleet duly arrived off Rochelle, and the army landed on the Isle of Rhé, but were driven back to their ships with great slaughter. Buckingham attempted nothing farther on behalf of the Rochellese. He returned to England with a disgraced flag and a murmuring fleet, amid the general discontent of the people. A second expedition sailed for the relief of the place, under the command of the Earl of Lindsay; but, though the fleet arrived in sight of Rochelle, it sailed back to England without even making an attempt on its behalf. The popular indignation rose to a still greater height than before. It was bruited abroad, and generally believed, that both expeditions had been a mere blind on the part of Charles I., and that, acting under the influence of his queen, Henrietta Maria, sister of the French king, he had never really intended that Rochelle should be relieved. However this might be, the failure was disgraceful; and when, in later years, the unfortunate Charles was brought to trial by his subjects, the abortive Rochelle expeditions were bitterly remembered against him.

Meanwhile Cardinal Richelieu vigorously prosecuted the war against the Huguenots wherever they stood in arms against the king. His operations were uniformly successful. The Huguenots were every where overthrown, and in the course of a few years they had ceased to exist as an armed power in France. Acting in a wise and tolerant spirit, Richelieu refrained from pushing his advantage to an extremity; and when all resistance was over, he advised the king to issue an edict granting freedom of worship and other privileges. The astute statesman was doubtless induced to adopt this course by considerations of state policy, for he had by this time entered into a league with the Swedish and German Protestant powers for the humiliation of the house of Austria, and with that object he sought to enlist the co-operation of the king's Protestant as well as Roman Catholic subjects. The result was, that, in 1629, "the Edict of Pardon" was issued by Louis XIII., granting to the Protestants various rights and privileges, together with liberty of worship and equality before the law.

From this time forward the Huguenots ceased to exist as a political party, and were distinguished from the rest of the people by their religion only. Being no longer available for purposes of faction, many of the nobles, who had been their leaders, fell away from them and rejoined the old Church, though a large number of the smaller gentry, the merchants, manufacturers, and skilled workmen continued Protestants as before. Their loyal conduct fully justified the indulgences which were granted to them by Richelieu, and confirmed by his successor Mazarin. Repeated attempts were made to involve them in the civil broils of the time, but they sternly kept aloof, and, if they took up arms, it was on the side of the government. When, in 1632, the Duke of Montmorency sought, for factious purposes, to reawaken the religious passions in Languedoc, of which he was governor, the Huguenots refused to join him. The Protestant inhabitants of Montauban even offered to march against him. During the wars of the Fronde, they sided with the king against the factions. Even the inhabitants of Rochelle supported the regent against their own governor. Cardinal Mazarin, then prime minister, frankly acknowledged the loyalty of the Huguenots. "I have no cause," he said, "to complain of the little flock; if they browse on bad herbage, at least they do not stray away." Louis XIV. himself, at the commencement of his reign, formally thanked them for the consistent manner in which they had withstood the invitations of powerful chiefs to resist the royal authority, while, at the same time, he professed to confirm them in the enjoyment of their rights and privileges.

The Protestants, however, continued to labor under many disabilities. They were in a great measure excluded from civil office and from political employment. They accordingly devoted themselves for the most part to industrial pursuits. They were acknowledged to be the best agriculturists, wine-growers, merchants, and manufacturers in France. "At all events," said Ambrose Paré, one of the most industrious men of his time, "posterity will not be able to charge us with idleness." No heavier crops were grown in France than on the Huguenot farms in Bearn and the southwestern provinces. In Languedoc, the cantons inhabited by the Protestants were the best cultivated and most productive. The slopes of the Aigoul and the Eperon were covered with their flocks and herds. The valley of Vaunage, in the diocese of Nismes, where they had more than sixty temples, was celebrated for the richness of its vegetation, and was called by its inhabitants "the Little Canaan." The vine-dressers of Berri and the Pays Messin, on the Moselle, restored those districts to more than their former prosperity; and the diligence, skill, and labor with which they subdued the stubborn soil and made it yield its increase of flowers and fruits, and corn and wine, bore witness in all quarters to the toil and energy of the men of The Religion.

The Huguenots of the towns were similarly industrious and enterprising. At Tours and Lyons they prosecuted the silk manufacture with great success, making taffetas, velvets, brocades, ribbons, and cloth of gold and silver, of finer qualities than were then produced in any other country in Europe. They also carried on the manufacture of fine cloth in various parts of France, and exported the article in large quantities to Germany, Spain, and England.* They estab-

---

* The wool used in the manufacture of the French cloth was, for the most part, brought from England, notwithstanding the heavy duties then levied on its export. When prices became excessive, the export was wholly prohibited. But this did not prevent the smuggling of wool outward on a large scale. It was carried on all round the coast, but principally by the *owlers* (as the smugglers of wool were called) of Romney Marsh. Men were always to be found ready to risk their necks for a shilling a day. The writer of a pamphlet published in 1671, entitled *England's Interest by Trade Asserted, showing the Necessity and Excellency thereof*, says: "The methods or ways of these evils are, first, in Rumny-Marsh in Kent, where the greatest part of rough wool is exported from England, put aboard French shallops by night, ten or twenty men, well armed, to guard it; some other parts there are, as in Sussex, Hampshire, and Essex, where the same methods may be used, but not so conveniently. The same for combed wool from Canterbury; they will carry it ten or fifteen miles at night towards the sea, with the like guard as before" (p. 16). In two years forty thousand packs were sent to Calais alone. The Romney Marsh men not only shipped their own wool, but large quantities brought from the inland counties. In 1677, Andrew Marvel described the wool-men as a militia that, in defiance of authority, conveyed their wool to the shallops in such strength that the officers of the crown dared not offend them. The coast-men, at shearing-time, openly carried

lished magnificent linen manufactories at Vire, Falaise, and Argentine, in Normandy; manufactories of bleached cloth at Morlaix, Landerman, and Brest; and manufactories of sail-cloth at Rennes, Nantes, and Vitré, in Brittany, great part of whose produce was exported to Holland and England.*

The Huguenots also carried on large manufactories of paper in Auvergne and the Angoumois. In the latter province they had no fewer than six hundred paper-mills, and the article they produced was the best of its kind in Europe. The mills at Ambert supplied the paper on which the choicest books which emanated from the presses of Paris, as well as Amsterdam and London, were then printed. The celebrated leather of Touraine, and the fine hats of Caudebec, were almost exclusively produced by the Protestant manufacturers, who also successfully carried on, at Sedan, the fabrication of articles of iron and steel, which were exported abroad in large quantities.

Perhaps one reason why the Huguenots were so successful in conducting these great branches of industry consisted in the fact that their time was much less broken in upon by saints' days and festival days, and that their labor was thus much more continuous, and consequently more effective, than in the case of the Roman Catholic portion of the population.†

their wool on horses' backs to the sea-shore, where French vessels were ready to receive it, attacking fiercely any one who ventured to interfere.

* "Such was the extent of this manufacture," says Weiss (*History of the French Protestant Refugees*), "that the English every year bought at Morlaix 4,500,000 livres' worth of these cloths—a fact verified by the register of the duties they paid for the stamp on their exit from the kingdom." Indeed, the English were at that time among the largest purchasers of French manufactures of all kinds. The writer of a pamphlet, entitled *An Inquiry into the Revenue, Credit, and Commerce of France, in a Letter to a Member of Parliament* (London, 1742), says: "We formerly took from France to the value of £600,000 per annum in silks, velvets, and satins; £700,000 in linen, canvas, and sail-cloth; £220,000 in beaver, demicastor, and felt hats; and 400,000 reams of paper; besides numerous other articles."

† "The working year of the Protestants consisted of 310 days, because they dedicated to repose only the fifty-two Sundays and a few solemn festivals, which gave to their industry the superiority of one sixth over that of the Catholics, whose working year was 260 days, because they devoted more than 105 to repose."—WEISS, *History of the French Protestant Refugees*, 27.

Besides this, however, the Protestants were almost of necessity men of stronger character; for they had to swim against the stream, and hold by their convictions in the face of obloquy, opposition, and very often of active persecution. The sufferings they had endured for religion in the past, and perhaps the presentiment of heavier trials in the future, made them habitually grave and solemn in their demeanor. Their morals were severe as their piety was rigid. Their enemies called them sour and fanatical, but no one called in question their honesty and integrity.* "If the Nismes merchants," once wrote Baville, intendant of that province, and one of the bitterest persecutors of the Protestants, "are bad Catholics, at any rate they have not ceased to be very good traders." The Huguenot's word was as good as his bond, and to be "honest as a Huguenot" passed into a proverb. This quality of integrity—which is essential in the merchant who deals with foreigners whom he never sees—so characterized the business transactions of the Huguenots, that the foreign trade

---

* It is worthy of note, that while the Huguenots were stigmatized, in contemporary Roman Catholic writings, as "heretics," "atheists," "blasphemers," "monsters vomited forth of hell," and the like, not a word is to be found in them as to their morality and integrity of character. The silence of their enemies on this head is perhaps the most eloquent testimony in their favor.

What the Puritan was in England, and the Covenanter in Scotland, that the Huguenot was in France; and that the system of Calvin should have developed precisely the same kind of men in these three several countries, affords a remarkable illustration of the power of religious training in the formation of character.

The French Protestants' Confession of Faith, framed in 1559, was based on that of Geneva. Two sacraments only were recognized—Baptism and the Lord's Supper. Christ crucified was the centre of their faith, their cardinal doctrines being justification by faith and Christ the only mediator with the Father.

The Huguenot form of worship was simple, consisting in prayer and praise, followed by exhortation. The sermon was a principal feature in the French Protestant service, and their ministers were chosen principally because of their ability as preachers.

Their church government resembled that of the Scotch Church, being based on popular election. Each congregation was governed by its *consistoire* or kirk-session; the congregations elected deputies, lay and clerical, to represent them in the provincial synod, and *colloque* or provincial assembly; and, finally, the whole congregations of France were represented in like manner by delegates in the *Synode Nationale*, or General Assembly.

of the country fell almost entirely into their hands. The English and Dutch were always found more ready to open a correspondence with them than with the Roman Catholic merchants, though religious affinity may possibly have had some influence in determining the preference. And thus at Bordeaux, at Rouen, at Caen, at Metz, at Nismes, and the other great centres of commerce, the foreign business of France came to be almost entirely conducted by the Huguenot merchants.

The enlightened minister Colbert gave every encouragement to these valuable subjects. Entertaining the conviction that the strength of states consisted in the number, the intelligence, and the industry of their citizens, he labored in all ways to give effect to this idea. He encouraged the French to extend their manufactures, and at the same time held out inducements to skilled foreign artisans to settle in the kingdom and establish new branches of industry. The invitation was accepted, and considerable numbers of Dutch and Walloon Protestants came across the frontier and settled as cloth manufacturers in the northern provinces. Colbert was the friend, so far as he dared to be, of the Huguenots, whose industry he encouraged, as the most effective means of enriching France, and enabling the nation to recover from the injuries inflicted upon it by the devastations and persecutions of the preceding century. With that object, he granted privileges, patents, monopolies, bounties, and honors, after the old-fashioned method of protecting industry. Some of these expedients were more harassing than prudent. One merchant, when consulted by Colbert as to the best means of encouraging commerce, answered curtly, "Laissez faire et laissez passer:" "Let us alone and let our goods pass"—a piece of advice which was not then appreciated or followed.

Colbert also applied himself to the improvement of the internal communications of the country. With his active assistance and co-operation, Riquet de Bonrepos was enabled to construct the magnificent canal of Languedoc, which connected the Bay of Biscay with the Mediterranean.* He restored the old roads of the country and constructed new ones. He established free ports, sent consuls to the Levant, and secured a large trade with the Mediterranean. He bought Dunkirk and Mardyke from Charles II. of England, to the disgust of the English people. He founded dock-yards at Brest, Toulon, and Rochefort. He created the French navy; and, instead of possessing only a few old ships lying rotting in harbors, in the course of thirty years France came to possess 190 vessels, of which 120 were ships of the line.

Colbert, withal, was an honest man. His predecessor Mazarin had amassed a gigantic fortune, while Colbert died possessed of a modest fortune, the fruits of long labor and rigid economy. His administration of the finances was admirable. When he assumed office, the state was overburdened by debt and all but bankrupt. The public books were in an inextricable state of confusion. His first object was to get rid of the debt by an arbitrary composition, which was tantamount to an act of bankruptcy. He simplified the public accounts, economized the collection of the taxes, cut off unnecessary expenditure, and reduced the direct taxation, placing his chief dependence upon indirect taxes on articles of consumption. After thirty years' labor, he succeeded in raising the revenue from thirty-two millions of livres to ninety-two millions net—one half only of the increase being due to additional taxation, the other half to better order and economy in the collection.

At the same time, Colbert was public-spirited and generous. He encouraged literature and the arts, as well as agriculture and commerce. He granted £160,000 in pensions to men of letters and science, among whom we find the names of the two Corneilles, Molière, Racine, Perrault, and Mezerai. Nor did he confine his liberality to the distinguished men of France, for he was equally liberal to foreigners who had set-

* For an account of this great work, and Colbert's part in it, see *Brindley and the Early Engineers*, p. 301.

tled in the country. Thus Huyghens, the distinguished Dutch natural philosopher, and Vossius, the geographer, were among his list of pensioners. He granted £208,000 to the Gobelins and other manufactures in Paris, besides other donations to those in the provinces. He munificently supported the Paris Observatories, and contributed to found the Academy of Inscriptions, the Academy of Sciences, and the Academy of Painting and Sculpture. In short, Colbert was one of the most enlightened, sagacious, liberal, and honorable ministers who ever served a monarch or a nation.

But behind the splendid ordonnances of Colbert there stood a superior power, the master of France himself—" the Most Christian King," Louis XIV. Richelieu and Mazarin had, by crushing all other powers in the state—nobles, Parliament, and people—prepared the way for the reign of this most absolute and uncontrolled of French monarchs.* He was proud, ambitious, fond of power, and believed himself to be the greatest of men. He would have every thing centre in the king's majesty. At the death of Mazarin in 1661, when his ministers asked to whom they were thenceforward to address themselves, his reply was, " A moi." The well-known saying, " L'etat, c'est moi," belongs to him. And his people took him at his word. They bowed down before him —rank, talent, and beauty—and vied with each other who should bow the lowest.

While Colbert was striving to restore the finances of France by the peaceful development of its industry, the magnificent king, his mind far above mercantile considerations, was bent on achieving glory by the conquest of adjoining territories. Thus, while the minister was, in 1668, engaged in laboriously organizing his commercial system, Louis

* The engrained absolutism and egotism of Louis XIV., M. Feuillet contends, were at their acme from his earliest years. In the public library at St. Petersburg, under a glass case, may be seen one of the copy-books in which he practiced writing when a child. Instead of such maxims as " Evil communications corrupt good manners," or " Virtue is its own reward," the copy set for him was this: " Les rois font tout ce qu'ils veulent."—*Edin. Review.*

wrote to Charles II. with the air of an Alexander the Great, saying, "If the English are satisfied to be the merchants of the world, and leave me to conquer it, the matter can be easily arranged: of the commerce of the globe, three parts to England, and one part to France."* Nor was this a mere whim of the king; it was the fixed idea of his life.

Louis went to war with Spain. He overran Flanders, won victories, and France paid for the glory in an increase of taxes. He next made war with Holland. There were more battles, and less glory, but the same inevitable taxes. War in Germany followed, during which there were the great sieges of Besançon, Salin, and Dôle; though this time there was no glory. Again Colbert was appealed to for money. But France had already been taxed almost to the utmost. The king told the minister in 1673 that he must find sixty millions of livres more; "if he did not, *another would*." Thus the war had become a question mainly of money, and money Colbert must find. Forced loans were then had recourse to, the taxes were increased, honors and places were sold, and the money was eventually raised.

The extravagance of Louis knew no bounds. Versailles was pulled down, and rebuilt at enormous cost. Immense sums were lavished in carrying out the designs of Vauban, and France was surrounded with a belt of three hundred fortresses. Various other spendthrift schemes were set on foot, until Louis had accumulated a debt equal to £100,000,000 sterling. Colbert at last succumbed, crushed in body and mind. He died in 1683, worn out with toil, mortified and heart-broken at the failure of all his plans. The people, enraged at the taxes which oppressed them, laid the blame at the door of the minister; and his corpse was buried at night, attended by a military escort to protect it from the fury of the mob.†

* MIGNET—*Negoc. de la Success. d'Esp.*, iii., 63.
† Il etait mort de la ruine publique, mort de ne pouvoir rien et d'avoir perdu l'espérance. On lui cherchait de querelles ridicules. Le roi lui reprochait la dépense de Versailles, fait malgré lui. Il lui citait Louvois, ces

THE KING'S ENMITY TO THE HUGUENOTS.

Colbert did not live to witness the more disgraceful events which characterized the later part of the reign of Louis XIV. The wars which that monarch waged with Spain, Germany, and Holland, for conquest and glory, were carried on against men with arms in their hands, capable of defending themselves. But the wars which he waged against his own subjects—the dragonnades and persecutions which preceded and followed the Revocation of the Edict of Nantes, of which the victims were defenseless men, women, and children—were simply ferocious and barbarous, and must ever attach the reputation of Infamous to the name of Louis XIV., in history miscalled "The Great."

One of the king's first acts, on assuming the supreme control of affairs at the death of Mazarin, was significant of his future policy with regard to the Huguenots. Among the representatives of the various public bodies who came to tender him their congratulations, there appeared a deputation of Protestant ministers, headed by their president Vignole; but the king refused to receive them, and directed that they should be ordered to leave Paris forthwith. Louis was not slow to follow up this intimation by measures of a more positive kind, for he had been carefully taught to hate Protestantism; and, now that he possessed unrestrained power, he flattered himself with the idea of compelling the Huguenots to abandon their convictions and adopt his own. His minister Louvois wrote to the governors throughout the provinces that "his majesty will not suffer any person in his kingdom but those who are of *his* religion;" and orders were shortly after issued that Protestantism must cease to exist, and that the Huguenots must every where conform to the royal will.

travaux de maçonnerie et des tranchées faits pour rien par le soldat, le paysan, comme si les travaux d'art d'un palais étaient même chose. Il l'acheva en le querillant sur le prix de la grille de Versailles. Colbert reutra, s'alita, ne se leva pas. . . . L'immense malédiction sous laquelle il mourait, le troubla à son lit de mort. Un lettre du roi lui vint, et il ne voulat pas la lire: "Si j'avais fait pour Dieu," dit il, "ce que j'ai fait pour cet homme, je serais sûr d'etre sauvé, et je ne sais pas où je vais . . . ."—MICHELET—*Louis XIV.*, p. 276–282.

A series of edicts was accordingly published with the object of carrying the king's purposes into effect. The conferences of the Protestants were declared to be suppressed. Though worship was still permitted in their churches, the singing of psalms in private dwellings was declared to be forbidden. Spies were sent among them, to report the terms on which the Huguenot pastors spoke of the Roman Catholic religion, and if any fault could be found with them, they were cited before the tribunals for blasphemy. The priests were authorized to enter the chambers of sick Protestants, and entreat them whether they would be converted or die in their heresy. Protestant children were invited to declare themselves against the religion of their parents. Boys of fourteen and girls of twelve years old might, on embracing Roman Catholicism, become enfranchised and entirely free from parental control. In that case the parents were further required to place and maintain their children in any Roman Catholic school into which they might wish to go.*

The Huguenots were again debarred from holding public offices, though a few, such as Marshal Turenne and Admiral Duquesne, who were Protestants, broke through this barrier by the splendor of their services to the state. In some provinces, the exclusion was so severe that a profession of the Roman Catholic faith was required from simple artisans—shoemakers, carpenters, and the like—before they were permitted to labor at their callings.†

Colbert, while he lived, endeavored to restrain the king, and to abate these intolerable persecutions, which dogged the Huguenots at every step. He continued to employ them

---

* Ordinance of 24th March, 1661.
† A ludicrous instance of this occurred at Paris, where the corporation of laundresses laid a remonstrance before the council that their community, having been instituted by St. Louis, could not admit heretics, and this reclamation was gravely confirmed by a decree of the 21st of August, 1665. The corporation nevertheless notoriously contained many abandoned women, but the orthodox laundresses were more distressed by heresy than by profligacy.—DE FELICE—*History of the Protestants of France*, p. 296—*Transl*, London. 1853.

in the departments of finance, finding no honester nor abler servants. He also encouraged the merchants and manufacturers to persevere in their industrial operations, which he regarded as essential to the prosperity and well-being of the kingdom. He took the opportunity of cautioning the king lest the measures he was enforcing might tend, if carried out, to the impoverishment of France and the aggrandizement of her rivals. "I am sorry to say it," said he to Louis, "that too many of your majesty's subjects are already among your neighbors as footmen and valets for their daily bread; many of the artisans, too, are fled from the severity of your collectors; they are at this time improving the manufactures of your enemies." But all Colbert's expostulations were in vain; the Jesuits were stronger than he was, and the king was in their hands; besides, Colbert's power was on the decline, and he, too, had to succumb to the will of his royal master, who would not relieve even the highest genius from that absolute submission which he required from his courtiers.

In 1666 the queen-mother died, leaving to her son, as her last bequest, that he should suppress and exterminate heresy within his dominions. The king knew that he had often grieved his royal mother by his notorious licentiousness, and he was now ready to atone for the wickedness of his past life by obeying her wishes. The Bishop of Meaux exhorted him to press on in the path his sainted mother had pointed out to him. "Oh kings!" said he, "exercise your power boldly, for it is divine—ye are gods!" Louis was not slack in obeying the injunction, which so completely fell in with his own ideas of royal omnipotence.

The Huguenots had already taken alarm at the renewal of the persecution, and such of them as could readily dispose of their property and goods were beginning to leave the kingdom in considerable numbers for the purpose of establishing themselves in foreign countries. To prevent this, the king issued an edict forbidding French subjects from proceeding abroad without express permission, under penalty of confiscation of their goods and property. This was followed by a succession of severe measures for the conversion or extirpation of such of the Protestants—in numbers about a million and a half—as had not by this time contrived to make their escape from the kingdom. The kidnapping of Protestant children was actively set on foot by the agents of the Roman Catholic priests, and their parents were subjected to heavy penalties if they ventured to complain. Orders were issued to pull down the Protestant places of worship, and as many as eighty were shortly destroyed in one diocese.

The Huguenots offered no resistance. All that they did was to meet together and pray that the king's heart might yet be softened toward them. Blow upon blow followed. Protestants were forbidden to print books without the authority of magistrates of the Romish communion. Protestant teachers were interdicted from teaching children any thing more than reading, writing, and arithmetic. Such pastors as held meetings amid the ruins of the churches which had been pulled down were condemned to do penance with a rope round their neck, after which they were to be banished the kingdom. Protestants were only allowed to bury their dead at daybreak or at nightfall. They were prohibited from singing psalms on land or on water, in workshops or in dwellings. If a priestly procession passed one of their churches while the psalms were being sung, they must stop instantly on pain of the fine or imprisonment of the officiating minister.

In short, from the pettiest annoyance to the most exasperating cruelty, nothing was wanting on the part of the "Most Christian King" and his abettors. Their intention probably was to exasperate the Huguenots into open resistance, with the object of finding a pretext for a second massacre of St. Bartholomew. But the Huguenots would not be exasperated. They bore their trials bravely and patiently, hoping and praying that the king's heart would yet relent, and that they might still be permitted to worship God according to conscience.

All their patience and resignation were however in vain, and from day to day the persecution became more oppressive and intolerable. In the intervals of his scandalous amours the king held conferences with his spiritual directors, to whom he was from time to time driven by bilious disease and the fear of death. He forsook Madame de la Valliere for Madame de Montespan, and Madame de Montespan for Madame de Maintenon, ever and anon taking counsel with his Jesuit confessor, Père La Chaise. Madame de Maintenon was the instrument of the latter, and between the two the "conversion" of the king was believed to be imminent. In his recurring attacks of illness his conscience became increasingly uneasy; confessor and mistress co-operated in turning his moroseness to account; and it was observed that every royal attack of bile was followed by some new edict of persecution against the Huguenots.

Madame de Maintenon, the last favorite, was the widow of Scarron, the deformed wit and scoffer. She belonged to the celebrated Huguenot family of D'Aubigny, her grandfather having been one of the most devoted followers of Henry IV. Her father led a profligate life, but she herself was brought up in the family faith. A Roman Catholic relative, however, acting on the authority conferred by the royal edict of abducting Protestant children, had the girl forcibly conveyed to the convent of Ursulines at Niort, from which she was transferred to the Ursulines at Paris, where, after some resistance, she abjured her faith and became a Roman Catholic. She left the convent to enter the world through Scarron's door. When the witty cripple married her, he said " his bride had brought with her an annual income of four louis, two large and very mischievous eyes, a fine bust, an exquisite pair of hands, and a large amount of wit."

Scarron's house was the resort of the gayest and loosest as

well as the most accomplished persons of the time, and there his young wife acquired that knowledge of the world, and conversational accomplishment, and probably social ambition, which she afterward turned so artfully and unscrupulously to account. One of her intimate friends was the notorious Ninon de l'Enclos, and it is not improbable that the sight of that woman, courted by the fashionable world after thirty years of polished profligacy, exercised a powerful influence on the subsequent career of Madame Scarron.

At Scarron's death, his young widow succeeded in obtaining the post of governess to the children of Madame de Montespan, the king's then mistress, whom she speedily superseded. She secured a footing in the king's chamber, to the exclusion of the queen, who was dying by inches,"* and by her adroitness, tact, and pretended devotion, she contrived to exercise an extraordinary influence over Louis—so much so that at length even the priests could only obtain access to him through her. She undertook to assist them in effecting his "conversion," and labored at the work four hours a day, reporting progress from time to time to Père la Chaise, his confessor. She early discovered the king's rooted hatred toward the Huguenots, and conformed herself to it accordingly, increasing her influence over him by artfully fanning the flames of his fury against her quondam co-religionists; and fiercer and fiercer edicts were issued against them in quick succession.

Before the extremest measures were however resorted to, an attempt was made to buy over the Protestants wholesale. The king consecrated to this traffic one third of the revenue of the benefices which fell to the crown during the period of their vacancy, and the fund became very large through the benefices being purposely left vacant. A "converted" Hu-

* Le roi tua la reine, comme Colbert, sans s'en apercevoir. . . . . Elle mourut (30 juillet, 1683). Madame de Maintenon la quittait expirée et sortait de la chambre, lorsque M. de la Rochefoucauld la prit par les bras, lui dit: "Le roi a besoin de vous." Et il la poussa chez le roi. A l'instant tous le deux partirent pour Saint-Cloud.—MICHELET, 273-4.

guenot named Pelisson was employed to administer the fund, and he published long lists of " conversions" in the *Gazette*, but he concealed the fact that the takers of his bribes belonged to the dregs of the people. At length many were detected undergoing " conversion" several times over, upon which a proclamation was published that persons found guilty of this offense would have their goods and property forfeited, and be sentenced to perpetual banishment.

The great body of the Huguenots remaining immovable and refusing to be converted, it was found necessary to resort to more violent measures. They were next attacked in their tenderest place—through their affections. Children of seven years old were empowered to leave their parents and become converted; and many were forcibly abducted from their homes, and immured in convent-prisons for education in the Romish faith at the expense of their parents. Another exquisite stroke of cruelty followed. While Huguenots as conformed were declared to be exempt from supplying quarters for the soldiery, the obstinate and unconverted were ordered to have an extra number quartered on them. Louvois wrote to Marillac, intendant of Poitou, in March, 1681, that he was about to send a regiment of horse into that province. " His majesty," he said, " has heard with much joy of the great number of persons who continue to be converted in your department. He wishes you to persist in your endeavors, and desires that the greater number of horsemen and officers should be billeted upon the Protestants. If, according to a just distribution, ten would be quartered upon the members of the Reformed religion, you may order them to accommodate twenty."* The opposition of Colbert for a time delayed the execution of this project, but not for long. It was the first attempt at the dragonnades.

Two years later, in 1683, the year of Colbert's death, the military executions began. Pity, terror, and anguish had by turns agitated the minds of the Protestants, until at length

* DE FELICE—*History of the Protestants of France*, p. 315.

they were reduced to a state almost of despair. Life was made almost intolerable to them. All careers were closed against them, and Protestants of the working class were under the necessity of abjuring or starving. The mob, observing that the Protestants were no longer within the pale of the law, took the opportunity of wreaking all manner of outrages on them. They broke into their churches, tore up the benches, and, placing the Bibles and hymn-books in a pile, set the whole on fire; the authorities usually setting their sanction on the proceedings of the rioters by banishing the burned-out ministers, and interdicting the further celebration of worship in the destroyed churches.

The Huguenots of Dauphiny were at last stung into a show of resistance, and furnished the king with the pretext which he wanted for ordering a general slaughter of those of his subjects who would not be "converted" to his religion. A large congregation of Huguenots assembled one day amid the ruins of a wrecked church to celebrate worship and pray for the king. The Roman Catholics thereupon raised the alarm that this meeting was held for the purpose of organizing a rebellion. The spark thus kindled in Dauphiny burst into flame in the Viverais and even in Languedoc, and troops were brought from all quarters to crush the apprehended outbreak. Meanwhile the Huguenots continued to hold their religious meetings, and a number of them were found one day assembled outside Bordeaux, where they had met to pray. There the dragoons fell upon them, cutting down hundreds, and dispersing the rest. "It was a mere butchery," says Rulhières, "without the show of a combat." Several were apprehended and offered pardon if they would abjure; but they refused, and were hanged.

Noailles, then governor, seized the opportunity of advancing himself in the royal favor by ordering a general massacre. He obeyed to the letter the cruel orders of Louvois, the king's minister, who prescribed *desolation*. Cruelty raged for a time uncontrolled from Grenoble to Bordeaux. There were massacres in the Viverais and massacres in the Cévennes. An entire army had converged on Nismes, and there was so horrible a dragonnade that the city was "converted" in twenty-four hours. Noailles wrote to the king that there had indeed been some slight disorder, but that every thing had been conducted with great judgment and discipline, and he promised with his head that before the next 25th of November there would be no more Huguenots in Languedoc.*

Like cruelties followed all over France. More Protestant churches were pulled down, and the property that belonged to them was confiscated for the benefit of the Roman Catholic hospitals. Many of the Huguenot land-owners had already left the kingdom, and others were preparing to follow them. But this did not suit the views of the monarch and his advisers; and the ordinances were ordered to be put in force which interdicted emigration, with the addition of condemnation to the galleys for life of heads of families found attempting to escape, and a fine of three thousand livres against any person found encouraging or assisting them. By the same ordinance all contracts for the sales of property made by the Reformed one year before the date of their em, igration were declared nullified. The consequence was that many landed estates were seized and sold, of which Madame de Maintenon, the king's mistress, artfully improved the opportunity. Writing to her brother, for whom she had obtained from the king a gratuity of 800,000 francs, she said: "I beg of you carefully to use the money you are about to receive. Estates in Poitou may be got for nothing; the desolation of the Huguenots will drive them to sell more. You may easily acquire extensive possessions in Poitou."*

Thus were the poor Huguenots trodden under foot—persecuted, maltreated, fined, flogged, hanged, or sabred; nevertheless, many of those who survived still remained faithful. Toward the end of 1684 a painful incident occurred at Maren-

* *Memoires de Noailles*, 15; MICHELET—*Louis XIV.*, 275-6.
† DE FELICE—Book iii., chap. xv., p. 317.

nes, in Saintonge, where the Reformed religion extensively prevailed, notwithstanding the ferocity of the persecution. The church there comprised from 13,000 to 14,000 persons; but on the pretense that some children of the new converts to Romanism had been permitted to enter the building (a crime in the eye of the law), the congregation was ordered, late one Saturday evening, to be suppressed. On the Sunday morning a large number of worshipers appeared at the church doors, some of whom had come from a great distance—their own churches being already closed or pulled down — and among them were twenty-three infants brought for baptism. It was winter; the cold was intense; and no shelter being permitted within the closed church, the poor things were mostly frozen to death on their mothers' bosoms. Loud sobbing and wailing rose from the crowd; all wept, even the men; but they found consolation in prayer, and resolved, in this their darkest hour, to be faithful to the end, even unto death.

A large body of troops lay encamped in Bearn in the early part of 1685, to watch the movements of the Spanish army; but a truce having been agreed upon, the Marquis de Louvois resolved to employ his regiment in converting the Huguenots of the surrounding districts after the methods adopted by Noailles at Nismes. Some hundreds of Bearnese Protestants having been driven by force into a church where the Bishop of Lescar officiated, the doors were closed, and the poor people compelled to kneel down and receive the bishop's absolution at the point of the sword. To escape their tormentors, the Reformed fled into the woods, the wildernesses, and the caverns of the Pyrenees. They were pursued like wild beasts, brought back to their dwellings by force, and compelled to board and lodge their persecutors. The dragoons entered the houses with drawn swords, shouting "Kill, kill, or become Catholics." The scenes of brutal outrage which occurred during these dragonnades can not be described. These soldiers were among the roughest, loosest, cruelest of men.* They suspended their victims with ropes, blowing tobacco-smoke into their nostrils and mouths, and practicing upon them a hundred other nameless cruelties, until they reduced their hosts to a condition of not knowing what they did, and of promising every thing to rid themselves of their tormentors.† No wonder that the constancy of the Bearnese at length yielded to the prolonged rigor of these torments, and that they hastened to the priests in crowds to abjure their religion.

The success of the dragonnades in enforcing conversion in Bearn encouraged the king to employ the same means elsewhere, and in the course of four months, Languedoc, Guienne, Saintonge, Poitou, Viverais, Dauphiny, Cevennes, Provence, and Gex were scoured by the new missionaries of the Church. Neither age nor sex was spared. The men who refused to be converted were thrown into dungeons, and the women were immured in prison-convents. Louvois thus reported the results of his operations, in September, 1685: "Sixty thousand conversions have been made in the district of Bor-

* Michelet says the word given to them by their commander, Luxembourg, when in Holland, was, "Amusez vous, enfants! pillez et violez!" and he adds the following description of "M. le dragon:" "Rossé par l'officier, il le rendit au paysan. Vrai singe, il aimait à mal faire, et plus mal que les autres; c'était son amour-propre. Il était ravi d'être craint, criait, cassait, battait, tenait à ce qu'on dit. Le dragon c'est le diable à quatre."—*Louis XIV. et la Révocation de l'Edit de Nantes*, p. 304–5. Such were the soldiery who proceeded to persecute the men, women, and children of the province of Bearn; and every torture which they could inflict without killing them outright, they inflicted on the Huguenots.

† Elie Benoit, in his *History of the Edict of Nantes*, fills page after page with descriptions of the cruelties perpetrated by the dragoons on the poor Huguenots. In one passage he says: "The horsemen fastened crosses to the mouth of their musquetoons to compel the people to kiss them by force, and when they met with any resistance, they thrust their crosses into the face and stomach of their unhappy victims. They spared children as little as persons of more advanced age, and, without the slightest regard for their years, they loaded them with blows with the flat of their swords, or with the butt-end of their musquetoons; and such was their violence, that many were made cripples for life. These infamous wretches took a pleasure in maltreating women. They beat them with whips; they struck them on the face with canes in order to disfigure them; they dragged them by their hair in the mud and over the stones. Sometimes the soldiers, meeting laborers on the road, or with their carts, drove them to the Roman Catholic churches, pricking them like cattle with their spurs to hasten their unwilling march."

deaux, and twenty thousand in that of Montauban. So rapid is the progress, that before the end of the month ten thousand Protestants will not be left in the district of Bordeaux, where there were one hundred and fifty thousand on the 15th of last month." Noailles wrote to a similar effect from Nismes: "The most influential people," said he, "abjured in the church the day following my arrival. There was a slackening afterward, but matters soon assumed a proper shape with the help of some billetings on the dwellings of the most obstinate."

In the mean time, while these forced conversions of the Huguenots were being made by the dragoons of De Louvois and De Noailles, Madame de Maintenon continued to labor at the conversion of the king himself. She was materially assisted by her royal paramour's bad digestion, and by the qualms of conscience which from time to time beset him at the dissoluteness of his past life. Every twinge of pain, every fit of colic, every prick of conscience, was succeeded by new resolutions to extirpate heresy. Penance must be done for his incontinence, but not by himself. It was the virtuous Huguenots that must suffer vicariously for him; and, by punishing them, he flattered himself that he was expiating his own sins. "It was not only his amours which deserve censure," says Sismondi, "although the scandal of their publicity, the dignities to which he raised the children of his adultery, and the constant humiliation to which he subjected his wife, add greatly to his offense against public morality. . . He acknowledged in his judgments, and in his rigor toward his people, no rule but his own will. At the very moment that his subjects were dying of famine, he retrenched nothing from his prodigalities. Those who boasted of having converted him had never represented to him more than two duties—that of renouncing his incontinence, and that of extirpating heresy in his dominions."*

The farce of Louis's "conversion" went on. In August, 1684, Madame de Maintenon wrote thus: "The king is pre-

* DE SISMONDI—*Histoire de France*, t. xxv., p. 481.

pared to do every thing that shall be judged useful for the welfare of religion; this undertaking will cover him with glory before God and man!" The dragonnades were then in full career throughout the southern provinces, and a long wail of anguish was rising from the persecuted all over France. In 1685 the king's sufferings increased, and his conversion became imminent. His miserable body was already beginning to decay; but he was willing to make a sacrifice to God of what the devil had left of it. Not only did he lose his teeth, but caries in the jaw-bone developed itself; and when he drank the liquid passed through his nostrils.* In this shocking state Madame de Maintenon became his nurse.

The Jesuits now obtained all that they wanted. They made a compact with Madame by which she was to advise the king to revoke the Edict of Nantes, while they were to consent to her marriage with him. Pere la Chaise, his confessor, advised a private marriage, and the ceremony was performed at Versailles by the archbishop of Paris, in the presence of the confessor and two more witnesses. The precise date of the transaction is not known; but it is surmised that the edict was revoked one day, and the marriage took place the next.†

The Act of Revocation was published on the 22d of October, 1685. It was the death-knell of the Huguenots.

* Michelet cites as his authority for this statement *Journal MS. des Medecins*, 1685.

† Madame dit (*Memoires*, ii., 108) que le marriage eut lieu *deux ans après la mort de la reine*, donc dans les derniers mois de 1685. M. de Noailles (ii, 121) établit la même date. Pour le jour précis, on l'ignore. On doit conjecturer qu'il eut lieu après le jour de la Revocation déclarée a la fin d'Octobre, ce jour où le roi tint parole, accorda l'acte qu'elle avait consenti, et où elle fut ainsi engagée sans retour.—MICHELET—*Louis XIV. et la Revocation*, p. 300.

CHAPTER VIII.

RENEWED FLIGHT OF THE HUGUENOTS.

GREAT was the rejoicing of the Jesuits on the Revocation of the Edict of Nantes. Rome sprang up with a shout of joy to celebrate the event. Te Deums were sung, processions went from shrine to shrine, and the Pope sent a brief to Louis conveying to him the congratulations and praises of the Romish Church. Public thanksgivings were held at Paris, in which the people eagerly took part, thus making themselves accomplices in the proscription by the king of their fellow-subjects. The provost and sheriffs had a statue of Louis erected at the Hotel de Ville, bearing the inscription *Luduvico Magno, victori perpetuo, ecclesia ac regum, dignitatis assertori*.* Leseuer was employed to paint the subject for the gallery at Versailles, and medals were struck to commemorate the extinction of Protestantism in France.

The Roman Catholic clergy were almost beside themselves with joy. The eloquent Bossuet was especially fervent in his praises of the monarch: "Touched by so many marvels," said he (15th of January, 1686), "let us expand our hearts in praise of the piety of the Great Louis. Let our acclamations ascend to heaven, and let us say to this new Constantine, this new Theodosius, what the six hundred and thirty fathers said in the Council of Chalcedon, 'You have strengthened the faith, you have exterminated the heretics: King of Heaven, preserve the king of earth.'" Massillon also indulged in a like strain of exultation: "The profane temples," said he, "are destroyed, the pulpits of seduction are cast down, the prophets of falsehood are torn from their flocks. At the first blow dealt to it by Louis, heresy falls, disappears, and is reduced

* The statue was pulled down in 1792, and cast into cannon which thundered at Valmy.

either to hide itself in the obscurity whence it issued, or to cross the seas, and to bear with it into foreign lands its false gods, its bitterness, and its rage."

Let us now see what the Revocation of the Edict of Nantes involved. The demolition of all the remaining Protestant temples throughout France, and the entire proscription of the Protestant religion; the prohibition of even private worship under penalty of confiscation of body and property; the banishment of all Protestant pastors from France within fifteen days; the closing of all Protestant schools; the prohibition of parents to instruct their children in the Protestant faith; the injunction upon them, under a penalty of five hundred livres in each case, to have their children baptized by the parish priest, and brought up in the Roman Catholic religion; the confiscation of the property and goods of all Protestant refugees who failed to return to France within four months; the penalty of the galleys for life to all men, and of imprisonment for life to all women, detected in the act of attempting to escape from France.

Such were a few of the cruel, dastardly, and inhuman provisions of the Edict of Revocation. Such were the marvels of the piety of the Great Louis, which were so eloquently eulogized by Bossuet and Massillon. The Edict of Revocation was a proclamation of war by the armed against the unarmed—a war against peaceable men, women, and children —a war against property, against family, against society, against public morality, and, more than all, against the rights of conscience.

The military jacquerie at once began. The very day on which the Edict of Revocation was registered, steps were taken to destroy the great Protestant church at Charenton, near Paris. It had been the work of the celebrated architect Debrosses, and was capable of containing 14,000 persons. In five days it was leveled with the ground. The great temple of Quevilly, near Rouen, of nearly equal size, in which the celebrated minister Jacques Basnage preached, was in like manner demolished. At Tours, at Nismes, at Montauban, and all over France, the same scenes were enacted, the mob eagerly joining in the work of demolition with levers and pickaxes. Eight hundred Protestant churches were thus thrown down in a few weeks.

The provisions of the Edict of Revocation were rigorously put in force, and they were succeeded by numerous others of like spirit. Thus Protestants were commanded to employ only Roman Catholic servants, under penalty of a fine of 1000 livres, while Protestant servants were forbidden to serve either Protestant or Roman Catholic employers. If any men-servants were detected violating this law, they were to be sent to the galleys; whereas women-servants were to be flogged and branded with a *fleur-de-lis*—the emblazonment of the "Most Christian King." Protestant pastors found lurking in France after the expiry of the fifteen days were to be condemned to death; and any of the king's subjects found giving harbor to the pastors were to be condemned— the men to be galley-slaves, the women to imprisonment for life. The reward of 5500 livres was offered for the apprehension of any Protestant pastor.

The Huguenots were not even permitted to die in peace, but were pursued to death's door and into the grave itself. They were forbidden to solicit the offices of those of their own faith, and were required to confess and receive unction from the priests, on penalty of having their bodies when dead removed from their dwelling by the common hangman and flung into the public sewer.* In the event of the sick Prot-

* The body of the distinguished M. de Chenevix was subjected to this brutal indignity. He was a gentleman illustrious for his learning and piety, and had been councilor to the king in the court of Metz. In 1686 he fell dangerously ill, when the curate of the parish, forcing himself into his presence, importuned him to confess, when he replied that he declined to confess to any but God, who alone could forgive his sins. The archbishop next visited him, urging him to communicate before he died, at the same time informing him of the penalties decreed by the king against such as died without receiving the sacrament. He refused, declaring that he would never communicate after the popish manner. At his death, shortly after, orders were given that his body should be removed by the executioner; and his corpse was accordingly taken, dragged away on a hurdle, and cast upon a dunghill. About

estant recovering, after having rejected the viaticum, he was to be condemned to perpetual confinement at the galleys, or imprisonment for life, with confiscation of all his property. Such were the measures by which the Great Louis sought to win back erring souls to Rome.

Crushed, tormented, and persecuted by these terrible enactments, the Huguenots felt that life in France had become almost intolerable. It is true there was one alternative—conversion. But Louis XIV., with all his power, could not prevail against the impenetrable rampart of conscience, and a large proportion of the Huguenots persistently refused to be converted. They would not act the terrible lie to God, and seek their personal safety at the price of hypocrisy. They would not become Roman Catholics; they would rather die. There was only one other means of relief—flight from France. Yet it was a frightful alternative, to tear themselves from the country they loved, from friends and relatives, from the homes of their youth and the graves of their kindred, and fly—they knew not whither. The thought of self-banishment was so agonizing that many hesitated long and prepared to endure much before taking the irrevocable step; and many more prepared to suffer death rather than leave their country and their home.

Indeed, to fly in any direction became increasingly difficult from day to day. The frontiers were strongly patroled by troops and gensdarmes; the coast was closely watched by an

---

four hundred of his friends, of whom the greater number were women, proceeded thither by night to fetch the body away. They wrapped it in linen; four men bore it aloft on their shoulders, and they buried it in a garden. While the corpse was being let down into the grave, the mourning assembly sang the 79th Psalm, beginning, "Save me, O God, for the waters are come into my soul." The brother of M. de Chenevix was a Protestant pastor, who was forced to fly at the Revocation, and took refuge in England. His son was a distinguished officer in the British army, and his grandson was made bishop of Killaloe in 1745, and afterward of Waterford and Lismore. The present Archbishop of Dublin, Richard Chenevix Trench, is his great grandson by the mother's side, being also descended, by the father's side, from another Huguenot family, the Trenches or De la Tranches, of whom the Earl of Clancarty is the head, who emigrated from France and settled in England shortly after the massacre of St. Bartholomew.

armed coast-guard; while ships of war cruised at sea to intercept and search outward-bound vessels. The law was strictly enforced against all persons taken in the act of flight. Under the original edict, detected fugitives were to be condemned to the galleys for life, while their denouncers were to be rewarded with half their goods. But this punishment was not considered sufficiently severe; and, on the 7th of May, 1686, the king issued another edict, proclaiming that any captured fugitives, as well as any person found acting as their guide, would be condemned to death.

But even these terrible penalties were not sufficient to prevent the flight of the Huguenots. Many of the more distinguished literary and scientific men of France had already escaped into other countries. When the Protestant University of Sedan was arbitrarily closed by the king in 1681, Jurieu, Professor of Hebrew and Theology, and Bayle, Professor of Philosophy, fled into Holland and obtained asylum there. The magistrates of Rotterdam expressly founded a new college for education, in which the fugitives were both appointed to professorships. Huyghens also, the distinguished astronomer and mathematician, who had been induced by Colbert to settle in Paris, made haste to take refuge in Holland. Though not much of a Protestant, and indeed not much of a Christian, Huyghens would not be a hypocrite, and he renounced all honors and emoluments rather than conform to an institution and system which he detested.

Amid the general proscription, a few distinguished exceptions were made by the king, who granted permission to several laymen, in return for past public services, to leave the kingdom and settle abroad. Among these were Marshal Schomberg, one of the first soldiers of France, who had been commander-in-chief of its armies, and the Marquis de Ruvigny, one of her ablest embassadors—whose only crime consisted in their being Protestants. The gallant admiral Duquesne also, the first sailor of France, was a Huguenot. The king sent for him and urged him to abjure his religion. But the old hero, pointing to his gray hair, replied, "For sixty years, sire, have I rendered unto Cæsar the things which are Cæsar's; suffer me still to render unto God the things which are God's." Duquesne was permitted to end his few remaining days in France, for he was then in his eightieth year; but his two sons were allowed to emigrate, and they shortly after departed into Holland.*

The banished pastors were treated with especial severity. Fifteen days only had been allowed them to fly beyond the frontier, and if they tarried longer in their agonizing leavetaking of their flocks they were liable to be sent to the galleys for life. Yet, with that exquisite malignity which characterized the acts of the monarch and his abettors, they were in some cases refused the necessary permits to pass the frontier, in order that they might thereby be brought within the range of the dreadful penalties proclaimed by the Act of Revocation. The pastor Claude—one of the most eloquent preachers of his day, who had been one of the ministers of the great church of Charenton, was ordered to quit France within twenty-four hours, and he set out forthwith, accompanied by one of the king's footmen, who saw him as far as Brussels. The other pastors of Paris were allowed two days to make their preparations for leaving. More time was allowed to those in the provinces; but they were permitted to carry nothing with them, not even their children—all under seven years of age being taken from them to be brought up in the religion of their persecutors. Even infants at the

* The eldest son, Henry, Marquis Duquesne, subsequently went to Switzerland to organize a flotilla on Lake Leman for the defense of the country against the Duke of Savoy who then threatened it. "Henry had secretly carried off from Paris the heart of his father, whose memory Louis XIV. refused to honor by a public monument. The body of that great man had been refused to his son, who had prepared for it a burial-place in a foreign land. He had the following words engraved on the mausoleum he had erected to him in the church of Aubonne : *This tomb awaits Duquesne's remains. You, who pass by, question the court, the army, the Church, and even Europe, Asia, Africa, and the two oceans ; ask them why a superb mausoleum has been raised to the valiant Ruyter, and not to his conqueror Duquesne? . . . . . I see that, out of respect for the Great King, you dare not speak.*"—WEISS—*History of the French Protestant Refugees,* 509.

breast must be given up; and many a mother's heart was torn by conflicting feelings—the duty of following a husband on the road to banishment, or remaining behind to suckle a helpless infant.

It may be asked, Why rake up these horrors of the past, these tortures inflicted upon innocent women and children in times long since past and gone? Simply because they are matters of history, which can not be ignored or suppressed. They may be horrible to relate, it is true, but they were far more horrible to suffer. And, however revolting they may now appear, any description of them, no matter how vivid or how detailed, must necessarily fall far short of the dreadful reality to those who endured them. They are, indeed, historical facts, full of significance and meaning, without a knowledge of which it were impossible to understand the extraordinary exodus of the French people which shortly followed, and which constituted one of the most important historical events of the seventeenth century. And, if we mistake not, they are equally necessary to an intelligent appreciation of the causes which led to the success of the English Revolution of 1688 and the events which followed it, as well as of the still more recent French Revolution of 1789.

When all the banished pastors had fled, those of their flocks who still remained steadfast prepared to follow them into exile, for they felt it easier to be martyrs than apostates. Those who possessed goods and movables made haste to convert them into money in such a way as to excite the least suspicion; for spies were constantly on the watch, ready to denounce intended fugitives to the authorities. Such of them as were engaged in trade, commerce, and manufactures were surrounded by difficulties; yet they were prepared to dare and risk all rather than abjure their religion. They prepared to close their workshops, their tanneries, their paper-mills, their silk manufactories, and the various branches of industry which they had built up, and to fly with the merest wreck of their fortunes into other countries. The owners of land had still greater difficulties to encounter. They were, in a measure, rooted to the soil; and, according to the royal edict, if they emigrated without special permission, their property was liable to immediate confiscation by the state. Nevertheless, many of these, too, resolved to brave all risks and fly.

When the full tide of the emigration set in, it was found difficult to guard the extensive French frontier so as effectually to prevent the escape of the fugitives. The high roads as well as the by-ways were regularly patroled day and night, and all the bridges leading out of France were strongly guarded. But the fugitives avoided the frequented routes, and crossed the frontier through forests, over trackless wastes, or by mountain paths, where no patrols were on the watch, and thus they contrived to escape in large numbers into Switzerland, Germany, and Holland. They mostly traveled by night, not in bands, but in small parties, and often singly. When the members of a family prepared to fly, they fixed a rendezvous in some town across the nearest frontier; then, after prayer and taking a tender leave of each other, they set out separately, and made for the agreed point of meeting, usually traveling in different directions.

Many of the fugitives were of course captured by the king's agents. Along so wide a frontier, it was impossible always to elude their vigilance. To strike terror into such of the remaining Huguenots as might be contemplating their escape, the prisoners who were taken were led as a show through the principal towns, with heavy chains round their necks, in some cases weighing over fifty pounds. "Sometimes," says Benoit, "they were placed in carts with irons on their feet, and the chains were made fast to the cart. They were forced to make long marches; and, when they sank under fatigue, blows compelled them to rise."[*] After they had been thus driven through the chief towns by way of example, the prisoners were sent to the galleys, where there were

[*] ELIE BENOIT—*Histoire de l'Edit de Nantes*, v., p. 964.

already more than a thousand by the end of 1686. The galley-slaves included men of all conditions—pastors and peasants; old men with white hairs and boys of tender years; magistrates, officers, and men of gentle blood, mixed with thieves and murderers; and no discrimination whatever was made in their classification, or in the barbarity of their treatment.

These cruelties were, however, of no avail in checking the emigration. The Huguenots continued to fly out of France in all directions. The Great Louis, still bent on their "conversion," increased his guards along the frontiers. The soldiers were rewarded in proportion to the captures they effected. The aid of the frontier peasantry was also invited, and thousands of them joined the troops in guarding the highways, the bridges, the ferries, and all the avenues leading out of France. False statements were published by authority, to the effect that such of the emigrants as had reached foreign countries were destitute and starving. It was stated that ten thousand of them had died of misery in England, and that most of those who survived were imploring permission to return to France and abjure.*

In vain! the emigration continued. Some bought their way across the frontier; others fought their way. They went in all sorts of disguises—some as peddlers, others as soldiers, huntsmen, valets, and beggars. Some, to disarm suspicion, even pretended to sell chaplets and rosaries. The Huguenots conducted the emigration on a regular system. They had itineraries prepared and secretly distributed, in which the safest routes and hiding-places were described in detail—a sort of "underground railroad," such as existed in the United States before the abolition of slavery there. Many escaped through the great forest of Ardennes into Luxembourg; others through the Vosges Mountains into Germany; and others through the passes of the Jura into Switzerland. Some were shot by the soldiers and peasant-

* WEISS—*History of the French Protestant Refugees*, p. 76.

ry; a still greater number were taken prisoners and sent to the galleys; yet many thousands of them nevertheless contrived to make their escape.

The flight of men was accompanied by that of women, old and young; often by mothers with infants in their arms. The hearts of the women were especially lacerated by the cruelties inflicted on them through their affections; by the tearing of their children from them for the purpose of being educated in convents; by the quartering of dragoons in their dwellings; and by the various social atrocities which preceded as well as followed the Edict of Revocation.* While many Protestant heads of families were ready to conform, in order to save their families from insult and outrage by a lawless and dissolute soldiery, the women often refused to follow their example, and entreated their husbands to fly from the land where such barbarities had become legalized, and where this daily war was being carried on against womanhood and childhood—against innocence, morality, religion, and virtue. To women of pure feelings, life under such circumstances was more intolerable even than death.

Every where, therefore, were the Huguenot women as well as the men found fleeing into exile. They mostly fled in disguise, often alone, to join their husbands or fathers at the appointed rendezvous. Benoit says that they cut off their hair, disfigured their faces with dyes, assumed the dress of peddlers or lackeys, and condescended to the meanest employments, for the purpose of disarming suspicion and insuring

* The frightful cruelty of these measures shocked the Roman Catholic clergy themselves, and, to their honor be it said, in many districts they refrained from putting them in force. On discovering this, Louis XIV., furiously zealous for the extirpation of heresy, ordered his minister De Portchartrain to address a circular to the bishops of France, charging them with want of zeal in carrying his edicts into effect, and calling upon them to require the curates of their respective dioceses to enforce them without fail.—COQUEREL, *Histoire des Eglises du Desert*, i., p. 68. The priests who visited the slaves at the galleys were horribly shocked at the cruelties practiced on them. The Abbé Jean Bion shed tears at the sight of the captives covered with bleeding wounds inflicted by the whip, and he could not resist the impression: "Their blood preached to me," says he in his *Relation*, "and I felt myself a Protestant."

L

their escape.* Young women, in many cases of gentle birth, who under other circumstances would have shrunk from the idea of walking a few miles from home, prepared to set out upon a journey on foot of some hundreds of miles, through woods, by unfrequented paths, across mountain ranges, braving all dangers so that they might but escape, though it were with their bare lives, from the soil of France. Jean Marteilhe, of Bergerac, describes a remarkable incident of this kind.† He had himself been taken prisoner in his attempt to escape across the French frontier near Marienbourg, and was lodged in the jail at Tournay to wait his trial. While lying there, five other Huguenot fugitives, who had been captured by the dragoons, were ushered into his cell. Three of these he at once recognized, through their disguise, as gentlemen of Bergerac; but the other two he failed to recognize. They eventually proved to be two young ladies, Mesdemoiselles Madras and Conceil of Bergerac, disguised as boys, who had set out, though it was winter, to make their escape from France through the forest of Ardennes. They had traveled

* Women of quality, even sixty and seventy years of age, who had, so to speak, never placed a foot upon the ground except to cross their apartments or stroll in an avenue, traveled a hundred leagues to some village which had been indicated by a guide. Girls of fifteen, of every rank, exposed themselves to the same hazard. They drew wheelbarrows, they bore manure, panniers, and other burdens. They disfigured their faces with dyes to embrown their complexion, with ointments or juices that blistered their skins and gave them a wrinkled aspect. Women and girls were seen to counterfeit sickness, dumbness, and even insanity. Some went disguised as men; and some, too delicate to pass as grown men, donned the dress of lackeys, and followed on foot, through the mud, a guide on horseback, who assumed the character of a man of importance. Many of these females reached Rotterdam in their borrowed garments, and hastening to the foot of the pulpit, before they had time to assume a more decent garb, published their repentance of their compulsory signature.—ELIE BENOIT—*Histoire de l'Edit de Nantes*, v., 554, 953.

† The narrative of Jean Marteilhe, entitled *Mémoires d'un Protestant condamné aux Galéres de France pour cause de Religion, écrits par lui meme*, gives a most interesting account of the adventures and sufferings of those condemned to the galleys because of their Protestantism. The book originally appeared at Rotterdam in 1755, and was translated into English by Oliver Goldsmith, under the fictitious name of "J. Willington," in the following year, Goldsmith receiving twenty guineas for making the translation. It has since been republished by the Religious Tract Society, under the title of *Autobiography of a French Protestant condemned to the Galleys for the sake of his Religion*, and is well worthy of perusal.

thirty leagues on foot, under dripping trees, along broken roads, and by almost trackless paths, enduring cold, hunger, and privations "with a firmness and constancy," says Marteilhe, "extraordinary for persons brought up in refinement, and who, previous to this expedition, would not have been able to walk a league." They were, however, captured and put in jail; and when they recognized in their fellow-prisoners other Huguenot fugitives from Bergerac, they were so happy that they wept for joy. Marteilhe strongly urged that the jailer should be informed of their sex, to which the young ladies assented, when they were removed to a separate cell. They were afterward tried, and condemned to be immured in the Convent of the Repentants at Paris, where they wept out the rest of their lives and died.

Marteilhe himself refused all the tempting offers, as well as the dreadful threats, made to induce him to abjure his religion, and he was condemned to be sent to the galleys at seventeen years of age. Marched from jail to jail, and from town to town, loaded with chains like his fellow-prisoners, he was first placed in the galleys at Dunkirk, where he endured the most horrible hardships* during twelve years; after which, on the surrender of Dunkirk to the English, he was marched, with twenty-two other Protestant galley-slaves, still loaded with chains, through Paris and the other principal towns, to Marseilles, to serve out the remainder of his sentence. There were other galley-slaves of even more tender years than Marteilhe. Andrew Bosquet was only sixteen, and he remained at the galleys twenty-six years. Francis Bourry and Matthew Morel were but fifteen; and only a few years since, Admiral Baudin, maritime prefect at Toulon, in turning over the ancient records of his department, discovered the register of a child who had been sent

* What life at the galleys was may be learned from Marteilhe's own narrative above cited, as well as from a highly interesting account of the Protestants sent to the galleys, by Athanase Coquerel fils, entitled *Les Forçats pour la Foi* (Galley-slaves for the Faith), recently published at Paris by Lévy Brothers.

to the galleys at twelve years of age "for having accompanied his father and mother to the preaching!"*

On the other hand, age did not protect those found guilty of adhering to their faith. David de Caumont, baron of Montbelon, was seventy years old when sent to the galleys. Antoine Astruc was of the same age when condemned; and Antoine Morlier seventy-one. Nor did distinction in learning protect the hapless Protestant; for the celebrated counselor of the king, Louis de Marolles, was sent to the galleys with the rest. At first, out of regard for his eminence, the jailer chained him by only one foot; but next day, by the express orders of Louis the Great, a heavy chain was fixed around his neck. It was while chained with all sorts of malefactors that Marolles compiled his *Discourse on Providence*, which was afterward published and translated into English. Marolles was also a profound mathematician—the author of one of the best treatises on algebra; and, while chained in his dungeon, he proposed a problem to the mathematicians of Paris which was afterward inserted in the works of Ozanam.

Another distinguished galley-slave was John Huber, father of three illustrious sons—Huber of the Birds, Huber of the Ants, and Huber of the Bees! The following touching incident is from the elder Huber's journal: "We arrived one night at a little town, chained, my wife and my children, with fourteen galley-slaves. The priests came to us, offering freedom on condition that we abjured. We had agreed to preserve a profound silence. After them came the women and children of the place, who covered us with mud. I made my little party fall on their knees, and we put up this prayer, in which all the fugitives joined: 'Gracious God, who seest the wrongs to which we are hourly exposed, give us strength to support them, and to forgive in charity those who wrong us. Strengthen us from good even unto better.' They had expected to hear complaints and outcries: our words astonished them. We finished our little act of wor-

* *Les Forçats pour la Foi*, p. 91.

ship by singing the hundred and sixteenth psalm. At this, the women began to weep. They washed off the mud with which our children's faces had been covered, and they sought permission to have us lodged in a barn separate from the other galley-slaves, which was done."

To return to the fugitives who evaded the dragoons, police, and coast-guard, and succeeded in making their escape from France. Many of them fled by sea, for it was difficult to close that great highway, or to guard the coast so strictly as to preclude the escape of those who dared to trust themselves upon it. Some of the fugitives from inland places, who had never seen the sea in their lives before, were so appalled at sight of the wide and stormy waste of waters, and so agonized by the thought of tearing themselves from their native land forever, that their hearts sank within them, and they died in sheer despair, without being able to accomplish their purpose. Others, stronger and more courageous, prepared to brave all risks; and on the first opportunity that offered, they put out to sea, from all parts of the coast, in open boats, in shallops, in fishing-smacks, and in trading ships, eager to escape from France in any thing that would float.

"The Protestants of the sea-board," says Weiss, "got away in French, English, and Dutch merchant vessels, whose masters hid them under bales of goods and heaps of coals, and in empty casks, where they had only the bung-hole to breathe through. There they remained, crowded one upon another, until the ship sailed. Fear of discovery and of the galleys gave them courage to suffer. Persons brought up in every luxury, pregnant women, old men, invalids, and children, vied with each other in constancy to escape from their persecutors, often risking themselves in open boats upon voyages the thought of which would in ordinary times have made them shudder. A Norman gentleman, Count de Marancé, passed the Channel, in the depth of winter, with forty persons, among whom were several pregnant women, in a vessel of seven tons' burden. Overtaken by a storm, he remained long at sea, without provisions or hope of succor, dying of hunger; he, the countess, and all the passengers reduced, for sole sustenance, to a little melted snow, with which they appeased their burning thirst, and moistened the parched lips of their weeping children, until they landed, half dead, upon England's shores."*

* WEISS—*History of the French Protestant Refugees*, p. 79, 80.

The Lord of Castelfranc, near Rochelle, was less fortunate than the Count de Marancé. He was captured at sea, in an open boat, while attempting to escape to England with his wife and family. Three of his sons and three of his daughters thus taken were sent to the Caribbee Islands as slaves. His three other daughters were detained in France in strict confinement; and after much suffering, during which they continued steadfast to their faith, they were at length permitted to depart for Geneva. The father contrived in some way afterward to escape from France and reach London, where he lived for many years in Bunhill Fields. The six slaves in the Caribbee Islands were eventually liberated by the crew of an English vessel, and brought to London. The three young men entered the English army under William III. Two of them were killed in battle in Flanders, and the third retired on half pay, settling at Portarlington in Ireland, where he died.*

Among the many who escaped in empty casks may be mentioned the Misses Raboteau, of Pont-Gibaud, near Rochelle. Their relatives had become "new Catholics," by which name the converts from Protestantism, often pretended, were called; but the two young ladies refused to be converted, and they waited an opportunity for making their escape from France. The means were at length provided by an exiled relative, John Charles Raboteau, who had emigrated long before, and settled as a wine-merchant in Dublin. He carried on a brisk trade with the French wine-growers, and occasionally sailed in his own ship to Rochelle, where he became the temporary guest of his relatives. At one of his visits the two young ladies confided to him that they had been sentenced to adopt the alternative of either marrying two Roman Catholic gentlemen selected for their husbands,

* AGNEW—*Protestant Exiles from France* [printed for private circulation], London, 1866. A work containing a large amount of curious and interesting information relative to the descendants of the French Protestant refugees in England and Ireland. We are glad to learn that the work is about to appear in a generally accessible form.

or being shut up in a convent for life. There was one other alternative—flight—upon which they resolved, if their uncle would assist them. He at once assented, and made arrangements for their escape. Two horses were obtained, on which they rode by night to Rochelle, where lodgings had been taken for them at the house of a widow. There was still, however, the greater difficulty to be overcome of getting the delicate freight put on board. Raboteau had been accustomed to take to Ireland, as part of his cargo, several large casks of French apples, and in two of such casks the young ladies were carried on board of his ship. They reached Dublin in safety, where they settled and married, and their descendants still survive.*

The Rev. Philip Skelton mentions the case of a French gentlewoman brought from Bordeaux to Portsmouth by a sea-captain of his acquaintance, which shows the agonies of mind which must have been endured by these noble women before they could bring themselves to fly alone across the sea to England for refuge. This lady had sold all the property she could convert into money, with which she purchased jewels, as being the easiest to carry. She contrived to get on board of the Englishman's ship by night, bringing with her the little casket of jewels—her sole fortune. She remained in a state of the greatest fear and anxiety till the ship was under sail. But no sooner did she find herself fairly out at sea and the land disappearing in the distance, than she breathed freely, and began to give way to her feelings of joy and gratitude. This increased in proportion as she neared England, though about to land there an exile, a solitary woman, and a foreigner; and no sooner did she reach the shore than she threw herself down and passionately kissed the

* One of them married Alderman Peter Barre, whose son was the famous Isaac Barré, M.P. and Privy Councilor; the other married Mr. Stephen Chaigneau, descended from an ancient family in the Charente, where their estate of Labelloniére was confiscated and sold as belonging to " Religionaires fugitifs du royaume pour cause de la religion." Several of their descendants have filled important offices in the state, army, and Church of England and Ireland.

ground, exclaiming, "Have I at last attained my wishes? Yes, gracious God! I thank thee for this deliverance from a tyranny exercised over my conscience, and for placing me where Thou alone art to reign over it by Thy word, till I shall finally lay down my head upon this beloved earth!"*

All the measures adopted by the French king to prevent the escape of fugitives by sea proved as futile as those employed to prevent their escape by land. The coast-guard was increased, and more tempting rewards were offered for the capture of the flying Protestants. The royal cruisers were set to watch every harbor and inlet to prevent any vessel setting sail without a most rigid search of the cargo for concealed Huguenots. When it became known that many had escaped in empty casks, provision was made to meet the case; and the royal order was issued that, before any ship was allowed to sail for a foreign port, the hold should be fumigated with deadly gas, so that any hidden Huguenot who could not be detected might thus be suffocated.† But this expedient was only of a piece with the refined and malignant cruelty of the Great Louis, and it failed like the rest, for the Huguenots still continued to make their escape.

It can never be known, with any thing approaching to accuracy, how many persons fled from France in the great exodus. Vauban, the military engineer, writing only a few years after the Revocation, said that "France had lost a hundred thousand inhabitants, sixty millions of money, nine thousand sailors, twelve thousand tried soldiers, six hundred officers, and its most flourishing manufactures." But the emigration was not then by any means at its height, and for many years after the Huguenots continued to swarm out of France, and join their exiled compatriots in other lands.

* PHILIP SKELTON [Rector of Fintona, county Tyrone]—*Compassion for the French Protestant Refugees recommended*, 1751.

† "On se servait d'une composition qui, lorsq'on y mettait le feu, développait une odeur mortelle dans tous les recoins du navire, de sorte que, en la 1espirant, ceux qui s'etaient cachés trouvaient une mort certaine!"—ROYER —*Histoire de la Colonie Française en Prusse*, p. 153.

Sismondi computed the total number of emigrants at from three to four hundred thousand; and he was farther of opinion that an equal number perished in prison, on the scaffold, at the galleys, and in their attempts to escape.*

The emigration gave a death-blow to several great branches of French industry. Hundreds of manufactories were closed, whole villages were depopulated, many large towns half deserted, and a large extent of land went altogether out of cultivation. The skilled Dutch cloth-workers, whom Colbert had induced to settle at Abbeville, emigrated in a body, and the manufacture was extinguished. At Tours, where some 40,000 persons had been employed in the silk manufacture, the number fell to little more than 4000; and instead of 8000 looms at work, there remained only about 100; while of 800 mills, 730 were closed. Of the 400 tanneries which had before enriched Lorraine, Weiss says there remained but 54 in 1698. The population of Nantes, one of the most prosperous cities of France, was reduced from 80,000 to less than one half; and a blow was struck at its prosperity from which it has not to this day recovered.

The Revocation proved almost as fatal to the prosperity of Lyons as it did to that of Tours and Nantes. That city had originally been indebted for its silk manufactures to the civil and religious wars of Sicily, Italy, and Spain, which occasioned numerous refugees from those countries to settle there and carry on their trade. And now, the same persecutions which had made the prosperity of Lyons threatened to prove its ruin. Of about 12,000 artisans employed in the silk manufacture of Lyons, about 9000 fled into Switzerland and other countries. The industry of the place was for a time completely prostrated. More than a hundred years passed before it was restored to its former prosperity, and then only to suffer another equally staggering blow from the

* Boulainvillers states that, under the intendancy of Lamoignon de Baville, a hundred thousand persons were destroyed by premature death in the single province of Languedoc, and that one tenth of them perished by fire, strangulation, or on the wheel.—DE FELICE, p. 340.

violence and outrage which accompanied the outbreak of the French Revolution.

Without pursuing the subject of the sufferings of the Huguenots who remained in France, of whom there remained more than a million, notwithstanding the frightful persecutions to which they continued to be subjected,* let us now follow the fugitives into the countries in which they found a refuge, and observe the important influence which they exercised, not only on their industrial prosperity, but also on their political history.

* Although Protestantism seemed to be utterly stamped out in France during the century which followed the Revocation of the Edict of Nantes—although its ministers were banished, its churches and schools suppressed, and it was placed entirely beyond the pale of the law—it nevertheless continued to have an active existence. Many of the banished ministers from time to time returned secretly to minister to their flocks, and were seized and suffered death in consequence—as many as twenty-nine Protestant pastors having been hanged between 1684 and 1762. During the same period, thousands of their followers were sent to the galleys, and died there. The names of 1546 of these illustrious galley-slaves are given in *Forçats pour la Foi*, but the greater number have been long forgotten on earth. The principal offense for which they were sent to the galleys was attending the Protestant meetings which continued to be held; for the Protestants, after the Revocation, constituted a sort of underground church, regularly organized, though its meetings were held by night, in forests, in caves among the hills, or in unsuspected places even in the heart of large towns and cities, in all parts of France. The "Churches of the Desert," as they were called, continued to exist down to the period of the French Revolution, when Protestantism in France was again allowed openly to show itself. A most interesting account of the Protestant Church in France during this "underground" period is to be found in CHARLES COQUEREL's *Histoire des Eglises du Désert*, in 2 vols., Paris, 1841.

CHAPTER IX.

THE HUGUENOTS AND THE ENGLISH REVOLUTION OF 1688.

THE flight of the French Protestants exercised a highly important influence on European politics. Among its other effects, it contributed to establish religious and political freedom in Switzerland, and to render it in a measure the Patmos of Europe; it strengthened the foundations of liberty in the then comparatively insignificant electorate of Brandenburg, which has since become developed into the great monarchy of Prussia; it fostered the strength and increased the political power and commercial wealth of the States of Holland; and it materially contributed to the success of the English Revolution of 1688, and to the establishment of the British Constitution on its present basis.

Long before the Revocation of the Edict of Nantes, the persecutions of the French Protestants had excited the general commiseration of Europe, and Switzerland and the northern nations vied with each other in extending to them their sympathy and their help. The principal seats of Protestantism being in Languedoc, Dauphiny, and the southwestern provinces of France, the first emigrants readily passed across the frontier of the Jura and Savoy into Switzerland, mostly making for the asylum of Geneva. That city had been in a measure created by the organization of Calvin, who had striven to make it a sort of Christian Sparta, and in a great degree succeeded. Under his regimen the place had become entirely changed. It had already emancipated itself from the authority of the Duke of Savoy, and established alliances with adjoining cantons for the purpose of insuring its independence, when Calvin undertook the administration of its ecclesiastical policy, to which the civil power shortly became entirely subordinate. There can be no doubt as to the rigor as well as the severity of Calvin's rule; but Geneva was surrounded by ferocious enemies, and had to struggle for very life. The French historian Mignet has in a few words described the rapid progress made by this remarkable community:

"In less than half a century the face of Geneva had become entirely changed. It passed through three consecutive revolutions. The first delivered it from the Duke of Savoy, who lost his delegated authority in the attempt to convert it into an absolute sovereignty. The second introduced into Geneva the Reformed worship, by which the sovereignty of the bishop was destroyed. The third constituted the Protestant administration of Geneva, and the subordination to it of the civil power. The first of these revolutions gave Geneva its independence of the ducal power; the second, its moral regeneration and political sovereignty; the third, its greatness. These three revolutions did not only follow each other; they were linked together. Switzerland was bent on liberty, the human mind on emancipation. The liberty of Switzerland made the independence of Geneva, the emancipation of the human mind made its reformation. These changes were not accomplished without difficulties nor without wars. But if they troubled the peace of the city, if they agitated the people's hearts, if they divided families, if they occasioned imprisonments, if they caused blood to be shed in the streets, they tempered characters, they awoke minds, they purified morals, they formed citizens and men, and Geneva issued transformed from the trials through which it passed. It had been subject, and it had grown independent; it had been ignorant, and it had become one of the lights of Europe; it had been a little town, and it was now a capital of the great Cause. Its science, its constitution, its greatness, were the work of France, through its exiles of the sixteenth century, who, unable to realize their ideas in their own country, had carried them into Switzerland, whose hospitality they repaid by giving them a new worship, and the spiritual government of many peoples."*

---

* MIGNET—*Memoires Historiques*, Paris, 1854, p. 385-7. In one of his letters to the Duke of Savoy in 1594, Francis de Sales urged the speedy suppression of Geneva as the capital of heresy and Calvinism. "All the heretics," said he, "respect Geneva as the asylum of their religion: this very year a person came out of Languedoc to visit it as a Catholic might visit Rome. There is not a city in Europe which offers more facilities for the encouragement of heresy, for it is the gate of France, of Italy, and Germany, so that one finds there people of all nations—Italians, French, Germans, Poles, Spaniards, English, and of countries still more remote. Besides, every one knows the great number of ministers bred there. Last year it furnished

Geneva having thus been established as a great Protestant asylum and strong-hold, mainly through the labors of Frenchmen—Calvin, Farel, De Beza, D'Aubigny, and many more—the fugitive Protestants naturally directed their steps thither in the first place. In 1685, hundreds of them were arriving in Geneva daily; but as the place was already crowded, and the accommodation it provided was but limited, the greater number of the new arrivals traveled onward into the interior cantons. Two years later, the refugees were arriving in thousands, mostly from Dauphiny and Lyons, the greater number of them being Protestant artisans. As the persecution began to rage in Gex, close upon the Swiss frontier, it seemed as if the whole population were flying. Geneva became so crowded with fugitives that they had to camp out in the public squares.

The stream of emigrants was not less considerable at Basle, Zurich, Berne, and Lausanne. The embassador of Louis XIV. wrote to his royal master, "The fugitives continue to crowd to Zurich; I met a number of them on the road from Basle to Soleure." A month later he informed his court that all the roads were full of French subjects making for Berne and Zurich; and a third dispatch informed Louis that carts laden with fugitives were daily passing through the streets of Basle. As the fugitives were mostly destitute, the Protestant cantons provided a fund* to facilitate the transit of those

twenty to France; even England obtains ministers from Geneva. What shall I say of its magnificent printing establishments, by means of which the city floods the world with its wicked books, and even goes the length of distributing them at the public expense? . . . All the enterprises undertaken against the Holy See and the Catholic princes have their beginning at Geneva. No city in Europe receives more apostates of all grades, secular and regular. From thence I conclude that Geneva being destroyed would necessarily lead to the dissipation of heresy."—*Vie de Ste. François de Sales*, par son neveu; Lyons, 1633, p. 120-1.

* The city of Geneva was superbly bountiful. In 1685, the citizens contributed 88,161 florins to the Protestant refugee fund. As the emigration increased, so did their bounty, until, in 1707, they contributed as much as 234,672 florins toward the expenses of the emigration. "Within a period of forty years," says Graverol, in his *History of the City of Nismes* (London, 1703), "Geneva furnished official contributions toward the assistance of the refugees of the Edict of Nantes amounting to not less than 5,143,266 florins."

whom the country was unable to maintain. And thus 15,591 persons were forwarded to Germany at the expense of the League.

Louis XIV. beheld with vexation the departure of so large a portion of his subjects, who preferred flight with destitution rather than French citizenship with "conversion;" and he determined to interpose with a strong hand, so as, if possible, to prevent their farther emigration. Accordingly, when the people of Gex went flying into Geneva in crowds, Louis called upon the magistrates at once to expel them. The republican city was then comparatively small and unarmed, and unable to resist the will of a monarch so powerful and with such long arms as Louis. The magistrates, therefore, made a show of compliance with his orders, and directed the expulsion of the fugitives by sound of trumpet. The exiles left by the French gate in a long and sad procession; but at midnight the citizens went forth and led them round the walls, bringing them into Geneva again by the Swiss gate. On this proceeding being reported to him, Louis vowed vengeance upon Geneva for thus trifling with his express orders, and giving refuge to his contumacious subjects. But Berne and Zurich having hastened to proffer their support to Geneva, the French king's threats remained unexecuted. The refugees, accordingly, remained in Switzerland, and settled in the various Protestant cantons, where they founded many important branches of industry, which continue to flourish to this day.

The Protestant refugees received a like cordial welcome in the provinces of North Germany, where they succeeded in establishing many important and highly flourishing colonies. The province of Brandenburg, which formed the nucleus of modern Prussia, had been devastated and almost ruined by the Thirty Years' War. Its trade and manufactures were de-

The sums expended by the cantons of Berne and Vaud during the same period exceeded 4,000,000 florins. This expenditure was altogether exclusive of the individual contributions and private hospitality of the Swiss people, which were alike liberal and bountiful.

stroyed, and much of its soil lay uncultivated. The elector Frederick William was desirous of restoring its population; and, with that view, he sought to attract into it men of skill and industry from all quarters. The Protestants whom the King of France was driving out of his kingdom were precisely the men whom the elector desired for subjects, and he sent repeated invitations to the persecuted Huguenots to settle in Brandenburg, with the promise of liberty of worship, protection, and hospitality. As early as 1661, numerous refugees embraced his offer and settled in Berlin, where they prospered, increased, and eventually founded a flourishing French church.

The Revocation of the Edict of Nantes furnished the elector with an opportunity for renewing his invitation with greater effect than before; and the promulgation of the Edict of Paris was almost immediately followed by the promulgation of the Edict of Potsdam. By the latter edict, men of the Reformed religion, driven out of France for conscience' sake, were offered a free and safe retreat through all the dominions of the elector, and promised rights, franchises, and other advantages on their settlement in Brandenburg, "in order to relieve them, and in some sort to make amends for the calamities with which Providence has thought fit to visit so considerable a part of His Church."* Facilities were provided to enable the emigrants from France to reach the Prussian states. Those from the southern and eastern provinces of France were directed to make for the Rhine, and thence to find their way by boats to Frankfort-on-the-Maine, or to Cleves, where the Prussian authorities awaited them with subsidies and the means of traveling eastward. Free shipping was also provided for them at Amsterdam, from whence they were to proceed to Hamburg, where the Prussian resident was directed to assist them in reaching their intended destinations.

These measures shortly had the effect of attracting large

* WEISS—*History of the French Protestant Refugees,* p. 100.

numbers of Huguenots into the northern provinces of Germany. The city of Frankfort became crowded with those arriving from the eastern provinces of France. The fugitives were every where made welcome, taken by the hand, succored and helped. The elector assisted them with money out of his own private means. "I will sell my plate," he said, "rather than they should lack assistance."

On arriving in Brandenburg, the emigrants proceeded to establish their colonies throughout the electorate. Nearly every large town in Prussia had its French church, and one or more French pastors. The celebrated Ancillon was pastor of the church at Berlin; and many of the Protestant gentry resorted thither, attracted by his reputation. The Huguenot immigration into Prussia consisted of soldiers, gentlemen, men of letters and artists, traders, manufacturers, and laborers. "All received assistance," says Weiss, "in money, employments, and privileges; and they contributed, in their turn, in a proportion very superior to their number, to the greatness of their adopted country."*

Numerous other bodies of the refugees settled in the smaller states of Germany, in Denmark, in Sweden, and even in Russia. A considerable body of them crossed the Atlantic and settled in the United States of America; others, led by a nephew of Admiral Duquesne, emigrated to the Cape of Good Hope;† while a colony settled as remote from France

* The personal history and particulars of the refugees who settled in Prussia are given at full length in the work published at Berlin, in 9 vols. 8vo, by Messrs. Erman and Réclam, entitled *Mémoires pour servir à l'Histoire des Refugiés François dans les Etats du Roi.*

† According to WEISS (book v., chap. v.), there are now in Cape Colony some 4000 descendants of Huguenot refugees, residing in French Valley. In 1739 the Dutch government proscribed the French language, and their language is therefore now Dutch; but they continue to be known by their surnames (such as Cocher, Dutoit, Malherbe, Retif), by their personal appearance, and by their religious habits. On each parlor table is one of those great folio Bibles which the French Protestants were wont to hand down from father to son, and in which the dates of birth and the names of all the members of the family are invariably inscribed. Clement Marot's Psalms and religious books are often to be found among them. Night and morning the members of each family assemble for prayer and the reading of the Bible. Every Sunday at sunrise the farmers set out in their rustic vehicles, covered

as Surinam, in Dutch Guiana. But Holland and England constituted the principal asylums of the exiled Huguenots—Holland in the first instance, and England in the next; many of them passing from the one country to the other in the course of the great political movements which followed close upon the Revocation of the Edict of Nantes.

Holland had long been a refuge for the persecuted Protestants of Europe. During the religious troubles of the sixteenth century, exiles fled to it from all quarters—from Germany, Flanders, France, and England. During the reign of Queen Mary thirty thousand English Protestants fled thither, who for the most part returned to England on the accession of Elizabeth. There were colonies of foreign exiles settled in nearly all the United Provinces—of Germans in Friesland and Guelderland, and of Walloons in Amsterdam, Haerlem, Leyden, Delft, and other towns in North and South Holland. And now these refugees were joined by a still greater influx of persecuted Protestants from all parts of France. Bayle designated Holland "the great ark of the fugitives." It became the chief European centre of free thought, free religion, and free industry. A healthy spirit of liberty pervaded it, which awakened and cultivated the best activities and energies of its people.

The ablest minds of France, proscribed by Louis XIV., took refuge in the Low Countries, where they taught from professors' chairs, preached from pulpits, and spoke to all Europe through the medium of the printing-press. Descartes, driven from France, betook himself to Holland, where he spent twenty years,* and published his principal philosophical works. It was the retreat of Bayle, Huyghens, Jurieu,

---

with hides or with coarse cloth, to attend divine service, and at night they return to their peaceful homes. The news of the world takes a long time to reach them. In 1828, when evangelical missionaries told them that religious toleration had existed in France for forty years, the old men shed tears, and long refused to believe that their brethren could be so favorably treated in a country from which their ancestors had been so cruelly expelled.

* He died in 1650 at Stockholm, whither he had proceeded and settled on the express invitation of Christina, queen of Sweden.

and many more of the best men of France, who there uttered and printed freely what they could do nowhere else. Among the most stirring books which emanated from the French press in Holland were those of Jurieu—formerly professor of theology and Hebrew in the University of Sedan—who now sought to rouse the indignation of Europe against the tyranny of Louis XIV. His writings were not permitted to pass into France, where all works hostile to the king and the Jesuits were seized and burnt; but they spread over Northern Europe, and fanned the general indignation into a fiercer flame.

Among the celebrated French Protestant divines who took refuge in Holland were Claude, Basnage, Martin, Benoit, and Saurin. Academies were expressly established at Leyden, Rotterdam, and Utrecht, in which the more distinguished of the banished ministers were appointed to professors' chairs, while others were distributed throughout the principal towns and placed in charge of Protestant churches. A fund was raised by voluntary subscription for the relief of the fugitives, to which all parties cheerfully and liberally contributed—not only Lutherans and Calvinists, but Jews, and even Roman Catholics.

The public, as well as the private hospitality of Holland toward the fugitives was indeed splendid. The magistrates of Amsterdam not only freely conferred on them the rights of citizenship, with liberty to exercise their respective callings, but granted them exemption from local taxes for three years. The States of Holland and the province of Friesland granted them similar privileges, with an exemption from all imposts for a period of twelve years. Every encouragement was given to the immigration. Not a town but was ready to welcome and help the destitute foreigners. The people received them into their houses as guests, and when the private dwellings were filled, public establishments were opened for their accommodation. All this was not enough. The Dutch, hearing of the sufferings of the poor exiles in Switzerland, sent invitations to them to come into Holland, where they held out that there was room for all.

The result was an immense increase of the emigration from France into Holland of men of all ranks—artisans, cloth-makers, silk-weavers, glass-makers, printers, and manufacturers. They were distributed, on their arrival, throughout the various towns and cities, where they settled to the pursuit of their respective callings, and in course of a short time they more than repaid, by the exercise of their industry and their skill, the splendid hospitality of their benefactors.

Another important feature of the immigration into Holland remains to be mentioned. This was the influx of a large number of the best sailors of France, from the coasts of Guienne, Saintonge, La Rochelle, Poitou, and Normandy, together with a still larger number of veteran officers and soldiers of the French army. This accession of refugees had the effect of greatly adding to the strength both of the Dutch navy and army, and, as we shall hereafter find, exercised a most important influence on the political history both of Holland and England.

Louis XIV. endeavored to check the emigration of his subjects into Holland, as he had tried to stop their flight into Switzerland and England, but in vain. His envoy expostulated against their reception by the States; and the States reiterated their proclamations of privileges to the refugees. It came to be feared that Louis would declare war against Holland; but the Prince of Orange had once before arrested the progress of Louis in his invasion of the provinces in 1672, and he longed for nothing so much as for another encounter with the French tyrant.

William, prince of Orange and stadtholder of Holland, hated France as his grandfather had hated Spain. Under an appearance of physical weakness and phlegmatic indifference he concealed an ardent mind and an indomitable will. He was cool and taciturn, yet full of courage and even daring. He was one of those rare men who never know despair. When the great French army of 100,000 men, under Condé and Turenne, swept over Flanders in 1672, capturing city after city, and approached Amsterdam, the inhabitants became filled with dread. De Witt proposed submission; but William, then only twenty-two years of age, urged resistance, and his view was supported by the people. He declared that he would die in the last ditch rather than see the ruin of his country, and, true to his word, he ordered the dikes to be cut and the country laid under water. The independence of Holland was thus saved, but at a frightful cost; and William never forgot, perhaps never forgave, the injury which Louis thereby caused him to inflict upon Holland.

William had another and more personal cause of quarrel with Louis. The prince took his title from the small but independent principality of Orange, situated in the southeast of France, a little to the north of Avignon. Though Orange was a fief of the imperial and not of the French crown, Louis, disregarding public law, overran it, dismantled the fortifications of the principal town, and subjected the Protestants of the districts to the same cruelties which he practiced upon his own subjects of that faith. On being informed of these outrages, William declared aloud at his table that the Most Christian King "should be made to know one day what it was to have offended a Prince of Orange." Louis's embassador at the Hague having questioned the prince as to the meaning of the words, the latter positively refused either to retract or explain them.

It may not be unimportant to remark that William was, like the other princes of his race, an intense Protestant. The history of his family was identified with the rise and progress of the new views, as well as with the emancipation of the United Provinces from the yoke of Spain and the Inquisition. His grandfather had fallen a victim to the dagger of Gérard, the agent of the Jesuits, and expired in the arms of his wife, who was a daughter of Admiral Coligny, the renowned victim of Saint Bartholomew. Thus the best Huguenot blood flowed in the veins of the young Prince of Orange, and his sympathies were wholly on the side of the fugitives who sought the asylum of Holland against the cruelty of their persecutor.

At the same time, William was doubly related to the English royal family. His mother was the daughter of Charles I., and his wife was the daughter of James II., then reigning king of England. James being then without male issue, the Princess of Orange was thus the heiress-presumptive to the British throne. Though William may have been ambitious, he was cautious and sagacious, and probably had not the remotest idea of anticipating the succession of his wife by the overthrow of the government of his father-in-law, but for the circumstance about to be summarily described, and which issued in the Revolution of 1688.

Although the later Stuart kings, who were Roman Catholics more or less disguised, had no love for Protestantism, they nevertheless felt themselves under the necessity of continuing the policy initiated by Queen Elizabeth, of giving a free asylum in England to the persecuted French Huguenots. In 1681, Charles II. was constrained by public opinion to sanction a bill granting large privileges to such of the refugees as should land on our shores. They were to have free letters-patent granted them; and on their arrival at any of the outports, their baggage and stock in trade—when they had any—were to be landed duty free. But the greater number arrived destitute. For example, a newspaper of the day thus announced the landing of a body of the refugees at Plymouth:

"Plymouth, 6th September, 1681.—An open boat arrived here yesterday, in which were forty or fifty Protestants who resided outside La Rochelle. Four other boats left with this, one of which is said to have put into Dartmouth, but it is not yet known what became of the other three."

Large numbers of the fugitives continued to land at all the southern ports—at Dover, at Rye, at Southampton, Dartmouth, and Plymouth; and, wherever they landed, they received a cordial welcome. Many were pastors, who came ashore hungering and in rags, lamenting the flocks, and some the wives and children they had left behind them in France. The people crowded round the venerable sufferers with indignant and pitying hearts; they received them into their dwellings, and hospitably relieved their wants. Very soon, the flocks followed in the wake of their pastors; and the landings of the refugees continued for many years, during which they crowded all the southern ports. The local clergy led and directed the hospitality of the inhabitants; and they usually placed the parish church at their disposal during a part of each Sunday, until they could be provided with special accommodation of their own.*

The sight of so much distress, borne so patiently and uncomplainingly, deeply stirred the heart of the nation, and every effort was made to succor and help the poor exiles for conscience' sake. Public collections were made in the churches, and a fund was raised for the relief of the most necessitous, and for enabling the foreigners to proceed inland to places where they could pursue their industry. Many were thus forwarded from the sea-coast to London, Canterbury, Norwich, and other places, where they eventually formed prosperous settlements, and laid the foundations of important branches of industry.

Meanwhile James II. succeeded to the British throne at

* At Rye, the refugees were granted the use of the parish church from eight to ten in the morning, and from twelve to two in the afternoon—the appropriation being duly confirmed by the Council of State. Reports having been spread abroad that the fugitives were persons of bad character, disaffected, and Papists in disguise, the vicar and principal citizens of Rye drew up and published the following testimonial in their behalf:

"These are to certifie to all whom it may concern, that the French Protestants who are settled inhabitants of this town of Rye are a sober, harmless, innocent people, such as serve God constantly and uniformly, according to the usage and custom of the Church of England. And further, that we believe them to be falsely aspersed for Papists and disaffected persons, no such thing appearing unto us by the conversations of any of them. This we do freely and truly certifie for and of them. In witness whereof, we have hereunto set our hands, the 18th day of April, 1682. Wm. Williams, Vicar; Thos. Tournay," etc., etc.—*State Papers, Domestic Calendar*, 1682, No. 65. See also *Sussex Archæological Collection*, xiii., 201.

the death of his brother Charles II., on the 6th of January, 1685—the year memorable in France as that in which the Edict of Nantes was revoked. Charles and James were both Roman Catholics—Charles when he was not a scoffer, James always. The latter had long been a friend of the Jesuits in disguise; but no sooner was he king than he threw off the mask, and exhibited himself in his true character. James was not a man to gather wisdom from experience. During the exile of his family he had learned nothing and forgotten nothing; and it shortly became clear to the English nation that he was bent on pursuing almost the identical course which had cost his father his crown and his head.

If there was one feeling that characterized the English people about this time more than another, it was their aversion to popery—not merely popery as a religion, but as a policy. It was felt to be contrary to the whole spirit, character, and tendency of the nation. Popery had so repeatedly exhibited itself as a persecuting policy, that not only the religious, but the non-religious; not only the intelligent few, but the illiterate many, regarded it with feelings of deep aversion. Great, therefore, was the public indignation when it became known that one of the first acts of James, on his accession to the throne, was to order the public celebration of the mass at Westminster, after an interval of more than a century. The king also dismissed from about his person clergymen of the English Church, and introduced well-known Jesuits in their stead. He degraded several of the bishops, though he did not yet venture openly to persecute them. But he showed his temper and his tendency by actively reviving the persecutions of the Scotch Presbyterians, whom he pursued with a cruelty only equaled by Louis XIV. in his dealings with the Huguenots.*

James II. was but the too ready learner of the lessons in

* In Scotland, whoever was detected preaching in a conventicle or attending one was punishable with death and the confiscation of all his property. Macaulay says the Scotch Act of Parliament (James VII., 8th May, 1685) enacting these penalties was passed at the special instance of the king.

despotism taught him by Louis XIV., whose pensioner* he was, and whose ultimate victim he proved to be. The two men, indeed, resembled each other in many respects, and their actions ran in almost parallel lines, though those who concede to Louis the title of "Great" will probably object that the English king was merely the ape of the French one.† They were both dissolute, and both bigots, vibrating alternately between their mistresses and their confessors. What La Valliere, Montespan, and Maintenon were to Louis XIV., that Arabella Churchill and Catharine Sedley were to James II., while the queens of both were left to pine in sorrow and neglect. The principal difference between them in this respect was, that Louis sinned with comely mistresses, and James with ugly ones.‡ Louis sought absolution from Pere la Chaise, as James from Father Petre; and when penance had to be done, both laid it alike upon their Protestant subjects—Louis increasing the pressure of persecution on the Huguenots, and James upon the Puritans and Covenanters. Both employed military missionaries in carrying out their designs of conversion; the agents of Louis being the "dragons" of Noailles, those of James the dragoons of Claverhouse. Both were despisers of constitutional power, and sought to

---

* James II. was from the first the pensioner of Louis XIV. One of his first acts on the death of Charles was to supplicate Barillon, the representative of Louis at the English court, for money. Rochester, James's prime minister, said to Barillon, "The money will be well laid out; your master can not employ his revenues better. Represent to him strongly how important it is that the King of England should be dependent, not on his own people, but on the friendship of the King of France alone." Louis had already anticipated the wishes of James by remitting to him bills of exchange equal to £37,500 sterling. James shed tears of joy on receiving them. In the course of a few weeks Barillon obtained a further remittance from France of about £12,000 sterling, and he was instructed to furnish the English government with the money for the purpose of corrupting members of the new House of Commons.—See Macaulay's *Hist. of England*, ed. 1849, p. 458, 463.

† Thus James aped Louis even in his worship, introducing four-and-twenty fiddlers in his church choir after the French king's model.

‡ Charles II. used to say that one might fancy his brother's mistresses were given to him by his father's confessor as penances, they were all so ugly. Catharine Sedley herself wondered what James chose them for. "We were none of us handsome," she said, "and if we had wit, he had not enough to find it out."

centre the government in themselves. But, while Louis succeeded in crushing the Huguenots, James ignominiously failed in crushing the Puritans. Louis, it is true, brought France to the verge of ruin, and paved the way for the French Revolution of 1792; while, happily for England, the designs of James were summarily thwarted by the English Revolution of 1688, and the ruin of his kingdom was thus averted.

The designs of James upon the consciences of his people were not long in developing themselves. The persecution of the Scotch Covenanters was carried on with increased virulence until resistance almost disappeared, and then he turned his attention to the English Puritans. Baxter, Howe, Bunyan, and hundreds of nonconformist ministers were thrown into jail; but there were as yet no hangings and shootings of them as in Scotland. To strengthen his power, and enable him to adopt more decisive measures, James next took steps to augment the standing army—a measure which exposed him to increased public odium. Though contrary to law, he in many cases dismissed the Protestant officers of regiments, and appointed Roman Catholics in their stead. To render the appointments legal, he proposed to repeal the Test Act, as well as the Habeas Corpus Act; but his minister Halifax refusing to concur in this course, he was dismissed, and Parliament adjourned. Immediately before its reassembling came the news from France of the Revocation of the Edict of Nantes and the horrible cruelties perpetrated on the Huguenots. The intelligence caused a thrill of indignation to run throughout England; and very shortly, crowds of the destitute fugitives landed on the southern coast, and spread abroad the tale of horror.

Shortly after, there came from France the report of a speech addressed by the Bishop of Valance to Louis XIV. in the name of the French clergy. "The pious sovereign of England," said the orator, "looked to the Most Christian King, the eldest son of the Church, for support against a heretical nation." The natural inference drawn was, that what Louis had done in France, James was about to imitate in England by means of his new standing army, commanded by Roman Catholic officers.

To allay the general alarm which began to prevail, James pretended to disapprove of the cruelties to which the Huguenots had been subjected; and, in deference to public opinion, he granted some relief to the exiles from his privy purse, and invited his subjects to imitate his liberality by making a public collection for them in the churches throughout the kingdom. His acts, however, speedily belied his words. At the instigation of Barillon, he had the book published in Holland by the banished Huguenot pastor Claude, describing the sufferings of his brethren, burnt by the hangman before the Royal Exchange; and when the public collection was made in the churches, and £40,000 was paid into the chamber of London, James gave orders that none should receive a farthing of relief unless they first took the sacrament according to the Anglican ritual. Many of the exiles who came for help, when they heard of the terms on which alone it was to be granted, went away, unrelieved, with sad and sorrowful hearts.

James proceeded steadily on his reactionary course. He ordered warrants to be drawn, in defiance of the law, authorizing priests of the Church of Rome to hold benefices in the Church of England; and various appointments were made in conformity with his royal will. A Jesuit was quartered as chaplain in University College, Oxford, and the Roman Catholic rites were there publicly celebrated. The deanery of Christchurch was presented to a minister of the Church of Rome, and mass was duly celebrated there. Roman Catholic chapels and convents rose all over the country; and Franciscan, Carmelite, and Benedictine monks appeared openly, in their cowls, beads, and conventual garb. The king made no secret of his intention to destroy the Protestant Church; and he lost no time in carrying out his measures, even in the face of popular tumult and occasional rioting, placing his reliance mainly upon his standing army, which was then encamped on Hounslow Heath. At the same time, Tyrconnel was sent over to Ireland to root out the Protestant colonies there, and one of his first acts was to cast adrift about 4000 Protestant officers and soldiers, supplanting them by as many stanch Papists. Those in his confidence boasted that in a few months there would not be a man of English race left in the Irish army. The Irish Protestants, indeed, began to fear another massacre, and a number of families, principally gentlemen, artificers, and tradesmen, left Dublin for England in the course of a few days.

At length resistance began to show itself. The Parliaments both of England and Scotland pronounced against the king's policy, and he was unable to carry his measures by constitutional methods. He accordingly resolved, like Louis XIV., to rule by the strong hand, and to govern by royal edict. Such was the state of affairs, rapidly verging on anarchy or civil war, when the English nation, sick of the rule of James II., after a reign of only three years, and longing for relief, looked abroad for help, and, with almost general consent, fixed their eyes upon William, Prince of Orange, as the one man capable of assisting them in their time of need.

The Prince of Orange had meanwhile been diligently occupied, among other things, with the reorganization of his army; and the influx of veteran officers and soldiers of the French king, banished from France because of their religion, furnished him with every facility for this purpose. He proposed to the States of Holland that they should raise two new regiments, to be composed entirely of Huguenots; but the States were at first unwilling to make such an addition to their army. They feared the warlike designs of their young prince, and were mainly intent on reducing the heavy imposts that weighed upon the country, occasioned by the recent invasion of Louis XIV., from the destructive effects of which they were still suffering.

William, fearing lest the veterans whom he so anxiously

desired to retain in his service should depart into other lands, then publicly proclaimed that he would himself pay the expenses of all the military refugees rather than that they should leave Holland. On this the States hesitated no longer, but agreed to pension the French officers until they could be incorporated in the Dutch army, and 180,000 florins a year were voted for the purpose. Companies of French cadets were also formed and maintained at the expense of the state. The Huguenot officers and men were drafted as rapidly as possible into the Dutch army; and before long William saw his ranks swelled by a formidable body of veteran troops, together with a large number of officers of fusiliers from Strasburg, Metz, and Verdun. Whole companies of Huguenot troops were drafted into each regiment under their own officers, while the principal fortresses at Breda, Maestricht, Bergen-op-Zoom, Bois-le-Duc, Zutphen, Nimeguen, Arnheim, and Utrecht were used as so many dépôts for such officers and soldiers as continued to take refuge in Holland.

William's plans were so carefully prepared, and he conducted his proceedings with such impenetrable mystery, that both James II. and Louis XIV. were kept entirely in the dark as to his plans and intentions. At length the prince was ready to embark his army, and England was ready to receive him. It forms no part of our purpose to relate the circumstances connected with the embarkation of William, his landing in England, and the revolution which followed, farther than to illustrate the part which the banished Huguenots played in that great political transaction. The narrative will be found brilliantly narrated in the pages of Macaulay, though that historian passes over with too slight notice the services of the Huguenots.

Michelet, the French writer, observes with justice: "The army of William was strong precisely in that Calvinistic element which James repudiated in England—I mean in our Huguenot soldiers, the brothers of the Puritans. I am astonished that Macaulay has thought fit to leave this circumstance in the background. I can not believe that great England, with all her glories and her inheritance of liberty, is unwilling nobly to avow the part which we Frenchmen had in her deliverance. In the Homeric enumeration which the historian gives of the followers of William, he reckons up English, Germans, Dutch, Swedes, Swiss, with the picturesque detail of their arms, uniforms, and all, down even to the two hundred negroes, with their black faces set off by embroidered turbans and white feathers, who followed the body of English gentry led by the Earl of Macclesfield. But he did not see our Frenchmen. Apparently the proscribed Huguenot soldiers who followed William did not do honor to the prince by their clothes! Doubtless many of them wore the dress in which they had fled from France—and it had become dusty, worn, and tattered."*

There is, indeed, little reason to doubt, notwithstanding Macaulay's oversight, that the flower of the little army with which William landed at Torbay, on the 15th of November, 1688, consisted of Huguenot soldiers trained under Schomberg, Turenne, and Condé. The expedition included three entire regiments of French infantry numbering 2250 men, and a complete squadron of French cavalry. These were nearly all veteran troops, officers and men, whose valor had been proved on many a hard-fought field. Many of them were gentlemen born, who, unable to obtain commissions as officers, were content to serve in the ranks. The number of French officers was very large in proportion to the whole force—736, besides those in command of the French regiments, being distributed through all the battalions. It is, moreover, worthy of note that William's ablest and most trusted officers were Huguenots. Schomberg, the refugee Marshal of France, was next in command to the prince himself; and such was the confidence which that skillful general inspired, that the Princess of Orange gave him secret instruc-

* MICHELET—*Louis XIV. et la Revocation*, p. 418-19.

tions to assert her rights, and carry out the enterprise should her husband fall.* William's three aids-de-camp, De l'Etang, De la Meloniére, and the Marquis d'Arzilliers, were French officers, as were also the chiefs of the engineers and the artillery, Gambon and Goulon, the latter being one of Vauban's most distinguished pupils. Fifty-four French gentlemen served in William's regiment of horse-guards, and thirty-four in his body-guard. Among the officers of the army of liberation, distinguished alike by their birth and their military skill, were the cavalry officers Didier de Boncourt and Chalant de Remeugnac, colonels; Danserville, lieutenant colonel; and Petit and Picard, majors; while others of equal birth and distinction as soldiers served in the infantry.†

Marshal Schomberg was descended from the old Dukes of Cleves, whose arms he bore; and several of his ancestors held high rank in the French service. One of them was killed at the battle of Ivry on the side of Henry IV., and another commanded under Richelieu at the siege of Rochelle. The marshal, whose mother was an Englishwoman of the noble house of Dudley, began his career in the Swedish army in the Thirty Years' War, after which he entered the service of the Netherlands, and subsequently that of France. There he led an active and distinguished life, and rose by successive steps to the rank of marshal. The great Condé had the highest opinion of his military capacity, comparing him to Turenne. He commanded armies successfully in Flanders, Portugal, and Holland; but on the Revocation of the Edict, being unable to conform to popery, he felt compelled to resign his military honors and emoluments, and leave France forever.

Schomberg first went into Portugal, which was assigned to

* WEISS, *History of the French Protestant Refugees*, p. 232.
† Weiss mentions among the captains of horse Massole de Montant, Petit, De Maricourt, De Boncourt, De Fabricè, De Lauray, Baron d'Entragues, Le Coq de St. Leger, De Saumaise, De Lacroix, De Dampierre; while among the captains of infantry we find De Saint Sauveur, Rapin (afterward the historian), De Cosne-Chavernay, Danserville, Massole de Montant, Jacques de Baune, Baron d'Avejan, Nolibois, Belcastel, Jaucourt de Villarnoue, Lislemaretz, De Montazier, and the three brothers De Batz.—*Ibid.*, p. 232.

him as his place of exile; but he shortly after left that country to take service, with numerous other French officers, under Frederick William of Brandenburg. His stay at Berlin was, however, of short duration; for when he heard of the intentions of William of Orange with respect to England, he at once determined to join him. Offers of the most tempting kind were held out by Frederick William to induce him to remain in Prussia. The elector proposed to appoint him governor general, minister of state, and member of the privy council; but in vain. Schomberg felt that the interests of Protestantism, of which William of Orange was the recognized leader, required him to forego his own personal interests; and, though nearly seventy years of age, he quitted the service of Prussia to enter that of Holland. He was accompanied by a large number of veteran Huguenot officers, full of bitter resentment against the monarch who had driven them forth from France, and who burned to meet their persecutors in the field, and avenge themselves of the cruel wrongs which they had suffered at their hands.

What the embittered feelings of the French Protestant gentry were, and what was the nature of the injuries they had suffered because of their religion, may, however, be best explained by the following narrative of the sufferings and adventures of a Norman gentleman who succeeded in making his escape from France, joined the liberating army of William of Orange as captain of dragoons, took part in the expedition to England, served with the English army in the Irish campaigns, and afterward settled at Portarlington in Ireland, where he died in 1709.

CHAPTER X.

DUMONT DE BOSTAQUET.—HIS ESCAPE FROM FRANCE INTO HOLLAND.

ISAAC DUMONT DE BOSTAQUET was a Protestant gentleman possessing considerable landed property near Yerville, in Normandy, about eight leagues from Dieppe. He had been well educated in his youth, and served with distinction in the French army as an officer of Norman horse. After leaving the army he married and settled on his paternal estates, where he lived the life of a retired country gentleman.*

It was about the year 1661 that the first mutterings of the coming storm reached De Bostaquet in his ancient chateau of La Fontelaye. The Roman Catholics, supported by the king, had begun to pull down the Protestant churches in many districts, and now it began to be rumored abroad that several in Normandy were to be demolished; among others the church of Lindebœuf, in which De Bostaquet and his family worshiped. He at once set out for Paris, to endeavor, if possible, to prevent this outrage being done. He saw his old commander Turenne, and had interviews with the king's ministers, but without any satisfactory result; for on his return to Normandy he found the temple at Lindebœuf had been demolished during his absence.

When De Bostaquet complained to the local authorities of

* The account given in this chapter is mainly drawn from the *Mémoires Inédits de Dumont de Bostaquet, Gentilhomme Normand*, edited by MM. Read and Waddington, and published at Paris in 1864. The MS. was in the possession of Dr. Vignolles, Dean of Ossory, a lineal descendant of De Bostaquet, and was lent by him to Lord Macaulay for perusal while the latter was engaged on his *History of England*. Lord Macaulay did not make much use of the MS., probably because it was difficult to read in the old French; but the references made to it in the foot-notes of his work induced the French editors to apply for a copy of the MS. to the Dean of Ossory, who courteously acceded to their request, and hence its recent publication.

the outrage, he was told that the king was resolved to render the exercise of the Protestant worship so difficult, that it would be necessary for all Protestants throughout France to conform themselves to the king's religion. This, however, De Bostaquet was not prepared to do; and a temporary place of worship was fitted up in the chateau at La Fontelaye, where the scattered flock of Lindebœuf reassembled, and the seigneur himself on an emergency preached, baptized, and performed the other offices of religion. And thus he led an active and useful life in the neighborhood for many years.

But the persecution of the Protestants became increasingly hard to bear. More of their churches were pulled down, and their worship was becoming all but proscribed. De Bostaquet began to meditate emigration into Holland; but he was bound to France by many ties—of family as well as property. By his first wife he had a family of six daughters and one son. Shortly after her death he married a second time, and a second family of six children was added to the first. But his second wife also died, leaving him with a very large family to rear and educate; and, as intelligent female help was essential for this purpose, he was thus induced to marry a third time; and a third family, of two sons and three daughters, was added to the original number.

At last the edict was revoked, and the dragoons were let loose on the provinces to compel the conversion of the Protestants. A body of cuirassiers was sent into Normandy, which had hitherto been exempt from such visitations. On the intelligence of their advance reaching De Bostaquet, he summoned a meeting of the neighboring Protestant gentry at his house at La Fontelaye, to consider what was best to be done. He then declared to them his intention of leaving France should the king persist in his tyrannical course. Although all who were present praised his resolution, none offered to accompany him—not even his eldest son, who had been married only a few months before. When the ladies of the household were apprised of the resolution he had expressed, they implored him, with tears in their eyes, not to leave them; if he did, they felt themselves to be lost. His wife, on the eve of another confinement, joined her entreaties to those of his children, and he felt that under such circumstances flight was impossible.

The intelligence shortly reached La Fontelaye that the cuirassiers had entered Rouen sword in hand, under the Marquis de Beaupré Choiseul; that the quartering of the troops on the inhabitants was producing "conversions" by wholesale; and that crowds were running to M. de Marillac, the intendant, to sign their abjuration, and thus get rid of the soldiers. De Bostaquet then resolved to go over to Rouen himself, and see with his own eyes what was going on there. He was greatly shocked both by what he saw and by what he heard. Sorrow sat on all countenances except those of the dragoons, who paraded the streets with a truculent air. There was a constant moving of them from house to house, where those quartered remained, swearing, drinking, and hectoring, until the inmates had signed their abjuration, when they were withdrawn for the purpose of being quartered elsewhere. De Bostaquet was ineffably pained to find that these measures were generally successful; that all classes were making haste to conform; and that even his brother-in-law, M. de Lamberville, who had been so stanch but a few days before, had been carried along by the stream and abjured.

De Bostaquet hastened from the place and returned to La Fontelaye sad at heart. The intelligence he brought with him of the dragonnades at Rouen occasioned deep concern in the minds of his household; but only one feeling pervaded them—resignation and steadfastness. De Bostaquet took refuge in the hope that, belonging as he did to the noblesse, he would be spared the quartering of troops in his family. But he was mistaken. At Rouen, the commandant quartered thirty horsemen upon Sieur Chauvel, until he and his lady, to get rid of them, signed their abjuration; and an intimation was shortly after made to De Bostaquet, that unless he and his family abjured, a detachment of twenty-five dragoons would be quartered in his chateau. Fearing the effects on his wife in her then delicate state of health, as well as desiring to save his children from the horrors of such a visitation, he at once proceeded to Dieppe with his eldest son, and promised to sign his abjuration, after placing himself for a time under the instruction of the reverend penitentiary of Notre Dame de Rouen.

No sooner had he put his name to the paper than he felt degraded in his own eyes. He felt that he had attached his signature to a falsehood, for he had no intention of attending mass or abjuring his religion. But his neighbors were now abjuring all round. His intimate friend, the Sieur De Boissé, had a company of musketeers quartered on him until he signed. Another neighbor, the Sieur de Montigny, was in like manner compelled to abjure—his mother and four daughters, to avoid the written lie, having previously escaped into Holland. None were allowed to go free. Old M. de Grosménil, De Bostaquet's father-in-law, though laid up by gout and scarce able to hold a pen, was compelled to sign. In anticipation of the quartering of the dragoons on the family, his wife had gone into concealment, the children had left the house, and even the domestics could with difficulty be induced to remain. The eldest daughter fled through Picardy into Holland; the younger daughters took refuge with their relatives in Rouen; the son also fled, none knew whither. Madame de Grosménil issued from her concealment to take her place by her suffering husband's bed, and she too was compelled to sign her abjuration; but she was so shocked and grieved by the sin she felt she had committed that she shortly after fell ill and died. "All our families," says De Bostaquet, "succumbed by turns." A body of troops next made their appearance at La Fontelaye, and required all the members of the household to sign their abjuration. De Bostaquet's wife, his mother—whose gray hairs did not protect her—his sons, daughters, and domestics, were all required to sign.

"The sad state to which my soul was reduced," continues De Bostaquet, "and the general desolation of the Church, occasioned me the profoundest grief. . . . . . All feeling equally criminal, we no longer enjoyed that tranquillity of mind which before had made us happy. God seemed to have hid himself from us; and though by our worship, which we continued publicly to celebrate, we might give evidence of the purity of our sentiments and the sincerity of our repentance, my crime never ceased to weigh upon my mind, and I bitterly reproached myself for having set so bad an example before my family as well as my neighbors. . . . . But I could not entertain without grief the thought of my children being exposed to the danger of falling a prey to these demons, who might any moment have carried them away from me. I was constantly meditating flight; but the flesh fought against the spirit, and the fear of abandoning this large family, together with the difficulty I saw before me of providing a subsistence for them in a foreign land, held me back; though I still watched for a favorable opportunity for escaping from France, by which time I hoped to be enabled to provide myself with money by the sale of my property."*

The whole family now began seriously to meditate flight from France—De Bostaquet's mother, notwithstanding her burden of eighty years, being one of the most eager to escape. Attempts were first made to send away the girls singly, and several journeys were made to the nearest port with that object; but no ship was to be met with, and the seacoast was found strictly guarded. De Bostaquet's design having become known to the commandant at Dieppe, he was privately warned of the risk he ran of being informed against, and of having his property confiscated and himself sent to the galleys. But the ladies of the family became every day more urgent to fly, declaring that their consciences would not allow them any longer hypocritically to conform to a church which they detested, and that they were resolved to escape from their present degradation at all risks.

At length it was arranged that an opportunity should be taken of escaping during the fêtes of Pentecost, when there was to be a grand review of the peasantry appointed to guard

* DE BOSTAQUET—*Mémoires Inédits*, p. 111.

the coast, during which they would necessarily be withdrawn from their posts as watchers of the Huguenot fugitives. The family plans were thus somewhat precipitated, before De Bostaquet had been enabled to convert his property into money, and thereby provide himself with the means of conducting the emigration of so large a family. It was first intended that the young ladies should endeavor to make their escape, their father accompanying them to the coast to see them safe on board ship, and then returning to watch over his wife, who was approaching the time of her confinement.

On the morning of Pentecost Sunday, the whole family assembled at worship, and besought the blessing of God on their projected enterprise. After dinner the party set out. It consisted of De Bostaquet, his aged mother, several grown daughters, and many children. The father had intended that the younger son should stay behind, but with tears in his eyes he implored leave to accompany them. The cavalcade first proceeded to the village of La Haliére, where arrangements had been made for their spending the night, while De Bostaquet proceeded to Saint Aubin to engage an English vessel lying there to take them off the coast.

The following night, about ten o'clock, the party set out from Luneray, accompanied by many friends and a large number of fugitives, like themselves making for the seacoast. De Bostaquet rode first, with his sister behind him on a pillion. His son-in-law De Renfreville, and his wife, rode another horse in like manner. De Bostaquet's mother, the old lady of eighty, was mounted on a quiet pony, and attended by two peasants. His son and daughter were also mounted, the latter on a peasant's horse which carried the valises. De Renfreville's valet rode another nag, and was armed with a musketoon. Thus mounted, after many adieus the party set out for Saint Aubin. On their way thither they were joined by other relatives—M. de Montcornet, an old officer in the French army, and De Bostaquet's brother-in-law, M. de Béquigny, who was accompanied by a German valet with another young lady behind him on a pillion.

"We found before us in the plain," says De Bostaquet, "more than three hundred persons—men, women, and children—all making for the sea-coast, some for Saint Aubin, and others for Quiberville. Nearly the whole of these people were peasants, there being very few of the better class among them; and none bore arms but ourselves and the two valets of De Béquigny and De Renfreville, who carried musketoons. The facility with which fugitives had heretofore been enabled to escape, and the belief that there was no danger connected with our undertaking, made us travel without much precaution. The night was charming, and the moon shone out brightly. The delicious coolness which succeeded the heat of the preceding day enabled the poor peasants on foot to march forward with a lighter step; and the prospect of a speedy deliverance from their captivity made them almost run toward the shore with as much joy as if they had been bound for a wedding-party.

"We passed by the end of the village of Avremenil, where a great number of the inhabitants had assembled to see us pass. They wished us *bon voyage*, and all things seemed favorable for our design. On the way, M. de Béquigny, who had remained behind, spurred on to the head of the troop where I was to inform me that Madame de Roncheraye, my sister-in-law, had come to join us in her carriage, with her three children and my daughter, from Ribœuf, together with a young lady from Rouen, named Duval, and that they begged me to wait for them. I accordingly checked the cavalcade, and we went forward more slowly.

"Those who intended to embark at Quiberville now left us, while those who were bound for Saint Aubin proceeded in that direction. As yet we had encountered no obstacle. We passed through Flainville without any one speaking to us; and, flattering ourselves that every thing was propitious, we at length reached the shore. We found the coast-guard station empty; no one appeared; and without fear we alighted to rest our horses. We seated the ladies on the shingle by the side of my mother, a tall girl from Caen keeping them company.

"I was disappointed at seeing no signs of the vessel in which we were to embark. I did not know that they were waiting for some signal to approach the land. While I was in this state of anxiety, my son came to inform me that his aunt had arrived. Her carriage had not been able to reach the shore, and she waited for me about a gun-shot off. I went on foot, accompanied by my son, to find her. She and her children were bathed in tears at the thought of their separation. She embraced me tenderly, and the sight of herself and little ones afflicted me exceedingly. My daughter from Ribœuf alighted from the carriage to salute me, as well as Mademoiselle Duval.

"I had been with them for a very little while, when I perceived there was a general movement down by the margin of the sea, where I had left my party. I asked what it was, and fearing lest the vessel might appear too far off, I proposed to have the carriage brought nearer to the shore; but I was not left long in uncertainty. A peasant called out to me that there was a great disturbance going forward; and soon after I heard the sound of drums beating, followed by a discharge of musketry. It immediately occurred to me that it must be the coast-guard returned to occupy their post, who had fallen on our party, and I began to fear that we were irretrievably lost. I was on foot alone, with my little son, near the carriage. I did not then see two horsemen coming down upon us at full speed, but I heard voices crying with all their might, 'Help! help!' I found myself in a strange state of embarrassment, without means of defense, when my lackey, who was holding my horses on the beach, ran toward me with my arms.

"I had only time to throw myself on my horse and call out to my sister-in-law in the carriage to turn back quickly, when I hastened, pistol in hand, to the place whence the screams proceeded. Scarce was I clear of the carriage when a horseman shouted 'Kill! kill!' I answered, 'Fire, rascal!' At the same moment he fired his pistol full at me, so near that the discharge flashed along my left cheek and set fire to my peruke, but without wounding me. I was still so near the carriage that both the coachman and lackey saw my hair in a blaze. I took aim with my pistol at the stomach of the scoundrel, but, happily for him, it missed fire, although I had primed it afresh on leaving Luneray. The horseman at once turned tail, accompanied by his comrade. I then took my other pistol, and followed them at the trot, when the one called out to the other, 'Fire! fire!' One of them had a musket, with which he took aim at me, and as it was nearly as light as day, and I was only two or three horse-lengths from him, he fired and hit me in the left arm, with which I was holding my bridle. I moved my arm quickly to ascertain whether it was broken, and putting spurs to my horse, gained the crupper of the man who had first fired at me, who was now on my left, and as he bent over his horse's neck I discharged my pistol full into his haunch. The two horsemen at once disappeared and fled.

"I now heard the voice of De Béquigny, who, embarrassed by his assailants on foot, was furiously defending himself; and, without losing time in pursuing the fugitives, I ran up to him sword in hand, encountering on the way my son-in-law, who was coming toward me. I asked him whither he was going, and he said he was running in search of the horses, which his valet had taken away. I told him it was in vain, and that he was flying as fast as legs could carry him, for I had caught sight of him passing as I mounted my horse. But I had no time to reason with him. In a moment I had joined De Béquigny, who had with him only old Montcornet, my wife's uncle; but, before a few minutes had passed, we had scattered the canaille, and found ourselves masters of the field. De Béquigny informed me that his horse was wounded, and that he could do no more; and I told him that I was wounded in the arm, and that it was necessary, without loss of time, to ascertain what had become of the poor women.

"We found them almost in the same place that we had left them, but abandoned by every body; the attendants and the rest of the troop having run away along the coast, under the cliffs. My mother, who was extremely deaf through age, had not heard the shots, and did not know what to make of the disturbance, thinking only of the vessel, which had not yet made its appearance. My sister, greatly alarmed, on my reproaching her with not having quietly followed the others, answered that my mother was unable to walk, being too much burdened by her dress; for, fearing the coldness of the night, she had clothed herself heavily. M. de Béquigny then suggested that it might yet be possible to rally some of the men of our troop, and thereby rescue the ladies from their peril. Without loss of time I ran along the beach for some distance, supposing that some of the men might have hidden under the cliffs through fear; but my labors were useless—I saw only some girls, who fled away weeping. Considering that my presence would be more useful to our poor women, I rejoined them at the gallop. M. de Béquigny, on his part, had returned from the direction of the coast-guard station, to ascertain whether there were any persons lurking there, for we entertained no doubt that it was the coast-guard that had attacked us; and the two horsemen with whom I had the affair confirmed me in this impression, for I knew that such men were appointed to patrol the coasts, and visit the posts, all the night through. On coming up to me, Béquigny said he feared we were lost; that the rascals had rallied to the number of about forty, and were preparing for another attack.

"We had no balls remaining with which to reload our pistols. Loss of blood already made me feel very faint. De Béquigny's horse had been wounded in the shoulder by a musket-shot, and had now only three legs to go on. In this extremity, and not knowing what to do to save the women and children, I begged him to set my mother on horseback. He tried, but she was too heavy, and he set her down again. M. de Montcornet was the only other man we had with us, but he was useless. He was seventy-two, and the little nag he rode could not be of much service. De Béquigny's valet had run away, after having in the skirmish fired his musketoon and wounded a coast-guardsman in the shoulder, of which the man died. The tide, which began to rise, deterred me from leading the women and children under the cliffs; besides, I was uncertain of the route in that direction. My mother and sister conjured me to fly instantly, because, if I was captured, my ruin was certain, while the worst that could happen to them would be confinement in a convent.

"In this dire extremity my heart was torn by a thousand conflicting emotions, and overwhelmed with despair at being unable to rescue those so dear to me from the perils which beset them. I knew not what course to take. While in this state of irresolution, I found myself becoming faint through loss of blood. Taking out my handkerchief, I asked my sister to tie it round my arm, which was still bleeding; but wanting the nerve to do so, as well as not being sufficiently tall to reach me on horseback, I addressed myself to the young lady from Caen, who was with them, and whom they called La Rosiére. She was tall, and by the light of the moon she looked a handsome girl. She had great reluctance to approach me in the state in which I was; but at last, after entreating her earnestly, she did me the service which I required, and the farther flow of blood was stopped.

"After resisting for some time the entreaties of my mother and sister to leave them and fly for my life—seeing that my staying longer with them was useless, and that De Montcornet and De Béquigny also urged me to fly—I felt that at length I must yield to my fate, and leave them in the hands of Providence. My sister, who feared being robbed by the coast-guard on their return, gave me her twenty louis d'ors to keep, and praying heaven to preserve me, they forced me to leave them and take to flight, which I did with the greatest grief that I had ever experienced in the whole course of my life."*

De Bostaquet and his friend De Béquigny first fled along the shore, but the shingle greatly hindered them. On their way they fell in first with De Béquigny's valet, who had fled with the horses, and shortly after with Judith-Julie, Dumont's little daughter, accompanied by a peasant and his wife. She was lifted up and placed in front of the valet, and they rode on. Leaving the sea-shore by a road which led from the beach inland, Dumont preceded them, his drawn sword in his hand. They had not gone far when they were met by six horsemen, who halted and seemed uncertain whether to attack or not; but, observing Dumont in an attitude of defense, they retired, and the fugitives fled as fast as De Béquigny's wounded horse would allow them to Luneray, to the house from which they had set out the previous night. There he left his little daughter, and again De Béquigny and he rode out into the night. As day broke they reached Saint Laurent. They went direct to the house of a Huguenot surgeon, who removed Dumont's bloody shirt, probed the wound to his extreme agony, but could not find

* *Mémoires Inédits*, p. 121–5.

the ball, the surgeon concluding that it was firmly lodged between the two bones of the fore-arm. The place was too unsafe for Dumont to remain, and, though suffering much and greatly needing rest, he set out again, and made for his family mansion at La Fontelaye. But he did not dare to enter the house. Alighting at the door of one of his tenants named Malherbe, devoted to his interest, he dispatched him with a message to Madame de Bostaquet, who at once hastened to her husband's side. Her agony of grief may be imagined on seeing him, pale and suffering, his clothes covered with blood, and his bandaged arm in a sling. Giving her hasty instructions as to what she was to do in his absence, among other things with respect to the sale of his property and every thing that could be converted into money, and after much weeping, and taking many tender embraces of his wife and daughters, committing them to the care of God, he mounted again, and fled northward for liberty and life.

De Bostaquet proceeds in his narrative to give a very graphic account of his flight across Normandy, Picardy, Artois, and Flanders, into Holland, in the course of which he traversed woods, swam rivers, and had many hairbreadth escapes. Knowing the country thoroughly, and having many friends and relatives in Normandy and Picardy, Roman Catholics as well as Protestants, he often contrived to obtain a night's shelter, a change of linen, and sometimes a change of horses for himself and his friend, Saint-Foy, who accompanied him. They lodged the first night at Varvannes with a kinsman on whom he could rely, for M. de Verdun, says De Bostaquet, "was a good man, though a papist and even a bigot." A surgeon was sent for to dress the fugitive's arm, which had become increasingly painful. The surgeon probed the wound, but still no ball could be found. Mounting again, the two rode all day, and by nightfall reached Grosmésnil. Sending for a skilled army surgeon, the wound was probed again, but with no better result. Here the rumor of the affair at Saint Aubin, greatly magnified, reached De Bostaquet; and, finding that his only safety lay in flight, he started again with his friend, and took the route for Holland through Picardy. They rode onward to Belozane, then to Neufchâtel, where he took leave of Saint-Foy.

The fugitive reached Foucarmont alone by moonlight in great pain, his arm being exceedingly swollen and much inflamed. He at once sent for a surgeon, who dressed the wound, but feared gangrene. Next morning the inflammation had subsided, and he set out again, reaching the outskirts of Abbeville, which he passed on the left, and, arriving at Pont-de-Remy, he there crossed the Somme. He was now in Picardy. Pressing onward, he arrived at Prouville, where he was kindly entertained for the night by a Protestant friend, M. de Monthuc. The pain and inflammation in his arm still increasing, the family surgeon was sent for. The wound, when exposed, was found black, swollen, and angry-looking. The surgeon sounded again, found no ball, and concluded by recommending perfect rest and low diet. The patient remained with his friend for two days, during which M. Montcornet arrived, for the purpose of accompanying him in his flight into Holland. Next day, to De Bostaquet's great surprise, the ball, for which the surgeons had so often been searching in vain, was found in the finger of one of his gloves, into which it had fallen. He was now comparatively relieved; and, unwilling to trespass longer upon the kindness of his friends, after a few more days' rest he again took the road with his aged relative. They traveled by Le Quesnel and Doullens, then along the grand high road of Hesdin, and through the woods of the Abbey of Sercan; next striking the Arras road (where they were threatened with an attack by footpads), they arrived at La Guorgues, and, crossing the frontier, they at last, after many adventures and perils, arrived in safety at Courtrai, where they began to breathe freely. But Dumont did not feel himself safe until he had reached Ghent, for Courtrai was still under the dominion of Spain; so again pushing on, the fugitives halted not until they arrived at Ghent late at night, where the two wayworn travelers at length slept soundly. Next day, Montcornet, who, though seventy-two years old, had stood the fatigues of the journey surprisingly well, proceeded to join his son, then lying with many other refugee officers in garrison at Maestricht, while De Bostaquet went forward into Holland to join the fugitives who were now flocking thither in great numbers from all parts of France.

Such is a rapid outline of the escape of Dumont de Bostaquet into the great Protestant asylum of the North. His joy, however, was mingled with grief, for he had left his wife and family behind him in France under the heel of the persecutor. After many painful rumors of the severe punishments to which his children had been subjected, he was at length joined by his wife, his son, and one of his daughters, who succeeded in escaping by sea. The ladies, taken prisoners by the coast-guard at Saint Aubin, besides being heavily fined, were condemned to be confined in convents, some for several years each, and others for life; the gentlemen and men-servants who accompanied them were condemned to the galleys for life, and their property and goods were declared forfeited to the king. This completed the ruin of Dumont de Bostaquet so far as worldly wealth was concerned; for by the law of Louis XIV., the property not only of all fugitives, but of all who abetted fugitives in their attempt to escape, was declared confiscated, while they were themselves liable, if caught, to suffer the penalty of death.

Dumont de Bostaquet now had no home save under the flag of the Prince of Orange; and when such sufferings as those which we have so briefly and imperfectly described are taken into account, we need not wonder at the ardor with which the banished French soldiers and gentry took service under the prince who so generously gave them protection, and the fury with which they fought against the despot who had ruined them, driven them forth from France, and continued to persecute themselves and their families even to the death.

CHAPTER XI.

DE BOSTAQUET IN ENGLAND.—THE IRISH CAMPAIGNS OF 1689-90.

DUMONT DE BOSTAQUET was hospitably received by the Prince of Orange, and, on his application for employment, was appointed to the same rank in the Dutch army that he had before held in that of Louis XIV. When the expedition to England was decided upon, such of the refugee officers as were disposed to join William were invited to send in their names, and De Bostaquet at once volunteered, with numbers more. Fifty of the French officers were selected for the purpose of being incorporated in his two dragoon regiments, red and blue, and De Bostaquet was appointed to a captaincy in the former regiment, of which De Louvigny was colonel.

The fleet of William had already been assembled at Maasluis, and with the troops on board shortly spread its sails for England. But the expedition, consisting of about five hundred sail, had scarcely left the Dutch shores before it was dispersed by a storm, which raged for three days. One ship, containing two companies of French infantry, commanded by Captains de Chauvernay and Rapin-Thoyras (afterward the historian), was driven toward the coast of Norway. Those on board gave themselves up for lost; but the storm abating, the course of the vessel was altered, and she afterward reached the Maas in safety. Very few ships were missing when the expedition reassembled; but among the lost was one containing four companies of a Holstein regiment and some sixty French officers and volunteers. When De Bostaquet's ship arrived in the Maas, it was found that many of the troop horses had been killed, or were so maimed as to be rendered unfit for service. After a few days' indefatigable labor, however, all damages were made good, the fleet was refitted anew, and again put to sea, this time with better prospect of success.

"Next day," says De Bostaquet, in his Memoirs, "we saw the coasts of France and England stretching before us on either side. I confess that I did not look upon my ungrateful country without deep emotion, as I thought of the many ties of affection which still bound me to it—of my children, and the dear relatives I had left behind; but as our fleet might even now be working out their deliverance, and as England was drawing nearer, I felt that one must cast such thoughts aside, and trust that God would yet put it into the heart of our hero to help our poor country under the oppressions beneath which she was groaning. The fleet was beheld by the people on the opposite shores with very different emotions. France trembled at the sight; while England, seeing her deliverer approaching, leaped with joy. It seemed as if the prince took pleasure in alarming France, whose coasts he long kept in sight. But at length, leaving France behind us, we made for the opposite shore, and all day long we held along the English coast, sailing toward the west. Night hid the land from farther view, and next morning not a trace of it was to be seen. As the wind held good, we thought that by this time we must have passed out of the English Channel, though we knew not whither we were bound. Many of our soldiers from Poitou hoped that we might effect a landing there. But at three in the afternoon we again caught sight of the English land on our right, and found that we were still holding the same course. M. de Bethencour, who knew the coast, assured us that we were bound for Plymouth; and it seemed to me that such was the prince's design. But the wind having shifted, we were astonished to see our vanguard put about, and sail as if right down upon us. Nothing could be more beautiful than the evolution of the immense flotilla which now took place under a glorious sky. The main body of the fleet and the rear-guard lay to, in order to allow the prince's division to pass through them, on which every ship in its turn prepared to tack. There were no longer any doubts as to where we were to land. We distinctly saw the people along the heights watching, and doubtless admiring, the magnificent spectacle, but there appeared to be no signs of alarm at sight of the multitude of ships about to enter their beautiful bay."*

De Bostaquet proceeds to describe the landing at Torbay, and the march of the little army inland, through mud and mire, under heavy rain and along villainous roads, until they entered Exeter amid the acclamations of the people. De

* *Mémoires Inédits de Dumont de Bostaquet*, p. 214–15.

Bostaquet found that many of his exiled countrymen had already settled at Exeter, where they had a church and minister of their own. Among others, he met with a French tailor from Lintot in Normandy, who had become established in business, besides other refugees from Dieppe and the adjoining country, who were settled and doing well. De Bostaquet expressed himself much gratified with his short stay in Exeter, which he praised for its wealth, its commerce, its manufactures, and the hospitality of its inhabitants.*

After resting six or seven days at Exeter, William and his army marched upon London through Salisbury, being daily joined by fresh adherents—gentry, officers, and soldiers. The army of James made no effort at resistance, but steadily retired; the only show of a stand being made at Reading, where five hundred of the king's horse, doubtless fighting without heart, were put to flight by a hundred and fifty of William's dragoons, led by the Huguenot Colonel Marouit. Not another shot was fired before William arrived in London, and was welcomed as the nation's deliverer. By this time James was making arrangements for flight, together with his Jesuits. He might easily have been captured and made a martyr of; but the mistake made in the case of Charles I. was not repeated, and James, having got on board a smack in the Thames, was allowed to slink ignominiously out of his kingdom and take refuge in France, there to seek the consolation of his royal brother Louis the Great, whose policy he had so foolishly and so wickedly attempted to imitate.†

* While in Exeter, De Bostaquet for the first time attended the English service in the Cathedral, as conducted in the time of James II. He found it very different from the plain Calvinistic worship of the Huguenots, and thus recorded his impressions of it: "What surprised me was to find that it seemed to retain nearly all the externals of popery. The churches have altars, two great candles at each side, and a basin of silver or silver-gilt between them. The canons, dressed in surplice and stole, occupy stalls on both sides of the nave. They have a choir of little boys in surplices who sing with them; the music seems to me fine, and they have charming voices. But as all this is very much opposed to the simplicity of our Reformed religion, I confess I was by no means edified with it" (p. 223).

† Little more than a month elapsed between the landing of the Prince of

The Huguenot officers and soldiers of William's army found many of their exiled countrymen already settled in London. Soho in the west, and Spitalfields in the east, were almost entirely French quarters. Numbers of new churches were about this time opened for the accommodation of the immigrants, in which the service was conducted in French by their own ministers, some of the most eminent of whom had taken refuge in England. The exiles formed communities by themselves; they were, for the most part, organized in congregations, and a common cause and common sufferings usually made them acquainted with each other. De Bostaquet and his compatriots, therefore, did not find themselves so much strangers in London as they expected to be, for they were daily encountering friends and brothers in misfortune.

A distinguished little circle of exiles had by this time been formed at Greenwich, of which the aged Marquis de Ruvigny formed the centre. That nobleman had for many years been one of the most trusted servants of the French government. He held various high offices in his own country, being a general in the French army and a councilor of state; and he had on more than one occasion represented France as envoy

Orange in Torbay and the flight of James II. The landing took place on the 5th of November, 1688, and the abdication of James on the 10th of December following. One of James's Jesuit followers addressed the following characteristic letter to his Provincial at Rome on the last-mentioned date:

"Signor William, my reverend Father,—Behold the end of all the good hopes of the progress of our holy religion in this country. The king and the queen are fugitives; all their adherents have abandoned them; a new prince has arrived, with a foreign army, without the slightest opposition; a thing the like of which has never been seen or heard of, and which is without example in history. A king, the peaceful possessor of his throne, with an army of thirty thousand soldiers and forty ships of war, is flying from his kingdom without firing so much as a pistol-shot. . . . *The greatest evil has come from ourselves:* our imprudence, our avarice, and our ambition, have occasioned all this. The king is served by weak men, knaves and fools, and the great minister you have sent hither has had his share in it. . . . Enough, my dear friend; all is over. . . . The confusion is great; neither faith nor hope remain; we are done for this time, and the fathers of our holy society have contributed their part toward the disaster. All the others—bishops, confessors, priests, and monks—have conducted themselves with but little prudence."

This letter (in Italian) is quoted by M. Guizot in his *Collection des Memoirs relatifs à la Revolution d'Angleterre.*

at the English court. But he was a Protestant, and therefore precluded from holding public office subsequent to the Revocation of the Edict of Nantes. "Had the marquis," says Macaulay, "chosen to remain in his native country, he and his household would have been permitted to worship God privately according to their own forms. But Ruvigny rejected all offers, cast in his lot with his brethren, and, at upward of eighty years of age, quitted Versailles, where he might still have been a favorite, for a modest dwelling at Greenwich. That dwelling was, during the last months of his life, the resort of all that was most distinguished among his fellow-exiles. His abilities, his experience, and his munificent kindness made him the undisputed chief of the refugees. He was at the same time half an Englishman, for his sister had been Countess of Southampton, and he was uncle of Lady Russell. He was long past the time of action. But his two sons, both men of eminent courage, devoted their swords to the service of William."*

A French church had been founded by the Marquis of Ruvigny at Greenwich in 1686,† of which M. Severin, an old and valued friend of De Bostaquet and his wife, had been appointed pastor, so that our Huguenot officer at once found himself at home. He was cordially received by the aged marquis, who encouraged him to bring over his family from Holland and settle them in the place. De Bostaquet accordingly proceeded to the Hague in the spring of 1689, and was received with great joy by his wife after their five months' separation. Accompanied by their two children, they set out for England, and, after a tempestuous voyage, landed at Greenwich, where they were cordially welcomed by the Ruvigny circle. Here De Bostaquet remained for only three months, enjoying the society of his family and the hospitality of his friends. "The

* MACAULAY—*History of England*, vol. iii., ch. xiv.
† The French chapel at Greenwich is still in existence, and now used as a Baptist chapel. It is situated in London Street, behind the shop of Mr. Harding, oilman. The commandments were written up in French on each side of the pulpit until the year 1814, when they were effaced.

O

time," says he, "passed like a dream, as much because of the joy I experienced at being reunited to my wife, as because of the beauties of the place and the good society I met there, but, above all, by the kindness of the Ruvigny family, whose generosity and charity toward the unfortunate exiles is unfailing, and command the respect and veneration of all who have the honor to know them."*

During de Bostaquet's sojourn at Greenwich his wife presented him with another son, his nineteenth child, to which the Marquis de Ruvigny stood godfather, and after whom he was named. Only a month later the good old marquis died, and De Bostaquet, with many other illustrious exiles, followed his remains to his tomb in the church of the Savoy, in the Strand, where he was buried.

Meanwhile William had been occupied in consolidating his government and reducing the disaffected parts of the kingdom to obedience. With Scotland this was comparatively easy, but with Ireland the case was widely different. The Irish Roman Catholics remained loyal to James because of his religion, and when he landed at Kinsale in March, 1689, he saw nearly the whole country at his feet. Only the little Presbyterian colony established in Ulster made any show of resistance. James had arrived in Ireland with substantial help in arms and money obtained from the French king, and before many weeks had elapsed 40,000 Irish stood in arms to support his authority. The forces of William in Ireland were few in number and bad in quality, consisting, for the most part, of raw levies of young men suddenly taken from the plow. They were therefore altogether unequal to cope with the forces of James, Tyrconnel, and the French Marshal de Rosen, and, but for vigorous measures on the part of William and his government, it was clear that Ireland was lost to the English crown.

The best troops of William had by this time been either sent abroad or disbanded. The English and Dutch veteran

* *Mémoires Inédits*, p. 246.

regiments had for the most part been dispatched to Flanders to resist the French armies of Louis, who threatened a diversion in favor of James in that quarter; while, in deference to the jealousy which the English people naturally entertained against the maintenance among them of a standing army—especially an army of foreigners—the Huguenot regiments had been disbanded almost immediately after the abdication of James and his flight into France. So soon, however, as the news of James's landing in Ireland reached London, measures were immediately taken for their re-embodiment, and four excellent regiments were at once raised—one of cavalry and three of infantry. The cavalry regiment was raised by Schomberg, who was its colonel, and it was entirely composed of French gentlemen—officers and privates. The infantry regiments were raised with the help of the aged Marquis de Ruvigny; and at his death in July, 1689, the enterprise was zealously prosecuted by his two sons—Henry, the second marquis, and Pierre de Ruvigny, afterward better known as La Caillemotte. These regiments were respectively commanded by La Caillemotte, Cambon, and La Melonière.

The French regiments were hastily dispatched to join the little army of about 10,000 men sent into the north of Ireland to assist the Protestants in arms there the same month in which they were raised. Their first operation was conducted against the town of Carrickfergus, which fell after a siege of a week, but not without loss, for the Huguenot regiments who led the assault suffered heavily, the Marquis de Venours and numerous other officers being among the killed.

Shortly after, the Huguenot regiment of cavalry arrived from England, and, joined by three regiments of Enniskilleners, the army marched southward. De Bostaquet held his former rank of captain in Schomberg's horse, and he has recorded in his memoirs the incidents of the campaign with his usual spirit. The march lay through burnt villages and a country desolated by the retiring army of James. They passed through Newry and Carlingford, both of which were found in ashes, and at length arrived in the neighborhood of Dundalk, where they encamped. James lay at Drogheda with an army of 20,000 men, or double their number. But the generals of neither force wished for battle—Schomberg, because he could not rely upon his troops, who were ill fed and (excepting the Huguenot veterans) ill disciplined, and Count Rosen, James's French general, because he did not wish to incur the risk of a defeat. The raw young English soldiers* in the camp at Dundalk, unused to campaigning, died in great numbers. The English foot were mostly without shoes and very badly fed; yet they were eager to fight, thinking it better to die in the field than in the camp. When they clamored to be led into action, Schomberg good-humoredly said, "We English have stomach enough for fighting; it is a pity that we are not equally fond of some other parts of a soldier's business."

At length, after enduring great privations, and leaving many of his men under the sod at Dundalk,† Schomberg decided to follow the example of the Jacobite army, and go

---

* Schomberg found that the greater number of them had never before fired a gun. "Others can inform your majesty," he wrote to William (12th Oct., 1689), "that the three regiments of French infantry and their regiment of cavalry do their duty better than the others." And a few months later he added, "From these three regiments, and from that of cavalry, your majesty has more service than from double the number of the others."

† "Our camp was on the edge of a morass," says De Bostaquet, "sheltered on one side by horrible mountains, from whence there arose a perpetual vapor as from a furnace. The scarcity of provisions, together with the bad weather, occasioned frightful disease. The English died by thousands." [It is stated in the *Memoirs of Dalrymple*, that of 15,000 men who at different times joined the camp, 8000 died.] "The colonels, captains, and soldiers of the French regiments did not escape. Many officers and privates died. A friend and relative of my own, named Bonel, son of Fresné-Cantbrun, of Caen, whose mother, daughter of Secretary Cognart, was a kinsman of my first wife, died, much to my sorrow. Our regiment was attacked by disease. Captain de Brugière and Cornet Baucelin both died; the loss of the latter, who was betrothed to a beautiful Norman girl, occasioned many tears. Des Saint-Hermine and Brasselaye, though they had only been a short time in camp, both left ill. The first died at Chester, and the other almost immediately on his reaching Windsor. In short, there remained in the camp only the dead and the dying."—*Mémoires Inédits de Dumont de Bostaquet*, p. 260–1.

into winter quarters. His conduct of the campaign occasioned much dissatisfaction in England, where it was expected that he should meet and fight James with a famished army of less than half the number, and under every disadvantage. It had now, however, become necessary to act with vigor if the policy initiated by the Revolution of 1688 was to be upheld; for a well-appointed army of 7300 excellent French infantry, commanded by the Count of Lauzun, with immense quantities of arms and ammunition, were on their way from France, with the object of expelling the Protestants from Ireland and replacing James upon the British throne.

William felt that this was the great crisis of the struggle, and he determined to take the field in person. He at once made his arrangements accordingly. He ordered back from Flanders his best English and Dutch regiments. He also endeavored, so far as he could, to meet Frenchmen by Frenchmen; and dispatched agents abroad, into all the countries where the banished Huguenot soldiers had settled, inviting them to take arms with him against the enemies of their faith. His invitation was responded to with alacrity. Many of Schomberg's old soldiers, who had settled in Brandenburg, Switzerland, and the provinces of the Lower Rhine, left their new homes and flocked to the standard of William. The Baron d'Avejan, lieutenant colonel of an English regiment, wrote to a friend in Switzerland, urging the immediate enlistment of expatriated Protestants for his regiment. "I feel assured," said he, "that you will not fail to have published in all the French churches in Switzerland the obligations under which the refugees lie to come and aid us in this expedition, which is directed to the glory of God, and ultimately to the re-establishment of His church in our country."*

These stirring appeals had the effect of attracting a large number of veteran Protestant soldiers to the army of Wil-

* Quoted by WEISS—*History of the French Protestant Refugees*, p. 238, from an unpublished memoir by Anthony Court, in the Geneva Library.

liam. Sometimes four or five hundred men left Geneva in a week for the purpose of enlisting in England. Others were dispatched from Lausanne, where they were provided by the Marquis d'Arzilliers with the means of reaching their destination. Many more, scattered along the shores of Lake Leman, were drilled daily under the flag of Orange, notwithstanding the expostulations of Louis's agents, and sent to swell the forces of William.

By these means, as well as by energetic efforts at home,* William was enabled, by the month of June, 1690, to assemble in the north of Ireland an army of 36,000 men—English, French, Dutch, Danes, and Germans; and putting himself at their head, he at once marched southward.† Arrived at the Boyne, about three miles west of Drogheda, he discerned the combined French and Irish army drawn up on the other side, prepared to dispute the passage of the river. The Huguenot regiments saw before them the flags of Louis XIV. and James II. waving together—the army of the king who had banished them from country, home, and family, making common cause with the persecutor of the English Protestants; and when it became known among them that every soldier in the opposing force bore the same badge—the white cross in their hat—which had distinguished the assassins of their forefathers on the night of St. Bartholomew, they burned to meet them in battle.

On the morning of the 1st of July, the Count Ménard de

* DE FELICE—*History of the French Protestants* (p. 339), says that "England raised eleven regiments of French volunteers;" but he does not give his authority. It is probable this number is an exaggeration.

† William landed at Carrickfergus on the 14th of June, 1690. From thence he proceeded to Belfast. On his way southward to join the army at Loughbrickland, when passing through the village of Lambeg, near Lisburn, he was addressed by one René Bulmer, a Huguenot refugee, then residing in a house now known as The Priory. René explained to his majesty the cause of his being settled there; and as the king was about to pass on, he asked permission to embrace him. To this William at once assented, receiving the Huguenot's salute on his cheek, after which, stooping from his horse toward Bulmer's wife, a pretty Frenchwoman, he said, "And thy wife too;" and saluted her heartily. The name Bulmer has since been changed to Boomer, but the Christian name René or Rainey is still preserved among the descendants of the family.—*Ulster Journal of Archæology*, i., 135, 286–94.

Schomberg, one of the old marshal's sons, was ordered to cross the river on the right by the bridge of Slane, and turn the left flank of the opposing army. This movement he succeeded in accomplishing after a sharp but short conflict, upon which William proceeded to lead his left, composed of cavalry, across the river, considerably lower down. At the same time, the main body of infantry composing the centre was ordered to advance. The Dutch guards led, closely followed by the Huguenot foot. Plunging into the stream, they waded across, and reached the opposite bank under a storm of cannon and musketry. Scarcely had they struggled up the right bank, than the Huguenot colonel, La Caillemotte, was struck down by a musket-shot. As he was being carried off the field, covered with blood, through the ranks of his advancing men, he called out to them, "A la gloire, mes enfans! à la gloire!"

A strong body of Irish cavalry charged the advancing infantry with great vigor, shook them until they reeled, and compelled them to give way. Old Marshal Schomberg, who stood eagerly watching the advance of his troops from the northern bank, now saw that the crisis of the fight had arrived, and he prepared to act accordingly. Placing himself at the head of his Huguenot regiment of horse which he had held in reserve, and pointing with his sword across the river, he called out, "*Allons, mes amis! rappelez votre courage et vos ressentements:* VOILA VOS PERSECUTEURS !"* and plunged into the stream. On reaching the scene of contest a furious struggle ensued. The Dutch and Huguenot infantry rallied; and William, coming up from the left with his cavalry, fell upon the Irish flank and completed their discomfiture. The combined French and Irish army was forced through the pass of Duleek, and fled toward Dublin—James II. being the first to carry thither the news of his defeat.† William's loss did

* Rapin, who relates this incident in his *History of England*, was present at the battle of the Boyne as an officer in one of the Huguenot regiments.
† On reaching Dublin Castle, James was received by Lady Tyrconnel, the wife of his viceroy. "Madame," said he, "your countrymen can run well."

not exceed 400 men; but, to his deep grief, Marshal Schomberg was among the fallen, the hero of eighty-two having been cut down in the melée by a party of Tyrconnel's horse, and he lay dead upon the field, with many other gallant gentlemen.

"Not quite so well as your majesty," was her retort, "for I see you have won the race."

CHAPTER XII.

HUGUENOT OFFICERS IN THE BRITISH SERVICE.

IT forms no part of our purpose to describe the military operations in Ireland which followed the battle of the Boyne farther than to designate the principal Huguenot officers who took part in them. Among these, one of the most distinguished was Henry, second Marquis de Ruvigny. At the date of the Revocation he had attained the rank of brigadier in the army of Louis XIV., and was esteemed an excellent officer, having served with great distinction under Condé and Turenne. Indeed, it is believed that the French army in Germany would have been lost but for the skill with which he reconciled the quarrels of the contending chiefs who aspired to its command on the death of Turenne. Louis XIV. anxiously desired to retain Ruvigny in his service, but all his offers of individual toleration were refused, and, casting in his lot with the exiled Protestants, he left France with his father and settled with him at Greenwich, dispensing hospitality and bounty. Being allowed the enjoyment of his French property, he did not join the British army which fought in Ireland. But when he heard that his only brother, De la Caillemotte, as well as Marshal Schomberg, had been killed at the Boyne, he could restrain his ardor no longer, and offered his services to King William, who appointed him major general, and farther gave him the colonelcy of Schomberg's regiment of Huguenot horse.

Ruvigny immediately joined the army of General Ginkell in Ireland, while engaged in the siege of Athlone. There a Huguenot soldier was the first to mount the breach, in which he fell, cheering on his comrades. That place taken, the French general Saint Ruth retired with the Irish army to

Aughrim, where he took up an almost impregnable position. Notwithstanding this advantage, Ginkell attacked and routed the Irish, the principal share in the victory being attributed to the Marquis de Ruvigny and his horse, who charged impetuously and carried every thing before them. That the brunt of the battle was borne by the Huguenot regiments is shown by the extent of their loss. Ruvigny's regiment lost 144 men killed and wounded; that of Cambon, 106; and that of Belcastle, 85—being about one fifth of the total loss on the side of the victors. "After the battle," says De Bostaquet, "Ginkell came up and embraced De Ruvigny, declaring how much he was pleased with his bravery and his conduct; then advancing to the head of our regiment, he highly praised the officers as well as soldiers. M. Casaubon, who commanded, gained great honor by his valor that day."* For the services rendered by De Ruvigny on this occasion, William raised him to the Irish peerage under the title of Earl of Galway.

In 1693 Lord Galway joined William in Flanders, and was with him in the severe battle of Neerwinden, where the combined Dutch and English army was defeated by Marshal Luxemburg. The Huguenot leader fought with conspicuous bravery at the head of his cavalry, and succeeded in covering William's retreat. He was shortly after promoted to the rank of lieutenant general.

The war with France was now raging all round her borders—along the Flemish and the German frontiers, and as far south as the country of the Vaudois. The Vaudois were among the most ancient Protestant people in Europe; and Louis XIV., not satisfied with exterminating Protestantism in his own dominions, sought to carry the crusade against it beyond his own frontiers into the territories of his neighbors. He accordingly sent to the young Duke of Savoy, requiring him to extirpate the Vaudois unless they would conform to the Roman Catholic religion. The duke refused to obey the

* *Mémoires Inédits de Dumont de Bostaquet*, p. 303.

French king's behest, and besought the help of the Emperor of Germany and the Protestant princes of the North to enable him to resist the armies of Louis. The Elector of Brandenburg having applied to William for one of his generals, Charles, duke of Schomberg, whose father fell at the Boyne, was at once dispatched to the aid of the Savoy prince with an army consisting for the most part of Huguenot refugees. William also undertook to supply a subsidy of £100,000 a year as the joint contribution of England and Holland to the cause of Protestantism in Savoy.

Schomberg, on his arrival at Turin, found the country in a state of the greatest consternation, the French army under Catinat overrunning it in all directions. With his vigorous help, however, the progress of the French army was speedily checked; but, unfortunately, Schomberg allowed himself to be drawn into a pitched battle on the plains of Marsiglia in October, 1693, in which he suffered a complete defeat, at the same time receiving a mortal wound, of which he died a few days after the battle.

On this untoward result of the campaign being known in England, the Earl of Galway was dispatched into Savoy to take the command, as well as to represent England and Holland as embassador at the court of Turin. To his dismay, he shortly discovered that the Duke of Savoy was engaged in a secret treaty with the French government for peace, on which Lord Galway at once withdrew with his contingent, the only object he had been able to accomplish being to secure a certain degree of liberty of worship for the persecuted Vaudois.

On his return to England the earl was appointed one of the Lords Justices of Ireland; and during the time that he held the office, he devoted himself to the establishment of the linen trade, the improvement of agriculture, and the reparation of the losses and devastations from which the country had so severely suffered during its civil wars. Among his other undertakings was the founding of the French colony of Portarlington. By his influence he induced a large number of the best class of the refugees—principally consisting of exiled officers and gentry and their families—to settle at that place; and he liberally assisted them out of his private means in promoting the industry and prosperity of the town and neighborhood. He erected above a hundred new dwellings of a superior kind for the accommodation of the settlers. He built and endowed two churches for their use— one French, the other English — as well as two excellent schools for the education of their children. Thus the little town of Portarlington shortly became a centre of polite learning, from which emanated some of the most distinguished men in Ireland, while the gentle and industrious life of the colonists exhibited an example of patient labor, neatness, thrift, and orderliness, which was not without beneficial effects on the surrounding population.

But, much though he did for Portarlington, Lord Galway was not permitted to complete what he had so well begun. It so happened that as soon as Louis XIV. heard that Ruvigny had joined the army of William, he ordered the immediate confiscation of all his property in France. To compensate his devoted follower for his loss, William conferred upon him the confiscated estate of Portarlington. This appropriation by the king was, however, violently attacked in the English Parliament; a bill was passed annulling all grants of the kind that he had made; the Earl of Galway's career as an Irish landlord was thus brought to an end; and Ruvigny, like many of his fellow-exiles, was again landless.

Nothing, however, could shake the king's attachment to Lord Galway, or Lord Galway's to him. Being unable, as King of England, to reward his faithful follower, William appointed him general in the Dutch army, and colonel of the Dutch regiment of Foot-guards (blue). In 1701, Evelyn thus records in his diary a visit made to the distinguished refugee on his arrival in London from Ireland: "*June* 22. I went to congratulate the arrival of that worthy and excellent person, my Lord Galway, newly come out of Ireland, where he had behaved himself so honestly and to the exceeding satisfaction of the people; but he was removed thence for being a Frenchman, though they had not a more worthy, valiant, discreet, and trusty person on whom they could have relied for conduct and fitness. He was one who had deeply suffered, as well as the marquis his father, for being Protestants."

From this time Lord Galway was principally employed abroad on diplomatic missions and in the field. The war against France was now in progress on the side of Spain, where the third Duke of Schomberg, Count Ménard, who led the attack in the battle of the Boyne, was in 1704 placed in command of the British troops in Spain, then fighting against the Bourbon Philip V., in conjunction with a Portuguese army. Philip was supported by a French army under command of the Duke of Berwick, the natural son of the dethroned James II. The campaign languished under Schomberg, and the government at home becoming dissatisfied with his conduct of it, the Earl of Galway was sent out to Portugal to take the command.

The campaigns which followed were mostly fought over the ground since made so famous by the victories of Wellington. There was the relief of Gibraltar, the storming of Alcantara, the siege of Badajos—in which the Earl of Galway lost an arm—the capture of Ciudad Rodrigo, and the advance upon Madrid. Then followed the defection of the Portuguese, and a succession of disasters; the last of which was the battle of Almanza, where the British, ill supported by their Portuguese allies, were defeated by the French army under the Duke of Berwick. Shortly after, the British forces returned home, and the Earl of Galway resided for the rest of his life mostly at Rookley, near Southampton, taking a kindly interest to the last in the relief of his countrymen suffering for conscience' sake.*

---

* It was when on a visit at Stratton House that the good Earl of Galway was summoned to his rest. He probably sank under the "bodily pains" to which he was so long subject, namely, gout and rheumatism. His mind was

When the refugees first entered the service of the Elector of Brandenburg, doubts were expressed whether they would fight against their former fellow-soldiers. When they went into action at Neuss, one of the Prussian generals exclaimed, "We shall have these knaves fighting against us presently." But all doubts were dispelled by the conduct of the Huguenot musketeers, who rushed eagerly upon the French troops, and by the fury of their attack carried every thing before them. It was the same at the siege of Bonn, where a hundred refugee officers, three hundred Huguenot cadets, with detachments of musketeers and horse grenadiers, demanded to be led to the assault; and on the signal being given, they rushed forward with extraordinary gallantry. "The officers," says Ancillon, "gave proof that they preferred rather to rot in the earth after an honorable death, than that the earth should nourish them in idleness while their soldiers were in the heat of the fight." The outer works were carried, and the place was taken. But nowhere did the Huguenots display such a fury of resentment against the troops of Louis as at the battle of Almanza, above referred to, where they were led by Cavalier, the famous Camizard chief.

Jean Cavalier was the son of a peasant, of the village of Ribaute, near Anduze, in Languedoc. Being an ardent Protestant, he took refuge from the persecutions in Geneva and Lausanne, where he worked for some time as a journeyman baker. But his love for his native home drew him back to Languedoc; and he happened to visit it in 1702, at the time when the Abbé du Chayla was engaged in directing the extirpation of the Protestant peasantry in the Cevennes. These poor people continued, in defiance of the law, to hold religious meetings in the woods, and caves, and fields, in conse-

---

entire to the last. He died on the 3d of September, 1720, aged seventy-two. He was the last of his family. Lady Russell was his nearest surviving relative, and became his heiress at the age of eighty-four. The property of Stratton has passed out of Russell hands; and Lord Galway's grave-stone [in Micheldever church-yard, where he was buried] can not now be recognized.—AGNEW—*Protestant Exiles from France in the reign of Louis XIV.*, p. 149.

quence of which they were tracked, pursued, sabred, hanged, or sent to the galleys, wherever found.

The peasants at length revolted. From forty to fifty of the most determined among them assembled at the Abbé du Chayla's house at Pont-de-Montvert, and proceeded to break open the dungeon in which he had penned up a band of prisoners, among whom were two ladies of rank. The abbé ordered his servants to repel the assailants with fire-arms; nevertheless they succeeded in effecting an entrance, and stabbed the priest to death. Such was the beginning of the war of the Blouses, or Camizards. The Camizards were only poor peasants driven to desperation by cruelty, without any knowledge of war, and without any arms except such as they wrested from the hands of their enemies, yet they maintained a gallant struggle against the French armies for a period of nearly five years.

On the outbreak of the revolt, Jean Cavalier assembled a company of volunteers to assist the Cevennes peasantry, and before long he became their recognized leader. Though the insurrection spread over Languedoc, their entire numbers did not exceed 10,000 men. But they had the advantage of fighting in a mountain country, every foot of which was familiar to them. They carried on the war by surprises, clothing and arming themselves with the spoils they took from the royal troops. They supplied themselves with balls made from the church-bells. They had no money, and needed none, the peasantry and herdsmen of the country supplying them with food. When they were attacked, they received the first fire of the soldiers on one knee, singing the sixty-eighth psalm: "Let God arise, let his enemies be scattered." Then they rose, precipitated themselves on the enemy, and fought with all the fury of despair. If they succeeded in their onslaughts, and the soldiers fled, they then held assemblies, which were attended by the Huguenots of the adjoining country; and when they failed, they fled into the hills, in the caverns of which were their magazines and hospitals.

Great devastation and bloodshed marked the course of the war of the Camizards. No mercy was shown either to the peasantry taken in arms or to those who in any way assisted them. Whole villages were destroyed; for the order was issued that wherever a soldier or priest perished, the place should immediately be burned down. The punishment of the stake was revived. Gibbets were erected and kept at work all over Languedoc. Still the insurrection was not suppressed, and the peasantry continued to hold their religious meetings wherever they could. One day, on the first of April, 1703, the intelligence was brought to Marshal Montrevil, in command of the royal troops, that some three hundred persons had assembled for worship in a mill near Nismes. He at once hastened to the place with a strong force of soldiers, ordered the doors to be burst open, and the worshipers against law slaughtered on the spot. The slowness with which the butchery was carried on provoked the marshal's indignation, and he ordered the mill to be fired. All who had not been murdered were burnt—all, excepting one solitary girl, who was saved through the humanity of the marshal's lackey; but she was hanged next day, and her salvor narrowly escaped the same fate.

Even this monstrous cruelty did not crush the insurrection. The Camizards were from time to time re-enforced by the burned-out peasants; and, led by Cavalier and his coadjutor Roland, they beat the detachments of Montrevil on every side—at Nayes, at the rocks of Aubais, at Martignargues, and at the Bridge of Salindres. The "Most Christian King" was disgusted at the idea of a Marshal of France, supported by a royal army completely appointed, being set at defiance by a miserable horde of Protestant peasants, and he ordered the recall of Montrevil. Then Marshal Villars was sent to take the command.

The new marshal was an honorable man, and no butcher. He shuddered at the idea of employing means such as his predecessor had employed to reduce the king's subjects to obedience, and one of the first things he did was to invite Cavalier to negotiate. The quondam baker's boy of Geneva agreed to meet the potent Marshal of France and listen to his proposals. Villars thus described him in his letter to the minister of war: "He is a peasant of the lowest rank, not yet twenty-two years of age, and scarcely seeming eighteen; small, and with no imposing mien, but possessing a firmness and good sense that are altogether surprising. He has great talent in arranging for the subsistence of his men, and disposes his troops as well as the best trained officers could do. From the moment Cavalier began to treat up to the conclusion, he has always acted in good faith."

In the negotiations which ensued, Cavalier stipulated for liberty of conscience and freedom of worship, to which, it is said, Villars assented, though the Roman Catholics subsequently denied this. The result, however, was, that Cavalier capitulated, accepted a colonel's commission, and went to Versailles to meet Louis XIV.; his fellow-leader, Roland, refusing the terms of capitulation, and determining to continue the struggle. At Paris, the mob, eager to behold the Cevennol rebel, thronged the streets he rode through, and his reception was almost tantamount to a triumph. At Versailles Louis exhorted him in vain to be converted, Cavalier even daring in his presence to justify the revolt in the Cevennes. He was offered the rank of major general in the French army, and a pension of 1500 livres for his father as the price of his apostasy; but still he refused; and he was dismissed from court as "an obstinate Huguenot."

Though treated with apparent kindness, Cavalier felt that he was under constant surveillance, and he seized the earliest opportunity of flying from France and taking refuge in Switzerland. From thence he passed into Holland, and entered the service of William of Orange, who gave him the rank of colonel. The Blouses, or Camizards, who had fled from the Cevennes in large numbers, flocked to his standard, and his regiment was soon full. But a difficulty arose. Cavalier insisted on selecting his own officers, while the royal commissioners required that all the companies should be commanded by refugee gentlemen. The matter was compromised by Cavalier selecting half his officers, and the commissioners appointing the other half—Cavalier selecting only such as had thoroughly proved their valor in the battles of the Cevennes. The regiment, when complete, proceeded to England, and was dispatched to Spain with other re-enforcements at the end of 1706.

Almost the only battle in which Cavalier and his Huguenots took part was on the field of Almanza, where they distinguished themselves in a remarkable degree. Cavalier found himself opposed to one of the French regiments, in whom he recognized his former persecutors in the Cevennes. The soldiers on both sides, animated by a common fury, rushed upon each other with the bayonet, disdaining to fire. The carnage which followed was dreadful. The papist regiment was annihilated, while of Cavalier's regiment, 700 strong, not more than 300 survived. Marshal Berwick, though familiar with fierce encounters, never spoke of this tragical event without deep emotion.* Cavalier himself was severely wounded, and lay for some time among the slain, afterward escaping through the assistance of an English officer. His lieutenant colonel, five captains, six lieutenants, and five ensigns, were killed, and most of the other officers were wounded or taken prisoners.

Cavalier returned to England, where he retired upon a small pension, which barely supported him, and he fell into debt.† He entreated to be employed in active service, but it was not until after the lapse of many years that his application was successful. He was eventually appointed governor of Jersey, and held that office for some time; after

* WEISS, p. 250.
† While he resided in London, Cavalier employed part of his leisure in dictating to another refugee, Galli of Nismes, the memoirs of his early adventures, which were published under the title of *Memoirs of the Wars of the Cevennes:* London, 1726.

which he was made brigadier in 1735, and farther promoted to be major general in 1739. He died at Chelsea in the following year, and his remains were conveyed to Dublin for interment in the French refugee cemetery near that city.

Another illustrious name among the Huguenot refugees is that of Paul de Rapin-Thoyras, better known as the historian of England than as a soldier, though he bore arms with the English in many a hard-fought field. He belonged to a French noble family, and was Lord of Thoyras, near Castres. The persecution drove him and his family into England; but, finding nothing to do there, he went over to Holland, and joined the army of William as a cadet. He accompanied the expedition to Torbay, and took part in the transactions which followed. Rapin was afterward sent into Ireland with his regiment, and, distinguishing himself by his gallantry at the siege of Carrickfergus, he was promoted to the rank of lieutenant. He afterward fought at the Boyne, and was wounded at the assault of Limerick. At Athlone he was one of the first to enter the place at the head of the assailing force. He was there promoted to a company, and remained at Athlone, doing garrison duty, for about two years. His intelligence and high culture being known, Rapin was selected by the king, on the recommendation of the Earl of Galway, as tutor to the Earl of Portland's eldest son, Viscount Woodstock. He accordingly took leave of the army with regret, making over his company to his brother, who afterward attained the rank of lieutenant colonel. From this time Rapin lived principally abroad in company with his pupil. While residing at the Hague, he resumed his favorite study of history and jurisprudence, which had been interrupted by his flight from France at the Revocation. After completing Lord Woodstock's education, Rapin settled at Wesel, where a number of retired refugee officers resided, and formed a very agreeable society. There he wrote his *Dissertation on Whigs and Tories*, and his well-known *History of England*, founded on Rhymer's *Fœdera*, a work of much labor and research, and long regarded as a standard work. Rapin died in 1725, at the age of sixty-four, almost pen in hand, worn out by hard study and sedentary confinement.

Among the many able Huguenot officers in William's service, John de Bodt was one of the most distinguished. He had fled from France when only in his fifteenth year, and shortly after joined the Dutch artillery. He accompanied William to England, and was made captain in 1690. He fought at the Boyne and at Aughrim, and eventually rose to the command of the French corps of engineers. In that capacity he served at the battles of Steinkirk and Nerwinde, and at the siege of Namur he directed the operations which ended in the surrender of the castle to the allied army. The fort into which Boufflers had thrown himself was assaulted and captured a few days later by La Cave at the head of 2000 volunteers, and William III. generously acknowledged that it was mainly to the brave refugees that he owed the capture of that important fortress.

All through the wars in the Low Countries, under William III., Eugene, and the Duke of Marlborough, the refugees bore themselves bravely. Wherever the fighting was hardest, they were there. Henry de Chesnoi led the assault which gave Landau to the allies. At the battles of Hochstedt, Oudenarde, Malplaquet, and at the siege of Mons, they were conspicuous for their valor. Le Roche, the Huguenot engineer, conducted the operations at Lisle, " doing more execution," says Luttrell, " in three days, than De Meer, the German, in six weeks."

The refugee Ligoniers served with peculiar distinction in the British army. The most eminent was Jean Louis, afterward Field Marshal Earl Ligonier, who fled from France into England in 1697. He accompanied the army to Flanders as a volunteer in 1702, where his extraordinary bravery at the storming of Liege attracted the attention of Marlborough. At Blenheim, where he next fought, he was the only captain of his regiment who survived. At Menin he led the grenadiers who stormed the counterscarp. He fought at Malplaquet, where he was major of brigade, and in all Marlborough's great battles. At Dettingen, as lieutenant general, he earned still higher distinction. At Fontenoy the chief honor was due to him for the intrepidity and skill with which he led the British infantry. In 1746 he was placed in command of the British forces in Flanders, but was taken prisoner at the battle of Lawfield. Restored to England, he was appointed commander-in-chief and colonel of the First Foot Guards; and in 1770 the Huguenot hero died full of honors, at the ripe age of ninety-two.

Of the thousands of Protestant sailors who left France at the Revolution, many settled in the ports along the south and southeastern coast of England; but the greater number entered the Dutch fleet, while a portion took service in the navy of the Elector of Brandenburg. Louis XIV. took the same steps to enforce conversion upon his sailors that he did upon the other classes of his subjects; but, so soon as the sailors arrived in foreign ports, they usually took the opportunity of deserting their ships, and thus reasserting their liberty. In 1686, three French vessels, which had put into Dutch ports, were entirely deserted by their crews, and in the same year more than 800 experienced mariners, trained under Duquesne, entered the navy of the United Provinces. When William sailed for England in 1688, the island of Zealand alone sent him 150 excellent French sailors, who were placed, as picked men, on board the admiral and vice-admiral's ships. Like their Huguenot fellow-countrymen on land, the Huguenot sailors fought valiantly at sea under the flag of their adopted country, and they emulated the bravery of the English themselves at the great naval battle of La Hogue a few years later. Many of the French naval officers rose to high rank in William's service, and acquired distinction by their valor on that element which England has been accustomed to regard as peculiarly her own. Among these may be mentioned the Gambiers, descended from a Huguenot refugee, one of whom rose to be a vice-admiral, and the other an admiral, the latter having also been raised to the peerage for his distinguished public services.

CHAPTER XIII.

HUGUENOT SETTLERS IN ENGLAND.—MEN OF SCIENCE AND
LEARNING.

OF the half million of French subjects who were driven into exile by the Revocation of the Edict of Nantes, more than 120,000 are believed to have taken refuge in England. The refugees were of all ranks and conditions—landed gentry, ministers of religion, soldiers and sailors, professional men, merchants, students, mechanics, artisans, and laborers. The greater number were Calvinists, and continued such; others were Lutherans, who conformed to the English Church; but many were Protestants merely in name, principally because they belonged to families of that persuasion. But, however lightly their family religion might sit upon them, these last offered as strenuous a resistance as the most extreme Calvinists to being dragooned into popery. This was especially the case with men of science, professional men, and students of law and medicine. Hence the large proportion of physicians and surgeons to be found in the ranks of the refugees.

It was not merely free religious thought that Louis XIV. sought to stifle in France, but free thought of all kinds. The blow struck by him at the conscience of France, struck also at its mind. Individualism was crushed wherever it asserted itself. An entire abnegation of the will was demanded. Men must abjure their faith, and believe as they were ordered. They must become part of a stereotyped system—profess adherence to a church to which they were indifferent, if they did not actually detest it—pretend to believe what they really did not believe, and in many cases even deny their most deeply-rooted convictions.

To indolent minds such a system would no doubt save an infinity of trouble. Once induce men to give up their individuality, to renounce the exercise of their judgment, to cease to think, and entertain the idea that a certain set of men, and no other, held in their hands the keys of heaven and hell, and conformity became easy. But many of the French king's subjects were of another temperament. They would think for themselves in matters of science as well as religion; and the vigorous, the independent, and the self-reliant—Protestant as well as non-Protestant—revolted against the intellectual tyranny which Louis attempted to establish among them, and fled for liberty of thought and worship into other lands.

We have already referred to such men as Huyghens and Bayle, who took refuge in Holland, and there found the freedom denied them in their own country. These men were not Protestants so much as philosophers; but they could not be hypocrites, and they would not conform: hence they fled from France. Others of like stamp took refuge in England. Among these latter were some of the earliest speculators as to that wonderful motive power which eventually became embodied in the working steam-engine. One of these fugitives was Solomon de Caus, a native of Caux, in Normandy. He was a man of encyclopædic knowledge. He studied architecture in Italy, and was an engineer, a mechanic, and a natural philosopher. Moreover, he was a Huguenot, which was fatal to his existence in France as a free man, and he took refuge in England. There he was employed about the court for a time, and, among other works, designed and erected hydraulic works for the palace gardens at Richmond. Shortly after he accompanied the Princess Elizabeth to Heidelberg, in Germany, on her marriage to the Elector Palatine, and there he published several works descriptive of the progress he had made in his inquiries as to the marvelous powers of steam.

But still more distinguished among the Huguenot refugees

was Dr. Denis Papin, one of the early inventors of the steam-engine, and probably also the inventor of the steam-boat. He was born at Blois in 1650, and studied medicine at the University of Paris, where he took his degree as physician. He began the practice of his profession, in which he met with considerable success; but, being attracted to the study of mechanics, and having the advantage of the instruction of the celebrated Huyghens, he made rapid progress, and promised to become one of the most eminent scientific men of his country. But Papin was a Protestant; and when the practice of medicine by Protestant physicians came to be subjected to serious disabilities,* finding the door to promotion or even to subsistence closed against him unless he abjured, Papin determined to leave France; and in 1681, the same year in which Huyghens took refuge in Holland, Papin took refuge in England. Arrived in London, he was cordially welcomed by the men of science there, and especially by the Honorable Robert Boyle, under whose auspices he was introduced to the Royal Society.

In the year of his arrival in London, Papin published a work descriptive of his new digester, which excited considerable interest. By means of this digester—in which the heat of the water was raised much above the boiling-point by preventing the escape of the steam—Papin was enabled to extract all the nutritious matter from the bones of animals, which had until then been thrown away as useless. The Fellows of the Royal Society had a supper cooked by the digester, of which Evelyn gives an account in his diary. The king commanded a digester to be made for Whitehall, and

---

* In 1680, Protestant lawyers and medical men were declared excluded from holding any public employment; and in the following year, physicians, surgeons, and others, called to assist the sick of the Reformed religion, were commanded to give notice thereof, under penalty of a fine of five hundred livres; and on the notice being given, the magistrates were required to visit the sick, with or without a priest, and ask them if they would abjure. Protestant midwives were absolutely forbidden to exercise their vocation, "because they did not believe baptism to be necessary, and could not christen children on emergency."

the invention shortly came into general use. In the preface to the second edition of his work, Papin announces that he "will let people see the Machines try'd once a week, in Blackfriars, in Water Lane, at Mr. Boissonet's [doubtless another Huguenot refugee], over against the Blew Boot, every Monday at three of the clock in the afternoon; but, to avoid confusion and crowding in of unknown people, those that will do me the honour to come are desired to bring along with them a recommendation from any of the members of the Royal Society."

In 1684 Papin was appointed temporary curator of the Royal Society, with a salary of £30 a year. It formed part of his duty, in connection with his new office, to produce an experiment at each meeting of the society, and this led him to prosecute his inquiries into the powers of steam, and ultimately to invent his steam-engine.* Papin's reputation having extended abroad, he was invited to fill the office of professor of mathematics in the University of Marburg, which he accepted; and he left England in the year 1687. But he continued, until his death, many years later, to maintain a friendly correspondence with his scientific friends in England; and one of the last things he did was to construct a model steam-engine fitted in a boat—"une petite machine d'un vaisseau à roues"—for the purpose of sending it over to England for trial on the Thames.† But, unhappily for Papin, the little vessel never reached England. To his great grief, he found that when it had reached as far as Münden, on the Weser, it was seized by the boatmen of the river and barbarously destroyed. Three years later the illustrious exile died, worn out by work and anxiety, leaving it to other inventors

---

* For an account of Solomon de Caus, as well as of the life and labors of Dr. Papin, see "Historical Memoir of the invention of the Steam-engine," given in the *Lives of Boulton and Watt*, p. 8, 30–8.

† "It is important," he wrote to Leibnitz, on the 7th of July, 1707, "that my new construction of vessel should be put to the proof in a sea-port like London, where there is depth enough to apply the new invention, which, by means of fire, will render one or two men capable of producing more effect than some hundreds of rowers."

to realize the great ideas he had conceived as to locomotion by steam-power.

Dr. Desaguliers was another refugee who achieved considerable distinction in England as a teacher of mechanical philosophy. His father, Jean des Aguliers, was pastor of a Protestant congregation at Aitré, near Rochelle, from which he fled about the period of the Revocation. His child, the future professor, is said to have been carried on board the ship by which he escaped concealed in a barrel.* The pastor first took refuge in Guernsey, from whence he proceeded to England, took orders in the Established Church, and became minister of the French chapel in Swallow Street, London. This charge he subsequently resigned, and established a school at Islington, at which his son received his first education. From thence the young man proceeded to Oxford, matriculating at Christ Church, where he obtained the degree of B.A., and took deacon's orders. Being drawn to the study of natural philosophy, he shortly after began to deliver lectures at Oxford on hydrostatics and optics, to which he afterward added mechanics.

His fame as a lecturer having reached London, Desaguliers was pressingly invited thither, and he accordingly removed to the metropolis in 1713. His lectures were much admired, and he had so happy a knack of illustrating them by experiments that he was invited by the Royal Society to be their demonstrator. He was afterward appointed curator of the society; and in the course of his connection with it communicated a vast number of curious and valuable papers, which were printed in the transactions. The Duke of Chandos gave Desaguliers the church living of Edgeware; and the king (before whom he gave lectures at Hampton Court) presented

---

* The statement is made in the "House and Farm Accounts of the Shuttleworths of Gawthorpe Hall."—*Cheetham Society's Papers*, 1856–8. The Shuttleworths were related by marriage to the Desaguliers family; Robert Shuttleworth, one of the successors to Gawthorpe, having married Anne, the second daughter of General Desaguliers (son of the above Dr. Desaguliers), who was one of the equerries of George III.

him with a benefice in Essex, besides appointing him chaplain to the Prince of Wales.

In 1734 Desaguliers published his *Course of Experimental Philosophy* in two quarto volumes—the best book of the kind that had until then appeared in England. It would appear from this work that the doctor also designed and superintended the erection of steam-engines. Referring to an improvement which he had made on Savery's engine, he says: "According to this improvement, I have caused seven of these fire-engines to be erected since the year 1717 or 1718. The first was for the late Czar Peter the Great, for his garden at Petersburg, where it was set up." Dr. Desaguliers died in 1749, leaving behind him three sons, one of whom, the eldest, published a translation of the *Mathematical Elements of Natural Philosophy*, by Gravesande, who had been a pupil of his father's; the second was a beneficed clergyman in Norfolk; and the third was a colonel of artillery and lieutenant general in the army, as well as equerry to George III.

Among other learned refugees who were elected members of the Royal Society were David Durand, the editor of *Pliny's Natural History, The Philosophical Writings of Cicero*, and other classical works, and the author of a *History of the Sixteenth Century*, as well as of the continuation of *Rapin's History of England;* Peter des Maiseaux, the intimate friend of Saint Evremonde, whose works he edited and translated into English; and Abraham de Moivre, the celebrated mathematician.

De Moivre was the son of a surgeon at Vitry in Champagne, and received his principal education at the Protestant seminary of Sedan. From the first he displayed an extraordinary genius for arithmetic; and his chief delight in his by-hours was to shut himself up with Le Gendre's arithmetic and work out its problems. This led one of his classical masters to ask on one occasion, "What that little rogue meant to do with all these ciphers?" When the college of Sedan was suppressed in 1681, De Moivre went to Saumur to pursue his studies in philosophy there, and afterward to Paris to prosecute the study of physics. By this time his father, being prohibited practicing as a surgeon because of his religion, left Vitry to join his son at Paris; but they were not allowed to remain long together. The agents of the government, acting on their power of separating children from their parents and subjecting them to the process of conversion, seized young De Moivre in his nineteenth year, and shut him up in the priory of St. Martin. There his Jesuit masters tried to drill him into the Roman Catholic faith; but the young Protestant was stanch, and refused to be converted. Being pronounced an obstinate heretic, he was discharged after about two years' confinement, on which he was ordered forthwith to leave the country.

De Moivre arrived in London with his father* in 1687, at the age of twenty, and immediately bestirred himself to earn a living. He had no means but his knowledge and his industry. He first endeavored to obtain pupils, to instruct them in mathematics; and he also began, like others of the refugees, to give lectures on natural philosophy. But his knowledge of English was as yet too imperfect to enable him to lecture with success, and he was, besides, an indifferent manipulator, so that his lectures were shortly discontinued. It happened that the *Principia* of Newton was published about the time that De Moivre arrived in England. The subject offering great attractions to a mind such as his, he entered upon the study of the book with much zest, and succeeded before long in mastering its contents, and arriving at a clear understanding of the views of the author. So complete was his knowledge of Newton's principles, that it is said, when Sir Isaac was asked for explanations of his writings, he would say, "Go to De Moivre; he knows better than I do."

* We find, from the *Lists of Foreign Protestants* published by the Camden Society (1862), that Abraham and Daniel de Moivre obtained letters of naturalization on the 16th of December, 1687.

Thus De Moivre acquired the friendship and respect of Newton, of Halley, and the other distinguished scientific men of the time; and one of the best illustrations of the esteem in which his intellectual qualifications were held is afforded by the fact that in the contention which arose between Leibnitz and Newton as to their respective priority in the invention of the method of fluxions, the Royal Society appointed De Moivre to report upon their rival claims.

De Moivre published many original works on his favorite subject, more particularly on analytical mathematics. Professor De Morgan has observed of them that "they abound with consummate contrivance and skill; and one, at least, of his investigations has had the effect of completely changing the whole character of trigonometrical science in its higher departments."* One of the works published by him, entitled *The Doctrine of Chances*, is curious, as leading, in a measure, to the development of the science of life assurance. From the first edition it does not appear that De Moivre intended to do more than illustrate his favorite theory of probabilities. He showed in a variety of ways the probable results of throwing dice in certain numbers of throws. From dice-throwing he proceeded to lotteries, and showed how many tickets ought to be taken to secure the probability of drawing a prize. A few years later he applied his views to a more practical purpose—the valuation of annuities on lives; and though the data on which he based his calculations were incorrect, and his valuations consequently unreliable, the publication of his *Doctrine of Chances*, applied to the valuation of annuities on lives, was of much use at the time it appeared, and it formed the basis of other and more accurate calculations.

De Moivre's books were on too abstruse subjects to yield him much profit, and during the later years of his life he had to contend with poverty. It is said that he derived a precarious subsistence from fees paid him for solving questions

* Art. "De Moivre" in *Penny Cyclopædia*.

relative to games of chance and other matters connected with the value of probabilities. He frequented a coffee-house in St. Martin's Lane, of which he was one of the attractions, and there his customers sought him to work out their problems. The occupation could not have been very tolerable to such a man; but he was growing old and helpless in body, and his power of calculating was his only capital. He survived to the age of eighty-seven, but during the last month of his life he sank into a state of total lethargy. Shortly before his decease the Academy of Berlin elected him a member. The French Academy of Sciences also elected him a foreign associate; and on the news of his death reaching Paris, M. de Fouchy drew up an eloquent *eloge* of the exiled Huguenot, which was duly inserted in the records of the Academy.

For the reasons above stated, the number of refugee physicians and surgeons who sought the asylum of England was very considerable. Many of them settled to practice in London and other towns in the south, while others obtained appointments in the army and navy. Weiss says it was to the French surgeons especially that England was in a great measure indebted for the remarkable perfection to which English surgical instruments arrived. The College of Physicians in London generously opened their doors to the admission of their foreign brethren. Between the years 1681 and 1689 we find nine French physicians admitted, among whom we observe the name of the eminent Sebastian le Fevre.* One of the members of the same family subsequently settled in Spitalfields as a silk manufacturer, from whom the late Speaker of the House of Commons, now Viscount Eversley, is lineally descended.

Among the literary men of the emigration were the brothers Du Moulins—Louis, for some time Camden professor of

* The family were of long and eminent standing in Anjou as medical men. Joshua le Fevre obtained letters of naturalization in 1681; but before that date Nicasius le Fevre, a member of the same family, was appointed chemist to Charles II., with a fee of £150 a year.—DURRANT COOPER—*Lists of Foreign Protestants*, p. xxvi.

history at Oxford, and Peter, prebendary of Canterbury—both authors of numerous works; Henry Justel, the learned secretary to Louis XIV., who sold off his valuable library and fled to England some years before the Revocation, when he was appointed king's librarian; Peter Anthony Motteaux, an excellent linguist, whose translations of Cervantes and Rabelais first popularized the works of those writers in this country; Maximilian Misson, author of *A New Voyage to Italy, Theatre Sacré des Cevennes*, and other works; Michel de la Roche, author of the *Memoirs of Literature*, and *A Literary Journal*, which filled up a considerable gap in literary history;* Michel Maittaire, M.A. Oxon, one of the masters of Westminster School, an able philologist, the author of several learned works on typography as well as theology; De Souligne, grandson of Du Plessis Mornay (the Huguenot leader), author of *The Desolation of France Demonstrated, The Political Mischiefs of Popery*, and other works; John Gagnier, the able Orientalist, professor of Oriental languages at Oxford University, and the author of many learned treatises on Rabbinical lore and kindred subjects; John Cornaud de la Croze, author of the *Bibliothèque Universelle, The Works of the Learned*, and *The History of Learning;* Abel Boyer, the annalist, author of the well-known *French and English Dictionary*, who pursued a successful literary career in England for nearly forty years; Mark Anthony de la Bastide, author of several highly-esteemed controversial works; and Grav-

---

* In his *Literary Journal* De la Roche says, "I was very young when I took refuge in England, so that most of the little learning I have got is of an English growth.... 'Tis in this country I have learned to have a right notion of religion, an advantage that can never be too much valued. Being a studious man, it was very natural to me to write some books, which I have done, partly in English and partly in French, for the space of twenty years. The only advantage I have got by them is that they have not been unacceptable, and I hope I have done no dishonor to the English nation by those French books printed beyond sea, in which I undertook to make our English learning better known to foreigners than it was before. I have said just now that I took refuge in England. When I consider the continual fear I was in for a whole year of being discovered and imprisoned to force me to abjure the Protestant religion, and the great difficulties I met with to make my escape, I wonder I have not been a stupid man ever since."

erol of Nismes, one of the founders of the academy of that city, a poet and jurisconsult, who published in London a history of his native place, addressed to "Messieurs les Réfugiés de Nîmes qui sont établis dans Londres." The last pages of this book contain a touching narrative of the sufferings of the Protestants of Languedoc, and it concludes as follows: "We, who are in a country so remote from our own only for the sake of God's Word, and for the testimony of Jesus Christ, let us study to render our confession and our faith glorious by discreet and modest conduct, by an exemplary life, and by entire devotion to the service of God. Let us ever bear in mind that we are the sons and the fathers of martyrs. Let us never forget this glory, but strive to transmit it to our posterity."*

But the most eminent of the refugees were unquestionably the pastors, some of whom were men highly distinguished for their piety, learning, and eloquence. Such were Abbadie, considered one of the ablest defenders of Christianity in his day; Saurin, one of the most eloquent of preachers; Allix, the learned philologist and historian; and Delange, his colleague; Pineton, author of *Les Larmes de Chambrun*, characterized by Michelet as "that beautiful but terrible recital;" Du Moulin, Drelincourt, Marmet, and many more.

Jacques Abbadie was the scion of a distinguished Bearnese family. After completing his studies at Sedan and Saumur, he took his doctor's degree at the age of seventeen. While still a young man, he was invited to take charge of the French church in Berlin, to which he acceded; and his reputation served to attract large numbers of refugees to that city. His *Treatise on the Truth of the Christian Religion* greatly increased his fame, not only at Berlin, but in France and throughout Europe. Madame de Sevigné, though she rejoiced at the banishment of the Huguenots, spoke of it in a high strain of panegyric as the most divine of all books: "I do not believe," she said, "that any one ever spoke of re-

* WEISS, p. 267.

ligion like this man!" Even Bussy Rabutin, who scarce passed for a believer, said of it, "We are reading it now, and we think it the only book in the world worth reading." A few years later, Abbadie published his *Treatise on the Divinity of Jesus Christ*. It is so entirely free from controversial animus, that the Roman Catholics of France even hoped to win him over to their faith, and they held out their hand to help him within their pale. But they only deceived themselves; for, on the death of the elector, Abbadie, instead of returning to France, accompanied his friend Marshal Schomberg to Holland, and afterward to England, in the capacity of chaplain. He was with the marshal during his campaigns in Ireland, and suffered the grief of seeing his benefactor fall mortally wounded at the Boyne. Returning to London, Abbadie became attached as minister to the church of the Savoy, where crowds flocked to his preaching. While holding this position, he wrote his *Art of Knowing One's Self*, in which he powerfully illustrated the relations of the human conscience to the duties inculcated by the Gospel. He also devoted his pen to the cause of William III., and published his *Defense of the British Nation*, in which he justified the deposition of James II. and the Revolution of 1688 on the ground of right and morality. In 1694 he was selected to pronounce the funeral oration of Queen Mary, wife of William III.—a sermon containing many passages of great eloquence; shortly after which he entered the English Church, and was appointed to the deanery of Killaloe, in which office he ended his days.

Jacques Saurin was the greatest of the Protestant preachers. He was the son of an advocate at Nismes, whose three sons all took refuge in England—Jacques, the pulpit orator; Captain Saurin, an officer in William's army; and Louis, some time minister of the French church in the Savoy, and afterward Dean of St. Patrick's, Ardagh.* Jacques Saurin was,

---

* From him were lineally descended the Right Reverend James Saurin, Bishop of Dromore, and the Honorable William Saurin, Attorney General for Ireland from 1807 to 1821.

in the early part of his life, tempted to the profession of arms; and when only seventeen years of age he served as an ensign in the army of Savoy, under the Marquis de Ruvigny, earl of Galway. Returning to his studies at Geneva, he prepared himself for the ministry; and having proceeded to England in 1701, he was appointed one of the ministers of the French church in Threadneedle Street. He held that office for four years, after which he was called to the Hague, and there developed that talent as a preacher for which he became so distinguished. He was made minister extraordinary to the French community of nobles, and held that office until his death. "Nothing," says Weiss, "can give an idea of the effect produced by his inspired voice, which for twenty-five years resounded beneath the vaulted roof of the temple at the Hague, unless it be the profound veneration and pious worship with which the memory of the great author, continually revived by the perusal of his writings, has remained surrounded in Holland."[*]

Scarcely less distinguished was Peter Allix, for some time minister of the great Protestant church at Charenton, near Paris, and afterward of the temple of the French Hospital in Spitalfields, London. His style of preaching was less ornate, but not less forcible, than that of Saurin. His discourses were simple, clear, and persuasive. The great object at which he aimed was the enforcement of union among Protestants. Louis XIV. tried every means to induce him to enter the Roman Catholic Church, and a pension was offered him if, in that case, he would return to France. But Allix resisted all persuasions, and died in exile. His great erudition was recognized by the University of Oxford and Cambridge, who conferred upon him the degree of doctor of divinity; and, on the recommendation of Bishop Burnet, he was made canon and treasurer of Salisbury Cathedral. Allix left behind him many published works, which in their time were highly esteemed.

[*] WEISS, p. 397.

Jacques Pineton was another of the refugee pastors who illustrated his faith by his life, which was pure and beautiful. He had personally suffered more than most of his brethren, and he lived to relate the story of his trials in his touching narrative entitled *Les Larmes de Chambrun*. He was pastor of a Protestant church in the village of that name, situated near Avignon, in the principality of Orange, when the district was overrun by the troops of Louis XIV. The dragonnade was even more furiously conducted here than elsewhere, because of the hatred entertained by the king toward the Protestant prince who took his title from the little principality. The troops were under the command of the Count of Tessé, a ferocious and profane officer. Pineton was laid up at the time by an attack of the gout, the suffering from which was aggravated by the recent fracture of a rib which he had sustained. As he lay helpless on his couch, a party of forty-two dragoons burst into his house, entered his chamber, lit a number of candles, beat their drums round his bed, and filled the room with tobacco-smoke, so as almost to stifle him. They then drank until they fell asleep and snored; but their officers, entering, roused them from their stupor by laying about among them with their canes. While the men were asleep, Pineton had urged his wife to fly, which she attempted to do, but was taken in the act and brought before Tessé, who brutally told her that she must regard herself as the property of the regiment. She fell at his feet distracted, and would have been lost, but that a priest, to whom Pineton had rendered some service, offered himself as surety for her. The priest, however, made it a condition that she and her husband should abjure their religion; and, in a moment of agony and despair, they succumbed. Remorse immediately followed, and they determined to take the first opportunity to fly. Upon the plea that Pineton, still in great pain, required surgical aid, he obtained leave to proceed to Lyons. He was placed in a litter, the slightest movement of which caused him indescribable pain. When the people saw him carried away, they all wept, Catholic as well as Protestant. Even the dragoons were moved. The sufferer contrived to reach Lyons, where he was soon cured and convalescent. It appeared that the frontier was less strictly guarded near Lyons; and with the assistance of a friend, Pineton shortly after contrived to escape in the disguise of a general officer. He set out in a carriage with four horses, attended by a train of servants in handsome liveries. At the bridge of Beauvoisin, where a picket of dragoons was posted, he was allowed to cross without interruption, the soldiers having previously been informed that "my lord" was a great officer traveling express into Switzerland. There was, however, still the frontier-guard of the Duke of Savoy to pass. It commanded the great road across the Alps, and was maintained for the express purpose of preventing the flight of refugees. By the same bold address, and feigning great indignation at the guard attempting to obstruct his passage, Pineton was allowed to proceed, and shortly after reached Chambery. Next morning he entered the French gate of Geneva, giving expression to his feelings by singing the eighth verse of the twenty-sixth Psalm—

> "Que j'aime ce saint lieu
> On Tu parois, mon Dieu," etc.

Madame Pineton was less fortunate in her flight. She set out for the Swiss frontier accompanied by three ladies belonging to Lyons. The guides whom they had hired and paid to conduct them had the barbarity to desert them in the mountains. It was winter. They wandered and lost their way. They were nine hours in the snow. They were driven away from Cardon, and were pursued along the Rhone. The Lyons ladies, vanquished by cold, fatigue, and hunger, wished to return to Lyons and give themselves up; they could endure no longer. But Madame Pineton hoped that by this time her husband had reached Geneva, and she found courage for them all. She would not listen to the proposal to go back; she must go forward; and the contest ended in their proceeding, and arriving at last at Geneva, and finding there safety and liberty.

The pastor Pineton, after remaining for a short time in that city, proceeded toward Holland, where he was graciously received by the Prince of Orange. Having been appointed one of the princess's chaplains, he accompanied Mary to London, and was appointed a canon of Windsor. He did not, however, live long to enjoy that dignity, for he died in 1689, the year after his arrival in England, though he lived to give to the world the touching narrative of his adventures and sufferings.*

Many of the most distinguished of the French pastors were admitted to degrees in the Universities of Oxford and Cambridge,† and several, besides the above, held benefices in the

* Those who would know the whole details of this exciting story must refer to *Les Larmes de Jacques Pineton de Chambrun, qui contiennent les Persecutions arrivées aux Eglises de la Principauté d'Orange depuis* 1660, *la chute et le rélévement de l'Auteur, avec le retablissement de S. Pierre en son Apostolat sur les Paroles de notre Seigneur Jesus Christ, selon S. Jean, xxi.* 14, recently republished at Paris by Meyrueis.

† Among the learned foreigners mentioned by Anthony Wood, in his *Athena Oxoniensis*, as having been admitted to the University of Oxford in acknowledgment of their learning, may be named the following :

1625. John Verneuil, M.A., Oxford (formerly of the University of Montauban).
1625–6. Thomas Levet, Bachelor of Civil Law, Oxford (formerly of the University of Orleans).
1638. Daniel Brevint, M.A., Oxford (formerly of the University of Saumur).
1648–9. Abraham Stuard, M.D., Oxford (formerly of the University of Caen).
1649. Louis du Moulin, M.D., Oxford and Cambridge (son of the French Protestant pastor Pierre du Moulin, and educated at the University of Leyden).
1655. Ludovic de Lambermont, M.D., Oxford (formerly of the University of Valence).
1656. Pierre du Moulin, D.D., Oxford and Cambridge (brother of the above-mentioned Louis).
1656–7. Theophilus de Garencieres, M.D., Oxford (formerly of the University of Caen).
1656. Pierre Vasson, M.B., Oxford.
1656–7. Abraham Conyard, Bachelor of Divinity, Oxford (formerly of the University of Rouen).
1676. Stephen le Moine, D.D., Oxford (formerly of Rouen, and subsequently Professor of Theology at Leyden).
1682–3. Samuel de l'Angle, D.D., Oxford (formerly of Rouen and Paris).
1685. James le Prix, D.D., Oxford (formerly Professor of Divinity in the University of Saumur).

English Church. In 1682, when the learned Samuel de l'Angle was created D.D. of Oxford without payment of the customary fees, he was conducted into the House of Convocation by the king's professor of divinity, and all the masters stood up to receive him. De l'Angle had been the chief preacher in the church of Charenton, near Paris; and after thirty-five years of zealous work there, he fled from France with his family to end his days in England. He was afterward made Prebendary of Canterbury and Westminster. Peter Drelincourt, son of the famous French divine, whose work on *Death** has been translated into nearly all the languages of Europe, was another refugee who entered the Church, and became Dean of Armagh; and Dr. Hans de Veille, a man of great learning, having also entered the Church, was made library-keeper at Lambeth Palace by Dr. Tillotson, then Archbishop of Canterbury.

Though many of the most eminent French ministers joined the Established Church of England, others equally learned and able became preachers and professors among the Dissenters. While Pierre du Moulin was a Prebendary of Canterbury, his brother Louis was a stout Presbyterian. Charles Marie du Veil, originally a Jew, was first converted to Roman Catholicism, next to Protestantism, and ended by becoming a Baptist minister. But the most eminent of the refugees who joined the Dissenters was the Reverend James Capell, who had held the professorship of Hebrew in the University of Saumur at the early age of nineteen. He fled into

---

1686. René Bertheau, D.D., Oxford (formerly of the University of Montpellier).
1686-7. James d'Allemagne, D.D., Oxford (a French minister of the Protestant Church).
1687. Elias Boherel, Bachelor of Civil Law, Oxford (formerly of the University of Saumur).
1689. John Mesnard, D.D., Oxford (formerly minister of Charenton, and subsequently chaplain to William III.).
1689. John Deffray, M.A., Oxford (formerly of the University of Saumur), etc., etc., etc.

* *Les Consolations de l'Ame fidelle contre les Frayeurs de la Mort* has been printed more than forty times in French, and many times in England in its translated form.

England shortly after the Revocation, and in 1708 he accepted a professor's chair at the Dissenters' College in Hoxton Square. There he long continued to teach the Oriental languages and their critical application in the study of the Scriptures, and he performed his duties with such distinguished ability that the institution came to enjoy a very high repute. Many of the ablest ministers of the next generation, churchmen as well as dissenters, studied under Mr. Capell, and received from him their best education. He held the office for fourteen years, and died at eighty-three, the last of his family.

Of the ministers of the French churches in London, besides those already named, the most distinguished were the Reverend Charles Bertheau, minister of the French church in Threadneedle Street, who officiated in that capacity with great ability for a period of forty-six years; the Reverend Henri Chatelain, minister of the French church in St. Martin's Lane;* the Reverend Cæsar Pegorier, minister of the Artillery and the Tabernacle churches, and author of numerous controversial works; the Reverend Henri Rochblave, minister of the refugee church at Greenwich, and afterward of the French Chapel Royal, St. James's; the Reverend Daniel Chamier, minister of the French church in Leicester Fields; and the Reverend Jean Graverol, minister of the French churches of Swallow Street and the Quarré, a voluminous and eloquent writer. The Reverend Antoine Pérès (formerly professor of Oriental languages in the University of Montauban) and Ezekiel Marmet were ministers of other French churches, and were greatly beloved—Marmet's book of meditations on the words of Job, "I know that my Redeemer liveth," being prized by devout readers of all persuasions.

* Henri Chatelain was the great-grandson of Simon Chatelain, the famous Protestant manufacturer of gold and silver lace. This lace was a much-prized article. It procured for the steadfast Huguenot the toleration of his religion, in which he was zealous from the fifteenth year of his age to the eighty-fifth, which was his last. He died in 1675, leaving more than eighty descendants, who all paid fines for openly attending his funeral.—AGNEW—*French Protestant Exiles*, 237.

The Reverend Claude de la Mothe and Jean Armand du Bourdieu were ministers of the French church in the Savoy, the principal West-end congregation, frequented by the most distinguished of the refugees. Both these ministers were eminent for their learning and their eloquence. The former was of a noble Huguenot family named Grostête, and studied law when a youth at Orleans, his native city, where he took the degree of Doctor of Civil Law. He was also a member of the Royal Society of Berlin. He practiced for some time at Paris as an advocate, but subsequently changed law for divinity, and was appointed pastor of the church at Lisy in 1675. At the Revocation he fled to England with his wife, and was appointed one of the ministers of the church in the Savoy. He was the author of numerous works, which enjoyed a high reputation in their day, and, besides, devoted much of his spare time to correspondence, with the object of obtaining the release of Protestant martyrs from the French galleys.

Jean Armand du Bourdieu, the colleague of De la Mothe, though celebrated as a preacher, was still more distinguished as an author. Like himself, his father was a refugee divine, and preached in London until his ninety-fifth year. Jean Armand had been pastor of a church at Montpellier, which he left on the Revocation, and came into England, followed by a large number of his flock. He was chaplain to the three dukes of Schomberg in succession, and was by the old duke's side when he fell at the Boyne. In 1707 he preached a sermon in London, which was afterward published, wherein he alluded to Louis XIV. as a Pharaoh to the oppressed Protestants of France. The French king singled him out from the many refugee preachers in England, and demanded, through his minister, that he should be punished. Louis's complaint was formally referred to the Bishop of London— the French church in the Savoy being under his jurisdiction— and Du Bourdieu was summoned before his grace at Fulham Palace to answer the charge. After reading and considering the memorial of the French embassador, the pastor was asked what he had to say to it. He replied that " during the war he had, after the example of several prelates and clergymen of the Church of England, preached freely against the common enemy and persecutor of the Church; and the greatest part of his sermons being printed with his name affixed, he was far from disowning them; but since the proclamation of peace [of Utrecht], he had not said any thing that did in the least regard the French king." No farther steps were taken in the matter.

Du Bourdieu continued indefatigably active on behalf of his oppressed brethren in France during the remainder of his life. His pen was seldom idle, and his winged words flew abroad and kept alive the indignation of the Protestant north against the persecutors of his countrymen. In 1717 he published two works, one "A Vindication of our Martyrs at the Galleys;" another, "A Comparison of the Penal Laws of France against Protestants with those of England against Papists;" and, in the following year, "An Appeal to the English Nation." He was now an old man of seventy; but his fire burned bright until the last. Two years later he died, beloved and lamented by all who knew him.*

There is little reason to doubt that the earnestness, eloquence, and learning of this distinguished band of exiles for conscience' sake exercised an influence not only on English religion and politics, but also on English literature, which continues to operate until this day.

* A great-grandson of Du Bourdieu, Captain Saumarez Dubourdieu, was an officer in the British army at the capture of Martinique from the French in 1762, and received the sword of the French commandant, who said, on presenting it, "My misfortune is the lighter, as I am conquered by a Dubourdieu, a beloved relative. *My* name is Dubourdieu!"

CHAPTER XIV.
HUGUENOT SETTLEMENTS IN ENGLAND.—MEN OF INDUSTRY.

WE now come to the immigration and settlement in England of Huguenot merchants, manufacturers, and artisans, which exercised a still greater influence on English industry than the immigration of French literati and divines did upon English literature.

It is computed that about 100,000 French manufacturers and workmen fled into England in consequence of the Revocation, besides those who took refuge in Switzerland, Germany, and Holland. When the Huguenot employers shut up their works in France, their men usually prepared to follow them. They converted what they could into money, whatever the loss might be, and made for the coast, accompanied by their families. The paper-makers of Angoumois left their mills; the silk-makers of Touraine left their looms, and the tanners their pits; the vine-dressers and farmers of Saintonge, Poitou, and La Rochelle left their vineyards, their farms, and their gardens, and looked out into the wide world, seaward, for a new home and a refuge, where they might work and worship in peace.

The principal emigration into England was from Normandy* and Brittany. Upward of 10,000 of the industrial class left Rouen; and several thousand persons, principally engaged in the maritime trade, set out from Caen, leaving that city to solitude and poverty. The whole Protestant population of Coutances emigrated, and fine linen manufactures of the place were at once extinguished. There was a similar flight of masters and men from Elbœuf, Alençon,

* FLOQUET, the accredited historian of Normandy (*Histoire du Parlement de Normandie*), calculates that not less than 184,000 Protestants took advantage of the vicinity of the sea, and of their connection with England and Holland, to abandon their country.

Caudebec, Havre, and other northern towns. The makers of *noyal* and white linen cloths, for which a ready market had been obtained abroad, left Nantes, Rennes, and Morlaix in Brittany, and Le Mans and Laval in Maine, and went over to England to carry on their manufactures there. The provinces farther north also contributed largely to swell the stream of emigration into England : the cloth-makers departed from Amiens, Abbeville, and Doullens; the gauze-makers and lace-makers from Lille and Valenciennes; and artisans of all kinds from the various towns and cities of the interior.

Notwithstanding the precautions taken by the French government, and the penalty of death, or the galleys for life, to which those were subject who were taken in the act of flight, the emigration could not be stopped. The fugitives were helped on their way by their fellow-Protestants, and often by the Roman Catholics themselves, who pitied their sad fate. The fugitives lay concealed in barns and farm-yards by day, and traveled by night toward the coast. There the maritime population, many of whom were Protestants like themselves, actively connived at their escape. France presented too wide a reach of sea-frontier, extending from Bayonne to Calais, to be effectively watched by any guard, and not only the French, but the English and Dutch merchant-ships, which hovered about the coast waiting for the agreed signal to put in and take on board their freight of fugitives, had usually little difficulty in carrying them off in safety.

Of those fugitives who succeeded in making good their escape, the richest took refuge in Holland, while the bulk of those who settled in England were persons of comparatively small means. Yet a considerable sum of ready money must have been brought by the refugees, as we find the French embassador writing to Louis XIV. in 1687 that as much as 960,000 louis d'ors had already been sent to the Mint for conversion into English money.* This was, however, the prop-

* Many of the refugees were eminent merchants and manufacturers, and did

erty of a comparatively small number of the more wealthy families, for the greater proportion of those who landed in England were altogether destitute.

Steps were immediately taken for the relief of the poorer immigrants. Collections were made in the churches; public subscriptions were raised; and Parliament voted considerable sums from the public purse. Thus a fund of nearly £200,000 was collected, and invested for the benefit of the refugees—the annual interest, about £15,000, being intrusted to a committee for distribution among the most necessitous, while about £2000 a year was applied toward the support of the poor French ministers and their respective churches. The pressure on the relief fund was of course the greatest in those years immediately following the Revocation of the Edict of Nantes, before the destitute foreigners had been able to maintain themselves by their respective callings. There was also a large number of destitute landed gentry, professional men, and pastors, to whom the earnings of a livelihood was even more difficult; and these also had to be relieved out of the fund.

From the first report of the French Relief Committee, dated December, 1687—that is, only fourteen months after the Revocation—it appears that 15,500 refugees had been relieved in the course of the year. "Of these," says Weiss, "13,050 were settled in London, and 2000 in the different sea-port towns where they had disembarked. Among them the committee distinguishes 140 persons of quality with their families; 143 ministers; 144 lawyers, physicians, traders, and burghers. It designates the others under the general denomination of artisans and workmen. The persons of quality received weekly assistance in money throughout the whole of that year. Their sons were placed in the best commercial

undoubtedly bring along with them much money and effects. I have seen a computation, at the lowest supposition, of only 50,000 of those people coming to Great Britain, and that, one with another, they brought £60 each in money or effects, whereby they added three millions sterling to the wealth of Britain.—MACPHERSON—*Annals of Commerce*, ii., 617.

houses. About 150 of them entered the army, and were provided, at the cost of the committee, with a complete outfit. The ministers obtained for themselves and their families pensions which were regularly paid. Their sons found employment in the houses of rich merchants or of persons of quality. Weekly assistance was granted to the sick, and to those whose great age prevented them earning their own living by labor. The greater part of the artisans and workmen were employed in the English manufactories. The committee supplied them with the necessary implements and tools, and provided, at the same time, for all their other wants. Six hundred of them, for whom it could not find employment in England, were sent at its cost to America. Fifteen French churches were erected out of the proceeds of the national subscription — three in London, and twelve in the various counties where the greater number of the refugees had settled."*

The help thus generously given to the distressed refugees by the nation was very shortly rendered in a great measure unnecessary by the vigorous efforts which they made to help themselves.† They sought about in all directions for em-

---

* WEISS—*History of the French Protestant Refugees*, p. 224.

† The emigration from France, however, did not come to an end until about the middle of the eighteenth century. Every revival of religious persecution there was followed by a fresh influx of fugitives into England. In 1718, the Rev. J. A. Dubourdieu, one of the ministers of the Savoy church, published *An Appeal to the English Nation*, in vindication of the body of the French Protestants against the calumnies of one Mallard and his associates, as to the alleged misapplication of the national bounty. It appears that the number of poor foreign Protestants relieved out of the fund in that year was 5194. M. Dubourdieu says, "There are some among the refugees who, having been over here twenty or thirty years, have by their industry and labor maintained themselves without being burdensome to any one; others who, not being bred to work for their living, brought over a small matter with them, and spent it by degrees. Both these, being overcome by age and infirmities, and incapable of doing any thing for themselves, are obliged to have recourse to this beneficence. The number of these is certainly very great, and is farther increased by those that come daily from France, more especially since the last peace; these come destitute of every thing. There are persons of all ages and degrees among them. The old and infirm persons must be relieved; and as for those that are young and in a condition to work, they want some assistance to put them forward, and enable them to get their livelihood some way or other." It is farther incidentally mentioned that "there are 80 min-

ployment, and being ingenious, intelligent, and industrious, they gradually succeeded in obtaining it. They were satisfied with small gains, provided they were honestly come by. French work-people are better economists than English, and less sufficed for their wants. They were satisfied if they could keep a roof over their heads, a clean fireside, and the *pot-au-feu* going. What English artisans despised as food, they could make a meal of. For they brought with them from France the art of cooking—the art of economizing nutriment and at the same time presenting it in the most savory forms — an art almost entirely unknown even at this day in the homes of English workmen, and a source of enormous national waste. Before the arrival of the refugees, the London butchers sold their bullocks' hides to the fellmongers, always with the tails on. The tails were thrown away and wasted. Who would ever dream of eating ox-tails? The refugees profited by the delusion. They obtained the tails, enriched their *pots-au-feu* with them, and reveled in the now well-known delicacy of ox-tail soup.

The refugees were also very helpful of one another. The richer helped the poorer, and the poor helped each other. The Marquis de Ruvigny almost kept open house, and was equally ready to open his purse to his distressed countrymen. Those who had the means of starting manufactories and workshops employed as many hands as they could; and the men who earned wages helped to support those who remained unemployed. Being of foreign birth, and having no claim upon the poor-rates, the French artisans formed themselves into societies for mutual relief in sickness and old age. These were the first societies of the kind established by workmen

---

isters who, with their families, are partakers of the charity, besides 60 ministers' widows who have a charge of children." Further on, the writer says: "There are but two French churches in this city [London] that are able to give £100 a year to their ministers, and but four in all that can maintain the ministry without some allowance out of the royal benefaction." At the head of the French committee were, it is stated, the Archbishop of Canterbury and the Bishop of London. The total number of "French refugees" M. Dubourdieu then estimated at "near 100,000 persons in the two kingdoms."

in England, though they have since been largely imitated;* and the Odd Fellows, Foresters, and numerous other benefit societies of the laboring class, though they may not know it, are but following in the path long since tracked out for them by the French refugees.

The working-class immigrants very soon settled down to the practice of their respective callings in different parts of the country. A large proportion of them settled in London, and several districts of the metropolis were almost entirely occupied by them. Spitalfields, Bethnal Green, and Soho were the principal French quarters, where French was spoken in the workshops, in the schools and churches, and in the streets. But the immigrants distributed themselves in other districts, many of them settling in Aldgate, Bishopsgate, Shoreditch, and the quarter adjoining Thames Street. A little colony of them settled in one of the streets leading from Broad Street to the Guildhall, which came to be called "Petty France," from the number of French who inhabited it. Others settled in Long Acre, the Seven Dials, and the neighborhood of Temple Bar. Le Mann, the famous biscuit-maker, opened his shop and flourished near the Royal Exchange. Some opened shops for the manufacture and sale of cutlery and mathematical and surgical instruments in the Strand; while others began the making of watches, the fabrication of articles in gold and silver, and the cutting and mounting of jewelry, in which the French artisans were then admitted to be the most expert in Europe.

France had long been the leader of fashion, and all the world bought dress and articles of vertu at Paris. Colbert was accustomed to say that the fashions were worth more to

---

* One of the oldest of the French benefit societies was the "Norman Society" of Bethnal Green, which only ceased to exist in 1863, after a life of upward of 150 years. Down to the year 1800, the whole of the society's accounts were kept in French, the members being the descendants of French Protestants, mostly bearing French names; but at length the foreign element became so mixed with the English that it almost ceased to be recognizable, and the society may be said to have died out with the absorption of the distinctive class for whose benefit it was originally instituted.

France than the mines of Peru were to Spain. Only articles of French manufacture, with a French name, could find purchasers among people of fashion in London. "The fondness of the nation for French commodities was such," said Joshua Gee, "that it was a very hard matter to bring them into love with those made at home."* Another writer, Mr. Samuel Fortrey, describing the international trade between England and France in 1663, set forth the great disadvantages at which the English manufacturers were then placed, and how seriously the balance of trade was against England. Goods to the amount of above two and a half millions sterling were annually imported from France, whereas the value of English goods exported thither did not amount to a million. "The chief manufactures amongst us at this day," said he, "are only woollen cloths, woollen stuffs of various sorts, stockings, ribandings, and perhaps some few silk stuffs, and some other small things, scarce worth the naming; and those already mentioned are so decayed and adulterated, that they are almost out of esteem both at home and abroad."

The principal articles imported from France previous to that time were velvets and satins from Lyons; silks and taffetas from Tours; silk ribbons, galloons, laces, gloves, and buttons from Paris and Rouen; serges from Chalons, Rheims, Amiens, and various towns in Picardy; beaver and felt hats from Paris, Rouen, and Lyons; paper of all sorts from Auvergne, Poitou, Limousin, Champagne, and Normandy; ironmongery and cutlery from Forrests, Auvergne; linen cloth from Brittany and Normandy; salt from Rochelle and Oleron, Isle of Rhé; wines from Gascony, Nantes, and Bordeaux; and feathers, fans, girdles, pins, needles, combs, soap, aquavitæ, vinegar, and various sorts of household stuffs, from different parts of France.†

---

* JOSHUA GEE—*The Trade and Navigation of Great Britain considered.*
† The following are the items as given by Mr. Fortrey in his *Account of Trade between Great Britain, France, Spain,* etc., 1663:
Velvets, satins, etc., made at Lyons............................. £150,000
Silks, taffetas, and other articles made at Tours.................. 300,000

So soon as the French artisans settled in London, they proceeded to establish and carry on the manufactures which they had practiced abroad, and a large portion of the stream of gold which before had flowed into France, now flowed into England. They introduced all the manufactures connected with the fashions, so that English customers became supplied with French-made articles without requiring to send abroad money to buy them; while the refugees obtained a ready sale for all the goods they could make, at remunerative prices. "Nay," says a writer of the time, "the English have now so great an esteem for the workmanship of the French refugees, that hardly any thing vends without a Gallic name."* The French beavers, which had before been imported from Caudebec in France, were now made in the borough of Southwark and at Wandsworth, where several hat-makers began their operations on a considerable scale.†

Silk ribbons, galloons, laces, and buttons, made at Paris, Rouen, etc. £150,000
Serges, made at Chalons, Rheims, Amiens, Crèvecœur, and towns in Picardy.. 150,000
Beaver and felt hats, made at Paris, Rouen, and Lyons............. 120,000
Feathers, fans, girdles, etc... 150,000
Pins, needles, tortoise-shell combs, etc................................. 20,000
Gloves, made at Paris, Rouen, etc....................................... 10,000
Paper of all sorts, made in Auvergne, Poitou, Limousin, Champagne, and Normandy... 100,000
Ironmongery wares, made in Forrests, Auvergne, etc............... 40,000
Linen cloth, made in Brittany and Normandy......................... 400,000
Household stuff, such as beds, mattresses, coverlets, hangings, fringes, etc.. 100,000
Wines from Gascony, Nantes, Bordeaux, etc.......................... 600,000
Aquavitæ, vinegar, etc.. 100,000
Soap, honey, almonds, olives, prunes, etc............................. 160,000
500 or 600 vessels of salt from Rochelle, Oleron, Isle of Rhé, etc.

* *History of the Trade in England*: London, 1702.

† Hat-making was one of the most important manufactures taken into England by the refugees. In France it had been almost entirely in the hands of the Protestants. They alone possessed the secret of the liquid composition which serves to prepare rabbit, hare, and beaver skins, and they alone supplied the trade with fine Caudebec hats in such demand in England and Holland. After the Revocation most of them went to London, taking with them the secret of their art, which was lost to France for more than forty years. It was not until the middle of the eighteenth century that a French hatter named Mathieu, after having long worked in London, stole the secret the refugees had carried away, took it back to his country, generously communicated it to the Paris hatters, and founded a large manufactory in the Faubourg St.

R

Others introduced the manufacture of buttons of wool, silk, and metal, which before had been made almost exclusively in France. The printing of calicoes was introduced by a refugee, who established a manufactory for the purpose near Richmond. Other print-works were started at Bromley in Essex, from whence the manufacture was afterward removed into Lancashire. A French refugee named Passavant purchased the tapestry manufactory at Fulham, originally established by the Walloons, which had greatly fallen into decay. His first attempts at reviving the manufacture not proving successful, he removed the works to Exeter, and eventually made them prosper with the assistance of some workmen whom he obtained from the Gobelins at Paris.

But the most important branch of manufacture to which the refugees devoted themselves, and in which they achieved both fame and wealth, was the silk manufacture in all its branches. The silk fabrics of France—its satins, its brocades, velvets, padausoys, figured and plain — were celebrated throughout the world, and were eagerly purchased. As much as 200,000 livres worth of black lustrings were bought by the English annually, made expressly for their market, and known as "English taffeties." Shortly after the Revocation, not only was the whole of this fabric made in England, but large quantities were manufactured for exportation abroad.

The English government had long envied France her possession of the silk manufacture, which gave employment to a large number of her people, and was a great source of wealth to the country. An attempt was made in the reign of Elizabeth to introduce the manufacture in England, and it was repeated in the reign of James I. The king issued instructions to the deputy lieutenants of counties that they should require the landowners to purchase and plant mulberry-trees

Antoine. Before this lucky larceny, the French nobility, and all persons making pretensions to elegance in dress, wore none but English hats; and the Roman cardinals themselves got their hats from the celebrated manufactory at Wandsworth established by the refugees.—WEISS, p. 260.

for the feeding of silkworms; and he granted a license for twenty-one years to one William Stallenge to print a book of instructions for their guidance.* It appears that M. de Verton, Sieur de la Forest, commissioned by the king, traveled all over the midland and eastern counties selling mulberry-trees at a low fixed price (6s. the hundred), and giving directions as to their cultivation.† The corporation of the city of London also encouraged the first attempts at introducing the manufacture; and we find from their records that in 1609 they admitted to the freedom of the city one Robert Therie or Thierry, on account of his skill and invention, and as "being the first in England who hath made stuffs of silke, the which was made by the silk-worms nourished here in England."‡ One M. Brumelach was also invited over from France, with sundry silk-throwsters, weavers, and dyers, and thus a beginning was made in the manufacture; but it was not until the influx of the Protestant refugees after the Revocation that the manufacture took root and began to flourish.

The workmen of Tours and Lyons brought with them the arts which had raised the manufactures of France to such a height of prosperity. They erected their looms in Spitalfields, and there practiced their improved modes of weaving

---

* *Domestic Papers*, James I., January 5, 1607. The book was entitled *Instructions for the increasing of mulberrie-trees and the breeding of silkewormes for the making of silk in this kingdom, whereunto is annexed his Majesty's letter to the Lord Lieutenants*, etc. : 4to, London, 1609.

† Doubts seem to have been entertained as to the ability of the Sieur de la Forest, on which he addressed the Earl of Salisbury in a "remonstrance against a suspicion of his ability to fulfill his contract for the supply of mulberry-trees." He stated that he "had in France a nursery of 500,000 trees," and detailed the pains he had taken in sending for them and inducing the people to buy, by showing them spinners of silk at work. *Domestic Papers*, James I., 1609, 110. The remonstrance is in French.

‡ The corporation were not alike liberal in other cases; for we find them, in the same year in which they admitted Thierry a freeman and citizen, expelling one John Cassell "for using the trade or art of twisting worsted yarn in Bartholomew Within, in the liberties of the city, he being no freeman, but a stranger born, contrary to the custom of the city. It is therefore thought fit, and so ordered by this court, that Mr. Chamberlain shall forthwith shut up the shop-windows of the said John Cassell's shop, and shall remove within a month all his goods, furniture, etc., to other places, which he promised to do."—*Corporation Records*, 1609.

—turning out large quantities of lustrings, velvets, and mingled stuffs of silk and wool, of such excellence as to insure for them every where a ready sale. Weiss says that the figured silks which proceeded from the London manufactories were due almost exclusively to the skill and industry of three refugees — Lanson, Mariscot, and Monceaux. The artist who supplied the designs was another refugee named Beaudoin. A common workman named Mongeorge brought them the secret, recently discovered at Lyons, of giving lustre to silk taffeta; and Spitalfields thenceforward enjoyed a large share of the trade for which Lyons had been so famous.*

To protect the English manufactures, the import duties on French silks were at first trebled. In 1692, five years after the Revocation, the manufacturers of lustrings and alamode silks were incorporated by charter under the name of the Royal Lustring Company; shortly after which, they obtained from Parliament an act entirely prohibiting the importation of foreign goods of like sorts. Strange to say, one of the grounds on which they claimed this degree of protection was, that the manufacture of these articles in England had now reached a greater degree of perfection than was attained by foreigners—a reason which ought to have rendered them independent of all legislative interference in their favor. Certain it is, however, that by the end of the century the French manufacturers in England were not only able to supply the whole of the English demand, but to export considerable quantities of their goods to those countries which France had formerly supplied.

One of the most remunerative branches of business was the manufacture of silk stockings†, in which the English

* WEISS, p. 253.
† The first pair of silk stockings brought into England from Spain was presented to Henry VIII., who highly prized them. In the third year of Elizabeth's reign, her tiring-woman, Mrs. Montague, presented her with a pair of black silk stockings as a New Year's gift; whereupon her majesty asked if she could have any more, in which case she would wear no more cloth stockings. Silk stockings were equally rare things in the royal court of Scotland,

shared with the French artisans. This trade was due to the invention of the stocking-frame by William Lee, M.A., about the year 1600. Not being able to find any encouragement for his invention in England, he went over to Rouen in 1605, on the invitation of the French minister Sully, to instruct the French operatives in the construction and working of the machine. Nine of the frames were in full work, and Lee enjoyed the prospect of honor and competency, when, unhappily for him, his protector, Henry IV., was assassinated by the fanatic Ravaillac. The patronage which had been extended to him was at once withdrawn, on which Lee proceeded to Paris to press his claims upon the government. But he had the misfortune to be a foreigner, and, worse than all, a Protestant; so his claims were disregarded, and he shortly after died at Paris in extreme distress.

Two of Lee's machines were left at Rouen; the rest were brought over to England; and in course of time considerable improvements were made in the invention. The stocking-trade became so considerable a branch of business, that in 1654 we find the framework-knitters petitioning Oliver Cromwell to grant them a charter of incorporation. The memorialists set forth the great utility of the knitting-frame, its exquisite workmanship, and the value of the materials it turned out. "Not only," say they, "is it able to serve your highness's dominions with the commodities it mercantably works, but also the neighboring countries round about, where it has gained so good repute that the vent thereof is now more foreign than domestic, and has drawn covetous eyes upon it, to undermine it here, and to transport it beyond the seas."* The

for it appears that before James VI. received the embassadors sent to congratulate him on his accession to the English throne, he requested one of the lords of his court to lend him his pair of silken hose, that he "might not appear as a scrub before strangers."

* The memorialists refer to the two stocking-frames of Lee's construction left at Rouen, with their workmen, and say—"Of the two which remained in France, only one is yet surviving; but so far short of the perfection of his trade (as it is used here), that of him, or what can be done by him, or his means, these petitioners are in no apprehension of fear." The petitioners go on to ascribe to Divine Providence the good fortune that has hitherto attend-

Protector did not grant the prayer of the framework-knitters that he would confer on them the monopoly of manufacture which they sought; accordingly, when the French refugees settled among us, they were as free to make use of Lee's invention as the English themselves were. Hence the manufacture of silk hosiery by the stocking-frame shortly became a leading branch of trade in Spitalfields, and English hose were in demand all over Europe. Keysler, the traveler, writing as late as 1730, remarks that "at Naples, when a tradesman would highly recommend his silk stockings, he invariably protests that they are right English."

In a petition presented to Parliament by the Weavers' Company in 1713, it was stated that, owing to the encouragement afforded by the crown and by divers acts of the Legislature, the silk manufacture at that time was twenty times greater in amount than it had been in 1664; that all sorts of black and colored silks, gold and silver stuffs, and ribbons, were made here as good as those of French fabric; that black silk for hoods and scarfs, which, twenty-five years before, was all imported, was now made here to the annual value of £300,000, whereby a great increase had been occasioned in the exportation of woolen and other manufactured goods to Turkey and Italy, whence the raw silk was imported. Such, among others, were the effects of the settlement in London of the French refugee artisans.

Although the manufacture of glass had been introduced into England before the arrival of the French refugees, it made comparatively small progress until they took it in hand. The first glass-work in London was begun by a Venetian, in Crutched Friars Hall, in 1564, after which two Flem-

---

ed their labors, and congratulate themselves on having concealed their mystery from "the nimble spirits of the French, the fertile wits of the Italians, and the industrious inclination of the Dutch." Their commercial success, they add, "has vindicated our nation against that old proverbial expression, *The stranger buys of the Englishman the case of the Fox for a groat, and sells him the tail again for a shilling;* for we may now invert the saying, and retort that *the Englishman buys silk of the stranger for twenty marks, and sells him the same again for one hundred pounds.*"

ings, driven over by the persecutions in the Low Countries, started a second glass-work at Greenwich in 1567;* but Mr. Pellatt, in his lecture on the manufacture of glass, delivered before the Royal Institution, attributes the establishment of the manufacture to the French Protestant refugees, most of the technical terms still used in glass-making being derived from the French.† Thus the "found" is the melting of the materials into glass, from the French word *fondre*. The "siege" is the place or seat in which the crucible stands. The "kinney" is the corner of the furnace, probably from *coin* or *cheminée*. The "journey," denoting the time of making glass from the beginning of the "found," is obviously from *journée*. The "foushart," or fork used to move the sheet of glass into the annealing-kiln, is from *fourchette*. The "marmre" is the slab, formerly of marble, but now of iron, on which the ball of hot glass is rolled. And so on with "cullet" (*coulé* — glass run off, or broken glass), "pontil" (*pointèe*), and other words obviously of French and Flemish origin.

The first French glass-makers who came into England began their operations in Savoy House in the Strand; but they

---

* See Appendix I.—*Immigration of Flemish and other foreign artisans into England.*

† It appears, from documents in the State Paper Office (*Dom. Eliz.*, 9th of August, 1567), that two refugees, Antoine Bequer and Jean Quarré, petitioned the queen for permission to establish works for the making of all such sort of table-glass as was then brought into England "out of Burgundy, Lorrayne, and France." They offered to pay the same duties as were levied on foreign glass, and to bind themselves "to retain Englishmen in their service, and teach them the art of making glass," provided only they were not required to retain more than were found needful for the purpose of the manufacture. The privilege sought was granted by the queen for twenty-one years; and the two first furnaces were required to be erected and set to work within a year from the date of the grant. Bequer and Quarré appear to have commenced their operations within the stipulated period, for we find that on the 6th of September, 1568, they memorialized the queen for permission to cut wood to make charcoal in Windsor Great Park, and to convey it from thence to their glass factory. This application, most probably, was unsuccessful, for nearly six years later the Bishop of Chichester incidentally mentions, in one of his letters (25th of April, 1574) to the Lord Treasurer Burghley, that there was " a combination to rob the French glass-makers;" and it would seem that they had established themselves in Sussex, which in the 16th century was one of the most wooded counties in England.

afterward removed into Sussex, because of the greater conveniency of finding fuel; and the art made such progress there, and in other parts of England, that Evelyn, in his Diary, spoke of the glass blown in this country as being "of finer metal than that of Murano at Venice." The Parisian glass-makers were especially celebrated for the skill with which they cast large plates for mirrors; and, shortly after the Revocation, when a large number of these valuable workmen took refuge in England, a branch of that manufacture was established by Abraham Thevenart, which proved highly successful. Other works were started for the making of crystal, in which the French greatly excelled; and before long, not only were they able to supply the home market, but to export large quantities of glass wares of various sorts to Holland and other European countries.

For the improvement of the English paper manufacture, also, we are largely indebted to the refugees—to the Protestant employers and artisans who swarmed over to England from the paper-mills of Angoumois. Before the Revocation, the paper made in this country was of the common "whitey-brown" sort—coarse and inelegant. All the best sorts were imported from abroad, mostly from France. But shortly after the Revocation the import of paper ceased, and the refugees were able to supply us with as good an article as could be bought elsewhere. The first manufactory for fine paper was established by the refugees in London in 1685; but other mills were shortly after started by them in Kent—at Maidstone and along the Darent—as well as in other parts of England.* That the leading workmen employed in the first fine

* The Patent Office records clearly show the activity of the French exiles in the province of invention, in the numerous patents taken out by them for printing, spinning, weaving, paper-making, and other arts. Such names as Blondeau, Dupin, De Cardonels, Le Blon, Ducleu, Pousset, Gastineau, Couran, Paul, etc., are found constantly recurring in the lists of patentees for many years subsequent to the Revocation. In 1686 we find M. Dupin, A. de Cardonels, C. R. M. de Crouchy, J. de May, and R. Shales taking out a patent for making writing and printing paper, having "lately brought out of France excellent workmen, and already set up several new-invented mills and engines for making thereof, not heretofore used in England."—[See *Abridgment of Specifications relating to Printing*, p. 82.]

paper-mills were French and Flemish is shown by the distinctive terms of the trade still in use. Thus, in Kent, the man who lays the sheets on the felts is the *coucher;* the fateman, or vatman, is the Flemish *fassman;* and the room where the finishing operations are performed is still called the *salle.*

One of the most distinguished of the refugee paper manufacturers was Henry de Portal. The Portals were an ancient and noble family in the south of France, of Albigeois descent, who stood firm by the faith of their fathers, and several of them suffered death rather than prove recreant to it. Toulouse was for many generations the home of the Portals, where they held and exercised the highest local authority. Several of them in succession were elected "Capitoul," a position of great dignity and power in that city. When the persecution of the Albigeois set in, the De Portals put themselves at their head; but they were unable to make head against the tremendous power of the Inquisition, and they fled from Toulouse in different directions—some to Nismes, and others into the neighborhood of Bordeaux. Some of them perished in the massacres which occurred throughout France subsequent to the night of the Saint Bartholomew at Paris; and they continued to suffer during the long century that ended in the Revocation, yet still they remained constant to their faith.

When the reign of terror under Louis XIV. began in the south of France, Louis de Portal was residing at his Château de la Portalerie, seven leagues from Bordeaux. To escape the horrors of the dragonnades, he set out with his wife and five children to take refuge on his estate in the Cevennes. The dragoons pursued the family to their retreat, overtook them, cut down the father and mother and one of the children, and burnt to the ground the house in which they had taken refuge. The remaining four children had concealed themselves in an oven outside the building, and were thus saved.

The four orphans—three boys and a girl—immediately determined to make for the coast and escape from France by sea. After a long and perilous journey on foot, exhausted by fatigue and wanting food, they at length reached Montauban, where little Pierre, the youngest, fell down fainting with hunger at the door of a baker's shop. The humane baker took up the child, carried him into the house, and fed and cherished him. The other three—Henry, William, and Mary de Portal—though grieving to leave their brother behind them, again set out on foot, and pressed forward to Bordeaux.

There they were so fortunate as to secure a passage by a merchant vessel, on board of which they were shipped concealed in barrels. They were among the last of the refugees who escaped previous to the issue of the infamous order to fumigate all departing vessels, so as to stifle any Protestant fugitives who might be concealed among the cargo. The youthful refugees reached Holland, where they found friends and foster parents, and were shortly in a position to assert the dignity of their birth. Miss Portal succeeded in obtaining a situation as governess in the family of the Countess of Finkenstein, and afterward married M. Lenornant, a refugee settled at Amsterdam; while Henry and William followed the fortunes of the Prince of Orange, accompanying him into England, and establishing the family of De Portal in this country.*

Henry, the elder brother, having learned the art of paper-making, started a mill of his own at Laverstoke, on the Itchin, near Whitchurch in Hampshire, where he achieved high reputation as a paper manufacturer. He carried on his business with great spirit, gathering round him the best French and Dutch workmen; and he shortly brought his work to so high a degree of perfection that the Bank of England gave him the privilege, which a descendant of the family still enjoys, of supplying them with the paper for bank-notes.†

* William entered the Church late in life. He was nominated tutor to Prince George, afterward George III., and held the livings of Clowne in Derbyshire, and Farnbridge in Essex. Abraham Portal, whose poetic works were published in 1781, was his grandson.

† William Cobbett, writing in 1825, says, "From this to Whitchurch is not more than about four miles, and we soon reached it, because here you begin to descend into the vale in which this little town lies, and through which there

Henry de Portal had resolved to rebuild the fortunes of his house, though on English ground, and nobly he did it by his skill, his integrity, and his industry. The De Portals of Freefolk Priors re-established themselves among the aristocratic order to which they originally belonged, and sons and daughters of the family formed alliances with some of the noblest families in England. The youngest brother, Pierre de Portal, who had been left fainting at the door of the baker at Montauban, was brought up to manhood by the baker, held to his Protestantism, and eventually set up as a cloth manufacturer in France. He prospered, married, and his sons grew up around him, one of them eventually becoming Lord of Pénardières. His grandson Alberèdes, also faithful to the creed of his fathers, rose to high office, having been appointed minister of marine and the colonies, councilor of state, and a peer of France, at the restoration of the Bourbons. The present baron, Pierre Paul Frederick de Portal, maintains the ancient reputation of the family; and to his highly interesting work, entitled *Les Descendants des Albigeois et des Huguenots, ou Mémoires de la Famille de Portal* (Paris, 1860), we are mainly indebted for the above facts relating to the family.

Various other branches of manufacture were either established or greatly improved by the refugees. At Canterbury they swelled the ranks of the silk manufacturers, so much so that in 1694 they possessed 1000 looms, giving employment

runs that stream which turns the mill of Squire Portal, and which mill makes the Bank of England note-paper. Talk of the Thames and the Hudson, with their forests of masts; talk of the Nile and the Delaware bearing the food of millions on their bosoms; talk of the Rio de la Plata and the other rivers, their beds pebbled with silver, and gold, and diamonds! What, as to their effect on the condition of mankind—as to the virtues, the vices, the enjoyments, and the sufferings of men—what are all these rivers put together compared with the river at Whitchurch, which a man of threescore may jump across dry-shod, which moistens a quarter of a mile wide of poor, rushy meadow . . . . . and which is, to look at it, of far less importance than any gutter in the Wen! Yet this river, by merely turning a wheel—which wheel sets some rag-tearers, and grinders, and washers, and recompressors in motion—has produced a greater effect on the condition of men than has been produced by all the other rivers, all the seas, all the mines, and all the continents in the world."—*Rural Rides*, p. 308–9.

to nearly 3000 workmen—though, for the convenience of the trade, the greater number of them subsequently removed to Spitalfields. Many of the immigrants also found their way to Norwich, where they carried on with great success the manufacture of lustrings, brocades, paduasoys, tabinets, and velvets, while others carried on the making of cutlery, clocks, and watches. The fifty years that followed the settlement of the French refugees in Norwich was the most prosperous period known in the history of that city. Another body of refugees settled at Ipswich in 1681, where they began the manufacture of fine linen, before then imported from France. The elders and deacons of the French church in Threadneedle Street raised the necessary funds for their support until they could maintain themselves by their industry. They were organized and superintended by a refugee from Paris named Bonhomme,* one of the most skilled manufacturers in France. To the manufacture of linen, one of sail-cloth was added, and England was shortly enabled entirely to dispense with any farther supply of the foreign-made article.

The lace manufacture, introduced originally by the Walloon refugees, was also greatly increased and improved by the influx of Huguenot lace-makers, principally from Burgundy and Normandy. Some established themselves in London, and others betook themselves to the adjoining counties, settling at Buckingham, Newport-Pagnell, and Stony Stratford, from whence the manufacture extended into Oxford, Northampton, Cambridge, and the adjoining counties.†

Some of the exiles went as far north as Scotland, and set-

---

* In 1681, Savil wrote from Paris to Jenkins, then Secretary of State, to announce the approaching departure of Bonhomme and all his family, adding, "This man will be able to give you some lights into the method of bringing the manufacture of sail-cloth in England."

† Speaking of Bedfordshire, De Foe, in his *Tour through the whole Island of Great Britain*, writes, "Through the whole south part of this country, as far as the borders of Buckinghamshire and Hertfordshire, the people are taken up with the manufacture of bone-lace, in which they are wonderfully exercised and improved within these few years past," most probably in consequence of the arrival of the French settlers after the Revocation of the Edict of Nantes.—MRS. PALLISER—*History of Lace*, p. 353.

tled there. Thus a colony of weavers from Picardy, in France, began the manufacture of linen in a suburb of Edinburg near the head of Leith Walk, long after known as "Little Picardy"—the name still surviving in Picardy Place.* Others of them built a silk factory, and laid out a mulberry plantation on the slope of Moultrie Hill, then an open common. The refugees were sufficiently numerous in Edinburg to form a church, of which the Rev. Mr. Dupont was minister; and William III., in 1693, granted to the city a duty of two pennies on each pint of ale, out of which 2000 merks were to be paid yearly toward the maintenance of the ministers of the French congregation. At Glasgow, one of the French refugees succeeded in establishing a paper-mill, the first in that part of Scotland. The Huguenot who erected it escaped from France accompanied only by his little daughter. For some time after his arrival in Glasgow he maintained himself by picking up rags in the streets. But, by dint of thrift and diligence, he eventually contrived to accumulate means sufficient to enable him to start his paper-mill, and thus to lay the foundation of an important branch of Scottish industry.

In short, there was scarcely a branch of trade in Great Britain but at once felt the beneficial effects of the large influx of experienced workmen from France. Besides improving those manufactures which had already been established, they introduced many entirely new branches of industry; and by their skill and intelligence, and their laboriousness, they richly repaid England for the hospitality and the asylum which had been so generously extended to them in their time of need.

* It has been surmised that Burdie House—a corruption of Bordeaux House, near Edinburg, was so called because inhabited by another body of French refugees at the same period. But this is a mistake: the place having been so called by the Frenchman who built the original house—most probably one of the followers of Mary Stuart, on her coming over to Scotland to take possession of the Scottish throne. The village of "Little France," near Craigmillar Castle, the residence of Queen Mary, was so called from being the quarters of her French guards.

CHAPTER XV.
THE HUGUENOT CHURCHES IN ENGLAND.

THE vast number of French Protestants who fled into England on the Revocation of the Edict of Nantes led to a large increase in the number of French churches. This was especially the case in London, which was the principal seat of the immigration. It may serve to give the reader an idea of the large admixture of Huguenot blood in the London population when we state that about the beginning of last century, at which time the population of the metropolis was not one fourth of what it is now, there were no fewer than thirty-five French churches in London and the suburbs.* Of these, eleven were in Spitalfields, showing the preponderance of the French settlers in that quarter.

The French church in Threadneedle Street, the oldest in London, was in a manner the cathedral church of the Huguenots. Thither the refugees usually repaired on their arrival in London, and such of them as had temporarily abjured their faith before flying, to avoid the penalty of death or condemnation to the galleys, made acknowledgment of their repentance, and were again received into membership. During the years immediately following the Revocation, the consistory of the French Church met at least once in every week in Threadneedle Street chapel for the purpose of receiving such acknowledgments or "reconnaissances." The ministers heard the narrative of the trials of the refugees, examined their testimony, and, when judged worthy, received them into communion. At the sitting of the 5th of March, 1686, fifty fugitives from various provinces of France abjured the Roman Catholic religion, to which they had pretended to be convert-

* Mr. Burn, in his *History of the Foreign Protestant Refugees*, gives the names of nearly forty French churches in London; but several of these were old churches merely translated or rebuilt with new names.

ed; and at one of the sittings in May, 1687, not fewer than 497 members were again received into the church which they had pretended to abandon.*

While the church in Threadneedle Street was thus resorted to by the Huguenot Calvinists, the French Episcopal church in the Savoy, opened about the year 1641, was similarly resorted to by the foreign Protestants of the Lutheran persuasion. This was the fashionable French church of the West End, and was resorted to by many of the nobility, who were attracted by the eloquence of the preachers who usually ministered there,† among whom we recognize the great names of Durrel, Severin, Abbadie, Saurin, Dubourdieu, Majendie, and Durand. There were also the following French churches in the western parts of London: the chapel of Marylebone, founded about the year 1656; the chapel, in Somerset House, originally granted by Charles I. to his queen Henrietta as a Roman Catholic place of worship, but which was afterward appropriated by Parliament, in 1653, for the use of the French Protestants; Castle Street Chapel, in Leicester Square, erected at the expense of the government in 1672 as a place of worship for the refugees; the Little Savoy Chapel in the Strand, granted for the same purpose in 1675; and Hungerford Chapel in Hungerford Market, which was opened as a French church in 1687.

After the Revolution of 1688, a considerable addition was made to the French churches at the West End. Thus three new congregations were formed in the year 1689—those of La Patente, in Soho, first opened in Berwick Street, from whence it was afterward removed to Little Chapel Street, Wardour Street; Glass House Chapel, Golden Square, from

* We find the following entry relating to the same subject in the Register of Glass House Street Chapel: "Le Dimanche, 13 May, 1688, Elizabeth Cautin de St. Martin de Retz, Susanne Cellier et Marie Cellier sa Souer de la Rochelle ont fait recognoissance publique au presche du Matin, l'une pour avoir esté au Sermon feignant d'estre de l'Eglise Romaine, les autres deux por avoir signé leur Abjuration. Mon Coutet les a receues."

† Evelyn mentions his attending it in 1649, the following entry appearing in his journal of that year: "In the afternoon I went to the French church in the Savoy, where I heard M. d'Espagne catechize."

whence it was afterward removed to Leicester Fields; and La Quarré (Episcopal) Chapel, originally of Berwick Street, and afterward of Little Dean Street, Westminster.

Another important French church at the West End was that of Swallow Street, Piccadilly.* This congregation had originally worshiped in the French embassador's chapel in Monmouth House, Soho Square, from whence they removed to Swallow Street in 1690. From the records of the church, which are preserved at Somerset House, it would appear that Swallow Street was also in the west what Threadneedle Street Church was in the east of London—the place first resorted to by the refugee Protestants to make acknowledgment of their backslidings, and claim readmission to church membership. Hence the numerous "reconnaissances" found recorded in the Swallow Street register. The following is a specimen: " On Friday, the first day of the year 1692, Claude Richier, a refugee from Montpellier, has given testimony in presence of this church of his repentance at having succumbed to the pressure of persecution in abjuring our holy religion, which he has confirmed by signing this present record." There are also entries of conversions, of which the following is an instance: " On Sunday, the fifth day of May, the day of Pentecoste, Susan Auvray, a native of Paris, has made public abjuration in this church of the errors and superstitions of Papism, after having given proofs of solid instruction, of her piety and good morals, which she has confirmed by signing this record."†

About the year 1700, there was another large increase in the number of French churches in London, six more being added to those already specified, namely, L'Eglise du Tabernacle, afterward removed to Leicester Fields Chapel; the French Chapel Royal, St. James's; Les Grecs, in Hog Lane,‡

---

* The chapel was sold to Dr. James Anderson in 1710, and is now used as a Scotch church.
† See Appendix, *Registers of French Churches in England.*
‡ Hogarth has given a representation of the old chapel in Hog Lane, in his picture of "Noon," and the figure coming out of the chapel is said to have

now Crown Street, Soho; Spring Gardens Chapel, or the Little Savoy; La Charenton, in Grafton Street, Newport Market; and La Tremblade, or West Street Chapel, St. Giles's. About the same date, additional church accommodation was provided for the refugees in the city, one chapel having been opened in Blackfriars, and another in St. Martin's Lane, of which the celebrated Dr. Allix was for some time pastor. With the latter chapel, known as the church of St. Martin Ongars, that of Threadneedle Street was eventually united.

But the principal increase in the French churches about this time was in the eastern parts of London, where the refugees of the manufacturing class had for the most part settled. The large influx of foreign Protestants is strikingly shown by the amount of new chapels required for their accommodation. Thus, in Spitalfields and the adjoining districts, we find the following: L'Eglise de St. Jean, Swan Fields, Shoreditch (1687); La Nouvelle Patente, Crispin Street, Spitalfields (1689); L'Eglise de l'Artillerie, Artillery Street, Bishopsgate (1691);* L'Eglise de Crispin Street, Spitalfields (1693); Petticoat Lane Chapel, Spitalfields (1694); L'Eglise de Perle Street, Spitalfields (1697), afterward incorporated with Crispin Street Chapel; the French Church of Wapping (1700); L'Eglise de Bell Lane, Spitalfields (1700); L'Eglise de Wheler Street, Spitalfields (1703), afterward incorporated with La Nouvelle Patente; L'Eglise de Swan Fields, Slaughter Street, Shoreditch (1721); L'Eglise de l'Hôpital, afterward L'Eglise Neuve, Church Street, Spitalfields (1742). Here we have no

---

been a very good likeness of the Rev. Thomas Hervé, who was minister there from about 1727 to 1731. This chapel, as the representative of the Savoy, has been considered as the mother-church of the French congregations at the West End of London. The congregations of the Savoy, Les Grecs, and Spring Gardens were united—the two former about 1721, and the latter subsequently. The congregation of La Patente en Soho was also united at a later period.—BURN—*History of Foreign Protestant Refugees*, 114.

* This church boasted of some of the most eloquent French preachers in the metropolis. Among these may be mentioned Cæsar Pegorier, the first minister of the congregation; and among his successors were Daniel Chamier, Pierre Rival, Joseph de la Mothe, Ezekiel Barbauld, Jacob Bourdillon, all men of high repute in their time.

fewer than eleven French churches opened east of Bishopsgate Street, providing accommodation for a very large number of worshipers. The church last named, L'Eglise Neuve, was probably the largest of the French places of worship in London, being capable of accommodating about 1500 persons. It is now used as a chapel by the Wesleyan Methodists, while the adjoining church of the Artillery is used as a poor Jews' synagogue.

In addition to the French churches in the city, at the West End, and in the Spitalfields district, there were several thriving congregations in the suburban districts of London in which the refugees had settled. One of the oldest of these was that of Wandsworth, where a colony of Protestant Walloons settled about the year 1570. Having formed themselves into a congregation, they erected a chapel for worship, which is still standing, nearly opposite the parish church. The building bears this inscription on its front: "Erected 1573—enlarged 1685—repaired 1809, 1831." Like the other refugee churches, it has ceased to retain its distinctive character, being now used as a Congregational chapel. The French there had also a special burying-ground, situated at the London entrance to Wandsworth, in which several distinguished refugees have been interred—among others, David Montolieu, Baron de St. Hyppolite, in 1761, aged ninety-three.

Several other French churches were established in the suburbs after the Revocation. At Chelsea the refugees had two chapels—one in Cook's Grounds (now used by the Congregationalists), and another in Little Chelsea. There were French churches also at Hammersmith, at Hoxton,* at Bow, and at Greenwich. The last named was erected through the influence of the Marquis de Ruvigny, who formed the centre of a select circle of refugee Protestants, who long continued to live in the neighborhood. Before their little church was

---

* Of this church Jacob Bourdillon was the last pastor. Among the names appearing in the Register are those of Romilly, Cossart, Faure, Durand, Hankey, Vidal, and Fargues.

ready for use, the refugees were allowed the use of the parish church at the conclusion of the forenoon service on Sundays. Evelyn, in his Diary, makes mention of his attending the French service there in 1687, as well as the sermon which followed, in which he says, "The preacher pathetically exhorted to patience, constancy, and reliance on God, amidst all their sufferings." The French church, which was afterward erected in London Street, not far from the parish church, is now used as a Baptist chapel.

The other French chapels throughout the kingdom, like those of London, received a large accession of members after the Revocation of the Edict of Nantes, and in many cases became too small for their accommodation. Hence a second French church was opened at Canterbury in a place called "The Malthouse,"* situated within the cathedral precincts. It consisted at first of about 300 persons; but the Canterbury silk trade having become removed to Spitalfields, the greater number of the French weavers followed it thither, on which the Malthouse Chapel rapidly fell off, and at length became extinct about the middle of last century.

The old French church of "God's House" at Southampton also received a considerable accession of members, chiefly fugitives from the provinces of the opposite sea-board. The original Walloon element had by this time almost entirely disappeared, the immigrants of a century before having become gradually absorbed into the native population. Hence nearly all the entries in the registers of the church subsequent to the year 1685 describe the members as "François refugiez," some being from "Basse Normandie," others from "Haute Languedoc," but the greater number from the province of Poitou.

Numerous refugee military officers, retired from active

* See Appendix—*Records of Huguenot Churches in England*. The Rev. M. Charpentier was one of the early ministers of the Malthouse Chapel. In a petition to the Archbishop of Canterbury he states that his family had suffered very much for the Protestant religion, especially his father, who was put to death by the dragoons, and died a martyr in the year 1683.—BURN, p. 53.

service, seem to have settled in the neighborhood of Southampton about the beginning of last century. Henry de Ruvigny, the venerable Earl of Galway, then lived at Rookley, and formed the centre of a distinguished circle of refugee gentry. The Baron de Huningue also lived in the town, and was so much respected and beloved that at his death he was honored with a public funeral.* We also find the families of the De Chavernays and De Cosnes settled in the place. The register of "God's House" contains frequent entries relating to officers in "Colonel Mordant's regiment." On one occasion we find Brigadier Mordant standing sponsor for the twin sons of Major François du Chesne de Ruffanes, major of infantry; and on another, the Earl of Galway standing sponsor for the infant son of Pierre de Cosne, a refugee gentleman of La Beauce. From the circumstance of Gerard de Vaux, the owner of a paper-mill in South Stoneham, being a member of the congregation, we also infer that several of the settlers in the neighborhood of Southampton were engaged in that branch of manufacture.

Among the new French churches formed in places where before there had been none, and which mark the new settlements made by the fresh influx of refugees, may be mentioned those of Bristol, Exeter, Plymouth, Stonehouse, Dartmouth, Barnstaple, and Thorpe-le-Soken in Essex.

The French Episcopal Church at Bristol seems at one time to have been of considerable importance. It was instituted in 1687, and was first held in what is called the Mayor's Chapel of St. Mark the Gaunt; but in 1726 a chapel was built for the special use of the French congregation on the ground of Queen Elizabeth's Hospital for the Red Maids, situated in Orchard Street. The chapel, at its first opening, was so crowded with worshipers, that the aisles, as well as the altar-place, had to be fitted with benches for their accommodation. From the register of the church, it would appear that the refugees consisted principally of seafaring persons—

* See Appendix—*Records of Huguenot Churches in England.*

captains, masters, and sailors—chiefly from Nantes, Saintonge, Rochelle, and the Isle of Rhé.

The congregations formed at Plymouth and Stonehouse,* as well as Dartmouth, were in like manner for the most part composed of sailors, while those at Exeter, on the other hand, were principally trades-people and artisans employed in the tapestry manufacture carried on in that city. M. Majendie, grandfather of Dr. Majendie, bishop of Chester, was one of the ministers of the Exeter congregation; and Tom D'Urfey, the song-writer, was the son of one of the refugees settled in the place.

The settlement at Thorpe-le-Soken, in Essex, seems to have been a comparatively small one, consisting principally of refugee gentry and farmers; but they were in sufficient numbers to constitute a church, of which M. Severin, who afterward removed to Greenwich, was the first minister. The church was closed "for want of members" about the year 1726. As was the case at many other places, the Thorpe-le-Soken refugees gradually ceased to be French. Year by year the foreign churches declined, even though fed, from time to time, by fresh immigrations from abroad. It was in the very nature of things that the rising generation should fall away from them, and desire to become completely identified with the nation which had admitted them to citizenship. Hence the growing defections in country places, as well as in the towns and cities where the refugees had settled, and hence the growing complaints of the falling off in the numbers of their congregations which we find in the sermons and addresses of the refugee pastors.

About the middle of last century, the thirty-five French churches in London and its suburbs had become reduced to

---

* It seems to have been the practice of the minister of the Stonehouse church to require all who were present at baptisms, as well as marriages, to sign the register as witnesses; and as nearly all were able to sign their names —not more than about five in the hundred requiring to sign with a mark—it would thereby appear that the refugees were, as a whole, an educated class, so far, at least, as elementary instruction was concerned.

a comparatively small number, and the French pastors were full of lamentations as to the approaching decadence of those which remained. This feeling was given eloquent utterance to by the Rev. Jacob Bourdillon, minister of the Artillery Church in Spitalfields, on the occasion of the jubilee sermon which he preached there in 1782, in commemoration of his fifty years' pastorate.* He had been appointed minister of the congregation when it was a large and thriving one in 1731, and he now addressed but a feeble remnant of what it had been. The old members had died off; but their places had not been supplied by the young, who had gone in search of other pastures. But it was the same with all the other French churches. When he was appointed minister of "The Artillery," fifty years before, there had, he said, been twenty†

---

* During these fifty years M. Bourdillon had to lament the loss of many dear friends. No fewer than fifty-two pastors of London refugee churches had in that time ended their course, and of these, six had been his colleagues. The deceased ministers, whose names he gives, and the places in which they ministered, are as follows:

Chapel Royal, St. James's.—The Rev. Messieurs Menard, Aufrére, Serces, Rocheblave, De Missy, Barbauld, Muisson.

The Savoy.—Olivier, Du Cros, Durand, Deschamps.

The Walloon Church, Threadneedle Street.—Bertheau, Besombes, De St. Colombe, Bonyer, Barbauld, Convenant, La Douespe, Duboulai.

Leicester Fields, Artillery, and La Patente.—Blanc, Barbauld, Stehelin, Mieg, Barnauin.

La Tremblade.—Gillet, Yver.

Castle Street and La Quarré.—Laval, Bernard, Cantier, Robert, Coderc.

La Patente in Spitalfields.—Forestier, Manuel, Balquerie, Masson.

Brown's Lane.—Le Moyne.

St. John Street.—Vincent, Palairet, Beuzeville.

Wapping.—Gally de Gaujac, Le Beaupin, Say, Guyot, Prelleur.

Swan Fields.—Briel.

Pastors of other churches who had died in London — Forent, Majendie, Esternod, Montignac, Du Plessis, Villette, Duval.

Pastors of French churches in London who had died abroad—Des Mazures, Bobineau, Boullier, Eynard, Dagneau, Marcombe, Patron, Romilly.

† From this it would appear that a considerable number of the French churches which existed in London at the beginning of the century had either been closed or become united with others. The French churches closed between 1731 and 1782, when this sermon was preached, were these: The church of the Savoy (La Grande), Spring Gardens, Rider's Court, La Tremblade, Castle Street, Wheeler Street, Crispin Street, Swan Fields, and Marylebone. The churches which still survived were these: St. James's, Les Grecs, Leicester Fields, La Patente, Le Quarré, Threadneedle Street (Londres), L'Eglise Neuve, St. Martin, L'Artillerie, La Patente, and St. Jean

flourishing French churches in London, nine of which had since been altogether closed; while of the remaining eleven some were fast drawing to their end, others were scarcely able to exist even with extraneous help, while very few were in a position to support themselves.

The causes of this decadence of the churches of the refugees were not far to seek. The preacher found them in " the lack of zeal and faithfulness in the heads of families in encouraging their children to maintain them—churches which their ancestors had reared, a glorious monument of the generous sacrifice which they had made, of their country, their possessions, and their employments, in the sacred cause of conscience, for the open profession of the truth; whereas now," said he, " through the growing aversion of the young for the language of their fathers, from whom they seem almost ashamed to be descended—shall I say more?—because of inconstancy in the principles of the faith, which induces so many, by a sort of infatuation, to forsake the ancient assemblies in order to follow novelties unknown to our fathers, and listen to pretended teachers whose only gifts are rapture and babble, and whose sole inspiration consists in self-sufficiency and pride. Alas! what ravages have been made here, as elsewhere, during this jubilee of fifty years!"

But there were other causes besides these to account for the decadence of the refugee churches. Nature itself was working against them. Year by year the children of the refugees were becoming less and less French, and more and more English. They lived and worked among the English, and spoke their language. They intermarried with them; their children played together; and the idea of remaining foreigners in the country in which they had been born and bred became year by year more distasteful to them. They were not a " peculiar people," like the Jews; but Protestants, like the nation which had given them refuge, and into

Street. Of these only three remain in existence, in two of which the ritual of the Church of England has been adopted.

which they naturally desired to become wholly merged. Hence it was that by the end of the eighteenth century nearly all the French churches, as such, had disappeared, and the places of the French ministers became occupied in some cases by clergymen of the Established Church, and in others by ministers of the different dissenting persuasions.

The Church of the Artillery, in which the Rev. Mr. Bourdillon preached the above sermon so full of lamentations, is now occupied as a poor Jews' synagogue. L'Eglise Neuve is a chapel of the Wesleyan Methodists. L'Eglise de St. Jean, Swan Fields, Shoreditch, has become one of the ten new churches of St. Matthew, Bethnal Green. Swallow Street Chapel is used as a Scotch Church. Leicester Fields, now called Orange Street Chapel, is occupied by a congregation of Independents; whereas Castle Street Chapel, Leicester Square, was, until quite recently, used as a Court of Requests.

The French churches at Wandsworth and Chelsea are occupied by the Independents, and those at Greenwich and Plymouth by the Baptists. The Dutch church at Maidstone is used as a school, while the Walloon church of Yarmouth was first converted into a theatre, and has since done duty as a warehouse.

Among the charitable institutions founded by the refugees for the succor of their distressed fellow-countrymen in England, the most important was the French Hospital. This establishment owes its origin to M. De Gastigny, a French gentleman who had been master of the buckhounds to William III. in Holland, while Prince of Orange. At his death in 1708 he bequeathed a sum of £1000 toward founding a hospital in London for the relief of distressed French Protestants. The money was placed at interest for eight years, during which successive benefactions were added to the fund. In 1716, a piece of ground in Old Street, St. Luke's, was purchased of the Ironmongers' Company, and a lease was taken from the city of London of some adjoining land, forming altogether an area of about four acres, on which a building was erected and fitted up for the reception of eighty poor Protestants of the French nation. In 1718, George I. granted a charter of incorporation to the governor and directors of the hospital, under which the Earl of Galway was appointed the first governor. Shortly after, in November, 1718, the opening of the institution was celebrated by a solemn act of religion, and the chapel was consecrated amid a great concourse of refugees and their descendants, the Rev. Philip Menard, minister of the French chapel of St. James's, conducting the service on the occasion.

From that time the funds of the institution steadily increased. The French merchants of London, who had been prosperous in trade, liberally contributed toward its support, and legacies and donations multiplied. Lord Galway bequeathed £1000 to the hospital at his death in 1720; and in the following year, Baron Hervart de Huningue gave a donation of £4000. The corporation were placed in the possession of ample means; and they accordingly proceeded to erect additional buildings, in which they were enabled by the year 1760 to give an asylum to 234 poor people.*

Among the distinguished noblemen and gentlemen of French Protestant descent who have officiated as governors of the institution since the date of its foundation may be mentioned the Earl of Galway, the Baron de Huningue, Robethon (privy councilor), the Baron de la Court, Lord Ligonier, and several successive Earls of Radnor; while among the list of directors we recognize the names of Montolieu, Baron de St. Hippolite, Gambier, Bosanquet, Colombies, Majendie (D.D.), Colonel de Cosne, Dalbiac, Gaussen, Dargent, Blaquiere, General Ruffane, Lefevre, Boileau (Bart.), Colonel Vignolles, Romilly, Turquand, Pechel (Bart.), Travers, Lieut. General de Villetes, Major General Montresor, Devisme,

* The French hospital has recently been removed from its original site to Victoria Park, where a handsome building has been erected as a hospital for the accommodation of 40 men and 20 women, after the designs of Mr. Robert Lewis Roumieu, architect, one of the directors; Mr. Roumieu being himself descended from an illustrious Huguenot family—the Roumieus of Languedoc.

Chamier (M. P.), Major General Layard, Bouverie, Captain Dumaresq (R. N.), Duval, the Hon. Philip Pusey, André (Bart.), De Hochepied Larpent (Bart.), Jean Sylvestre (Bart.), Cazenove, Dollond, Petit (M.D.), Le Mesurier, Landon, Martineau, Baron Maseres, Chevalier, Durand, Hanbury, Labouchere, De la Rue (F. R. S.); and many other names well known and highly distinguished in the commerce, politics, literature, and science of England.

CHAPTER XVI.

HUGUENOT SETTLEMENTS IN IRELAND.

It had long been the policy of the English monarchs to induce foreign artisans to settle in Ireland and establish new branches of skilled industry there. It was hoped that the Irish people might be induced to follow their example, and that thus the unemployed population of that country, instead of being a source of national poverty and weakness, might be rendered a source of national wealth and strength.

We have already seen the Earl of Strafford engaged in an attempt to establish the linen trade in the north of Ireland. But his term of office was cut short, and the country shortly after fell a prey to civil war and all its horrors. At the Restoration, Charles II. endeavored to pursue the same policy; and many of the French refugees, so soon as they landed in England, were forwarded into Ireland at the expense of the state. In 1674, the Irish Parliament passed an act offering letters of naturalization to the refugees, and free admission to all corporations. The then viceroy, the Duke of Ormond, zealously encouraged this policy; and under his patronage, colonies of French refugees were planted at Dublin, Waterford, Cork, Kilkenny, Lisburn, and Portarlington, where they introduced glove-making, silk-weaving, lace-making, and manufactures of cloth and linen. The refugees were prosperously pursuing their respective trades when the English Revolution of 1688 occurred, and again Ireland was thrown into a state of civil war, which continued for three years, but was at length concluded by the peace of Limerick in 1691.

No sooner was the war at an end than William III. took steps to restore the prostrate industry of the country. The Irish Parliament again revived their bill of 1674 (which the

Parliament of James had suspended), granting naturalization to such of the refugees as should settle in Ireland, and guaranteeing them the free exercise of their religion. A large number of William's foreign officers at once availed themselves of the privilege, and settled at Youghal, Waterford, and Portarlington; while colonies of foreign manufacturers at the same time planted themselves at Dublin, Cork, Lisburn, and other places.

The refugees who settled at Dublin established themselves for the most part in "The Liberties," where they began the manufacture of tabinet, since more generally known as "Irish poplin."* The demand for the article became such that a number of French masters and workmen left Spitalfields and migrated to Dublin, where they largely extended the manufacture. The Combe, Pimlico, Spitalfields, and other streets in Dublin, named after corresponding streets in London, were built for their accommodation; and Weavers' Square became a principal quarter in the city. For a time the trade was very prosperous, and gave employment to a large number of persons; but about the beginning of the present century, the frequent recurrence of strikes among the workmen paralyzed the employers of labor; the manufacture in consequence became almost lost, and "The Liberties," instead of the richest, became one of the poorest quarters of Dublin. So long as the French colony prospered, the refugees had three congregations in the city. One of these was an Episcopal congregation, attached to St. Patrick's Cathedral, which worshiped in St. Mary's Chapel, granted to them by the dean and chapter; and it continued in existence until the year 1816. The other two were Calvinistic congregations, one of which had their place of worship in Peter Street,

* There are no certain records for fixing the precise date when silk-weaving was commenced in Dublin; but it is generally believed that an ancestor of the present respected family of the Latouches commenced the weaving of tabinets or poplins and tabbareas, in the liberties of Dublin, about the year 1693.—DR. W. COOKE TAYLOR, in *Statistical Journal* for December, 1843, p. 354.

and the other in Lucas Lane. The refugees also had special burying-places assigned them—the principal one adjoining St. Stephen's Green, and the other being situated on the southern outskirts of the city.

But the northern counties of Down and Antrim were, more than any other parts of Ireland, regarded as the sanctuary of the refugees. There they found themselves among men of their own religion—mostly Scotch Calvinists, who had fled from the Stuart persecutions in Scotland to take refuge in the comparatively unmolested districts of Ulster. Lisburn, formerly called Lisnagarvey, about ten miles southwest of Belfast, was one of the favorite settlements of the refugees. The place had been burnt to the ground in the civil war of 1641; but, with the help of the refugees, it was before long restored to more than its former importance, and shortly became one of the most prosperous towns in Ireland.

The government of the day, while they discouraged the woolen manufacture of Ireland because of its supposed injury to England, made every effort to encourage the trade in linen. An act was passed with the latter object in 1697, containing various enactments calculated to foster the growth of flax and the manufacture of linen cloth. Before the passing of this act, William III. proceeded to invite Louis Crommelin, a Huguenot refugee, then temporarily settled in Holland, to come over into Ireland and undertake the superintendence of the new branch of industry.

Crommelin belonged to a family who had carried on the linen manufacture in its various branches in France for upward of 400 years, and he had himself been engaged in the business for more than 30 years at Armandcourt, near Saint Quentin, in Picardy, where he was born. He was singularly well fitted for the office to which the king called him, being a person of admirable business qualities, of excellent good sense, and of remarkable energy and perseverance. Being a Protestant, and a man of much foresight, he had quietly realized what he could of his large property in the neighborhood of

St. Quentin shortly before the revocation of the Edict of Nantes, and migrated across the frontier into Holland before the bursting of the storm.

In 1698, Crommelin, having accepted the invitation of William, left Holland, accompanied by his son, and shortly after his arrival in England he proceeded into the north of Ireland to fix upon the site best adapted for the intended undertaking. After due deliberation, he pitched upon the ruined village of Lisnagarvey as the most suitable for his purpose.* The king approved of the selection, and authorized Crommelin to proceed with his operations, appointing him "Overseer of the Royal Linen Manufactory of Ireland." In consideration of Crommelin advancing £10,000 out of his own private fortune to commence the undertaking, a grant of £800 per annum was guaranteed to him for twelve years, being at the rate of 8 per cent. on the capital invested. At the same time, an annuity of £200 was granted him for life, and £120 a year for two assistants, whose duty it was to travel from place to place and superintend the cultivation of the flax, as well as to visit the bleaching-grounds and see to the proper finishing of the fabric.†

* Crommelin's first factory was at the foot of the wooden bridge over the Lagan, and his first bleaching-ground was started at the place called Hilden.
† The following is the substance of the patent granted by King William to Louis Crommelin:

"In consequence of a proposal by Louis Crommelin to establish a linen manufacture in Ireland, and the design and method in said memorial being approved of by the Commissioners of Treasury and Trade, the following grant was made: That £800 be settled for ten years as interest on £10,000 advanced by said Louis Crommelin for the making of a bleaching-yard and building a pressing-house, and for weaving, cultivating, and pressing hemp and flax, and making provision of both to be sold ready prepared to the spinners at reasonable rate and upon credit; providing all tools and utensils, looms, and spinning-wheels, to be furnished at the several costs of persons employed, by advances to be paid by them in small payments as they are able; advancing sums of money necessary for the subsistence of such workmen and their families as shall come from abroad, and of such persons of this our kingdom as shall apply themselves in families to work in the manufactories; such sums to be advanced without interest, and to be repaid by degrees. That £200 per annum be allowed to said Crommelin during pleasure for his pains and care in carrying on said work, and that £120 per annum be allowed for two assistants, together with a premium of £60 per annum for the subsistence of a French minister, and that letters patent be granted accordingly. Dated 14th of February, 1699."

Crommelin at once sent invitations abroad to the Protestant artisans to come over and join him, and numbers of them responded to his call. A little colony of refugees of all ranks and many trades soon became planted at Lisburn, and the place shortly began to exhibit an appearance of returning prosperity. With a steadiness of purpose which distinguished Crommelin through life, he devoted himself with unceasing zeal to the promotion of the enterprise which he had taken in hand. He liberally rewarded the toil of his brother-exiles, and cheered them on the road to success. He imported from Holland a thousand looms and spinning-wheels of the best construction, and gave a premium of £5 for every loom that was kept going. Before long, he introduced improvements of his own in the looms and spinning-wheels, as well as in the implements and in the preparation of the material. Every branch of the operations made rapid progress under the Huguenot chief, from the sowing, cultivating, and preparing of the flax through the various stages of its manipulation, to the finish of the cloth at the bleach-fields. And thus, by painstaking, skill, and industry, zealously supported as he was by his artisans, Crommelin was shortly enabled to produce finer sorts of fabrics than had ever before been made in Britain.*

* A linen board was established by the Duke of Ormond in October, 1711. In a petition to this board, L. Crommelin recounted all he had done, and requested a renewal of the patent. The board reported favorably. Crommelin had now been fourteen years at work. The colony of refugees, about 70 at first, had increased to 120 in 1711. In 1703, November 20, Parliament voted confidence in Crommelin, and again, in October, 1707, by vote declared that he had been eminently useful. In his petition, Crommelin states that "by the first patent, granted by the late King William, the whole sum of £800 was granted to your petitioner for the settlement of himself and colony for ten years, over and above £380 per annum for pension for your petitioner and his three assistants, and the minister, during pleasure, which said patent was not put in execution, but instead thereof, after the said King William's death, the Honorable Trustees obtained a second from our most gracious Queen Anne, authorizing them to dispose of the said sums of £800 and £380, both to your petitioner and his colony, and the natives of the country, both which sums were limited for ten years, whereas by the first the pensions were granted during pleasure; so that your petitioner was reduced to £400, which was a great discouragement, and produced not 3 per cent. instead of the 8 per cent. they were to have by the first patent. . . . . . The present patent will

Crommelin, among his other labors for the establishment of the linen trade, wrote and published at Dublin, in 1705, *An Essay toward the improving of the Hempen and Flaxen Manufacture of the Kingdom of Ireland*, so that all might be made acquainted with the secret of his success, and be enabled to go and do likewise. The treatise contained many useful instructions for the cultivation of flax, in the various stages of its planting and growth to perfection, together with directions for the preparation of the material, in the several processes of spinning, weaving, and bleaching.

Though a foreigner, Crommelin continued throughout his life to take a warm interest in the prosperity of his adopted country; and his services were recognized, not only by King William, who continued his firm friend to the last, but by the Irish Parliament, who from time to time voted grants of money to himself, and his assistants, and his artisans,[*] to enable him to prosecute his enterprise; and in 1707 they voted him the public thanks for his patriotic efforts toward the establishment of the linen trade in Ireland, of which he

determine on the 24th of June next, and unless the same be renewed for a certain term of years, your petitioner and his colony will be reduced to great extremities, and rendered incapable of continuing a settlement begun with so much difficulty." The prayer of the petition was for a renewal of the patent for ten years or other term, and for Crommelin a pension of £500 per annum, which was granted.—*Ulster Journal of Archæology*, i., 286–9.

[*] In the papers of the Irish House of Commons the following account occurs:
Pensions paid to the French colony at Lisburn:

1704–5, Feb. 16.	Paid to Lewis Crommelin, for three years..............	£600
	To French minister for two years.......................	102
	To flax-dresser for two and a quarter years............	27
	To the reed-maker for the like term....................	18
1705–6, Jan. 18.	To Louis Crommelin for one year.......................	280
Nov. 26.	To same for nine months................................	210
1707, Aug. 22.	To same for like term.......................................	210
	To the arrears of two assistants..........................	360
Nov. 20.	To Louis Crommelin, minister, etc., for three months	80
1708, June 19.	To do. do. do. for six months...	160
Dec. 11.	To same..	26

The "reed-maker" referred to in this account was one Mark Henry Dupré, a skilled workman who fled from France shortly after the Revocation, and landed in the south of Ireland. From thence he made his way to Lisburn, and joined Crommelin, to whom he proved of great service. His descendants are still to be found in Belfast.

was unquestionably the founder. Crommelin died in 1727, and was buried beside other members of his family who had gone before him, in the church-yard at Lisburn.

The French refugees long continued a distinct people in that neighborhood. They clung together, associated together, and worshiped together, frequenting their own French church, in which they had a long succession of French pastors.[*] They carefully trained up their children in their native tongue and in the Huguenot faith, cherishing the hope of some day being enabled to return to their native land. But that hope at length died out, and the descendants of the Crommelins eventually mingled with the families of the Irish, and became part and parcel of the British nation.

Among the other French settlers at Lisburn was Peter Goyer, a native of Picardy. He owned a large farm there, and also carried on an extensive business as a manufacturer of cambric and silk at the time of the Revocation; but when the dragonnades began, he left all his property behind him and fled across the frontier. The record is still preserved in the family of the cruelties practiced upon Peter's martyred brother by the ruthless soldiery, who tore a leaf from his Bible and forced it into his mouth before he died. From Holland Goyer proceeded to England, and from thence to Lisburn, where he began the manufacture of the articles for which he had acquired so much reputation in his own country. After a short time he resolved on returning to France, in the hope of being able to recover some of his property. But the persecution was raging more fiercely than ever, and he found that, if captured, he would probably be condemned to the

[*] The Rev. Saumarez Dubourdieu, grandson of the celebrated French pastor of the Savoy Church in London, was minister of the French church at Lisburn for forty-five years, and was so beloved in the neighborhood that at the insurrection of 1798 he was the only person in Lisburn whom the insurgents agreed to spare. The French congregation having become greatly decreased by deaths as well as intermarriages with Irish families, the chapel was at length closed—it is now used as the court-house of Lisburn—and the pastor Dubourdieu having joined the Established Church, he was presented with the living of Lambeg. His son, rector of Annahelt, County Down, was the author of *A Statistical Survey of the County Antrim*, published in 1812.

T

galleys for life. He again contrived to make his escape, having been carried on board an outward-bound ship concealed in a wine-cask. Returned to Lisburn, he resumed the manufacture of silk and cambric, in which he employed a considerable number of workmen. The silk manufacture there was destroyed in the rebellion of 1798, which dispersed the workpeople; but that of cambric survived, and became firmly founded at Lurgan, which now enjoys a high reputation for the perfection of its manufactures.

Other colonies of the refugees were established in the south of Ireland, where they carried on various branches of manufacture. William Crommelin, a brother of Louis, having been appointed one of his assistants, superintended the branch of the linen trade which was established at Kilkenny through the instrumentality of the Marquis of Ormonde. Another settlement of refugees was formed at Cork, where they congregated together in a quarter of the town forming part of the parish of St. Paul, the principal street in which is still called French Church Street. Though the principal refugees at Cork were merchants and traders, there was a sufficient number of them to begin the manufacture of woolen cloth, ginghams, and other fabrics, which they carried on for a time with considerable success.

The woolen manufacture at Cork was begun by James Fontaine, a member of the noble family of De la Fontaine, in France, a branch of which embraced Protestantism in the sixteenth century, and continued to adhere to it down to the period of the Revocation. The career of James Fontaine was singularly illustrative of the times in which he lived. His case was only one among thousands of others, in which persons of rank, wealth, and learning were suddenly stripped of their all, and compelled to become wanderers over the wide earth for conscience' sake. His life farther serves to show how a clever and agile Frenchman, thrown upon a foreign shore, a stranger to its people and its language, without any calling or resources, but full of energy and courage, could contrive to earn an honest living and achieve an honorable reputation.

James Fontaine was the son of a Protestant pastor of the same name, and was born at Royan in Saintonge, a famous Huguenot district. His father was the first of the family to drop the aristocratic prefix of " de la," which he did from motives of humility. When a child, Fontaine met with an accident through the carelessness of a nurse which rendered him lame for life. When only eight years old, his father died, and little was done for his education until he arrived at about the age of seventeen, when he was placed under a competent tutor, and eventually took the degree of M.A. with distinction at the College of Guienne when in his twenty-second year. Shortly after his mother died, and he became the possessor of her landed property near Pons, on the Charente.

Young Fontaine's sister, Marie, had married a Protestant pastor named Forestier, of St. Mesme in Angoumois. Jacques went to live with them for a time, and study theology under the pastor. The persecutions having shortly set in, Forestier's church was closed, and he himself compelled to fly to England. The congregation of St. Mesme was consequently left without a minister. Young Fontaine, well knowing the risk he ran, nevertheless encouraged the Protestants to assemble in the open air, and himself occasionally conducted their devotions. For this he was cited to appear before the local tribunals. He was charged with the crime of attending one of such meetings in 1684, contrary to law, and though he had not been present at the meeting specified, he was condemned and imprisoned. He appealed to the Parliament at Paris, whither he carried his plea of *alibi*, and was acquitted.

Early in 1685, the year of the Revocation, the dragoons were sent into the Huguenot district of Royan to carry out the mission of the " Most Christian King." In anticipation of their visit, shiploads of Huguenots had sailed for Holland and England a few days before, but Fontaine did not accompany them. He fled from his home, however, and remained concealed among his friends and relatives until he felt that he could no longer remain in France with safety. In the month of October, when the intelligence reached him that the Edict of Revocation was proclaimed, he at once determined to make his escape. A party of Protestant ladies had arranged to accompany him, consisting of Janette Forestier, the daughter of the pastor of St. Mesme (now a fugitive in England), his niece, and the two Mesdemoiselles Boursignot, to one of whom he was betrothed.

At Marennes, Fontaine found the captain of an English ship who was willing to give the party a passage to England. It was at first intended that they should rendezvous on the sands near Tremblade, and then proceed privily on shipboard. But the coast was very strictly guarded, especially between Royan and La Rochelle, where the Protestants of the interior were constantly seeking outlets for escape; and this part of the plan was given up. The search of vessels leaving the ports had become so strict, that the English captain feared that even if Fontaine and his ladies succeeded on getting on board, it would not be possible for him to conceal them or prevent their falling into the hands of the king's detectives. He therefore proposed that his ship should set sail, and that the fugitives should put to sea and wait for him to take them on board. It proved fortunate that this plan was adopted, for scarcely had the English merchantman left Tremblade than she was boarded and searched by a French frigate on the look-out for fugitive Protestants. No prisoners were found, and the captain of the merchantman was ordered to proceed at once on the straight course for England.

Meanwhile, the boat containing the fugitives having put to sea, as arranged, lay to waiting the approach of the English vessel. That they might not be descried from the frigate, which was close at hand, the boatman made them lie down in the bottom of his boat, covering them with an old sail. They all knew the penalties to which they were liable if detected in the attempt to escape—Fontaine, the boatman, and his son, to condemnation to the galleys for life, and the three ladies to imprisonment for life. The frigate bore down upon the boat and hailed the boatman, who feigned drunkenness so well as completely to deceive the king's captain, who, seeing nothing but the old sail in the bottom of the boat, ordered the ship's head to be put about, when the frigate sailed away in the direction of Rochefort. Shortly after, while she was still in sight, though distant, the agreed signal was given by the boat to the merchantman (that of dropping the sail three times in the apparent attempt to hoist it), on which the English vessel lay to, and took the exiles on board. After a voyage of eleven days they reached the welcome asylum of England, and Fontaine and his party landed at Barnstaple, North Devon, his sole property consisting of twenty pistoles and six silver spoons, which had belonged to his father, and bore upon them his infantine initials, I. D. L. F.—Jacques de la Fontaine.

Fontaine and the three ladies were hospitably received by Mr. Donne of Barnstaple, with whom they lived until a home could be prepared for their reception. One of the first things which occupied Fontaine's attention was how to earn a living for their support. A cabin biscuit, which he bought for a halfpenny, gave him his first hint. The biscuit would have cost twopence in France; and it at once occurred to him that, such being the case, grain might be shipped from England to France at a profit. Mr. Donne agreed to advance the money requisite for the purpose, taking half the profits. The first cargo of corn exported proved very profitable; but Fontaine's partner afterward insisting on changing the consignee, who proved dishonest, the speculation eventually proved unsuccessful.

Fontaine had by this time married the Huguenot lady to whom he was betrothed, and who had accompanied him in his flight to England. After the failure of the corn speculation he removed to Taunton in Somerset, where with difficulty he made shift to live. He took pupils, dealt in provisions, sold brandy, groceries, stockings, leather, tin and copper wares, and carried on wool-combing, dyeing, and the making of calimancoes. In short, he was a "jack-of-all-trades;" and his following so many callings occasioned so much jealousy in the place, that he was cited before the mayor and aldermen as an interloper, and required to give an account of himself.* This and other circumstances determined him to give up business in Taunton—not, however, before he had contrived to save about £1000 by his industry—and to enter on the life of a pastor. He had already been admitted to holy orders by the French Protestant synod at Taunton, and in 1694 he left that town for Ireland in search of a congregation.

Fontaine's adventures in Ireland were still more remarkable than those he had experienced in England. The French refugees established at Cork had formed themselves into a congregation, of which he was appointed pastor in January,

* When Fontaine was brought before the mayor (who was a wool-comber), he was asked if he had served an apprenticeship to all the trades he carried on. Fontaine replied, "Gentlemen, in France a man is esteemed according to his qualifications, and men of letters and study are especially honored by every body if they conduct themselves with propriety, even though they should not be worth one penny. . . . . . All the apprenticeship I have ever served, from the age of four years, has been to turn over the pages of a book. I took the degree of Master of Arts at the age of twenty-two, and then devoted myself to the study of the Holy Scriptures. Hitherto I had been thought worthy of the best company wherever I had been; but when I came to this town, I found that science without riches was regarded as a cloud without water, or a tree without fruit—in a word, a thing worthy of supreme contempt; so much so, that if a poor ignorant wool-comber or a hawker amassed money he was honored by all, and looked up to as first in the place. I have therefore, gentlemen, renounced all speculative science; I have become a wool-comber, a dealer in pins and laces, hoping that I may one day attain wealth, and be also one of the first men in the town."

The recorder laid down the law in favor of Fontaine: "If the poor refugees," said he, "who have abandoned country, friends, property, and every thing sweet and agreeable in this life for their religion and the glory of the Gospel—if they had not the means of gaining a livelihood, the parish would be burdened with their maintenance, for you could not send them to their birthplace. The parish is obliged to Mr. Fontaine for every morsel of bread he earns for his family. In the desire he has to live independently, he humbles himself so far as to become a tradesman, a thing very rarely seen among learned men, such as I know him to be from my own conversation with him. There is no law that can disturb him."

Fontaine retired from the court amid showers of benedictions.

1695. They were, however, as yet too poor to pay him any stipend; and, in order to support himself, as well as to turn to account the £1000 which he had saved by his industry and frugality at Taunton, he began a manufactory of broadcloth. This gave much welcome employment to the laboring poor of the city, besides contributing toward the increase of its general trade, in acknowledgment of which the corporation presented him with the freedom. He still continued to officiate as pastor; but one day, when expounding the text of "Thou shalt not steal," he preached so effectively as to make a personal enemy of a member of his congregation, who, unknown to him, had been engaged in a swindling transaction. The result was so much dissension in the congregation that he eventually gave up the charge.

To occupy his spare time—for Fontaine was a man of an intensely active temperament, unhappy when unemployed—he took a farm at Bearhaven, situated at the entrance to Bantry Bay, nearly at the extreme southwest point of Munster, the very Land's End of Ireland, for the purpose of founding a fishery. The idea occurred to him, as it has since to others, that there were many hungry people on land waiting to be fed, and shoals of fish at sea waiting to be caught, and that it would be a useful enterprise to form a fishing company, and induce the idle people to put to sea and catch the fish, selling to others the surplus beyond what was necessary to feed them. Fontaine succeeded in inducing some of the French merchants settled in London to join him in the venture, and he himself went to reside at Bearhaven to superintend the operations of the company.

Fontaine failed, as other Irish fishing companies have since failed. The people would rather starve than go to sea, for Celts are by nature averse to salt water; and the consequence was that the company made no progress. Fontaine had even to defend himself against the pillaging and plundering of the natives. He then brought some thirteen French refugee families to settle in the neighborhood, having previously taken small farms for them, including Dursey Island; but the Irish gave them no peace nor rest, and they left him before the end of three years. The local court would give Fontaine no redress when any injury was done to him. If his property was stolen, and he appealed to the court, his complaint was referred to a jury of papists, who invariably decided against him; whereas, if the natives made any claim upon him, they were sure to recover.

Notwithstanding these great discouragements, Fontaine held to his purpose, and determined, if possible, to establish his fishing station. He believed that time would work in his favor, and that it might yet be possible to educate the people into habits of industry. He was well supported by the government, who, observing his zealous efforts to establish a new branch of industry, and desirous of giving him increased influence in his neighborhood, appointed him justice of the peace. In this capacity he was found very useful in keeping down the "Tories,"[*] and breaking up the connections between them and the French privateers who then frequented the coast. Knowing his liability to attack, Fontaine converted his residence into a sod fort, and not without cause, as the result proved. In June, 1704, a French privateer entered Bantry Bay and proceeded to storm the sod fort. The lame Fontaine, by the courage and ability of his defense, showed himself a commander of no mean skill. John Macliney, a Scotchman, and Paul Roussier, a French refugee, showed great bravery on the occasion; while Madame Fontaine, who acted as aid-de-camp and surgeon, distinguished herself by her quiet courage. The engagement lasted from eight in the morning until four in the afternoon, when the French decamped with the loss of three killed and seven wounded, spreading abroad a very wholesome fear of Fontaine and his sod fort.

---

[*] The Tories were Irish robbers or banditti who lived by plunder; the word being derived from the Irish word TORUIGHUIN, "to pursue for purposes of violence."

When the refugee's gallant exploit was reported to the government, he was rewarded by a pension of five shillings a day for beating off the privateer, and supplied with five guns, which he was authorized to mount on his battery.

Fontaine was now allowed to hold his post unmolested. It was at the remotest corner of the island, far from any town, and surrounded by a hostile population, in league with the enemy, whose ships were constantly hovering about the coast. In the year following the above engagement, while Fontaine himself was absent in London, a French ship entered Bantry Bay and cautiously approached Bearhaven. Fontaine's wife was, however, on the look-out, and detected the foreigner. She had the guns loaded and one of them fired off to show that the little garrison was on the alert. The Frenchman then veered off and made for Bear Island, where a party of the crew landed, stole some cattle, which they put on board, and sailed away again.

A more serious assault was made on the fort about two years later. A company of soldiers was then quartered at the Half Barony in the neighborhood, the captain of which boarded with the refugee family. On the 7th of October, 1708, during the temporary absence of Fontaine as well as the captain, a French privateer made his appearance in the haven, and hoisted English colors. The ensign residing in the fort at the time, deceived by the stratagem, went on board, when he was immediately made a prisoner. He was plied with drink and became intoxicated, when he revealed the fact that there was no officer in command of the fort. The crew of the privateer were principally Irish, and they determined to attack the place at midnight, for which purpose a party of them landed. Fontaine had, however, by this time returned, and was on the alert. He hailed the advancing party through a speaking-trumpet, and no answer being returned, he ordered fire to be opened on them. The assailants then divided into six detachments, one of which set fire to the offices and stables; the household servants under the direction of Madame Fontaine, protecting the dwelling-house from conflagration. The men within fired from the windows and loopholes, but the smoke was so thick that they could only fire at random. Some of the privateer's men succeeded in making a breach with a crowbar in the wall of the house, but they were saluted with so rapid a fire through the opening that they suspected there must be a party of soldiers in the house, and they retired. They advanced again, and summoned the besieged to surrender, offering fair terms. Fontaine approached the French for the purpose of parley, when one of the Irish lieutenants took aim and fired at him. This treachery made the Fontaines resume the defensive, which they continued without intermission for some hours; when, no help arriving, Fontaine found himself under the necessity of surrendering, conditional upon himself and his two sons, with their two followers, marching out with the honors of war. No sooner, however, had the house been surrendered, than Fontaine, his sons, and their followers were at once made prisoners, and the dwelling was given up to plunder.

Fontaine protested against this violation of the treaty, but it was of no use. The leader of the French party said to him, "Your name has become so notorious among the privateers of St. Malo that I dare not return to the vessel without you. The captain's order was peremptory to bring you on board, dead or alive." Fontaine and his sons were accordingly taken on board as prisoners; and when he appeared on the deck, the crew set up a shout of "Vive le Roi." On this, Fontaine called out to them, "Gentlemen, how long is it since victories have become so rare in France that you need to make a triumph of such an affair as this? A glorious feat indeed! Eighty men, accustomed to war, have succeeded in compelling one poor pastor, four cowherds, and five children, to surrender upon terms!" Fontaine again expostulated with the captain, and informed him that, being held a prisoner in breach of the treaty under which he had surrendered, he must be prepared for the retaliation of the English government upon

French prisoners of war. The captain would not, however, give up Fontaine without a ransom, and demanded £100. Madame Fontaine contrived to borrow £30, and sent it to the captain, with a promise of the remainder; but the captain could not wait, and he liberated Fontaine, but carried off his son Pierre to St. Malo as a hostage for the payment of the balance.

When the news of this attack of the fort at Bearhaven reached the English government, and they were informed of the violation of the conditions under which Fontaine had surrendered, they ordered the French officers at Kinsale and Plymouth to be put in irons until Fontaine's son was sent back. This produced an immediate effect. In the course of a few months Pierre Fontaine was set at liberty and returned to his parents, and the balance of the ransom was never claimed. The commander of the forces in Ireland made Fontaine an immediate grant of £100, to relieve him in the destitute state to which he had been reduced by the plunder of his dwelling; the county of Cork afterward paid him £800 as damages on its being proved that Irishmen had been principally concerned in the attack and robbery; and Fontaine's two sons were awarded the position and rights of half-pay officers, while his own pension was continued. The fort at Bearhaven, having been completely desolated, was abandoned; and Fontaine, with the grant made him by government, and the sum awarded him by the county, left the lawless neighborhood which he had so long labored to improve and to defend, and proceeded to Dublin, where he settled for the remainder of his life as a teacher of languages, mathematics, and fortification. The school proved highly successful, and he ended his days in peace. His noble wife died in 1721, and he himself followed her shortly after, respected and beloved by all who knew him.*

* Nearly all Fontaine's near relatives took refuge in England. His mother and three of his brothers were refugees in London. One of them afterward became a Protestant minister in Germany. One of his uncles, Peter, was pastor of the Pest House Chapel in London. Two aunts—one a widow, the

We return to the subject of the settlements made by other refugees in the southern parts of Ireland. In 1697, about fifty retired officers, who had served in the army of William III., settled with their families at Youghal, on the invitation of the mayor and corporation, who offered them the freedom of the town on payment of the nominal sum of sixpence each. It does not appear that the refugees were sufficiently numerous to maintain a pastor, though the Rev. Arthur d'Anvers for some time privately ministered to them. From the circumstance principally of their comparatively small number, they speedily ceased to exist as a distinctive portion of the community, though names of French origin are still common in the town, and many occur in the local registers of births, marriages, and deaths, of about a hundred years ago.

The French refugee colony at Waterford was of considerably greater importance. Being favorably situated for trade near the mouth of the River Suir, with a rich agricultural country behind it, that town offered many inducements to the refugee merchants and traders to settle there. In the act passed by the Irish Parliament in 1662, and re-enacted in 1672, "for encouraging Protestant strangers and others to inhabit Ireland," Waterford is specially named as one of the cities selected for the settlement of the refugees. Some twenty years later, in 1693, the corporation of Waterford, being desirous not only that the disbanded Huguenot officers and soldiers should settle in the place, but also that those skilled in arts and manufactures should become citizens, ordered "that the city and liberties do provide habitations for fifty families of

---

other married to a refugee merchant—were also settled in London. Fontaine's sons and daughters mostly emigrated to Virginia, where their descendants are still to be found. His daughter Mary Anne married the Rev. James Maury, Fredericksville Parish, Louisa County, Virginia, from whom Matthew Fontaine Maury, LL.D., lately Captain in the Confederate States Navy, and author of *The Physical Geography of the Sea*, is lineally descended. The above facts are taken from the "*Memoirs of a Huguenot Family*, translated and compiled from the original Autobiography of the Rev. James Fontaine, and other family manuscripts, by ANN MAURY" (another of the descendants of Fontaine): New York, 1853.

the French Protestants to drive a trade of linen manufacture, they bringing with them a stock of money and materials for their subsistence until flax can be sown and produced on the lands adjacent; and that the freedom of the city be given them *gratis*." At the same time, the choir of the old Franciscan monastery was assigned to them, with the assent of the bishop, for the purpose of a French church, the corporation guaranteeing a stipend of £40 a year toward the support of a pastor.

These liberal measures had the effect of inducing a considerable number of refugees to establish themselves at Waterford, and carry on various branches of trade and manufacture. Some of them became leading merchants in the place, and rose to wealth and distinction. Thus John Espaignet was sheriff of the city in 1707, and the two brothers Vashon served, the one as mayor in 1726, the other as sheriff in 1735. The foreign wine-trade of the south of Irelend was almost exclusively conducted through Waterford by the French wine-merchants, some of their principal stores being in the immediate neighborhood of the French church. The refugees also made vigorous efforts to establish the linen manufacture in Waterford, in which they were encouraged by the Irish Parliament; and for many years linen was one of the staple trades of the place, though it has ceased since the introduction of power-looms.

Another colony of the refugees was established at Portarlington, which town they may almost be said to have founded. The first settlers consisted principally of retired French officers as well as privates, who had served in the army of King William. We have already referred to the circumstances connected with the formation of this colony by the Marquis de Ruvigny, created Earl of Galway, to whom William granted the estate of Portarlington, which had become forfeited to the crown by the treason and outlawry of Sir Patrick Grant, its former owner. Although the grant was revoked by the English Parliament, and the earl ceased to own the Portarlington estate, he nevertheless continued to take the same warm interest as before in the prosperity of the refugee colony.*

Among the early settlers at Portarlington were the Marquis de Paray, the Sieur de Hauteville, Louis le Blanc, Sieur de Percé, Charles de Ponthieu, Captain d'Alnuis and his brother, Abel Pelissier, David d'Arripe, Ruben de la Rochefoucauld, the Sieur de la Boissiere, Guy de la Blachière de Bonneval, Dumont de Bostaquet, Franquefort, Châteauneuf, La Beaume, Montpeton du Languedoc, Vicomte de Laval, Pierre Goulin, Jean la Ferriere, De Gaudry, Jean Lafaurie, Abel de Ligonier de Vignolles,† Anthoine de Ligonier, and numerous others.

The greater number of these noblemen and gentlemen had served with distinction under the Duke of Schomberg, La Melonniere, La Caillemotte, Cambon, and other commanders, in the service of William III. They had been for the most part men of considerable estate in their own country, and were now content to live as exiles on the half-pay granted them by the country of their adoption. When they first came into the neighborhood the town of Portarlington could scarcely be said to exist. The village of Cootletoodra, as it was formerly called, was only a collection of miserable huts

---

* The *Bulletin de la Société de l'Histoire du Protestantisme Français* (1861, p. 69) contains a letter addressed by the Earl of Galway to David Barbut, a refugee residing at Berne, in January, 1693, wherein he informs him that King William is greatly concerned at the distress of the French refugees in Switzerland, and desires that 600 families should proceed to Ireland and settle there. He adds that the king has recommended the Protestant princes of Germany and the States-General of Holland to pay the expense of the transport of these families to the sea-board, after which the means would be provided for their embarkation into Ireland. "The king," said he, "is so touched at the misery with which these families are threatened where they are, and perceives so clearly how valuable their settlement would be in his kingdom of Ireland, that he is resolved to provide all the money that may be required for the purpose. We must not lose any time in the matter, and I hope that by the month of April, or May at the latest, these families will be on their way to join us."

† The Des Vignolles were of noble birth, descended from the celebrated Estienne des Vignolles of Languedoc, where the family possessed large estates. Two brothers of the name were Huguenot officers who served under William III. Charles Vignolles, C. E., is descended from the elder brother, and the Dean of Ossory from the younger.

unfit for human residence; and until the dwellings designed for the reception of the exiles by the Earl of Galway could be built, they resided in the adjoining villages of Doolough, Monasterevin, Cloneygown, and the ancient village of Lea.

The new Portarlington shortly became the model town of the district. The dwellings of the strangers were distinguished for their neatness and comfort, and their farms and gardens were patterns of tidiness and high culture. They introduced new fruit-trees from abroad; among others, the black Italian walnut and the jargonelle pear, specimens of which still flourish at Portarlington in vigorous old age. The original planter of these trees fought at the Boyne as an ensign in the regiment of La Melonniere. The immigrants also introduced the "espalier" with great success, and their fruit became widely celebrated. Another favorite branch of culture was flowers, of which they imported many new sorts, while their vegetables were unmatched in Ireland.

The exiles formed a highly select society, composed as it was of ladies and gentlemen of high culture, of pure morals, and of gentle birth and manners, so different from the roystering Irish gentry of the time. Though they had suffered grievous wrongs at the hands of their country, they were contented, cheerful, and even gay. Traditions still exist of the military refugees, in their scarlet cloaks, sitting in groups under the old oaks in the market-place, sipping tea out of their small china cups. They had also their balls, and ordinaries, and "ridottos" (places of pleasant resort), and a great deal of pleasant visiting went on among them. They continued to enjoy their favorite wine of Bordeaux, which was imported for them in considerable quantities by their fellow-exiles, the French wine-merchants of Waterford and Dublin.[*]

[*] Thus we find Monsieur Pennetes, a Dublin wine-merchant, sending to a Portarlington colonist in 1726 " 3 gals. Frontignac at 6s.; oxhead of clarate, prise agreed, £11; a dousen of wine, 11s.; oxhead of Benicarlo at 2s. 6d. per gal., allowing 64 gals., coms to £8; une demy-barrique de selle de France, 6s." In 1757, Joshua Pilot, a retired paymaster and surgeon in Battereau's regiment, imported largely direct from Messrs. Barton and Co. of Bordeaux.—Sir E. D. BUROUGH in *Ulster Journal of Archæology.*

There were also numerous refugees of humbler class settled in the place, who carried on various trades. Thus the Fouberts carried on a manufacture of linen, and many of the minor tradesmen were French — bakers, butchers, masons, smiths, carpenters, tailors, and shoemakers. The Blancs, butchers, transmitted the business from father to son for more than 150 years; and they are still recognizable at Portarlington under the name of Blong. The Micheaus, farmers, had been tenants on the estates of the Robillard family in Champagne, and they were now tenants of the same family at Portarlington. One of the Micheaus was sexton of the French church of the town until within the last few years. La Borde the mason, Capel the blacksmith, and Gautier the carpenter, came from the neighborhood of Bordeaux; and their handiwork, much of which still exists at Portarlington and the neighborhood, bears indications of their foreign training.

The refugees, as was their invariable practice where they settled in sufficient numbers, early formed themselves into a congregation at Portarlington, and a church was erected for their accommodation, in which a long succession of able ministers officiated, the last of whom was Charles de Vignolles,[*]

---

[*] The register of the French church at Portarlington is still preserved. It commenced in 1694, and records the names, families, and localities in France from whence the refugees came. "The first volume of the register," says Sir E. D. Burough, "still wears the coarse and primitive brown paper cover in which it was originally invested by its foreign guardians 161 years since. One side bears the following inscription in large capitals: LIVR. . . . . . DES BAPT. . . . . MARIAG. . . . . ET ENTERREMENTS, 1694."
The following is the list of pastors of the French church:

    Depuis 1694—1696, Gillet.
  5 Octre. 1696—   Belaquiere.
  1 Decre. 1696—1698, Gillet.
 15 May, 1698—1698, Durassus.   }Calvinists.
    ...   ...   Ducasse.
26 Juin, 1698—1702, Daillon.

  3 Octre. 1702—1729, De Bonneval.
14 Augt. 1729—1739, Des Vœux.
16 Febre. 1739–40—1767, Caillard.
  2 Sep. 1767—1793, Des Vœux.   }Anglicans.
   Jan. 1793—1817, Vignolles *père*.
      1817—   Charles Vignolles *fils*.

afterward Dean of Ossory. The service was conducted in French down to the year 1817, since which it has been discontinued, the language having by that time become an almost unknown tongue in the neighborhood.

Besides a church, the refugees also possessed a school, which enjoyed a high reputation for the classical education which it provided for the rising generation. At an early period the boys seem to have been clothed as well as educated, the memorandum-book of an old officer of the Boyne containing an entry, April 20th, 1727, " making six sutes of cloths for ye blewbois, at 18 pce. per sute, 00 : 09 : 00." M. Le Fevre, founder of the Charter Schools, was the first schoolmaster in Portarlington. He is said to have been the father of Sterne's "poor sick lieutenant."* The Bonnevaux and Tersons were also among the subsequent teachers, and many of the principal Protestant families of Ireland passed under their hands. Among the more distinguished men who received the best part of their education at Portarlington may be mentioned the Marquis of Wellesley and his brother the Earl of Mornington, the Marquis of Westmeath, the Honorable John Wilson Croker, Sir Henry Ellis (of the British Museum), Daniel W. Webber, and many others.

Lady Morgan, referring in her *Memoirs* to the French colony at Portarlington, observes: "The dispersion of the French Huguenots, who settled in great numbers in Ireland, was one of the greatest boons conferred by the misgovernment of other countries upon our own. Eminent preachers, eminent lawyers, and clever statesmen, whose names are not unknown to the literature and science of France, occupied high places in the professions in Dublin. Of these I may

---

* The Portarlington Register contains the following record : " Sepulture du Dimanche 23ᵉ Mars, 1717–18. Le Samedy 22ᵉ du present mois entre minuet et une heure, est mort en la foy du Seigneur et dans l'espérance de la glorieuse resurrection, Monsieur Favre, Lieutenant à la pention, dont l'ame estait allée a Dieu, son corps a eté enterré par Monsieur Bonneval, ministre de cette Eglise dans le cemitiere de ce lieu. A. Ligonier Bonneval, min. Louis Buliod."

mention, as personal acquaintances, the Saurins, the Le Fanus, Espinasses, Favers, Corneilles, Le Bas, and many others, whose families still remain in the Irish metropolis."*

It is indeed to be regretted that the settlements of the refugee French and Flemings in Ireland were so much smaller than those which they effected in different parts of England, otherwise the condition of that unfortunate country would probably have been very different from what we now find it. The only part of Ireland in which the Huguenots left a permanent impression was in the north, where the branches of industry which they planted took firm root, and continue to flourish with extraordinary vigor to this day. But in the south it was very different. Though the natural facilities for trade at Cork, Limerick, and Waterford were much greater than those of the northern towns, the refugees never obtained any firm footing or made any satisfactory progress in that quarter, and their colonies there only maintained a sickly existence, and gradually fell into decay. One has only to look at Belfast and the busy hives of industry in that neighborhood, and note the condition of the northern province of Ulster—existing under precisely the same laws as govern the south—to observe how seriously the social progress of Ireland has been effected by the want of that remunerative employment which the refugees were so instrumental in providing in all the districts in which they settled, wherever they found a population willing to be taught by them, and to follow in the path which they undeviatingly pursued, of peaceful, contented, and honorable industry.

* LADY MORGAN—*Memoirs*, i., 106.

CHAPTER XVII.

DESCENDANTS OF THE REFUGEES.

ALTHOUGH 300 years have passed since the first religious persecutions in Flanders and France compelled so large a number of Protestants to fly from those countries and take refuge in England, and although 180 years have passed since the second great emigration from France took place in the reign of Louis XIV., the descendants of the "gentle and profitable strangers" are still recognizable among us. In the course of the generations which have come and gone since the dates of their original settlement, they have labored diligently and skillfully, greatly to the advantage of British trade, commerce, and manufactures, while there is scarcely a branch of literature, science, and art in which they have not distinguished themselves.

Three hundred years form a long period in the life of a nation. During that time many of the distinctive characteristics of the original refugees must necessarily have become effaced in the persons of their descendants. Indeed, by far the greater number of them before long became completely Anglicized, and ceased to be traceable except by their names, and even these have for the most part become converted into names of English sound.

So long as the foreigners continued to cherish the hope of returning to their native country on the possible cessation of the persecutions there, they waited and worked on with that end in view; but as the persecutions only waxed hotter, they at length gradually gave up all hope of return. They claimed and obtained letters of naturalization; and though many of them continued for several generations to worship in their native language, they were content to live and die English subjects. Their children grew up amid English associations, and they desired to forget that their fathers had been fugitives and foreigners in the land. They cared not to remember the language or to retain the names which marked them as distinct from the people among whom they lived, and hence many of the descendants of the refugees, in the second or third generation, abandoned their foreign names, while they gradually ceased to frequent the distinctive places of worship which their fathers had founded.

Indeed, many of the first Flemings had no sooner settled in England and become naturalized than they threw off their foreign names and assumed English ones instead. Thus, as we have seen, Hoek, the Flemish brewer in Southwark, assumed the name of Leeke; while Haestricht, the Flemish manufacturer at Bow, took that of James. Mr. Pryme, formerly professor of political economy in the University of Cambridge, and representative of that town in Parliament, whose ancestors were refugees from Ypres, in Flanders, has informed us that his grandfather dropped the "de la" originally prefixed to the family name in consequence of the strong anti-Gallican feeling which prevailed in this country during the Seven Years' War of 1756–63, though his son has since assumed it; and the same circumstance doubtless led many others to change their foreign names to those of English sound.

Nevertheless, a large number of purely Flemish names, though it may be with English modifications, are still to be found in various parts of England and Ireland where the foreigners originally settled. These have been, on the whole, better preserved in rural districts than in London, where the social friction was greater, and more speedily rubbed off the foreign peculiarities. In the lace towns of the west of England, such names as Raymond, Spiller, Brock, Stocker, Groot, Rochett, and Kettel are still common, and the same trade has continued in their families for many generations. The Walloon Goupés, who settled in Wiltshire as cloth-makers more than 300 years since, are still known there as the Guppys.

In the account of the early refugee Protestants given in the preceding pages, it has been pointed out that the first settlers in England came principally from Lille, Turcoing, and the towns situated along both sides of the present French frontier—the country of the French Walloons, but then subject to the crown of Spain. Among the first of these refugees was one Laurent des Bouveryes,* a native of Sainghin, near Lille. He first settled at Sandwich as a maker of serges in 1567, after which, in the following year, he removed to Canterbury to join the Walloon settlement there. The Des Bouveryes family prospered greatly. In the third generation, we find Edward, grandson of the refugee, a wealthy Turkey merchant of London. In the fourth generation, the head of the family was created a baronet; in the fifth, a viscount; and in the sixth, an earl; the original Laurent des Bouveryes being at this day represented in the House of Lords by the Earl of Radnor.

About the same time that the Des Bouveryes came into England from Lille, the Hugessens arrived from Dunkirk and settled at Dover. They afterward removed to Sandwich, where the family prospered; and in course of a few generations we find them enrolled among the country aristocracy of Kent, and their name borne by the ancient family of the Knatchbulls. It is not the least remarkable circumstance connected with this family that a member of it now represents the borough of Sandwich, one of the earliest seats of the refugees in England.

Among other notable Flemish immigrants may be numbered the Houblons, who gave the Bank of England its first governor, and from one of whose daughters the late Lord Palmerston was lineally descended.† The Van Sittarts, Jan-

---

* The Bouveries were men of mark in their native country. Thus, in the *Histoire de Cambray et du Cambrensis*, published in 1664, it is stated, "La famille de Bouverie est reconnu passer plusiers siecles entre les patricés de Cambray."

† Anne, sister and heir of Sir Richard Hublon, was married to Henry Temple, created Lord Palmerston in 1722.

sens, Courteens, Van Milderts, Vanlores, Corsellis, and Vannecks* were widely and honorably known in their day as London bankers or merchants. Sir Matthew Decker, besides being eminent as a London merchant, was distinguished for the excellence of his writings on commercial subjects, then little understood; and he made a useful member of Parliament, having been elected for Bishop's Castle in 1719.

Various members of the present landed gentry trace their descent from the Flemish refugees. Thus Jacques Hoste, the founder of the present family (represented by Sir W. L. S. Hoste, Bart.), fled from Bruges, of which his father was governor, in 1569; the Tyssens (now represented by W. G. Tyssen Amhurst, Esq., of Foulden) fled from Ghent; and the Crusos of Norfolk fled from Hownescout in Flanders, all to take refuge in England.

Among artists, architects, and engineers of Flemish descent we find Grinling Gibbons, the wood sculptor; Mark Gerrard, the portrait painter; Sir John Vanbrugh, the architect and play-writer; Richard Cosway, R.A.,† the miniature painter; and Sir Cornelius Vermuyden and Westerdyke, the engineers employed in the reclamation of the drowned lands in the Fen districts. The Tradescants, the celebrated antiquarians, were also of the same origin.‡

One of the most distinguished families in the Netherlands was that of the De Grotes or Groots, of which Hugo Grotius was an illustrious member. When the Spanish persecutions were at their height in the Low Countries, several of the Protestant De Grotes, who were eminent as merchants at

* The Vanneck family is now represented in the peerage by Baron Huntingfield.

† Cosway belonged to a family, originally Flemish, long settled at Tiverton, Devon. His father was master of the grammar-school there.

‡ *The Tatler*, vol. i., ed. 1786, p. 435, in a note, says, "John Tradescant senior is supposed to have been of Dutch or Flemish extraction, and to have settled in this kingdom probably about the end of Queen Elizabeth's reign, or in the beginning of the reign of James I." Father and son were very ingenious persons, and worthy of esteem for their early promotion and culture of the science of natural history and botany. The son formed the Tradescant Museum at Oxford.

Antwerp, fled from that city, and took refuge, some in England and others in Germany. Several of the Flemish De Grotes had before then settled in England. Thus, among the letters of denization contained in Mr. Brewer's *Calendar of State Papers*, Henry VIII., we find the following:

"Ambrose de Grote, merchant, of the Duchy of Brabant (Letters of Denization, Patent 11th of June, 1510, 2 Henry VIII.).

"12 Feby., 1512-13. Protection for one year for Ambrose and Peter de Grote, merchants of Andwarp, in Brabant, going in the retinue of Sir Gilbert Talbot, Deputy of Calais."

One of the refugee Grotes is supposed to have settled as a merchant at Bremen, from which city the grandfather of the present Mr. Grote, the historian of Greece, came over to London early in the last century, and established first a mercantile house and afterward a banking house, both of which flourished. But Mr. Grote is also of Huguenot blood, being descended by his mother's side from Colonel Blosset, commander of "Blosset's Foot," the scion of an ancient Protestant family of Touraine, an officer in the army of Queen Anne, and the proprietor of a considerable estate in the county of Dublin, where he settled subsequent to the Revocation of the Edict of Nantes.

The great French immigration which ensued on the last-named event, being the most recent, has left much more noticeable traces in English family history and nomenclature notwithstanding the large proportion of the refugees and their descendants who threw aside their French names and adopted them in an English translation. Thus L'Oiseau became Bird; Le Jeune, Young; Le Blanc, White; Le Noir, Black; Le Maur, Brown; Le Roy, King; Lacroix, Cross; Le Monnier, Miller; Dulau, Waters; and so on. Some of the Lefevres changed their name to the English equivalent of Smith, as was the case with the ancestor of Sir Culling Eardley Smith, Bart., a French refugee whose original name was Le Fevre. Many names were strangely altered in their conversion from French into English. Jolifemme was freely translated into Pretyman—a name well known in the Church; Momerie became Mummery, a common name at Dover; and Planché became Plank, of which there are instances at Canterbury and Southampton. At Oxford, the name of Willamise was traced back to Villebois; Taillebois became Talboys; Le Coq, Laycock; Bouchier, Butcher or Boxer; Coquerel, Cockerill; Drouet, Drewitt; D'Aeth, Death; D'Orleans, Dorling; and Sauvage, Savage and Wild. Other pure French names were dreadfully vulgarized. Thus Condé became Cundy; Chapùis, Shoppee; De Preux, Diprose; De Moulins, Mullins; Pelletier, Pelter; Huyghens, Huggins or Higgins; and Beaufoy, Boffy !*

Many pure French names have, however, been preserved; and one need only turn over the pages of a *London Directory* to recognize the large proportion which the descendants of the Huguenots continue to form of the modern population of the metropolis. But a short time since, in reading the report of a meeting of the district board of works at Wandsworth—where the refugees settled in such numbers as to form a considerable congregation—we recognized the names of Lobjoit, Baringer, Fourdrinier, Poupart, and others, unmistakably French. Such names are constantly "cropping out" in modern literature, science, art, and manufactures. Thus we recognize those of Delaine† and Fonblanque in the press; Rigaud and Roget in science; Dargan (originally Dargent) in railway construction; Pigou in gunpowder; Gillott in steel pens; Courage in beer; and Courtauld in silk.

* Mr. Lower, in his *Patronymica Britannica*, suggests that Richard Despair, a poor man buried at East Grinstead in 1726, was, in the orthography of his ancestors, a Despard.

Among other conversions of French into English names may be mentioned the following: Letellier, converted into Taylour; Brasseur into Brassey; Batcheler into Bachelor; Lenoir into Lennard; De Leau into Dillon; Pigou into Pigott; Breton into Britton; Dieudonné into Dudney; Baudoir into Baudry; Guilbert into Gilbert; Koch into Cox; Renalls into Reynolds; Merineau into Meryon; Petit into Pettit; Reveil into Revill; Saveroy into Savery; Gebon into Gibbon; Scardeville into Sharwell; Levereau into Lever; and so on with many more.

† Peter de Laine, Esq., a Protestant refugee, French tutor to the children of the Duke of York, obtained letters of naturalization dated 14th of October, 1681.—DURRANT COOPER'S *Lists*, etc.. 30-1.

That the descendants of the Huguenots have vindicated and continued to practice that liberty of thought and worship for which their fathers sacrificed so much, is sufficiently obvious from the fact that among them we find men holding such widely different views as the brothers Newman, Father Faber and James Martineau, Dr. Pusey and the Rev. Hugh Stowell. The late Rev. Sydney Smith was a man of a different temperament from all these. He was himself accustomed to attribute much of his constitutional gayety to the circumstance of his grandfather having married Maria Olier, the daughter of a French Protestant refugee—a woman whom he characterizes as "of a noble countenance and as noble a mind."

From the peerage to the working class, the descendants of the refugees are to this day found pervading the various ranks of English society. The Queen of England herself is related to them, through her descent from Sophia Dorothea, granddaughter of the Marquis d'Olbreuse, a Protestant nobleman of Poitou. The marquis was one of the numerous French exiles who took refuge in Brandenburg on the Revocation of the Edict of Nantes. The Duke of Zell married his only daughter, whose issue was Sophia Dorothea, the wife of George Louis, Elector of Hanover, afterward George I. of England. The son of Sophia Dorothea succeeded to the English throne as George II., and her daughter married Frederick William, afterward King of Prussia; and thus Huguenot blood continues to run in the royal families of the two great Protestant states of the North.

Several descendants of French Huguenots have become elevated to the British peerage. Of these the most ancient is the family of Trench, originally De la Tranche, the head of which is the Earl of Clancarty. Frederick, lord of La Tranche in Poitou, took refuge in England about the year 1574, shortly after the massacre of St. Bartholomew. He settled for a time in Northumberland, from whence he passed over into Ireland. Of his descendants, one branch founded the peerage of Clancarty, and another that of Ashtown. Several members of the family have held high offices in Church and State, among whom may be mentioned Power le Poer Trench, the last Archbishop of Tuam, and the present Archbishop of Dublin, in whom the two Huguenot names of Trench and Chenevix are honorably united.

Among other peers of Huguenot origin are Lord Northwick, descended from John Rushout, a French refugee who established himself in London in the reign of Charles I.; Lord de Blaquiere, descended from John de Blacquire, a scion of a noble French family, who settled as a merchant in London shortly after the Revocation; and Lord Rendlesham, descended from Peter Thelusson, grandson of a French refugee who about the same time took refuge in Switzerland.

Besides these elevations to the peerage of descendants of Huguenots in the direct male line, many of the daughters of distinguished refugees and their offspring formed unions with noble families, and led to a farther intermingling of the blood of the Huguenots with that of the English aristocracy. Thus the blood of the noble family of Ruvigny mingles with that of Russell* (Duke of Bedford) and Cavendish (Duke of Devonshire); of Schomberg with that of Osborne (Duke of Leeds); of Champagné (neé De la Rochefoucauld) with that of Forbes (Earl of Granard); of Portal and Boileau with that of Elliot (Earl of Minto); of Auriol with that of Hay Drummond (Earl of Kinnoul); of D'Albiac† with that of Innes-Ker (Duke of

---

* Rachel, daughter of Daniel de Massue, Seigneur de Ruvigny, married Thomas Wriothesley, Earl of Southampton, in 1634. The countess died in 1637, leaving two daughters, one of whom, Elizabeth, afterward married the Earl of Gainsborough, and the other, Rachel, married, first Lord Vaughan, and secondly William Lord Russell, known as "the patriot." Every one has heard of his celebrated wife, the daughter of a Ruvigny, whose son afterward became second Duke of Bedford, and whose two daughters married, one the Duke of Devonshire, and the other the Marquis of Granby.

† The D'Albiacs were a noble Protestant family of Nismes, who were almost exterminated at the Revocation. The father, mother, four sons, and three daughters were murdered. Two sons escaped death, one of whom abjured Protestantism to save the family estate, the other sent his two children to England, dispatching them in hampers. They arrived safely, and founded two families. The late Lieutenant General Sir J. C. Dalbiac was the lineal

Roxburghe); of La Touche with that of Butler-Danvers (Earl of Lanesborough); of Montolieu with that of Murray (Lord Elibank); and so on in numerous other instances.

Among recent peerages are those of Taunton, Eversley, and Romilly, all direct descendants of Huguenots. The first Labouchere who settled in England was Peter Cæsar Labouchere. He had originally taken refuge from the persecution in Holland, where he joined the celebrated house of Hope at Amsterdam, and he came over to London as the representative of that firm. He eventually acquired wealth and distinction, and the head of the family now sits in the House of Lords as Baron Taunton.

The Lefevres originally came from Poitou, where Sebastian Lefevre, M.D., was distinguished as a physician. Pierre, one of his sons, suffered death for his religion. The father, with his two other sons, John and Isaac, took refuge in England. The former entered the army, and rose to the rank of lieutenant colonel, serving under Marlborough all through his campaigns in the Low Countries. The second son, Isaac, from whom Lord Eversley (late Speaker of the House of Commons) is lineally descended, commenced and carried on successfully the business of a silk manufacturer in Spitalfields. John Lefevre, the last of the Spitalfields branch in the male line, possessed considerable property at Old Ford, which is still in the family; and his only daughter Helena having married Charles Shaw, of Lincoln's Inn, in 1789, their descendants have since borne the name and arms of the Lefevres.*

The story of the Romilly family is well known through the admirable autobiography left by the late Sir Samuel Romilly, and published by his sons.† The great-grandfather

---

descendant of one of them, and his only daughter married the present Duke of Roxburghe.

* DURRANT COOPER—*Lists of Foreign Protestants and Aliens:* Camden Society, 1862.
† *Memoirs of the Life of Sir Samuel Romilly, written by himself.* Edited by his Sons. 3 vols. London, 1840.

of Sir Samuel was a considerable landed proprietor in the neighborhood of Montpellier. Though a Protestant by conviction, he conformed to Roman Catholicism, with the object of saving the family property for the benefit of his only son. Yet he secretly worshiped after his own principles, as well as brought up his son in them. The youth, indeed, imbibed Protestantism so deeply, that in the year 1701, when only seventeen, he went to Geneva for the sole purpose of receiving the sacrament—the administration of the office by Protestant ministers in France rendering them liable, if detected, to death or condemnation to the galleys for life. At Geneva young Romilly met the celebrated preacher Saurin, then in the height of his fame, who happened to be there on a visit. The result of his conversations with Saurin was the formation in his mind of a fixed determination to leave forever his native country, his parents, and the inheritance which awaited him, and trust to his own industry for a subsistence in some foreign land, where he might be free to worship God according to conscience.

Young Romilly accordingly set out for London, and it was not until he had landed in England that he apprised his father of the resolution he had formed. After a few years' residence in London, where he married Judith de Monsallier, the daughter of another refugee, Mr. Romilly began the business of a wax-bleacher at Hoxton, his father supplying him from time to time with money. But a sad reverse of fortune ensued on the death of his father, which shortly after took place. A distant relative, who was a Catholic, took possession of the family estate, and farther remittances from France came to an end. Then followed difficulty, bankruptcy, and distress; and the landowner's son, unable to bear up under his calamities, sank under them at an early age, leaving a widow and a family of eight children almost entirely unprovided for.

His youngest son, Peter, father of the future Sir Samuel, was bound apprentice to a French refugee jeweler, named Lafosse, whose shop was in Broad Street. On arriving at manhood he went to Paris, where he worked as a journeyman, saving money enough to make an excursion as far south as Montpellier to view the family estate, now in the possession of strangers and irrecoverably lost, since it could only be redeemed, if at all, by apostasy. The jeweler eventually returned to London, married a Miss Garnault, like himself descended from a Protestant refugee, and began business on his own account. He seems to have enjoyed a moderate degree of prosperity, living carefully and frugally, bringing up his family virtuously and religiously, and giving them as good an education as his comparative slender means would admit, until the death of a rich relative of his wife, a Mr. de la Haize, who left considerable legacies to each member of the family, enabled Mr. Romilly to article his son Samuel to a clerk in chancery, and enter upon the profession in which he eventually acquired so much distinction. It is unnecessary to describe his career, which has been so simply and beautifully related by himself, or to trace the farther history of the family, the head of which now sits in the House of Lords under the title of Baron Romilly.

The baronetage, as well as the peerage, includes many descendants of the Huguenots. Jacques Boileau was Lord of Castelnau and St. Croix, near Nismes, in the neighborhood of which the persecution long raged so furiously. He was the father of a family of twenty-two children, and could not readily leave France at the Revocation; but, being known as a Protestant, and refusing to be converted, he was arrested and placed under restraint, in which condition he died. His son Charles fled, first into Holland, and afterward into England, where he entered the army, obtained the rank of captain, and commanded a corps of French gentlemen under Marlborough at the battle of Blenheim. He afterward settled as a wine-merchant at Dublin, and was succeeded by his son. The family prospered; and the great-grandson of Marlborough's captain was promoted to a baronetcy, the present wearer of the title being Sir John Boileau.

The Crespignys also belonged to a noble family in Lower Normandy. Claude Champion, Lord of Crespigny, was an officer in the French army; and at the Revocation he fled into England, accompanied by his wife, the Comtesse de Vierville, and a family of eight children, two of whom were carried on board the ship in which they sailed in baskets. De Crespigny entered the British army, and served as colonel under Marlborough. The present head of the family is Sir C. W. Champion Crespigny, Bart.

Elias Bouhérau, M.D., an eminent physician in Rochelle, being debarred the practice of his profession by the edict of Louis XIV., fled into England with his wife and children, and settled in Ireland, where his descendants rose to fame and honor, the present representative of the family being Sir E. R. Borough, Bart.

Anthony Vinchon de Bacquencourt, a man eminent for his learning, belonged to Rouen, of the Parliament of which his father was president. He was originally a Roman Catholic, but, being incensed at the pretended miracles wrought at the tomb of the Abbé Paris, he embraced Protestantism, and fled from France. He settled in Dublin under the name of Des Vœux (the family surname), and became minister of the French church there; afterward joining the Rev. John Peter Droz, another French refugee, in starting the first literary journal that ever appeared in Ireland. The present representative of the family is Sir C. Des Vœux, Bart.

Among other baronets descended from French refugees may be mentioned Sir John Lambert, descended from John Lambert, of the Isle of Rhé; Sir J. D. Legard, descended from John Legard, of ancient Norman lineage; Sir A. J. de Hochepied Larpent, descended from John de Larpent, of Caen; and Sir G. S. Brooke Pechell, descended from the Pechells of Montauban, in Languedoc. One of the members of the last-mentioned family having embraced Roman Catholicism, his descendants still hold the family estate in France.

Many of the refugees and their descendants have also sat in

Parliament, and done good service there. Probably the first Huguenot member of the House of Commons was Philip Papillon, who sat for the city of London in 1695. The Papillons had suffered much for their religion in France, one of them having lain in jail at Avranches for three years. Various members of the family have since sat in Parliament for Dover, Romney, and Colchester.

Of past members of Parliament, the Pechells have sat for Essex; the Fonneraus for Aldborough; the Durants for St. Ives and Evesham; the Devagnes for Barnstaple; the Maugers for Poole; the La Roches for Bodmin; and the Amyands for Tregony, Bodmin, and Camelford. The last member of the Amyand family was a baronet, who assumed the name of Cornewall on marrying Catharine, the heiress of Velters Cornewall, Esq., of Moccas Court, Herefordshire; and his only daughter, having married Sir Thomas Frankland Lewis, became the mother of the late Sir George Cornewall Lewis, Bart.

Many descendants of the Huguenots who had settled in Ireland also represented constituencies in the Irish Parliament. Thus the La Touches sat for Catherton; the Chaigneaus for Gowran; and the celebrated William Saurin, who filled the office of Irish attorney general for fourteen years, may be said to have represented all Ireland. He was a man of great ability and distinguished patriotism, and, but for his lack of ambition, would have been made a judge and a peer, both of which dignities he refused. Colonel Barré, who belonged to the refugee family of the name settled in Ireland, is best known by his parliamentary career in England. He was celebrated as an orator and a patriot, resisting to the utmost the passing of the American Stamp Act, which severed the connection between England and her American colonies. In 1776 he held the office of Vice-Treasurer of Ireland, and afterward that of Paymaster to the Forces for England.

Among more recent members of Parliament may be mentioned the names of Dupré, Gavin, Hugessen, Jervoise, Labouchere, Layard, Lefevre, Lefroy, Paget (of the Leicestershire family, formerly member for Nottingham), Pusey, Tomline, Rebow, and Vandeleur. Mr. Chevalier Cobbold is descended by the female side from Samuel le Chevalier, minister of the French church in London in 1591, one of whose descendants introduced the well-known Chevalier barley. Mr. Du Cane is descended from the same family to which the great admiral belonged. The first Du Cane or Du Quesne who fled into England for refuge settled at Canterbury, and afterward in London. The head of this family was an alderman of the city in 1666, and in the next century his grandson Richard sat for Colchester in Parliament, the present representative of the Du Canes being the member for North Essex.

Of the descendants of refugees who were distinguished as divines may be mentioned the Majendies, one of whom—John James, son of the pastor of the French church at Exeter—was Prebendary of Sarum, and a well-known author; and another, son of the prebendary, became Bishop of Chester, and afterward of Bangor. The Saurins also rose to eminence in the Church, Louis Saurin, minister of the French church in the Savoy, having been raised to the Deanery of St. Patrick's, Ardagh; while his son afterward became Vicar of Belfast, and his grandson Bishop of Dromore. Roger du Quesne, grandson of the Marquis du Quesne, was Vicar of East Tuddenham in Norfolk, and a prebendary of Ely.

One of the most eminent scholars of Huguenot origin was the Rev. Dr. Jortin, Archdeacon of London. He was the son of René Jortin, a refugee from Brittany, who served as secretary to three British admirals successively, and went down with Sir Cloudesley Shovel in the ship in which he was wrecked off the Scilly Isles in 1707. The son of René was entered a pupil at the Charter-House, and gave early indications of ability, which were justified by the distinction which he shortly after achieved at Cambridge. On the recommendation of Dr. Thirlby, young Jortin furnished Pope with translations from the commentary of Eustathius on Homer, as well as with notes for his translation of the *Iliad;* but, though Pope adapted them almost verbatim, he made no acknowledgment of the labors of his young helper. Shortly after, on a fellowship becoming vacant at Cambridge by the death of William Rosen, the descendant of another refugee, Jortin was appointed to it. A few years later he was appointed to the vicarage of Swavesey, in Cambridgeshire, from whence he removed to the living of Kensington, near London. There he distinguished himself as the author of many learned works, of which the best known is his able and elaborate *Life of Erasmus.* He was eventually made Archdeacon of London, and died in 1770 at Kensington, where he was buried.

Another celebrated divine was the Rev. George Lewis Fleury, Archdeacon of Waterford—" the good old archdeacon" he was called—widely known for his piety, his charity, and his goodness. He was descended from Louis Fleury, pastor of Tours, who fled into England with his wife and family at the Revocation. Several of the Fleurys are still clergymen in Ireland.

The Maturins also have produced some illustrious men. The pastor Gabriel Maturin, from whom they are descended, lay a prisoner in the Bastile for twenty-six years on account of his religion. But he tenaciously refused to be converted, and was at length discharged, a cripple for life, having lost the use of his limbs through his confinement. He contrived, however, to reach Ireland with some members of his former flock, and there he unexpectedly found his wife and two sons, of whom he had heard nothing during the long period of his imprisonment. His son Peter arrived at some distinction in the Church, having become Dean of Killala; and his grandson Gabriel James became Dean of St. Patrick's, Dublin. From him descended several clergymen of eminence, one of them an eloquent preacher, who is also more generally known as the author of two remarkable works—*Melmoth the Wanderer*, and the tragedy of *Bertram*.

There were numerous other descendants of the refugees, clergymen and others, besides those already named, who distinguished themselves by their literary productions. Louis Dutens, who held the living of Elsdon, in Northumberland, produced a successful tragedy, *The Return of Ulysses*, when only about eighteen years of age. In his later years he was the author of numerous works of a more solid character, of which one of the best known is his *Researches on the Origin of Discoveries attributed to the Moderns*—a work full of learning and labor. He also wrote an *Appeal to Good Sense*, being a defense of Christianity against Voltaire and the Encyclopædists, besides numerous other works.

The Rev. William Romaine, Rector of St. Ann's, Blackfriars, was the son of a French refugee who had settled at Hartlepool as a merchant and corn-dealer. Mr. Romaine was one of the most popular of London clergymen, and his *Life, Walk, and Triumph of Faith* is to this day a well-known and popular book among religious readers. Romaine has been compared to " a diamond, rough often, but very pointed ; and the more he was broken by years, the more he appeared to shine." Much of his life was passed in polemical controversy, and in maintaining the Calvinistic views which he so strongly held. He was a most diligent improver of time; and, besides being exemplary and indefatigable in performing the duties of his office, he left behind him a large number of able works, which were collected and published in 1796, in eight octavo volumes.

The Rev. David Durand, F.R.S., was another voluminous writer on history, biography, philosophy, and science. Among his various works were those on *The Philosophical Writings of Cicero*, a *History of the Sixteenth Century*, and two volumes in continuation of Rapin's *History of England*.

We have already spoken of the distinction achieved by Saurin and Romilly at the Irish and English bar. But they did not stand alone. Of the numerous lawyers descended from the refugees, several have achieved no less eminence as judges than as pleaders. Of these, Baron Mazeres, appointed Curzitor Baron of the Exchequer in 1773, was one of the most illustrious. He was no less distinguished as a man of science than as a lawyer, his writings on arithmetic, algebra, and mathematics being still prized.* Justice Le Blanc and Sir John Bosanquet were also of like French extraction, the latter being descended from Pierre Bosanquet, of Lunel, in Languedoc. Chief Justice Lefroy and Justice Perrin, of the Irish bench, were in like manner descended from Huguenot families long settled in Ireland.

A long list might be given, in addition to those already mentioned, of persons illustrious in literature, science, and the arts, who sprang from the same stock; but we must be content with mentioning only a few. Peter Anthony Motteaux was not less distinguished for his enterprise as an East India merchant than for his ability as a writer; and Sir John Charden, the traveler and author, afterward jeweler to the court, was esteemed in his time as a man of great parts and of noble character. Garrick, the great English actor, was for the most part French, his real name being Garrigue, that of the Huguenot family to which he belonged. The French

* William Cobbett says of him, "I knew the baron well. He was a most conscientious man; he was, when I first knew him, still a very clever man; he retained all his faculties to a very great age. . . . He was the only man that I ever heard of who refused to have his salary augmented when an augmentation offered, and when all other such salaries were augmented. . . . The baron was a most implacable enemy of the Roman Catholics, as Catholics. There was rather a peculiar reason for this: his grandfather having been a French Huguenot, and having fled with his children to England at the time of the Revocation of the Edict of Nantes. . . . There was great excuse for the baron. He had been told that his father and mother had been driven out of France by the Catholics; and there was that mother dinning this in his ears, and all manner of horrible stories along with it, during all the tender years of his life. In short, the prejudice made part of his very frame. . . . The baron was a very humane man; his humanity made him assist to support the French emigrant priests; but, at the same time, he caused Sir Richard Musgrove's book against the Irish Cathòlics to be published at his own expense. He and I never agreed upon this subject; but this subject was, with him, a vital one. He had no asperity in his nature; he was naturally all gentleness and benevolence, and therefore he never resented what I said to him on this subject (and which nobody else ever, I believe, ventured to say to him); but he did not like it; and he liked it the less because I certainly beat him in the argument."—*Rural Rides*, ed. 1830, p. 251-3.

D'Aubignés have given us several eminent men, bearing the name of Daubeny, celebrated in natural history. Among other men of science we note the names of Rigaud, Sivilian professor of astronomy at Oxford, and Roget the physiologist, author of one of the Bridgewater treatises. The Rev. G. J. Faber also is descended from a French refugee who came over at the Revocation. The Martineaus, so well known in English literature, are descended from Gaston Martineau, a surgeon of Dieppe, who settled at Norwich in 1685; and the Barbaulds are sprung from a minister of the French church of La Patente in London. Some of our best novelists have been of like French extraction. Captain Marryatt and Captain Chamier, whose nautical tales have charmed so many English readers, were both descended from illustrious Huguenots, as was also Tom D'Urfey, the English song-writer; and Miss Burney and Mrs. Radcliffe* were in like manner descended by the female side from Protestant refugees. It has also been supposed that the family of De Foe (or Vaux) were of Huguenot origin.

Several men of considerable distinction in science and invention emanated from the Huguenot settlers in Spitalfields, which long continued to be the great French quarter of London. The French hand-loom weavers were in many respects a superior class of workmen, though their earnings were comparatively small in amount. Their employment was sedentary, and it was entirely of a domestic character, the workshop being almost invariably situated over the dwelling, and approached through it. All the members of the family took part in the work, which was of such a nature as not to prevent conversation; and when several looms were worked on the same floor, this was generally of an intellectual character. One of the young people was usually appointed to read to those at work, it might be a book on history, or frequently a controversial work, the refugee divines being among the

---

* Mrs. Radcliffe was descended from a Walloon family, the De Witts, settled at Hatfield Chase.

most prolific authors of their time. Nor were the sufferings of the Huguenots at the galleys and in the prisons throughout France forgotten in the dwellings of the exiles, who often spoke of them to their children, and earnestly enjoined them to keep steadfast in the faith for which their fathers had endured so much.

The circumstances in which the children of the Huguenot workmen were thus brought up—their domestic training, their religious discipline, and their school culture—rendered them for the most part intelligent and docile, while their industry was proverbial. The exiles indulged in simple pleasures, and were especially noted for their love of flowers. They vied with one another in the production of the finest plants, and wherever they settled they usually set up a floricultural society to exhibit their products. One of the first societies of the kind in England was that established by the exiles in Spitalfields; and when a body of them went over to Dublin to carry on the manufacture of poplins, they proceeded to set on foot the celebrated Flower Club which still exists in that city. Others of them, who settled in Manchester and Macclesfield, carried thither the same love of flowers and botany, which still continues so remarkably to characterize their descendants.

Among the hand-loom weavers of Spitalfields were also to be found occasional inquirers into physical science, as well as several distinguished mathematicians. They were encouraged in these studies by the societies which were established for their cultivation, a philosophical hall having been founded with that object in Crispin Street, Spitalfields.* Though Simpson and Edwards, both professors of mathematics at Woolwich, were not of French extraction, they were both silk-weavers in Spitalfields, and taught the mathematics there. The Dollonds, however, were of pure French origin. The parents of John Dollond were Protestant refugees from

* The building, which still exists, is now used as an earthenware-store.

Normandy, from whence they came shortly after the Revocation. His father was a silk-weaver, to which trade John was also brought up. From an early age he displayed a genius for construction, and he embraced every opportunity of reading and studying books on geometry, mathematics, and general science. He was, however, unable to devote more than his spare moments to such subjects; and when he reached manhood and married, his increasing family compelled him to work at his loom more assiduously than ever. Nevertheless, he went on accumulating information, not only on mathematics, but on anatomy, natural history, astronomy, and optics, reading also extensively in divinity and ecclesiastical history. In order to read the New Testament in the original, he even learned Greek, and to extend his knowledge of foreign literature, he also learned Latin, French, German, and Italian.

John Dollond apprenticed his eldest son Peter to an optician; and on the expiry of the young man's apprenticeship, at the age of twenty, he opened a shop in Vine Street, Spitalfields. The business proved so prosperous that, shortly after, the elder Dollond was induced to leave his loom at the age of forty-six, and enter into partnership with his son as an optician. He was now enabled to devote himself wholly to his favorite studies, and to pursue as a business the art which before had occupied him chiefly as an amusement.

One of the first subjects to which Dollond devoted himself was the improvement of the refracting telescope. He entered on a series of experiments, which extended over several years, at first without results; but at length, after " a resolute perseverance" (to use his own words), he made the decisive experiment which showed the error of Newton's conclusion as to the supposed law of refraction. The papers embodying Dollond's long succession of experiments were printed in the Transactions of the Philosophical Society, and for the last of them he was awarded the Royal Society's Copley medal. The result of the discovery was an immediate great improvement in the powers and accuracy of the telescope and microscope, of which the Dollond firm reaped the result in a large increase of business, which still continues in the family.

We might greatly enlarge the list of descendants of the Huguenots illustrious for their inventions in the arts, but will conclude with a brief account of the life of Lewis Paul, partly because it is little known, and also because his invention of spinning by rollers, subsequently revived and successfully applied by Sir Richard Arkwright, has exercised so extraordinary an influence on the manufacturing system of England and the world at large.

Lewis Paul was the son of a French refugee who carried on business as a druggist in St. Paul's Church-yard. By this calling he acquired a considerable property, and at his death he left his son under the guardianship of Lord Shaftesbury, and his brother the Honorable M. A. Cooper. We have no information as to his bringing up, but gather from his papers that Lewis led a gay life as a young man, fell into bad company, and, to pay his debts, mortgaged the valuable property in the parish of St. Bride's which his father had left him. He was evidently on the high road to ruin unless he reformed his habits, and that speedily. He had the courage to break off his connection with his former associates, though by that time his purse was nearly empty; and he proceeded to apply himself to business connected with invention.

In a letter addressed by him to the Earl of Shaftesbury, son of his guardian, many years later, Paul said: "As it too often happens with young sparks, I made but an ill use of my position and patronage. However, before the calamities I had laid the foundation of had reached me, I had exerted myself to the repair of my affairs with such ardor and success, that, notwithstanding the various impediments necessarily in the way of a person who had spent his time in every way so remote from the arts of trade, I nevertheless completed a machine of great value in the most extensive manufacture of the kingdom."* The machine to which he thus referred was that for spinning by rollers, on the principle subsequently adopted and completed by Sir Richard Arkwright.

It appears that the first invention of Paul was a machine for the pinking of crapes, tammies, etc., which brought him considerable profit. He employed a number of women to work the machine, among whom we find Mrs. Demoulins, a protegée of Dr. Johnson, frequently referred to in Boswell's *Life*. It is probable that Paul's connection with the French manufacturers of Spitalfields served to direct his attention to the invention of new methods of facilitating production, with the object of turning them to account in the raising of his depressed fortunes.

Shortly after we find him in communication with John Wyatt, of Weeford, near Lichfield, afterward of Birmingham, well known in his district as a highly ingenious and expert workman. It appears from the papers of Wyatt, which we have carefully examined,† that he had invented a file-cutting machine, which he agreed to dispose of, " when perfected," to one Richard Heely, of Birmingham, a gunmaker, for certain considerations. But Heely having become involved in difficulties, the agreement came to an end, and Wyatt looked out for another customer for his invention. Such he found in Lewis Paul; and in September, 1732, an agreement was entered into between them, in which Paul is described as " of the parish of St. Andrew's, Holborn, gentleman," and Wyatt as " of the parish of Weeford, county of Stafford, carpenter." By this agreement Paul bound himself to the same terms as Heely had done, though the machine was declared to be " not yet perfected and completed." Paul, however, being unable to pay the stipulated instalments, reconveyed the invention to Wyatt in the following year by a deed in which it is de-

* Paper read by Robert Cole, F.S.A., before the British Association at Leeds, 1858.
† These papers have been kindly lent us for examination by Mrs. Silvester, a descendant of John Wyatt.

scribed as "a certain tool or instrument intended to be used in and for the cutting of files."*

We next find Paul residing at Birmingham, and Wyatt employed under his directions in bringing out a new invention for spinning fibrous materials by machinery. It is said that Wyatt had before that time made a model of such a machine while residing at Sutton Coldfield, by means of which he was enabled to spin thread successfully; and probably Paul was only acting on the suggestion first thrown out by Wyatt, in proceeding to join him for the purpose of bringing the machine to perfection. Both were equally short of money, but Paul had greater facilities for raising means among his London friends, at the same time that he carried on his business of pinking crape and tammies. Both were men of hot temper, and being hampered for want of money and struggling with difficulties, they often quarreled violently, and usually ended by agreeing and working together again. The invention seems to have occupied the minds of both for more than four years, during which time they occasionally proceeded to London, Paul to try and raise money among his friends, and Wyatt to visit the manufacturers' shops in Spitalfields and obtain practical hints from the manufacturers for the purposes of the machine.

Paul returned to Birmingham, leaving Wyatt in London to proceed with "the work;" the former sending remittances in payment of Wyatt's agreed salary, according as the money could be raised. In one of Paul's letters, inclosing a remittance for salary and "work done," he says: "As to particulars, I dare say when you see Perriere's work you'll remember the whole design I have laid down." In a letter written two days later, Paul says: "When I wrote you last, being in a good deal of haste, I apprehend that I omitted some directions necessary. A principal was, that you should take a lodging either where you are not known, or where you can have the highest confidence to remove the tool to,

* Wyatt MSS.

and to prepare that work, for I would not have it seen by any body besides yourself for any reasons." Toward the end of the year 1737 Paul was still struggling with difficulties as to money, putting off Wyatt with excuses, assuring him that if it were possible to borrow he should be supplied forthwith, and that he himself was extremely anxious to be in town, but could not stir for want of the "*primum mobile.*" In his next letter, all that he could send Wyatt was two guineas, which he had raised " with much difficulty ;" but he hoped to have more soon, when he would immediately set out for London.

In the beginning of 1738, Paul wrote to Wyatt in great joy, having been at length enabled to obtain a sum of money from Mr. Warren, a Birmingham bookseller; but it had been advanced on the express condition that it was to be invested in Paul's crape business, over which Mr. Warren was to have control, excepting the sum of £70, which Paul was to be at liberty to employ for his own purposes. On the strength of this advance, he proceeded to ask Wyatt if he would engage to work on a salary for six months, with a view to the perfecting of the machine. Wyatt answered that he could give four days a week, at 5*s.* a day, to the forwarding of Paul's work, taking a payment of 17*s.* weekly on account, and leaving the rest to accumulate until Paul was able to pay him. This was a most generous offer on the part of Wyatt, who was laboring with self-denying zeal to perfect the invention, occasionally pawning his clothes to maintain himself and wife until remittances arrived from Birmingham, the suit which he wore being so ragged that he declared he was ashamed to be seen abroad in it.

In the mean time Paul was impatient for the completion of the model, which was delayed in consequence of the secrecy which was observed with respect to it, the whole of the work having to be done by Wyatt himself. At length the model was ready, and Paul proceeded to London to take out a patent for the invention of spinning wool and cotton by means of rollers. His petition was enrolled in January, 1738, and the patent was issued in the month of July following. The process detailed in the specification is clearly akin to that afterward revived by Arkwright, and by him turned to such profitable account. The sliver "is put between a pair of rollers," . . . and, "being turned round by their motion, draws in the raw mass of wool or cotton to be spun in proportion to the velocity of such rollers;" and "a succession of other rollers, moving proportionately faster than the rest, draw the rope, thread, or sliver into any degree of fineness that may be required;" in addition to which, "the bobbyn, spole, or quill, upon which the thread is spun, is so contrived as to draw faster than the first rollers give, and in such proportion as the sliver is supposed to be diminished." The whole principle of spinning by rollers is clearly embodied in this description; and that it was the invention of Lewis Paul is clear from a memorandum in the handwriting of John Wyatt, found among his papers, to the following effect:

"*Thoughts originally Mr. Paul's.*—1. The joining of the rolls. 2. Their passing through cylinders. 3. The calculation of the wheels, by which means the bobbin draws faster than those cylinders: this, I presume, was picked up somewhere before I knew him."

The rest of the details of the invention were claimed by Wyatt—"the horizontal and tracer, the conic whorves," the proportional size of the spindle and bobbin, and sundry other mechanical details of the machine.

But, though Paul secured a patent for his invention, and sold sundry licenses to manufacturers to spin wool and cotton after his process, it does not appear that it proved very successful. James Johnson, a manufacturer in Spitalfields, bought a license to use 150 spindles. Warren, the Birmingham bookseller, took a license for 50 spindles, in consideration of the money owing to him by Paul, being induced to do so by the favorable report of Dr. James, of fever-powder celebrity.* Edward Cave also, the printer of the *Gentleman's Magazine*, was tempted to embark in the speculation. He bought from Paul a license for 250 spindles, and in 1740 he started a spinning-mill on Turnhill Brook, a little to the north of Fleet Bridge, at the back of Field Lane, Holborn. John Wyatt was so sanguine as to the success of the invention that he too, like Warren, agreed to take a grant of 300 spindles in discharge of the debt of £820 which Paul by this time owed to him.

But all the attempts made to spin by Paul's machine proved comparatively unsuccessful as regarded profitable results. Johnson's mill in Spitalfields was accidentally burned down, and he did not care to repeat the experiment. Cave could not work his spindles to a profit, though the mill was superintended by Paul himself, and it was shortly given up. Wyatt was not more fortunate. He first started fifty spindles in a large warehouse near the Well in the Upper Priory, Birmingham. The movement was given to the machinery by two or more asses working round an axis, and required some ten girls to attend to the work. After a short trial, Wyatt found himself in difficulties and in debt, and a few months later we find him a prisoner in the Fleet. His assignees sold the spindles to a Mr. Samuel Touchet (a French refugee), of Northampton, whither they were removed from Birmingham; and Wyatt, having taken advantage of the Insolvent Debtors' Act, and obtained his discharge, went down to Northampton to superintend in person the erection and working of the spinning factory.

It is not necessary to describe the Northampton adventure. Suffice it to say, that after working for more than ten years,†

---

* Dr. James wrote to Mr. Warren thus: "Yesterday I went to see Mr. Paul's machine, which gave us all entire satisfaction, both in regard to the carding and spinning. You have nothing to do but to get a purchaser for your grant: the sight of the thing is demonstration enough. I am certain that if Paul could begin with ten thousand pounds, he must, or at least might, get more money in twenty years than the city of London is worth."

† In 1757 we find John Wyatt, disgusted with the results of the spinning adventure, sending the remainder of his spindles to the manager of the mill

the factory was given up as a failure, Paul alleging that the chief cause lay in the mismanagement of the owners. Touchet was glad to get out of the concern at a loss; on which Edward Cave, doubtless persuaded by Paul, entered upon a lease of the factory; but at his death shortly after, his brother Joseph, to whom the property devolved, became so disheartened that he resolved to abandon the enterprise. Paul, still firmly believing in the soundness of his project, next took a lease of the Northampton mill for twenty-one years; but, being unable to pay the rent, Cave put in a distress for the moneys due to him. On this and other occasions we find Dr. Johnson negotiating between Paul and the Caves, and endeavoring to bring them to terms.* The machinery of the mill at Northampton was eventually sold for the price of the materials; and the experiment, promising as it seemed, and embodying, as it did, the principles of an invention which has since enriched thousands, ended, for the time, in disaster to all concerned.†

Paul continued to add to his inventions. He invented a carding machine in 1748, which he patented; and, ten years

at Northampton: "You have herewith," he said, "a reversion of old gimcracks, which, by order of Mr. Yeo, I am directed to send to you. I most heartily wish Mr. Yeo better success than any of his predecessors have had."

* *Boswell's Life of Johnson*, by CROKER. 1 vol., ed. 1853, p. 43, 101-2-3.

† So far as we can judge from the Wyatt MSS., Paul was the inventor of the principle of spinning by rollers, and Wyatt the skilled mechanic who embodied the principle in a working machine. In a letter addressed by the latter to Sir H. Gough, he describes himself as "the principal agent, I might almost say the sole compiler, of the machine for spinning." Wyatt afterward proved his ability both as a mechanic and an inventor. The machine for weighing loaded carriages, still in use, was invented by him. Among his other inventions was a method of neutralizing the friction of wheels by surrounding the wearing parts of the axle with three or more cylinders inclosed in a steel box impervious to dust—an invention for which several patents have since been taken out, and in one of which Wyatt's expedient has been applied with success in railway turn-tables. Another of his contrivances was a double lathe, of beautiful construction and arrangement, for cutting out of bone the mould in which a peculiar kind of button was formed, which proved of much use in the Birmingham trade. During the later years of his life he was employed by Matthew Boulton, to whom he was of great service in erecting the machinery for Soho. He died in 1766, and his funeral was attended by the principal inhabitants of Birmingham—Baskerville, the printer (also descended from a French refugee), a man of eccentric character, arraying himself on the occasion in a splendid suit of gold lace.

later, he took out a second patent for a spinning machine, substantially the same as the first, embodying many improvements in detail, though not in principle. He did not, however, long survive the grant of this patent, but died shortly after, in April, 1759, at Brook Green, Kensington.

The invention at which Paul had labored with such unfortunate results was at length perfected and introduced into successful practice by Arkwright in 1768, his patent for spinning by rollers having been taken out in the following year. In course of time the invention was generally adopted, and the cotton manufacture became one of the great staple trades of the north of England. The invention of the steam-engine by Watt gave another great impulse to this branch of industry; and the further invention of the power-loom gave almost the death-blow to hand-loom weaving.

From that time the manufactures of Spitalfields, of Dublin, and the other places where the descendants of the refugee artisans had principally settled, fell into comparative decay. Many of the artisans, following the current of trade, left their looms in Spitalfields, and migrated to Coventry, Macclesfield, Manchester, and the other northern manufacturing towns, then rapidly rising in importance. The stronger and more self-reliant pushed out into the world; the more quiescent and feeble remained behind. The hand-loom trade could not be revived, and no amount of patient toil and industry could avert the distress that fell upon the poor silk-weavers, which, even to this day, from time to time sends up its wail in the eastern parts of London.*

* The Rev. Isaac Taylor, incumbent of St. Matthias, Bethnal Green, in a letter to the *Times* of the 14th of February last, thus describes the state of the district:

"This portion of Bethnal Green is the headquarters of what is known as the Spitalfields silk-trade. The silk-weavers, by whom the parish of St. Matthias is mainly populated, are descendants of those Huguenot exiles who, for the cause of God and truth, and liberty and life, fled from the sunny plains of their native France in the years which succeeded the massacre of St. Bartholomew, and who were encouraged by Queen Elizabeth and her advisers to bring their valuable industry to this country, and to settle on the lands adjacent to the Hospital of St. Mary—the Hospital or "Spital-fields,"

Owing to these circumstances, as well as to the gradual intermingling of the foreign with the native population, the French element year by year became less marked in Spitalfields, and in the course of a few generations the religious fervor which had distinguished the original Huguenot refugees entirely died out in their descendants. They might continue to frequent the French churches, but it was in constantly decreasing numbers. The foreign congregations, which had been so flourishing about the beginning of the eighteenth century, toward the end of it became the mere shadows of what they had been, and at length many of them were closed altogether, or were turned over to other denominations.

Sir Samuel Romilly, in his *Autobiography*, gives a touching account of the domestic life of his father's family—their simple pleasures, their reading, society, and conversation. Nearly all the visitors and friends of the family were of French descent. They associated together, worshiped together, and intermarried among each other. The children went to a school kept by a refugee. On Sunday mornings French was exclusively spoken in the family circle, and at least once in the day the family pew in the French Artillery Church was regularly filled. "My father," says Sir Samuel, "had a pew in one of the French chapels, which had been established when the Protestant refugees first emigrated into England, and he required us to attend alternately there and at the parish church [this was about the year 1770]. It was

---

as they were called, which were then just outside the walls of London. The descendants of these emigrants continue to inhabit the district. Many of them still cherish proud traditions of their ancestry; many of them, though now perhaps only clad in rags, bear the old historic names of France—names of distinguished generals, and statesmen, and poets, and historians—names such as Vendome, Ney, Racine, Defoe, La Fontaine, Dupin, Blois, Le Beau, Auvache, Fontaineau, and Montier. In addition to their surnames and their traditions, the only relic which these exiles retain of their former prosperity and gentle nurture is a traditional love of birds and flowers. Few rooms, however wretched, are destitute either of a sickly plant, struggling, like its sickly owner, for bare life, or a caged bird warbling the songs of heaven to the poor imprisoned weaver as he plies his weary labor."

a kind of homage which he paid to the faith of his ancestors, and it was a means of rendering the French language familiar to us; but nothing was ever worse calculated to inspire the mind of a child with respect for religion than such a kind of religious worship. Most of the descendants of the refugees were born and bred in England, and desired nothing less than to preserve the memory of their origin, and the chapels were therefore ill-attended. A large uncouth room, the avenues to which were crowded courts and dirty alleys, and which, when you entered it, presented to the view only irregular unpainted pews, and dusty, unplastered walls; a congregation consisting principally of some strange-looking old women, scattered here and there, two or three in a pew; and a clergyman reading the service and preaching in a monotonous tone of voice, and in a language not familiar to me, was not likely either to impress my mind with much religious awe, or to attract my attention to the doctrines which were delivered. In truth, I did not once attempt to attend to them; my mind was wandering to other subjects, and disporting itself in much gayer scenes than those before me, and little of religion was mixed in my reveries."*

Very few of the refugees returned to France. They long continued to sigh after the land of their fathers, hoping that the religious persecutions abroad would abate, so that they might return to live and die there. But the persecutions did not abate. They flared up again from time to time with increased fury, even after religion had become almost prostrate throughout France. Protestantism, though proscribed, was not, however, dead; and meetings of the Huguenots continued to be held in "the Desert"—by night, in caves, in the woods, among the hills, by the sea-shore, where a body of faithful pastors ministered to them at the hourly peril of their lives. The "Church in the Desert" was even regularly organized, had its stated elders, deacons, and ministers, and appointed circuit meetings. Very rarely were their secrets

* *Life of Sir Samuel Romilly*, i., 15.

betrayed, yet they could not always escape the vigilance of the Jesuits, who continued to track them with the aid of the soldiery and police, and succeeded in sending fresh victims to the galleys so long as they retained their power in France.

Down even to the middle of last century the persecution of the Protestants continued unabated. Thus, at Grenoble, in the years 1745 and 1746, more than three hundred persons were condemned to death, the galleys, or perpetual imprisonment because of their religion. Twenty-nine nobles were condemned to be deprived of their nobility; fourteen persons were banished; four were condemned to be flogged by the common hangman; six women were sentenced to have their heads shaved by the same functionary, and be imprisoned, some for different periods, others for life; two men were condemned to be placed in the pillory; thirty-four were sent to the galleys for from three to five years, six for ten years, and a hundred and sixteen, among whom were forty-six gentlemen and two chevaliers of the order of Saint Louis, were sent to the galleys for life; and four were sentenced to death.* The only crime of which these persons had been guilty was that they had been detected attending Protestant worship contrary to law.

The peace of Aix-la-Chapelle in 1750, which gave a brief repose to Europe, brought no peace to the Huguenots. There was even an increase in the persecutions for a time, for there was a large body of soldiery set at liberty, who became employed in hunting down the Protestants at their meetings in "the Desert." Between the years 1750 and 1762 fifty-eight persons were condemned to the galleys, many of them for life. In the latter year, more than six hundred fugitives fled across the frontier into Switzerland, and passed down the Rhine, through Holland and England, into Ireland, where they settled. It is a somewhat remarkable circumstance that, according to M. Coquerel, one of the last women imprisoned for her religion was condemned by an Irish Roman Catholic, then

* ANTOINE COURT—*Mémoires Historiques*, p. 94 et seq.

in the service of France: "Marguerite Robert, wife of Joseph Vincent, of Valeirarques, in the diocese of Uzès, was arrested in her house because of having been married by a Protestant pastor, and condemned in 1759 by *Monseigneur de Thomond . . . ce Lord Irlandois.*"*

The punishment of the galleys was also drawing to an end. The mutterings of the coming revolution were already beginning to be heard. The long uncontrolled rule of the Jesuits had paved the way for Voltaire and Rousseau, whose influence was beginning to penetrate French society. In 1764 the Jesuits were suppressed by Parliament, and the persecutions in a great measure ceased. In 1769, Alexander Chambon, of Praules, in the Viverais, the last galley-slave for the faith, was discharged from the convict-prison at Toulon through the intervention of the Prince of Beauveau. Chambon was then eighty years old, and had passed twenty-seven years at the galleys, to which he had been condemned for attending a religious meeting.

The last apprehension of a Protestant minister was that of M. Broca, of La Briè, as late as the year 1773; but the spirit of persecution had so much abated that he was only warned and required to change his residence. It began to be felt that while materialism and atheism were being openly taught even by priests and dignitaries of the French Church—by the Abbé de Prades and others—the persecution of the Protestants could no longer be consistently enforced, and they accordingly thenceforward enjoyed a degree of liberty in the exercise of their worship such as they had not experienced since the death of Mazarin.

But this liberty came too late to be of any use to the exiled Huguenots and their descendants settled in England, who had long since given up all hope of returning to the land of their fathers. The revolutionary period shortly followed, after which came the wars of the Republic, and the revival of the old feud between France and England. Many of the de-

* CHARLES COQUEREL—*Histoire des Eglesis du Desert*, ii., p. 428.

scendants of the exiles, no longer desiring to remember their origin, adopted English names, and ceased to be French. Since that time the fusion of the exiles with the English people has become complete, even in Spitalfields. There are still whole quarters of streets there in which the glazed garrets indicate the dwellings of the former silk-weavers, but most of them are unoccupied. There are still some of their old mulberry-trees to be seen in the gardens near Spital Square. Many pure French names may still be observed over the shop-doors in that quarter of London, and several descendants of the French manufacturers still continue to carry on the business of silk-weaving there. Even the *pot-au-feu* is still known in Spitalfields, though the poor people who use it know not of its origin. And although there are many descendants of the French operatives still resident in the east of London, probably by far the largest proportion of them have long since migrated to the more prosperous manufacturing districts of the North.

Throughout the country there was the same effacement of the traces of foreign origin among the descendants of the exiles. Every where they gradually ceased to be French.* The foreign manners, customs, and language probably held out the longest at Portarlington, in Ireland, where the old French of Louis Quatorze long continued to be spoken in society, while the old French service was read in church down to the year 1817, when it was finally supplanted by the English.

Thus the refugees of all classes at length ceased to exist as a distinctive body among the people who had given them a refuge, and they were eventually absorbed into and became an integral part of the British nation.

* The French mercantile houses in England and Ireland, who did business in London, long continued to have their special London bankers, among whom may be mentioned those of Bosanquet, Puget, etc. The house of Puget and Co., in St. Paul's Churchyard, recently wound up, kept all their books in French down to the beginning of the present century.

CHAPTER XVIII.

CONCLUSION.—THE FRENCH REVOLUTION.

WHILE such were the results of the settlement of the Protestant refugees in England, let us briefly glance at the effect of their banishment on the countries which drove them forth.

The persecutions in Flanders and France doubtless succeeded after a sort. Philip II. crushed Protestantism in Flanders as he did in Spain, to the temporary ruin of the one country and the debasement of the other. Flanders eventually became lost to the Spanish crown, though it has since entered upon a new and prosperous career under the constitutional government of Belgium; but Spain sank until she reached the very lowest rank among the nations of Europe. The Inquisition flourished, but the life of the nation decayed. Spain lost her commerce, her colonies, her credit, her intellect, her character. She became a country of émeutes, revolutions, pronunciamentos, repudiations, and intrigues. We have only to look at Spain now. If it be true that in the long run the collective character of a nation is fairly represented by its government and its rulers, the character of Spain must have fallen very low indeed.

And how fared it with France after the banishment of her Huguenots? So far as regarded the suppression of Protestantism, Louis XIV. may also be said to have succeeded. For more than a century, that form of religion visibly ceased to exist in France. The Protestants had neither rights nor privileges, and not even a vestige of liberty, for they were placed entirely beyond the pale of the law. Such of them as would not be dragooned into conformity to the Roman Catholic religion were cast into prison or sent to the galleys. If the Protestants were not stamped wholly out of existence, at least they were stamped out of sight; and if they continued to worship, it was in secret only—in caves, among the hills, or in "the Desert." Indeed, no measure of suppression could have been more complete. But now see with what results.

One thing especially strikes the intelligent reader of French history subsequent to the Act of Revocation, and that is the almost total disappearance of great men in France. After that date we become conscious of a dull, dead level of subserviency and conformity to the despotic will of the king.* Louis trampled under foot individuality, strength, and genius, and there remained only mediocrity, feebleness, and flunkyism. This feature of the time has been noted by writers so various as De Felice, Merivale, Michelet, and Buckle, the last of whom goes so far as to say that Louis XIV. "survived the entire intellect of the French nation."†

The Protestant universities of Saumur, Montauban, Nismes, and Sedan were suppressed, and the professors in them departed into other lands. All Protestant schools were closed, and the whole educational organization of the nation was placed in the hands of the Jesuits. War was declared against the books forbidden by the Church of Rome. Dom-

* In the reign of Louis XIV. a sonnet was privately circulated, from which the following is an extract:

"Ce peuple que jadis Dieu gouvernait lui-même
Trop las de son bonheur, voulait avoir un Roi,
He bien, dit le Seigneur, peuple ingrat et sans foi,
Tu sentiras bientôt le poids du diadème.
    *   *   *   *   *   *
Ainsi règne aujourd'hui par les vœux de la France
Ce Monarque absolu qu'on nomme Dieu-donné."

† M. Puaux, referring to the measures so servilely passed by the French Parliament legalizing and aggrandizing the illegitimate offspring of Louis XIV., and declaring them princes of the blood capable of succeeding to the throne, goes on to say: "At sight of these councilors of the red robe, who trembled before the old Sultan of Versailles in sanctioning the glaring scandals of his life, one is justified in asking whether Frenchmen continued to retain the courage displayed by them on so many a field of battle, and whether the cruel saying of Paul-Louis Courier be not true: 'Frenchmen, you are the most flunkyish of all peoples!' (*Français, vous êtes le plus valet de tous le peuples.*) We blush as we write the lines, at the same time avowing our belief, which we do with pride, that the Great King would never have obtained from a Huguenot court what was so servilely granted him by a Catholic one."
—PUAUX—*Histoire de la Reformation Française*, tom. vii., p. 64.

iciliary visits were paid by the district commanders to every person suspected of possessing them; and all devotional books of sermons and hymns, as well as Bibles and Testaments, that could be found, were ruthlessly burned.*

There was an end for a time of political and religious liberty in France. Freedom of thought and freedom of worship were alike crushed; and then the new epoch began—of mental stagnation, political depravity, religious hypocrisy, and moral decay. With the great men of the first half of Louis XIV.'s reign, the intellectual greatness of France disappeared for nearly a century. The Act of Revocation of 1685 cut the history of his reign in two: every thing before, nothing after. There was no great statesman after Colbert. At his death in 1683, the policy which he had so laboriously and so grandly initiated was summarily overthrown. The military and naval genius of France seemed alike paralyzed. The great victories of Condé and Turenne on land, and of Duquesne at sea, preceded the Revocation. After that, Louis's army was employed for years in hunting and dragonnading the Huguenots, which completely demoralized them, so that his next campaign, that of 1688, began in disaster and ended in disgrace.

---

* Louis XV., who succeeded to Louis XIV., pursued the same policy of book-burning. On the 25th of April, 1727, he issued an edict ordering all "new converts" [*i. e.*, Protestants who had been compelled to conform, or pretended to conform, to Popery] to deliver up all books relating to religion within fifteen days, for the purpose of being burnt in presence of the commandants of the respective districts. Those who did not so deliver up their books were heavily fined; and if found guilty a second time of withholding their books, they were to be sentenced to *three years' banishment* and a fine amounting to *not less than one third the value of their entire property*. This measure completed the destruction of the Protestant libraries. The dragoons were the Omars of the time, and ruthlessly carried out the royal edict for the destruction of Protestant literature. In most of the towns and villages throughout France great bonfires were lit, into which were cast thousands of volumes, including Bibles and Testaments. Hence the great rarity of some of the earlier editions of the Scriptures, which are now only to be met with out of France. The most considerable *auto-da-fé* of this kind took place at Beaucaire, where many thousand volumes of rare and valuable books were consumed on a great pile lit in front of the Hotel de Ville, in the presence of the municipal authorities, and of M. de Beaulieu, sub-delegate of the intendant of Languedoc.

The same barrenness fell upon literature. Molière, the greatest of French comedians, died of melancholy in 1674. Racine, the greatest of French poets and dramatists, died in 1697, but his genius may be said to have culminated with the production of *Phœdre* in 1676. Corneille died in 1684, but his last, though not his greatest work, *Surena*, was produced in 1674. La Fontaine published his last fables in 1679.

With Pascal, a man as remarkable for his piety as for his genius, expired in 1662 the last free utterance of the Roman Catholic Church in France. He died protesting to the last against the immorality and despotism of the principles of the Jesuits. It is true, after the Revocation there remained of the great French clergy Bossuet, Bourdaloue, and Fénélon. They were, however, the products of the first half of Louis's reign, and they were the last of their race; for we shall find that the effect of the king's policy was to strike with paralysis the very Church which he sought exclusively to establish and maintain.

After this period we seem to tread a dreary waste in French history. True loyalty became extinguished, and even patriotism seemed to have expired. Literature, science, and the arts almost died out, and there remained a silence almost as of the grave, broken only by the noise of the revelries at court, amid which there rose up from time to time the ominous wailings of the gaunt and famishing multitude.

The policy of Louis XIV. had succeeded, and France was at length "converted." Protestantism had been crushed, and the Jesuits were triumphant. Their power over the bodies and souls of the people was as absolute as law could make it. The whole education of the country was placed in their hands, and what the character of the next generation was to be depended in a great measure upon them. Not only the churches and the schools, but even the national prisons, were controlled by them. They were the confessors of the bastiles, of which there were twenty in France, where persons could be incarcerated for life on the authority merely of *lettres de cachet*, which were given away or sold.* Besides the bastiles and the galleys,† over which the Jesuits presided, there were also the state prisons, of which Paris alone contained about thirty, besides convents, where persons might be immured without any sentence. "Surely never," says Michelet, "had man's dearest treasure, liberty, been more lavishly squandered."

The Church in France had grown immensely rich by the property of the Protestants which was transferred to it, as well as by royal grants and private benefactions. So far as money went, it had the means and the power of doing all that it would in moulding the mind and conscience of the French nation. The clergy held in their hands one fifth of the whole landed property of the country, estimated to be worth about £160,000,000; and attached to these lands were the serfs, whom they continued to hold as such until the Revolution.‡

And now let us see what was the outcome of the action of this Church, so rich and so powerful, after enjoying a century of undisputed authority in France. All other faiths had been expelled to make way for it; Protestantism had been exterminated, and free thought of all kinds had shrunk for a time out of sight.

What was the result of this exclusive action upon the mind and conscience of the French people? The result was

* Saint Florentin alone gave away no fewer than 50,000. Many of the persons immured in these horrible places were forgotten, or, if they succeeded in obtaining their release, they sometimes issued from their dungeons with their ears and noses gnawed away by rats.

† In the reign of Louis XV., "The Well-Beloved," the galleys still contained many Protestants, besides persons who had been detected aiding Protestants to escape. They were regarded as veritable slaves, and were occasionally sold, the price of a galley-slave in the Well-Beloved's reign being about £120. Voltaire was presented with a galley-slave by M. de Choiseul.

‡ The clergy still possessed serfs in the time of the Revolution. The whole of the eighteenth century had passed away, together with all the liberators, both Rousseau and Voltaire, whose last thought was the enfranchisement of the Jura. Yet the priest had still his serfs. . . . Bondage was not expressly abolished till March, 1790.--MICHELET—*History of the French Revolution*.

utter emptiness: to use the words of Carlyle, "emptiness of pocket, of stomach, of head, and of heart." The Church which had claimed and obtained the sole control of the religious education of France saw itself assailed by its own offspring—desperate, ignorant, and so ferocious that in some places they even seized the priests and indecently scourged them in front of their own altars.*

The nation that would not have the Bayles, and Claudes, and Saurins of a century before, now cast themselves at the feet of the Voltaires, Rousseaus, and Diderots. Though France would not have the God of the Huguenot's Bible, behold now she accepts the evangel according to Jean Jacques, and a poor bedizened creature, clad in tawdry, is led through the streets of Paris in the character of the Goddess of Reason!

But a large number of the clergy of the Roman Catholic Church in France had themselves long ceased to believe in the truth of what they professed to teach. They had grown utterly corrupted and demoralized. Their monasteries were the abodes of idleness and self-indulgence. Their pulpits were mute: their books were empty. The doctors of the Sorbonne still mumbled their accustomed jargon, but it had become powerless. Instead of the great churchmen of the past — Bossuet, Bourdaloue, and Fénélon—there were such blind leaders of the blind as the Cardinal de Rohan, the profligate confederate of Madame la Motte in the affair of the diamond necklace; the Abbé Sièyes, the constitution-monger; the Abbé Raynal, the open assailant of Christianity in every form; and Father Lomenie, the avowed atheist.†

* CARLYLE—*French Revolution*, ii., p. 2.
† At the Revolution many of the priests openly abjured Christianity, and were applauded accordingly. The Bishop of Perigaux presented the woman whom he had married to the Convention, saying, "I have taken her from among the sans culottes." His speech was hailed with immense applause. Gobel, Archbishop of Paris, presented himself at the bar of the Convention, with his vicars and many of his curates, and desired to lay at the feet of the Assembly their sacerdotal garments. "Citizens," said the president in reply, "you are worthy of the Republic, because you have sacrificed at the altar of your country these Gothic bawbles." Gobel and his priests then donned the

The corrupt, self-condemned institution became a target for the wit of Voltaire and the encyclopædic philosophy of Diderot. It was next assailed by the clubs of Marat, Danton, and Robespierre. Then the unfed, untaught, desperate victims of centuries of oppression and misguidance rose up almost as one man, and cried "Away with it"—*Ecrasez l'Infame.* The churches were attacked and gutted, as those of the Huguenots had been a century before. The church-bells were cast into cannon, the church-plate coined into money; and at length Christianity itself was abolished by the Convention, who declared the Supreme People to be the only God!

The Roman Catholic clergy, who had so long witnessed the persecutions of the Huguenots, were now persecuted in their turn by their own flocks. Many of them were guillotined; others, chained together as the Huguenots had been, were sent prisoners to Rochelle and the Isle of Aix. As a body of them passed through Limoges on their way to the galleys, they encountered a procession of asses clothed in priests' dresses, a mitred sow marching at their head. Some 400 priests lay riding in Aix Roads, where the Huguenot galley-slaves had been before them—"ragged, sordid, hungry, wasted to shadows, eating their unclean rations on deck, circularly, in parties of a dozen, with finger and thumb; beating their scandalous clothes between two stones; choked in horrible miasmata, under close hatches, seventy of them in a berth through the night, so that the aged priest is found lying dead in the morning in an attitude of prayer."*

Such was the real outcome of the Act of Revocation of Louis the Great—Sansculottism and the Reign of Terror! There was no longer the massacre and banishment of Huguenots, but there was the guillotining and banishment of the

---

bonnet rouge in token of fraternization with the "Friends of Men." Numbers of priests came daily and gave up to the Convention their letters of priesthood. Puaux says, "Those of their predecessors who distinguished themselves in the crusades against the Huguenots had slipped their foot in blood; but these fell lower—their foot slipped in mud."

* CARLYLE—*French Revolution,* ii., 338.

successors of the priests whom Louis had set up. There was one other point in which 1793 resembled 1685. The fugitive priests fled in precisely the same direction in which the Huguenot pastors had done; and again the persecuted for religion's sake made for the old free land of England, to join the descendants of the Huguenots, driven out of France for altogether different reasons a century before.

But the Roman Catholic priests did not fly alone. They were accompanied by the nobles, the superintendents of the dragonnades. Never, since the flight of Huguenots which followed the Revocation of the Edict of Nantes, had there been such an emigration of Frenchmen from France. But there was this difference between the emigrations of 1685 and 1793, that whereas in the former period the people who emigrated consisted almost entirely of the industrious classes, in the latter period they consisted almost entirely of the idle classes. The men who now fled were the nobles and priests, who had so misguided and mistaught the people intrusted to their charge that in nearly all parts of France they had at length risen up in fierce rebellion against them.

The great body of the people had become reduced to absolute destitution. They had no possession whatever but their misery. They were literally dying of hunger. The Bishop of Chartres told Louis XV. that in his diocese the men browsed like sheep. For want of food, they filled their stomachs with grass. The dragoons, who had before been employed to hunt down the Huguenots because of their attending religious meetings, were now employed on a different duty. They were stationed in the market-places where meal was exposed for sale to keep back the famishing people. In Paris alone there were 200,000 beggars prowling about, with sallow faces, lank hair, and hung in rags. In 1789, crowds of them were seen hovering about the Palais Royal—spectral-looking men and starving women, delirious from fasting. Some were said not to have eaten for three whole days. The women wandered about like hungry lionesses, for they had children.

One Foulon, a member of the king's council, on being told of the famine endured by the people, said, "Wait till I am minister: I will make them eat hay; my horses eat it." The words were bitterly avenged. The hungry mob seized Foulon, hanged him *a là lanterne*, and carried his head about the streets, his mouth filled with hay.

From the provinces news came that the starving helots were every where rising, burning down the chateaus of the nobles, tearing up their title-deeds, and destroying their crops. On these occasions the church-bells were rung by way of tocsin, and the population of the parish turned out to the work of destruction. Seventy-two chateaus were wrecked and burnt in the Maçonnais and Beaujolais alone; and the conflagration spread throughout Dauphiny, Alsace, and the Lyonnais, the very quarters from which the Huguenots had been so ferociously driven out a century before.

There was scarcely a district in which the Huguenots had pursued their various branches of industry, now wholly suppressed, in which the starving and infuriated peasantry did not work wild havoc, and take revenge upon their lords. They had learned but too well the lessons of the sword, the dungeon, and the scaffold, which their rulers had taught them, and the Reign of Terror which followed was but the natural outcome of the massacre of Saint Bartholomew, the wars of the dragonnades, the cruelties which followed the Act of Revocation, and a long course of like teaching. But the victims had now changed places. Now it was the nobles who were persecuted, burnt out, had their estates confiscated, and were compelled to fly for their lives.

The dragonnades of the Huguenots became repeated in the noyades of the Royalists; and again Nancy, Lyons, Rouen, Bordeaux, Montauban, and numerous other places, witnessed a repetition of the cruelties of the preceding century. At Nantes, where the famous Edict of Toleration, afterward revoked, was proclaimed, the guillotine was worked until the headsman sank exhausted; and to hasten matters, a general fusillade in the plain of St. Mauve followed, of men, women, and children. At Paris, the hideous Marat called for "eight hundred gibbets," in convenient rows, to hang the enemies of the people. He would be satisfied with nothing short of "two hundred thousand aristocratic heads."

It is unnecessary to pursue the dreadful story farther. Suffice it to say that the nobles, like the priests, fled out of France to escape the fury of the people, and they too made for England, where they received the same asylum that had been extended to their clergy, and before them to the Huguenots. To prevent the flight of the noblesse, the same measures were adopted by the Convention which Louis XIV. adopted to prevent the escape of the Huguenots. The frontiers were strictly guarded, and all the roads patroled which led out of France. Severe laws were passed against emigration, and the estates of fugitive aristocrats were declared to be confiscated to the state. Nevertheless, many succeeded in making their escape into Switzerland, Germany, and England.

It fared still worse with Louis XVI. and his beautiful queen Marie Antoinette. They were the most illustrious victims of the barbarous policy of Louis XIV. That monarch had sowed the wind, and they now reaped the whirlwind. A mob of starving men and women, the genuine offspring of the Great King, burst in upon Louis and his consort at Versailles, shouting "Bread! bread!" They were very different from the plumed and garlanded courtiers accustomed to worship in these gilded saloons, and by no means so obsequious. They insisted on the king and queen accompanying them to Paris, virtually their prisoners. The royal family tried to escape, as the Huguenots had done before them, across the frontier into Germany. But in vain. The king's own highway was closed against him, and the fugitives were led back to Paris and the guillotine.

The last act of the unfortunate Louis was his attempt to address a few words to his subjects, when the drums were ordered to be beaten, and his voice was drowned by the noise. It was remembered that the last occasion on which a like scene had occurred in France was on the occasion of the execution of the young Huguenot pastor Fulcran Rey at Beaucaire. When he opened his mouth publicly to confess his faith, the drummers posted round the scaffold were ordered to beat, and his dying speech remained unheard. The slaughter of the martyred preacher was thus terribly avenged.

We think we are justified in saying that, but for the persecution and expulsion of the Huguenots at the Revocation of the Edict of Nantes in 1685, the Revolution of 1789 most probably never would have occurred. The Protestants supplied that enterprising and industrious middle class which gives stability to every state. They provided remunerative employment for the population, while at the same time they enriched the kingdom by their enterprise and industry. Moreover, they furnished that virtuous and religious element in society without which a nation is but so much chaff that is driven before the wind. When they were suppressed or banished, there was an end to their industrial undertakings. The farther growth of a prosperous middle class was prevented; and the misgovernment of the ruling class being unchecked, the great body of the working order were left to idleness, nakedness, and famine. Faith in God and in good died out; religion, as represented by the degenerate priesthood, fell into contempt, and the reign of materialism and atheism began. Frightful distress at length culminated in revolution and anarchy; and there being no element of stability in the state—no class possessing moral weight to stand between the infuriated people at the one end of the social scale, and the king and nobles at the other—the imposture erected by the Great Louis was assailed on all sides, and king, Church, and nobility were at once swept away.

As regards the emigration of the Huguenots in 1685, and of the nobles and clergy in 1789, it must be acknowledged that the former was by much the most calamitous to France. "Was the one emigration greater than the other?" says Michelet. "I do not know. That of 1685 was probably from three to four hundred thousand persons. However this may be, there was this great difference: France, at the emigration of '89, lost its idlers; at the other its workers. The terror of '89 struck the individual, and each feared for his life. The terror of the dragonnades struck at heart and conscience; then men feared for their all."

The one emigration consisted for the most part of nobles and clergy, who left no traces of their settlement in the countries which gave them asylum; the other emigration comprised all the constituent elements of a people—skilled workmen in all branches, manufacturers, merchants, and professional men; and wherever they settled they founded numerous useful establishments which were a source of prosperity and wealth.

Assuredly England has no reason to regret the asylum which she has in all times so freely granted to fugitives flying from religious persecution abroad; least of all has she reason to regret the settlement within her borders of so large a number of industrious, intelligent, and high-minded Frenchmen, who have made this country their home since the Revocation of the Edict of Nantes, and thereby not only stimulated, and in a measure created, British industry, but also influenced, in a remarkable degree, our political and religious history.

APPENDIX.

I. EARLY SETTLEMENT OF FOREIGN ARTISANS IN ENGLAND.

THE first extensive immigration of foreign artisans of which we have any account took place in the reign of Henry II. It was occasioned by an inundation in the Low Countries which dispossessed many of the inhabitants, when large numbers of them came over into England. They were well received by the king, who forwarded a body of them to Carlisle, for the purpose of planting them on the then unsettled and almost desert lands adjacent to the Scotch border. But the lawless state of the district was fatal to the quiet pursuits of the Flemings, and Henry subsequently directed their removal to the peninsula of Gower, in South Wales. There the Flemings began and successfully carried on their trade of cloth-weaving. They formed a community by themselves, and jealously preserved their nationality. The district long continued to be known as " Little England beyond Wales;" and to this day the community of Gower is to a great extent distinct and separate from that of the surrounding country.

Another colony of Flemings settled about the same time at Worsted, near Norwich, and "worsted" stuffs soon became common. These colonists were the first to introduce into England water-driven corn-mills, wind-mills, and fulling-mills. They also reintroduced the art of building in brick, which had not been practiced in England since the time of the Romans. Traces of their early brick-work are still observable in several of the old churches at Norwich and Worsted—Worsted church furnishing an unmistakable specimen of early Flemish architecture. Other colonies of Flemish fishermen settled at Brighton, Newhaven, and other places along the south coast, where their lineage is still traceable in local words, names, and places.*

Other Flemings established themselves still farther north.† At Berwick-upon-Tweed they occupied a large factory called the Red Hall, situated in the

---

* "Strombolo" or "stromballen" (stream-balls) is the pure Flemish name given here to pieces of black bitumen, charged with sulphur and salt, found along the coast. It is one of the many indications of an early Flemish colony of fishers.—MURRAY'S *Sussex*.

† A writer in the *Edinburg Review* (July, 1863) says, "During the twelfth and thirteenth centuries Flemish colonies have been traced in Berwick, St. Andrew's, Perth, Dumbarton, Ayr, Peebles, Lanark, Edinburg, and in the districts of Renfrewshire, Clydesdale, and Annandale These strangers lived under the protection of a special code of mercantile law; and recent investigations have established the fact that, a hundred years before the great Baltic Association came into being, we had a Hanseatic League in Scotland, small and unimportant comparatively, but known by that very name. This was in the time of David I., toward the middle of the twelfth century."

main street of the town. The principal business carried on by them there was the export of wool, wool-fells, and hides, and the import of iron, weapons, implements, and merchandise of various kinds. These Flemish traders were under the special protection of the Scotch king, to whom they rendered loyal service in return; for history relates that on the storming of Berwick by Edward I., in 1296, the Flemings barricaded themselves in the Red Hall, and defended themselves with such courage and obstinacy that, rather than surrender, they were buried to a man in the ruins.

A new impulse was given to the immigration of Flemish artisans into England by the protracted intestine feuds arising out of the dynastic quarrels of the Burgundian princes, which unsettled industry and kept the Low Countries in a state of constant turmoil. But perhaps a still more potent cause of Flemish emigration was the severity of the regulations enforced by the guilds or trades unions of Flanders, Ghent, Bruges, Liege, and the other great towns, which became so many centres of commercial monopoly. The rich guilds combined to crush the poorer ones, and the privileged to root out the unprivileged. Such artisans as would not submit to their exactions were liable to have their looms broken and their dwellings gutted, and to be themselves expelled with their families beyond the walls. If they took shelter in the neighboring villages, and began to exercise their calling there, they were occasionally pursued by the armed men of the guilds, who burned down the places which had given them refuge, and drove them forth into the wide world with no other possession than their misery.*

These persecuted artisans, who had earned their living for the most part by working up English wool into Flemish cloth, naturally turned their eyes in the direction of England, and all who could find the means of emigrating made haste to fly, and place the sea between them and the tyranny of the trades unions.

Although the early English kings had been accustomed to encourage the immigration of foreign artisans, it was not until the reign of Edward III., usually styled "the father of English commerce," that any decided progress was made by this country in manufacturing industry. That sagacious monarch held that, as regarded the necessaries of life, clothing as well as food, the people of his kingdom should be as much as possible independent of foreign supply. In the early part of his reign the English people relied mainly upon the Flemish manufacturers for the better sorts of clothing, while the English wool-growers looked to the Flemish wool-markets as the chief outlet for their produce. So long as peaceful relations existed between the two countries, the exchange of the raw produce for the manufactured articles went on, to the benefit of both. But when these were interrupted by civic broils in Flanders, by feuds among the guilds, or by war between the two countries, serious inconveniences were immediately felt. The English producer lost a market for his staple at the same time that the English consumer was deprived of the supply of clothing on which he had been accustomed to rely.

The question naturally occurred to the English king, Why not establish markets for the staple at home, and work up the wool into cloth by the hands

* See ALTMEYER's curious pamphlet illustrative of this subject, entitled *Notices Historiques sur la Ville de Poperinghen*, Ghent, 1840.

of our own people ? This appeared to him both reasonable and desirable ; and to accomplish both objects, Edward proceeded to invite Flemish artisans to come over in increased numbers and settle in England, with the view of teaching the English work-people the arts of spinning, dyeing, and weaving the best kinds of cloth. He accordingly sent abroad agents to induce them to come over to this country, promising them protection, and holding out liberal offers to such as should embrace his invitation.

Fuller, in his *Church History*, gives the following curious account of the means resorted to by Edward : " Englishmen," he says, " at this time knew no more what to do with the wool than the sheep that wear it, as to any artificial and curious drapery, their best cloths being no better than friezes, such was their coarseness from want of skill in the making. Unsuspected emissaries were employed by our king in those countries, who wrought themselves into familiarity with such Dutchmen as were absolute masters of their trade, but not masters of themselves, as journeymen and apprentices. They bemoaned the slavishness of these poor servants, whom their masters used rather like heathens than Christians ; yea, rather like horses than men ; early up, and late in bed, and all day hard work, and harder fare, as a few herrings and mouldy cheese, and all to enrich the churls their masters, with profit to themselves. But oh ! how happy should they be if they would but come into England, bringing their mystery with them, which would provide them welcome in all places. Here they should feed on fat beef and mutton till nothing but their fullness should stint their stomachs. Yea, they should feed on the labors of their own hands, enjoying a proportionable profit of their gains to themselves ; their beds should be good, and their bedfellows better, seeing the richest yeomen in England would not disdain to marry their daughters unto them, and such the English beauties that the most envious foreigner could not but commend them."

The representations made by Edward's agents were not without their effect in inducing many of the distressed Flemings to come over and settle in various parts of England. But another circumstance materially contributed to hasten the exodus of the foreign artisans. This was the sudden outbreak of war between England and France in 1336. Philip de Valois, the French king, artfully stirred up Louis de Nevers, Count of Flanders, to strike a blow against England in his behalf ; and an order was issued by him for the arrest of all the English then in the Low Countries. The order was executed ; but it was speedily felt that the blow had been struck at Flanders rather than at England.

Edward, on his part, was not slow to retaliate. He prohibited the export of English wool as well as the import of Flemish cloth. The Flemings thus found themselves at the same moment deprived of their indispensable supply of raw material, and shut out from one of the principal markets for the sale of their goods. At the same time Edward took the opportunity of reiterating, which he did with increased effect, his invitation to the Flemish artisans to come over to England, where they would be amply supplied with wool, and provided with ready markets for all the cloth they could manufacture. He granted a charter for the express purpose of protecting such foreign merchants and artisans as might settle in England, guaranteeing them security in the pursuit of their industry, freedom to trade within the realm, exemption from certain duties, good and prompt justice, good weight, and good measure.* These measures proved successful in a remarkable degree. Large numbers of Flemings forthwith migrated into England, bringing with them their tools, their skill, and their industry. The French king tried, when too late, to stop the emigration, but he found it impossible to stop the flight of the artisans through the ports of Flanders into the dominions of his enemy.

The great migrations of Flemings into England in the reign of Edward III. may be said, in some measure, to have laid the foundations of English manufacturing industry. The Dutch statesman De Witt, referring to it as matter of history, observed that before the removal of the cloth-trade to England the Netherlanders could deal well enough with the English, "they being only shepherds and wool-merchants."† Michelet also, reviewing the same events, says, "Before England was the great manufactory of ironware and woolens for the world, she was a manufactory of wool and meat. From time immemorial her people had been a cattle-breeding, sheep-rearing race. . . . . I take it that the English character has been seriously modified by these emigrations, which went on during the whole of the fourteenth century. Previously we find no indications of that patient industry which now distinguishes the English. By endeavoring to separate Flanders and England, the French king only stimulated Flemish emigration, and laid the foundation of England's manufactures."‡

The Flemish cloth-workers, as they came over, had special districts assigned to them, with special liberties and privileges. They were planted all over England—in London, in Kent, in Somerset, in Norfolk, in Nottinghamshire, in Yorkshire, in Lancashire, and as far north as Kendal in Westmoreland.

Seventy Walloon families from Brabant were settled in the ward of Candlewick, London, and two meeting-places were assigned to them—one in Laurence Pountney church-yard, the other in the church-yard of St. Mary, Somerset. Stow says they were weavers of drapery, tapery, and napery—in other words, of woolen and linen stuffs. Guilds were established in connection with the new branches of trade; and, with a view to their encouragement, the king himself joined them as a guild brother.

The name of the leader of one of the earliest bands of Flemish emigrants has been handed down to us—that of John Kempe, a Flemish woolen-weaver, to whom royal letters of protection were granted in 1330, to exercise his art, and "to teach it to such of our people as shall be inclined to learn it." The like protection was extended to his men, servants, and apprentices, and to all his goods and chattels whatsoever. Kempe eventually settled at Kendal, and there began the manufacture of cloths, which continues to this day, the descendants of Kempe being still traceable in Kendal and the neighborhood.§

Six years after Kempe came over, Edward granted similar protection to two Brabant weavers, who settled at York, and carried on their trade there. They are described in the royal letter as "Willielmus de Brabant et Hancheinus de Brabant, textores," after the latter of whom the *hank* or skein of worsted is said to have been called.

* RYMER—*Fœdera*, ii , 747. † DE WITT—*The True Interest of Holland.*
‡ MICHELET—*History of France*, book vi , ch. 1.
§ NICHOLSON—*Annals of Kendal*, 2d edition, p. 235.

The woolen-cloth trade seems early to have become established at Nottingham, and gave rise in the town and county to many considerable families, some of whose names indicate a Flemish origin. Thus there were the Bugges and Willoughbys, joint ancestors of the house of Willoughby (Lord Middleton), at Wollaton, near Nottingham; the Mappurleys, Thurlands, Amyases, Plumtres, Tamesleys, Binghams, and Hunts.*

Other Flemings planted themselves in the west of England, and in course of time their fulling-mills were busily at work along the streams of Wiltshire, Somerset, and South Gloucester, where the manufacture of cloth still continues to flourish.† Bath and Bristol also shared in the prosperity which followed the introduction of this new branch of trade. At the latter place, three brothers of the name of Blanket, taking advantage of the immigration of the foreign artisans, set up looms in their houses for the weaving of cloth. The magistrates, on hearing of their proceedings, tried to stop them by heavy fines, on which the brothers Blanket appealed to the king. Edward immediately wrote to the corporation that, "considering the manufactures may turn out to the great advantage of us and all the people of our kingdom, you are to permit the machines to be erected in their [the Flemings'] houses, without making on that account any reproach, hinderance, or undue exaction." This royal order had the effect of checking the oppressive interference of the corporation. The brothers Blanket were accordingly enabled to proceed with their operations, and blankets‡ soon became an important branch of Bristol manufacture.

Before the time of Edward III. the common people had been accustomed to wear coarse clothes made of hemp, but on the introduction of blankets they came into general use for purposes of clothing. The blankets were also used by travelers, soldiers, and sportsmen, instead of the loose mantle and puckered cloak and cape, which, with the long loose robe or gown, had been found very inconvenient. When bedsteads were introduced in the same reign —before which time people slept on rushes, straw, or fern, laid on the floor— blankets were introduced as part of the necessary bed-furniture; and repeated mention of them is made in the "Expenses of the Great Wardrobe of Edward III., 1347-9."§ A considerable demand being thus created for the new article, the brothers Blanket soon became rich men, and rose to honor and dignity. Thomas, the youngest brother, to whom the merit of introducing the manufacture was chiefly due, served as high bailiff of Bristol in 1349, and

* Mr. Felkin, of Nottingham, informs us that the woolen-cloth manufacture flourished in the town before the time of King John. That monarch staid in the place several times, in a building called King John's Palace, lately taken down. He granted a charter to Nottingham, in which persons within ten miles of it were forbidden to work woolen cloth except it was dyed in the borough.

† At a later date (20th Henry VII.) Anthony Bonvis, an Italian, introduced the art of spinning with the distaff in Devonshire, and began the making of Devonshire kerseys and coxal cloths. Before his time only friezes and plain coarse cloths were made in that county.

‡ It has been supposed by some that the brothers Blanket gave its distinctive name to the now familiar woolen bed-sheet. But, as the article was well-known abroad by the same name (*blanchet*—from the absence of color), it is more likely that the blanket gave its name to the brothers, than that the article was named after them. It was quite usual in those days for men to take the name of the article they manufactured or the trade they lived by. *Webb* cloth and *Clutterbucks* were, however, so called after the persons who first manufactured them in the west of England.

§ *Archæologia*, vol. xxxi.

the two other brothers successively represented the city in Parliament—Edward in 1362, and Edmund in 1369.

The cloth-manufactures of Kent, also, rose into importance by reason of the skill and enterprise of the Flemings. They planted their fulling-mills along the rivers Cray and Dart,* the weavers settling principally at Cranbrook, Goudhurst, and the neighboring villages. Many of the small freeholders of the Weald sent their sons to learn the trade, and they afterward set up as manufacturers on their own account. At county meetings the "Gray-coats of Kent" carried all before them—gray cloth being the prevailing color of the Kentish article, as that of Kendal was green. The cloth-trade has, however, long since departed from Cranbrook, then the centre of the Kentish trade—its manufactures, like so many others, having migrated northward; and the only indications remaining of the extinct branch of industry are the ancient factories, evidently of Flemish origin, which are still to be seen in the principal street of the town.

Norwich and the neighboring towns continued to derive increasing advantages from the influx of foreign artisans. To the trade of spinning worsted, that of manufacturing it into cloth was added in 1336, after which date the latter branch became the leading manufacture of the city. Norwich was appointed by royal edict one of the ten staple towns for the sale of wool, woolfells, and cloths, to which merchants resorted from all parts for purposes of business. Enjoying such privileges, Norwich became a centre of busy industry, and the adjoining towns of Worstead and Wymondham shared in its prosperity, "every one," says an ancient chronicler, "having combers, carders, spinsters, fullers, dyers, pressers, packers, and fleece-sorters."

While the Flemish artisans prospered, the English yeomen grew rich with them. "Happy the yeoman's house," says Fuller, "into which one of these Dutchmen did enter, bringing industry and wealth along with him. Such who came in strangers within the doors soon after went out bridegrooms and returned sons-in-law. Yea, those yeomen in whose houses they harbored soon proceeded gentlemen, gaining great estates to themselves, arms and worship to their families."†

Edward continued indefatigable in his efforts to promote the establishment and extension of the new branches of industry. Some of the measures which he adopted with this object, viewed by the light of the present day, may seem to display more zeal than wisdom. Thus he ordered that none but English-made cloth should be worn throughout England, except by himself and certain privileged persons of the higher classes. He not only fixed by edict the prices of cloth, but prescribed the kind to be worn by tradesmen, mechanics, and rustics respectively, as well as the quality of the woolen shrouds they were to be buried in!

To foster the home trade, Edward gave free license to all persons whatsoever to make English cloth, while at the same time he rigidly excluded that of foreign manufacture. He also endeavored to prohibit the export of English wool; but it was found difficult to enforce this measure, as it inflicted even

---

* Most of the paper-mills now situated on these streams were originally fulling-mills, as is shown by the title-deeds of the properties still extant.
† FULLER—*Church History*.

more injury on the English wool-grower than it did on the foreign manufacturer. The annual production of English wool was so large that it was impossible for the Flemish immigrants, helped though they were by their English journeymen and apprentices, to work it up into cloth. The English market accordingly became glutted with wool, at the same time that the Flemish and French weavers continued to famish for want of raw material from England. Nature set up her usual remedy under such circumstances, and established the Smuggler. All round the coast the law was set at defiance, and wool was surreptitiously sent abroad through every port.* As it was found impossible to maintain restrictions so rigid and so injurious, they were speedily relaxed. The export of wool was again legalized on payment of a duty of 40s. the pack, or equal to about £6 of our present money, and the extent of the trade may be inferred from the fact that the impost thus levied produced about £250,000 a year.

At the same time, Flemish cloth was again admitted on payment of duty, for it was found that the production of English cloth was as yet insufficient for the home consumption. This latter measure also had the effect of stimulating the English manufacturers to increased industry and enterprise, and the result was that, before long, cloth of English make was exported in large quantities, not only to France, Denmark,† and Germany, but to Flanders it-

---

* The restrictions on the exportation of English wool long continued in force, and "owling," or wool-smuggling, became the business of a large part of the coast population, especially along the shores of Sussex and Kent. There was always, however, a strong patriotic party at home, favorable to the encouragement of English manufactures by artificial methods, such as the prohibition of the export of English wool. The Lansdowne MSS. (796 f. 2, British Museum) contain a poem of the time of Henry IV., supposed to have been the composition of a monk, containing many curious references to this early branch of English industry. The writer says:

"Ther ys noother pope, emperowre, nor kyng,
Bysschop, cardynal, or any man levyng,
Of what condicion, or what maner degree,
Duryng theyre levyng thei must have thynges iij—
Mete, drynk, and cloth, to every manne's sustynaunce—
They leng alle iij, without varyaunce."

The writer goes on to say that in respect of the iij, England "of all the relmes in the worlde berythe the lanterne;" and he proceeds to show that not only English wool, but English cloths, were in demand abroad:

"Ffor the marchauntis comme owre wollys for to bye,
Or elles the cloth that is made thereoff sykyrly,
Oute of dyverse londes fer beyond the see,
To have thyse merchaundyss into theyr contré."

Toward the conclusion of the poem, the writer urges the withholding of wool from the foreigners as one of the most effectual means of promoting England's prosperity:

"And ffulle fayne that they may be subject to this lond,
Yf we kepe the woollys straytly owt of their hond,
For by the endraperyng thereoff they have theyre sustynaunce,
And thus owre enmys be supportyd to our gret hynderaunce.
And therefor, for the love of God in trinyté,
Conceyve well these mators, and scherysshe the comynalté,
That theyre pore levyng, synfulle and adversyté,
May be attratyd into welth, rychess, and prosperyté."

† In the year 1361 we find Edward III. addressing Magnus, king of Norway, on behalf of some English merchants of Norwich, Yarmouth, St. Edmund's Bury, and Colchester, who had sent out a ship bound for Schonen, laden with woolen cloths and other merchandise to the value of 2000 merks. The ship was lying in a harbor in Norway when a storm came on, and the crew carried the goods on shore for safety, upon which they were seized by the king's officers. Hence Edward's demand for immediate restitution of the goods, with damages to the owners, which was prompt'y complied with.

self. Indeed, the prosperity of the woolen-trade was such that the wealth it brought to the nation is said to have materially contributed to the military successes of Edward, and helped him to win the battles of Crecy and Poitiers, in like manner as the spinning-jenny of Arkwright and the steam-engine of Watt enabled us in later times successfully to contend with the gigantic military power of the first Napoleon.

Various other branches of industry were about the same time planted in England by the Flemish and other foreign artisans. In 1368 Edward III. induced three Dutch clock-makers to settle in London to practice their craft: John and William Uninam, and John Latuyt, of Delft. The kings who succeeded Edward pursued the same policy, and from time to time induced fresh bodies of foreign artisans to settle in England, and begin new branches of skilled industry. Thus Richard II. invited a colony of Flemish linen-weavers to London in 1387, and they took up their abodes for the most part in Cannon Street, where they long prospered.* He also induced a band of silk-weavers from Lucca to settle in the city, and teach his subjects their trade. That the art must have made progress is obvious from the fact that in 1463 the native silk-weavers turned round upon the foreigners and protested against their competition. There were then said to be about a thousand women, in nunneries and private dwellings, practicing the art of silk-throwing, and, in a petition presented by these silk-women to Parliament, they complain of the Lombards and other Italians, who, they say, "import such quantities of threads, ribbands, and other silken articles, that they are greatly impoverished thereby."

The art of metallurgy being a branch of industry systematically studied and practiced in Germany, repeated invitations, accompanied by liberal promises of reward, were held out to German miners to settle in England. Thus Edward III. invited a body of them to instruct his subjects in copper-mining, under a grant made to certain adventurers to work the mines of Shieldam in Northumberland, Alstone Moor in Cumberland, and Richmond in Yorkshire. Henry VI. pursued the same policy, and in 1430 we find him inviting three famous German miners, named Michael Gosselyn, George Harbryke, and Mathew Laweston, with thirty skilled workmen of Bohemia and Hungary, to superintend and work the royal tin-mines in Cornwall; and a few years later the same monarch invited John de Schieldame, a gentleman of Zealand, with sixty workmen, to come over and instruct his subjects in the manufacture of salt. Edward IV. also sought the aid of Flemish artisans for less peaceful purposes, for we find him in 1471 landing a corps of three hundred Flemish armorers at Ravenspurg, in Yorkshire, for the purpose of manufacturing hand-guns for his army.

Again, in the reign of Edward VI., we find a party of German miners, consisting of laborers, smiths, carpenters, assayers, drainers, and colliers, setting out from Frankfort and arriving at Antwerp, where they waited the arrival of a consignment of kerseys, the sale of which was to provide for their convey-

---

* In a pamphlet published in 1699, entitled *England's Advocate, Europe's Monitor*, being an entreaty in behalf of the English silk-weavers and silk-thrumsters, the writer, speaking of the decay of the trade, observes: "Sure I am, the case is extremely altered with the weavers, since Cannon Street, both sides the way, was nothing but weaver's workshops."—P. 36.

ance to England.* Elizabeth also invited skilled miners from Germany to settle in England, for the purpose of teaching the people the best methods of working. To two of these, named Hochstetter and Thurland, of Augsburg, the queen granted a patent to search for gold, silver, quicksilver, and copper, in eight counties, with power to convert the proceeds to their own use. Hochstetter first established copper-works at Keswick, in Cumberland, which were worked to great advantage. Their success was indeed such, that it was said of Queen Elizabeth that she left more brass than she had found iron ordnance in England. But when the German miners died out, the works fell into decay, and the mines ceased to be worked. Fuller, the Church historian, writing in 1684, after they had been "laid in," surmised that "probably the burying of so much steel in the bowels of men during the late civil wars hath hindered the further digging of copper out of the bowels of the earth." The same Hochstetter afterward proceeded to open out the silver-mines of Cardiganshire, in the township of Skibery Coed, and worked them to considerable profit. Letters-patent were also granted to Cornelius de Vos, a Dutchman, for working alum-mines; and to William Humphreys and Christopher Schutz, a German from Annaburg, in Saxony, to dig and work all mines besides those specified in the other patents. The companies formed under these grants are said to have turned out most advantageously both for the crown and the patentees.†

The first saw-mills, wire-mills, and paper-mills in England were, in like manner, set on foot by Dutch and Germans, then highly skilled in mechanical engineering, while the Flemings were more devoted to the various branches of the textile manufacture. Thus, in 1565, the Christopher Schutz above mentioned started the first wire-drawing mill in England. About the same time, Joseph Laban, a Dutchman, erected wire-works near Tintern Abbey, and the descendants of the family are still traceable in the neighborhood. Godfrey Box, of Liege, began the same business at Esher, in Surrey, where it was afterward continued by two Germans, Mommer and Demetrius. The art of needle-making was introduced by another German named Elias Crowse. Stow says that before his time a Spanish negro made needles in Cheapside, but held his art a secret. The Germans were more open, and taught other workmen the trade, thereby establishing a considerable branch of industry. "For," says the quaint Fuller, "the needle is woman's pencil, and embroidery is the masterpiece thereof. This industrious instrument—needle, *quasi ne idle*, as some will have it—maintaineth many millions; yea, he who desireth a blessing on the plough and the needle comprehends most employments, at home and abroad, by land and by sea."

Paper-making was another art introduced, like printing, from the Low Countries. Caxton brought over from Haarlem, about 1468, a Dutch printer

---

* *Calendar of State Papers*, Foreign Series, 1547–1553. It is not quite clear from the State Paper records that this mining party found kicking their heels on the Antwerp quays ever reached their intended destination.

† The art of *blasting* in mines is supposed to have been first practiced in England by Prince Rupert, another German, who was well acquainted with the methods practiced abroad. The prince for some years directed the Society of Mines Royal. Most of the mining terms still in use among miners indicate their German origin. Hence *smelt*, from *schmelzen*, to melt; *slag*, from *schlagen* or cinder; *sump* (the cavity below the shaft), from *sumpf*, a bog or pit; *spern*, a point or buttress; and so on with other terms familiar in mining operations.

named Frederick Corsellis,* who made his first essay at Oxford, and afterward set up presses at Westminster, St. Alban's, and Worcester. The first books printed by Caxton himself were printed on foreign-made paper; but in 1507 one William Tate erected a mill at Hertford, where the whitey-brown paper was made on which Wynkyn de Worde printed his edition of Bartholomew's *De Proprietatius Rerum*, the first book printed in England on English-made paper. Tate's mill, however, does not seem to have prospered, and the manufacture of paper was discontinued. Another was then started by one Remigius, a German, who was invited into England for the purpose; and a third venture was made by Sir Thomas Gresham, but all alike failed; and it was not until John Spilman, the German jeweler of Queen Elizabeth, erected his large paper-mill at Dartford, in 1598, that this branch of manufacture may be said to have become established in England. The queen granted him an exclusive patent to "buy lynnen ragges and make paper" thereof, and, judging from the number of men employed by Spilman, he must have carried on a large trade.† It may be added that the manufacture of paper still continues a thriving branch of industry at Dartford and the neighborhood.

The manufacture of felt hats was introduced by Spaniards and Dutchmen in 1524, before which time the ordinary covering for the head was knitted caps, cloth hoods, and "thromed hats," the common people for the most part going bare-headed as well as bare-legged. An old writer quaintly observes, "Spaniards and Dutchmen instructed us how to make Spanish felts, and the French taught us not only how to perfect the mystery of making hats, but also how to take them off;" and he adds, "'Twas in Elizabeth's reign the Dutch taught us to cloathe ourselves, as the French did, in another queen's reign, how to uncloathe ourselves."‡

Glove-making was, in like manner, taught us by foreigners, the first eminent glover being Andreas de Loos, who held a license from Queen Elizabeth for making 200,000 pelts yearly, paying her majesty 20s. the thousand.

The glass-manufacture was brought into England by Venetians. Jacob Venalini was the first who started a glass-work, in 1564, in Crutched Friars' Hall, but his operations were shortly put a stop to by a fire occasioned by the intense heat of his furnaces, and the building was burnt down. Queen Elizabeth also licensed two Flemings, Anthony Been and John Care, to erect furnaces for making window-glass, at Greenwich, in 1567; and two of their fellow-countrymen, Peter Briet and Peter Appell, continued the manufacture.

* In *The Danger of the Church and Kingdom from Foreigners considered* (London, 1721), it is stated: "From Holland the art of printing was brought into England by Caxton and Turner about the year 1471, whom King Henry VI. sent thither to learn that mystery. These two fellows, not being able to gain their ends there, cunningly wheedled into England one Frederick Corsellis, a Dutch printer at Haarlem. This mercenary foreigner, having made his first essay at Oxford, set up printing-houses at Westminster, St. Alban's, and Worcester."

† Thomas Churchyard, a poet of the sixteenth century, thus speaks of him:

"Then, he that made for us a paper-mill,
Is worthy well of love and worldes good will,
And though his name be *Spill*-man by degree,
Yet *Help*-man now, he shall be calde by me.
Six hundred men are set at work by him,
That else might starve, or seek abroad their bread;
Who nowe live well, and go full braw and trim,
And who may boast they are with paper fed."

‡ *The Danger of the Church and Kingdom from Foreigners considered* (London, 1721)

At that time glass was regarded as so precious, that during the Duke of Northumberland's absence from Alnwick Castle, the steward was accustomed to take out the glazed windows, and stow them away until his grace's return, the glass being apt to be blown out by the high winds. Even in the next century, or as late as 1661, glass had not been generally introduced; the royal palaces in Scotland being only glazed in their upper windows, the lower ones being provided with wooden shutters.

Another Italian, named James Verselyn, established a second glass-house at Greenwich, for manufacturing the better kinds of glass; and Evelyn, writing of this "Italian glass-house" more than a century later, says that "glass was then blown in England of finer metal than that of Murano at Venice." Another glass-house was erected at Greenwich in the reign of James I. Some refugee Flemings established a work at Newcastle-on-Tyne,* where the manufacture still flourishes; and some Venetians carried on the manufacture, helped by the French refugee workmen, at Pinner's Hall in Austin Friars, London, where the best descriptions of glass were then made. The Flemings excelled in glass-painting; one of them, Bernard van Linge, established in London in 1614, being the first to practice the art in England. This artist supplied the windows for Wadham College, the beautiful window of Lincoln's Inn Chapel, and several subjects for Lincoln's College Chapel.

It will thus be found that in all manufactures requiring special skill, our main reliance was upon foreigners down to the middle of the seventeenth century; and the finest fabrics of all kinds were, as a rule, made almost exclusively by foreign workmen. Even in masonry and carpentry, when work of a superior kind was required, as well as in drainage and engineering, the practice was to send abroad, not only for the master-builder or engineer, but for workmen and the principal materials. Thus, when Sir Thomas Gresham built the Royal Exchange in 1566, he brought from Flanders the requisite masons and carpenters to execute it, under the direction of Henryke, their master-builder. The foreigners also brought with them all necessary materials—the wainscot, the glass, the slates, the iron, and even much of the stone for the building. In short, as Holinshed relates, Gresham "bargained for the whole mould and substance of his workmanship in Flanders."† Only the laborers employed upon the structure were provided from among the London workmen, who do not seem to have been in great repute at the time, for Sir Stephen Soame says of the house-painters in Elizabeth's reign that "among the number of three hundred painters now in London, there are not twelve sufficient workmen to be found among them, and one of these (he being fifty years old, and such was his poverty) was fain for his relief to wear, upon Lord-mayor's day, a blue gown and red cap, and carry a torch!"

Although English manufactures were in gradual course of establishment in

---

* It is a curious fact that the manufacture of window-glass in England should have first been attempted at Newcastle-on-Tyne as early as the year 670. The Abbot Benedict then brought over some glass-blowers from Gaul, probably Italians, for the purpose of manufacturing the glass required for the church and monastery of Wearmouth Abbey; but when the glass had been made, the furnaces were extinguished, and remained so for more than 800 years.

† HOLINSHED, ed. 1807, i., 395. See also BURGON—*Life of Sir T. Gresham*, ii., 117.

the face of many difficulties,* arising principally from the non-industrial habits of the people—for skilled industry is a matter of habit, and the product, it may be, of centuries of education—the English markets continued to be supplied with the better sorts of manufactured articles principally from abroad. Our iron and steel wares came from Germany, France, Flanders, and Spain; our hats, paper, and linen (hollands), from Holland; our stone drinking-pots from Cologne; our glass from Italy and the Low Countries; and silks, bays, ribbons, gloves, lace, and other articles of wearing apparel, from Flanders and France. The writer of an old book, entitled *A Brief Account of English Poesy*, referring to the large trade in French, Spanish, Flemish, Milan, and Venetian articles in the reign of Edward VI., observed, "I mervail no man taketh heed to it what number of trifles come hither from beyond the seas that we might clean spare, or else make them within our realm; for the which we either pay inestimable treasure every year, or else exchange substantial wares and necessary for them, for the which we might receive great treasure."

Under these circumstances, it was natural that the English monarchs, seeing the great wealth and power, as well as profitable employment for the poorer classes, which followed the establishment of leading branches of industry among the population, should have systematically pursued the policy of inviting foreign artisans from all countries to settle in England, and protected them by royal patents, thereby enabling them to pursue their several callings without interference from the native guilds. This course seems to have been adopted at different times, with more or less effect, from the reign of Edward I. downward;† and as late as the reign of James I.—the industry of England being still in as much need as ever of foreign help—we find that monarch going so far as to employ agents to bring from Rochelle "three prime workmen," for the purpose of instructing his subjects in the process of manufacturing the alum used in dyeing; and the "three prime workmen" were smuggled out of the French port "*in hogsheads.*"‡

These efforts made by successive English monarchs to establish new branches of industry were not always successful. The patents which they granted for the purpose of encouraging them frequently proved oppressive monopolies,

* The flax-manufacture was eventually established at Bridport; an old charter conferring upon the town a monopoly in the supply of naval cordage. To be "stabbed with a Bridport dagger" passed into a proverb, signifying the use of Bridport rope at the yard-arm or the gallows. Northampton was said to stand chiefly on other men's legs, being early distinguished for its make of boots and shoes. Staffordshire was celebrated for its nails, Sheffield for its whistles, Bristol for its gray soap, Taunton for its serges, and Ripon for its spurs: hence the proverb, "As true steel as Ripon rowels."

† Henry VIII. seems to have been a great patron of foreigners, for we find his cutler to have been one Marinus Garet, a native of Normandy; his goldsmith, Henry Holtesweller, a native of Burg, in Germany; his tailor, Stepen Jesper, a native of Hainault; at the same time that the "chief surgeon of his body" was one John Veyreri, described as "Nemausan ex regione linguæ Auxitanæ."* In the same reign we find foreign "bere brewers" settling among us; one of these, bearing the appropriate name of Adam Barl, a native of Wesel, obtaining letters of denization in 1512. The king also, like several of his predecessors, induced a number of German armorers, principally from Nuremberg, to settle in England and instruct his subjects in the practice of their art.

‡ *Machinery and Manufactures of Great Britain*—Weale's Quarterly Papers on Engineering, 117.

* See Letters of Denization in Brewer's *Calendar of State Papers*, reg Henry VIII, 1509-14.

the immediate effect of which was to compel the public to pay excessive prices for the articles made by the protected foreigners, and still the manufactures often refused to take root among us. The growth of the new industries were also to a great extent hindered by the proceedings of the manufacturers themselves. Few in number, they were prone to combine for the purpose of keeping up the prices of their commodities; while the workmen, following their example, combined to keep up the rate of wages. Man seems by nature to be a bigot and monopolist in matters of trade; but this is only saying, in other words, that he is selfish and that he is human. No sooner was any new branch of industry started, than its members set up guilds and corporations for the purpose of confining its benefits as much as possible to themselves. Those who were within the pale of the protected craft combined together rigorously to exclude all who were outside it. Hence the repetition by the cloth-weavers of Norwich, at a very early period, of the same tyranny which had almost ruined the trade of Ghent and Bruges. The Flemish weavers, who had been the victims of monopoly in Brabant, had scarcely established themselves in Norfolk ere the hard lessons which their fathers had learned were forgotten, and the trades unions of the Low Countries were copied almost to the letter. The usual methods of maintaining prices and wages were enforced—long apprenticeships, limitation in the number of apprentices, and rigorous exclusion of all "strangers." And when the native population at length came to learn the secrets of the trade, they too, in their turn, sought to exclude the very Flemings who had taught it them. The "cursede forrainers" were repeatedly attacked by the native workmen, and in 1369 some of them even fell victims to the popular fury. On this King Edward, at whose invitation they had been induced to settle in the country, issued a proclamation declaring the Flemish workmen to be under his special protection, and the native violence was for a time held in check.

The evils arising from the absurd restrictions of the Norwich guilds were, however, less easy of correction; but they carried with them their own punishment, and in course of time they wrought their own cure. They drove away many workmen who could not, or would not comply with their regulations, and they prevented other workmen from settling in the place and carrying on their trade. The consequence was, that the artisans proceeded to other unprivileged places, mostly in the north of England, and there laid the foundations of the great manufacturing towns of Manchester, Leeds, and Sheffield; while the trade of Norwich itself languished, and many of its houses stood empty. To remedy these evils, which the cupidity of the Norwich guilds had brought upon their city, the Flemish artisans were appealed to, and urged by promises of favor and protection to settle again in the place, for it was clear that the guildmen could not yet dispense with the skill and industry of the strangers. These invitations had their effect; and with the increased settlements of Flemings (described in the text), the prosperity of the place was again restored.

The same native hostility to the foreigners displayed itself in London and other towns, and occasionally led to serious public commotions, notwithstanding their being under the protection of the crown. The vulgar and ignorant of all countries, as a rule, hate foreigners. Their dress is strange, and their language stranger; their manners and customs are unusual, and their habits peculiar; and they are almost invariably looked upon by the less educated classes with prejudice and suspicion, if not with hostility. This is especially the case where—as the ignorant poor are so ready to believe—the bread eaten by the foreigners is so much bread taken out of their own mouths. This native aversion to the Flemish workmen, originating in these causes, not unfrequently displayed itself in England, and was taken advantage of by demagogues. Thus, when Wat Tyler burst into the city with his followers in 1381, the Flemings were among the first to suffer from their fury. Thirteen of them were dragged from the church in Austin Friars, where they had taken refuge; seventeen from another church; while thirty-two were seized in the Vintry, besides others in Southwark. They were carried before Wat Tyler, who is said to have tested the nationality of the prisoners by their pronunciation of the words "bread and cheese." If it sounded any thing like "brod and cawse" they were pronounced Flemings, and executed forthwith. During the same revolt the Hanseatic merchants were in great peril;* but, fortunately for them, they had taken the precaution to surround their warehouse fortress in Dowgate with strong walls, and, having barred their iron-clamped doors, they effectually resisted the assaults of the rioters until the authorities had recovered from their panic, and proceeded to restore civil order by the strong arm of the law.

At a later period, in 1493, the mob were more successful in their attack upon the Steelyard, which they broke into and completely gutted. This riot was supposed to have been instigated by the native merchants, who were jealous of the privileges granted to the strangers, under which they conducted almost the entire foreign trade of the country. But the antipathy of the mob to the foreigners reached its height about the beginning of the reign of Henry VIII., when a formidable riot broke out (in 1517), which was long after known as "Evil May-day." Large numbers of foreign artisans then crowded the suburbs, where they made and sold a variety of articles, to the supposed prejudice of the London workmen. The Flemings abounded in Southwark, Westminster, Tottenham, and St. Catharine's, all outside the freedom of the city. Hall, in his *Life of Henry VIII.*, says, "There were such numbers of them employed as artificers that the English could get no work." It was also alleged that "they export so much wool, tin, and lead, that English adventurers can have no living;" and the Dutch were especially complained against because of their importations of large quantities of "iron, timber, and leather, ready manufactured, and nails, locks, baskets, cupboards, stools, tables, chests, girdles, saddles, and painted cloths." Probably the real secret of the outcry was that the foreign artisans were more industrious,

---

* The Hanseatic merchants, or "Steelyard Company of Foreign Merchants," occupied extensive premises in Downgard (now Dowgate) Ward, in Upper Thames Street. There they had their guildhall, dwellings, and warehouses, surrounded by a strong wall, with a wharf on the Thames. For a long time nearly the whole foreign trade of the country was conducted by these merchants, who exported English wool and imported foreign merchandise, paying toll at Billingsgate in fine cloth, gloves, pepper, and vinegar. The exclusive privileges of the Steelyard merchants at length became the subject of such general complaint, and were regarded as so prejudicial to the development of native commerce, that they were withdrawn in 1552. Their extensive premises occupied part of the site of the present Cannon Street Railway Station.

and manufactured better and cheaper things than the English could then do. One John Lincoln, a broker, was loudest of all in his complaints against the foreigners, and by his influence a popular preacher named Bell was led to denounce them from the pulpit; and he declaimed with so much eloquence on the hardships suffered by the native-born freemen in consequence of their competition, that the city was soon thrown into a ferment.

In this state of excitement, the apprentices, a rather turbulent class, encouraged each other to insult and abuse the foreigners whom they met in the streets. On the 28th of April, a body of them set upon and beat the Flemings in so shameful a manner that the lord-mayor found it necessary to interfere; and he, accordingly, had the offenders seized by the city watch, and lodged in the compter. The indignation of the populace became greater than ever, and a riot was apprehended. Cardinal Wolsey sent for the lord-mayor and aldermen, and told them that he would hold them responsible for the tranquillity of the city. Prompt measures were taken to provide against the apprehended rising of the mob, and on May-day-eve the magistrates resolved to issue orders to every householder in the city to keep themselves, their children, apprentices, and servants strictly within doors on the following day; but before the order could be issued the riot broke out, and the cry was raised of "'Prentices! 'prentices! clubs! clubs!" Several hundred watermen, porters, and idlers joined the rioters, who forthwith broke open the compter and released the prisoners. In the mean time, the foreigners, apprehending the outbreak, had for the most part taken the precaution to depart from the city to Islington, Hackney, and other villages outside the walls, so that the rioters could only expend their fury upon their dwellings, which were speedily pillaged and destroyed.

The Earls of Shrewsbury and Surrey then entered the city at the head of a strong body of troops, and aided the lord-mayor in capturing nearly 300 of the rioters. Lincoln the broker, and Bell the preacher, were also apprehended. These, with ten others, were found guilty and sentenced to death; but Lincoln only was hanged, and the others were reprieved until the king's pleasure should be known. Henry ordered the lord-mayor, the sheriffs and aldermen, with the prisoners, 278 in number, to appear before him at Westminster Hall. The former wore mourning in token of contrition for their negligence; the latter had halters round their necks. Wolsey addressed the magistrates in the king's name, and severely rebuked them for not having taken proper precautions to insure the peace of the city, and protect the lives and property of the strangers, who carried on their industry in the full reliance that they would be protected by the magistracy as well as by the law. Then addressing the prisoners, Wolsey asked them what they could plead in extenuation of their deep offense, and whereupon they should not one and all suffer death. Their sobs and cries for mercy softened the king's heart; some of the nobility around him besought the pardon of the unhappy culprits, which was granted, and the prisoners were discharged.

This severe lesson had its effect upon the unruly populace, and the foreign artisans returned to their homes, the city being compelled to make good the damage which had been done to them by the destruction of their dwellings and furniture, and the interruption of their industry.

On the whole, the authorities acted with creditable vigor on the occasion; and though discontent at the subsequent extensive immigration of foreign artisans frequently displayed itself, there was never such another wild outbreak of the London mob as that which happened on the long-remembered "Evil May-day."

II. REGISTERS OF FRENCH PROTESTANT CHURCHES IN ENGLAND.

THE records of most of the Huguenot churches have been lost. The congregations died out, and left no traces, except in contemporary accounts of them, which are imperfect. The registers of some of the more important have, however, been preserved, and are of a peculiarly interesting character.

A royal commission having been appointed, some twenty-five years since, to collect the non-parochial registers of baptisms, marriages, and burials, under the powers of the new Registration Act, a considerable number of the records of the extinct French churches were brought to light, collected, and placed in the custody of the Registrar General at Somerset House, where they now are. The greater number of these registers originally passed through the hands of Mr. J. Southernden Burn, secretary to the commission, who in 1846 published the results of a careful examination of them in his *History of the Foreign Protestant Refugees settled in England.*

Notwithstanding Mr. Burn's almost exhaustive treatise, the author has thought it desirable to have the registers re-examined for the purposes of the present work; and the following analysis, the result of a careful search, has been kindly made for him by Mr. Frederick Martin, author of *The Statesman's Year-Book.*

The registers of French Protestant churches preserved at Somerset House are as follow:

French Churches in London. Dates of Entries in Registers.

Threadneedle Street, City, removed to Founders Hall Chapel...... 1599-1753
St. Martin Ongar's, Cannon Street, removed to Threadneedle Street.. 1690-1762
French Chapel, Savoy, Strand... 1684-1822
Glasshouse Street Chapel... 1688-1699
Hungerford Chapel, Hungerford Market... 1688-1727
Le Temple... 1689-1782
Swallow Street Chapel... 1690-1709
Le Quarré, Little Deane Street.. 1690-1763
Le Tabernacle.. 1696-1710
Leicester Fields Chapel... 1699-1783
French Chapel Royal, St. James's.. 1700-1754
Ryder's Court Chapel, St. Ann's, Westminster................................. 1700-1750
La Charenton, Newport Market... 1701-1704
Les Grecs, Crown Street, afterward in Little Edward Street......... 1703-1731

FRENCH CHURCHES IN LONDON.

West Street Chapel, Soho.. 1706-1743
Berwick Street Chapel... 1720-1788
Castle Street Chapel, Leicester Square....................................... 1725-1754
Hoxton Chapel... 1748-1783
Eglise Neuve, Church Street, Spitalfields.................................. 1753-1809
Eglise de Swan Fields, do.. 1721-1735
Eglise de St. Jean, St. John Street, do.. 1687-1823
Eglise de l'Artillerie, Artillery Street, do................................... 1691-1786
Eglise de Wheeler Street, do... 1703-1741
Eglise de la Patente, do... 1689-1785
Eglise de Crespin Street, do.. 1694-1716
Perle Street. do... 1700-1701
Bell Lane, do... 1711-1716
Eglise de Marche, do.. 1719

French Churches in the Country.

Walloon Church, Canterbury.. 1581-1837
Malt House, do... 1709-1744
Norwich Walloon and French Church....................................... 1599-1611
Plymouth... 1733-1807
St. Julien, or God's House, Southampton................................. 1567-1799
Stonehouse, near Plymouth.. 1692-1791
Eglise de Thorpe-le-Soken, Essex.. 1684-1726
Thorney Abbey... 1654-1727

It will be observed, from the dates of the entries in the registers, that several of them are exceedingly imperfect. Many books have been altogether lost. Of those which have been preserved, the following present the principal features worthy of notice:

French Protestant Church of Threadneedle Street, London.
Established about 1546.

The registers of this church are in thirteen volumes, in a good state of preservation. The first volume, folio size, contains entries of baptisms and marriages from 1599 to 1636. Most of the entries are very short, giving nothing more than the names of the parties, and in some cases the places of their origin. The notices of baptism run: "Mardy, 29 Janvier, 1599, Jean le Quion, fils de Jean le Quion et d'Ester sa femme, fut presénté, au Ste Baptesme par Erhart Franco Anglois et Editho Ansolam, Mario Penart femme de Valentin Marchant et Marie Bigot femme d'Estienne Thierry;" while the marriages are mostly entered as follows: "Le dimanche 27 Janvier, 1599; Isidore fils de feu Jacques Pinchon natif d'Armentiers et Bastienne du Mont veuve de Lazare Martin native de Valenciennes, furent epousé le dict jour." As far as can be judged from the earlier entries, most of the persons whose names occur were natives of the north of France and of the Walloon provinces. The annual number of baptisms entered in the first volume averages from 80 to 150 during the period from 1599 to 1610, and from 140 to 100 in the years from 1611 to 1636.

A A

The second volume of the registers of Threadneedle Street Church has entries of baptisms from 1636 to 1691, and of marriages from 1636 to 1645. The latter fill not more than eight pages; but the baptisms are exceedingly numerous, including, as stated in the volume—a folio more than two inches thick—those of the chapel of L'Hôpital at Spitalfields. From the commencement of the year 1670 till the end of the year 1679, the number of baptisms entered amounts to 1123, comprising 578 boys and 545 girls. The notices are very meagre, giving nothing but the names of the parents and of the godfather and godmother.

The third volume contains only entries of baptisms, including, as before, those of L'Hôpital, commencing in 1698 and ending in 1711. The baptisms during this period number 7032, comprising 3522 boys and 3510 girls, or an average of 540 per annum. In most cases the occupation of the male parent is given, and in nine entries out of ten it is set down as "weaver," or, as frequently spelled, "wever." The word "ouvrier en soye" occurs up to the year 1699, after which the English term is substituted, not only here, but in reference to other trades mentioned, such as "watchmaker," "diamant-cutter," "haberdasher," "ivory-turner," and "cloth-printer." Toward the end of the book scarcely any other trade occurs but that of "weaver."

The fourth volume, a folio about an inch and a half thick, contains entries of baptisms from the beginning of 1691 till the end of 1727. All the entries are very short, mentioning merely the name of the parents and of godfather and godmother. There is much confusion in the dates, which spring forward and backward, making calculations of the numbers very difficult. No entries of any interest occur.

The whole of the remaining nine volumes—of various sizes, from the largest folio to the smallest duodecimo—are filled with mere index-like entries of baptisms and marriages, ranging over the period from 1650 to 1753. Against the cover of the fifth volume is pasted the official "certificate," describing the registers. It is as follows: "The thirteen accompanying books are the original register-books of baptisms and marriages which have been kept for the church called the London Walloon Church, being of the French Protestant denomination, situate in Threadneedle Street, in the city of London, founded about the year 1546. The books have been, from time to time, in the custody of the consistory for the time being of the congregation, and are sent to the commissioners from the immediate custody of the said consistory. Signed the 21st of October, 1840. F. Martin, minister."

Among the names which most frequently occur in the register are those of Du Bois, Denys, Primerose, Mahieu (Mayhew), Bultel, Brunet, Coppinger, Felles, Mariot (Mariott), Pinchon, Ducane or Du Quesne, Vincent, Leadbitter, Pontin, Waldo, De la Marre, and Papillon.

Among the ministers of the church were François La Riviere and Richard François, appointed in 1550; Samuel le Chevalier (1591); Gilbert Primerose, also king's chaplain (1623); Pierre Dumoulin (1624); Ezekiel Marmet (1631); Charles Bertheau (1687); Jacques Saurin (1701); Ezechiel Barbauld (1704); Jean Jacques Claude, grandson of the celebrated Claude (1711): David Henry Durand (1760); and Jean Romilly (1766).

French Church of the Savoy, Strand, London.

These registers are in two folios, the first with entries of marriages from 1684 to 1753, and the second, a much thinner volume, with entries of baptisms, marriages, banns, and sundry other notices, from 1699 to 1773. The title-page of the first book is " Livre des Mariages de l'Eglise françoise de la Savoye, commencé au nom de Dieu à Londres le premier May, 1684." In the earlier entries, only the names of the bridegroom and bride, together with that of the officiating minister, are given ; but the latter notices are a little fuller, mentioning frequently the origin and domicile of the married couple, as well as their trade and profession. This is the case particularly from the year 1700, the first entry of which notes the nuptials of "Jean Anthoine Laroche, chirurgien, demeurant en Panton Street, paroisse de St. Martin-in-the-Fields, à l'enseigne d'un baston de chirurgien."

In many of the descriptions of domicile there is a curious mixture of French and English. Under date of July 20, 1700, is entered the marriage of " Pierre Pinsun, lieutenant, logé en Berwick Street, nex door to Mr. Clerck, King's Messenger, paroisse St. James ;" and the entry after this, dated July 21, 1700, refers to "Jacob Bouchet, vermisseur, demeurant paroisse St. James, in St. James Street, chez un Sheesmonguer à l'enseigne de l'Indien." The next four entries record the nuptials of " Pierre Deconde de Largni, capitaine dans les troupes de Hollande, demeurant en Sofolstreet chez Madame Benoist, au milieu de la rue ;" of "Jean Maret, officier de Marine, logé en la paroisse de St. Anne, Westminster, in Bruce Street, joignent l'enseigne de Marocco ;" of " Paul Lescot, ministre de St. Evangille, demeurant en Ruperstreet aux deux piliers noirs, vis-à-vis une boutique de cuisinier ou rotisseur ;" and of " Michel Cauvin, menusier, demeurant en Contompt Street, proche l'enseigne des trois pigeons." The surgeons and physicians are rather numerously represented; and in 1704 there is one "Estienne Baron dit Dupont, operateur pour les dents."

Under date of Nov. 22, 1719, there is an entry of unusual length, differing in form from all others. It runs: "Je sousigné Saville Bradely, chapelain de Mylord duc de Richemont, recteur de Earnly dans la province de Sussex en Angleterre, certifie avoir aujourdhui marié Ecuyer Charles Theodore de Maxuel, capitain dans le regiment de Gauvain au service de sa Majesté Britannique, à la demoiselle Marthe Susanne Degennes, fille de Daniel Degennes sieur de la Picottière, et de dame Judith Ravenel, demeurant à Morlaix en Bretagne, dans l'hôtel de son Excellence Mylord Comte de Stair, ambassadeur extraordinaire du Roy de la Grande Bretagne à Paris ce neuf de Novembre, mille sept cens dix neuf." The entries from 1700 to 1726 average twenty per annum ; but subsequent to the latter date there is a gradual decline, till toward the end there are not more than two marriages a year. The last is dated October 14, 1753.

The second volume of the Savoy records, a very thin folio, is filled with entries of baptisms, most of them very short, interspersed with notices and letters relating to the same. There is great confusion among the whole of the entries, many of them are struck through with the pen, and queries attached to others. At the end is a certificate of the "Commissaires nommés par la compagnie du Consistoire de l'Eglise de la Savoie," stating that they have examined the registers, and "corrigé les fautes qui nous ont parus essentielles avec tout le soin et l'attention, dont nous avons été capables." The certificate seems to refer to many more books than those now at the General Register Office.

Among the celebrated ministers of this church were James Abbadie (1700), James Severin (1703), Claude de la Mothe (1705), John Dubourdieu (1709), Louis Saurin (1711), J. J. Majendie (1735), and David Durand, D.D., the well-known author.

Swallow Street Chapel, London.

The registers of this place of worship, bound in a thin folio, contain entries of baptisms and marriages, with various other notices chiefly relating to conversions and "reconnoissances," from the year 1690 to 1709. Nearly all the entries are of some length, with many particulars as to the birth, origin, and nationality of the individuals concerned. One of the first entries runs: "Le Dimanche dixhuitième jour de May, 1690, a esté baptisé Frideric fils de Guy Mesming, docteur en medecine et Anne Marie son épouse, ayant Monsieur Wolfgang de Schmettau ministre d'Estat et Envoyé Extraordinaire de sa Serenité Electorale de Brandebourg vers leur Majestés Britanniques et Monsieur Jean de Remy de Montigny gentilhomme de la Reyne pour parrain, et dam[le] Madeleine Olympe Beauchamp pour marraine, lesquels ont dit l'enfant être né le 12 jour de May dernier, present mois et an, et ont signe." Here follow the signatures of the parents, godfather and godmother, with "Lamothe, ministre," at the end. Almost all the entries of baptism are in a similar form, while of the marriages the following is a specimen: "Le Samedy septième jour de Novembre an 1691, a esté beny en ceste Eglise, Monsieur Mollet, ministre de l'Eglise françoise de Colchester, et Marguerite Bureau, presentée par Isaac Bureau son père en vertu d'une licence à eux accordée le vingt-neuvième jour d'Octobre dernier et ont signé." .... Here again follow the signatures of the persons mentioned, together with that of the minister.

The notices of "reconnoissance" (acknowledgment of sin or backsliding) are rather numerous, running usually as follows: "Vendredy premier jour de l'année 1692, Claude Richieu refugié de Montpellier a temoigné en presence de ceste Eglise sa repentance d'avoir succombé sous le faix de la persecution en abjurant notre sainte Religion, ce qu'il a confirmé en signant le present acte." There is the entry of a conversion on the next page: "Le Dimanche cinq jour de May, jour de la Pentecoste, Susanne Auvray, native de Paris, a fait abjuration publique en ceste Eglise des erreurs et superstitions du Papisme, après avoir adonné des preuves d'une solide instruction, de sa pieté et de ses bonnes moeurs, ce qu'elle a confirmé en signant cet acte." The notices of "reconnoissances" are most numerous in the years 1692–6, after which they gradually fall off, disappearing entirely with the end of the century.

Many names of distinguished persons occur among the baptismal entries. That of King William figures several times as godfather by proxy. The first time his majesty is mentioned it is as follows: "Le Mercredy 13 jour de Decembre an 1693 a esté baptisé par Monsieur de la Mothe l'un des pasteurs de cette église, Guillaume Rabault, fils de Messire Jean Rabault, chevalier seigneur de la Coudrière et de dame Nehenée Marguerite, née Jedouin, son epouse, ayant pour parrain le Très Haut et Très Puissant Seigneur Guillaume Roy d'Angleterre, d'Ecosse, de France, et d'Irlande, par Mylord Silskirque (Selkirk) l'un des gentilshommes ordinaires de la Chambre de sa Majesté, et Mylord Jaques Duc d'Ormord, et pour marraine Dame Caroline Elisabeth, Raugrave Palatine, duchesse de Schomberg." The name of "Monsieur Graverol, l'un de ministres de cette eglise," occurs first in January, 1691, in an entry of baptism, signed, in a beautiful handwriting, J. Graverol; while the next entry, dated February, 1691, mentions "Monsieur de Rocheblave, l'un des pasteurs de cette eglise." Both names occur again, at intervals, till 1698, most frequently that of Graverol. The names of the ministers change constantly, and sometimes as many as four appear in one entry.

The remaining registers of the French churches in London contain few entries worthy of particular notice. We therefore proceed to an examination of the registers of the country churches, more particularly that of the " God's House" at Southampton, which will be found of peculiar interest.

Church of St. Julien, or " God's House," Southampton.

The registers of this church are in one volume folio, about an inch thick, strongly bound, and very well preserved. The official certificate, pasted against the fly-leaf, states that the volume "is the original Register-book of baptisms, marriages, deaths, and other entries, which has been kept for the formerly Walloon Church, but now the Protestant Episcopal French Church, congregating in the chapel of God's House at Southampton, founded about the year 1567." It is farther stated that "the book has been from time to time in the custody of the ministers or elders for the time being, and is sent to the commissioners from the immediate custody of George Atherley, Esq., who has kept it since 1832 as elder and trustee." This certificate bears the date December 22, 1837, with " Frederick Vincent," minister, at the bottom.

The first series of entries in this volume, filling about thirty-six pages, are lists of persons who attended Holy Communion. The heading of the first page is " Ensuyt les noms de ceux qui ont faict professio de leur foy et admis a la Cene le 21 de Decebre, 1567." The number of communicants under this date is fifty-eight, the last eight in the list being distinguished as " Anglois." The second body of communicants, entered under date of April 5, 1568, number thirty-nine; and the third, under date of July, 1568, amount to ten. There is a great variation in the numbers set down for the following years; but the entries, which at first contain the mere names, become gradually more distinct, specifying the place of origin of the communicants, and at times, though very rarely, the trade or profession. The trades mentioned are " tisseran," " boulangier," " coustelier," and " brasseur;" and the professions " medecin" and " ministre." The medical men are comparatively numerous. Among the places of origin most frequently mentioned are Valenciennes, Lisle, Dieppe, " Gernese" (Guernsey), and " Jerse."

From many entries it appears that the Holy Communion was only administered to those newly arrived in the colony after they had furnished satisfactory proofs of being true Protestants. The words "témoignage par écrit," or simply "témoignage," are attached to a great many names. The withholding of the communion occurred often, and for various causes. Under date of 3d July, 1569, there is the entry, " Cene defendue a Martin Lietart pour avoir battu et mauré sa famme." Again, under date of 2d April, 1570, " Cene defendue a Jan Groza pour ivrognerie continuelle." Under date of October 1, 1570, the entry is " La Cene fut suspendue a Lille le Felu pour ivrognerie jusques a ce qon voiroit son repentance." Under date of the 5th of July, 1573, the reason for requiring "témoignages" is distinctly stated to be "pour ferre paroir qu'ils estoient de la religion auparavant estre sortie de la France, de poeur de quelque faux frère qui vien droit pour espier sous ombre de la religion." Subsequent to the year 1573 there are many entries with the word " messe" prefixed, as showing that the communicants had been forced to attend mass for a time. There is a note relating to this subject under date of January 3, 1574. It runs: " Tiebaut du Befroi, sa femme, son fils, et sa fille, apres avoir fect leur recognaissance publicque d'avoir esté a la messe, furent tous recus a la cene." The entries of "messe" become less numerous subsequent to 1577; but there are notices of having " communiqué avec les anglois."

There is visible confusion among the entries of the year 1583, explained by a note, dated the 7th of July, as follows: " Pour la peste quy estoit au milieu de nous fut le lendemain de la cene de Juilet les prieres publicques commencées du soir tous les jours hors presche, a 5 heures du soir." The short list of communicants of August, 1583, has a note attached—"pour nous fortifier en foi, en luy priant d'avoir pitié de nous." The ravages of the plague are visible for a long time in the small number of persons attending "la Cene," who, after the year 1605, are mostly strangers, producing "témoignages," or "avec attestation." In the whole year 1630 there are only nine communicants entered, six of them "jeunes filles;" in 1631 there are but five communicants; and in 1632 but two. Then there is a blank till 1662, when one name is entered, while three more follow in 1665. Here end the lists of communicants.

As a sort of appendix to these lists there follows, after a blank space, the entry of a conversion. It runs: " Le 12 Aoust, 1722. Monsieur Pierre Carpentier prêtre de l'eglise Romaine du troisième ordre des franciscains, natif de Paris, fit abjuration publicque des erreurs de la dite eglise et fut recu à la paix de l'Eglise par nous Pierre Denain, docteur en theologie, et ministre de cette Eglise."

After about sixteen blank leaves a new series of entries commences, headed " Registre des enfans qui ont este baptisees en l'eglise des estrangers Walons en la Ville de Hampton admise par la Magesté de la Royne Elizabeth l'an 1567." The baptisms commence in December, 1567, when there are two, the fathers entered as from Valenciennes and " Hampton," and the mothers from London and Valenciennes. In the year 1568 the baptisms number eight; in 1569, nine; in 1570, seventeen; in 1571, six; in 1572, ten; in 1573, fifteen; in 1574, twenty; in 1575, sixteen; in 1576, twenty-two; and from 1577 to the end of the century, they vary from twenty to thirty. But the lists do not appear to have been regularly kept, for there are many blank spaces, and the usual formula, "fut baptizé," with name of "parin" or "tesmoin," is often very incomplete. There are several entries "fut baptizé par Monsieur Hopkins, ministre anglois," in 1584. The place of origin of the parents is seldom given, but a description of trade or profession occurs in a few instances; among them Pierre Tiedet, "orfèvre;" Martin, "batteur d'estain;" and Philippe de la Motte, "ministre de la parole de Dieu," all of which names appear frequently. "Monsieur de Bouillon, ministre de la parolle de Dieu," is also entered more than once among the parents.

After the year 1600 the baptismal registers are more confused and irregular than before, the names of godfathers and witnesses being scarcely ever given. From 1634 to 1657 the entries entirely cease, to be resumed only in alternate years. Under date of the 23d of July, 1665, is the following note, signed "Couraud, Pasteur:" "Dieu ayant affligé notre ville du plus terrible de ses fleaux quj a obligé la plus part des habitans d'abandonner leurs maisons, et Monsieur Bernert leur pasteur estant detenu de maladie et ayant este contraint de quitter sa demoure pour changer d'air à la campagne, nous avons en son absense baptizé dans notre Eglise françoise un petit enfant Anglois appellé Nicolas, et ce par l'ordre de monsieur le Maire." (Among the death entries, farther on in the book, stands, under date of Sept. 21, 1865, "Monsieur Couraud, notre pasteur—peste.")

There are only seven entries of baptism in the year 1665, among them "Elizabeth, fille de Monsieur Couraud, notre pasteur." The next pastor mentioned is "Monsieur Anthoine Cougot, ministre de ceste Eglise et Docteur en medecine," described, in 1691, as married to one "Anthoinette," daughter of "Monseigneur Marc Anthoine de Fineste du Falga, gentilhomme françois de la province de Languedoc." The entries about this period are few in number, including, however, names of some distinction. A child of "Abraham Buillon de St. Hillaire, sur Lotize en Poitou," and another of "Jean Thomes, apoticaire et chirugien de la ville de Cauvisson en Languedoc"—the latter with "Charles Gajot de la Renaudiere, gentilhomme françois de la province de Poitou," as godfather—are entered in 1691. As far as the origin of the parents is stated, the natives of France predominate in the lists subsequent to 1697. Many are entered as "François refugiez;" some from "Basse Normandie," some from "Haut Languedoc," but the greater number from the province of Poitou. Under date of July, 1702, one "Gerard de Vaux, françois, de la ville de Castres en Haut Languedoc," is mentioned as possessed of a paper-mill, "demeurans au moulin à papier, dans la paroisse de South Stoneham," and both in 1699 and in 1705 there occurs names of officers "dans le regiment du Colonel Mordant," or "Brigadier Mordant;" while in 1711 "Monsieur le lieutenant general Mordant" figures as the godfather of twin sons of "Monsieur François du Chesne de Ruffanes, major infanterie de Chevreux en Poitou."

The entries of baptisms cease in 1779, after gradually declining in number, amounting to only twenty-one in the thirty-three years from 1744. During the whole of this period the Reverend "Isaac Jean Barnouin" figures as "ministre de cette eglise," and a note at the end, signed "Hugh Hill, D.D., vicar of Holy Rhood," states that "the Rev. Isaac John Barnouin died on the 30th of March, 1797, and was buried the 6th of April, 1797."

The lists of marriages commence in December, 1567, but for about 130 yeers, till near the end of the seventeenth century, the entries are irregular and somewhat confused. Subsequently they are full of details as to the birth, origin, and, at times, the profession of the bridegroom and bride. During the plague of 1665–6, many English couples were married in the French church, the English clergymen having all fled from the town. Hence such entries as the following: "Jacob Berger et Sara Baylie, tous deux Englois, receurent la Benediction de leut marriage p nostre pasteur en L'Eglise de St. Jean en cette ville, les Ministres Englois ayant abandoné leur tropeaux à cause de la peste qui ravagoit en ce lieu ce 4^{em} de Decembre, 1665." The following is a specimen of the ordinary entries: "Le 29 Novembre, 1702, a eté beni par moi Antoine Cougot le marriage de Jean Lefebre, orphevre de sa profession, demeurant a Londres, fils de feu Jean le Fabre, marchand de la ville de Chalons en Champagne et de Marie Conteneau sas père et mère, d'une part, et d'Esther Villeneau, fille de Charles Villeneau marchand dans l'Isle de Ré et d'Esther Sorré ses père et mère d'autre part. Lequel marriage a eté benit après la publication de trois annonces." The entries of marriages are never numerous, either before or after the year 1700—averaging, on the whole, not more than two a year. From 1710 to 1720 there are but six; from 1720 to 1730, but seven; and from the latter date till 1753, only three. The Rev. Isaac Jean Barnouin, in the whole of his long ministry, enters but two marriages—one in 1736, and the other in 1753. Very few of the names found in the lists of baptisms reoccur among the marriages, which appear to have taken place chiefly among persons settled at "Hamptone," or, quite as frequently, between natives of the Channel Islands.

The marriage-lists are followed by twenty-three blank pages, after which commences the death-register. It is headed "Registre de Ceux qui sont mors de l'eglise de Estrangers Walons admise par la Maiesté de la Royne Elizabeth en la Ville de Hamptone, 1567." The first entries are very short, giving merely the name; but in 1570 there is a lengthened notice of the death of one "Jherome Dentiere," native of "Lanbrechie aupres de Lille lez flandre," farther described as "souldat a monsieur de Bergne," who arrived ill, "et vint à Refuge de cette Eglise tant pour estre aidé en sa nesessité come pour avoir consollation, et fut gardé a la maison de foy le perre bien long-temps et au grand despens des poures, mais par la fin trespassa le 17 jour de May, 1570, et fut ensepulturé le mesme jour." The death-entries number not more than four or five times per annum for the first fifteen years, except in 1573, when there are nine, five of which are marked "passant" and "non de l'eglise," with farther notice, in some cases, that they were "mis aux depens des poures," or wayfarers kept by public charity. The burial of these poor took place nearly always the same day, and that of others the day after death. The place of nativity is very seldom given in the earlier entries, down to the middle of the seventeenth century.

There are long lists of the dead, giving nothing more than the names, which were apparently entered in a batch; the words "fut enterré le mesme jour" occur very frequently and regularly after the year 1600, when the first signs of the ravages of the plague became strongly visible. In 1604 long strings of names are followed by "peste," the entries throughout being of the shortest, such as " Catharine Martin mourut le 30 Aoust—peste," and " Pierre fils de Pierre Geulin mourut le jour susdit—peste." In the year 1604, 161 persons are set down as having died of the plague, the number amounting at times, in August and September, to four and five a day. In April, 1605, there is "non-peste" after a name; but no farther deaths are entered during the remainder of the year.

The first entry in 1617 is " Phillippe de la Motte, ministre de la parole de Dieu mourut le 6 de May et fust en terre le mesme jour en compaignie de tout le magistrat." There are but three deaths on the average of the years 1617-65, at which latter date the word "peste" again makes its appearance after the names. From the 15th of July, when the word first occurs, till the end of the year 1665, twenty-three deaths from the plague are recorded. One more person died of the plague in August, 1666, after which there stands "non-peste" to a name. The entries henceforth decrease farther in number, and greatly change in phraseology. The old form is "Guillaume Mansell trespassa le 26 de Auril au matin et fut mis en terre le mesme jour sur le soir;" while the entries after the great plague year of 1665 are mostly as follows: " Le sieur Mathieu Brohier françois refugié est mort le 29 de Juin est enterré le 30." The following entry occurs in 1661: "Ce grand Serviteur de Dieu, Paul Mercier, deceda le 22me d'Aoust, estant vendredi, et fut ensepultré dedans cette Eglize le Lundy ensuyvant. Iceluy estant un des grand Pilliers de cette Eglise et plaine d'aumosne."

There are no entries of any particular interest during the whole of the seventeenth century; the names are nearly all French, and the description "refugié" very frequently accompanies the name. From 1700 till 1712 there are but thirty-four deaths entered, and only one in 1713. The latter is of unusual length, as follows: " Demoiselle Antoinete de Ginesse de la ville de Puitaurens en Languedoc et femme du sieur Antoine Cougot, docteur en medicine, Recteur de Millbrook et ministre de cette Eglise, est morte le 21 May, 1713, et a eté enterre le 25e dans l'eglise de la Toussaint proche la table de la communion." There is no death entered in 1714, and but one in 1715, running, "Monsieur Samuel Dornam, gentilhomme refugié, né a Alençon est mort le 17 Juillet et enterré le 19e."

In 1721 we find the following obituary notice filling nearly half a page: " Monsieur Philibert d'Hervart, baron d'Hunniggen, français refugié, mourut en cette ville le 30 Avril, 1721, agé de 46 ans et fut enterré dans l'église paroissiale d'Holirood, auprès de M. Frédéric d'Hervart son fils, le mercredi suivant, son corps étant conduit à la sepulture par tous les ministres françois et anglois de cette ville et de St. Mary, et par une grande multitude de françois et d'anglois. Sous le règne de Guillaume troisième il fut envoyé extraordinaire à Genève, en Suisse, et s'étant retiré de cette ville il a laissé des marques de sa grande charité pour les pauvres en laissant à cette église un billet de £32 sterling, plus tard encore £50 sterling; aussy bien que de son zèle pour la gloire de Dieu en laissant pour l'entretien du ministère de cette église la somme de 12 livres sterling de rentes. Il avoir donné il y a environ 8 mois quatre mille livres sterling a l'hôpital des françois refugiés à Londres, vulgairement appellé la Providence. Les pauvres des deux nations françoise et angliose perdent beaucoup à sa mort. Du veuille avoir pitié d'eux, à leur susciter des personnes aussy charitables."

This entry is followed by another of some interest. It is: "Monsieur Antoine Cougot, cy-devant ministre de cette église mourut en cette ville le 14 de May, 1721, et fut enterré le Mercredy suivant dans l'église paroissiale de Millbrook dont il étoit recteur ; il avoit servi cette église avec édification pendant 30 ans." There are two more entries after this, the one stating the decease of "damoiselle la Cruce du Terme, fille de Monsieur le Colonnel du Terme," in August, 1721, and the other that of "Monsieur François du Rouré," in March, 1722. Here the death-register ends.

After an intervening space of thirty blank leaves, another, and exceedingly interesting series of entries commences, specifying the Fasts and Thanksgivings held at the church of "God's House." The heading of these entries is "Les jeusnes publicques quy se sont fectes en ceste Eglise Contre les tamps d'afliction selon la Coustume des Eglises de Dieu." The fasts, numbered in chronological order, extend from 1568 till the year 1667, or exactly a century. There are altogether sixty-eight "jeusnes," besides three thanksgivings, or "actions de graces," all of them containing reflections on contemporary events.

The first entry is as follows: "Lan 1568, le 3ᵉ jour de Setembre fut celebré le jeusne publicque, l'ocasion estoit que Monsigneur le Prince d'oreng descendoit dalemaigne aux paiis bas pour assaié, avec l'aide de Dieu de delivres les poures eglises dafliction, or pour prier plus ardamment le Seigneur a la delivrance de son peuple le jeusne fut celebré."

The second entry is as follows: "Lan 1570. Au 6ᵉ jour de May fut celebré le jeusne, l'ocasion estait que Monsieur le prince de Condé et Autres princes de la france estantes en guerre pour maintenir la vrai religion que le Roy voulait abolir, perdirent une grose bataille, de quoi toutes les Eglises se seroient fort desolées en pro chaines de calamité extreme. A cette cause on celebra le jeusne pour prier pour eux."

The third entry runs: "Lan 1572. Le 25 jour le Setembre fut celebré une jeusne publique, la raison estoit pour ce que Monsieur le Prince d'orenge estait venu aux paiis bas avec nouvelle armee dalemaigne pour asaier a deliverer le pais e les pauvres eglises hors de la main du duc d'Albe ce cruel tiran, et aussi principallement pour ce que les eglises de la France estoient en une merveilleuse et horrible calamité extreme. Une horrible massacre avoit esté fait a paris le 24 jour daout passe, un grand nombre de nobles et de fidelles furent tues en une nuit, environ de 12 ou 13 milles, la Presche deffendu par tout le roiaume et tous les biens des fidelles pilles par tout le roiaume, or pour la consollation d'eux et des paix bas, et pour prier le Seigneur a leur deliverance fut celebré ce jeusne solemmel."

The next six "jeusnes," numbered 4 to 10 (1574–5), were held to pray for the "pauvres eglises" of France and Holland; also for preservation against the plague. The next after this, marked 11, is as follows: "Le vingt et neuvieme d'aout 1576 fut celebré un jeusne public en ceste eglise priant Dieu de maintenir la maiesté de la Reine en bone Amitie et acord avec M. le prince d'orenge, a la gloire de dieu et au salut et conservation des eglises."

The next, the 12th entry, runs: "Le 22 Novembre, 1576, le jeusne fut celebré en ceste eglise et ce mesme jour aussi en firent autant toutes les eglises des estrangers refugiez en angleterre. Priant dieu pour la conservation des eglises de France quy se voient menachees et pour la delivrance plainiere de celles des pais de flandres et pour la consolassion des paures fidelles quy ont recu grand afliction a la destruction de la Ville d'anvers que l'espagnol a detruicte le 4ᵉ du present, et pour prier le Seigneur leur tenir la bride afin quy n'aillent point plus ontre afligat le peuple."

The 13th entry runs: "Au mois de feburier mil cinc cens septante et sept, le 4ᵉ jour fut celebre un jeusne public aves toutes les eglises estrangeres quy sont en Angleterre priant dieu pour les eglises quy sont en la france et flandres a ce quelles furent gardees cotre les menees qu'on etendait que l'ennemy faisoit pour les grener en rompant la paix."

The 14th fast relates to the war in the Netherlands, prayers being directed against the progress of the "frère bastard du Roy d'espaine." The 15th entry is to the same effect: "Pour cause que Dom Jan d'austrice avait une grosse armee au paiis de brabat." The 16th fast, dated March 30, 1579, likewise relates to the war in the Netherlands—"l'espagnol gouverné par le prince de parme" being prayed against. The 17th entry runs: "Le 28ᵉ Juilet, 1579, fut celebré le jeusne Apres la prinse de Mastrik par les espagnols priant dieu avoir pitie de son eglise des paiis bas, ou les afferres sont a present en horrible confusion, et aussy priat a dieu que les eglises en le paiis ne soient troublees par la venue du duc d'alencon de laquelle on parle beaucoup." [Duke d'Alençon, favored suitor of Queen Elizabeth.]

The next fast, the 18th, relates to an earthquake in England and France, as follows: "Le 28 d'Au il, 1580, le jeusne fut celebré pour prier dieu nous garder contre son ire quy le 6 de ce mois nous avoit esté monstré par un grand tremblemet de terre quy a esté non seulemet en tout ce Roiaume mes aussy Picardie et les paiis bas de la flandres. comme pour garder de guerre, de peste, et pour preserver les pauvres eglises de flandres e france des effors de leurs enemis quy requilloient leurs forces avec une grant armee d'espagne pour les tenir affaillir."

The 19th fast relates to the great comet of 1581. The entry runs: "Le 6ᵉ d'Auril, 1581, le jeusne fut celebré pour prier dieu nous garder cotre les effets des signes de son ire dequoy avons esté menachee en la Commette quy s'est commencee a monstrer le 8 d'octobre et a duree jusques au 12 decebre. puis aussi cotre les grands changemens et ressolutions aparentes en pais de flandres et ailleurs par de la, afin que de sa grace. Il luy pleut tout tourner a bien pour le profit de son eglise."

The 20th fast (January 25, 1852) relates again to the war in the Netherlands—"pour prier pour les eglises de flandres quo l'on voisit en grant confusion et afliction." Very similar is the entry of the 21st fast, dated 28th of February, 1583, held "pour prier dieu d'avoir pitie de ses eglises quy sont en la flandres."

The entry of the 22d fast runs: "Le 12 Septebre, 1583, Le jusne public fat celebré en priant dieu pour les pauvres eglises, premierement pour celles en la france quy sont en grande Menace d'affliction pour guerres. celles de flandres sont affliges par les espagnols et Malcontens quy gattent la flandres et remettent la papauté et idolatrie por toutes les villes quy prennent, et en troisieme lieu pour ceste eglise ici en ceste ville quy passé 5 ou 6 mois a este affligée de peste de la en est morte en ceste eglise environ 50 personnes et en ceste ville environ 400 et continue encore l'afliction, le seigneur la veuille faire cesser bientost et ici et ailleurs aussi."

The 23d fast again relates to the doings in Flanders—"les horribles guerres des espagnols et malcontents." The next four entries, fasts 24 to 28, are still concerning the wars in France and the Netherlands, and other great troubles, "desquels l'Eglise de dieu estoit menacee."

Between the 29th and 30th fasts there is an entry of thanksgiving concerning the great Armada of Spain. The entry is as follows: "Actions de graces. le 29ᵉ de Novebre, 1588. graces furet rendues publiquement an Seigneur pour la dissipation estrange de la flotte d'Espagne quy s'estoit rendue aux costes d'Angleterre peur conquester ledit royaume et le remettre sous la tyrannie du Pape." The 30th fast reflects upon the previous thanksgiving. The entry runs: "Le 5 de Decebre, 1588, le jeusne public fut celebré afin de prier le Seigneur qu'il luy plaise donner aux Eglises de france et de flandres semblable delivrance come celle de laquele il est cidessus fait mention."

The next entry is as follows: "Le 19ᵉ jour de May, 1589, le jeusne fut publis en noctre assembles pour le celebrer le 22 du mesme mois pour prier le Seigneur qu'il lui plaise benir l'armée navale de la Serenissime Elizabeth roine d'Angleterre quy avoit fait voile contre l'espagnol. Item pour supplier qu'il lui plaise aussi doner paix heureuse aux eglises de france et de flandres."

The 32d fast relates to the change of dynasty in France. The entry runs: "Le 21 d'Aout, 1589, le jusne publique fut celebre en ceste Eglise de Hamptone come par toutes les Eglises estrangeres de ce royaume pour les troubles et remuements de la france a cause du transport de la couronne en la maison de Bourbon et les maux dequels l'Eglise estoit menaçee, a cette fin que l'ire de Dieu estant appaisée il se montra favorable a l'Eglise."

This fast is followed by another thanksgiving registered as follows: "Le 20 de Mars, 1590, graces furent publiquement rendues au Seigneur pour la Victoire signalée que le Roy de France et de Navarre a obtenue par le faveur de l'Eternal des armées sur ses enemis le 14 de Mars stil nouveau aupres du village nommé St. André." The 33d and 34th fasts relate to the state of affairs in France, and the struggle of the new king to maintain both the Reformed religion and his crown, "choses que n'estoient point sans grandes difficultés."

The entry of the 34th fast is followed by a note recording a visit of Queen Elizabeth to Southampton. The note runs: "Le 4 de Septebre, 1591, la Serenissime Elizabeth Roine d'Angleterre vint a Hamptone avec toute sa court quy estoit tres grande et partit le 7ᵉ dudit mois envers le midi, et come elle partoit et estoit hors de la ville, n'ayans peut avoir acces vers sa Majesté en la ville, la remerciasmes de ce que passé vingt quatre ans avoit este nous maintenus en ceste ville en tranquillité e repos. Elle repondit fort humainement louant Dieu de ce qu'il luy avoit donné puissance de recueillir et faire bien aux poures estrangers."

The entries of the six fasts numbered 35–40 relate to the wars in France and the Netherlands, with prayers against "les nouveaux appareils du Duc de Parme cotre le Roy." The 41st fast speaks about a general dearth of food in England. The entry is: "Le 12 de Janvier, 1597, le jeusne publique fut celebré en cette eglise a cause de la chereté horrible par tout ce royaume de blés par la longue continuation des plages quy a gaté la moisson et la semaille." The 42d fast relates to the assistance given by Queen Elizabeth to Henry IV. The entry runs: "Le 25 de Juillette, 1597, le jusne publique fut celebré en ceste Eglise come aussi en les autres Eglises estrangeres pour prier le Seigneur qu'il luy plaise doner bons succes a l'armée de lay Royne." The next two entries are on the same subject, the fasts being "pour invocquer ardament l'Eternel qu'il luy plaise benir les armes de la Roine en Irlande cotre les rebelles fomantez par l'espagnol."

The 45th entry runs: "Le jeusne fut celebré en ceste eglise le 25^d Aout, 1599, par advis de la Compagnie, pour les bruits de guerre et apprehensions d'une flotte d'Espagne et autres remuements quy parassoient alors, afin d'induire le peuple à serieuse conversion au Seigneur." The next two entries relate again to the war in the Netherlands, notably "une bataille fort furieuse entre le comto Maurice et l'Archiduc."

In the 48th entry reference is made to a new outbreak of the plague, as follows. "Le jusne public fut celebré particulierement en ceste eglise le 8e de Feburier, 1604, à raison de la maladie cotagieuse de laquele nos estions menacez, Dieu ayant visité quelques deux à trois familles en ceste ville de cotagio." The 49th fast relates to the affairs of Flanders, and again to the plague. "Le jusne publicque fut celebré en ceste Eglise le 24e de May, 1604, come aussy aux autres Eglises de la langue françoise en ce royaume, tant à raison de l'estat de Flandres, le conte Maurice assiégant l'Escluse et s'efforçant de faire lever le siege de Ostende assiegée par l'Archiduc d'Autriche ; que pour l'Estat de ce pays, le parlement sestenant e reeluy, aussi pour les verges de grand chastiement de peste que Dieu monstroite à Londres et autres endroits du royaume, et outre tout cela pour ce qu'en nostre Eglise nos estions apres la confirmation et instalation du frère Timothée Blier au Saint Ministère de l'Evangile."

The next entry still refers to the plague. It runs: "Le jusne public fut celebré en ceste eglise le 11e de Juillette, 1604, a raison de la maladie cotagieuse laquele estoit bien affreuse au milieu de ceste Republique et de nostre Eglise."

The next is an entry of thanksgiving for the cessation of the plague, as follows: "Le 16 de Janvier, 1605, actions de graces publiques et solennelles furet rendues au Seigneur particulierement en nostre eglise de ce qu'il avoit pleu à Dieu de faire cesser le grand fléau de peste tant en nostre Assemblée qu'en la Republique de ceste ville."

The 51st fast is entered: "Le 30 May, 1605, le jeusne fut celebré en ceste Eglise come aussy en les autres Eglises estrangeres recueillis en ce royaume pour invocquer plus ardament le Seigneur pour la prosperité de cest Estat, et pour les estats de Hollande et autres provinces Unies qu'il plaise à Dieu benir leurs armes à sa gloire et au bien de toute son Eglise."

The 52d fast again refers to the plague. The entry runs: "Le 22e d'Octobre, 1606, le jusne publique fut celebré en ceste Eglise come le jour suivant il fust aux Eglises estrangeres recueillies en ce royaume à cette fin de prier le Seigneur à ce qu'il appaisat son ire embrazée cotre les frères de Londres lesquels il visitoit de grand fleau de peste, et semblablement pour le supplier d'accompagner les armées de Messeigneurs les Estats des Provinces Unies de ses faveurs accoustumées reprimant les gloires et triomphes profanes des ennemis de la verité."

The 53d fast, occurring after an interval of eight years, refers, for the first time, to the Protestants of Germany. The entry is as follows: "Le 14 de Sept., 1614, le jeusne fut celebré en cette Eglise au mesme jour que les autres estrangeres de ce royaume pour prier le Seigneur de dissiper les enterprises de l'empereur et du Pape et leurs confederes s'efforcants de ruiner les Eglises de l'Allemagne, et benir au contraire les armes de ceux qu'il suscitoit pour la conservation de son Eglise."

The 54th fast has reference to France, as follows: "Le 16 de November, 1615. Le jeusne fust celebré en ceste Eglise au mesme jour qu'en autres estrangeres de ce royaume a cause des troubles de la France et pour prier le Seigneur de conserver son Eglise à l'encontre de touts les attentats des ennemis de sa verité." The next two entries relate to the affairs of the Netherlands, notably "less troubles qui incommodent les Eglises des Provinces Unies." These "troubles" are more pointedly alluded to in the 57th fast, as follows: "Le 28 de Septembre, 1620. Le jusne fut encor celebré en ceste Eglise come en autres Eglises estrangeres en ce Royaume en consideration du Synode de divers pays qui estoit assemblé en Holland pour appaiser les troubles qui incommódoyent les Eglises des Provinces Unies."

The next entry principally refers to events in France: "Le 21 de Juin, 1621. Le jusne fut encor celebré en ceste eglise comme en autres Eglises estrangeres de ce Royaume en consideration des fascheux traittements qui sont faicts a ceux qui font profession de la mesme religion que nous en France et ailleurs." In the 59th and 60th fasts reference is made to the afflictions of the Protestant churches in Holland and in the German Palatinate.

The next entry, of the 61st fast, has once more reference to the plague: "Le 27 de Juillet, 1625. Ceste Eglise se joignit à celebrer le jusne public avec l'église Angloise tous les Mercredis selon le commandement du Roy en consideration de la peste ayant commencé a Londres et menassant tout le royaume."

The entry of the 62d fast runs: "Le second jour d'Aoust, 1626. Ceste Eglise se joignit encor à celebrer le jusne publique avec l'Eglise Angloise selon le commandement du Roy en consideration des dangers qui menassent ce royaume." The next entry has relation to the state of the Continental foreign churches, "l'affliction que souffrent les Eglises d'outre mer."

The deliberations of the English Parliament are referred to in the next fast, the 64th, as follows: "Le 21 d'Auril, 1628. Ceste Eglise se joingnit à celebrer le jusne publiq avec l'Eglise Angloise selon le commandement du Roy en consideration des dangers qui menasent ce royaume et pour prier Dieu qu'il face reussir à bien les deliberations du Parlement qui est assemblé." A fast to the same effect was held eleven months after. The entry runs: "Le 20 de Mars, 1629. Ceste Eglise se joignit encore avec l'Eglise Angloise pour celebrer un jusne publique par le commandement du Roy a mesme consideration que le precedent."

The fresh appearance of the plague is referred to in the next, the 66th, fast, held after an interval of thirty-six years: "Le 6 de Decembre, 1665. Le jusne fut celebré en ceste Eglise noste ville estant affligé de la peste les 5 mois passé estant mort de nostre petitt troupeau viron 20 personnes et des Englais 800. Le Seigneur voile bien Arrester cette vissitation et issy et ailleurs."

The next entry relates to the great fire of London. It is as follows: "Le 10 d'Octobre, 1666. Le jusne fut celebré en ceste Eglize par le commandement du Roy come aussy en toutes les Eglizes Engloizes pour prier le Seigneur d'appaiser son Ire et rester ses jugemens maintenant repandu sur ce Royaume la ville (capitale) de Londres estant la plus grande partié consumé par le feu."

In the 68th fast (June 19th, 1667), the last of the regular entries, prayers are offered for "notre roi et sa gloire," the occasion being "Monsieur Couraud notre Pasteur nous y ayant puissamment exhortez par ses predications."

After this fast the numbered entries cease; but there is a short appendix on the following page referring to two more "jeusnes" held on the 16th of December, 1720, and the 8th of December, 1721. Both took place, it is stated, "par ordre de sa majesté et de monseigneur notre evesque," the prayers being directed "pour preserver le royaume de la guerre."

At the end of the book, forming the conclusion of the records of the Southampton "God's House," are five entries, headed "Livre pour les aferres survenates en ceste Eglise." The entries chiefly relate to the collection of certain funds for the education of the children of the poorer members of the church. It was resolved, on the 19th of July, 1584, that "de trois mois en trois mois les anciens et diacres iront de maison en maison pour recuiller les deniers que chacun voudra doner." It appears from several of these entries that general assemblies were held, at stated times, of the heads of families, or "chefs de famille," of the French Protestant churches of Jersey, Guernsey, Alderney, and Sark, united with the congregation of "God's House." Among the names which most frequently occur in the register, we observe those of Guillaumott, Page, Baillehache, Barnouin, Cupin, Mariette, Teulin, Baucquart, Le Vasseur, Le Febure, Vincent, De la Motte, Prevost, Sequin, Durant, Hervieu, De Leau, De la Place, Sauvage, Durand, Duval, and Dupré.

French Protestant or Walloon Church, Canterbury.

These registers form nine volumes, or ten parts. The first two parts, bound in one volume—a long, thin, narrow octavo, the paper yellow with age, and the ink of rusty red—contains entries of baptisms, marriages, and deaths from the year 1583 to 1630. There are evidently many leaves wanting, particularly in the earlier portion. The entries commence in May, 1583, with "Le 5 fut celebré le marriage de Herbert . . . . . (family name illegible) à Marrie Du Mourrier." There are six marriages entered in May, 1583; four in June, four in July, two in August, none in September, four in October, one in November, and two in December. Nine more marriages are entered from January to June, 1584; then these cease, and entries of baptisms commence —the first under date of October, 1583, as follows: "Le 8 fut baptise l'enfant de Antoine Du Bois appelle Jay," followed by the names of the godfathers and godmothers. There are twenty-one entries of births from October 8 to the end of the year 1583, and twenty-three from the 5th of January to the 5th of October, 1584, when they come to an end.

After two blank leaves, there now come entries of deaths, beginning with the year 1581, as follows: "Le 27ᵈ de Juin mourut May Dulour, femme de . . . . ." (name illegible). There are forty-one death-entries in 1581, but most of them evidently made some time after the event occurred, less than a line being given to each, and the whole in a sort of tabulated form. Baptisms, marriages, and deaths, in very irregular order, fill up the rest of the first volume. There are no features worth noticing, save the general fact that the names are chiefly Hebrew, such as Abraham, Daniel, and Mary; but a very large proportion of the girls have the name Elizabeth given to them in baptism, doubtless after that of the English queen.

The second volume commences with the year 1630, and ends with 1715. The entries are all of deaths. The volume is in a most dilapidated state, the paper dark brown with age, the ink deep red, and many of the leaves moth-eaten and half-torn. A great many Dutch names occur in this volume, and there are frequent entries of the fact of a gravestone having been made for the deceased. The following is a specimen: "Jean Jacob Vanderfleet, Docteur en Medecine, mourut le 3ᵈ jour de Feburier, 163½ en Londres, apres avoir este taillé de la pierre." Many names are entered of persons dying at distant places in England and France, and even in the West Indies. The entries are very irregular; often a hundred seem to have been made at the same time, in a tabulated form.

A curious entry, throwing considerable light upon these irregularities, occurs in 1649. After "Le 6ᵉ Auril, 1649, mourut Charle Bénoit," are four lines as follows: "Les jours de incroyable troubles advenu par Pouiade è sa faction en la rupture è desciremient de l'eglise le Registre estè quelque temps dilaiex a estè redraisse le mieux la memoire la peu porter." The death-entries after these words sum up the years 1645–9; they are very short and clearly imperfect; the name Pouiade is not any where to be met with.

The internal disturbances of the church appear to have continued till 1715, for the lists are not only most irregular, but seemingly made by an inexperienced hand. The last entry in vol. ii. runs: "Le 27ᵈ October, 1715, mourout Habraham Hibau, agie de 57." The Hebrew names of baptism cease to a great extent in this volume, Jean and Jacques being the most common.

The third volume of the Canterbury records is the first that is tolerably perfect. It contains both baptisms and marriages. The fly-leaf on the front is inscribed "Livre des Baptesmes de l'eglise Valone de Cantorbery depuis le XXIIII. de Juillet, 1590, jusquau 15ᵈ de Mars, 1602." The following is the first entry of baptism: "Susanne fille de Daniel Veron fust presentée au Baptisme ayant pour tesmoings Josse des Rousseaux et Joseph de Sevart, item Anne femme de Loys Theuclin et Pasquette femme de Michel Aman." All the other entries are similar, but the names of witnesses are not always given. At the end of the year 1592 is the following entry: "Ce sont ceux qui ont este par le St. Baptesme mise en l'Aliance de Dieu en l'Eglise de Cantorbery en l'An 1592."

The number of children entered as baptized in 1591 is 119; while in the following year, 1592, it amounts to 148; in 1593, to 141; in 1594, to 132; in 1595, to 136; in 1596, to 107; in 1597, to 91; in 1598, to 72; in 1599, to exactly 100; in 1600, to 106; in 1601, to 68; and in 1602, to only 22, as far as the 15th of April. Here the entries of births cease.

The entries of marriages, at the other side of the volume, appear less complete than those of baptism. There are 27 marriages entered in 1591; 36 in 1592; 29 in 1593; 39 in 1594, 25 in 1595; 31 in 1596; 19 in 1597; 25 in 1598; 22 in 1599; 18 in 1600; 15 in 1601; and only 4 in the first four months of 1602—on January 24, February 14, March 14, and April 12. Here the entries of the third volume cease, a blank page being left in the middle of the book between the baptisms and marriages.

Neither the baptismal nor the marriage entries of this volume contain anything specially noteworthy beyond the fact that the settlers mostly intermarried. The following is a specimen of the marriage-entries: "Andrea Du Forest filz de Roger natif de Conty en Picardie et Marie Huchon fille de Adam natif de Armentieres." There are an extraordinary number of widows; in some years they form nearly one third of the whole entered in the marriage-lists. Widowers also are numerous.

The fourth volume of the Canterbury records is similar in arrangement to the third, the baptisms being entered on one side and the marriages on the other. There are no deaths either in this or the preceding volume. The entries of baptisms commence on the 18th of April, 1602, and end December 30, 1621. There are 40 baptisms entered in (the 8½ months of) 1602; 77 in 1603; 65 in 1604; 66 in 1605; 81 in 1606; 82 in 1607; 69 in 1608; 59 in 1609; 69 in 1610; 65 in 1611; 63 in 1612; 58 in 1613; 63 in 1614; 69 in 1615; 56 in 1616; 61 in 1617; and 59 in 1618. During the next three years the entries are very confused, large numbers being evidently made at the same time.

The marriage-entries, on the other side of the book, run from 1602 to 1620, and average about 21 a year. Most of the women of this period entered as married seem to have been of the second generation of settlers, "natif de Cantorbery." The following is a specimen of the form of most of the marriage-entries: "Le 5 de Auril Nicolas de Sentluns filz de feu Estienne natif da Cambray et Anthoinette de Naux, fille de Jacques natife de Cantorbery." It appears there were also, now and then, marriages of daughters of the settlement with Englishmen: two occur in June, 1608, of George Lowe with Marie Colée, and John Chandler with Judith Rousset, both marked as "mariés entre les Anglais." Unions where the bride is English are very rare. One specially marked as such is "Jehan Parmentier veuf et une Anglaise Jane Bachelar veufe de feu Regnant natif de Cantorbery."

The fifth volume, similar in arrangement to the preceding, contains baptisms and marriages from 1622 to 1644. There are 56 entries of baptisms in 1622; 50 in 1623; 54 in 1624; 72 in 1625; 72 in 1626; 81 in 1627; 98 in 1628; 81 in 1629; 110 in 1630; 100 in 1631; 101 in 1632; 124 in 1633; 85 in 1634; and 75 in 1635. For the remaining years, till 1644, the entries of baptisms are somewhat irregular, averaging from 70 to 80 per annum. The marriages entered during the period 1622 to 1644 average about 23 per annum. There is scarcely any influx of strangers visible during the period, both bride and bridegroom being set down, in nearly all cases, as "natifs de Cantorbery." The forms of entry are precisely the same as those in vol. iv.

B B

Notes of any other kind are not to be found, nor any features of special interest.

The sixth volume—a thick 8vo of above 400 pages—is almost entirely filled with entries of baptisms, there being only nine pages devoted to marriages at the end of the book—reversed. The baptisms extend from 1644 to 1704, and the marriages—most incomplete and fragmentary—from 1644 to 1666, with four more in 1672, 73, 74, and 75. Both baptisms and marriages were evidently entered long after the actual event, by the hundred. The baptisms, for the greater part of the period, do not average more than 50 per annum, and for many years they are considerably less, though the evident imperfection of the entries leaves little room for calculation. There are no entries of any particular interest. Many of them are by an illiterate hand, and a few seem to be made by a boy or girl, intermixed with scrawls and various ornaments. English names are becoming very numerous, and frequently the names are given double, in French and English, as " Le Munier or Miller." This is repeated several times, till, in the end, an entry runs simply " Miller," and another " Mellor." Of the baptisms registered in 1675 there are 34 boys and 34 girls; about one half the boys have the names " Jean," " Jacques," or " Pierre ;" while more than one third of the girls are called " Marie."

At the end of the year 1683 the registrar of baptisms signs his name for the first time : " Enregistré Abraham Didier." The entries of this year appear very complete ; there are 46 boys and 31 girls. The few pages of marriages show that the immigration from other parts into the colony had nearly ceased at this period ; almost the whole of the brides, as well as bridegrooms, are entered as " natifs de Canterbury." There are no entries of special interest.

The seventh volume consists of a number of loose leaves, not stitched together, or fastened in any way, but merely stuck into a leather case. The leaves, not quite 200, contain only entries of marriages and of banns of marriage, ranging from 1644 to 1704. Most of the leaves have suffered greatly from the ravages of time, but the entries are in a remarkably fine handwriting. The form is throughout as follows : " Le 16' Avril "(year not given), " Jacques Villers, fils d'Arnould, natif de Cantorbery et Marie Ferre fille de Vincent, native de Cantorbery." The banns run : " Il y a promesse de mariage entre Gedeon Despaigne fils de Jean natif de Canterbury, et Marie Le Leu fille de feu Jean natife de Canterbury." Often there are three strokes (either ııı or ₩ or ≠) against the entry of the banns, to denote that they have been proclaimed three times, in which cases an appendix is not uncommon, such as " Ils ont esté marié en l'eglise Wallonne de Cantorbery le 7' du December."

Owing to the scattered condition of the leaves—not chronologically arranged—it is impossible to say over what years the entries in this volume extend ; from various dates, here and there, the period 1644 to 1704 seems probable, making it appear that this was a supplementary volume to the one previously noticed. Entries of special interest are wanting.

The eighth volume is a stout folio, not half filled, bound in thick parchment and well preserved. It contains only entries of baptisms ranging from 1704 to 1837. The number of entries for the first fifteen years average about 30, but they gradually dwindle down until they cease with the family of Monsieur

Miette, pastor of the "Walloon Church," who appears as the last procreative member of the colony.

On the inside of the cover of this volume are some references to books relating to the settlement. They are: "The Undercroft of Canterbury Cathedral given to the Walloons, 1568; see *Kentish Companion*, 1787—to 18 families of Walloons by 2 Eliz.; see *Duncombe descrip. Cath.* 56, and pag. 5th; under the choir is a spacious church granted in the time of 2 Eliz. to 18 families of French refugees, and used by their descendants ever since. Committee or Royal Bounty first granted to the French refugees 1695; see *Tindall's contin. Rapin*, page 258 n., edit. octavo."

The ninth and last volume of the Canterbury Records is a small and very thin quarto, with four pages of marriage-entries on the one side, and eight pages of banns on the other. They extend over the time 1719 to 1747, and are exceedingly imperfect. There are no marriages entered between 1720 and 1736, which is the last in the list. The banns go to 1747. There are no entries of any interest in this little volume. Against the fly-leaf of the third volume of the Canterbury Registers is pasted the following " Certificate :"

"The annexed or accompanying books are the original Register-books of marriages and baptisms which have been kept for the Chapel or Meeting-house called the Walloon Congregation or French Protestant Church, situate in the Undercroft of Canterbury Cathedral, in the county of Kent, founded about the year 1568. The books have been from time to time in the custody of the scribe of the Elders, for the time being, of the Congregation, and are sent to the commissioners from the immediate custody of the minister of the said church in the Undercroft of said Cathedral, who has kept them since 1834 as minister of the Congregation. Signed the 12th of Sept., 1837. J. F. Miéville, minister; Chas. N. Miette, elder; M. T. Miette, deacon."

Malt-House Chapel, Canterbury.

These registers, which are in a large, thin folio of about thirty pages, are described in the official "certificate" annexed to the book as follows : " The original Register-book of marriages and baptisms of the Conformist French Chapel, commonly called the ' Malt-House,' being of the Episcopal Church denomination, situate in the precincts of Canterbury Cathedral, in the county of Kent, founded about the year . . . (1709), and now dissolved. The book has been from time to time in the custody of the scribe for the time being, and is sent to the commissioners from the same persons who held the registers of the Walloon Congregation of the Cathedral Undercroft, in the city of Canterbury, who kept it since 1817. Signed the 12th of September, 1837. J. F. Miéville, minister; Charles N. Miette, elder."

There are not more than thirty entries of baptisms and marriages in this book, the greater part of which is filled with matters relating to the discipline and government of the congregration. It appears from one of the first of these notices that the "Malt-House" dissenters formed themselves into a congregation in October, 1709, when forty-eight men and twelve women signed a public declaration, expressing their " unfeigned assent and consent to all and every thing contained and prescribed in and by the Book entitled ye Book of Common Prayer and Administration of ye Sacraments and other Rites and

Ceremonies of ye Church of England." The leading men of this congregation, who were chosen "Anciens," or elders, on its formation, appear to have been Jean de Cleve, Abraham de la Neuve Maison, Jean de Lon, Gabriel Pain, and Paschal Lardeau. The notices immediately following show that hot quarrels broke out at once between the members of the "Walloon Church" and the worshipers at the "Malt-House," chiefly on account of a sum of "one hundred and fourscore pounds," assigned from a charitable fund in London to the Canterbury refugees, and of which the new society claimed a fair share for its own poor. The dispute about this money was carried on with much bitterness, but how it ended is not stated. The first minister elected by the "Malt-House" congregation was Pierre Richard, who certifies, under date of July 30, 1710, that he has received the sum of fifty shillings from Monsieur de Cleve, as his monthly salary, declaring himself "fort content et satisfait." Pierre Richard left his charge soon after, and in September, 1710, Jean Lardeau was chosen minister, with no fixed pay, but on the understanding "qu'il jouira des benefices et priviledges de ceste Eglise." Whatever the privileges consisted of, the benefices probably were very small, for Jean Lardeau too quitted his post at the end of a few months, and after him came a quick succession of other pastors. Under date of January 25, 1713, there is an entry stating that the ministers and elders have learnt "avec douleur et un sensible deplaisir," of there being "une diminution considerable des deniers qui se recuillent a la porte de ceste Eglise;" and they exhort the members of the congregation to come forward more freely with their money, each "selon les moyens qu'il plaist à Dieu de lui fournir." The appeal seems to have had little effect, as far as can be judged from the next entries, which show a decline in the number of members. In 1716, Pierre le Sueur was chosen minister, succeeding Jean Charpentier, and retained his charge till 1744, when the entries cease. Pierre le Sueur made several conversions, which are noticed at great length; and baptized sixty-three children during the term of his ministry, or about two per annum. There is only one marriage-entry in the book. In very few of the entries of baptism is the origin of the parents given; but it appears, from the names which occur, that natives of France were most numerously represented in the congregation. This is farther shown in some of the notices, where the members of the old French church are referred to somewhat contemptuously as "Walloons." Among the names entered most frequently are Sequin, Tevelin, Blanchard, De l'Estang, Boré, Le Duc, Ricard, and Le Sueur. The name Layard occurs once in this entry: "Susanne Françoise de l'Estang, fille de Monsieur Louis de l'Estang a été batisée le 30 de Sept., 1728, et a eu pour parrain Monsieur Pierre Layard et pour marraine mademoiselle Françoise de St. Paul."

Walloon Church, Norwich.

The registers of this church are in one volume, described as follows in the official "certificate" pasted against the fly-leaf: "The annexed book is the original Register-book of baptisms and marriages which has been kept for the church or chapel called the French or Walloon Church, being of the French Protestant denomination, situated in the city of Norwich, founded about the year 1590, and now dissolved, and so declared by decree of the Court of Chancery in a suit of Attorney General *v.* Columbine in 1836. The book sent has been from time to time in the custody of the minister or deacons for the time being of the congregation, and is sent to the commissioners from the immediate custody of Edgar Tayler, of Bedford Row, in the county of Middlesex, who has kept it since 1834, as solicitor to Mr. Henry Martineau, the last deacon, from whom he received it for production in the said suit. Signed the 21st day of June, 1837. Edgar Tayler, solicitor."

The book, a long narrow folio, about five inches broad and rather more than an inch thick, is tolerably well preserved, with the exception of the first twenty pages, which are worm-eaten, torn, and illegible. The heading of the first page is "Baptesmes en l'Eglise Wallonne de Norwich depuis le 22 Juin, 1595." Under date of June 29, 1595, is the first legible entry: "Victor du Bois presente un enfans pour estre bapthise et le nom de lenfan sapellera Elizabeth." The next entry which can be deciphered runs: "Le 20 de Julet, 1595. Salut nous soit donne de par nostre Seigneur Jesus Christ. Moy Rournille Terrien et ma femme presente mon enfant pour estre baptiser en l'eglise de Dieu et donnons le nom David, et pour tesmoin Philippe Terrien mon frere et Guillame De Bonne et pour marine Ratelinne Gate et Jenne De Bonne. Dieu en fasse son serviteur." The same formula, with slight variations, continues throughout the whole of the entries of baptism.

There are fifty-five entries in the year 1595, commencing at the end of June; sixty-nine in 1596; and thirty-three in 1597. The chronological order is very imperfectly kept in these and all the following entries, and the whole registry seems incomplete. In scarcely any instance is the place of origin or nationality of the parents mentioned; but the names appear to be about one half Flemish and the other half French, with a tendency, in both cases, to Anglicize them.

The average number of baptisms during the first half of the seventeenth century is thirty per annum; but after this period they rapidly decline, till, at the end of another fifty years, they amount to but one or two per annum. In 1700 there are three baptisms entered; three again in 1701, two in 1702, three in 1703, two in 1704, and less than one for the average of the next five-and-twenty years.

In November, 1695, occurs for the first time the name Martineau, in the baptism of a son of "Gaston Martineau," also called Gaston, with David le Monnier for godfather. Gaston Martineau has another son, named Guillaume, baptized in October, 1700, with Anne Paon for witness; and a third son, to whom the name Elie is given, in April, 1707. At this last baptism there is entered as godfather "M. Baldy, ministre de ceste eglise."

The latter name reoccurs in the next entry, which is of unusual length. It runs: "Samedy matin 27 Mars, 1708, a trois quart d'heure apres minuit, ou environ, Dieu a doné une enfant à David Baldy ministre, elle a esté presente au bapteseme le dimanche suivant 28 dito dans l'eglise Waloone par Jude Havé, parrin, et Elysabet de Sauvage, marrine. La nom de l'enfant est Marie."

Gaston Martineau figures again as father of a daughter, named Marguerite, in August, 1711, the godfather and godmother being "Gaston Martineau le

Jeune et Marie Martineau aussy la Jeune." There are forty-one more baptisms entered from this date till the year 1752, when the register comes to an end.

The same names reoccur constantly in this list: Lecohie, Barbé, Colombine, Pigney, and Le Monnier or Miller. The final entry is "Pierre Le Monier, *anglice* Miller, fils de Pierre le Monier et de Marie Steward, nacquit à Norwich le 21 Juin, 1752, et fut baptisé le 30 du même mois. Il a eu pour parein son pere et sa mère pour meraine."

At the end of the register-book of the Norwich "Walloon Church" there is a list of marriages, filling eight pages, and extending from October, 1599, to May, 1611. The total number of marriages entered is ninety-five. Most of the notices are very short, merely stating the name of bridegroom and bride, though in some of the earlier ones the place of origin is given. In nearly every instance the places mentioned are in French Flanders—Valenciennes, Tournay, and Lisle occurring most frequently. There are no entries of any special interest.

Against the fly-leaf at the end of the book is pasted a sheet of paper, giving, as stated in the heading, "Copies of Inscriptions on the Monuments and Tombstones in the French Church, Norwich, arranged in order of date." There are thirty altogether, as follows:

Dates of Death.   Names, Ages, and Inscriptions.

1729. May 29. David Martineau, æt. 32. Artis chirurgiæ peritissimi qui vitam suis percaram quam plurimis proficientem at premature deposuit.

1759. July 20. Kervin Wright, aged 55 years. An eminent physician in this city, son of the Rev. Kervin Wright, of Debenham, Suffolk.

1765. Mary Colombine, an infant.

1766. April 22. Richard Willement, aged 52.

1766. Peter Colombine, aged 6.

1768. Nov. 19. David Martineau, aged 42 years. He was eminently distinguished as a surgeon, as a man of most amiable manners, and as the best of fathers.

1768. Nov. 28. John Hilyard, aged 17.

1769. Oct. 18. Richard Willement, aged 25.

1770. Dec. 11. Peter Colombine, aged 73.

1776. July 22. Ann, wife of John Hilyard, aged 56.

1779. Feb. 3. Esther, wife of Paul Colombine, and eldest daughter of Simeon Waller. A woman of singular merit and ingenuity, who lived with her husband near fifty years in perfect harmony and affection.

1780. May 6. Mary, wife of Peter Colombine, aged 86.

1783. March 27. John Hilyard, aged 59.

1784. Aug. 30. Paul Colombine, aged 85. Descended from an ancient family in the province of Dauphiny, in France, from whence his father, a man of piety, probity, and learning, withdrew at the Revocation of the Edict of Nantes; and having early taken a degree abroad, practiced physic in this city. This, his youngest son, whose temperance, industry, and moderation, through a long and blameless life, had merited and obtained the best and sweetest of human blessings—health, competence, and content.

1788. Dec. 7. Catharine Blomfield, aged 86.
1788. Dec. 19. Hewett Rand, aged 77.
1789. Jan. 14. Mary, wife of Hewett Rand, aged 62.
1790. March 14. Hannah Finch, aged 86.
1790. Sept. 8. Mary Miller, aged 83.
1797. Aug. 22. Margaret, relict of Richard Willement, aged 85.
1799. Nov. 3. Elizabeth, wife of Peter Colombine, aged 28.
1800. Nov. 26. Sarah, wife of David Martineau, aged 74. She was eminently distinguished for sound judgment, active conduct, and piety.
1805. E. B.
1807. Jan. 13. Margaret Villement, aged 38.
1810. Oct. 29. Peter Colombine, aged 73.
1816. Sept. 21. Theodora, wife of David Colombine, aged 73.
1817. Dec. 15. Sarah, daughter of David Colombine, aged 51.
1819. Nov. 2. David Colombine, aged 86.
1829. Jan. 13. Melea, wife of Peter Colombine, aged 78.
1829. Jan. 30. Melea Colombine, aged 48.

The above list is certified as correct by John W. Dowson, solicitor, Norwich, under date of January 13, 1838.

French Church, Bristol.

The registers of this church, in three volumes, are described in the official "certificate" as follows: "The accompanying books are the original Register-books which have been kept for the Chapel called the French Protestant Episcopal Chapel, the service of which was first held in what is called the Mayor's Chapel, St. Mark the Gaunt. In 1726 they built one on the ground of Queen Elizabeth's Hospital for the Red Maids. The books sent have been from time to time in the custody of the churchwardens and the ministers, and are sent to the commissioners from the immediate custody of Marienne de Soyres, who has kept them since 1791, as the widow of the Rev. Francis de Soyres, the last of said congregation. Signed the 7th of March, 1838. M$^{ne.}$ de Soyres." In a letter accompanying this certificate, also signed Marienne de Soyres, it is stated that "the French began to arrive in Bristol in 1687, as they could escape from France, being sorely persecuted and forced to attend mass." "They joined," Madame de Soyres continues, "those already settled here, most of them from Nantes, Saint-Onge, Rochelle, Poitou, and Guyenne; some of the very old people, alive when I came to Bristol, used to say the chapel was full to excess, the aisle filled with benches as well as altar; so there must have been several hundreds. In 1790, when we came, the congregation never amounted to more than sixty, and mostly of people fond of French, or those wishing to improve. . . . . Our own children, twelve in number, were all baptized in the parish church of St. Michael's. . . . Neither Mr. de Soyres nor self belonged to the Refuge so-called.

Mr. de Soyres came to this country in 1783, I in 1786." In another note Madame de Soyres states that "not a remnant is left of the numerous French families formerly settled in Bristol."

The first volume of the Bristol records, a folio about an inch thick, contains entries of baptisms, marriages, and burials, extending over the years 1687 to 1700. All the entries are more or less minute in their details, some of them filling a page or more, and the whole book is exceedingly well kept and as well preserved. Many of the notices are full of interest, as giving the origin, occupation, and other particulars of the members of the congregation. A remarkably large number of them are described as "mariniers," "capittaine de navire," or "maistre de navire," and nearly all are referred to as natives of the southern and western provinces of France, the neighborhood of La Rochelle and the Isle de Rhé being most numerously represented. Next to the seamen, the trades and professions chiefly occurring are "tisseran en laine," "ouvrier en laine," "orfevre," "serrurier," "tailleur d'habit," "cordier," and "chirurgien." There are scarcely any noble names, and the whole of the adults referred to are entered as belonging to some profession or trade.

The second volume contains entries of baptisms, marriages, and burials, ranging from 1701 to 1715. The notices are not quite as full as those of the first volume, but they also give, in most instances, the origin and occupation of the persons whose names occur. Among the burial-entries is the following: "Le mardy seizième Juin mil sept cens trois a esté enterré dans ceste Eglise appellée le Gant, Monsieur Descairac, un des nos ministres, agé denviron soixante six ans, apres avoir exercé le saint ministère et preché la pure parole de Dieu dans cette meme Eglise depuis le vingt neuvième May de l'année mil six cens quatre vingt sept, sans interruption jusqu'au Dimanche avant son decés qu'il fut ataqué d'une apoplexie sur la chaire en prechant sur les paroles du livre de Josué, chap. 24, parties du vers 15e, en ces mots: Choisissés vous aujourdhuy a quy vous voulez servir; mais quant a moy et à ma maison nous servirons a l'Eternel. . . . . . Le corps fut conduit a l'Eglise par tout le troupeau. Tinel, pasteur." Among the trades that most frequently occur are "ouvrier en laine," "chapellier," and "marinier." The entries greatly decrease in number toward the end of the volume, and many of the names are English or Anglicized.

The third volume contains short entries of baptisms, marriages, and burials, from 1715 to 1807. They only fill twenty-eight pages, and the rest of the book is blank. There are but three entries from 1762 to 1807—the first in 1762, stating the birth of a son of "Pierre Gautier, ministre de la chapelle François;" the second of May, 1791, mentioning the death of the same Pierre Gautier; and the third of February 15, 1807, the death of "François de Soyres, ministre."

French Church of Stonehouse, Plymouth.

The registers of this church are in four small volumes, described as follows in the official "certificate" pasted against the cover of volume the first: "The accompanying books are the original Register-books of births or baptisms, marriages and burials, which have been kept for the chapel called 'L'Eglise françoise de Stonehouse,' in the county of Devon, founded about the year

1692, and the congregation dissolved in the year 1810. The books sent have been from time to time in the custody of the minister for the time being, and are sent to the commissioners from the custody of the incumbent of East Stonehouse, who has kept them since the year 1829 ; Mr. Delacombe, of Stonehouse, trustee, having had charge of them in the interim. Signed the 3d of November, 1840. H. A. Greaves, inc. of Stonehouse."

The first volume contains entries of births, marriages, and deaths from 1692 to 1720. They follow each other irregularly; the baptisms and marriages are always signed by the minister, but the interspersed notices of death are seldom thus authenticated. There are nine entries of baptisms, one of marriage, and three of deaths, from July to December, 1692, and the same proportion continues throughout, with a great decline toward the end. It is very rarely that the place of origin is given, though, from the names and other indications, it appears that nearly all the members of the church were of French descent. An entry, under date of October 10, 1692, runs : " Suzanne Godineau, veuve, decedée le jour d'hier a esté ce jour enterré au nouveau cimitière donné pour la sepulture des françois refugiés en ceste ville de Stonehouse."

There is an entry of extraordinary length under date of September 13, 1697, stating the marriage of " Guillaume Henry Aures, Sieur de la Combes, filz naturel et legitime de feu M. Aures et damoiselle Marie de Gout natif de Saint-André de Valborgne, dans le Sevenes en France et après demeurant a Plymouth, d'une part, et damoiselle Louize Tordeux fille legitime et naturelle de feu Charles Tordeux Sieur de Belle Espine et damoiselle Anne Blaize natifue de Metz en Lorraine, d'autre part." The minister, Charles Delacombe, in this entry describes himself as "ministre de l'Eglize françoise conformiste de Stonehouse."

The whole of the entries, from October, 1697, to the end of the volume in July, 1710, are signed "Etienne Molenier, ministre," and bear evidence of great care, in the minuteness of many of the facts. Between the baptisms, marriages, and deaths are various notices of another character, such as " le 18 Janvier, 169$\frac{8}{9}$. Izaac Videau de la Trenblade en France a fait recognoissance publicque de la faute qu'il a fait." Another notice, following soon after, is more explicit. It runs : " Le 30 Juillet, 1699, Jean Gruseiller natif de St. George de Didonne a fait reconnoissance publicque de la faute qu'il avoit comise en france en ayant adheré à l'idolatrie de l'eglise romenne, par devant nous ministre de l'Eglise françoise de Stonhouse le jour et an que dessus. Molenier." There are altogether seven of these notices, the last in 1701. The name Delacombe reoccurs constantly in the latter part of the volume.

The second volume, a small thin quarto, like the previous one, contains entries of baptisms and marriages from 1720 to 1741. In nearly all these entries, the baptisms as well as the marriages, the individuals present have signed their names, in some instances as many as ten or twelve at a time. Most of the persons appear to have been able to write, for the "marks" are comparatively rare, amounting to scarcely more than five in a hundred. The total number of entries is not above 140, or at the rate of 7 per annum, about two thirds of them representing baptisms.

Interspersed are some curious notices, described in the heading as "deliberations du Consistoire," the longest of which, filling an entire page, is as follows: "Notre aide soit au nom de Dieu qui a fait le ciel et la terre. Amen. Nous pasteur de l'Eglise françoise de Stonehouse nous estant assemblés en consistoire avec les anciens de la ditte Eglise, sur la plainte a nous portée par Anne Ratton, veuve, contre Jacques Loiel, tous deux habitans de ce lieu et membres de la susditte Eglise, de ce que Jacques Loiel avoit scandaleusement procedé et agi enver elle et son honneur, estant alors seulle en sa chambre, tant de parolles que d'actions deshonnestes, avons apres avoir invoqués les lumières divines du Saint Esprit, et murement deliberez sur la plainte porte et sur les circonstances scandaleuses, trop connues de la plus grande partie des membres de la ditte Eglise, avons deja à cet egard procedez contre le delinquaut par censures ecclesiastiques, auquel nous avons fait prèmierment demander à genoux pardon a Dieu et à son Eglise de son scandale et de sa fautte devant les anciens et devant la ditte offensée à laquelle nous lui avons ensuitte après l'avoir fait relever fait faire excuse et reparation de son attendat devant les temoins choisis par elle, après quoi pour peinne et punition du scandal du dit Jacques Loiel, nous l'avons taxé à une amende pour les pauvres et l'avons suspendu de la St. Cene pour six mois à compter depuis Pacque jusqu'à la St. Michel, au quel temps après avoir fait paroitre sa repentance au Consistoire, et lui demander d'entree restitué, sera alors restitué sans reconnoissance publique; en foi de quoi nous avons signé la presente deliberation censure et suspension prononcé en Consistoire ce 28 Mars de la presente année 1721. J. De Maure, pasteur. T. Delacombe, secretaire. Jaques Lardeau, J. Delatorte, J. Guitton."

The next notice shows a similar exercise of judicial functions of the minister and elders against one François Alard, for "rebellion manifeste contre le Pasteur de l'Eglise," with the addition that, having made "reconnaissance de son scandal," he had been pardoned, "il a eté recu à la St. Cene et retablé comme membre fidel de la susditte Eglise." The whole of these entries are signed "Joseph De Maure, pasteur de Stonehouse et ministre du St. Evangile."

The third volume of the Stonehouse records, a very small octavo of about twenty leaves, in the shape of a pocket-book, contains a few entries of baptisms and burials, ranging from 1743 to 1760. All the entries are signed "Fauriel, ministre;" and the heading of the burials is "Memoire de ceux qui sont morts dans mon Eglise depuis l'année 1743." There are no notices of any interest, and the whole of the entries seem to have been made merely as personal memoranda for the use of the pastor.

The fourth volume, a thin quarto of about twenty-five pages, contains on the one side entries of baptisms from 1762 to 1791, and on the other of burials from 1762 to 1782. The first entry of baptism runs: "Le 24e Septembre, 1762, sur un Vendredi, a eté baptisée Anne fille legitime de monsieur Antoine Delacombe, ancien de notre Eglise et de Madame Jeane, née Delacombe sa femme. Parain, Monsier François Delacombe, ancien de notre Eglise. Maraine, Madame Jeane, femme de Jean Brock, lieutenant, pour Sa Majesté." The fourth entry of baptism is as follows: "Le 23 Septembre, 1764, a eté batisée, sur un Dimanche, Frederic Louis, fils legitime de Monsieur David Louis Monin, pasteur de cette Eglise et de Lydie née Droz sa femme. Parrain, Monsieur Jean Brock, lieutenant, pour Sa Majesté le Roi George. Maraine, Madame Jeane née Delacombe, femme de Monsieur Antoine Delacombe, Ancien de notre Eglise."

There are but two baptisms entered in 1764, one in 1765, one in 1766, one in 1767, and then none till 1770, when there is again one. Under date of 1772 is the notice, " Le service de notre ancienne Eglise françoise de Stonehouse a pris fin le vingt Septembre et j'ai convoqué le Seigneur pour la nouvelle Eglise le 18th Octobre, 1772, à deux heures après midi. Martin Guillaume Bataille, ministre du St. Evangile."

There are thirty-five more entries of baptisms from 1772 till 1791, when the list closes. Under date 1790 there is an entry marking the commencement of the French Revolution and the Vendée troubles. It runs: "George Marie Eugène, fils de François Bertrand et de Réné le Goff natife de Basse Bretagne en France fut né a Stonehouse et baptisée par moi a la maison le jour de sa naissance dix neuvième d'Avril, 1790. Le parain a été le très puissant Eugène Jacques Marie de Kerouatre, chevalier, et Maraine la très puissante Aline Yvesse Maria Quemper demoiselle de Lanascol. La ceremonie fut faite par moi Martin Guillaume Bataille, ministre."

The entries of burials are but nineteen in number during the years 1763 to 1782, or one per annum In nearly all cases it is stated that the deceased was "enterrée dans le cimetière de la Chapelle angloise." The first six entries were made, as stated in the heading, during the ministry of David Louis Monin, who became "pasteur" April 11, 1762, and the rest, commencing in 1770, are signed by Martin Guillaume Bataille. All the names that occur are French. There are no notices of special interest.

French Church of Thorpe-le-Soken, Essex.

The registers of this church, comprising baptisms, burials, and marriages, are in two parts, bound in one thin volume tolerably well preserved. In the first part the baptisms are entered on the one side, and the burials and marriages indiscriminately on the other. The second part of the book consists of an index of the baptisms and marriages arranged in chronological order, from 1684 to 1726, and followed by the notice "L'Eglise Françoise de Thorpe, faute de membres, fut fermée peu après ce tems-là."

The entries of baptisms are all of some length, each signed by the minister for the time being, but none of them stating the origin of the parents. There are thirteen entries signed "Severin, ministre," from March, 1684, to September, 1686; one signed Laporte, in March, 1687; ninety-nine signed Mestayer, from May, 1687, to May, 1707; ten signed Colin, from January, 1708, to November, 1713; and seven signed Richier, from March, 1717, to January, 1726, when the register ceases. It thus appears that the births, at the establishment of the colony and for some time after, averaged about five per annum, and fell down in the end to less than one.

There is evidence from the minute care of the entries that the register was very perfect. The first entry in the book is as follows: "Aujourd'huy 9 jour de Mars, 1684, a esté baptizé Marthe, fille de Jean Sionneau et d'Elizabeth Maistayer ses père et mère. De laquelle le Sieur Joan de L'estrille Sieur de la Clide a esté parrain et mlle. Marguerite Raillard, veuve de feu le sieur Estrang, maraine, qui ont dit que cet enfant est née le 6ᵉ jour du même mois et de la ditte année. Severin, ministre." All the other entries are similar, only varying in adding at times to the name of the parents the parish in which they live, most frequently "la Paroisse le Thorpe," and, in fewer instances, "la paroisse de Kirby," "de Tendring," and others.

The greater part of the members of the congregation were clearly agriculturists; a large proportion bear noble names—Charles de la Porte, Pierre le Febure, and Jacques de Mede, occur very frequently. Others, less numerous, are Abraham de Rivière, and Charles Fouquet de Bournizeau. "Paul Potier, maitre chirurgien," figures often in the earlier notices. From an entry under date of March, 168$\frac{5}{6}$, it appears that there was a French congregation at Harwich, as the godfather mentioned is " Le sieur Hypolite de Lazancy, ministre de la paroisse D'Harwich et Dovercourt."

The register of marriages and burials commences in 1684 and ends in 1718. As in the case of the births, every entry is signed by the minister. Marriages and burials succeed each other with curious regularity, and the notices throughout are very clear and precise. The first entry runs: "Aujourd'huy 13 jour de May, 1684, a esté beny le marriage dans l'Eglise de Thorp d'entre Charles de la Porte natif de St Jean de Gardomenque en la province de Sevenes, d'une part, et Louise Plumail fille de deffunct Theodore Plumail, vivant marchand demeurant a Rioid en Poitou et Louise de la Vaux, ses père and mère d'autre part. Severin, ministre." The next entry is "Aujourd'huy 1 jour de May, 1865, a esté enterré le corps de deffunt Isaac de Sevre dit La Chaboissière decedé au Seigneur le 29 d'Avril de cette année, agé d'environ soixante et treize ans. Severin."

The same forms continue throughout, though in many cases of burials the origin or occupation of the deceased is mentioned. In September, 1688, is the entry of the burial of " Samuel Bauchamp, cy devant avocat au Parlement de Paris, agé de 78 ans;" and in December, 1705, that of "Pierre Espinasse, de la paroisse de Thorpe, chirurgien." The marriages cease altogether in 1708, and there are but very few deaths after this period—two in 1709, two in 1711, one 1712, and one in 1718. The last entry is that of the death of "Susanne Grellet," and a notice at the end of the register-index states that the Grellet family kept the books of the congregation for a time. This notice, signed "Jacob Bourdillon, pasteur," and dated November 13, 1784, attests that " Monsieur Jacques Grellet séant retiré à Londres, m'à remis, il y a environ douze ans, le livre des actes et registres de Consistoire, aussi bien que celui des Batêmes, mariages et enterrements de l'Eglise française de Thorpe, lesquels j ai confié au Consistoire de mon Eglise de l'Artillerie au Spitalfields."

French Church at Thorney Abbey, Cambridgeshire.

Nothing is known of the origin of the French church at Thorney Abbey, which was established in 1652, and continued until 1727. The register of baptisms begins in 1654, and contains particulars of the names of the sponsors as well as parents of the children baptized.

It is supposed that the Thorney French church was formed shortly after the breaking up of the Walloon colony at Sandtoft, in the Level of Hatfield Chase, Yorkshire, during the wars of the Commonwealth, and that many of the settlers then came from the northern colony.

An abstract of the Sandtoft register (now lost) is given by the Rev. Joseph Hunter in his *History of the Deanery of Doncaster*, from which it would appear that out of seventy-one families at Sandtoft, fourteen removed to Thorney, bearing the names of Bentiland, Blancart, Descamps, Egar, Flahau, Le Haire, Hardiég, Harlay, De la Haye, De Lanoy, De Lespierre, Massingarbe, Du Quesne, and Taffin; as well as members of the following families: Amory, Beharelle, Blique, Du Bois, Clais, Le Conte, Coqueler, Desbiens, Desquier, La Fleur, Fontaine, Frouchart, Gouy, Hancar, Le Lieu, Marquillier, Renard, Ramery, Le Roux, Le Roy, Le Talle, and Vennin.

There are, however, numerous names in the Thorney register which do not occur in that of Sandtoft, more particularly those of De Bailleu, Lisy, De Seine (Dessein), Le Fevre, Sigié, Le Pla, Rio, Fauverque, De la Rue, Caillet, Wantier, Descou, Dournelle, Yserby, Vandebeck, Du Pont, Brasseur, Seneschal, etc.

The French congregation at Thorney does not appear to have received any accession of members in consequence of the Revocation of the Edict of Nantes. In the five years following the Revocation not a single baptism appears in any family which was not settled in Thorney before that event.

The average number of baptisms at this church from 1660 to 1670 was 39; in the following ten years, 32; from which time the number gradually declined, until, in the ten years ending 1727, the baptisms were only six.

Judge Bayley, of the Westminster County Court, to whom we are indebted for this analysis of the Thorney register, is descended from one of the foreign settlers, and informs us of the singular mutations which the name of his family has undergone in little more than two centuries—from the original De Bailleu, or De Bailleux, to Balieux, Balieu, Balieul, De Bailleul, Bailleul, Balieul, Bayly, Bailly, and eventually Bayley—all these successively appearing in the register, showing the tendency of foreign appellations gradually to assimilate themselves to those of the country in which they have become native, and illustrating the difficulty of preserving the spelling, and even the sound, of foreign family names during the course of a few generations.

III. HUGUENOT REFUGEES AND THEIR DESCENDANTS.

The following list of the more notable men among the refugees has been collated from Haag's *La France Protestante*; Agnew's *Protestant Exiles from France*; Durrant Cooper's *Lists of Foreign Protestants and Aliens*, 1618–1688; Burn's *History of the Foreign Refugees*; the *Ulster Journal of Archæology*; and from private sources of information. It is probable that important names have been omitted from the list, and that the facts may in certain cases be inaccurately stated. Should the opportunity be afforded him, the author will be glad to correct such defects in a future edition.

ABBADIE, JAMES, D.D., a native of Nay, in Bearn, where he was born in 1654. An able preacher and writer; first settled in Berlin, which he left to accompany the Duke of Schomberg into England. He was for some time minister of the Church of the Savoy, London, and was afterward made Dean of Killaloe in Ireland. He died in London in 1727. For farther notice, see p. 240.

ALLIX, PETER, an able preacher and controversialist. Born at Alençon 1641 ; died in London 1717. Was one of the ministers of the great church at Charenton, near Paris. At the Revocation he took refuge in England, where he was appointed canon and treasurer to the Cathedral of Salisbury. For farther notice, see p. 242.

AMAND, or AMYAND : a Huguenot refugee of this name settled in London in the beginnning of last century. His son Claude was principal surgeon to George II. ; and the two sons of the latter were Claudius, under secretary of state, and George (created a baronet in 1764), who sat in Parliament for Barnstaple. The second baronet assumed the name of Cornewall. His daughter married Sir Gilbert Frankland Lewis, Bart., and was the mother of the late Sir Cornewall Lewis, Bart., M.P.

ANDRE, the name of a French refugee family settled in Southampton, from whom the celebrated and unfortunate Major André was descended, though the latter was brought up at Lichfield.

AUBERTIN, PETER, a native of Neufchâtel, in Picardy, who fled into England about the middle of last century. He was for many years an eminent merchant in London. His son, the late Rev. Peter Aubertin, vicar of Chipstead, Surrey, died in 1861 at the age of 81, leaving a numerous family.

AUFRERE, GEORGE, M.P., descended from a Huguenot refugee; sat for Stamford in Parliament from 1761 to 1768.

AURIOL, PETER, a refugee from Lower Languedoc, who rose to eminence as a London merchant. The Archbishop of York, the Hon. and most Rev. R. N. Drummond, married his daughter and heiress, Henrietta, and afterward succeeded to the peerage of Strathallan. The refugee's daughter thus became Countess of Strathallan. The present head of the family is the Earl of Kinnoul, who continues to bear the name of Auriol. The Rev. Edward Auriol is rector of St. Dunstans-in-the-West, London.

BACQUENCOURT, see *Des Vœux.*

BARON, PETER, Professor in the University of Cambridge about 1575. He was originally from Etampes, and fled to England after the massacre of St. Bartholomew. He died in London, leaving behind him an only son, Samuel, who practiced medicine, and died at Lyme-Regis, in Norfolk.

BARRE, a Protestant family of Pont - Gibau, near Rochelle, several members of which settled in Ireland. Peter Barré married Miss Raboteau, also a refugee. He was an alderman of Dublin, and carried on a large business as a linen-draper. His son Isaac, educated at Trinity College, Dublin, entered the army, in which he rose to high rank. He was adjutant general of the British forces under Wolfe at Quebec. He afterward entered Parliament, where he distinguished himself by his eloquence and his opposition to the American Stamp Act. In 1776 Colonel Barré was made vice-treasurer of Ireland and privy councilor. He subsequently held the offices of treasurer of the navy and paymaster of the forces, in both of which he displayed eminent integrity and efficiency. He died in 1802.

BATZ, the name of a Huguenot family, the head of which was seigneur of Monan, near Nerac, in Guyenne. Three of the sons of Joseph de Batz, seigneur of Guay, escaped from France into Holland, entered the service of the Prince of Orange, whom they accompanied in his expedition to England. Two of them, captains of infantry, were killed at the Boyne.

BEAUFORT, DANIEL AUGUSTUS DE, a controversial writer, was pastor of the church of the New Patent in 1728; of the Artillery in 1728; and of the Savoy, and probably Spring Gardens, in 1741. He afterward went to Ireland, where he held the living of Navan, and was appointed Dean of Tuam. The descendants of the family are still in England. One is rector of Lymm in Cheshire; another is favorably known as a novelist.

BEAUVOIR, DE, the name of one of the most ancient families in Languedoc, several branches of which were Protestant. Francis, eldest son of Scipio du Roure, took refuge in England at the Revocation, and obtained a company in a cavalry regiment. His two sons also followed the career of arms with distinction. Alexander, the eldest, was colonel of the 4th Foot, governor of Plymouth, lieutenant general, commander-in-chief in Scotland, etc. He especially distinguished himself at the battle of Dettingen. He went into France for the benefit of his health, and died at Bareges, whither he had gone for the benefit of the waters. The French government having refused his body Christian burial, in consequence of his being the son of a refugee Protestant, the body was embalmed and sent to England to be buried. The second son, Scipio, was also the colonel of an English infantry regiment, and was killed at the battle of Fontenoy. Another family of the same name is sprung from Richard de Beauvoir, Esq., of the island of Guernsey, who purchased the manor of Balmes, in the parish of Hackney, and thus gave its name to De Beauvoir town.

BELCASTEL DE MONTVAILLANT, PIERRE, a refugee officer from Languedoc, who entered the service of William of Orange. After the death of La Caillemotte at the Boyne, he was made colonel of the regiment. Belcastel took a prominent part in the Irish campaigns of 1690-1. He was eventually raised to the rank of major general in the Dutch army. He was killed at the battle of Villa Viciosa, in Spain, in 1710.

BENEZET, ANTOINE, one of the earliest and most zealous advocates of negro emancipation. He was born in London in 1713, of an honest refugee couple from St. Quentin, and bred to the trade of a cooper. He accompanied his parents to America, and settled at Philadelphia. There he became a Quaker, and devoted himself with great zeal to the question of emancipation of the blacks, for whose children he established and supported schools in Philadelphia. He died there in 1784.

BENOIT, N., a refugee silk-weaver settled in Spitalfields. He was the author of several controversial works, more particularly relating to baptism, Benoit being of the Baptist persuasion.

BERNIÈRE, JEAN ANTOINE DE, a refugee officer who served under the Earl of Galway in Spain. He lost a hand at the battle of Almanza. His son was a captain in the 30th Foot; his grandson (Henry Abraham Crommelin de Bernière) was a major general in the British army; and his great-grandson, married to the sister of the present Archbishop of Canterbury, rose to the same rank.

BERTHEAU, REV. CHARLES, refugee pastor in London, a native of Montpellier, expelled from Paris, where he was one of the ministers of the great Protestant church of Charenton at the Revocation. He became minister of the Walloon church in Threadneedle Street, which office he filled for forty-four years. Several volumes of his sermons have been published.

BION, JEAN FRANÇOIS, a native of Dijon, Roman Catholic curate of Ursy, afterward appointed chaplain to the galley *Superbe* at Toulon, which contained a large number of galley-slaves condemned for their faith. Touched by their sufferings, as well as by the patience and courage with which they bore them, Bion embraced Protestantism, exclaiming, "Their blood preaches to me!" He left France for Geneva in 1704, and afterward took refuge in London, where he was appointed rector of a school, and officiated as minister of the French church at Chelsea. He subsequently proceeded to Holland, where he exercised the functions of chaplain of an English church. He was the author of several works, his best known being the *Relation des Tourmens que l'on fait souffrir aux Protestans qui sont sur les Galères de France*, published at London in 1708.

BLANC, ANTHONY, pastor of the French church of La Nouvelle Patente in 1692. Theodore and Jean Blanc were two other French refugee pastors in London about the same time, the latter being pastor of L'Artillerie. The Blancs were from Saintonge and Poitou.

BLAQUIÉRE, DE, a French noble family, of whom John de Blaquiére, a zealous Huguenot, took refuge in England in 1685. One of his sons became eminent as a London merchant; another settled at Lisburn, where his sister married John Crommelin, son of Louis. The fifth son, John, entered the army, and rose to be lieutenant colonel of the 17th Light Dragoons. He held various public offices—was secretary of Legation at Paris, secretary to the lord lieutenant of Ireland, was made a baronet in 1784, and raised to the peerage in 1800 as Lord de Blaquiére of Ardkill in Ireland.

BLONDEL, MOSES, a learned refugee scholar in London, circa 1621, author of a work on the Apocryphal writings.

BLONDEL, JAMES AUGUSTUS, a distinguished refugee physician in London, as well as an able scholar. The author of several learned and scientific treatises. Died in 1734.

BLOSSET, a Nivernais Protestant family, the head of which was the Sieur de Fleury. Several Blossets fled into Holland and England at the Revocation. Colonel Blosset, of "Blosset's Foot," who settled in Ireland, was the owner of a good estate in the county of Dublin. Sergeant Blosset, afterward Lord Chief Justice of Bengal, belonged to the family.

BOCHART, FRANÇOIS. Haag says that among the Protestant refugees in Scotland, Francis Bochart has been mentioned, who, in conjunction with Claude Paulin, established in 1730 the manufacture of cambric at Edinburg.

BODT or BOTT, JOHN DE, a refugee French officer, appointed captain of artillery and engineers in the British service in 1690. He distinguished himself by the operations conducted by him at the siege of Naumur, to which William III. mainly attributed the capture of the place. Bodt afterward entered the service of the King of Prussia, who made him brigadier and chief engineer. He was also eminent as an architect, and designed some of the principal public buildings at Berlin.

BOESMER DE LA TOUCHE, pastor of the French congregation at Winchelsea in 1700-6. His son, of the same name, was a surgeon in London in 1764.

BOILEAU DE CASTELNAU, an ancient Languedoc family, many of whose members embraced Protestantism and remained faithful to it. Charles, son of Jacques Boileau, councilor of Nismes, was a captain of infantry in the English service, who settled in England about the end of the seventeenth century, and was the founder of the English branch of the Boileau family, the present head of which is Sir John Boileau, Bart.

BOIREAU, see *Bouherau*.

BOISBELAU DE LA CHAPELLE, usually known as Aimand de la Chapelle, left France at the Revocation. He was destined for the ministry from an early age. At eighteen he was sent into Ireland to preach to the French congregations, and after two years, at the age of twenty, he was appointed pastor of the French church at Wandsworth. He subsequently officiated as minister of the Artillery Church, and of the French church at the Hague. He was a voluminous writer.

BONHOMME, a Protestant draper from Paris, who settled at Ipswich, and instructed the artisans there in the manufacture of sail-cloth, which shortly became a considerable branch of British industry.

BONNELL, THOMAS, a gentleman of good family near Ypres, in Flanders, who took refuge in England from the Duke of Alva's persecutions, and settled at Norwich, of which he became mayor. His son was Daniel Bonnell, merchant, of London, father of Samuel Bonnell, who served his apprenticeship with Sir William Courteen (a Flemish refugee), and established himself as a merchant at Leghorn. He returned to England, and at the Restoration was appointed accountant general for Ireland. He died at Dublin, and was succeeded in the office by his son, a man eminent for his piety, and whose life has been written at great length by Archdeacon Hamilton, of Armagh.

BOSANQUET, DAVID, a Huguenot refugee, naturalized in England in 1687. His grandson, Samuel, was a director of the Bank of England. Mary, the sister of the latter, was the celebrated wife of the Rev. Mr. Fletcher, vicar of Madeley. Other members occupied illustrious positions in society. One, William, founded the well-known bank in London. Sir John B. Bosanquet, the celebrated judge, also belonged to the family, which is now represented by Samuel Richard Bosanquet, of Dingeston Court, Monmouth.

BOSQUET, ANDREW, a refugee from Languedoc, who escaped into England after suffering fourteen years' slavery in the French king's galleys. He was the originator of the Westminster French Charity School, founded in 1747, for the education of children of poor French refugees.

BOSTAQUET, DUMONT DE. For notice of, see p. 192 et seq.

BOUFFARD, a refugee family from the neighborhood of Castres, of whom Bouffard, Sieur de la Garrigue, was the head. One of the family emigrated to England, and, in accordance with the usual practice, took the name of the family estate. David Garrick, the tragedian, is said to have been one of his descendants.

BOUHEREAU, ELIAS, M.D., D.D., a learned Huguenot refugee, who became secretary to the Earl of Galway in Ireland. When the earl left Ireland, he became pastor to one of the French congregations in Dublin; was afterward episcopally ordained, and officiated as chantor of St. Patrick's Cathedral. One of his sons, John, entered the Church; another was "town-major" of Dublin. The latter altered his name to Borough, and from him the present Sir E. R. Borough, of Baseldon Park, Berkshire, is lineally descended.

BOURDILLON, JACOB, an able and eloquent pastor of several French churches in London. For notice of, see p. 278.

BOUVERIES, LAURENCE DES, a refugee from Sainghen, near Lille, in 1568. He settled first at Sandwich and afterward at Canterbury, where began the business of a silk-weaver. Edward, the grandson of Laurence, established himself in London as a Levant merchant, and from that time the family greatly prospered. William was made a baronet in 1711, and Jacob was created a peer, under the title of Viscount Folkestone, in 1747. His son Philip assumed the name of Pusey on his marriage in 1798. The Rev. Dr. Pusey, of Oxford, is one of the sons by this marriage. For further notice, see p. 309.

BOYER, ABEL, a refugee from Castres, where he was born in 1664. He died, pen in hand, at Chelsea, in 1729. He was the author of the well-known *French and English Dictionary*, as well as of several historical works.

BRISSAC, B. DE, a refugee pastor from Châtellerault, who fled from France at the Revocation. We find one of his descendants, Captain George Brissac, a director of the French Hospital in London in 1773. Haag says that one of the female Brissacs became famous at Berlin for her sausages, and especially for her black puddings, which continue to be known there as "boudins français."

BRUNET, a numerous Protestant family in Saintonge. N. Brunet, a privateer of La Rochelle, was in 1662 condemned to suffer corporal punishment, and to pay a fine of 1000 livres, unless within a given time he produced before the magistrates thirty-six young Protestants whom he had carried over to America. Of course the refugee youths were never produced. At the Revocation the Brunets of Rochelle nearly all emigrated to London. We find frequent baptisms of children of the name recorded in the registers of the churches of Le Quarré and La Nouvelle Patente, as well as marriages at the same place, and at Wheeler Street Chapel and La Patente in Soho.

BUCER, MARTIN, a refugee from Alsace; one of the early reformers, an eloquent preacher as well as a vigorous and learned writer. He accepted the invitation of Archbishop Cranmer to settle in England, where he assisted in revising the English Liturgy, excluding what savored of popery, but not going so far as Calvin. He was appointed professor of theology at Cambridge, where he was presented with a doctor's diploma. But the climate of England not agreeing with him, Bucer returned to Strasburg, where he died in 1551.

BUCHLEIN, otherwise called FAGIUS, a contemporary of Martin Bucer, and, like him, a refugee at Cambridge University, where he held the professorship of Hebrew. While in that office, which he held for only a few years, he fell ill of fever, of which he died, but not without a suspicion of having been poisoned.

BUISSIÉRE, PAUL, a celebrated anatomist, F.R.S., and corresponding member of various scientific societies. He lived for a time in London, but eventually settled at Copenhagen, where he achieved a high reputation. We find one Paul Buissiére governor of the French Hospital in London in 1729, and Jean Buissiére in 1776.

CAILLEMOTTE, LA, younger son of the old Marquis de Ruvigny, who commanded a Huguenot regiment at the battle of the Boyne, where he was killed. See *Massue*, and notices at p. 211 and 215.

CAMBON, a refugee French officer, who commanded one of the Huguenot regiments raised in London in 1689. He fought at the Boyne and at Athlone, and died in 1693.

CAPPEL, LOUIS, characterized as the father of sacred criticism. He was born at Saint Elier in 1585; at twenty he was selected by the Duke of Bouillon as tutor for his son. Four years later, the church at Bordeaux furnished him with the means of visiting the principal academies of England, Holland, and Germany. He passed two years at Oxford, during which he principally occupied himself with the study of the Shemitic languages. He subsequently occupied the chair of theology in the University of Samur, until his death, which occurred in 1658. Bishop Hall designated Louis Cappel "the grand oracle of the Hebrasts." Louis's son James was appointed professor of Hebrew in the same University at the early age of nineteen. At the Revocation he took refuge in England, and became professor of Latin in the Nonconformist College, Hoxton Square, London. See notice at p. 246.

CARBONEL, JOHN, son of Thomas Carbonel, merchant of Caen: John was one of the secretaries of Louis XIV., and fled to England at the Revocation. His brother William became an eminent merchant in London.

CARLE, PETER, a native of Valleraugue in the Cevennes, born 1666; died in London 1730. He fled from France at the Revocation, passing by Geneva through Switzerland into Holland, and finally into England. He entered the corps of engineers in the army of William, and fought at the Boyne, afterward accompanying the army through all its campaigns in the Low Countries. He rose to be fourth engineer in the British service, and retired upon a pension in 1693. He afterward served under Lord Galway in Spain, when the King of Portugal made him lieutenant general and engineer-in-chief. In 1720 he returned to England, and devoted the rest of his life to the improvement of agriculture, on which subject he wrote and published many useful works.

CARRÉ, a Protestant family of

Poitou, of which several members emigrated to England, and others to North America. A M. Carré officiated as reader in the French church at Hammersmith, and another of the same name was minister of La Patente in London. We also find one Francis Carré a member of the consistory of New York in 1772.

CARTAUD or CARTAULT, MATTHEW, a Protestant minister who fled from France at the time of the Bartholomew massacre, and officiated as pastor of the little church of fugitives at Rye, afterward returning to Dieppe; and again (on the revival of the persecution) finally settling and dying in England. One of his sons was minister of La Nouvelle Patente in London in 1696.

CASAUBON, ISAAC, son of a French refugee from Bordeaux settled at Geneva, where he was born in 1559. His father returned to Paris on the temporary cessation of the persecution, became minister of a congregation at Crest, and proceeded with the education of his son Isaac, who gave signs of extraordinary abilities. At nine years of age he spoke Latin with fluency. At the massacre of St. Bartholomew the family fled into concealment, and it was while hiding in a cavern that Isaac received from his father his first lesson in Greek. At nineteen he was sent to the academy of Geneva, where he studied jurisprudence under Pacius, theology under De Beza, and Oriental languages under Chevalier; but no branch of learning attracted him more than Greek, and he was, at the age of twenty-four, appointed professor of that language at Geneva. His large family induced him to return to France, accepting the professorship of civil laws in the University of Montpellier; and there he settled for a time. On the revival of persecution in France at the assassination of Henry IV., Casaubon emigrated to England. He was well received by James I., who gave him a pension, and appointed him prebend of Westminster. He died at London in 1614, leaving behind him twenty sons and daughters, and a large number of works written during his lifetime, chiefly on classical and religious subjects. His son Florence Stephen Casaubon, D.D., having accompanied his father into England, was entered a student at Christ Church, Oxford, in 1614, where he greatly distinguished himself. In 1622 he took the degree of M.A. He was appointed rector of Ickham, and afterward prebendary of Canterbury. He was the author of many learned works. He died at Canterbury in 1671.

CAUX, DE: many refugees of this name fled from Normandy into England. Several of them came over from Dieppe and settled in Norwich, their names frequently occurring in the registers of the French church there, in conjunction with those of Martineau, Columbine, Le Monnier, De la Haye, etc. Solomon de Caus, the engineer, whose name is connected with the first invention of the steam-engine, spent several years as a refugee in England, after which he proceeded to Germany in 1613, and ultimately died in France, whither he returned in his old age. For notice of him, see p. 231.

CAVALIER, JOHN, tne Cevennol leader, afterward major general in the British army. For notice, see p. 222.

CHAIGNEAU, LOUIS, JOHN, AND STEPHEN, refugees from St. Sairenne, in the Charente, where the family held considerable landed estates. They settled in Dublin, and prospered. One of the sons of Louis sat for Gowram in the Irish Parliament; another held a benefice in the Church. John had two sons—Colonel William Chaigneau, and John, Treasurer of the Ordnance. The great-grandson of Stephen was called to the Irish bar in 1793, and eventually purchased the estate of Benown, in county Westmeath.

CHAMBERLAYNE, PETER, M.D., a physician of Paris, who fled into England at the massacre of St. Bartholomew. He was admitted a member of the college of physicians, and obtained an extensive practice in London, where he died.

CHAMIER, an eminent Protestant family, originally belonging to Avignon. Daniel Chamier, who was killed in 1621 in the defense of Montauban, then besieged by Louis XIII., was one of the ablest theologians of his time, and a leading man of his party. He drew up for Henry IV. the celebrated Edict of Nantes. Several of his descendants settled in England. One was minister of the French church in Glass-House Street, London, and afterward of the Artillery Church. His eldest son, also called Daniel, emigrated to Maryland, U. S., where he settled in 1753. A younger son, Anthony, a director of the French Hospital, sat for Tamworth in Parliament in 1772. See also *Des Champs*.

CHAMPAGNÉ, ROBILLARD DE, a noble family in Saintonge, several of whom took refuge in England and Ireland. The children of Josias de Robillard, chevalier of Champagné, under charge of their mother, escaped from La Rochelle concealed in empty wine-casks, and arrived safe at Plymouth. Their father went into Holland and took service with the Prince of Orange. He afterward died at Belfast on his way to join his regiment in Ireland. Madame de Champagné settled at Portarlington with her family. One of Champagné s sons, Josias, was an ensign in La Melonniére's regiment of French infantry, and fought at the Boyne. He afterward became major of the 14th Foot. Several of his descendants have served with distinction in the army, the Church, and the civil service, while the daughters of the family have intermarried with various titled families in England and Ireland.

CHAMPION, see *Crespigny*.

CHARDEVENNE, a Protestant family belonging to Casteljaloux. The first eminent person of the name was Antoine, doctor of medicine, who afterward became a famous preacher and pastor, first at Caumont, and afterward at Marennes. At the Revocation the members of his family became dispersed. Some of them went to North America; in 1724 we find Pierre (son of the pastor above named) a member of the French Church at New York, while others fled to England, and established themselves at Hungerford.

CHARLOT, CHARLES, better known under the name of D'Argenteuil, was a Roman Catholic curé converted to Protestantism, who took refuge in England, and officiated as pastor in several of the London churches. In 1699 he was minister of the Tabernacle, with Pierre Rival and Cæsar Pegorier for colleagues. He published several works through Duchemin, the refugee publisher.

CHARPENTIER, of Ruffec, in Angoumois, a martyr in 1685 to the brutality of the dragoons of Louis XIV. To force him to sign his abjuration they made him drink from twenty-five to thirty glasses of water; but this means failing, they next dropped into his eyes the hot tallow of a lighted candle. He died in great torture. His son John took refuge in England, and was minister of the Malthouse Church, Canterbury, in 1710.

CHASTELET, HIPPOLYTE, a monk of La Trappe, who left that monastery in 1672, and took refuge in England, where he acquired great fame as a Protestant preacher, under the name of Lusancy. He officiated for a time as pastor of the church in the Savoy, and was afterward appointed to the charge of the French church at Harwich. Lusancy wrote and published a life of Marshal Schomberg, together with other works, principally poetry.

CHATELAIN, HENRY, son of Zachariah Chatelain, a manufacturer of gold and silver lace (see notice at p. 247), who fled from Paris to Holland, and there introduced the manufacture. Zachariah had nine sons and two daughters. Henry, the eldest son, was born at Paris in 1684. He was educated at Leyden, and eventually decided to enter the Church. He came over to England in 1709, and was ordained by the Bishop of London. He became minister of the French church of St. Martin Ongars in 1711, and latterly accepted the pastorate of the church at the Hague, where he died in 1743. He was a most eloquent preacher, as well as a vigorous writer. He wrote the life of Claude, as well as of Bernard, and a work *On the Excellence of the Christian Religion*, besides six volumes of sermons.

CHENEVIX, a distinguished Lorraine family, which became dispersed throughout Europe at the Revocation. The Béville branch of the family settled in Brandenburg, and the Eply branch in England. Philip Chenevix was minister of the church of Limay, near Mantes, from which place he fled to London. One of his sons entered the King's Guards, of which he became colonel. The son of this last was for thirty years Bishop of Waterford. Another member of the family, Richard, was a distinguished chemist, member of the Royal Society in 1801, and author of many able works on science, including an *Essay on National Character*. For notice of Paul Chenevix of Metz, brother of the Rev. Philip Chenevix above named, see note to p. 154.

CHERON, LOUIS, a painter and engraver who took refuge in England at the Revocation, and died in London in 1723.

CHEVALIER, ANTOINE-RODOLPHE, a zealous Huguenot, born at Montchamps in 1507. When a youth he was compelled to fly into England for life. He completed his studies at Oxford, and being recommended to the Duke of Somerset, he was selected by him to teach the Princess (afterward Queen) Elizabeth the French language. Chevalier subsequently held the professorship of Hebrew at Cambridge, but resigned it in 1570 to return to France. He was again compelled to fly by the renewed persecution at the time of the Bartholomew massacre, and he died in exile at Guernsey in 1572. He was a voluminous author on classical subjects. During his short residence abroad, he left his son Samuel at Geneva, for the purpose of being educated for the Church, under Theodore de Beza. On the revival of the persecutions in France, Samuel took refuge in England, and was appointed minister of the French church in London in 1591, and afterward of the Walloon church at Canterbury in 1595. Mr. Chevalier Cobbold, M.P., belongs to this family.

CLAUDE, JEAN-JACQUES, a young man of remarkable talents, grandson of the celebrated French preacher at the Hague. He was appointed pastor of the Walloon church in Threadneedle Street in 1710, but died of smallpox a few years later, aged only twenty-eight.

COLIGNON, ABRAHAM DE, minister of Mens. At the Revocation he and several of his sons took refuge in Hesse, while Paul became minister of the Dutch church in Austin Friars, London. His son Charles became professor of anatomy and medicine at Cambridge, and was known as the author of several able works on those subjects.

COLLOT DE L'ESCURY, a refugee officer from Noyon, who escaped from France through Switzerland into Holland at the Revocation, and joined the army of William of Orange. He was major in Schomberg's regiment at the Boyne. His eldest son David was a captain of dragoons; another, Simeon, was colonel of an English regiment, both of whose sons were captains of foot. Their descendants still survive in Ireland.

COLOMIES, JEROME, the great pastor and preacher of Rochelle, belonged to a Bearnese family. His grandson, Paul, the celebrated author, came over to England in 1681, and was first appointed reader in the French church of the Savoy. Sancroft, Archbishop of Canterbury, afterward made him his librarian. Paul Colomiès was the author of numerous learned works, the titles of nineteen of which are given by Haag in *La France Protestante*. He died in London, 1692.

CONAUT, JOHN, son of a Protestant refugee from Normandy who had settled in Devonshire. He studied at Oxford, entered the Church, and was appointed vicar of Yealmpton, Devon, in which office Cromwell continued him during the Commonwealth. In 1654 he was appointed professor of theology, and in 1657 vice-chancellor of the University of Oxford. In 1676 he was archdeacon of Norwich, and in 1681 he was appointed a prebendary of Worcester. He died in 1693.

CONSTANT, a Protestant family of Artois. At the Revocation, several of them fled into Switzerland, others into Holland, and took service under the Prince of Orange. Samuel, known as Baron de Constant, served as adjutant general under Lord Albemarle in 1704, and afterward fought under Marlborough in all the great battles of the period. His son David-Louis, an officer in the same service, was wounded at Fontenoy. Benjamin Constant, the celebrated French author, belonged to this family.

CORCELLIS, NICHOLAS, son of Zeager Corcellis of Ruselier, in Flanders, who took refuge in England from the persecutions of the Duke of Alva. Nicholas became a prosperous London merchant. James was a physician in London, 1664.

CORNAUD DE LA CROZE, a learned refugee, author of *The Works of the Learned*, *The History of Learning*, and numerous other works.

COSNE, PIERRE DE, a refugee gentleman from La Beauce, Orleans, who settled at Southampton. His son Ruvigny de Cosne entered the Coldstream Guards, and rose to be lieutenant colonel in the British army. He was afterward secretary to the French embassy, and embassador at the Spanish court.

COSNE-CHAVERNEY, DE, another branch of the same family. Captain de Cosne-Chavernay came over with the Prince of Orange in command of a company of gentlemen volunteers. He was lieutenant colonel of Belcastel's regiment at the taking of Athlone in 1691.

COTTEREAU, N., a celebrated Protestant horticulturist, who fled into England at the Revocation, and was appointed one of the gardeners of William III. Having gone into France to look after a manufactory of pipes which he had established at Rouen, he was detected encouraging the Protestants there to stand fast in the faith. He had also the imprudence to write something about Madame de Maintenon in a letter, which was construed as a libel. He was thereupon seized and thrown into the Bastile, where he lay for many years, during several of which he was insane. The converters offered him liberty if he would abjure his religion. At last he abjured, but he was not released. "It was deemed just, as well as necessary, that Cottereau should remain in the Bastile and be forgotten there." He accordingly remained there a prisoner for eighteen years, until he died.

COULAN, ANTHONY, a refugee pastor from the Cevennes. He was for some time minister of the Glasshouse Street French church in London. He died in 1694.

COURTEEN, WILLIAM, the son of a tailor at Menin in Flanders, a refugee in England from the persecutions of the Duke of Alva. He established himself in business, with his son Peter Boudeau, in Abchurch Lane, and is said to have owed his prosperity to the manufacture of French hoods. His son became Sir William Courteen, a leading merchant of the city of London. His descendants also married with the Bridgewater and other noble families.

COUSIN, JEAN, a refugee pastor from Caen, one of the first ministers of the Walloon church in London about the year 1562. He returned to France, but again fled back to England after the massacre of St. Bartholomew, and died in London.

CRAMAHÉ, a noble family of La Rochelle. The three brothers, Cramahé, De L'Isle, and Des Roches, made arrangements to escape into England at the Revocation. The two former succeeded, and settled in this country. Des Roches was less fortunate; he was detected under the disguise in which he was about to fly; was flogged, maltreated, stripped of all the money he had, put in chains, and cast into a dungeon. After being transferred from one prison to another, and undergoing many cruelties, being found an obstinate heretic, he was, after twenty-seven months' imprisonment, banished the kingdom.

CRAMER, a refugee Protestant family of Strasburg, some of whom settled in Geneva, where Gabriel Cramer, a celebrated physician, became Dean of the College of Medicine in 1677. Jean-Louis Cramer held the rank of captain in the English army, and served with distinction in the Spanish campaign. When the French army occupied Geneva at the Revolution, Jean-Antoine, brother of the preceding, came over to England and settled. His second son, Jean-Antoine, was a professor at Oxford and Dean of Carlisle. He was the author of several geographical works. Another member of this family was Gabriel Cramer, of Geneva, the celebrated mathematician.

CREGUT, a refugee pastor from Montélimar, who officiated as minister of the French church in Wheeler Street, and afterward in that of La Nouvelle Patente, London.

CRESPIGNY, CLAUDE CHAMPION DE, a landed proprietor in Normandy, who fled from France into England with his family at the Revocation. He was related by marriage to the Pierpoints, who hospitably received the fugitives. Two of his sons entered the army; Gabriel was an officer in the Guards, and Thomas captain in Hotham's Dragoons. The grandson of the latter had two sons: Philip Champion de Crespigny, M.P. for Aldbough, 1803, and Sir Claude Champion de Crespigny, created baronet in 1805.

CROMMELIN, LOUIS, royal superintendent of the linen manufacture in Ireland, to which office he was appointed by William III. For notice of him, see p. 285.

CRUSO, JOHN, a refugee from Hownescoat in Flanders, who settled in Norwich. His son Timothy became a prosperous merchant in London, and founded the present Norfolk family of the Crusos.

DAILLON, JAMES DE, a member of the illustrious family of Du Lude. He entered the English Church, and held a benefice in Buckinghamshire toward the end of the 17th century; but, having declared in favor of James II., he was deposed from his office in 1693, and died in London in 1726. His brother Benjamin was also a refugee in England, and held the office of minister in the church of La Patente, which he helped to found.

D'ALBIAC: this family is said to derive its name from Albi, the capital of the country of the Albigenses, which was destroyed in the religious crusade against that people in the thirteenth century. The D'Albiacs fled from thence to Nismes, where they suffered heavily for their religion, especially after the Revocation. Two youthful D'Albiacs were sent to England, having been smuggled out of the country in hampers. They both prospered and founded families. We find the names of their descendants occurring among the directors of the French Hospital. The late Lieutenant General Sir J. C. Dalbiac, M.P., was lineally descended from one of the sons, and his only daughter became Duchess of Roxburghe by her marriage with the duke in 1836.

DALECHAMP, CALEB, a refugee from Sedan, who entered the English Church, and became rector of Ferriby in Lincolnshire.

DANSAYS, FRANCIS, a French refugee at Rye, in Sussex. William was a jurat of that town; he died in 1787. The family is now represented by the Stonhams.

DARGENT or DARGAN, a refugee family from Sancerre, some of the members of which settled in England and Ireland at the Revocation. Two of them served as officers in William III.'s Guards. Two brothers were directors of the French Hospital — John in 1756, and James in 1762.

D'ARGENTEUIL, see *Charlot*.

DAUDE, PETER, a member of one of the best families of Maruéjols in the Gévaudan. He came to England in 1680, and became a tutor in the Trevor family, after which he accepted a clerkship in the Exchequer, which he held for twenty-eight years. He was a very learned, but an exceedingly diffident and eccentric man. His nephew, also named Peter, was a minister of one of the French churches in London.

DAVID, a Protestant family of Rochelle, many members of which fled from France, some into England, and others to the United States of America. One, John David, was a director of the French Hospital in London in 1750.

DE JEAN, LOUIS, descended from a French refugee, was colonel of the 6th Dragoon Guards, and eventually lieutenant general.

DE LA CHEROIS, a noble family of Languedoc, seigneurs of Cherois, near Sens. Three brothers fled into Holland and took service under the Prince of Orange. Their two sisters afterward fled in disguise on horseback, accompanied by a faithful page, traveling always by night, and concealing themselves in the woods during the day. The brothers followed the fortunes of William III.; fought at the Boyne, where one of them was killed, and afterward in the Low Countries. The two remaining brothers, Nicholas and Daniel, eventually settled at Lisburn in Ireland, where they married two daughters of Louis Crommelin. Daniel was appointed governor of Pondicherry in the East Indies. Nicholas reached the rank of lieutenant colonel in the British army. Their descendants still exist in Ireland.

DE LAINE, PETER, a French refugee, who fled into England before the Revocation, and obtained letters of denization dated 1681. He was appointed French tutor to the children of the Duke of York, afterward James II.

DE LA MOTHE, see *Mothe*.

DELAUNE, a refugee family from Normandy, who took refuge in England as early as 1599, when a Delaune officiated as minister of the Walloon church in London. Another, in 1618, held the office of minister of the Walloon church at Norwich. Thomas Delaune was a considerable writer on religious and controversial subjects.

DE LAVALADE: this family possessed large estates in Languedoc. Several members of them succeeded in escaping into Holland, and afterward proceeded to Ireland, settling at Lisburn. M. de Lavalade was forty years pastor of the French church there.

DELEMAR, DE LA MER, DELMER, a Protestant refugee family of Canterbury, whose names are of frequent occurrence in the register of that church. Their descendants are numerous, and enjoy good positions in society.

DELMÉ, PHILIP, minister of the Walloon congregation, Canterbury, whose son Peter settled in London as a merchant, and whose grandson, Sir Peter, ancestor of the present family of Delmé Radcliffe, was lord-mayor of London in 1723.

DE LOVAL, VICOMTE, possessor of large estates in Picardy, who, after heavy persecution, fled at the Revocation, and took refuge in Ireland, settling at Portarlington. His son was an officer in the British army.

DE MOIVRE, ABRAHAM, F.R.S. For notice, see p. 235.

DESAGULIERS, DR. For notice, see p. 234.

DES CHAMPS, JOHN, a native of Bergerac, belonging to an ancient family established in Perigord. At the Revocation he took refuge, first in Geneva, and then in Prussia. Of his sons, one became minister of the church at Berlin, while another came over to England and became minister of the church of the Savoy, in which office he died in 1767. The son of the latter, John Ezekiel, entered the civil service of the East India Company, and became member of Council of the Presidency of Madras. He ultimately took the name of *Chamier*, having been left sole heir to Anthony Chamier. By his marriage with Georgiana Grace, daughter of Admiral Burnaby, he had a numerous family. One of his sons is Captain Frederick Chamier, the novelist and nautical annalist.

DES MAISEAUX, PETER, a native of Auvergne, born in 1666, the son of a Protestant minister who took refuge in England. Little is known of Des Maiseaux's personal history beyond that he was a member of the Royal Society, a friend of Saint Evremond, and a voluminous author. He died in 1745.

DES ORMEAUX, also named COLIN DES ORMEAUX, a Rochelle family. At the Revocation several members of it settled at Norwich. One Catharine Colin was married to Thomas le Chevalier in 1727. Gabriel Colin was minister of Thorpe-le-Soken from 1707 to 1714. A member of the family, Jacques Louis des Ormeaux, was elected a director of the French Hospital in 1798.

DES VŒUX, VINCHON, second son of De Bacquencourt, president of the Parliament of Rouen. He took refuge in Dublin, where he became minister of the French church. In conjunction with the Rev. Peter Droz, he commenced, about 1742, the publication of the first literary journal which appeared in Ireland. He afterward removed to Portarlington. The present head of the family is Sir C. Des Vœux, Bart.

DEVAYNES, WILLIAM, M.P., descended from a Huguenot refugee. He was a director of the East India Company, a director of the French Hospital, and was elected for Barnstaple in 1774.

DE VEILLE, HANS, a refugee who entered the English Church, and was made library keeper at Lambeth by Archbishop Tillotson. His son Thomas entered the English army as a private, and was sent with his regiment to Portugal. Then he rose by merit to the command of a troop of dragoons. On his return to London he was appointed a London justice, an office then paid by fees; and his conduct in the riots of 1735 was so much approved that he received the honor of knighthood. He was also colonel of the Westminster militia.

DOLLOND, JOHN. For notice, see p. 325.

DRELINCOURT, PETER, son of Charles Drelincourt, one of the ablest preachers and writers among the French Protestants. He was educated at Geneva, and afterward came to England, where he entered the English Church, and eventually became dean of Armagh.

DU BOIS or DU BOUAYS, a Protestant family of Brittany, of whom many members came over to England, and settled at an early period at Thorney, Canterbury, Norwich, and London. Others of the name came from French Flanders.

DUBOUCHET, an illustrious Huguenot family of Poitou, several of whose members took refuge in England. One of them, Pierre, officiated as minister of the French church at Plymouth between 1733 and 1737.

DU BOULAY, a family descended from the Marquis d'Argencon de Boulay, a Huguenot refugee in Holland in 1685. His grandson was minister of the French church in Threadneedle Street, London. The family is now represented by Du Boulay, of Denhead Hall, Wiltshire.

DUBOURDIEU, a noble Protestant family of Bearn. Isaac was for some time minister of the Savoy church, London. His son, John Armand, after having been minister at Montpellier, took refuge in England, and also became one of the ministers of the church in the Savoy. His grandson was the last pastor of the French church at Lisburn, and afterward rector of Annahilt in Ireland. For notice of the Dubourdieus, see p. 248, and notes to p. 253 and 289.

DU BUISSON, FRANCIS, a doctor of the Sorbonne. Becoming converted to Protestantism, he fled into England at the time of the massacre of

St. Bartholomew, and became minister of the French church at Rye.

DU CAREL, ANDREW-COLTÉE, a refugee who accompanied his parents from Caen into England at the revival of religious persecution in France in 1724. He studied at Eton and Oxford. In 1757 he was appointed archbishop's librarian at Lambeth, and in the following year he was sent to Canterbury, where he held an important appointment in the record office. He was a man of great antiquarian learning, and published numerous works on classical antiquities.

DU CROS, JOHN, a refugee from Dauphiny. In 1711 his son was minister of the Savoy.

DU JON, a noble family of Berri, several members of whom took refuge in England. Francis, son of a refugee at Leyden, where he studied, was appointed librarian to the Earl of Arundel, and held the office for thirty years. He was one of the first to devote himself to the study of Anglo-Saxon, and published several works on the subject.

DU MOULIN, an ancient and noble family of the Isle of France, that has furnished dignitaries to the Roman Church as well as produced many eminent Protestant writers. Charles du Moulin, the eminent French jurisconsult, declared himself a Protestant in 1542. Pierre du Moulin belonged to another branch of the family. He was only four years old at the massacre of St. Bartholomew, and was saved by an old servant of his father. In his youth he studied at Sedan, and afterward at Oxford and Leyden. At the latter University he was appointed professor of philosophy when only in his twenty-fourth year. Grotius was among his pupils. Seven years later he was "called" by the great Protestant church at Charenton, near Paris, and accepted the invitation to be their minister. He officiated there for twenty-four years, during which he often incurred great peril, having had his house twice pillaged by the populace. At the outbreak of the persecution in the reign of Louis XIII. he accepted the invitation of James I. to settle in England, where he was received with every honor. The king appointed him a prebendary of Canterbury, and the University of Cambridge conferred upon him the degree of D.D. He afterward returned to Paris to assist in the conferences of the Protestant Church, and died at Sedan at the age of ninety. His two sons, Peter and Louis, both settled in England. The former was preacher to the University of Oxford in the time of the Commonwealth. In 1660 Charles II. appointed him one of his chaplains as well as prebendary of Canterbury. Louis, on the other hand, who had officiated as Camden Professor of History at Oxford during the Commonwealth, was turned out of his office on the Restoration, and retired to Westminster, where he continued for the rest of his life an extreme Presbyterian. Both brothers were voluminous authors.

DUNCAN, a Scotch family naturalized in France at the beginning of the 17th century. Mark Duncan was Protestant professor of philosophy and Greek at Saumur. One of his sons, Sainte-Hélène, took refuge in London, where he died in 1697. Another descendant of the family, Daniel, was celebrated as a chemist and physician, and wrote several able works on his favorite subjects. His son Daniel was the last pastor of the French church at Bideford, where he died in 1761. He was also celebrated as a writer on religious subjects.

DUPIN, PAUL, an eminent paper manufacturer who established himself in England after the Revocation, and carried on a large paper-mill with great success.

DU PLESSIS, JACQUES, chaplain of the French Hospital in 1750. Another of the name, Francis, was minister of La Nouvelle Patente and Wheeler Street chapels, London—of the latter in 1720.

DU PORT, a Protestant family of Poitou, several members of whom took refuge in England. One of them, James, was pastor of the French Walloon church in London in 1590. His son, of the same name, filled the office of professor of Greek at the University of Cambridge with great distinction. In 1660 he was appointed dean of Peterborough and chaplain to the king. He was the author of several learned works, and died in 1679.

DU PUY, a Protestant family of Languedoc. At the Revocation, the brothers Philip and David entered the army of William of Orange. They were both officers in his guards, and were both killed at the Boyne. Another brother, Samuel, was also an officer in the British army, and served with distinction in the Low Countries.

DU QUESNE, ABRAHAM, second son of the celebrated admiral, a lieutenant in the French navy, settled in England after the Revocation, and died there. His son Thomas Roger was prebendary of Ely and vicar of East Tuddenham, Norfolk. Another branch of the family of Du Quesne or Du Cane settled in England in the sixteenth century. One of their descendants was an alderman of London. From this branch the Du Canes of Essex are descended, the head of whom is the present Charles du Cane, M. P., of Braxted Park.

DURAND, a noble family of Dauphiny. Several ministers of the name officiated in French churches in England—one at Bristol and others in London. One Francis Durand, from Alençon, a convert from Romanism, was minister of the French church at Canterbury in 1767.

DURANT: several members of this Huguenot family sat in Parliament. Thomas sat for St. Ives in 1768, and George for Evesham.

DURAS, BARON, see *Durfort*.

DURFEY, THOMAS, born at Exeter about the middle of the seventeenth century. The son of a French refugee from Rochelle, well known as a song-writer and dramatic author.

DURFORT DE DURAS, an ancient Protestant family of Guienne. Louis, marquis of Blanquefort, came over to England in the reign of Charles II., and was well received by that monarch, who created him Baron de Du-

ras, and employed him as embassador extraordinary at Paris. James II. created him, though a Protestant, Earl of Faversham, and gave him the command of the army which he sent against the Duke of Monmouth. He died in 1709. The French church which he founded at Faversham did not long survive him.

DUROURE, FRANCIS, scion of an ancient family in Languedoc. His two sons became officers in the English army. Scipio was lieutenant colonel of the 12th Foot, and was killed at Fontenoy. Alexander was colonel of the 4th Foot, and rose to be lieutenant general.

DURY, PAUL, an eminent officer of engineers, who entered the service of William III., from which he passed into that of the Elector of Hesse. Two of his sons served with distinction in the English army; the elder, of the regiment of La Melonniere, was killed at the Boyne.

DU SOUL, MOSES, a refugee from Tours, known in England as a translator and philologist about the beginning of the eighteenth century.

DU TEMS, LOUIS, a refugee from Tours, historiographer to the king of England, member of the Royal Society and of the French Academy of Inscriptions. Having entered the English Church, he was presented with the living of Elsdon in Northumberland. He was the author of many well-known works.

DUVAL. Many refugees from Rouen of this name settled in England, and several were ministers of French churches in London. Several have been governors of the French Hospital.

EMERIS. A refugee family of this name fled out of France at the massacre of St. Bartholomew, and purchased a small property in Norfolk, which descended from father to son, and is still in the possession of the family, at present represented by W. R. Emeris, Esq., of Louth, Lincolnshire.

ESPAGNE, JOHN D', a refugee from Dauphiny, some time minister of Somerset House French church, in London; the author of numerous religious works.

EVREMOND, CHARLES DE ST. DENYS, SEIGNEUR DE STE. EVREMOND, a refugee gentleman of wit and bravery, who served with distinction under Turenne and Condé. His satirical humor lost him the friendship of his patrons, and provoked the enmity of Louis XIV., who ordered his arrest. Having received timely notice, Evremond fled first into Germany and Holland, and afterward into England, where he became a great favorite with Charles II., who gave him a pension. In 1678, an order in Council was passed directing returns to be made of foreigners then in England, and among them appears the following, doubtless that of our French seigneur: "Nov. 23, 1678. Ste. Evremond, chassé de France il y a long temps, est venu d'abord en Angleterre, de la il est allé en Flandre, de Flandre en Allemagne, d'Allemagne en Hollande, de Hollande il est revenu en Angleterre, ou il est presentement, ne pouvant retourner en son pais; il n'a qu'un valet nommé Gaspard Girrard, flammand de nation. Je suis logé dans St. Alban's Street au coin.—Sr. Evremond."—[*State Papers, Domestic, various*, No. 694.] Ste. Evremond was not a Protestant, nor would he be a Catholic. Indeed, he seems to have been indifferent to religion. His letters are among the most brilliant specimens of that style of composition in which the French so much excel; but his other works are almost forgotten. Des Maiseaux, another refugee, published them in three vols. quarto in 1705, afterward translating the whole into English.

EYNARD, a refugee family of Dauphiny. Anthony entered the British army, and served with distinction, dying in 1739. His brother Simon began business in London, and acquired a considerable fortune by his industry. A sister, Louise, married the refugee Gideon Ageron, who also settled in England.

FARGUES, JACQUES DE, a wealthy apothecary, belonging to one of the best families of Montpellier. In 1569 his house was pillaged by the populace, while he himself was condemned to death because of his religion, and hanged. His family fled to England, where their descendants still exist.

FLEURY, LOUIS, Protestant pastor of Tours, who fled into England in 1683. His son, Philip Amauret, went over to Ireland as a Protestant minister, and settled there. His son, grandson of the refugee, became vicarchoral of Lismore; and the greatgrandson of the refugee, George Lewis Fleury, became archdeacon of Waterford.

FONNEREAU. Three members of this family, descended from a Huguenot refugee—Zachary Philip, Thomas, and Martin—sat in Parliament successively for Aldborough in 1768, 1773, and 1774.

FONTAINE, JAMES, M.A. and J. P. For notice of, see p. 291.

FORET, MARQUIS DE LA, a major general in the British army, who served in the Irish campaign of 1699.

FORRESTIER, or FORRESTER. There were several refugees of this name in England. Peter Forrester was minister of the French church, La Nouvelle Patente, in 1708. Paul was minister of the French church at Canterbury; and another was minister of that at Dartmouth. Alexander was a director of the French Hospital in 1735; and James was a captain in the British army.

FOURDRINIER, HENRY, the inventor of the paper-making machine. He was descended from one of the numerous industrial families of the north of France who fled into Holland at the Revocation. From Holland, Fourdrinier's father passed into England about the middle of the eighteenth century, and established a paper manufactory. The first idea of the paper-making machine belonged to France, but Fourdrinier fully developed it, and embodied it in a working plan. He labored at his invention for seven years, during which he was assisted by his brother Sealy and John Gamble. It was perfected in 1809.

GAGNIER, JOHN, a celebrated Orientalist scholar, who, becoming converted to Protestantism, fled from France into England. The Bishop of Worcester appointed him his chaplain. In 1715 he was appointed Professor of Oriental Languages at Oxford. His son took the degree of M. A., and was appointed rector of Stranton in the diocese of Durham. Durham

GALWAY, EARL OF. See p. 217, 301.

GAMBIER, a French refugee family settled at Canterbury, the name very frequently occurring in the registers of the French church there. James Gambier, born 1692, became distinguished as a barrister: he was a director of the French Hospital in 1729. He had two sons, James and John. The former rose to be a vice-admiral, the second became governor of the Bahama Islands, where his son James, afterward Lord Gambier, was born, 1756. He early entered the royal navy, and rose successively to the ranks of post-captain, vice-admiral, and admiral. He was created a peer for his services in 1807. His elder brother Samuel was a commissioner of the navy; and other members of the family held high rank in the same service.

GARENCIERES, THEOPHILUS DE, a doctor of medicine, native of Caen, who came over to England as physician to the French embassador, and embraced Protestantism. He was the author of several medical works.

GARRET, MARK, afterward called Gerrard, the portrait painter, a refugee from Bruges in Flanders, from whence he was driven over into England by the religious persecutions in the Low Countries. He was king's painter in 1618.

GARRIGUE, see *Bouffard*.

GASTIGNY, founder of the French Hospital in London. For notice, see p. 280.

GAUSSEN: there were several branches of this distinguished Protestant family in France. Haag mentions those of Saumur, Burgundy, Guienne, and Languedoc. David Gaussen, who took refuge in Ireland in 1685, belonged to the Guienne branch. His descendants still flourish at Antrim, Belfast, and Dublin. The Gaussens who settled in England were from Languedoc. John Gaussen fled to Geneva at the Revocation. Of his sons, Peter and Francis came to England, where we find the former a director of the French Hospital in 1741, treasurer in 1745, and sub-governor in 1756. A nephew of these two brothers, named Peter, joined them in 1739, in his sixteenth year. He rose to eminence as a merchant; became governor of the Bank of England, and a director of the East India Company. By his marriage with Miss Bosanquet he had a family of sons and daughters, among whom may be mentioned Samuel-Robert, colonel in the army, high sheriff of Hertford, and member of Parliament. Like other members of his family, he also held the office of director of the French Hospital. The Gaussens are still honorably known in London life.

GAUTIER, N., a physician of Niort, who took refuge in England at the Revocation. He was the author of several religious books.

GENESTE, LOUIS, the owner of a large estate in Guienne, which he forfeited by adhering to the Protestant religion. He first fled into Holland and took service under the Prince of Orange, whom he accompanied into England and Ireland, and fought in the battle of the Boyne in the regiment of Lord Lifford. After the pacification of Ireland, Geneste settled at Lisburn, and left behind him two sons and a daughter, among whose descendants may be particularized the names of Hugh Stowell and Geneste, well known in the Christian world.

GEORGES, PAUL. Two refugees of this name were ministers of the French church at Canterbury. One of them, from Chartres, was minister in 1630. The other a native of Picardy, died in 1689, after a ministry of 42 years.

GERVAISE, LOUIS, a large hosiery merchant at Paris, an elder of the Protestant church there. At the Revocation of the Edict, though seventy years of age, he was incarcerated in the Abbey of Gannat, from which he was transferred to that of Saint Magloire, then to the Oratory, and after that to the convent of Lagny and the castle of Angoulême. All methods of converting him having failed, he was finally banished from France in 1688, when he took refuge in London with his brother and his son, who had succeeded in escaping before him.

GIBERT, ETIENNE, one of the last refugees from France for conscience' sake. He labored for some time as a pastor of the "Church in the Desert;" but the Bishop of Saintes having planned his capture, he fled into Switzerland. Afterward, in 1763, we find him attending a secret synod in France as deputy of Saintonge; but at length, in 1771, he fled into England. He was minister of the French church of La Patente in London in 1776, and afterward of the Royal Chapel of St. James. He was finally presented with the rectory of St. Andrew's in the island of Guernsey, where he died in 1817.

GOSSET, a Huguenot family who took refuge in Jersey, and afterward in London. Isaac Gosset invented a composition of wax, in which he modeled portraits in an exquisite manner. His son, the Rev. Isaac Gosset, D.D., F.R.S., was eminent as a preacher, biblical critic, and book-collector. He died in 1812.

GOULARD, JAMES, MARQUIS OF VERVANS, a Huguenot refugee in England, who died there in 1700. The marchioness, his wife, was apprehended when about to set out to join her husband. She was shut up in the convent of the Ursulines at Angoulême, from which she was successively transferred to the Abbey of Puyberlan in Poitou, to the Abbey of the Trinity at Poitiers, and finally to Port-Royal. Her courage at length succumbed and she conformed, thereby securing possession of the estates of her husband.

GOYER, PETER, a refugee manufacturer from Picardy, who settled at Lisburn in Ireland. For notice of him, see p. 289.

GRAVEROL, JOHN, born at Nismes, 1647, of a famous Protestant family. He early entered the ministry, and became pastor of a church at Lyons. He fled from France at the Revocation, and took refuge in London. He was pastor of the French churches in Swallow Street and the Quarré. Graverol was a voluminous author.

GROSTÊTE, CLAUDE, a refugee pastor in London, minister of the French church in the Savoy.

GROTE or DE GROOT. For notice of family, see p. 310.

GUALY, a Protestant family of Rouergue. Peter, son of the Sieur de la Gineste, fled into England at the Revocation, with his wife and three children—Paul, Francis, and Margaret. Paul entered the English army, and died a major general. Francis also entered the army, and eventually settled at Dublin, where his descendants survive.

GUERIN, a French refugee family long settled at Rye, now represented by the Crofts.

GUIDE, PHILIP, a French physician of Paris, a native of Châlons-sur-Saône, who took refuge in London at the Revocation. He was the author of several medical works.

GUILLEMARD, JOHN, a refugee in London from Champdeniers, where he had been minister. His descendants have been directors of the French Hospital at different times.

GUILLOT. Several members of this family were officers in the navy of Louis XIV. They emigrated to Holland at the Revocation, and were presented by the Prince of Orange with commissions in his navy. Their descendants settled in Lisburn in Ireland. Others of the same name —Guillot and Gillett—of like French extraction, settled in England, where their descendants are still to be found at Birmingham and Sheffield, as well as at Glastonbury, Exeter, and Banbury.

GUYON DE GEIS, WILLIAM DE, son of the Sieur de Pampelona, a Protestant, fled into Holland at the Revocation. He took service under William of Orange, and saw much service in the campaigns in Piedmont and Germany, where he lost an arm. William III. gave him a retiring pension, when he settled at Portarlington, and died there in 1740. Several of his descendants have been officers in the English army. The last, Count Guyon, entered the Austrian service, and distinguished himself in the Hungarian rebellion of 1848.

HARENC, a refugee family from the south of France. Benjamin was a director of the French Hospital in 1765. He bought the estate of Footscray, Kent; his son married the daughter of Joseph Berens, Esq., and was a prominent county magistrate in Kent.

HAZARD or HASAERT, PETER, a refugee in England from the persecutions in the Low Countries under the Duchess of Parma. Returning on a visit to his native land, he was seized and burned alive in 1568. His descendants still survive in England and Ireland under the name of Hassard.

HERAULT, LOUIS, a refugee pastor from Normandy, who obtained a benefice in the English Church in the reign of Charles I. But he was so zealous a Royalist that he was forced to fly again into France, from which, however, he returned at the Restoration, and obtained a canonry at Canterbury, which he enjoyed until his death.

HERVART, PHILIBERT, BARON DE HUNINGUE, a refugee of high character and station. In 1690 William III. appointed him his embassador at Geneva. He afterward settled at Southampton. He became governor of the French Hospital in 1720, to which he gave a sum of £4000, dying in the following year.

HIPPOLITE, STE., see *Montolieu.*

HOUBLON, PETER, a refugee from Flanders because of his religion, who settled in England about the year 1568. His son John became an eminent merchant in London, his grandson James being the father of the Royal Exchange. Two sons of the latter, Sir James and Sir John, were aldermen of London; while the former represented the city in Parliament in 1698, the latter served it as lord-mayor in 1695. Sir John was the first governor of the Bank of England; he was also a commissioner of the Admiralty. Another brother, Abraham, was also a director and governor of the bank. His son, Sir Richard, left an only daughter, who married Henry Temple, created Lord Palmerston in 1722, from whom the late Lord Palmerston was lineally descended.

HUDEL or UDEL, pastor of "Les Grecs" French church, London, the eldest son of a zealous Huguenot, confined in prison for a quarter of a century, and who was only released at the death of Louis XIV.

HUGESSEN, JAMES, a refugee from Dunkirk, who settled at Dover. The family is now represented by E. Knatchbull Hugessen, M.P. For notice, see p. 309.

JANSEN, THEODORE, youngest son of the Baron de Heez. The latter was a victim to the cruelty of the Duke of Alva in the Netherlands, and suffered death at the hands of the public executioner. Theodore took refuge in France, from whence the family fled into England. His grandson, also named Theodore, was knighted by William III., and created a baronet by Queen Anne. The family were highly distinguished as merchants and bankers in London. Three of Sir Theodore's sons were baronets, two were members of Parliament, and one, Sir Stephen Theodore, was lord-mayor of London in 1755.

JUSTEL, HENRY, a great Protestant scholar, formerly secretary to Louis XIV., but a fugitive at the Revocation. On his arrival in England in 1684, the king appointed him royal librarian. He was the author of numerous works.

JORTIN, RENE, a refugee from Brittany. For notice of the family, see p. 320.

LABOUCHERE. For notice of, see p. 315.

LA CONDAMINE, an ancient and noble family belonging to the neighborhood of Nismes. André, the elder, was a Protestant, and held to his religion; Charles-Antoine abjured, and obtained possession of the family estate. André fled with his family, traveling by night only — the two youngest children swung in baskets across a horse or mule. They succeeded in reaching the port of St. Malo, and crossed to Guernsey. The boy who escaped in the basket founded a family of British subjects. His son John became king's comptroller of Guernsey, and colonel of the Guernsey militia; and his descendants still survive in England and Scotland.

LALO, of the house of De La in Dauphiny, a brigadier in the British army, killed at the battle of Malplaquet.

LA MELONNIÉRE, ISAAC DE MONCEAU, SIEUR DE, a lieutenant colonel in the French army, who fled from France at the Revocation, and joined the army of the Prince of Orange. He raised the regiment called after him "La Melonniére's Foot." He served throughout the campaigns in Ireland and Flanders, and was raised to the rank of major general. Several of his descendants have been distinguished officers in the British army.

LA MOTTE, FRANCIS, a refugee from Ypres, in Flanders, who settled at Colchester as a manufacturer of bays and sayes. His son John became an eminent and wealthy merchant of London, of which he was an alderman.

L'ANGLE, DE. For notice of, see p. 245.

LA PIERRE, a Huguenot family of Lyons. Marc-Conrad was a magistrate, and councilor to the Parliament at Grenoble—a man highly esteemed for his learning and integrity. He left France at the Revocation, and settled in England. One of his sons was the minister of Spring Gardens French church in 1724; and Pierre de la Pierre was a director of the French Hospital in 1740.

LA PILONNIERE, a Jesuit converted to Protestantism, who took refuge in England about 1716. He was the author of several works relating to his conversion, and also on English history.

LA PRIMAUDAYE, a great Protestant family of Anjou. Several of them took refuge in England. In 1740 Pierre de la Primaudaye was a governor of the French Hospital, and others of the same name afterward held that office.

LA ROCHE, a refugee from Bordeaux, originally named Crothaire, whose son became M. P. for Bodmin in 1727. His grandson, Sir James Laroche, Bart., also sat for the same borough in 1768.

LAROCHEFOUCALD (FREDERICK CHARLES DE), Count de Roye, an able officer of Louis XIV., field-marshal under Turenne, who served in the great campaigns between 1672 and 1683. He left France at the Revocation, first entering the Danish service, in which he held the post of grand marshal. He afterward settled in England. He died at Bath in 1690. His son Frederick-William was a colonel of one of the six French regiments sent to Portugal under Schomberg. He was promoted to the rank of major general, and was raised to the peerage (for life) under the title of Earl of Lifford, in Ireland.

LAROUCHEFOUCALD, FRANCIS DE, son of the Baron de Montendre. He escaped from the abbey of the Canons of Saint Victor, where he had been shut up for "conversion," and fled to England. He entered the English army, served in Ireland, where he was master general of artillery, and rose to the rank of field marshal.

LA ROCHE-GUILHEM, MELLE DE, a voluminous writer of romances

of the Scuderi school, and a Protestant, who first took refuge in Holland, and afterward settled in England about 1697, though his works continued to be published abroad, mostly in Amsterdam.

LARPENT, JOHN DE, a refugee from Caen, in Normandy, who fled into England at the Revocation. His son and grandson were employed in the Foreign Office. The two sons of the latter were F. S. Larpent, judge advocate general in Spain under the Duke of Wellington, and Sir George Gerard de Hochepied Larpent, Bart.

LA TOMBE, THOMAS, a Protestant refugee from Turcoigne, in the Low Countries, who settled at Norwich about 1558. His son, of the same name, was a thriving merchant in London in 1634.

LA TOUCHE, a noble Protestant family of the Blesois, between Blois and Orleans, where they possessed considerable estates. At the Revocation, David Digues de la Touche fled into Holland, and joined the army of the Prince of Orange. He served in the Irish campaigns, afterward settling in Dublin, where he founded the well-known bank which still exists. His sons David and James founded good families in Ireland. From them are descended the families of La Touche, of Marlay, of Harristown, of Sans-Souci, and of Bellevue. Many members of the family have sat in Parliament, and have intermarried with the nobility. N. Latouche, a refugee in London, was the author of an excellent French grammar.

LA TRANCHE, FRÉDÉRICK DE, a Huguenot gentleman, who took refuge in England shortly after the massacre of St. Bartholomew. He first settled in Northumberland, from whence the family afterward removed to Ireland, and founded the French family, the head of which is the Earl of Clancarty. Many high dignitaries of the Church, and officers in the army and civil service, have belonged to this family. The present Archbishop of Dublin is a Trench as well as a Chenevix (which see), thus being doubly a Huguenot by his descent. The Power-Keatings are a branch of the Trench family. The Earl of Ashtoun is the head of another branch.

LA TREMOUILLE, CHARLOTTE DE, wife of James Stanley, Earl of Derby. The countess was a Protestant—the daughter of Claude de la Tremouille and his wife the Princess of Orange. Sir Walter Scott incorrectly makes the countess to have been a Roman Catholic.

LAVAL, ETIENNE-ABEL, author of a *History of the Reformation and of the Reformed Churches of France*, and minister of the French church in Castle Street, London, about the year 1730.

LA VALLADE, pastor of the French church at Lisburn, in Ireland, during forty years. He left an only daughter, who married, in 1737, George Russell, Esq., of Lisburn, whose descendants survive.

LAYARD, originally LAJARD, a refugee family from Montpellier. Antoine de Lajard was controller general of the king's farms, and at his death in 1681, his family, being Protestants, fled from France into England. Pierre Layard became a major in the English army. His son Daniel-Peter was a celebrated doctor, and held the appointment of physician to the Dowager Princess of Wales. He was the author of numerous works on medicine; among others, of a treatise on the cattle distemper, which originally appeared in the *Philosophical Transactions*, and has since been frequently reprinted. The doctor had three sons —Charles-Peter, afterward prebendary of Worcester and dean of Bristol; Anthony-Lewis and John-Thomas, who both entered the army, and rose, the one to the rank of general, and the other to that of lieutenant general. Austin Layard, M. P., so well known for his exploration of the ruins of Nineveh, is grandson of the above dean of Bristol. Two cousins are in the Church. The head of the family is Brownlow Villiers Layard, Esq., of Riversdale, near Dublin.

LE COURRAYER, PIERRE-

FRANÇOIS, a canon of St. Geneviève, at Paris, afterward canon of Oxford. He was a very learned man, and a voluminous author. Having maintained as a Roman Catholic the validity of ordination by the bishops of the Anglican Church because of their unbroken succession from the apostles, he was denounced by his own Church as a heretic, and excommunicated. In 1728 Le Courrayer took refuge in England, and was cordially welcomed by Wake, then Archbishop of Canterbury. The University of Oxford conferred on him the degree of D.D. Although he officiated as canon of Oxford, he avowed to the last that he had not changed his religion; and that it was the Roman Catholic Church, and not he, that was in fault, in having departed from the doctrines and practices of the early Church. Le Courrayer died in London in 1776.

LE FANU, a Norman Protestant family. Etienne le Fanu, of Caen, having, in 1657, married a lady who professed the Roman Catholic religion, her relatives claimed to have her children brought up in the same religion. Le Fanu nevertheless had three of them baptized by Protestant ministers. The fourth was seized and baptized by the Roman Catholic vicar. At the mother's death the maternal uncle of the children claimed to bring them up, and to set aside their father, because of his being a Protestant, and the magistrates of Caen ordered Le Fanu to give up the children accordingly. He appealed to the Parliament of Rouen in 1671, and they confirmed the decision of the magistrates. Le Fanu refused to give up his children, and was consequently cast into prison, where he lay for three years. He eventually succeeded in making his escape into England, and finally settled in Ireland, where his descendants still survive.

LE FEVRE. Many refugees of this name settled in England. The Lefevres of Anjou were celebrated as chemists and physicians. Nicholas, physician to Louis XIV., and demonstrator of chemistry at the Jardin des Plantes, was invited over to England by Charles II., and made physician and chemist to the king in 1660. Sebastian Lefevre, M.D., of Anjou, was admitted licentiate of the London College of Physicians in 1684. A branch of the family settled in Spitalfields, where they long carried on the silk manufacture. From this branch the present Lord Eversley is descended. For farther notice, see p. 315.

LEFROY, ANTHONY, a native of Cambray, who took refuge in England from the persecutions in the Low Countries about the year 1579, and settled at Canterbury, where his descendants followed the business of silk-dying for about 150 years, until the trade was removed to Spitalfields. A descendant of the family, also called Anthony, was a merchant of Leghorn, and died in 1779. From him the Irish family of the name is descended. This Anthony was a great antiquary, his collection of 6600 coins being one of the finest ever made by a private person. He was an intimate friend of Thomas Hollis, and is frequently mentioned in his memoirs. Colonel Anthony Lefroy, of Limerick, represented the family during the latter half of last century. His son, the Right Hon. Thomas Lefroy, chief justice of Ireland, recently retired from the bench. Anthony Lefroy, M. P., and Brigade General Lefroy, R. A., are members of the same family.

LE GOULON, a pupil of Vauban, and a refugee at the Revocation; general of artillery in the army of William III. He served with distinction in Ireland, Germany, and Italy, dying abroad.

LE MOINE, ABRAHAM, son of a refugee from Caen. He was chaplain to the Duke of Portland and rector of Eversley, Wilts, the author of numerous works. He died in 1760.

L'ESCURY, see *Collot.*

LESTANG, a Protestant family of Poitou, one of whom acted as aid-de-camp to the Prince of Orange on his invasion of England. Another, Louis de Lestang, settled at Canterbury with his family.

LE SUEUR, the refugee sculptor who executed the fine bronze equestrian statue of Charles I. at Charing Cross. Another work of his, still preserved, is the bronze statue of the Earl of Pembroke in the picture-gallery at Oxford. The statue of Charles was sold by the Parliament for old metal, when it was purchased by Jean Rivet, supposed to be another refugee, and preserved by him until after the Restoration. A refugee (named Le Sueur) was minister of the French church at Canterbury.

LE THIEULLIER, JOHN, a Protestant refugee from Valenciennes. His grandson was a celebrated London merchant, knighted in 1687.

LE VASSOR, MICHAEL, a refugee from Orleans, who entered the English Church, and held a benefice in the county of Northampton, where he died. He was the author of several works, among others of a *History of Louis XIII.*, which gave great offense to Louis XIV.

LIGONIER, a Protestant family of Castres. Jean Louis was a celebrated general in the English service; he was created Lord Ligonier, Baron Inniskillen. During his life he was engaged in nineteen pitched battles and twenty-three sieges, without ever having received a wound. One of his brothers, Antoine, was a major in the English army; and another, who was raised to the rank of brigadier, was mortally wounded at the battle of Falkirk. For farther notice of Lord Ligonier, see p. 228.

LOGIER, JEAN-BERNARD, a refugee musician, inventor of the method of musical notation which bears his name; settled as a teacher of music at Dublin, where he died.

LOMBART, PIERRE, a celebrated French engraver, who took refuge in England in the reign of Charles I., and remained there until the early period of the Restoration. During that time he produced a large number of highly-esteemed engravings. He died at Paris, and was interred in the Protestant cemetery at Charenton a few years before the Revocation.

LUARD, ROBERT ABRAHAM, a Huguenot refugee from Caen, who settled in London. His son, Peter-Abraham, became a great Hamburg merchant. George Augustus Luard, Esq., of Blyborough Hall, is the present head of the family, to which Major Luard, of the Mote, Tunbridge, also belongs.

MAITTAIRE, MICHAEL, a celebrated philologist, linguist, and bibliographer, one of the masters of Westminster School at the beginning of the eighteenth century. He was an able writer, principally on classical and religious subjects. Haag gives a list of sixteen of his works.

MAJENDIE: several refugees from Bearn of this name fled into England at the Revocation. One of them became pastor of the French church at Exeter. His son Jean-Jacques Majendie, D.D., was pastor of the French church in St. Martin's Lane, and afterward of the Savoy. The son of this last became Bishop of Bangor, and afterward of Chester.

MANGIN: several refugees of this name from Metz settled in Ireland. Paul became established at Lisburn, where he married Madeleine, the daughter of Louis Crommelin.

MARCET, a refugee family from Meaux, originally settled at Geneva, from whence Alexander came over to London about the end of last century, and settled as a physician. He was one of the founders of the Medico-Chirurgical Society, physician to Guy's Hospital, and the author of many valuable works on medicine and chemistry. Mrs. Marcet was also the author of many esteemed works on political economy and natural history.

MARIE, JEAN, minister of the Protestant church at Lion-sur-Mer, who took refuge in England after the massacre of St. Bartholomew, and became pastor of the French church at Norwich. His son Nathaniel was minister of the French church in London.

MARION, ELIÉ, a refugee from the Cevennes. He joined his friend Cavalier in England. Francis Marion, the celebrated general in the

American War of Independence, is said to have been one of his descendants.

MARTINEAU, GASTON, a surgeon of Dieppe, who fled into England at the Revocation, and settled at Norwich. His son David was also a skillful surgeon. Many of their descendants still exist, and some of them are highly distinguished in modern English literature.

MASERES, FRANCIS, a celebrated judge and mathematician. At the Revocation, the grandfather of Maseres escaped into Holland, took service in the army of William of Orange, and came over to England in the regiment of Schomberg, in which he served as a lieutenant. He was afterward employed in Portugal, where he rose to the rank of colonel. His son studied medicine at Cambridge, took his degree of doctor, and practiced in London. Francis Maseres, the grandson of the refugee, also studied at Cambridge; and after distinguishing himself in the mathematics, he embraced the profession of the law. Besides his eminence as a judge, he was an able and industrious author. Haag gives the titles of fifteen books published by him on different subjects. For farther notice, see p. 323.

MASSUE, HENRI DE, Marquis de Ruvigny. For notice of, see p. 208, 314 (note); and of his son Henry, Earl of Galway, p. 217, 301.

MATHY, MATTHEW, a celebrated physician and author. After a residence in Holland, he settled in England about the middle of last century. He was admitted a fellow of the Royal Society, of which he was appointed secretary in 1758. He was afterward appointed librarian of the British Museum, in which office he was succeeded by his son.

MATURIN, GABRIEL, a refugee pastor who escaped from France after having been shut up in the Bastile for twenty-six years. He settled in Ireland, where he arrived a cripple. His son Peter became dean of Killala, and his grandson dean of Saint Patrick's, Dublin. From him descended the Rev. C. Maturin, senior fellow, Trinity College, Dublin, rector of Fanet; the Rev. C. R. Maturin, an eloquent preacher, author of *Bertram;* and Gabriel Maturin, Esq., Washington.

MAUDUIT, ISAAC, descended from a Norman refugee settled at Exeter as a merchant. Isaac was a dissenting minister at Bermondsey. He was the father of Jasper Mauduit, Esq., of Hackney.

MAURY, MATTHEW, a refugee gentleman from Castle Mauron, in Gascony, settled in London for a time, where his son James was ordained a minister. The family afterward emigrated to Virginia, U. S., where their descendants survive. Captain Maury, LL.D., belongs to the family.

MAYERNE, THEODORE DE, a celebrated physician, belonging to a Lyons family, originally from Piedmont. He studied medicine at Heidelberg and Montpellier, where he took his degree of M.D. in 1595. He opened a medical school at Paris, in which he delivered lectures, and obtained an extensive practice. Henry IV. appointed him his first physician. After the assassination of that prince, Marie de Medicis endeavored to convert Mayerne from Protestantism; but he was firm, and consequently lost the patronage of the court. James I. invited him over to England, and appointed him his first physician. The Universities of Oxford and Cambridge conferred honorary degrees upon him, and he obtained a large practice in London. After the execution of Charles I. he retired into private life, and died at Chelsea in 1655.

MAZIERES, DE, a Protestant family of Aunis, north of Saintonge, several members of whom fled from France at the Revocation. Peter was a lieutenant in the French army, and afterward joined the army of William of Orange. He settled at Youghal, in Ireland, where he died in 1746. Other members of the family settled at Cork, where they left numerous descendants.

MERCIER, PHILIP, a portrait painter, born at Berlin, of a French refugee family, and afterward settled in London, where he died in 1760. He was patronized by Frederick, Prince of Wales. Many of his portraits were engraved by Simon, Faber, Avril, and Heudelot (refugee engravers in London), as well as by English artists.

MESNARD, JEAN, one of the pastors of the Protestant church of Charenton, at Paris, from which he fled into Holland at the Revocation. His brother Philip, pastor of the Church of Saintes, was fined 10,000 livres and condemned to perpetual banishment; his church was demolished and a cross set up on its site. Mesnard was invited to Copenhagen by the queen, Charlotte Amelia, and appointed pastor of the French church there. He afterward came over to England, and became minister of the Chapel Royal of St. James in 1700. He was appointed a director of the French Hospital in 1718; he died in 1727.

METTAYER, JOHN, minister of the Patente in Soho; afterward minister of the French church at Thorpe-le-Soken, where he died in 1707.

MEUSNIER, PHILIP, a refugee painter of architectural subjects, who studied under Nicholas de Larquillière, another refugee artist.

MISSON, MAXIMILIEN, one of the Protestant judges in the "Chamber of the Edict" in the Parliament of Paris. At the Revocation he fled into England, and was selected by the Duke of Ormond as tutor to his grandson. Misson traveled with him through Europe, and afterward published several books of travels.

MISSY, CÆSAR DE, son of a refugee merchant from Saintonge established at Berlin, who studied for the ministry, and came over to England in 1731, when he was appointed minister of the French church of the Savoy, in London, and afterward of St. James's. He was the author of many highly-prized works.

MOIVRE, ABRAHAM. For notice of, see p. 235.

MOLENIER, STEPHEN, a refugee pastor from the Isle of Jourdain, who fled into England, and became minister of the French church at Stonehouse, Plymouth.

MONCEAU, ISAAC DE, see La Melonniére.

MONTENDRE, DE, see Larochefoucauld.

MONTOLIEU, DE SAINT HIPPOLITE. Of this noble family, David came to England with the army of William III., under whom he also served in Flanders. He was made a colonel and afterward a brigadier general. His descendants still survive in several noble and gentle families.

MOTHE, CLAUDE DE LA, refugee minister of the church in the Savoy. For notice of, see p. 248.

MOTTEAUX, PETER ANTHONY, poet and translator, a refugee from Rouen, who fled into England, and settled in London in 1660. He first translated and published Don Quixote and Rabelais into English, which were received with great favor. He also published several volumes of poetry and a tragedy, "Beauty in Distress." Notwithstanding his success as an English author, he abandoned literature for commerce, and made a considerable fortune by a series of happy speculations. He died in 1717.

NADAULD, a Huguenot family who settled at Ashford-in-the-Water, in Derbyshire, shortly after the Revocation. The grandson of the original refugee was the Rev. Thomas Nadauld, for upward of fifty years incumbent of Belper and Turnditch. One of the members of the family was a celebrated watch-maker and silversmith. Another was a sculptor, who was employed by the Duke of Devonshire to execute some of the most important works at Chatsworth Palace. Others were clergymen, surgeons, and officers in the British army.

OUVRY, JAMES, a refugee from the neighborhood of Dieppe about the period of the Revocation. His family became settled in Spitalfields, and were owners of freeholds there in the early part of last century. Francis Ouvry, treasurer of the Society of Antiquaries, belongs to the family; also

Francisca I. Ouvry, author of *Henri de Rohan, or the Huguenot Refugee,* and other works.

PAGET, VALERIAN, a refugee from France after the massacre of St. Bartholomew, who settled in Leicestershire and founded a flourishing family, the head of which is Thomas Paget, Esquire, of Humberstown. Charles, lately M. P. for Nottingham, belongs to the family.

PAPILLON, DAVID, a refugee from Avranches, where he was imprisoned for three years because of his religion. He afterward fled into England, where his family prospered. Different members of them have since represented the city of London, Dover, Romney, and Colchester in Parliament. The present head of the family is David Papillon, Esquire, of Crowhurst, Sussex.

PAPIN, DENIS. For notice of, see p. 232.

PAUL, LEWIS, inventor of spinning by rollers. For notice of, see p. 327.

PECHELL, SAMUEL, a refugee from Montauban, in Languedoc, who settled in Dublin. From him have descended Samuel Pechell, Master in Chancery, and Lieutenant Colonel Paul Pechell, of Pagglesham, Essex, created a baronet in 1797. Two other descendants of the family have been rear-admirals, and occupied seats in the House of Commons.

PERRIN, COUNT, a Huguenot refugee from Nouere, where he had large possessions. He originally settled at Lisburn, in Ireland, from which he afterward removed to Waterford, and founded the family to which Justice Perrin, of the Irish Bench, belonged.

PETIT, LE SIEUR, an officer in the Red Dragoons of the Prince of Orange on his expedition to England. Many descendants of the family have served in the British army, and held offices in Church and State.

PINETON, REV. JAMES, DE CHAMBRUN. For notice of, see p. 243.

PORTAL, an ancient noble Protestant family of Toulouse. For notice of the refugees of the name in England, see p. 265.

PRELLEUR, PETER, a musical composer, born in London of a French refugee family. He began life as a writing-master in Spitalfields, after which he applied himself exclusively to music. He composed a number of pieces for the theatre in Goodman's Fields, in which David Garrick, or Garrigue, the son of another French refugee, made his first appearance as an actor. Prelleur also held the office of organist of the church of St. Alban's, and afterward of Christ Church, Middlesex.

PRIMROSE, GILBERT, of Scotch origin, who settled in France in 1601 as minister of the Protestant church of Mirambeau, and afterward of Bourdeaux. In 1623 Louis XIII. ordered his banishment from France, when he proceeded to London, and became minister of the French church in Threadneedle Street; after which we find him appointed chaplain to the king, next Canon of Windsor, and eventually Bishop of Ely. His two sons, David and James, were remarkable men in their time, the one as a theologian, the other as a physician. Both were authors of numerous works.

PRYME, MATTHEW DE LA, a refugee from Ypres, in Flanders, during the persecutions of the Duke of Alva. He settled, with many others of his countrymen, in the Level of Hatfield Chace, after the same had been drained by Vermuyden. His son was the Rev. Abraham de la Pryme. George Pryme, Esq., late M. P., and professor of political economy at Cambridge, is lineally descended from the above.

PUISSAR, LOUIS JAMES, Marquis of, was appointed colonel of the 24th regiment in 1695, and afterward served in Flanders.

PUSEY, see *Bouveries.*

RABOTEAU, JOHN CHARLES, a refugee from Pont-Gibaud, near Rochelle, who settled in Dublin, and prospered as a wine-merchant. For notice of his nieces, the Misses Raboteau, see p. 166.

RADNOR, EARL OF, see *Bouveries.*

RAPIN DE THOYRAS, PAUL. For notice of, see p. 227.

RAVANEL, SAMUEL DE, son of a Protestant gentleman of Picardy who came into England before the Revocation. He afterward married the niece of Marlborough. Hozier supposes that Edward Ravenel, director of the French Hospital in 1740, was his son.

REBOW : a refugee of this name from Flanders, settled at Colchester, from whom Sir Isaac Rebow, knighted by King William (whom he entertained), was descended. Several members of the family have since represented the town in Parliament.

RIVAL, PETER, pastor of several of the French churches in London, and lastly of that of the Savoy. He was a copious author and a vehement controversialist. He died about 1728.

ROBETHON, the Right Hon. JOHN, a French refugee in London. His brother remained in Paris, and was attorney general of the Mint in 1722. William III. made John Robethon his private secretary. He was afterward made secretary to the embassies and privy councilor. In 1721 he was elected governor of the French Hospital. He died in the following year.

ROCHE, LOUIS, a refugee manufacturer who settled at Lisburn at the same time that Louis Crommelin established himself there. He became an extensive merchant; and his descendants are now among the first inhabitants of Belfast.

ROCHEBLAVE, HENRY DE, pastor in succession of the French churches at Greenwich, Swallow Street, Hungerford, the Quarré, St. James's, and, last of all, of Dublin, where he died in 1709.

ROMAINE, a Huguenot refugee who settled at Hartlepool as a corn-dealer; father of the celebrated Rev. W. Romaine, author of the *Triumph of Faith*, for notice of whom, see p. 322.

ROMILLY. For notice of this family, see p. 315, 335.

ROUBILLARD, see *Champagné*.

ROUBILLIAC, LOUIS - FRANCIS, the sculptor; born at Lyons about 1695. Haag says he was probably the son of a "new convert," and that he only returned to the religion of his fathers. His works in England are well known. He was buried in the French church of St. Martin's-le-Grand in 1762.

ROUMIEU, a Huguenot refugee in England, descended from Roumieu, the Albigensian hero. The present representative of the family is Robert-Lewis Roumieu, the celebrated architect.

ROUQUET, JAMES, son of a French Protestant condemned to the galleys for life. The young man reached London, and was educated at Merchant Tailors' school. He entered the Church, but became a follower of Wesley, and superintended Wesley's school at Kingswood. He eventually accepted the curacy of St. Werburgh, Bristol, where he labored with great zeal in reclaiming outcasts, and died in 1776.

ROUQUET, N., a painter in enamel, belonging to a French refugee family of Geneva, who spent the greater part of his life in England. He was an author as well as an artist, and wrote an account of *The State of Art in England*, which was published at Paris in 1755.

ROUSSEAU, JAMES, an excellent landscape painter, mostly in fresco, son of a joiner at Paris, where he was born in 1630. He studied art in Italy, and on his return to France his reputation became great. He was employed in decorating the palaces at Versailles and Marley, and in other important works. In 1662 he was admitted a member of the Royal Academy of Painting, and was afterward elected a member of the council. But in 1661, when the persecution of the Protestants set in with increased severity, Rousseau was excluded from the Academy because of his being a Huguenot. At the same time, eight other Protestant artists were expelled. At the Revocation of the Edict, Rousseau first took refuge in Switzerland, from whence he proceeded to Holland, and afterward to England, where he settled. The Duke of Montague employed him to execute the decorations of his town house, on the site of the present British Museum. It is also said that he superintended the erection of the building. He executed other fresco-paintings on the walls of Hampton Court, where they are still to be seen. Died in London in 1693.

ROUSSEAU, SAMUEL, an Orientalist scholar, the son of a French refugee settled in London. He was an extensive contributor to the *Gentleman's Magazine* on classical subjects, as well as the author of several works on the Persian and Hindostanee languages.

ROUSSELL, ISAAC, a French Protestant refugee from Quillebœuf, in Normandy, who fled into England in 1699. He settled in London, and became a silk manufacturer in Spitalfields. The present representative of the family is John Beuzeville Byles, Esq., of Henley-on-Thames.

ROYE, DE, see *Larochefoucauld.*

RUVIGNY, MARQUIS OF. For notice of, see p. 208 and 314 (*note*).

SAURIN, JACQUES. For notice of, as well as other members of the family, see p. 241, 320.

SAY, a French Protestant family of Languedoc, of whom several members settled in England. One of them, Samuel Say, who died in 1743, was a dissenting minister in London; another, Francis-Samuel, was minister of the French church in Wheeler Street. Thomas Say emigrated to America, and joined the Quakers; and his son was the celebrated natural historian of the United States. Jean Baptiste Say, the celebrated writer on political economy, belonged to the same family.

SCHOMBERG, DUKES OF. For notices of Frederick-Armand, 1st duke, see p. 189, 211, 216; Charles, 2d duke, p. 219; Ménard, 3d duke, p. 214-15, 221.

SIMON, a family of artists originally from Normandy, who belonged to the Protestant Church of Charenton, near Paris. John, a refugee in London, acquired great reputation as an engraver. He was employed by Sir Godfrey Kneller to engrave the portraits painted by him, a long list of which, as well as of his other works, is given by Haag. Simon died at London in 1755.

TASCHER: several refugees of this name were ministers of French churches in London at the beginning of the eighteenth century. Pierre de Tascher was a director of the French Hospital in 1727.

TEULON or THOLON, an ancient family of Nismes, descended from Marc Teulon, Sieur de Guirnal. Peter and Anthony fled from France at the time of the Revocation, and settled at Greenwich. Peter went into Ireland, and founded the Cork branch of the family, to which the late Colonel George Teulon, one of the aids-de-camp to the Duke of Wellington at Waterloo, Lieutenant Colonel Charles Teulon, and Major Peter Teulon, belonged. The present representatives of the family in Ireland are B. Teulon, Esq., of Bandon; Thomas, a major in the army; and Charles-Peter, a barrister. Anthony Teulon, of Greenwich, married Frances de la Roche, and left descendants. Among the present representatives of this branch may be named Samuel Saunders and William Milford Teulon, the eminent architects, and Seymour Teulon, Esq., of Limpsfield Park, Surrey. Another branch is settled in Scotland, represented by Captains James and John Teulon. Pierre Emile Teulon, of Nismes, president of the council under the government of Louis Philippe, is supposed to belong to a branch of the family remaining in France.

TEXTARD, LEON, SIEUR DES MESLARS, a refugee who feigned to abjure under the terror of the dragonnades, and at length fled to England with his wife, a sister of James Fontaine, whom no terror could shake. They settled in London, together with other members of the family.

TEXTAS: two ministers of this name, related to the family of Chamier, took refuge in England after the Revocation.

THELUSSON, originally a Protestant family of Lyons, who took refuge in Geneva. Peter Thelusson, son of John (an illustrious citizen of the Republic), settled in London in 1750, and acquired a large fortune by trade. He sat in Parliament some time for Malmesbury. His son, Peter-Isaac, was created Baron Rendlesham.

THORIUS, RAPHAEL, a physician and celebrated Latin poet, born in France, but a refugee in England because of his religion. He died in 1625, leaving behind him a son, John, who studied medicine at Oxford, and became fellow of the College of Physicians of Dublin in 1627. He was the author of several medical works.

TRENCH, see *La Tranche*.

TRYON, PETER, a wealthy refugee from Flanders, driven out by the persecutions of the Duke of Alva. He succeeded in bringing with him into England so large a sum as £60,000. The family made many alliances with English families of importance. Samuel, son of the original refugee, was in 1621 made a baronet of Layer Marney, in Essex. The baronetcy expired in 1724.

TURQUAND, PETER, a Protestant refugee from Châtelherault, near Poitiers, who settled in London, where his descendants still flourish.

TYSSEN, FRANCIS, a refugee from Ghent, in Flanders. His son, of the same name, became a thriving merchant of London. The family is at present represented by W. G. Tyssen Amhurst, of Foulden, in Norfolk, lord of the manor of Hackney.

VANACKER, JOHN, a refugee from Lille, in Flanders, who became a merchant in London. His grandson Nicholas, a Turkey merchant, was created a baronet in 1700.

VANDERPUTT, HENRY, born in Antwerp; fled to England from the religious persecution in the Low Countries in 1568, and became a London merchant. His great-grandson Peter, also a London merchant, was sheriff of London in 1684, and created a baronet in 1723.

VANLORE, PETER, a Protestant refugee from Utrecht. He became a celebrated London merchant, and was created a baronet in 1628.

VARENNES, JOHN DE, a French refugee, whose descendants remain in England. Ezekiel G. Varennes is a surgeon in Essex.

VERNEUIL, JOHN, a native of Bordeaux, from which city he fled, on account of his religion, to England. He was a learned man, and was appointed sub-librarian at Oxford, where he died in 1647.

VICOSE, GUY DE, Baron de la Court, a Protestant noble, who suffered frightful cruelties during the dragonnades. He took refuge in London, where we find him a director of the French Hospital in 1718, and governor in 1722.

VICTORIA, QUEEN. For notice of her Huguenot descent, see p. 313.

VIGNOLLES, a noble Protestant family in Languedoc. Charles de Vignolles was a military officer, who fled with his wife into Holland at the Revocation. He afterward accompanied the Prince of Orange into England, fought in the Irish campaigns, and settled at Portarlington. Many members of the family have distinguished themselves in the army, the Church, and the civil service. Dr. Vignolles, Dean of Ossory, and Charles Vignolles, F.R.S., the eminent engineer, are among the living representatives of two branches of the family.

VILETTES, SEBASTIAN DE, a country gentleman, lord of Montledier, near Castres. Like his ancestors, he was a Protestant, and suffered heavy persecutions at the Revocation. The family fled from France, and took refuge in foreign lands; some in England, and others in Germany. The names of the De Vilettes frequently occur in the list of directors of the French Hospital. Among others we observe those of Lieut. Gen. Henry Clinton de Vilettes in 1777, and of Major William de Vilettes in 1779.

VILLETTE, C. L. DE, minister of the French church in Dublin, and the author of numerous religious works.

VINCENT: numerous refugees of this name settled in England, though none were men of any particular mark.

WITTENRONG, JACOB, a Protestant refugee from Ghent, in Flanders, who earned his bread in London as a notary. His son became a brewer in London, and greatly prospered. He was knighted by Charles I. in 1640, and created a baronet, of Stantonbury, county Bucks, in 1662.

YVER, JOHN, a refugee pastor, who officiated as minister in several of the churches of the refuge in London. He afterward went into Holland, where he died.

THE HUGUENOTS IN AMERICA.

BY THE HON. G. P. DISOSWAY.

As the author of the "Huguenots, their Settlement, Churches, and Industries in England and Ireland," does not include in his plan any account of the emigration of the same persecuted people to America, it seems proper, especially for the benefit of the American reader, to append this chapter. The history of American Huguenots given in detail would fill a volume. In this connection we can only contribute a mite toward the illustration of this portion of our national history.

As early as the year 1555 the French Huguenots attempted to make a settlement in America at Brazil, and a few years afterward in Florida. Both attempts, however, failed, on account of the bitter hostility of the Spanish and Portuguese. Philip II., a proud and bigoted Romanist, was on the throne of Spain, and would not permit the heresy of Calvinism to be planted in his American provinces. Charles IX., too, son of the intriguing and dissolute Catharine de Medici, had ascended the French throne. Both this monarch and his mother entertained the most bitter enmity toward the Huguenots, or French Protestants. The mother, an Italian, not more by her lineage than her subtlety, became the actual mistress and ruler of the French empire.

Among the most devoted friends of Pope Pius V. were these three royal personages. This pope made France the theatre of his most sanguinary persecutions. Excepting Innocent III., his predecessor, no pontiff, perhaps, ever caused the Protestant world so great sorrow. The bloody Inquisition was his nursery and school, and his opposition to Protestant Christianity knew no bounds.

The Huguenots in 1569 lost the hard-fought battle of Jarnac, where six or seven thousand Protestants contended against a Romish army four times as strong. During the fight the Prince of Condé, a brave and distinguished leader of the Reformers, was killed, and his dead body, borne by an ass, became an object of derision to many who before had trembled at the very mention of his name. Pius V. greatly exulted over this Huguenot defeat, and he left seven letters, written on this sorrowful occasion, to Catharine, the queen mother, which will ever remain as monuments of his unholy zeal and vindictiveness. He commanded that his enemies should be "*massacred*" and "*totally exterminated.*"* The holy father went still further, and struck a medal to commemorate the battle, representing himself uncovered and kneeling, returning thanks to Heaven for the triumph.

This pontiff would have extirpated the Protestants from every land; but, happily for the Christian world, he died in 1572. Yet he aroused the diabolical spirit which, soon after his death, caused the St. Bartholomew massa-

* Delitis omnibus.

cre—a wholesale human butchery never to be forgotten in the memory of man, nor ever remembered except with horror. This massacre may be pronounced the most foul and bloody of ancient or modern times, and our author has graphically described the bloody scenes of that terrific night. Gregory XIII., then pope, had a medal struck to celebrate the atrocious event. On the obverse it has, as usual, a head of the pope. The reverse exhibits a destroying angel, with a cross in one hand and a sword in the other, pursuing and slaying a band of prostrate and flying heretics. Its legend is "UGONOTIUM STRAGES,* 1572." Strange and bloody work for an angel! This rare historical medal tells its own terrible tale.

Then followed the malignant, desolating religious wars which raged in France during the seventeenth century, and of which history affords no parallel. Wearied with increasing persecutions, the Huguenots began to emigrate, and many left France even before the revocation of the Edict of Nantes. The edict was finally revoked, October 18, 1685, at Fontainebleau, without the least pretext or necessity. Why the act should be termed the "Revocation," we know not, for all its provisions had long been repealed by several ordinances forbidding the profession of the Reformed faith under severe penalties. This celebrated Edict of Nantes, to speak accurately, had been a new confirmation of former treaties between the French government and the Protestants, or *Huguenots*—in fact, a royal act of indemnification for all past offenses. The verdicts against Protestants were erased from the rolls of the Superior Courts in France, and their unlimited liberty of conscience was recognized. This solemn and important edict marked the close of the Middle Ages, and the true commencement of modern times. It was sealed with the great seal of green wax, to indicate its perpetuity, and in signing this great document the illustrious Henry IV. granted to the Huguenots all their civil and religious rights, which had been refused them by their enemies. But a state policy so novel could not fail to excite the clamors of the more violent factions. The sovereign, however, remained firm, declaring to Parliament that he had pronounced the edict as king, and as king would be obeyed. "My predecessors," he said to the clergy, "have given you good words, but I, with my gray jacket, will give you good deeds. I am all gray on the outside, but I'm all gold within." It was due to these noble royal sentiments that peace was for a time maintained in the French realm.

But the French Protestants did not long enjoy the privileges granted to them by the Edict of Nantes, for twelve years after its promulgation Henry was assassinated, when religious discord again broke out, and the persecutions against the Reformed became so violent, bloody, and intolerable, that flight from their native land became inevitable. Many, however, prepared to suffer martyrdom rather than to leave their country and their homes. When the full tide of emigration set in from the extended frontier of France, it became impossible to prevent the escape of thousands of the fugitives into England, Switzerland, Germany, and Holland. Holland! glorious Protestant Holland! was the favorite ark of the refugees. In this land of our noble Dutch forefathers they received the most generous private and public hospitality, with the most precious privileges of religious freedom.

* Massacre of the Huguenots.

During the last twenty years of the seventeenth century the French emigration into that Holland became a marked political event. In the single year of the "Revocation" more than two hundred and fifty Huguenot preachers reached the free soil of the United Provinces. Amsterdam alone obtained sixteen. The Protestant Frenchmen greatly advanced all the branches of human learning in Holland, for here no fetters embarrassed genius, and there was no secret censorship over intellect. The refugees also increasing the commerce, manufactures, and agriculture of the Netherlands, after a while rendered Amsterdam one of the most famed cities of the world. Like ancient Tyre, named the "perfection of beauty" by the prophet, her merchant princes traded with all islands and nations.

Until the close of the eighteenth century, the descendants of the Huguenots in Holland united among themselves by intermarriage and the bonds of mutual sympathies. But a fusion with the Dutch in time became inevitable in Holland, as was the case, also, in Germany and England. Many refugees, adopting a new nationality, changed their French names into Dutch. The Leblancs, for instance, called themselves De Witt; the Deschamps, Van der Velde; the Dubois, Van der Bosch; the Chevaliers, Ruyter; the Le Grands, De Groot, etc. With this change of names, Huguenot churches began to disappear in the Netherlands, so that out of sixty-two which existed in 1688 among the seven provinces, only eleven now remain.

This rapid review of the Holland Huguenots seems necessary for a better understanding of our subject. The Dutch made the earliest settlements in New Netherlands, and with them soon came the French Protestants.

THE WALLOONS.

Staten Island, that beautiful spot in our New York Bay, has the honor of having offered the first safe home in America to the Walloons. As early as the year 1622 several Walloon families from the frontier, between Belgium and France, turned their attention to America. They applied to Sir Dudley Carleton for permission to settle in the colony of Virginia, with the privilege of erecting a town and governing themselves by magistrates of their own election. This application was referred to the Virginia Company,[*] but its conditions were too republican for their taste. Many of these emigrants looked toward New Netherlands, where some had arrived in 1624 with Minuit, the early Dutch director. At first they settled on Staten Island, and built a little church near Richmond, as tradition relates, but afterward removed to *Wahle Bocht*, L. I., or the "Bay of Foreigners," since corrupted into Wallabout. This settlement subsequently extended toward "Breukelen," named after an ancient Dutch village on the River Veght, in the province of Utrecht. The name of Walloon itself is said to be derived either from Wall (water or sea), or more probably the old German word *Wahle*, signifying a foreigner.

It must be remembered that this is a page in the earliest chapter of New Netherlands, a region which the West India Company now resolved to erect into a province. To the Chamber of Amsterdam the superintendence of this extensive and newly-discovered country was committed, and that body had

[*] London Doc., i., 24.

sent out an expedition, in a vessel called the "New Netherlands," whereof Cornelius Jacobs, of Hoorn, was skipper, with *thirty* families, mostly Walloons, to plant a colony in America. They arrived in the beginning of May (1623), and the old London document from which we obtain this information adds :

"God be praised ; it hath so prospered that the honorable Lords Directors of the West India Company have, with the consent of the noble, high, and mighty Lords States-General, undertaken to plant some colonies.* . . . . . The honorable Daniel van Leuckebeeck, for brevity called ' Beeck,' was commissary here, and so did his duty that he was thanked."

The Walloons had passed through the fires of religious persecutions. They inhabited the southern Belgic Provinces, and spoke the old French language. In the year 1579 the northern provinces of the Netherlands formed their political union at Utrecht ; the southern attached themselves to the Roman Church, and declined joining the confederation. Many, however, professed the principles of the Reformation, and against these the Spanish government exercised inquisitorial vengeance. Thus mercilessly persecuted, they emigrated by thousands into Holland, where strangers of every race and creed obtained a hearty welcome.

The Hollanders were much indebted to the Walloons for many branches of useful manufacture, and the fame of the New World reaching the ears of these French artisans of Amsterdam, their attention was directed thither. In the year 1625 three ships and a yacht arrived at Manhattan with more families, farming implements, and one hundred and three head of cattle. Hitherto the government of the Dutch settlement had been quite simple, but now a proper director from Holland was appointed—Peter Minuit—and instructed to organize a provincial government. He arrived in May, 1626. There was no regular clergyman as yet in the infant colony, but two "Visitors of the Sick" were appointed, who also read the Scriptures on Sundays to the people. Thus more than two centuries ago was laid the corner-stone of the Empire State on the sure and firm foundations of justice, morality, and religion. The Dutch and Huguenot colonists were grave, persevering men, who brought with them the simplicity, integrity, and industry of their Belgic sires, and to those eminent virtues were added the light of the civil law and the purity of the Protestant faith.

The Rev. Johannes Megapolensis as early as the year 1642 became dominie of the Dutch Reformed Church in Albany, under the patronage of Van Rensselaer, the patroon, and five years afterward he took charge of the congregation at Manhattan. He selected in 1652 for a colleague Samuel Drissius, on account of his knowledge of French and English ; and from his letters we learn that he went once a month to preach to the French Protestants on Staten Island ; these, it is related, were Vaudois or *Waldenses*, who had found a home in Holland from the severe persecutions of Piedmont, and by the liberality of the city of Amsterdam were settled in New Netherlands. This ministry continued from 1652 to 1697. and this is all the information we have found about this early minister and his little Huguenot flock upon Staten Island. The New York Consistory, about the year 1690, invited the

* *Wassemaer's Historie van Europa*, Amsterdam, 1621–3.

Rev. Peter Daille, who had ministered among the Massachusetts Huguenots, to preach occasionally on the island.

During the month of August, 1661, a small colony of Dutch and French emigrants from the Palatinate obtained grants of land on the south side of Staten Island, where the site of a village was surveyed. To protect them from the Indians, a block-house was erected and garrisoned with three guns and ten soldiers. This region became a favorite asylum for the French refugees, where they arrived in considerable numbers about 1675. Their pious descendants are among the influential members of the numerous Christian churches there, and the Disosways and Guions yet occupy the same farms which their pious French ancestors settled a century and a half ago. Here the French language was formerly spoken, and was as common as the English is in our day.

ULSTER.

At an early period in our colonial history the Huguenots made a settlement in that part of New York now known as Ulster County. Abraham Hasbrouck, one of the first patentees, was a native of Calais, France, and the first emigrant of the family to America, arriving in 1675 with a party of French Huguenots. They had resided a while on the banks of the Rhine, in the Palatinate. To commemorate the kindness of the Hollanders when they reached our shores, the new settlement was called "*De Paltz*" (now "*New Paltz*"), as the Palatinate was always styled by the Dutch. The beautiful stream also flowing through this region was known as the "*Walkill*," after the River Wael, a branch of the Rhine running into Holland. The first twelve patentees, or the "*Duzine*," as long as they lived managed the affairs of the infant settlement, and after their death for a long period all the important papers and land-titles were kept in one chest. To the pastor, or oldest man, was intrusted its key, and reference was made to this depository for the settlement of all difficulties about boundaries. We can trace to this simple and judicious plan the well-known harmony among the descendants of the early settlers in this region, the fidelity of their landmarks, and the absence of litigation about property. From their earliest settlement there has been a constant intermarriage among the French and Dutch and their descendants, many of whom continue to reside upon the venerable homesteads of their pious forefathers.

Devoted as the Huguenots ever had been to the worship of God, it is not strange that one of their first enterprises at New Paltz was the erection of a church. It was built of logs, and afterward gave place to a substantial one constructed of brick brought from Holland, the place answering the double purpose of a house of worship and of a fort. Their third tabernacle was an excellent stone building, in which they worshiped for eighty years, when it was demolished in the year 1839; the present splendid edifice was erected on its venerable site.

For some time after their emigration to Ulster the Frenchmen used their own tongue, but afterward they adopted not only the language, but also the customs and habits of the Dutch. Some of their descendants in New Paltz still write their names in the style of their old French ancestors two centuries ago. Bevier, Dubois, Deyeau, Hasbroque, Le Fevre, are well-known instances. After the destruction of the Protestant churches at Rochelle in 1685, the colonists from that brave city came to the settlements of the New York colony, and it became necessary sometimes to print the public documents not only in Dutch and English, but also in French.

WESTCHESTER.

Westchester County, New York, was settled by emigrants seeking safety from religious persecution in New England and France. As early as the year 1642 John Throckmorton, with thirty-five associates, having been driven from New England by the violent Hugh Peters, commenced the first settlement in this region with the approbation of the Dutch authorities. They called the place *Vredeland,* or *Land of Peace,* a beautiful name for the home of those seeking rest from the violence of persecutors. Twelve years afterward this little Puritan colony was increased by the arrival of more emigrants from Connecticut.

New Rochelle is situated near the shore of Long Island Sound, and in September, 1689, a body of exiled Huguenots here purchased *six thousand* acres of land; the purchasers, their heirs, and assigns, as an acknowledgment, were to pay "*one fat calf on every four-and-twentieth day of June, yearly, and every year forever, if demanded.*" It is a well-known fact, that every Huguenot on the festival of St. John the Baptist, as long as the claim endured, paid his proportion of the fat calf. During the year 1690 Governor Leisler released to these banished French Protestants the lands thus purchased for them. They named their settlement New Rochelle, and were themselves a portion of the 50,000 who found safety in that old noble Protestant land four years before the Revocation of the Edict of Nantes. According to tradition, they landed from a royal vessel on the present Davenport's Neck, then called Bonnefoy's Point.

Simultaneously with the foundation of their village, they organized a church, "according to the usage of the Reformed Church in France." Their house of worship was built of wood, about 1692–93, and was destroyed soon after the Revolutionary War. David Bonrepos, D.D., who accompanied the earliest Huguenots in their flight to this land, was the first pastor, 1695. He also preached to the French refugees on Staten Island. The Rev. Daniel Bondet, A.M., who arrived at Boston in 1688, was the next minister at New Rochelle. At first he used the French prayers, but subsequently, every third Sunday, the liturgy of the English Church. Following the example of their Reformed French brethren in England, this congregation conformed in 1709 to the English Church, as then established by law, in the New York colony.

This organization increasing, a new sacred stone edifice was completed in 1710. After nearly twenty-seven years of faithful labor, Mr. Bondet died in 1722, greatly lamented, and was buried beneath the chancel of his church. Here are also entombed the ashes of his successor, the Rev. Pierre Stouppe, A.M., who departed 1760, and of the Rev. Michael Houdin, A.M., who succeeded Stanhope, and died 1766. Since the removal of the old edifice, the ashes of these very early Protestant missionaries sleep beneath the common highway to Boston, and not a stone tells where they lie.

Among the emigrants to New Rochelle were the ancestors of John Jay and Bishop De Lancey. Mr. Jay's family originally came from La Guienne.

NEW YORK CITY.

Such was the increase of the French refugees into the colony of New York, that the French church of our city for some time became the metropolis of Calvinism in the New World. During the year 1685 there was a large addition of French Protestants to the population. Many of these, having sojourned in the islands of St. Christopher and Martinique, made a final settlement among our tolerant citizens, bringing with them wealth, industry, and the useful arts. By the year 1695 their families had reached nearly two hundred in number, and were among the most influential of the city. At first they worshiped in a small building on Marketfield Street; then a more commodious chapel was built upon Pine—"*L'Eglise du Saint Esprit*," the Church of the Holy Spirit. It was built of stone, was seventy by fifty feet in size, and there was attached to it a burying-ground. At the conclusion of the public services the minister always said "*Souvenez vous les pauvres,*" "Remember ye the poor," when old and young dropped their benefactions into the "poor-box" behind the church doors. The next morning, at 9 o'clock regularly, the beneficiaries came to receive this pious gift. The Huguenots always remembered and aided their poor brethren. Here for one hundred and thirty years the French Protestants worshiped God after "Calvin's way," as did the Reformed churches of France and Geneva. They thus used the religious forms of their fathers until the year 1804, when the old congregation conformed to the Protestant Episcopal Church, except in language, to this day retaining the French. "L'Eglise," on Pine, was sold, and the elegant white marble sacred edifice erected at the corner of Franklin and Church Streets, where the congregation maintained their religious services for some years, but has recently erected a beautiful edifice in the upper part of the city. Since the establishment of the original church, fourteen ministers have been its pastors. James de Lancey was its most generous benefactor. In 1729 he was a member of the Colonial Council, and subsequently justice of the Supreme Court, and lieutenant governor of the state.

Bancroft, writing of early New York (1656), says, "Its settlers were relics of the first-fruits of the Reformation, chosen from the Belgic provinces and England, from France and Bohemia, from Germany and Switzerland, from Piedmont and the Italian Alps." . . . . "When the Protestant churches in Rochelle were razed, the colonists of that city were gladly admitted, and the French Protestants came in such numbers that the public documents were sometimes issued in French as well as in English."

MASSACHUSETTS.

As early as the year 1662, John Touton, a doctor of Rochelle, applied to the Court of Massachusetts, asking that he and other French Protestants who had been expelled from their homes on account of their faith might come to New England, and that American colony generously received them. They became useful and honorable citizens of the state. *Faneuil Hall*, Boston, where so early was heard the plea for national independence, was the generous gift of a Huguenot's son, and the time-honored edifice still retains his name, and its venerable walls are adorned with his full-length portrait.

The General Court of Massachusetts granted a tract of land eight miles square, some 12,000 acres, to the French refugees for their village of Oxford in 1686. The region was then a howling wilderness, but is now the busy town of Worcester. One of the first acts of these settlers was the settlement of a minister at £40 a year. Surrounded by savages, the new settlers erected a fort, traces of which are still to be seen in our day, though the site is overgrown with currant-bushes, roses, and other shrubbery. Mrs. Sigourney, during a visit to this venerable spot, wrote these beautiful lines:

> "Green vine! that mantlest in thy fresh embrace
> Yon old gray rock, I hear that thou, with them,
> Didst brave the ocean surge.
>   Say, drank thy germ
> The dews of Languedoc? . . . .
> At fair Rochelle!
> Hast thou no tale for me?" etc.

This fortification not making their forest home safe from the murderous savages, the colonists in 1696 repaired to Boston, where vestiges of their industry and agricultural taste long remained. This region has been celebrated for its delicious pears, many of which retain their French names to this day. A refugee minister of France, Daillé, and a Mr. Lawrie, are named as early pastors to this little flock.

PENNSYLVANIA, MARYLAND, AND VIRGINIA.

Pennsylvania furnished an asylum for many hundreds of the French Protestants who had first established themselves in England, but who, when the ascent of James II. to the throne threatened their liberties, emigrated to America.

In 1690 Maryland also received quite a large number of Huguenots, and during the same year King William III. sent to the Virginia colony a body of these refugees who had followed him from Holland into England, and doubtless had also taken part in the Irish war. Lands were assigned to them twenty miles above Richmond, upon the southern bank of James River, near an old Indian place, "Mannikin," after which they named their settlement, afterward known as the "Parish of King William." About three hundred families in 1699, just escaped from France, greatly strengthened this infant colony, and was increased still more the next year by two hundred, and soon afterward by one hundred other French families. Claude Philippe de Richebourg, their pastor, had been driven from France by the Revocation of the Edict of Nantes, and for a long time was the faithful guide and spiritual counselor of these expatriated Christians.

Our author, Mr. Smiles, refers to the romantic and noble life of James Fontaine, who was a striking example of a true Huguenot. About the year 1716 three of his sons, emigrating to the colony of Virginia, became eloquent and useful ministers in the Established Church. A grandson also, the Rev. James Maury, settled in St. Margaret's Parish, King William County, and from him descended Matthew Fontaine Maury, LL.D., late of the National Observatory, Washington, and author of "The Physical Geography of the

Sea." From this Fontaine stock alone have descended hundreds of the best citizens in Virginia, and the late Dr. Hawks estimated their relations in the United States at not less than 2000.

SOUTH CAROLINA.

South Carolina was styled "the Home of the Huguenots," and became their principal retreat in the New World. Richebourg conducted thither part of his flock from Virginia. Nearly a thousand fugitives successively embarked for Carolina in the ports of Holland alone. One historian in 1686 states that "more than a hundred persons are buying a frigate, half resolved on going to Carolina. . . . . There will be about four hundred persons, resolved to fight well in case of attack, and set fire to the vessel should they be reduced to extremity. . . . . These gentlemen can not accommodate themselves with a vessel in this country. There is one carrying fifty cannon which has been chartered for them in England," and fifty guns, fifty musquetoons, and thirty pairs of pistols were purchased at Utrecht for this vessel. The same writer continues: "Our Carolinians of Amsterdam are about to join themselves to those of Rotterdam, in which they are going to England. At London they have many associates, who will go with them. . . . . The two barks which belong to them, and in which they will make their voyage to England, will serve them also for going to Carolina. They will load them with Malmsey wine, and other merchandise, in the island of Madeira. The two barks, and their ship of from forty-five to fifty guns, which they have chartered in England, will be manned by four hundred well-armed persons." In their flight, doubtless, if an attempt had been made to arrest them, these well-armed emigrants would have dearly sold their lives.

Isaac Mazicq, one of the French refugees, a merchant from the island of Rhé, opposite La Rochelle, reached Charleston in the year 1686, accompanied by many other Huguenots, and became the progenitor of one of the most respectable families in South Carolina. He established a commercial house in the capital of that province, laying the foundation of an immense fortune, which he most generously devoted to his new and adopted country.

A number of Englishmen, during the reign of James II., fearing the restoration of the Roman Catholic religion, emigrated to Carolina, accompanied by many Huguenots, refugees in England, apprehensive as to the protection of a prince who openly attached himself to the Romanist faith. All here found a home where, although the English form of worship was dominant, still the kind tolerance of Shaftesbury had opened a religious asylum to Christians of all denominations. The most considerable emigration took place in 1687, when, through the royal bounty, six hundred French Protestants were sent to America, most of them locating in Carolina. These were generally mechanics and laborers, to whom also had been given the necessary tools for their trades and pursuits.

The refugees established three colonies in South Carolina—Orange Quarter, on the Cooper River, Santee, and that at Charleston. Amid these primitive forests the exiles worshiped God without fear of man or of royal edicts, and their psalms mingled with the free winds of heaven. From Orange

Quarter the colonists repaired on Sundays in their light canoes to their church at Charleston. Ten families from the Orange Quarter made a settlement upon the site of the modern town of Strawberry Ferry, and built a church, of which Florent Philippe Trouillart became the first pastor.

In this until then uninhabited country another settlement at Jamestown was commenced in 1705, and contained one hundred French families. Their earliest pastor is said to have been Pierre Robert, a Swiss, who doubtless accompanied a party of the fugitives in their escape from France. Next to the colony at the capital, this became the most flourishing. The richest and most populous Huguenot settlement in South Carolina was that of Charleston, where entire streets were built by them. One still bears the name of its founder, Gabriel Guignard. Here Elias Prioleau became the first pastor, a descendant of Antoine Prioli, the Doge of Venice in 1618.

The adventures, trials, and misfortunes of some of these pious emigrants in leaving their native land for a safe home in this province are full of romance, and can not be read except with painful interest. Judith Manigault, a young married woman, at once a Christian and a true heroine, has left this record of the flight of her family from France :

" We quitted our home in the night, leaving the soldiers in their beds, and abandoning to them our house and all that it contained. Well knowing that we should be sought for in every direction, we remained ten days concealed at Romans, in Dauphiny, at the house of a good woman who had no thought of betraying us." Making a long circuit through Holland and Germany, and after suffering many misfortunes, the family embarked for America at London. Then she continues: " The red fever broke out on board the ship; many of us died of it, and among them our aged mother. We touched at the island of Bermuda, where the vessel which carried us was seized. We spent all our money there, and it was with great difficulty that we procured a passage on board of another ship. New misfortunes awaited us in Carolina. At the end of eighteen months we lost our eldest brother, who succumbed to such unusual fatigues ; so that after our departure from France we endured all that it was possible to suffer. I was six months without tasting bread, working besides like a slave ; and during three or four years I never had the wherewithal completely to satisfy the hunger which devoured me." "Yet," adds this admirable woman, with most Christian resignation, "God accomplished great things in our favor by giving us the strength necessary to support these trials." From this fragment of history we can well imagine the untold sufferings which thousands of other refugee emigrants endured in their flight from their own to other and more tolerant lands.

In 1764 two hundred and twelve exiles from France added new strength to the refugee settlements in Carolina. Their pastor, named Gilbert, accompanied them, the English government furnishing their passage. Vacant lands were distributed among them, and soon a town raised itself, to which its founders gave the name of New Bordeaux, in honor of the capital of Guienne, where most of them were born. The foreign Protestants who had settled in Carolina up to the year 1782 had increased to no less than sixteen thousand, of whom a good portion were French. In the two Carolinas the Lords Proprietors not only granted lands to the French Protestants upon the condition of a penny an acre yearly payment, but they likewise conferred upon them all the civil and military offices in their power to bestow. They also gave them the most unlimited religious freedom. They became naturalized in 1697, and were legally admitted into the great body of the American people. From the French colonists in Carolina we find the descendants of many honorable families—the Ravenels, Trevezants, Pèronneaus, Neuvilles, Manigaults, Marions, Laurenses, Legares, Hugers, Gaillards, Duboises, Duprés, Chevaliers, Bacots, Benoits, Bayards, etc.

That never-dying sentiment, attaching man to his native land, notwithstanding the advantages of their home in America, inspired some of the emigrants with a new and strange project, which, if the royal monarch had any of the nobler feelings of human nature, must have touched the heart of Louis XII. Not at all disposed, like their expatriated brethren in Europe, to return to France, they yet indulged the hope of settling on the French lands of America. They requested Bienville, the Governor of Louisiana, to send their petition to the court at Versailles. This was signed by 400 families, who had taken refuge, after the "Revocation," in Carolina, and who only solicited permission to settle in Louisiana on the simple condition that they should enjoy liberty of conscience. With Romanism this is entirely out of the question, and the Count de Pontchartrain informed the petitioners that his royal master the king had not driven them from his kingdom to form a Protestant republic in his American possessions. While entire liberty of conscience prevailed in the American colonies and churches, Louisiana alone was founded under the dark and malign shadow of intolerant despotism. That beautiful region languished during one hundred years in a sad and feeble infancy. Nor did she awaken from this stupor until after her entrance into the Protestant American family. Then the State of Louisiana rapidly doubled her population, and free from obstacles, developed the immense riches she carried in her bosom. This refusal of Louis XIV. destroyed every hope of the refugees remaining Frenchmen, and they became more than ever attached to their newly-adopted homes and country.

In conclusion, let us briefly refer to the effects of the Huguenot migration upon American history.

The American colonies were largely remunerated for the generous hospitalities they extended to the French Protestants. In Massachusetts the latter cleared the forests then surrounding the Boston and Oxford settlements, and introduced the culture of the pear, quince, and grape. The founders of New Rochelle reclaimed smiling fields and fruitful gardens from a savage wilderness; and thus, too, were the uncultivated lands of the James River transformed into fruitful farms and rich harvests. Along the banks of the Cooper, in South Carolina, they planted the olive, the vine, and the mulberry, with most other productions of Southern France. When Charles II., in 1680, sent the first band of French Protestants to Carolina, his principal object was to introduce into that colony the excellent modes of cultivation which they had followed in their own country. Their lands, an early traveler (Lawson) states, presented the aspect of the most cultivated portions of France and England; and he adds, "They live like a tribe, like one family, and each one rejoices at the prosperity and elevation of his brethren."

The mechanics and merchants chose Charleston for their residence, and they became a valuable addition to the then newly-founded American colony. They established silk and woolen manufactories, and made the cotton *Romalls*, so much demanded in America, and similar to our universally-used bleached muslins. Thus the refugees added greatly to the national prosperity and wealth of the United States.

Nor were their political influences and services less numerous and important to the American colonies. They often fought in the ranks of the American militia during the first half of the eighteenth century. Naturally enemies to political despotism and religious intolerance, in the Revolutionary contest the French Protestants ran to arms, and displayed the energy and bravery which they had inherited from their noble ancestors. As before remarked, Faneuil Hall, the "Cradle of Liberty," was offered by the son of a Huguenot to the orators of New England for their patriotic deliberations.

Many scions of the Huguenot families on the field of battle led the Americans to victory, or distinguished themselves in the councils of the infant republic. Amid the more radiant glory of Washington, Franklin, Hamilton, Lafayette, and Rochambeau, the names of John Bayard, Francis Marion, Henry and John Laurens, John Jay, Elias Boudinot, and the two Manigaults, should ever be gratefully remembered for their eminent and patriotic services to our common country. Henry Laurens, John Jay, and Elias Boudinot, of the seven presidents who directed the deliberations of our earliest Congress during the War of Independence, descended from French ancestors.

The services of Henry Laurens to his country were truly brilliant. A native of Charleston, born in 1724, when solicited not to take part in the coming American contest, he replied, "I am determined to stand or fall with my country;" and by accepting the presidency of the Committee of Safety in 1775, he risked his fortune and life in the common cause. A member of the first national Congress in 1776, as we have remarked, he was elected its presiding officer, manifesting rare ability, with nobility and dignity of thought and language. In the archives of Congress his official letters have been preserved, and are doubly marked with the stamp of a statesman and patriot, bearing the impress of manly energy and elevated sentiment. In 1778, voluntarily resigning his high office, Congress presented him a vote of public thanks, with their declaration that he deserved well of the country. The next year, appointed minister from the United States to Holland, on his voyage to that land he was captured by a British ship, and imprisoned in the Tower of London. At the age of fifty-six years, and infirm, he was confined to a cell, and no one was permitted to visit him. After a month's confinement he was informed that if he would serve the interests of England in her conflict with the colonies he should be set at liberty, but he rejected the proposition with the most lively indignation. "I will never," he replied, "subscribe my name to my own infamy and to the dishonor of my family." His firmness did not forsake him for an instant. "Nothing," he added, "can move me." Here was the noble old Huguenot spirit of his forefathers. In the year 1781 he was brought before the Court of the King's Bench, and the judge addressing him in the usual form, "The king, your sovereign master," etc., Laurens interrupted him and cried, "He is not my sovereign." After a rigorous imprisonment of more than fourteen months, he was set at liberty with impaired health. Nevertheless, he again, and for the last time, served his now independent country. With Franklin, Adams, and Jay, Mr. Laurens, in 1782, repaired to Paris and signed the memorable treaty which secured independence to the thirteen American provinces, and placed them among the nations of the world.

John Laurens, his son, was born at Charleston in 1755, was educated a lawyer, and when the War of Independence broke out, became an aid-de-camp to General Washington. He was wounded at the battle of Germantown, and took a glorious part at Monmouth in June, 1778. When Charleston capitulated to the British he became a prisoner of war, but, being exchanged for an English officer, Congress sent him to France as embassador extraordinary to Louis XVI. He was charged to represent the critical condition of the country, solicit a loan and the assistance of the king's fleet. Succeeding in this important mission, he returned home in six months, having obtained every thing he requested—a subsidy of six millions, the French king's security for ten millions borrowed from Holland, and a strong re-enforcement to the American naval and land forces. Thus the son of a Huguenot refugee obtained important aid for his native land from the country of his ancestors, and, having accomplished this, he hastened to resume his place again among General Washington's aids-de-camp. Afterward elevated to the rank of colonel, he confirmed the confidence of his superiors by one of the most brilliant acts of the campaign. At the siege of Yorktown two formidable redoubts had to be taken at all hazards, and within 300 paces of the British intrenchments. The French were ordered to storm one and the Americans the other. Young Laurens commanded the latter, and his soldiers marched to the assault with unloaded muskets, and, scaling the palisades, in a few minutes carried the redoubt. The French took the other redoubt, and Cornwallis, vainly defending foot by foot the approaches to his camp, was compelled to surrender with 8000 men. Washington designated John Laurens to draw up the articles of capitulation, and, strange to add, while arranging the conditions which made a British army prisoners of war, at that very moment his father was a close prisoner in the Tower of London.

But military operations were not yet entirely suspended; for, although the English had met with this great reverse, they still held Charleston, and Colonel Laurens, with General Greene's army, determined to share the last dangers yet to be encountered for the independence of their country. At the noise of the firing made by a sally of the enemy from Charleston, Colonel Laurens left his sick-chamber and followed General Gist, with 300 men, to repel the advance of a strong detachment. Engaging a very superior force, and in the expectation of speedy relief, after great valor he received a mortal wound, and died gloriously on the field of battle, August 27th, 1782, scarcely twenty-seven years of age. Thus was this brave and noble young man struck down in the moment of triumph. At the time he was the idol of his country, the glory of the American army, an ornament to human nature, his talents shining with no less brilliancy in the legislative halls than upon the battle-field.

Although less illustrious than the two Laurenses the two Manigaults should be recorded among the Americans of French Protestant origin who aided in the triumph of the Revolution, thus in a measure paying the debt of hospitality incurred by their ancestors. Gabriel Manigault, born in Charleston, 1704, of a family formerly living at La Rochelle, became one of the most wealthy merchants in America, and most loyal to the cause of American liberty. Too old to take up arms, with his fortune he assisted the cause by loaning $220,000 to the State of South Carolina; and when General Prevost threatened Charleston, the brave old man took his grandson, a child of only fifteen years, by the hand, and fell into the volunteer ranks to fight their country's battle. Two years after he died, leaving a fortune of $500,000 honorably acquired, and an unstained record.

The history of this patriotic family does not end here; his son, Gabriel Manigault, was born in Charleston, 1731. He was appointed a judge, and was elected a delegate to the Provincial Congress. In 1766 he was president of the Carolina Assembly, which prepared the way for Revolutionary movements. He was able and eloquent, and, in the midst of a useful and brilliant career, died at the early age of forty-two years, at the moment when the "Liberty Boys" of Boston were throwing the British cargo of tea into their harbor.

John Jay, the descendant of an original Huguenot family, and of illustrious memory, was born in New York. In 1774 he signed the act of association between the thirteen colonies to suspend the importation of British merchandise, and during 1774 was chosen president of Congress. He drew up an eloquent circular for that body, when the temporary success of the British arms at the South had occasioned great despondency, and caused the depreciation of the Continental paper money. He ably proved that the United States, from their resources and natural riches, would be able to meet their engagements, and implored his fellow-citizens to resume their confidence in themselves and their infant government. Like Laurens, Mr. Jay represented his country at the court of Louis XVI., and, on November 30, 1782, was one of the commissioners to sign the Treaty of Versailles, which secured American independence.

Faithful to the traditions of the French Protestants, he was always a great lover and student of the Bible, and in advanced life was chosen president of the American Bible Society. Every morning his whole family was regularly summoned to religious worship, and precisely at nine in the evening he read to them a chapter of God's Word, and concluded the day with prayer. Nothing ever interfered with these holy services. At an early period of our national history was published by Mr. Madison and Colonel Alexander Hamilton the well-known *Federalist*. Mr. Jay had contributed the second, third, fourth, and fifth numbers, when he was obliged to discontinue writing from a dangerous wound inflicted on his forehead while endeavoring to preserve the public peace at an alarming riot in New York during the year 1787. Afterward, however, he added the sixty-fourth number, upon the then important treaty-making powers, a most appropriate subject for his consideration, who was perhaps the most competent man in the country to discuss it. He died on the 14th of May, 1829, in his eighty-fourth year, and the public journals the courts, and all parties united in proper tributes to his exalted virtues. Congress ordered his bust, as the first chief justice of the United States, to be placed in the Supreme Court room. The whole life of this Huguenot descendant exhibited the rare and sublime picture of the patriot, statesman, and Christian united, and justified the universal respect and honor ever bestowed upon him.

Elias Boudinot, another eminent Huguenot by descent, preceded John Jay in the presidency of the American Bible Society. He was born in Philadelphia, March 2d, 1740, of a French Protestant family which had emigrated after the Revocation of the Edict of Nantes. He was considered one of the most eminent lawyers in Pennsylvania. He filled the office of chief justice of New Jersey when the War of Independence broke out, and, following the example of nearly all the descendants of the French refugees, he embraced the cause of the American patriots. Congress appointed him to the important trust of commissary general of prisoners, the duties of which office he discharged with great prudence and humanity. In the year 1777 his fellow-citizens elected him a member of Congress, and in 1782 he was chosen its president, and had the honor of signing the treaty of peace which secured the national independence. Upon the adoption of the Federal Constitution in 1789, Mr. Boudinot was honored with a seat in the House of Representatives, and occupied the important trust for six successive years. General Washington appointed him director of the Mint in 1796, and he continued to discharge the duties of this office until 1805, when he retired from public life, settling at Burlington, N. J. During his last years, Mr. Boudinot devoted his leisure to the study of Biblical literature, and the exercise of a public and private charity. While in its infancy, the American Bible Society was by his large donations placed upon a firm foundation. A trustee of Princeton College, he founded its cabinet of Natural History at a cost of $3000. Mr. Boudinot early married a daughter of Richard Stockton. He left an only daughter, and after suitably providing for her, bequeathed the most of his large estate to those excellent objects which through life had been dearest to his heart.

Mr. Boudinot wrote several works, and among them an able reply ("The Age of Revelation") to Tom Paine's "Age of Reason." His principal publication was the "Star of the West," or an attempt to discover the long-lost tribes of Israel, which at the time was read with much interest. He reached the advanced age of eighty-one, and died in the city of Burlington, N. J., Oct. 24, 1821. On his tomb-stone is inscribed this sentence:

"Mark the perfect man and behold the upright, for the end of that man is peace!"

Although the literary influence of the French Protestants in America was less than that which they exercised in political affairs, nevertheless it should not be passed over in entire silence. They have often appeared with distinction upon the seats of our tribunals, as well as in the sacred desk. Elias Prioleau, the first pastor of the Huguenot church at Charleston, was both an eloquent preacher and a writer of merit. His manuscript works are said to possess great purity of doctrine, elegance of style, and vigorous thought. Bancroft says, referring to Bowdoin, "The name of the oldest college recalls to mind the wise liberality of a descendant of a Huguenot." The same historian also recognizes in the French Protestants that moral elevation of which they gave so many proofs in every country where they were dispersed, and he adds, "The children of the French colonists have certainly good reason to hold the memory of their fathers in great honor."*

To the earliest settlements in the colony of New York can be traced the Huguenot element mingling with the excellent Dutch population. It is a remarkable fact that the first white child born in the New Netherlands, June 9, 1625, was Sarah, daughter of George Jansen de Rapelje, an expatriated Huguenot after the St. Bartholomew's, who emigrated first to Holland, and then to New Netherlands. The Indians, it is stated, commemorated her birth by presenting to the father and his fellow-countrymen a liberal grant of lands around Wallabout, Long Island.

Johannes Delamontagnie, a Huguenot refugee, came to New Amsterdam in 1637, and was honored by Governor Kieft as a member of the council, at that period the second in the colonial government. He purchased a farm of 200 acres at Harlem for $720, naming it "Vredendal," or Valley of Peace. Numerous and respectable descendants are still to be found from this early Protestant settler. The original French families have long since disappeared from Flushing, Long Island, but the fruit-trees they introduced still remain, especially the apple and the pear, so famous in that highly-cultivated region.

At the present time, descendants of the Huguenots may be found in all the United States, particularly in New York, Maryland, Virginia, and the Carolinas. It is not so easy to recognize their names, altered as they have been by a bad pronunciation, or translated into English. The sons and grandsons of the French refugees, little by little, have become mingled with the society which gave a home to their fathers in the same way as in England, Holland, and Germany. As their Church disappeared in America, the members became attached to other evangelical denominations, especially the Episcopal, Reformed Dutch, Methodist, and Presbyterian. The French language, too, has long since disappeared with their Church services, which used to call to mind the country of their ancestors. French was preached in Boston until the close of the last century, and at New York the Huguenot services were celebrated both in French and English as late as 1772. Here, at the French Protestant church, which succeeded the Huguenot years since, the Gospel is preached in the same language in which the prince of French pulpit orators, Saurin, used to declare divine truth two centuries ago. The Huguenot church at Charleston, South Carolina, alone has retained in its primitive purity, in their public worship, the old Calvinistic liturgy of its forefathers.

The greater part of the exiled French families have long since disappeared, and their scattered communities have been dissolved by amalgamation with the other races around them. These pious fugitives have become public blessings throughout the world, and have increased in Prussia, Germany, Holland, and England the elements of power, prosperity, and Christian development. In our land, too, they helped to lay the firm corner-stones of the great republic, whose glory they most justly share.

The Clove, S. I., Oct., 1867.

---

* Bancroft, vol. ii., p. 183.

INDEX.

A.

Abbadie, Huguenot pastor, dean of Killaloe, 240.
Allix, Huguenot pastor, 242.
Alva, Duke of, interview with Catharine de Medicis, 59; persecutions in Flanders conducted by, 62; plots against Queen Elizabeth, 74.
America, flight of refugees to, 111, 176.
Antwerp, printing of Bibles at, 23; prosperity of, 61; sack of, 81.
Armada, Sacred, 81, 118, 380
Artisans, refugee, in England—Flemish, 63, 86-109, 353-68; French, 250-69.
Assassination of William of Orange, 75 (note); plots to assassinate Elizabeth, 72, 75-80.
Austin Friars, Dutch church in, 113 (note), 114 and note.

B.

Barnstaple, French refugees at. 293.
Baronets, English, of Huguenot descent, 317.
Barré, family of, 167 (note), 31J.
Bartholomew, massacre of Saint, 65
Bearhaven, Ireland, James Fontaine's endeavors to establish a fishing-station at, 295.
Bearn, massacre of Protestants in, 128; dragonnades in, 148.
Benefit societies established by French refugees, 254.
Bermondsey, Flemings in, 94, 95
Bethnal Green, descendants of refugees in, 334 (note).
Beza, Theodore de, 53, 55.
Bible, dearness of MS., 13; first printed, 15; early editions, 18; prohibited, 18; value of, 20; influence on literature, 21 (note); Luther's translation of, 22; Tyndale's translation, 23: effects of its circulation, 24; burning of, 30, 146, 342.
Bidassoa, interview at, 59.
Blanket, the brothers, their manufacture, 357-8.
Bodt, John de, engineer, 228.
Boileau, family of, 317.
Bonrepos, Riquet de, 135.
Books, burning of, 29, 146, 342.
Bossuet, his praise of Louis XIV. for revoking the Edict of Nantes, 152.
Bostaquet, Dumont de—family of, 192; escape from France, 196; flight into Holland, 202; expedition to England, 205; campaign in Ireland, 211.
Bordeaux, Huguenots at, 146.
Bourdieu, John du. (See *Dubourdieu.*)
Bourdillon, French pastor, on decay of the churches, 278.

Bouveries, family of, 309.
Bow, Flemings at, 96.
Boyne, battle of the, 214.
Brandenburg, French refugees in, 175.
Briçonnet, bishop of Meaux, 26.
Briot, introduces the coining press, 96 (note).
Bristol, French church at, 276, 391.
Burleigh, Cecil Lord, conspiracy against, 78; mayor of Rye's letters to, 78, 89.
Burning of printers, 28; of Bibles and books, 29, 146, 342.

C.

Caillemotte, La, 211; killed at the Boyne, 215.
Calvin in Saintonge, 38; his care for psalmody, 43 (note); his influence on the organization of Geneva, 171.
Cambric manufacture introduced in Ireland, 290.
Camizards, war of the, 222-6
Canterbury, first arrival of Walloon refugees at, 120; their church in the Under Croft, 123; church still in existence, 126; silk manufacture at, 267; Malthouse Church at, 275, 287; registers of churches at, 383-8.
Cape of Good Hope, Huguenots' colony at, 176 (note).
Capell, James, French pastor, 246.
Castelfranc, Lord de, attempted escape of, 166.
Catharine de Medicis, letter to the pope, 53 (note); interview with the Duke of Alva at Bidassoa, 59; connection of, with the massacre of Saint Bartholomew, 64.
Caus, Solomon de, engineer, 231.
Cavalier, John, Camizard general; his origin, 222; leader in the Cevennes, 223; at the battle of Almanza, 226; major general in the English army, 227.
Cave, Edward, his speculation in spinning-mills with Paul's machine, 332.
Chaise, Père la, confessor to Louis XIV., 143-4, 151.
Chambon, Alexander, the last galley-slave for the faith, 338.
Champion, family of, 318.
Changes of foreign names, 96 (note).
Character of the Protestants—of the Flemish refugees, 73, 81, 92, 103, 120; of the French Huguenots, 134, 182 (note).
Charles I, his policy toward the refugees, 110; sends a fleet to Rochelle, 129.
Charles II., privileges granted by him to the Protestant refugees, 181.
Charles IX., state of France at accession of, 51; proposes an edict of amnesty, 51; witness of the massacre of St. Bartholomew, 65; death of, 68.

INDEX.

Chenevix, M. de, of Metz, burial of, 154 (note), 314.
Chevalier family, 320.
Churches, French, in England—Threadneedle Street, London, 114, 270, 369; at Sandwich, Rye, etc., 114, 182 (note); at Norwich, 115, 388; at Southampton, 115, 275, 373; Canterbury, 120, 383, 387; in Exeter, 207, 277; in Bristol, 276, 391; Stonehouse, Plymouth, 276, 392; the Savoy, London, 271, 371; in Swallow Street, 272, 372; in Spitalfields, 273; in the London suburbs, 274; Thorpe-le-Soken, Essex, 277, 395; Thorney Abbey, 396; decadence of the churches, 278; Church of the Artillery, Spitalfields, 278–80, 335.
Churches, French, in Ireland—Portarlington, 220, 304; Dublin, 284; Kilkenny, 285; Lisburn, 285–9; Cork, 204; Waterford, 300.
Churches, French, Registers of the, 368.
Church government of the Huguenots, 134 (note).
Church in the Desert, 170 (note), 336.
Churches, Protestant, in France—demolished, 56; destroyed by Louis XIV., 142; state of Protestants under Louis XIV., 344.
Churches, Walloon, in England—Austin Friars, 87, 113 (note), 114 and note; Sandwich, Rye, etc, 114; Norwich, Southampton, etc., 115; Canterbury, 120.
Civil Wars—in Flanders, 62, 63; in France, 57, 128.
Claude, French pastor, 157.
Clement VIII., Pope, 70.
Clergy of Roman Catholic Church, 19, 25, 42, 152, 161 (note), 345; at the French Revolution, 345–6 (note).
Cloth manufacture introduced into England, 85, 353–60.
Colbert, his policy, 135–6; character, 136–8.
Coligny, Admiral, 57; attempt to assassinate, 65; his murder, 66.
Coligny, Odo—his tomb in Canterbury Cathedral, 123 (note).
Colchester, Flemish colony at, 104 (note).
Collections made for refugees, 90 and note.
Colporteurs, French, 40 (note).
Condé, Prince of, 51, 57.
Conversion of Louis XIV., 150–1; forced conversions of Protestants, 194.
Copying of the Bible, its costliness, 13, 16.
Cork, French settlement at, 290.
Coster, Laurence, and invention of printing, 15.
Council of Trent, 58.
Courand, French pastor, Southampton, 120.
Cranmer's Bible, 23 (note).
Crommelin, Louis, at Lisburn, 285–7.

D.

Dauphiny, Huguenots of, 146
Descendants of the refugees, 307, 397.
Desaguliers, Dr., 234–5.
Desert, church in the, 170 (note), 336.
Des Vœux, family of, 318.
Dissenters, French pastors become, 246.
Divines, celebrated Huguenot, 240–9; of Huguenot descent, 320.
Dollond, John, his life and labors, 326.
Dover, refugees at, 91.

Dragonnades, first attempt at, 145; at Bordeaux, 146; in Bearn, 148; at Rouen, 194.
Dreux, battle of, a turning-point, 58 (note).
Dublin, settlement of refugees at, 107; manufactures established in, 284; churches, 284.
Dubourdieu, John, French pastor, 248–9, 253 (note), 289 (note).
Ducane, or Du Quesne, Admiral—his constancy, 157; family of, 320.
Durand, David, F.R S, 235.
Dutens, Rev. Louis, 322.

E.

Edicts—of 1559, 44; of Nantes, 70; of Pardon, 130; of Louis XIV. against Protestantism, 140; of the Revocation, 151; of Potsdam, 175.
Edinburg, French refugees in, 269
Edward III., first settlements of foreign artisans in the reign of, 86, 354–7.
Edward VI., immigration of Protestant Flemings in the reign of, 87, 360; churches granted to, by, 113.
Elizabeth, Queen, difficulties of her position, 71; plots against her, 74, 80; Pope's bull against, 75, 82; policy and religion of, 78, 83; protection given by her to the refugees, 87, 97, 101; visit to Sandwich, 92; Southampton, 119.
Emigration of foreign Protestants — from Flanders, 62, 63, 86; from France, 88, 141, 152; of French manufactures, 250.
Emigration of French priests and nobles, 347.
England, the asylum of the persecuted foreign Protestants, 63, 72; numbers of the fugitives in, 88; settlements of the refugees in, 85, 250.
Evil May-day, 366.
Exeter—settlement of Huguenots at, 207; cathedral service at, 207 (note); French church at, 277.

F.

Farel, follower of Lefevre, 26; escape, 27.
Farmers, the Huguenots as, 132.
Faust, John, of Mentz, 16.
Fens, reclamation of, 107.
Fishing settlements of refugees, 106, 353 (note).
Flanders, religious persecutions in, 61, 78, 81, 340.
Flax manufactures in Ireland founded by refugees, 108, 285.
Flemish refugees in England, 63, 72; their character defended by Bishop Jewell, 74 (note); settlement at Sandwich, 91–4; in Southwark, 95; various settlements, 96; numbers of, in London, 97, 98, 110; at Norwich, 100–103; in Ireland, 107; in Scotland, 109, 353; churches, 113–27; names existing, 308; distinguished descendants of, 308–10; early settlements of Flemings in England, 353.
Fleury, Archdeacon, 321.
Fontaine, James, French Protestant refugee, life and adventures in England and Ireland, 290–96.
France—the Bible in, 214; persecutions of the Reformed, 28; at the accession of Charles IX., 51; massacre of Vassy, 55,

of Saint Bartholomew, 65; renewal of persecution, 128; flight of the Huguenots from, 152, articles imported into England from, 256; at the Revolution, 340
Frederick William, elector of Brandenburg, 175.
French embassador, reception of, by Elizabeth after the massacre of Saint Bartholomew, 79.
French Hospital, London, 280.
French mechanics in London, Henry VIII's reign, 94, 95
French refugees (See *Huguenots*.)
Fruit-trees introduced by refugees, 94, 303.
Fund, French refugee relief—collections in aid of, 89-90; at Geneva, 173 (*note*); in Holland, 178, in England, 186, 252.

G.

Galley-slaves for the faith, 159-61; their youth, 163; their age and eminence, 164; the last, 338; sale of, 344 (*note*).
Galway, Earl of, his career, 218-221; his settlement of Portarlington, 301; descendants of, 314.
Gambier, Admiral, 229.
Gardening introduced by Flemish refugees, 93.
Gastigny, De, founds the French Hospital, 280.
Geneva, its independence, and bounty to the refugees, 172-3.
German Bible, 23
German miners in England, 360.
Germany, refugees in, 174
Glass manufacture introduced in England by Protestant refugees, 262, 263-4, 362.
Glastonbury, Flemish weavers at, 104 (*note*).
God's House, Southampton, 115, 275, 373
Gols, Gerard de, Sandwich, 114 (*note*).
Gospel, translated, 26; preaching of, forbidden, 52.
Gospellers at Meaux, 27: at Saintes, 38, 39.
Goujon, Jean, French sculptor, 50, 68 (*note*).
Goyer, Peter, refugee at Lisburn, 289.
Graverol, French pastor, 240.
Greenwich, refugee settlement at, 208; church at, 274; glass-house at, 362-3.
Grenoble, last persecutions at, 337.
Grenvelle, Cardinal, inquisitor in Flanders, 61
Grote, family of, and descendants, 310.
Guise, Duke of, at Vassy, 53; in the massacre of Saint Bartholomew, 66; corresponds with Mary Stuart, 74
Gutenberg and invention of printing, 15.

H.

Hamburg, Bible printed at, 23 (*note*).
Hamelin, Philebert, early martyr, 39 (*note*).
Hat-making introduced by refugees, 257, 362.
Henry II of England, early settlement of foreign artisans in reign of, 353.
Henry III of France visits Palissy, 49; civil war in the reign of, 69.
Henry IV. of France—marriage, 64; becomes king, 69; promulgates the Edict of Nantes, 70; assassination, 70, 198
Henry VIII. of England—French mechanics in reign of, 86, 94; his protection of Flemish artisans, 364 (*note*), 365; Evil Mayday, 366.
Hervart, Baron de Huningue, 281, 377.
Holland, the great ark of the fugitives, 177; its splendid hospitality to the refugees, 178.
Hops introduced by Flemings, 94 (*note*).
Hospital, the French, 280.
Houblons, family of, and descendants, 309.
Huber, John, a galley-slave, 164.
Hugessen, family of, 309.
Huguenots, origin of, 29; first persecution of, 27, 44; spread of "The Religion," 50; massacre of Vassy, 55; civil war, 57; massacre of St Bartholomew, 65; renewal of civil war, 69; flight into England, 87; renewal of civil war, 128; siege of Rochelle, 129; the Huguenots crushed as a political power by Richelieu, and the Edict of Pardon issued, 130; Huguenots as men of industry, 132-4: form of worship and church government, 134 (*note*); Colbert befriends, 135; persecution of, by Louis XIV, 139; cruel edicts against, 140; emigration of, forbidden. 141; attempt to purchase conversions of, 144; dragonnades in Dauphiny and at Bordeaux, 146; dragonnades in Bearn, 148; Revocation of the Edict of Nantes, 151; general flight of the, 155; sent to the galleys, 159; flight by sea of, 165: number supposed to have escaped, 168; refuge of, in Prussia, 175; in Holland, 177; soldiers and officers in the army of the Prince of Orange, 188; at the battle of the Boyne, 214; officers in British service, 217; men of learning settled in England, 229; men of industry, 250; settlements in Ireland, 283; descendants of, in England and Ireland, 307; the last persecutions of, in France, 337; consequences to France of banishment of, 340.

I.

Iconoclasts, the, in France, 57.
Ignatius Loyola, 60.
Indulgences, sale of, 25.
Industry, branches of, established by refugee Flemings—bays and says making at Sandwich, 88, 91; other manufactures at, 91, 93; gardening introduced, 93 (*note*), 94; carpentry, 95; brewing, 96; dyeing, 96; felt and hat making, etc, 96; bombazine manufacture at Norwich, 100; woolen weaving in west of England, 103; thread and lace making, 104; mining, 105; iron and steel manufactures, 106; fishing at Yarmouth, 106; fen-drainage, 107; various branches in Ireland, 108; in Scotland, 109; early manufactures, 360-3.
Industry, branches of, established by refugee French—engine-making, 255; instrument-making, 255; beaver hats, 257; buttons, 258; calico-printing, 258; tapestry manufacture, 258; silk manufacture, 258; silk stockings, 260-1; glass-making, 262-3; paper-making, 264, 269; lustrings, brocades, etc., 260; fine linen, 268; lace-making, 268; Iri h poplins, 284; Irish linen manufactures, 285; Irish cambric, 289; Irish woolen manufacture, 290.

INDEX.

Industry, Huguenot, in France, 132.
Inquisition in Flanders, 61; in Spain, 82-3.
Inventors, French refugee, 264 (note), 326, 328.
Ireland, refugees in—Flemish, 107; French, 219, 283, 306.
Iron and steel makers—at Shotley, 105; Sheffield, 106.

J.

James I. of England—grants of naturalization to refugees in Ireland, 108; his protection of the refugees, 110; attempts to introduce silk manufacture, 258; smuggling of French artisans into England in hogsheads, 364.
James II. of England—his accession, 182-3; introduces the Jesuits, 183; persecution of Scotch Presbyterians and English Puritans, 183-5; comparison of, with Louis XIV., 184; opposed by the nation, 187; flight to France, 207; return to Ireland with a French army, 210; defeated at the battle of the Boyne, 215.
Jesuits—Order of, instituted by Loyola, 60; in Flanders, 61, 75 (note); Mary Queen of Scots in league with, 79, 80; in France, 143, 151, 338, 343; in England, 183, 208 (note).
Jewell, Bishop, defense of the Flemish refugees, 73; his works proscribed by Laud, 111 (note).
Jortin, Archdeacon, 320.

K.

Kempe, John, Flemish woolen manufacturer, 356.
Kendal, settlements of refugees in, 104, 356.
Kent, settlements of Flemings in, 91, 105, 264, 358.

L.

Labouchere, family of, 315.
Lace manufacture introduced by refugees, 104, 105, 268.
Lasco, John A', superintendent of refugee churches in Edward VI., 113 and note.
Laud, Archbishop, his policy with respect to Protestant refugees, 110 and note, 111 (note), 112.
Lawyers, eminent, sprung from French refugees, 322-3.
Lee, William, his invention of the stocking-frame, 261.
Lefevre, Jacques, his French translation of the Bible, 24.
Lefevre, family of, 315.
Ligonier, Lord, 228.
Linen manufacture introduced in England by refugees, 268; in Scotland, 269; in Ireland, 108, 285.
Lisburn, settlement of refugees at, 285-8.
Literary men, distinguished, of Huguenot origin, 322.
Literature and printing, 13; influence of the Bible on, 21 (note); depression of, in France, Louis XIV., 342.
London, settlements of refugees in—Flemings, 86, 94; in Southwark and Bermondsey, 95; at Bow, Wandsworth, etc., 96; census of foreigners in 1571, 98; Walloon churches in, 113; French refugees in, 1687, 252; French churches in, 270; descendants of refugees in Spitalfields, 324-34; Flemings in, in the reign of Edward III., 354; riots against foreigners, 365-6.
Louis XIII. of France—war against the Huguenots, 128; issues Edict of Pardon, 130.
Louis XIV. of France, absolutism of, 137; his ambition for military glory, 137, 138; persecution of the Huguenots, 139; his amours, 143; his Revocation of the Edict of Nantes, 151; cruelty of his rule, 153, 164; requires the refugees to be expelled from Geneva, 174; compared with James II. of England, 284; results of Louis's rule in France, 341.
Louis XIV. of France—persecutions in reign of, 337; suppression of Protestant literature and burning of books, 342.
Louis XVI. of France a victim to the despotism of Louis XIV., 349.
Loyola, Ignatius, 60.
Luther, Martin, his first perusal of the Bible, 21; his translation of Bible, 22; on music, 42 (note).
Lyons, massacre at, 66; Protestant emigration from, 169.

M.

Maintenon, Madame de, and Louis XIV.— her early life, 143; her intrigues, 150; marriage with Louis XIV., 151.
Majendie, family of, 320.
Manufactures. (See Industry.)
Manuscript literature, dearness of, 13, 16.
Marie Antoinette, victim of Louis XIV., 349.
Marolles, Louis de, a galley-slave, 164.
Marteilhe, Jean, his sufferings as a galley-slave, 162.
Martineau, family of, 324, 389-90.
Mary Queen of Scots. 74-80.
Massacres—of Vassy, 55; throughout France, 57; of St. Bartholomew, 65; at Lyons, 66; in Dauphiny and Bordeaux, 146; at Nismes, 224; of the Revolution, 348.
Massillon, his praises of Louis XIV., 152.
Maturin, Gabriel, and descendants, 321.
Mazarin, Bible, 15 (note); the cardinal, acknowledges the loyalty of the Huguenots, 131.
Mazeres, Baron, 323 and note.
Meaux, the Reformation at, 25.
Medicis, Catharine de, 51; letter to the Pop, 53 (note); interview with Alva, 59; her connection with the massacre of St. Bartholomew, 64.
Medicis, Marie de, 128, 141.
Mentz, origin of printing at, 15, 17, 18.
Merchants, Flemish, in London, 97.
Merchants, the Huguenots as, 134 and note.
Millinery, origin of the word, 85 (note).
Miners, German, in England, 360.
Moivre, Daniel de, 235-8.
Montmorency, Duke of, 45, 56.
More, Sir Thomas, his sentence on John Tyndale, 18 (note).
Mothe, Claude de la, pastor, 243.
Motteaux, refugee author, 323.
Mutual benefit societies of refugees, 254.

INDEX. 447

N.

Names of manufactured articles, origin of, 85 (*note*); changes of, by Flemings and French, 96, 304, 308, 311.
Nantes, Edict of, 151; Revocation of, 151; depopulation of, 169; massacre at, 349.
Navarre, Henry of. (See *Henry IV.*)
Newcastle-on-Tyne, steel and iron makers at, 105; early glass-makers at, 362, 363 and *note*.
Nonconformist emigrants to America, 111.
Norman (benefit) society, Bethnal Green, 255 (*note*).
Norwich, settlement of Flemings at, 90; conspiracy against refugees, 101; Walloon church at, 115, 388; silk manufacture at, 268; early settlements of Flemings at, 354, 358, 365.
Numbers of Alva's victims in the Netherlands, 63; killed in the massacres in France, 1572, 67; of strangers in London, 1550 and 1571, 87, 97-8; of foreign workmen in Norwich, 100, 103; of Huguenots in France, Louis XIV , 142; of refugees from France, 168; of refugees in England, 230, 250.

O.

Officers, Huguenot, in army of William III., 189; at the Boyne, 217.
Orange, principality of, 180. (See *William III. of Orange*.)
Ormonde, patronage of refugees by Duke of, 108 (*note*), 287 (*note*), 290.

P.

Palissy, Bernard, life and history, 31-40.
Paper, manufacture of, introduced by refugees, 109, 133, 264; early manufacture, 361-2.
Papillon, family of, 319.
Papin, Dr Denis, 232.
Paré, Ambrose, 50, 65, 67.
Paris, burning of printers at, 28; Palissy at, 48; Protestant churches destroyed at, 56; massacre at, 65; rejoicings at, 67; rejoicings on the Revocation, 152; destruction of Protestant churches at, 153; Protestant pastors banished from, 157; at the Revolution, 347-9.
Parliament, Huguenots in, 319.
Pastors, celebrated Huguenot, 240-9; list of deceased, 278 (*note*).
Paul, Lewis, inventor of spinning by rollers, 327-33.
Pauli, Dr , on the French church at Canterbury, 127.
Peers of Huguenot descent, 313.
Persecutions. (See *Flanders* and *Huguenots*.)
Philip II. of Spain, 59, 61; laughs at news of the great massacre of Protestants at Paris, 67; plot against Elizabeth's life, 77; his Sacred Armada, 81; contrasted with Elizabeth, 83.
Philip II of Spain, 59, 61, 83, 340.
Physicians, Huguenot, proscribed, 232, 235.
Pineton, Jacques, pastor, his escape from France, 243.

Plots against life of Queen Elizabeth, 74, 77, 80 and *note*.
Plymouth, landing of refugees at, 181; church at, 277.
Popery, popular aversion to, in England, 183.
Popes—Alexander VI., prohibition of printing, 18; Paul IV. issues the first *Index Expurgatorius*, 29; Pius IV. attempts to suppress heresy, 43, 44; Pius V. refuses assent to marriage of Henry of Navarre, 64; his bull against Elizabeth, 75; Clement VIII , his denunciation of the Edict of Nantes, 70; Sixtus V. reissues bull against Elizabeth, 82; Innocent XI., his rejoicing at the Revocation of the Edict, 152.
Portal, family of De, 265.
Portarlington, settlement of refugees at, 220, 301, 339.
Potters, refugee, at Sandwich, 93; at Norwich 100 (*note*); Staffordshire, 100 (*note*).
Prices of manuscripts, 13.
Printing, invention of, 13; of the Bible 15-24; attempts to suppress, 28, 29; in Scotland, 109-10 (*note*); in England, 362 (*note*).
Protestantism in England, 71, 78, 110, 183.
Protestants, foreign. (See *Flanders* and *Huguenots*)
Prussia, Huguenot refugees in, 175.

Q.

Queen of England, her Huguenot descent, 313.

R.

Raboteau, escape of the Misses, 166.
Radnor, Earl of, 309.
Ramus, Peter, 50, 68 (*note*)
Rapin-Thoyras, the soldier-historian, 205, 227.
"Reconnaissances" of French refugees, 270.
Reformation heralded by printing, 18; at Meaux, 27; at Saintes, 39; supporters of, 33; in Flanders, 61; in England, 72.
Reformed. (See *Flemings* and *Huguenots*.)
Refugees, foreign, defense of, by Bishop Jewell, 74 (*note*); Flemish, in England, and settlements, 85-110; refugee churches, 113-27; French in Switzerland, 171; in Prussia, 175; in Africa, 176; in Holland, 177; in England, 181 *et seq.*; religion of, 230 , trades of, 250; aid given to, 251; benefit societies of, 254; industry of, 263; churches of, 270; in Ireland, 283; descendants of, 307; effects of settlement on England, 351; early, 353.
Refugee relief fund, 186, 251-2.
Relations of England with France and Spain, 71.
Revolution, French, and its causes, 346.
Richard II., foreign artisans in London, times of, 360.
Richelieu, Cardinal, his policy, 120; at siege of Rochelle, 120; his toleration of Huguenots, 124
Ridolfi, agent in plots against life of Elizabeth, 76
Riots in London against foreigners, 97; in Norwich, 101; in Canterbury Cathedral, 125 and *note;* at Norwich, 365; in London, 336.

INDEX.

Roche, M. de la, refugee author, 239 and *note.*
Rochelle, sieges of, 69, 129.
Romaine, Rev. W., 322.
Roman Catholics in England, 75; priests persecuted at the French Revolution, 346.
Romilly family, the, 315, 335.
Ross, Bishop of, plot against Elizabeth, 76.
Russell, Lady Rachel, her descent, 314 (*note*).
Ruvigny, Marquis de, at Greenwich, 208, 314 and *note.* (See *Galway, Earl of.*)
Rye, landing of refugees at, 88; testimony to their good character, 182 (*note*).

S.

Sacred Armada, 81, 82, 118, 380.
Sail-cloth manufacture introduced, 133 and *note.*
Sailors, refugee, 179, 229, 277.
Saintes, gospellers under Palissy at, 38, 39.
Saintonge, painful incident at, 148.
Saint Germain's, treaty of, 58.
Sancerre, siege of, 63.
Sandwich, settlement of Flemings at, 87, 91–93.
Saurin, Jacques, refugee pastor, 241.
Saurin, Irish Attorney General, 319.
Savoy, Protestants of, aided by William III., 219.
Savoy, Church in the, Strand, 248, 253 (*note*), 271, 371.
Schœffer, and invention of printing, 15, 17.
Schomberg, Marshal, 156, 189, 190; campaign in Ireland, 211; death at the Boyne, 216; Charles, second Duke of, 219; Menard, third duke, in Ireland, 214–15; in Spain, 221.
Science, refugee men of, 230, 323.
Scotland, Flemings in, 109, 353 (*note*); French refugees in, 268.
Settlements of refugees. (See *Flemish, Huguenots,* and *Industry.*)
Sheffield, settlement of Flemings at, 106.
Sieges of Huguenot towns, 128, 129; of Rochelle, 129.
Silk manufacture attempted in England, 258; established by the French refugees, 259; at Canterbury and Norwich, 267–8.
Soldiers, Huguenot, emigration of, 179; in army of William III., 189; in Ireland, 211; recruited in Switzerland, 213; at the Boyne, 215; at Athlone and Aughrim, 217–18; campaign in Savoy, 219; in Spain, 221; in the Low Countries, 228
Southampton, early refugees at, 115; their church, 115–18; influx of refugees, 276; church of "God's House," 373
Southwark, Flemish refugees in, 95, 366–7.
Spain under Philip II., 83; modern condition, 340.
Spinning by rollers, invention of, by Lewis Paul, 331.
Spitalfields, refugee manufacturers in, 259; churches in, 270; hand-loom-weavers of, 324; descendants of refugees in, 334, 339.
Steel and iron manufactures introduced in England by refugees, 105, 360.
Stonehouse, Plymouth, French church at, 276, 392.

Strafford, Earl of, encourages linen manufacture in Ireland, 108.
Surgeons, refugee, in England, 238.
Swallow Street French church, 272, 372.
Switzerland, refugees in, 171–3, 213.

T.

Taunton, French refugees at, 293
Taxes of the Roman Chancery, 25 (*note*).
Thorney Abbey, French church at, 396.
Thorpe-le-Soken, French church at, 277, 395.
Threadneedle Street, French church in, 114, 270, 369.
Throgmorton, leader of conspiracy at Norwich, 101.
Trade in French goods, 256.
Trades established by refugees. (See *Industry.*)
Tours, massacre at, 57; depopulation of, 169.
Trench, family of, 313.
Trent, Council of, 58.
Tyndale's translation of Bible, 18 (*note*); martyrdom, 23 (*note*).

U.

Undercroft, French church of the, Canterbury Cathedral, 122–3.

V.

Vassy, massacre of, 55.
Vaudois, massacre of, 28; Bible committed to memory by Vaudois youth, 38 (*note*); crusade against, by Louis XIV., 218.
Vermuyden, Dutch engineer in the Fens, 107.
Vignolles, family of, 192 (*note*), 302 and *note,* 304
Villars, Marshal, interview with Cavalier, 224–5.
Vitelli, Chapin, offers to assassinate Queen Elizabeth, 77.
Volumes printed in fifteenth century, 28 (*note*).

W.

'Walkers" of cloth, Flemish derivation of the word, 104 (*note*).
Walloons. (See *Flemings.*)
Wandsworth, Flemish gardens at, 94; manufactures at, 96; French church at, 274.
Waterford, refugee settlement at, 300.
William III. of Orange, 179; recruits his army with Huguenot officers and soldiers, 188; expedition to England, 205; campaign in Ireland, 211; assists the Protestants in Savoy, 219.
Winchelsea, settlement of refugees at, 90.
Wolsey, Cardinal, on printing, 19 (*note*).
Women, sufferings of Huguenot, 145, 149 (*note*), 161, 167.
Wool of England, 85, 352; smuggling of, 132, 133 (*note*), 359.
Worsted, Flemish settlement at, 353.
Wyatt, his partnership with Lewis Paul, 328-33.
Wyckliffe's translations of Bible, 18 (*note*).

Y.

Yarmouth, Flemish fishery at, 106.

THE END.

CPSIA information can be obtained
at www.ICGtesting.com
Printed in the USA
LVHW031148200319
611264LV00001B/1/P

9 781410 203588